Walter Simson, James Simson

A history of the Gipsies: with specimens of the Gipsy language

Walter Simson, James Simson

A history of the Gipsies: with specimens of the Gipsy language

ISBN/EAN: 9783742823229

Manufactured in Europe, USA, Canada, Australia, Japa

Cover: Foto ©Andreas Hilbeck / pixelio.de

Manufactured and distributed by brebook publishing software (www.brebook.com)

Walter Simson, James Simson

A history of the Gipsies: with specimens of the Gipsy language

A

HISTORY OF THE GIPSIES:

WITH

Specimens of the Gipsy Language,

BY WALTER SIMSON.

EDITED WITH

PREFACE, INTRODUCTION, AND NOTES, AND A DISQUISITION ON THE PAST, PRESENT AND FUTURE OF GIPSYDOM.

BY JAMES SIMSON.

"Hast thou not noted on the bye-way side,
Where aged saughs lean o'er the lazy tide,
A vagrant crew, far straggled through the glade,
With trifles busied, or in slumber laid;
Their children lolling round them on the grass,
Or pestering with their sports the patient ass?
The wrinkled beldame there you may espy,
And ripe young maiden with the glossy eye;
Men in their prime, and striplings dark and dun,
Scathed by the storm and freckled with the sun;
Their swarthy hue and mantle's flowing fold,
Bespeak the remnant of a race of old.
Strange are their annals—list! and mark them well—
For thou hast much to hear and I to tell."—[illegible]

LONDON:
SAMPSON LOW, SON, AND MARSTON,
MILTON HOUSE, LUDGATE HILL,
EDINBURGH:—MENZIES.

1865.

[THE RIGHT OF TRANSLATION IS RESERVED.]

CONTENTS.*

* The Contents of these Chapters will be found detailed in the Index, forming an epitome of the work, for reference, or studying the subject of the Gipsies.

EDITOR'S PREFACE.

This work should have been introduced to the world long ere now. The proper time to have brought it forward would have been about twenty years ago,* when the subject was nearly altogether new, and when popular feeling, in Scotland especially, ran strongly toward the body it treats of, owing to the celebrity of the writings of the great Scottish novelist, in which were depicted, with great truthfulness, some real characters of this wayward race. The inducements then to hazard a publication of it were great; for by bringing it out at that time, the author would have enjoyed, in some measure, the sunshine which the fame of that great luminary cast around all who, in any way, illustrated a subject on which he had written. But for Sir Walter Scott's advice—an advice that can only be appreciated by those who are acquainted with the vindictive disposition which the Gipsies entertain toward those whom they imagine to have injured them—our author would have published a few magazine articles on the subject, when the tribe would have taken alarm, and an end would have been made to the investigation. The dread of personal danger, there is no doubt, formed a considerable reason for the work being so long withheld from the public: at the same time, our author, being a timid and nervous man, not a little dreaded the spleen of the party opposed to the literary society with which he identified himself, and the idea of being made the subject of one of the slashing criticisms so characteristic of the times. But now he has descended into the tomb, with most of his generation, where the abuse of a reviewer or the ire of a wandering Egyptian cannot reach him.

Since this work was written there has appeared one by

* It has been brought down, however, to the present time.

Mr. Borrow, on the *Gitanos* or Spanish Gipsies. In the year 1838, a society was formed in Scotland, under the patronage of the Scottish Church, for the reformation of the wandering portion of the body in that country, with some eminent men as a committee of management, among whom was a reverend gentleman of learning, piety, and worth, who said that he himself was a Gipsy, and whose fine swarthy features strongly marked the stock from which he was descended. There are others in that country of a like origin, ornaments to the same profession, and many in other respectable walks of life, of whom I will speak in my Disquisition on the Gipsies, at the end of the work.

Although a few years have elapsed since the principal details of this work were collected, the subject cannot be considered as old. The body in Scotland has become more numerous since the downfall of Napoleon; but the improved system of internal order that has obtained since that period, has so very much suppressed their acts of depredation and violence toward the community, and their savage outbursts of passion toward those of their own race who had offended them, that much which would have met with only a slight punishment before, or in some instances been passed over, as a mere Gipsy scuffle, would now be visited with the utmost penalty the law could inflict. Hence the wild spirit, but not the number, of the body has been very much crushed. Many of them have betaken themselves to regular callings of industry, or otherwise withdrawn from public observation; but, in respect to race, are as much, at heart, Gipsies as before. Many of the Scottish wandering class have given way before an invasion of swarms of Gipsies from Ireland.

It is almost unnecessary to give a reason why this work has been introduced here, instead of the country in which it was written, and of which, for the most part, it treats. Suffice it to say, that, having come to this country, I have been led to bring it out here, where it may receive, sooner or later, more attention from those at a distance from the place and people it treats of, than from those accustomed to see and hear of them daily, to many of whom they appear as mere vagabonds; it being a common feature in the human mind, that that which comes frequently under our observation is but little thought of, while that at a distance, and unknown to us, forms the subject of our investigations and desires.* In taking this view of the subject, the language of Dr. Bright may be used, when he says: "The condition and circumstances of the Gipsy nation throughout the whole of Europe, may truly be considered amongst the most curious phenomena in the history of man." And although this work, for the most part, treats of Scottish Gipsies, it illustrates the history of the people all over Europe, and, it may be said, pretty much over the world; and affords materials for reflection on so singular a subject connected with the history of our common family, and so little known to mankind in general. To the American reader generally, the work will illustrate a phase of life and history with which it may be reasonably assumed he is not much conversant; for, although he must have some knowledge of the Gipsy race generally, there is no work, that I am aware of, that treats of the body like the present. To all kinds of readers the words of the celebrated Christopher North, as quoted in the author's Introduction, may be addressed:

> "Few things more sweetly vary civil life
> Than a barbarian, savage Tinkler† tale."

It is a singular circumstance that, until comparatively lately, little was known of this body in Scotland, beyond their mere existence, and the depredations which they committed on their neighbours; no further proof of which need

* "Men of letters, while eagerly investigating the customs of Otaheite or Kamschatka, and losing their tempers in endless disputes about Gothic and Celtic antiquities, have witnessed, with apathy and contempt, the striking spectacle of a Gipsy camp—pitched, perhaps, amidst the mouldering entrenchments of their favourite Picts and Romans. The rest of the community, familiar from infancy with the general character and appearance of these vagrant hordes, have probably never regarded them with any deeper interest than what springs from the recollected terrors of a nursery tale, or the finer associations of poetical and picturesque description."—*Blackwood's Magazine.*

† *Tinkler* is the name generally applied to the Scottish Gipsies. The wandering, tented class prefer it to the term Gipsy. The settled and better classes detest the word: they would much rather be called Gipsies; but the term Egyptian is the most agreeable to their feelings. Tinkler has a peculiar meaning that can be understood only by a Scotchman. In its radical sense it means Tinker. The verb tink, according to Jamieson's Scottish Dictionary, means to "rivet, including the idea of the noise made in the operation of riveting; a Gipsy word."

be given than a reference to the letters of Sir Walter Scott and others, in the introduction to the work, and the avidity with which the few articles of our author in Blackwood's Magazine were read.

The higher we may rise in the scale of general information and philosophic culture, the greater the attractions will this moral puzzle have for our contemplation—the phenomenon of a barbarous race of men, free as the air, with little but the cold earth for a bed, and the canopy of heaven for a covering, obtruding itself upon a civilized community, and living so long in the midst of it, without any material impression being made on the habits of the representative part of it; the only instance of the kind in the modern history of the world. In this solitary case, having nothing from which to reason analogously as to the result, observation alone must be had recourse to for the solution of the experiment. It is from this circumstance that the subject, in all its bearings, has been found to have such charms for the curious and learned; being, as it were, a study in history of the most interesting kind. It may be remarked that Professor Wilson, the Christopher North of Blackwood, is said to have accompanied some of the tribe in their peregrinations over parts of England and Wales. Without proceeding to the same length, our author, in his own peculiar way, prosecuted his researches with much indefatigability, assiduity, and patience. He kept an open house for them at all times, and presented such allurements as the skillful trapper of vermin will sometimes use in attracting the whole in a neighbourhood; when if one Gipsy entered, many would follow; although he would generally find them so shy in their communication as sometimes to require years of such baiting to ensure them for the elucidation of a single point of their history. In this way he made himself appear, in his associations with them, as very odd, and perhaps not of very sound mind, in the estimation of the wise ones around him.

The popular idea of a Gipsy, at the present day, is very erroneous as to its extent and meaning. The nomadic Gipsies constitute but a portion of the race, and a very small portion of it. A gradual change has come over their outward condition, all over Europe, from about the commencement of the first American war, but from what time previous to that, we have no certain data from which to form an opinion. In the whole of Great Britain they have been very much mixed with the native blood of the country, but nowhere, I believe, so much so as in Scotland. There is every reason to suppose that the same mixture has taken place in Europe generally, although its effects are not so observable in the southern countries—from the circumstance of the people there being, for the most part, of dark hair and complexion—as in those lying further toward the north. But this circumstance would, to a certain extent, prevent the mixture which has taken place in countries the inhabitants of which have fair hair and complexions. The causes leading to this mixture are various.

The persecutions to which the Gipsies were exposed, merely for being Gipsies, which their appearance would readily indicate, seem to have induced the body to intermarry with our race, so as to disguise theirs. That would be done by receiving and adopting males of our race, whom they would marry to females of theirs, who would bring up the children of such unions as members of their fraternity. They also adopted the practice to give their race stamina, as well as numbers, to contend with the people among whom they lived. The desire of having servants, (for Gipsies, generally, have been too proud to do menial work for each other,) led to many children being kidnapped, and reared among them; many of whom, as is customary with Oriental people, rose to as high a position in the tribe as any of themselves.*

Then again, it was very necessary to have people of fair complexion among them, to enable them the more easily to carry on their operations upon the community, as well as to contribute to their support during times of persecution. Ow-

* Mr. Borrow labours under a very serious mistake when he asserts that "The unfounded idea, that Gipsies steal children, to bring them up as Gipsies, has been the besetting sin of authors, who have attempted to found works of fiction on the way of life of this most singular people." The only argument which he advances to refute this belief in regard to Gipsies, which is universal, is the following: "They have plenty of children of their own, whom they can scarcely support; and they would smile at the idea of encumbering themselves with the children of others." This is rather inconsistent with his own words, when he says, "I have dealt more in facts than in theories, of which I am, in general, no friend." As a matter of fact, children have been stolen and brought up as Gipsies, and incorporated with the tribe.

ing to these causes, and the occasional occurrence of white people being, by more legitimate means, received into their body, which would be more often the case in their palmy days, the half, at least, of the Scottish Gipsies are of fair hair and blue eyes. Some would naturally think that these would not be Gipsies, but the fact is otherwise; for, owing to the dreadful prejudice which has always attached to the name of Gipsy, these white and parti-coloured Gipsies, imagining themselves, as it were, banished from society, on account of their descent, cling to their Gipsy connection; as the other part of their blood, they imagine, will not own them. They are Gipsies, and, with the public, they think that is quite enough. They take a pride in being descended from a race so mysterious, so ancient, so universal, and cherish their language the more from its being the principal badge of membership that entitles them to belong to it. The nearer they approach the whites as regards blood, the more acutely do they feel the antipathy which is entertained for their race, and the more bitter does the propinquity become to them. The more enlightened they become, the stronger becomes their attachment to the sept in the abstract, although they will despise many of its members. The sense of such an ancient descent, and the possession of such an ancient and secret language, in the minds of men of comparatively limited education and indifferent rearing, brought up in humble life, and following various callings, from a tinker upward, and even of men of education and intelligence, occupying the position of lawyers, medical doctors, and clergymen, possess for them a charm that is at once fascinating and enchanting. If men of enlightened minds and high social standing will go to such lengths as they have done, in their endeavours to but look into their language, how much more will they not cling to it, such as it is, in whose hearts it is? Gipsies compounded for the most part of white blood, but with Gipsy feelings, are, as a general thing, much superior to those who more nearly approach what may be called the original stock; and, singularly enough, speak the language better than the others, if their opportunities have been in any way favourable for its acquisition.

The primitive, original state of the Gipsies is the tent and tilted cart. But as any country can support only a limited number in that way, and as the increase of the body is very large, it follows that they must cast about to make a living in some other way, however bitter the pill may be which they have to swallow. The nomadic Gipsy portion resembles, in that respect, a water trough; for the water which runs into it, there must be a corresponding quantity running over it. The Gipsies who leave the tent resemble the youth of our small seaports and villages; for there, society is so limited as to compel such youth to take to the sea or cities, or go abroad, to gain that livelihood which the neighbourhood in which they have been reared denies to them. In the same manner do these Gipsies look back to the tent from which they, or their fathers, have sprung. They carry the language, the associations, and the sympathies of their race, and their peculiar feelings toward the community, with them; and, as residents of towns, have generally greater facilities, from others of their race residing near them, for perpetuating their language, than when strolling over the country.

The prejudice of their fellow creatures, which clings to the race to which they belong, almost overwhelms some of them at times; but it is only momentary; for such is the independence and elasticity of their nature, that they rise from under it, as self-complacent and proud as ever. They in such cases resort to the *tu quoque*—the *tit for tat* argument as regards their enemies, and ask, "What is this white race, after all? What were their forefathers a few generations ago? the Highlands a nest of marauding thieves, and the Borders little better. Or society at the present day—what is it but a compound of deceit and hypocrisy? People say that the Gipsies steal. True; some of them steal chickens, vegetables, and such things; but what is that compared to the robbery of widows and orphans, the lying and cheating of traders, the swindling, the robberies, the murders, the ignorance, the squalor, and the debaucheries of so many of the white race? What are all these compared to the simple vices of the Gipsies? What is the ancestry they boast of, compared, in point of antiquity, to ours? People may despise the Gipsies, but they certainly despise all others not of their own race: the veriest beggar Gipsy, without shoes to his feet, considers himself better than the queen that sits upon the throne. People say that Gipsies are blackguards. Well, if some of them are blackguards, they are at least illustrious blackguards as regards descent, and so in fact; for they never rob each other, and far less do they rob or ruin those of their own family." And they conclude that the odium which clings to the race is but a prejudice. Still, they will deny that they are Gipsies, and will rather almost perish than let any one, not of their own race, know that they speak their language in their own households and among their own kindred. They will even deny or at least hide it from many of their own race.

For all these reasons, the most appropriate word to apply to modern Gipsyism, and especially British Gipsyism, and more especially Scottish Gipsyism, is to call it a caste, and a kind of masonic society, rather than any particular mode of life. And it is necessary that this distinction should be kept in mind, otherwise the subject will appear contradictory.

The most of these Gipsies are unknown to the public as Gipsies. The feeling in question is, for the most part, on the side of the Gipsies themselves; they think that more of them is known than actually is. In that respect a kind of nightmare continually clings to them; while their peculiarly distant, clannish, and odd habits create a kind of separation between them and the other inhabitants, which the Gipsy is naturally apt to construe as proceeding from a different cause. Frequently, all that is said about them amounts only to a whisper among some of the families in the community in which they live, and which is confidentially passed around among themselves, from a dread of personal consequences. Sometimes the native families say among themselves, "Why should we make allusion to their kith and kin? They seem decent people, and attend church like ourselves; and it would be cruel to cast up their descent to them, and damage them in the estimation of the world. Their cousins, (or second cousins, as it may be,) travel the country in the old Tinkler fashion, no doubt; but what has that to do with them?" The estimate of such people never, or hardly ever, goes beyond the simple idea of their being "descended from Tinklers;" few have the most distant idea that they are Gipsies, and speak the Gipsy language among themselves. It is certain that a Gipsy can be a good man, as the world goes, nay, a very good man, and glory in being a Gipsy, but not to the public.

He will adhere to his ancient language, and talk it in his own family; and he has as much right to do so, as, for example, a Highlander has to speak Gaelic in the lowlands, or when he goes abroad, and teach it to his children. And he takes a greater pride in doing it, for thus he reasons: "What is English, French, Gaelic, or any other living language, compared to mine? Mine will carry me through every part of the known world: wherever a man is to be found, there is my language spoken. I will find a brother in every part of the world on which I may set my foot; I will be welcomed and passed along wherever I may go. Freemasonry indeed! what is masonry compared to the brotherhood of the Gipsies? A language—a whole language—is its pass-word. I almost worship the idea of being a member of a society into which I am initiated by my blood and language. I would not be a man if I did not love my kindred, and cherish in my heart that peculiarity of my race (its language) which casts a halo of glory around it, and makes it the wonder of the world!"

The feeling alluded to induces some of these Gipsies to change their residences or go abroad. I heard of one family in Canada, of whom a Scotchman spoke somewhat in the following way: "I know them to be Gipsies. They remind me of a brood of wild turkeys, hatched under a tame bird; it will take the second or third descent to bring them to resemble, in some of their ways, the ordinary barn-door fowl. They are very restless and queer creatures, and move about as if they were afraid that every one was going to tramp on their corns." But it is in large towns they feel more at home. They then form little communities among themselves; and by closely associating, and sometimes huddling together, they can more easily perpetuate their language, as I have already said, than by straggling, twos or threes, through the country. But their quarrelsome disposition frequently throws an obstacle in the way of such associations. Secret as they have been in keeping their language from even being heard by the public while wanderers, they are much more so since they have settled in towns.

The origin of the Gipsies has given rise, in recent times, to many speculations. The most plausible one, however, seems to be that they are from Hindostan; an opinion our author supports so well, that we are almost bound to acquiesce in it. In these controversies regarding the origin of the Gipsies, very little regard seems to have been had to what they say of themselves. It is curious that in every part of Europe they have been called, and are now called, Egyptians. No trace can now be found of any enquiry made as to their origin, if such there was made, when they first appeared in Europe. They seem then to have been taken at their word, and to have passed current as Egyptians. But in modern times their country has been denied them, owing to a total dissimilarity between their language and any of the dialects of modern Egypt. A very intelligent Gipsy informed me that his race sprung from a body of men—a cross between the Arabs and Egyptians—that left Egypt in the train of the Jews.* In consulting the record of Moses, I find it said, in Ex. xii. 38, "and a mixed multitude went up also with them" (the Jews, out of Egypt). Very little is said of this mixed multitude. In Lev. xxiv. 10, mention is made of the son of an Israelitish woman, by an Egyptian, being stoned to death for blasphemy, which would almost imply that a marriage had taken place previous to leaving Egypt. After this occurrence, it is said in Num. xi. 4, "and the mixed multitude that was among them fell a lusting" for flesh. That would imply that they had not amalgamated with the Jews, but were only among them. The scriptures say nothing of what became of this mixed multitude after the Jews separated from them (Neh. xiii. 3), and leave us only to form a conjecture relative to their destiny.

We naturally ask, what could have induced this mixed multitude to leave Egypt? and the natural reply is, that their motive was the same that led to the exodus of the Jews—a desire to escape from slavery. No commentator that I have read gives a plausible reason for the mixed multitude leaving Egypt with the Jews. Scott, besides venturing four suppositions, advances a fifth, that "some left because they were distressed or discontented." But that seems to fall infinitely short of the true reason. Adam Clark says, "Probably they were refugees who came to sojourn in Egypt, because of the dearth which had obliged

* The intelligent reader will not differ with me as to the weight to be attached to the Gipsy's remark on this point.

them to emigrate from their own countries." But that dearth occurred centuries before the time of the exodus; so that those refugees, if such there were, who settled in Egypt during the famine, could have returned to their own countries generations before the time of that event. Scott says, "It is probable some left Egypt because it was desolate;" and Henry, "Because their country was laid waste by the plagues." But the desolation was only partial; for we are told that "He that feared the word of the Lord among the servants of Pharaoh, made his servants and his cattle flee into the houses;" by which means they escaped destruction from the hail, which affected only those remaining in the field. We are likewise told that, although the barley and flax were smitten by the same hail-storm, the wheat and rye, not being grown up, were left untouched. These two latter (besides fish, roots and vegetables) would form the staples of the food of the Egyptians; to say nothing of the immense quantities in the granaries of the country. If the Egyptians could not find bread in their own country, how were they to obtain it by accompanying the Jews into a land of which they knew nothing, and which had to be conquered before it could be possessed? Where were they to procure bread to support them on the journey, if it was not to be had at home?

The other reasons given by these commentators for the departure of the mixed multitude from Egypt are hardly worth controverting, when we consider the social manners and religious belief of the Egyptians. We are told that, for being shepherds, the Israelites were an abomination unto the Egyptians (Gen. xlvi. 34); and that the Egyptians considered it an abomination to eat bread with a Hebrew, (Gen. xliii. 32,) so supreme was the reign of caste and of nationality at that period in Egypt. The sacrifices of the Jews were also an abomination to the Egyptians (Ex. viii. 26). The Hebrews were likewise influenced by feelings peculiar to themselves, which would render any alliances or even associations between them and their oppressors extremely improbable; but if such there should have been, the issue would be incorporated with the Hebrews.

There could thus be no personal motive for any of the Egyptians to accompany the Hebrews; and as little could there be of that which pertains to the religious; for, as a people, they had become so "vain in their imaginations," and had "their foolish hearts so darkened," as to worship almost every created thing—bulls, birds, serpents, leeks, onions and garlic. Such a people were almost as well nigh devoid of a motive springing from a sense of elevated religion, as were the beasts, the reptiles and the vegetables which they worshipped. A miracle performed before the eyes of such a people would have no more salutary or lasting influence than would a flash of lightning before the eyes of many a man in every day life; it might prostrate them for a moment, but its effects would be as transitory. Like the Jews themselves, at a subsequent time, they might credit the miracle to Beelzebub, the prince of devils; and, like the Gergesenes, rise up in a body and beseech Moses and his people to "depart out of their coasts." Indeed, after the slaying of the first-born of the Egyptians, we are told that "the Egyptians were urgent upon the people that they might send them out of the land in haste; for, they said, We be all dead men." Considering how hard a matter it was for Moses to urge the Jews to undertake the exodus; considering their stiff-necked and perverse grumbling at all that befell them; notwithstanding that to them "pertained the fathers, the adoption, the glory and the covenant;" the commands and the bones of Joseph; the grievous bondage they were enduring, and the almost daily recourse to which Moses had for a miracle to strengthen their faith and resolution to proceed; and we will perceive the impossibility of the "mixed multitude" leaving Egypt on any ground of religion.

This principle might even be urged further. If we consider the reception which was given to the miracles of Christ as "a son over his own house, and therefore worthy of more glory than Moses, who was but a servant," we will conclude that the miracles wrought by Moses, although personally felt by the Egyptians, would have as little lasting effect upon them as had those of the former upon the Jews themselves; they would naturally lead to the Hebrews being allowed to depart, but would serve no purpose of inducing the Egyptians to go with them. For if a veil was mysteriously drawn over the eyes of the Jews at the advent of Christ, which, in a negative sense, hid the Messiah from them (Mark iv. 11, 12; Matt. xi. 25, 26; and John xii. 39,

40), how much more might it not be said, "He hath blinded their eyes, and hardened their hearts, that they should not see with their eyes, nor understand with their hearts," and let the people of Israel go, "till they would thrust them out hence altogether;" and particularly so when the object of Moses' mission was to redeem the Israelites from the bondage of Egypt, and spoil and smite the Egyptians.

The only reasonable conclusion to which we can come, as regards a motive for the "mixed multitude" leaving Egypt along with the Jews, is, that being slaves like themselves, they took advantage of the opportunity, and slipped out with them.*

The Jews, on being reduced to a state of bondage, were employed by Pharaoh to "build treasure cities, and work in mortar and brick, and do all manner of service in the field," besides being "scattered abroad through all the land of Egypt, to gather stubble in place of straw," wherewith to make their tale of bricks. In this way they would come much in contact with the other slaves of the country; and, as "adversity makes strange bed-fellows," they would naturally prove communicative to their fellow-sufferers, and expatiate on the history of their people, from the days of Abraham downward, were it only from a feeling of vanity to make themselves appear superior to what they would consider the ordinary dross around them. They would also naturally allude to their future prospects, and the positive promise, or at least general idea, which they had of their God effecting their deliverance, and leading them into a country (Gen. l. 24, 25) where all the miseries they were then enduring would be forgotten. They would do that more especially after Moses had returned from his father-in-law in Midian, to bring them out of Egypt; for we are told, in Ex. iv. 29–31, that the elders of the children of Israel were called together and informed of the intended redemption, and that all the people believed. By such means as these would the minds of some of the other slaves of Egypt be inflamed at the very idea of freedom being perhaps in immediate prospect for so many of their fellow-bondsmen.

* Since the above was written, I have read Hengstenberg on the Pentateuch, who supposes that the "mixed multitude" were an inferior order of workmen, employed, like the Jews, as slaves, in the building of the pyramids.

Thereafter happened the many plagues; the causes of which must have been more or less known to the Egyptians generally, from the public manner in which Moses would make his demands (Ex. x. 7); and consequently to their slaves; for many of the slaves would be men of intelligence, as is common in oriental countries. Some of these slaves would, in all probability, watch, with fear and trembling, the dreadful drama played out (Ex. ix. 20). Others would perhaps, give little heed to the various sayings of the Hebrews at the time they were uttered; the plagues would, perhaps, have little effect in reminding them of them. As they experienced their effects, they might even feel exasperated toward the Hebrews for being the cause of them; still it is more probable that they sympathized with them, as fellow-bondsmen, and murmured against Pharaoh for their existence and greater manifestation. But the positive order, nay the entreaty, for the departure of the Israelites, and the passage before their eyes of so large a body of slaves to obtain their freedom, would induce many of them to follow them; for they would, in all likelihood, form no higher estimate of the movement than that of merely gaining that liberty which slaves, in all nations, and under all circumstances, do continually sigh after.

The character of Moses alone was a sufficient guarantee to the slaves of Egypt that they might trust themselves to his leadership and protection (not to speak of the miraculous powers which he displayed in his mission); for we are told that, besides being the adopted son of Pharaoh's daughter, he was learned in all the wisdom of the Egyptians, and mighty in word and deed. Having been, according to Josephus, a great commander in the armies of Egypt, he must have been the means of reducing to bondage many of the slaves, or the parents of the slaves, then living in Egypt. At the time of the exodus we are told that he was "very great in the land of Egypt, in the sight of Pharaoh's servants, and in the sight of the people" (Ex. xi. 3). The burying of the "first-born" was not a circumstance likely to prevent a slave gaining his freedom amid the dismay, the moaning, and groaning, and howling throughout the land of Egypt. The circumstance was even the more favourable for his escape, owing to the Hebrews being allowed to go, till it pleased God again to harden and stir up Pharaoh to pursue them

(Ex. xiv. 2–5 and 8), in order that his host might be overthrown in the Red Sea.

The Jews, while in Egypt, seem to have been reduced to a state of serfdom only—crown slaves, not chattels personal; which would give them a certain degree of respect in the eyes of the ordinary slaves of the country, and lead them, owing to the dignity of their descent, to look down with disdain upon the "mixed multitude" which followed them. While it is said that they were "scattered over the land of Egypt," we are told, in Ex. ix. 4, that the murrain touched not the cattle of Israel; and in the 26th verse, that "in the land of Goshen, where the people of Israel were, there was no hail." And Moses said to Pharaoh, "our cattle also shall go with us; there shall not an hoof be left behind; for thereof we must take to serve the Lord our God" (Ex. x. 26) From this we would naturally conclude, that such of the Jews only as were capable of work, were scattered over the land of Egypt to do the work of Pharaoh, while the rest were left in the land of Goshen. By both the Egyptians and their slaves, the Hebrews would be looked upon as a mysterious people, which the former would be glad to send out of the land, owing to the many plagues which they had been the cause of being sent upon them; and while they got quit of them, as they did, there would be no earthly motive for the Egyptians to follow them, through a wilderness, into a country of which the Hebrews themselves knew nothing. But it would be different with their slaves; they had everything to hope from a change of condition, and would readily avail themselves of the chance to effect it.

The very term "mixed multitude" implies slaves; for the Hebrew word *hasaphsuph*, as translated by Bochartus, means *populi colluvies undecunque collecta*—" the dregs or scum of the people gathered together from all parts." But this interpretation is most likely the literal meaning of a figurative expression, which was intended to describe a body of men such as the slaves of Egypt must have been, that is, a mixture that was compounded of men from almost every part of the world known to the Egyptians; the two principal ingredients of which must have been what may be called the Egyptian and Semitic. Moses seems to have used the word in question in consequence of the vexation and snare which the mixed multitude proved to him, by bringing upon the camp of his people the plague, inflicted, in consequence of their sins, in the midst of them. At the same time the Hebrews were very apt to term "dregs and scum" all who did not proceed from the loins of their father, Abraham. But I am inclined to believe that the bulk or nucleus of the mixed multitude would consist of slaves who were located in Goshen, or its neighbourhood, when the Jews were settled there by Pharaoh. These would be a mixture of the shepherd kings and native Egyptians, held by the former as slaves, who would naturally fall into the hands of the Egyptian monarch during his gradual reconquest of the country; and they would be held by the pure Egyptians in as little esteem as the Jews themselves, both being, in a measure, of the shepherd race. In this way it may be claimed that the Gipsies are even descendants of the shepherd kings.

After leaving Egypt, the Hebrews and the "mixed multitude," in their exuberance of feeling at having gained their freedom, and witnessed the overthrow of their common oppressor in the Red Sea, would naturally have everything in common, till they regained their powers of reflection, and began to think of their destiny, and the means of supporting so many individuals, in a country in which provisions could hardly be collected for the company of an ordinary caravan. Then their difficulties would begin. It was enough for Moses to have to guide the Hebrews, whose were the promises, without being burdened and harassed by those who followed them. Then we may reasonably assume that the mixed multitude began to clamour for flesh, and lead the Hebrews to join with them; in return for which a plague was sent upon the people. They were unlikely to submit to be led by the hand of God, and be fed on angels' food, and, like the Hebrews, leave their carcasses in the wilderness; for their religious sentiments, if, as slaves of Egypt, they had religious sentiments, would be very low indeed, and would lead them to depend upon themselves, and leave the deserts of Arabia, for some other country more likely to support them and their children. Undoubtedly the two people then separated, as Abraham and Lot parted when they came out of Egypt.

How to shake off this mixed multitude must have caused Moses many an anxious thought. Possibly his father-in-law, Jethro, from the knowledge and sagacity which he displayed in forming the government of Moses himself, may have assisted him in arriving at the conclusion which he must have so devoutly wished. To take them into the promised land with him was impossible; for the command of God, given in regard to Ishmael, the son of Abraham, by Hagar the Egyptian, and which was far more applicable to the mixed multitude, must have rung in his ears: "Cast out this bondwoman and her son, for the son of this bondwoman shall not be heir with my son, Isaac;" "for in Isaac shall thy seed be called." As slaves of Egypt they would not return to that country; they would not go north, for that was the heritage of the people of Israel, which had to be wrested from the fierce tribes of Palestine; they would not go north-east, for there lay the powerful empire of Assyria, or the germs out of which it sprung; they could not go south, for the ocean hemmed them in, in that direction; and their only alternative was to proceed east, through Arabia Petrea, along the gulf of Persia, through the Persian desert, into northern Hindostan, where they formed the Gipsy caste, and whence they issued, after the lapse of so many centuries, in possession of the language of Hindostan, and spread themselves over the earth. What a strange sensation passes through the mind, when such a subject is contemplated! Jews and Gipsies having, in a sense, the same origin, and, after such vicissitudes, meeting each other, face to face, under circumstances so greatly alike, in almost every part of the world, upward of 3000 years after they parted company. What destiny awaited the Jews themselves on escaping from Egypt? They had either to subdue and take the place of some other tribe, or be reduced to a state of slavery by it and perhaps others combined; or they might possibly have been befriended by some great empire as tributaries; or failing these three, what remained for them was the destiny that befell the Gipsies.

On leaving Egypt, the Gipsies would possess a common language, which would hold them together as a body; as slaves under the society of an Egyptian monarchy, they would have few, if any, opinions of a religious nature; and they would have but little idea of the laws of *meum* and *tuum*. The position in which they would find themselves placed, and the circumstances surrounding them, would necessitate them to rob, steal, or appropriate whatever they found to be necessary to their existence; for whether they turned to the right hand or to the left, they would always find territory previously occupied, and property claimed by some one; so that their presence would always be unwelcome, their persons an intrusion everywhere; and having once started on their weary pilgrimage, as long as they maintained their personal independence, they would never attain, as a body, to any other position than they have done in popular estimation, for the last four hundred and fifty years in Europe.

In entering Hindostan they would meet with a civilized people, governed by rigid caste, where they would have no alternative but to remain aloof from the other inhabitants. Then, as now, that country had many wandering tribes within its borders, and for which it is peculiarly favourable. Whatever might have been the amount of civilization which some of the Gipsies brought with them from Egypt, it could not be otherwise than of that *quasi* nature which generally characterizes that of slaves, and which would rapidly degenerate into a kind of barbarism, under the change of circumstances in which they found themselves placed. As runaway slaves, they would naturally be shy and suspicious, and be very apt to betake themselves to mountains, forests and swamps, and hold as little intercourse with the people of the country in which they were, as possible. Still, having been reared within a settled and civilized state, they would naturally hang around some other one, and nestle within it, if the face of the country, and the character and ways of the people, admitted of it. Having been bondsmen, they would naturally become lazy after gaining their freedom, and revel in the wild liberty of nature. They would do almost anything for a living rather than work; and whatever they could lay their hands on would be fairly come by, in their imagination. But to carry out this mode of life, they would naturally have recourse to some ostensible employment, to enable them to travel through the country, and secure the toleration of its inhabitants. Here their Egyptian origin would come to their assistance; for as slaves of that country, they must have had many among them who would be familiar with horses, and working in metals, for which ancient Egypt was famous; not to speak of some of the occult sciences which they would carry with them from that country. In the first generation their new habits and modes of life would become chronic; in the second generation they would become hereditary; and from this strange phenomenon would spring a race that is unique in the history of the human family. What origin could be more worthy of the Gipsies? What origin more philosophical?

Arriving in India a foreign caste, the Gipsies would naturally cling to their common origin, and speak their common language, which, in course of ages, would be forgotten, except occasional words, which would be used by them as catch-words. At the present day my Gipsy acquaintances inform me that, in Great Britain, five out of every ten of their words are nothing but common Hindostanee. How strange would it be if some of the other words of their language were those used by the people of Egypt under the Pharaohs. Mr. Borrow says: "Is it not surprising that the language of *Petulengro*, (an English Gipsy,) is continually coming to my assistance whenever I appear to be at a loss with respect to the derivation of crabbed words. I have made out crabbed words in Æschylus by means of his speech; and even in my Biblical researches I have derived no slight assistance from it." "Broken, corrupted and half in ruins as it is, it was not long before I found that it was an original speech, far more so, indeed, than one or two others of high name and celebrity, which, up to that time, I had been in the habit of regarding with respect and veneration. Indeed, many obscure points connected with the vocabulary of these languages, and to which neither classic nor modern lore afforded any clue, I thought I could now clear up by means of this strange, broken tongue, spoken by people who dwell among thickets and furze bushes, in tents as tawny as their faces, and whom the generality of mankind designate, and with much semblance of justice, as thieves and vagabonds."

A difficulty somewhat similar to the origin of the Gipsies has been started in reference to their language; whether it is a speech distinct from any other surrounding it, or a few slang words or expressions connected together by the usual languages of the countries in which the race is to be found. The slightest consideration will remove the doubt, and lead us to the former conclusion. It is true there must needs be some native words mixed up with it; for what language, in ancient or modern times, has come down free of a mixture with others? If that be the case with languages classified, written, and spoken in a community, with no disturbing element near it to corrupt it, is it to be expected that the speech of a people like the Gipsies can be free of similar additions or substitutions, when it possesses none of these advantages for the preservation of its entirety and purity? From the length of time the people have been in Europe, and the frequency of intercourse which they have been forced by circumstances, in modern times especially, to have with its natives, it would appear beyond measure surprising that even a word of their language is spoken at all. And this fact adds great weight to Sir Walter Scott's remark, when he says that "their language is a great mystery;" and to that of Dr. Bright, when he speaks of its existence as being "little short of the miraculous." But when we consider, on strictly philosophical principles, the phenomenon of the perpetuation of the Gipsy language, we will find that there is nothing so very wonderful about it after all. The race have always associated closely and exclusively together; and their language has become to them like the worship of a household god—hereditary, and is spoken among themselves under the severest of discipline. It is certain that it is spoken at the present day, by some of the race, nearly as well as the Gaelic of many of the immediate descendants of the emigrants in some of the small Highland settlements in America, when it has not been learned by book, even to the extent of conversing on any subject of ordinary life, without apparently using English words. But, as is common with people possessing two languages, the Gipsies often use them interchangeably in expressing the smallest idea. Besides the way mentioned by which the Gipsy language has been corrupted, there is another one peculiar to all speeches and which is, that few tongues are so copious as not to stand in need of foreign words, either to give names to things or wants unknown in the place where the language originated, or greater meaning or elucidation to a thing than it is capable of; and preëminently so in the case of a barbarous people, with few ideas beyond the commonest wants of daily life, entering states so far advanced toward that point of civilization which they have now reached. But the question as to the extent of the Gipsy language never can be conclusively settled, until some able philologist has the unrestricted opportunity of daily intercourse with the race; or, as a thing more to be wished than obtained, some Gipsy take to suitable learning, and confer a rarity of information upon the reader of history everywhere: for the attempt at getting a single word of the language from the Gipsies, is, in almost every case, impracticable. Sir Walter Scott seems to have had an intention of writing an account of the Gipsies himself; for, in a letter to Murray, as given by Lockhart, he writes: "I have been over head and ears in work this summer, or I would have sent the Gipsies; indeed I was partly stopped by finding it impossible to procure a few words of their language." For this reason, the words furnished in this work, although few, are yet numerous, when the difficulties in the way of getting them are considered. Under the chapter of Language will be found some curious anecdotes of the manner in which these were collected.

Of the production itself little need be said. Whatever may be the opinion of the public in regard to it, this may be borne in mind, that the collecting of the materials out of which it is formed was attended with much trouble, and no little expense, but with a singular degree of pleasure, to the author; and that but for the urgent and latest request of him whom, when alive or dead, Scotchmen have always delighted to honour, it might never have assumed its present form. It is what it professes to be—a history, in which the subject has been stripped of everything pertaining to fiction or even colouring; so that the reader will see depicted, in their true character, this singular people, in the description of whom, owing to the suspicion and secrecy of their nature, writers generally have indulged in so much that is trifling and even fabulous.

Such as the work is, it is offered as a contribution toward the filling up of that void in literature to which Dr. Bright alludes, in the introduction to his travels in Hungary, when, in reference to Hoyland's Survey, and some scattered notices of the Gipsies in periodicals, he says: "We may hope at some time to collect, satisfactorily, the history of this extraordinary race." It is likewise intended as a response to the call of a writer in Blackwood, in which he says: "*Our* duty is rather to collect and store up the *raw materials* of literature—to gather into our repository scattered facts, hints and observations—which more elaborate and learned authors may afterwards work up into the dignified tissue of history or science."

I deem it proper to remark that, in editing the work, I have taken some liberties with the manuscript. I have, for example, recast the Introduction, re-arranged some of the materials, and drawn more fully, in some instances, upon the author's authorities; but I have carefully preserved the facts and sentiments of the original. I may have used some expressions a little familiar and perhaps not over-refined in their nature; but my excuse for that is, that they are illustrative of a subject that allows the use of them.

EDITOR'S INTRODUCTION.

The discovery and history of barbarous races of men, besides affording exquisite gratification to the general mind of civilized society, have always been looked upon as important means toward a right understanding of the history of our species, and the relation in which it stands to natural and revealed theology; and in their prosecution have produced, in latter times, many instances of the most indefatigable disinterestedness and greatest efforts of true courage of which our nature is capable; many, in the person of the traveller, philanthropist and missionary, cheerfully renouncing in their pursuit every comfort of civilized life, braving death itself in every variety of form, and leaving their bones on the distant shore, or far away in the unknown interior of the dreary continent, without a trace of their fate to console those most dearly attached to them. The result of the discoveries hitherto made has invariably confirmed the conclusions of a few superior minds, formed without the assistance drawn from such a source, that under whatever circumstances man is placed, and whatever advantages he may enjoy, there is very little real difference between the characters, intrinsically considered, of the savage and man in what is considered a civilized community. There is this difference between what may be called barbarism, not unfrequently to be met with in a civilized community, springing from the depravity natural to man, and what obtains in a barbarous tribe or nation as such, that, in the former, it forms the exception; the brother, the father, or the son of the person of it often exhibiting the most opposite nature and conduct; while, in the latter, it forms the rule, and what the individual cannot, in a sense, avoid. But, in making this distinction, is there nothing to be found within the former sphere somewhat anomalous to the position thus presented?

The subject of the following enquiry forms the exception,

and from its being the only instance to be met with in the history of Europe, it may be said to merit the greatest consideration of the statesman, the historian, the philosopher, and the Christian.

It does not appear possible, from the peculiar mould in which the European mind has been cast, for it to have remained in that state of immobility which, from the remotest antiquity, seems to have characterized that of Asia; in which continent society has remained torpid and inactive, contented with what it has inherited, without making any effort at change or advancement. This peculiarity of character, in connexion with the influences of the Christian religion, seems to have had the effect of bringing about that thorough amalgamation of races and ideas in the various countries of Europe in which more than one people happened to occupy the same territory, or come under the jurisdiction of the same government, when no material difference in religion existed. In no country has such an amalgamation been more happily consummated than in our own; if not altogether as to blood, at least as to feeling, the more important thing of the two; the physical differences, in occasional instances, appearing in some localities, on the closest observation of those curious individuals who make such a subject the object of their learned researches.

Notwithstanding what has been said, how does it happen that in Europe, but especially in our own country, there exists, and has for four hundred years existed, a pretty numerous body of men distinct in their feelings from the general population, and some of them in a state of barbarism nearly as great as when they made their appearance amongst us? Such a thing would appear to us in no way remarkable in the stationary condition so long prevalent in Asia; where, in the case of India, for example, are to be found, inhabiting the same territory, a heterogeneous population, made up of the remnants of many nations; where so many languages are spoken, and religions or superstitions professed, and the people divided into so many castes, which are separated from each other on the most trivial, and, to Europeans, ridiculous and generally incomprehensible points; some eating together, and others not; some eating mutton, and others not; some beef and fowls, others vegetables, milk, butter and eggs, but no flesh or fish; those going to sea not associating with those remaining at home; some not following the occupation of others; and all showing the most determined antipathy to associate with each other;—where, from the numerous facilities so essential toward the perpetuation of peculiar modes of life, and the want of the powerful elements of assimilation and amalgamation so prominent in our division of the human race, a people may continue in a stereotyped state of mind and habits for an indefinite length of time. But in a country that is generally looked upon as the bulwark of the Reformation, and the stronghold of European civilization, how does it happen that we find a people, resembling in their nature, though not in the degree, the all but fabulous tribe that was lately to be found in the dreary wastes of Newfoundland, flying from the approach, and crossing the imagination of the fishermen like a spectre? Or like the wild men of the jungle, in some of the oceanic parts of Asia, having no homes, roaming during the dry season in the forests, and sleeping under or on the branches of trees, and in the rainy season betaking themselves to caves or sheltering beneath rocks, making their beds of leaves, and living on what they can precariously find, such as roots and wild honey; yet, under the influence of the missionary, many of them now raising crops, building dwellings, erecting school-houses, keeping the Sabbath, and praising God? But some of the Gipsies with us may be said to do few of these things. They live among us, yet are not of us; they come in daily contact with us, yet keep such distance from the community as a wild fowl, that occasionally finds its way into the farm-yard, does in shrinking from the close scrutiny of the husbandman. They cling like bats to ruined houses, caves, and old lime-kilns; and pitch their tents in dry water-courses, quarry-holes, or other sequestered places, by the way-side, or on the open moor, and even on dung-heaps for the warmth to be derived from them during the winter season, and live under the bare boughs of the forest during the summer;—yet amid all this apparent misery, through fair means or foul, they fare well, and lead what some call a happy life; while everything connected with them is most solicitously wrapt up in inscrutable mystery. These Gipsies exhibit to the European mind the most inexplicable moral problem on record; in so far as such phenomena are naturally expected to be found among a people whom the rays of civilization have never reached; while, in the case of the Gipsies, the first principles of nature would seem to be set at defiance.

> "And thus 'tis ever; what's within our ken,
> Owl-like, we blink at, and direct our search
> To fartherest Inde, in quest of novelties;
> Whilst here at home, upon our very thresholds,
> Ten thousand objects hurtle into view,
> Of interest wonderful."

But to give a fair description of the tented Gipsy life, I cannot employ more appropriate language than that of Doctor Bright, when, in reference to the English Gipsies, he says: "I am confident that we are apt to appreciate much too lightly the actual happiness enjoyed by this class of people, who, beneath their ragged tents, in the pure air of the heath, may well excite the envy of many of the poor, though better provided with domestic accommodation, in the unwholesome haunts of the town. At the approach of night, they draw around their humble but often abundant board, and then retiring to their tent, leave a faithful dog to guard its entrance. With the first rays of morning, they again meet the day, pursue their various occupations, or, rolling up their tents and packing all their property on an ass, set forward to seek the delights of some fresh heath, or the protection of some shaded copse. I leave it to those who have visited the habitations of the poor, to draw a comparison between the activity, the free condition, and the pure air enjoyed by the Gipsy, and the idleness, the debauchery, and the filth in which the majority of the poorer classes are enveloped."—"No sooner does a stranger approach their fire on the heath, than a certain reserve spreads itself through the little family. The women talk to him in mystic language; they endeavour to amuse him with secrets of futurity; they suspect him to be a spy upon their actions; and he generally departs as little acquainted with their true character as he came. Let this, however, wear away; let him gain their confidence, and he will find them conversable, amusing, sensible and shrewd; civil, but without servility; proud of their independence; and able to assign reasons for preferring their present condition to any other in civilized society. He will find them strongly attached to each other, and free from many cares which too often render the married life a source of discontent."

In what direction may we look for the causes of such an anomaly in the history of our common civilization? This question, however, will be discussed by and by: in the meantime let us consider the fact itself.

In the early part of the fifteenth century there first appeared in Europe large hordes of a people of singular complexion and hair, and mode of life—apparently an Asiatic race—which, in spite of the sanguinary efforts of the governments of the countries through which they passed, continued to spread over the continent, and have existed in large numbers to this day; many of them in the same condition, and following the same modes of life, now as then; and preserving their language, if not in its original purity, yet without its having lost its character. This circumstance has given rise in recent times to several researches, with no certain result, as to the country which they left on entering Europe, and still less as to the place or the circumstances of their origin. The latter is not to be wondered at, when it is considered that, in the instances of even the most polished nations of antiquity, nothing is to be found as to their origin beyond what is contained in the myths and fables of their earliest poets and historians. But considering the traces that have been left of the origin and early history of the people and kingdoms of Europe, subsequent to the fall of the Roman Empire, amid the barbarism and confusion attending their establishment, and, in many respects, the darkness immediately and for a long time following it, we would naturally think that, for an event happening so recently as the fifteenth century, some reliable traces would have been discovered and bequeathed to us on a subject that has baffled the antiquarians of modern times.

If, however, there is any doubt as to the country which they left on entering Europe, and their place of origin, there remains for us to consider the people generally, and in an especial manner those who have located themselves in Scotland; and give an account of their subsequent history in its various aspects, and their present condition. But before doing that, it would be well to take a general but cursory view of the political as well as social condition of Europe at the time they made their appearance in it, so as, in some measure, to account for the circumstance of no trace being left of their previous history; form an estimate of the relative position in which they have stood to its general population since; and attempt to realize the feeling with which they have always been regarded by our own people, so as to account for that singular degree of dread and awe which have always been associated with the mention of their name; the foundation of which has been laid in infancy.

That which most forcibly strikes the mind of the student, in reading the history of the age in which the Gipsies entered Europe, is the political turmoil in which nearly the whole of the continent seems to have been embroiled for the greater part of a century. The desperate wars waged by England against what has been termed her natural enemy, for the recovery and retention of her ancient continental possessions, and the struggle of the other for her bare existence; the long and bloody civil wars of England, and the distracted state of France, torn with dissensions within, and menaced at various points from without; the long and fanatical struggle of religion and race, between the Spaniards and their invaders, for the possession of the peninsula; the brave stand made by the Swiss for that independence so much theirs by nature; the religious wars of the Hussites, and the commotions throughout central Europe; the perpetual internal feuds of the corrupt and turbulent southern republics; the approaching dissolution of the dissolute Byzantine empire; the appalling progress of that terrible power that had emerged from the wilds of Asia, subdued the empire, and threatened Europe from its vulnerable point; all these seem to have been enough to have engrossed the mental energies of the various countries of Europe, and prevented any notice being taken of the appearance of the race in question.

But over and above these convulsions, sufficient as they were to exclusively engage the attention of the small amount of cultivated intellect then in the world, there was one that was calculated even to paralyze the clergy, to whom, in that age, fell the business of recording passing events, and which seems to have prevented their even taking notice of important matters in the history of that time. I mean the schism that for so long rent the church into fragments, the greatest schism, indeed, that the world ever saw, when, for so many years, two and even three Popes reigned at once, each anathematizing and excommunicating the other, for a schism which, after an infinity of intrigues, was ultimately so happily patched up to the comfort of the church. On the death of Urban V, Gregory XI became Pope, but soon after died, and was succeeded by Urban VI; but the Cardinals, who were in the French interest, after treating him as Pope for a short time, annulled the whole proceedings, on the plea of having been constrained in the election by the turbulence of the Roman populace, but really on account of the extraordinary harshness with which he began his reign, and chose one of themselves in his stead, under the name of Clement VII. The former remained at Rome, and was supported by Italy, the Empire, England and the North; while Clement proceeded to Avignon, and was acknowledged by France, Spain, Scotland, and Sicily. Urban was respectively succeeded by Boniface IX, Innocent VI, and Gregory XII; and Clement, at his death, in 1394, by Benedict XIII, the most implacable spirit in prolonging the schism, from whose authority France for a time withdrew, without acknowledging any other head, but afterwards returned, at the same time urging his resignation of the chair. At last the Cardinals, disgusted with the unprincipled dissimulation of both, and at their wits' end in devising a way to stay the scandal, and build up the influence of the whole church, then so rapidly sinking in the estimation of the world, amidst such unheard of calamities, deserted both, and summoned a council, which met at Pisa, and in which both were deposed, and another, in the person of Alexander V, elected to fill the chair. But in place of proving a remedy, the step rendered the schism still more furious. After that, John XXIII, successor to Alexander V, was reluctantly prevailed on to call a council, which accordingly met at Constance, in 1414, but in which he himself was deposed. Martin V being chosen, was succeeded by Eugenius IV. But the Fathers of Basle elected Felix V, thus renewing the schism, and dividing the church for some years, from France and the Empire observing a neutrality, while England adhered to Eugenius, Aragon and the smaller states to Felix; but the partisans of Felix gradually losing their influence, Nicholas V, the successor of Eugenius, after much cajolery, prevailed on him to resign his claim, and thus restored peace to the world.

At that time the kinds of learning taught were, in the

greater part of Europe, confined to few, being almost entirely monopolised by the clergy and a few laymen; by the former for the dogmatism of the schools and the study of the canon law, and by the latter for civil jurisprudence and medicine. Even the sons of nobles were generally wholly illiterate, one of them, only, being educated, to act as the clerk of the family. We are even told of a noble, when a conspiracy was detected, with the name of his son attached to it, saying, "Thank God, none of my children were ever taught to write." The great mass of the people, and especially those of the lower classes, were as ignorant of direct educational training as a tribe of semi-barbarians at the present day. Many of the nobility, although as scantily educated as the lowest of our own people, and having as much difficulty in inditing an epistle as some of these would now have, would still admirably maintain their position in such a state of society, by the influence which their high birth and breeding, elevated bearing, superiority of character, and possession of domain, gave them; and by the traditionary feudal awe that had sunk so deeply into the feelings of their comparatively, and often absolutely, abject dependents and followers, extending itself, when unaccompanied by overt acts of oppression, to the inhabitants of the smaller towns, where so many restraints surrounded their personal independence, from their precarious modes of living, owing to all so much depending on each other for a subsistence, and the endless jealousies prevailing among them.

At the same time all classes, although frequently possessing a sufficiency, if not an abundance, of the rough necessaries of life, enjoyed nothing of the comfort and elegancies of subsequent times. The house of many a noble presented such a plainness in furnishing as a person, in very moderate circumstances, would now be almost ashamed to possess. The circumstances of the middle classes were much more lowly; plain boards and wooden trenchers, few beds, but many *shake-downs*, rough stools and no chairs, with wonderfully few apartments relative to the size of the family, and much sleeping on straw-heaps in the *cock-loft*, marked the style of living of a class now deemed very respectable. The huts of the poorest class were as often composed of "sticks and dirt" as any other material, with *plenishing* to correspond. There was a marked exception to this state of comparative barbarism to be found, however, in some of the cities of Italy, and other parts of the Mediterranean, the seats of the flourishing republics of the middle ages; arising not only from the affluence which follows in the wake of extended commerce and manufactures, but also from the feelings with which the wreck of a highly polished antiquity inspired a people in whom the seeds of the former civilization had not died out; heightened, as it must have been, by the influence of the once celebrated, but then decaying, splendour which the court of the long line of eastern emperors shed over the countries lying contiguous to it. The inhabitants of the cities of the north, on the other hand, were marked by a degree of substantial wealth and comfort, sense and ease, civility and liberality, which were apt to distinguish a people situated as they were, without the traditions and objects, meeting the eye at every step in the south, of the greatest degree of culture in the polite arts of life unto which a people can attain. But, with the exception of the inhabitants of these cities, and some of those in a few of the cities of western Europe, the clergy and some of the laity, the people, as such, were sunk in deep ignorance and superstition, living in a state of which, in our favoured times, we can form no adequate conception. Then, life and property were held in little respect, and law trampled upon, even if it existed under more than the shadow of its present form; and no roads existed but such as were for the greater part of the year impassable, and lay through forests, swamps and other uncultivated wastes, the resorts of numerous banditti. Then, almost no intercourse existed between the people of one part of a country and another, when all were exceedingly sanguinary and rude.

What wonder, then, that, under such circumstances, the race in question should have stolen into Europe unobserved, without leaving a trace of the circumstances connected with the movement? The way by which they are supposed to have entered Western Europe was by Transylvania, a supposition which, if not true, is at least most likely. Although, when first publicly taken notice of in Europe, they were found to move about in large bands, it is unlikely that they would do that while entering, but only after having experienced the degree of toleration and hospitality which the representation of their condition called forth; at least if we judge from the cunning which they have displayed in moving about after their true character became known. Asia having been so long their home, where from time immemorial they are supposed to have wandered, they would have no misgiving, from their knowledge of its inhabitants, in passing through any part of it. But in contemplating an entry into Europe they must have paused, as one, without any experience of his own or of others, would in entering on the discovery of an unknown continent, and anxiously examined the merchants and travellers visiting Europe, on the various particulars of the country most essential to their prospects, and especially as to the characteristics of the people. There seems no reason for thinking that they were expelled from Asia againts their will; and as little for supposing that they fled rather than submit to a particular creed, if we judge from the great readiness with which, in form, they have submitted to such in Europe, when it would serve their purpose. The only conclusion, in regard to their motive of migration, to which we can come, is, that having, in the course of time, gradually found their way to the confines of Western Asia, and most likely into parts of Northern Africa, and there heard of the growing riches of modern Europe, they, with the restlessness and unsettledness of their race, longed to reach the Eldorado of their hopes—a country teeming with what they were in quest of, where they would meet with no rivals of their own race to cross their path. The step must have been long and earnestly debated, possibly for generations, ere it was taken; spies after spies may have surveyed and reported on the country, and the movement been made the subject of many deliberations, till at last the influence, address, or resolution of some chief may have precipitated them upon it, possibly at a time when some accidental or unavoidable cause urged them to it. Nor would it be long ere their example was followed by others of the tribe; some from motives of friendship; others from jealousy at the idea of all the imagined advantages being reaped by those going before them; and others from the desire of revenging unsettled injuries, and jealousy combined. After the die had been cast, their first step would be to choose leaders to proceed before the horde, spy out the richness of the land, and organize stations for those to follow; and then continue the migration till all the horde had passed over. Considering that the representative part of the Gipsies have retained their peculiarities almost uncontaminated, it is in the highest degree probable, it may even be assumed as certain, that this was the manner in which they entered Europe : at first stragglers, with systematic relays of stations and couriers, followed up by such small, yet numerous and closely following, companies, as almost to escape the notice of the authorities of the countries through which they passed ; a mode of travelling which they still pursue in Great Britain. But when any special obstacle was to be encountered in their journey —such, for example, as the hostility of the inhabitants of any particular place—they would concentrate their strength, so as to force their way through. Their next step would be to arrange among themselves the district of country each tribe was to occupy. After their arrival, they seem to have appeared publicly in large bands, growing emboldened by the generous reception which they met with for some time after their appearance ; and they seem to have had the sagacity to know, that if they secured the favour of the great, that of the small would necessarily follow.

But if the first appearance of the Gipsies in Europe had a different complexion from what I have conjectured, there are other causes to which may be attributed the fact of its not being known. Among these is to be found the distracted state of the Eastern Empire in its struggles with the Turks, which led to the capture of its capital, and the subversion of the Greek rule in the East. The literary and other men of note, scattered over the provinces, likely to chronicle such an event as the appearance of the Gipsies, must necessarily have betaken themselves to the capital, as each district submitted to the conquerors, and so lost the opportunity of witnessing the migration, under such circumstances as would have made it observable, assuming that the Gipsies travelled in large companies, which, under all the circumstances of the case, was not, on all occasions, likely. The surrounding countries having been the theatre of so many changes in the history of the human family, and the inhabitants having undergone so many changes of masters, leading to so many distinct races, from the intellectual and cultivated Greek to the barbarous Arab and dusky Moor, of so various hues and habits, many of whom would be found in such a city as Constantinople, what peculiarity was there about the Gipsies to attract the notice of the haughty Greek, characterized as he was by all the feelings of disdain which his ancestors displayed in not even naming the Jews and early Christians? Then, if we consider the peculiar turn which the new-born literary pursuits of learned men assumed during that age—how it was exclusively confined to the restoration of the classics, and followed in Europe by the influx of the Greeks during the troubles of their country, we will find another reason for the manner of the first appearance of the Gipsies not being known. Nor is it to be expected that any light would be thrown on the subject by the memoirs of any of our own countrymen, visiting the East at a time when so little intercourse existed between the West and that part of the world; nothing perhaps beyond a commercial or maritime adventurer, under the flag of another nation, or one whose whole acquirements consisted in laying lance in rest and mounting the breach in an assault; it being a rare thing even to see an English ship in the Mediterranean during the whole of the fifteenth century.

That the Gipsies were a tribe of Hindoo *Sudras*, driven, by the cruelty of Timour, to leave Hindostan, is not for a moment to be entertained; for why should that conqueror have specially troubled himself with the *lowest* class of Hindoos? or why should they, in particular, have left Hindostan? It would have been the *ruling*, or at least the *higher*, classes of Hindoo society against which Timour would have exercised any acts of cruelty; the *lowest* would be pretty much beneath his notice. Not only do we not read of such a people as the Hindoos ever having left their country on any such account—for it is contrary to their genius and feelings of caste to do so—but the opinion that the Gipsies left India on Timour's account rests on no evidence whatever, beyond the simple circumstance that they were first taken notice of in Europe *about* the time of his overrunning India. Mr. Borrow very justly remarks: "It appears singular that if they left their native land to escape from Timour, they should never have mentioned, in the western world, the name of that scourge of the human race, nor detailed the history of their flight and sufferings, which assuredly would have procured them sympathy; the ravages of Timour being already but too well known in Europe." Still, Mr. Borrow does not venture to give reasons for the trustworthiness or untrustworthiness of a passage in Arabschah's life of Timour, in which it is said that Gipsies were found in Samarcand at a time before that conqueror had even directed his thoughts to the invasion of India. The description given of these Zingarri or Gipsies of Samarcand is as applicable to the Gipsies as possibly can be; for in it it is said, "Some were wrestlers, others gladiators, others pugilists. These people were much at variance, so that hostilities and battling were continually arising amongst them. Each band had its chief and subordinate officers." How applicable this description is to the Scottish Gipsies, down to so late a period as the end of last century!

If there is little reason for thinking that the Gipsies left India owing to the cruelties of Timour, there is less for supposing, as Mr. Borrow supposes, that their being called Egyptians originated, not with themselves, but with others; for he says that the tale of their being Egyptians "probably originated amongst the priests and learned men of the east of Europe, who, startled by the sudden apparition of bands of people foreign in appearance and language, skilled in divination and the occult arts, endeavoured to find in Scripture a clue to such a phenomenon; the result of which was that the Romas (Gipsies) of Hindostan were suddenly transformed into Egyptian penitents, a title which they have ever since borne in various parts of Europe." Why should the priests and learned men of the east of Europe go to the Bible to find the origin of such a people as the Gipsies? What did priests and learned men know of the Bible at the beginning of the fifteenth century? Did every priest, at that time, know there even was such a book as the Bible in existence? The priests and learned men of the east of Europe were more likely to turn to the eastern nations for the origin of the Gipsies, than to Egypt, were the mere matter of the skill of the Gipsies in divination and the occult arts to lead them to make any enquiry into their history. But what could have induced the priests and learned men to take any such particular interest in the Gipsies? When the Gipsies entered Europe, they would feel under the necessity of saying who they were. Having committed themselves to that point, how could they afterwards call themselves by that name which Mr. Borrow supposes the priests and learned men to have given them? Or, I should rather say, how could the priests and learned men think of giving them a name after they themselves had said who they were? And did the priests and learned men invent the idea of the Gipsies being pilgrims, or bestow upon their leaders the titles of dukes, earls, lords, counts and knights of Little Egypt? Assuredly not; all these matters must have originated with the Gipsies themselves. The truth is, Mr. Borrow has evidently had no opportunities of learning, or, at least, has not duly appreciated, the real mental acquirements of the early Gipsies, an idea of which will be found in the history of the race on their first general arrival in Scotland, about a hundred years after they were first taken notice of in Europe, during which time they are not supposed to have made any great progress in mental condition. I may venture to say that the prophecy of Ezekiel,* in regard to the scattering of the Egyptians, does not apply to the Gipsies, for this reason, that such of these Egyptians as were *carried away captive* would become lost among other nations, while the "mixed multitude" which left Egypt with the Jews, travelled East, *their own masters*, and became the origin of the Gipsy nation throughout the world. If we could but find traces of an Egyptian origin among the Gipsies of Asia, say Central and Western Asia, the question would be beyond dispute. But that might be a matter of some trouble. I am inclined to believe that the people in India corresponding to the Gipsies in Europe, will be found among those tented tribes who perform certain services to the British armies; at all events there is such a tribe in India, who are called Gipsies by the Europeans who come in contact with them. A short time ago, one of these people, who followed the occupation of a camel driver in India, found his way to England,

* Ezek. xxix. 12,-14, and xxx. 10, 23, and 26.—The scattering of the Egyptians, here foretold, is a subject about which very little is known. Scott, in commenting on it, says: "History informs us that Nebuchadnezzar conquered Egypt, and carrying multitudes of prisoners hence, dispersed them in different parts of his dominions: and doubtless great numbers perished, or took shelter in other nations at the same time. But we are not sufficiently informed of the transactions of those ages, to show the exact fulfilment of this part of the prophecy, as has been done in other instances."

The bulk of the Egyptians were doubtless restored to their country, as promised in Ezek. xxix. 13, 14, and it is not impossible that the Gipsies are the descendants of such as did not return to Egypt. The language which they now speak proves nothing to the contrary, as, since the time in question, they have had opportunities to learn and unlearn many languages.

and "pulled up" with some English Gipsies, whom he recognized as his own people; at least he found that they had the ways and ceremonies of them. But it would be unreasonable to suppose that such a tribe in India did not follow various occupations. Bishop Heber, on several occasions, speaks of certain tents of people whom he met in India, as Gipsies. But I can conceive nothing more difficult than an attempt to elucidate the history of any of the infinity of sects, castes, or tribes to be met with in India.* What evidently leads Mr. Borrow and others astray, in the matter of the origin of the Gipsies, is, that they conclude that, because the language spoken by the Gipsies is apparently, or for the most part, Hindostanee, therefore the people speaking it originated in Hindostan; as just a conclusion as it would be to maintain that the Negroes in Liberia originated in England because they speak the English language!

The leaders of the Gipsies, on the arrival of the body in Europe, and for a long time afterwards, seem to have been a superior class to those known as Gipsies to-day; although, if the more intelligent of the race were observable to the general eye, they would, in many respects, compare most

* Abbé Dubois says: "In every country of the Peninsula, great numbers of foreign families are to be found, whose ancestors had been obliged to emigrate thither, in times of trouble or famine, from their native land, and to establish themselves amongst strangers. This species of emigration is very common in all the countries of India; but what is most remarkable is, *that in a foreign land, these emigrants preserve, from generation to generation, their own language and national peculiarities.* Many instances might be pointed out of such foreign families, settled four or five hundred years in the district they now inhabit, without approximating in the least to the manners, fashions, or even to the language, of the nation where they have been for so many generations naturalized. They still preserve the remembrance of their origin, and keep up the ceremonies and usages of the land where their ancestors were born, without ever receiving any tincture of the particular habits of the countries where they live."—Preface xvii.

At page 470, he gives an instance of a wandering tribe in the Mysore and Telinga country, originally employed in agriculture, who, a hundred and fifty years previously, took up their vagrant and wandering life, in consequence of the severe treatment which the governor of the province was going to inflict upon some of their favourite chiefs. To this kind of life they have grown so much accustomed, that it would be impossible to reclaim them to any fixed or sedentary habits; and they have never entertained a thought of resuming their ancient manners. They sojourn in the open fields, under small tents of bamboo, and wander from place to place as humour dictates. They amount to seven or eight thousand individuals, are divided into tribes, and are under the government of chiefs, and maintain a great respect for the property of others.

favourably with many of our middle classes. If the leaders of the Gipsies, at that time, fell behind some of even the nobility, in the pittance of the education of letters which the latter possessed, they made up for it in that practical sagacity, the acquisition of which is almost unavoidable in the school in which, from infancy, they had been educated—that of providing for the shifts and exigencies of which their lives, as a whole, consisted; besides showing that superior aptitude for many of the things of every-day life, so inseparable from the success to which a special pursuit will lead. A Gipsy leader stood, then, somewhat in the position towards a gentleman that a swell does to-day; with this difference, that he was not apt to commit himself by the display of that ignorance which unmasks the swell; an ignorance which the gentleman, in spite of his little learning, no less shared in. If the latter happened to be well educated, the Gipsy could still pass muster, from being as well, or rather as ill, informed as many with whom the gentleman associated. The Gipsy being alert, capable of playing many characters, often a good musician, an excellent player at games of hazard, famous at tale and repartee, clever at sleight of hand tricks, ready with his weapon, at least in the boast of it, apt at field and athletic sports, suspicious of everything and everybody around him, the whole energies of his mind given to, and his life spent in, circumventing and plundering those around him, while, in appearance, "living in peaceable and catholic manner," and "doing a lawful business," and having that thorough knowledge of men acquired by mixing with all classes, in every part of the country—he became even more than a match for the other, whose life was spent in occasional forays, field sports and revellings, with so little to engage his intellectual nature, from his limited education, the non-existence of books, and the forms of government and social institutions, with those beautifully complicated bearings and interests towards general society which the present age displays. At such a time, conversation must have been confined to the ordinary affairs of common life, the journal of much of which, beyond one's own immediate neighbourhood, would be found in the conversation of the accomplished Gipsy, who had the tact of ingratiating himself, in a manner peculiar to himself, with all kinds of society, even sometimes the very best. And it is remarkable that, when the Gipsies were persecuted, it was seldom, if ever, at the instance of private individuals, but almost always by those acting under authority. If they were persecuted by a private individual, they would naturally leave for another district, and place themselves, for a time, in the nominal position of a clansman to such barons as would be always ready to receive them. The people at large generally courted their friendship, for the amusement which they afforded them, and the various services which they rendered them, the most important of which was the safety of property which followed from such an acquaintance. That being the case even with people of influence, it may be judged what position the Gipsies occupied towards the various classes downwards; the lowest of which they have always despised, and delighted to tyrannize over. In coming among them, the Gipsies, from the first, exhibited ways of life and habits so dissimilar to those of the natives, and such tricks of legerdemain so peculiar to Eastern nations, and such claims of seeing into the future, as to cause many to believe them in league with the evil one; a conclusion very easily arrived at, in the darkness in which all were wrapped. Although the rabble of the Gipsies is said to have presented, in point of accoutrements, a most lamentable appearance, that could much more have been said of the same class of the natives, then, and long after, if we judge of a Highland "tail," of a little more than a century ago, as described by the author of Waverly; or even of the most unwashed of what has been termed the "unwashed multitude" of to-day. In point of adaptability to their respective modes of life, the poorest of the Gipsies far excelled the others. To carry out the character of pilgrims, the bulk of the Gipsies would go very poorly dressed; it would only be the chiefs who would be well accoutred.

But the Gipsies that appear to the general eye have fallen much from what they were. The superior class of Scottish Gipsies, possessing the talents and policy necessary to accommodate themselves to the change of circumstances around them, have adopted the modes of ordinary life to such an extent, and so far given up their wandering habits, as to baffle any chance of discovery by any one unacquainted with their history, and who will not, like a bloodhound, follow them into the retreats in which they and their descendants are now to be found. Such Gipsies are still a restless race, and nourish that inveterate attachment to their blood and language which is peculiar to all of them. When we consider the change that has come over the face of society during the last hundred years, or even during a much shorter time, we will find many causes that have contributed to that which has come over the Gipsy character in its more atrocious aspect. All classes of our own people, from the highest to the lowest, have experienced the change; and nowhere to a greater extent than in the Highlands, where, in little more than a hundred years, a greater reformation has been effected, than took almost any other part of the world perhaps three centuries to accomplish; and where the people, as a body, have emerged, from a state of sanguinary barbarism, into the most lawful and the most moral and religious subjects of the British Empire. The Gipsies have likewise felt the change. Even the wildest of them have had the more outrageous features of their character subdued; but it is sometimes as an animal of prey, sans teeth, sans claws, sans everything. Officials, in the zeal of their callings, often greatly distress those that go about—compelling them, in their wanderings, to "move on;" and look after them so closely, that when they become obnoxious to the inhabitants, the offence has hardly occurred, ere, to use an expression, they are snapped up before they have had time to squeak. Amid such a state of things, it is difficult for Gipsies to flourish in their glory; still, such of them as go about in the olden form are deemed very annoying.

The dread which has always been entertained toward the Gipsies has been carefully fostered by them, and has become the principal means contributing to their toleration. They have always been combined in a brotherhood of sentiment and interest, even when deadly feuds existed among them; an injury toward one being generally taken up by others; and have presented that union of sympathy, and lawless violence toward the community, which show what a few audacious and desperate men, under such circumstances, will sometimes do in a well regulated society. Sir Walter Scott, relative to the original of one of his heroines, says: "She was wont to say that she could bring, from the remotest parts of the island friends, to revenge her quarrel, while she sat motionless in her cottage; and frequently boasted that there was a time when she was of still more considerable importance, when there were at her wedding fifty saddled asses, and unsaddled asses without number." But of their various crimes, none have had such terrors for the grown-up person as those of fire-raising and child-stealing. The Gipsy could easily steal into a well guarded but scattered premises, by night, and, in an instant, spread devastation around him, and irretrievable ruin to the rural inhabitant. But that which has, perhaps, contributed most to the feeling in question, has been their habit of child-stealing, the terrors of which have grown up with the people from infancy. This trait in the Gipsy character has certainly not been so common, in latter times, as some others; still, it has taken place. As an instance, it may be mentioned that Adam Smith, the author of the great work called "An Enquiry into the Causes of the Wealth of Nations," was actually carried off by the Gipsies, when a child, and was some hours in their possession before recovery. It is curious to think what might have been the political state of so many nations, and of Great Britain in particular, at the present time, if the father of political economy and free-trade, as he is generally called, had had to pass his life in a Gipsy encampment, and, like a white transferred to an Indian wigwam, under similar circumstances, acquired all their habits, and become more incorrigibly attached to them than the people themselves; tinkering kettles, pots, pans and old metal, in place of separating the ore of a beautiful science from the débris which had been for generations accumulating around it, and working it up into one of the noblest monuments of modern times.

When a child will become unruly, the father will often say, in the most serious manner, "Mother, that canna be our bairn—the Tinklers must have taken ours, and left theirs—are you sure that this is ours? Gie him back to the Gipsies again, and get our ain." The other children will look as bewildered, while the subject of remark will instantly stop crying, and look around for sympathy; but meeting nothing but suspicion in the faces of all, will instinctively flee to its mother, who as instinctively clasps it to her bosom, quieting its terrors, as a mother only can, with the lullaby,

"Hush nae, hush nae, dinna fret ye;
The black Tinkler winna get ye."*

* The Gipsies frighten their children in the same manner, by saying that they will give them to the *Gorgio*.

And the result is, that it will remain a "good bairn" for a long time after. This feeling, drawn into the juvenile mind, as food enters into the growth of the body, acts like the influence of the stories of ghosts and hobgoblins, often so inconsiderately told to children, but differs from it in this respect, that what causes it is true, while its effects are always more or less permanent. It has had this effect upon our youth—in connection with the other habits of the people, so outlandish when compared with the ways of our own—that should they happen to go a little distance from home, on such expeditions as boys are given to, and fall in with a Gipsy camp, a strange sensation of fear takes possession of them. The camp is generally found to be pitched in some little dell or nook, and so hidden from view as not to be noticed till the stranger is almost precipitated into its midst ere he is aware of it. What with the traditionary feeling toward the Gipsies, and the motley assemblage of wild looking men, and perhaps still wilder looking women, ragged little urchins, ferocious looking dogs, prepared for an assault with an instinct drawn from the character of their masters, and the droll appearance of so many *cuddies* (asses,) startled in their browsing—animals that generally appear singly, but, when driven by Gipsies, come in battalions;—the boys, at first rivetted to the spot with terror, will slip away as quietly as possible till a little way off, and then run till they have either arrived at home, or come within the reach of a neighbourhood or people likely to protect them, although, it might be, the Gipsies had not even noticed them.* Curiosity is so strong in our youth, in such cases, as often to induce them to return to the spot, after being satisfied that the Gipsies have decamped for another district. They will then examine the débris of the encampment with a great degree of minuteness, wreaking their vengeance on what is left, by turning up with their feet the refuse of almost everything edible, particularly as regards the bones and feathers of fowl and game, and, if it happened to be near the sea, crab, limpet, and whelk shells, and heaps of tin clippings and horn scrapings. In after life, they will often think of and visit the scenes of such adventures. At other times, our youth, when rambling, will often make a

* As children, have we not, at some time, run, affrighted, from a Gipsy? —*Grellmann on the Hungarian Gipsies.*

detour of several miles, to avoid falling in with the dreaded Gipsies. The report of Gipsies being about acts as a salutary check upon the depredatory habits of the youth of our country towns on neighbouring crops; for, as the farmers make up their minds to lose something by the Gipsies, at any rate, the wholesome dread they inspire, even in grown-up lads, is such as, by night especially, to scare away the thieves from those villages, whose plunderings are much greater, and more unwillingly submitted to, from the closeness of residence of the offenders; so that the arrival of the Gipsies, in some places, is welcomed, at certain times of the year, as the lesser of two evils; and, to that extent, they have been termed the "farmers' friends." And if a little encouragement is given them—such as the matter of "dogs' payment," that is, what they can eat and drink, and a mouthful of something for the *cuddy*, for the first day after their arrival—the farmer can always enlist an admirable police, who will guard his property against others, with a degree of faithfulness that can hardly be surpassed. I heard of a Scottish farmer, very lately, getting the Gipsies to take up their quarters every year on the corner of a potato or turnip field, with the express purpose of using them, as half constables half scare-crows, against the common rogues of the neighbourhood. "Now," said he to the principal Gipsy, "I put you in charge of this property. If you want anything for yourselves, come to the barn." Whatever might have been the experience of farmers near by, this farmer never missed anything while the Gipsies were on his premises.

But a greater degree of awe is inspired by the females than the males of the Gipsies. In their periodical wanderings, they will generally, with their fortune-telling, turn the heads of the country girls in matters of matrimony—setting them all agog on husbands; and render them, for the time, of but little use to their employers. In teaching them the "art of love," they will professedly so instruct them as to have as many lovers at once as their hearts can desire. But if a country girl, with her many admirers, has one to get quit of, who is "no' very weel faured, but a clever fellow," or another, who is "no' very bright in the upper story, but strapping enough to become the dish-clout," she will call in the assistance of the strolling Gipsy; who, after carefully weighing the circumstances of the case, will sometimes, after ordinary means have failed, collect, unknown to her, a bucket full of everything odious about a dwelling, wait at the back door the return of the rustic Adonis, and, ere he is aware, dash it full in his face; then fold her arms akimbo, and quietly remark, "That will cool your ears, and your courting too, my man!" Such Gipsy women are peculiarly dreaded by the males of our own people, who will much sooner encounter those of the other sex; for, however much some of them may be satisfied, in their cooler moments, that these Gipsy women will not attempt what they will sometimes threaten, they generally deem them "unco uncanny," at any time, and will flee when swearing that they will *gut* or *skin alive* all who may have anything to say to them.

To people unacquainted with the peculiarities of the Gipsies, it may appear that this picture is overdrawn. But Sir Walter Scott, who is universally allowed to be a true depicter of Scottish life, in every form, says, in reference to the original of Meg Merrilees, in Guy Mannering: "I remember to have seen one of her grand-daughters; that is, as Dr. Johnson had a shadowy recollection of Queen Anne—a stately lady in black, adorned with diamonds; so my memory is haunted by a solemn remembrance of a woman, of more than female height, dressed in a long, red cloak, who commenced acquaintance by giving me an apple, but whom, nevertheless, I looked on with as much awe as the future Doctor could look upon the Queen." And he approvingly quotes another writer, as to her daughter, as follows: "Every week, she paid my father a visit for her *awmons*, when I was a little boy, and I looked on her with no common degree of awe and terror." The same feeling, somewhat modified, I have heard expressed by Germans, Spaniards, and Italians. In England, the people do not like to trouble the Gipsies, owing to their being so "spiteful," as they express it. The feeling in question cannot well be realized by people reared in towns, who have, perhaps, never seen Gipsies, or heard much about them; but it is different with youths brought up in the country. When the Gipsies, in their peregrinations, will make their appearance at a farmer's house, especially if it is in the pastoral districts, and the farmer be a man of information and reflection, he will often treat them kindly, from the interest with which their singular history inspires him; and others, not unkindly, from other motives. The farmer's sons, who are young and hasty, probably but recently returned from a town, where they have been jeered at for their cowardice in being afraid to meddle with the Gipsies, will show a disposition to use them roughly, on the cry arising in the house, that "the Tinklers are coming." But the old father, cautious with the teachings of years gone by, will become alarmed at such symptoms, and, before the Gipsies have approached the premises, will urge his children to treat them kindly. "Be canny now, bairns—be canny; for any sake dinna anger them; gie them a' they want, and something more." With this, a good fat sheep will sometimes be killed, and the band regaled with *kail*, and its accompaniments; or, if they are very *nice gabbit*, it will be served up to them in a roasted form. Thereafter, they will retire to the barn, and start in the morning on something better than an empty stomach.

And yet it is singular that, if the Gipsies are met in the streets of a town, or any considerably frequented place, people will, in passing them, edge off a little to the side, and look at them with a degree of interest, which, on ordinary occasions, the Gipsies will but little notice. But if a person of respectable appearance will scrutinize them in an ominous way, they will observe it instantly; and, as a swell-mobsman, on being stared at by a detective, on the mere suspicion of his being such, generally turns the first cross street, and, in turning, anxiously looks after his enemy, who, after calculating the distance, has also turned to watch his movements, so the Gipsy will become excited, soon turning round to watch the movements of the object of his dread; a fear that will be heightened if any of his band has been spoken to. And such is the masonic secrecy with which they keep their language, that should they at the time have rested on the road-side, and the stranger assume the most impressive tone, and say: "*Sallah, jaw drom*"—(curse you, take the road), the effects upon them are at first bewildering, and followed by a feeling of some dire calamity that is about to befall them. When any of the poorest kind can be prevailed upon to express a candid sentiment, and be asked how they really do get on, they will reply, "It's only day and way we want, ye ken—what a farmer body ne'er can miss; foreby selling a spoon, and tinkering a kettle now and then."

In viewing the effects of civilization upon a barbarous

race, we are naturally led to confine our reflections to some of the instances in which the civilized race has carried its influence abroad to those beyond its pale, to the exclusion of those instances, from their infrequency of occurrence, in which the barbarous race, of its own accord or otherwise, has come within its circle. There are but two instances, in modern times, in which the latter has happened, and they are well worthy of our notice. The one is, the existence of the Gipsies, in the very heart of civilization; the other, that of the Africans in the various European settlements in the New World; and between these a short comparison may be instituted, although at the risk of it being deemed a digression.

The forcible introduction of barbarous men into the colonies of civilized nations, in spite of the cruelties which many of them have undergone, has greatly improved their condition—their moral and intellectual nature—at the expense of the melancholy fact of it being advanced as a reason of justification for that sad anomaly in the history of our times. The African, it is admitted, was forcibly brought under the influence of the refinement, religion, and morals of the whites, whether as a domestic under the same roof, a field labourer, in the immediate vicinity of the master, or in some other way under his direct control and example. Not only was he, as it were, forced to become what he is, but his obedient, light-hearted, and imitative nature, even under many bodily sufferings, instinctively led him to enter immediately into the spirit of a new life, presenting to his barbarous imagination, so destitute of everything above the grossest of animal wants and propensities, those wonderfully incessant and complicated employments of a being, appearing to him as almost a god, when compared with his own savage and unsophisticated nature. The importations comprised Negroes of many dialects, which were distributed on arrival in every direction. A large proportion would live singly with the poorer classes of the colonists, as domestics; two or three would be the limited number with many others, and the remainder would be disposed of, in larger or smaller numbers, for the various services necessary in civilized life. Single domestics would be under the necessity of learning the language of the master; and, having none speaking their own dialect to commune with, or only occasionally meeting such, momentarily, they would soon forget it. When several of different dialects lived together, they would naturally follow the same course, to communicate with each other. All these circumstances, with the frequent changes of masters and companions, and the general influence which the whites exercised so supremely over them, have had the effect of almost erasing every trace of the language, customs, and superstitions of Africa, in part of the United States of America, in little more than one generation. The same may especially be said of what pertains to the religious; for a race of men, in a state of nature, or but slightly civilized, depending for such instruction on the adjunct of a superior grade, in the person of a priest, would, on being deprived of such, soon lose recollection of what had been taught them. Such an instance as to language, and, I understand, to a great extent as to religion, is to be found in St. Domingo; French and Spanish being spoken in the parts of that island which belonged to these countries respectively. Still, such traces are to be found in Cuba; but, were importations of Africans into that island to cease, the same result would, in course of time, follow. From such causes as those stated, the Negroes in the United States have, to a very great extent, nay, as far as their advantages and opportunities have gone, altogether, acquired the ways of civilized life, and adopted the morals and religion of the white race; and their history compares favourably with that of a portion of the Gipsy race, which, being unique, and apparently incomprehensible, I will institute a short enquiry into some of the causes of it.

While the language and common origin of the Gipsies hold them together as a body, their mode of life has taken such a hold on the innate nature of the representative part of them, as to render it difficult to wean them from it. Like the North American Indians, they have been incapable of being reduced to a state of servitude;* and, in their own peculiar way, have been as much attached to a life of unrestricted freedom of movement. Being an Oriental people, they have displayed the uniformity of attachment to habit, that has characterized the people of that part of the world. Like the maidens of Syria, wearing to-day the identical kind of veil with which Rebecca covered herself when she met

* There is an exception, however, to this rule in the Danubian Principalities, to which I will again refer.

Isaac, they have, with few exceptions, adhered to all that originally distinguished them from those among whom they are found. In entering Europe, they would meet with few customs which they would willingly adopt in preference to their own. Their chiefs, being men of ambition, and fond of a distinguished position in the tribe, would influence the body to remain aloof from the people at large; and society being divided between the nobles and their various grades of dependents, and the restrained inhabitants of towns, with what part of the population could the Gipsies have been incorporated? With the lowest classes only, and become little better than serfs—a state to which it was almost impossible for a Gipsy to submit. His habits rendered him unfit to till the soil; the close and arbitrary laws of municipalities would debar him from exercising almost any mechanical trade, in a way suitable to his disposition; and, no matter what might have been his natural propensities, he had almost no alternative left him but to wander, peddle, tinker, tell fortunes, and "find things that nobody ever lost." His natural disposition was to rove, and partake of whatever he took a liking to; nothing coming so acceptably and so sweetly to him, as when it required an exercise of ingenuity, and sometimes a degree of danger, in its acquisition, and caused a corresponding chagrin to him from whom it was taken, without affording him any trace of the purloiner. He must also enjoy the sports of the river and lake, the field, hill and forest, and the pleasure of his meal, cooked after his own fashion, in some quiet spot, where he would pitch his tent, and quench his thirst at his favourite springs. Then followed the persecution of his race; both by law and society it was declared outcast, although, by a large part of the latter, it was, from selfish motives, tolerated, and, in a measure, courted. The Gipsy's mode of life; his predatory habits; his vindictive disposition toward his enemies; his presumptuous bearing toward the lower classes, who had purchased his friendship and protection; his astuteness in doubling upon and escaping his pursuers; his audacity, under various disguises and pretences, in bearding justice, and the triumphant manner in which he would generally escape its toils; his utter destitution of religious opinions, or sentiments; his being a foreigner of such strongly marked appearance, under the legal and social ban of proscription;

and the hereditary name which has, in consequence, attached to his race, have created those broad and deep-drawn lines of isolation, fear and antipathy, which, in the popular mind, have separated him from other men. To escape from the dreadful prejudice that is, in consequence, entertained toward his race, the Gipsy will, if it be possible, hide the fact of his being a Gipsy; and more especially when he enters upon settled life, and mixes with his fellow-men in the world.

In the general history of Europe, we can find nothing to illustrate that of the Gipsies. But if we take a glance at the history of the New World, we will find, in a mild and harmless form, something that bears a slight resemblance to it. In various parts of the eastern division of North America are to be found remnants of tribes of Indians, living in the hearts of the settlements, on reserves of lands granted to them for their support; a race bearing somewhat the same resemblance to the European settlers that the Gipsies, with their dark complexion, and long, coarse, black hair, seem to have borne to the natives of Europe. Few of these Indians, although in a manner civilized, and professing the Christian religion, and possessing houses, schools and churches, have betaken, or, if they support their numbers, will ever betake, themselves to the ways of the other inhabitants. They will engage in many things to make a living, and a bare living; in that respect very much resembling some of the Gipsies. They will often leave their home, and build their wigwams whenever and wherever they have a mind, and indulge in the pleasures of hunting and laziness; and often make numerous small wares for sale, with the proceeds of which, and of the timber growing on their lots of land, they will manage to pass their lives in little better than sloth, often accompanied by drunkenness. If it prove otherwise, it is generally from the Indian, or rather half or quarter breed, having been wholly or partly reared with whites, or otherwise brought up under their immediate influence; or from the ambition of their chiefs to raise themselves in the estimation of the white race, leading, from the influence which they possess, to some of the lower grades of the tribes following their example. It may be that the "poor Indian" has voluntarily exiled himself, in a fit of melancholy, from the wreck of his patrimony, to make a miserable shift for himself elsewhere, as he best may. In this respect the resemblance fails: that the Indian in America is aboriginal, the Gipsy in Europe foreign, to the soil; but both are characterized by a nature that renders them almost impervious to voluntary change. In this they resemble each other: that they are left to live by themselves, and transmit to their descendants their respective languages, and such of their habits as the change in their outward circumstances will permit. But in this they differ: that these Indians really do die out, while the Gipsies are very prolific, and become invigorated by a mixture of the white blood; under the cover of which they gradually leave the tent, and become scattered over and through society, enter into the various pursuits common to the ordinary natives, and become lost to the observation of the rest of the population.

The peculiar feeling that is entertained for what is popularly understood to be a Gipsy, differs from that which is displayed toward the Negro, in that it attaches to his traditional character and mode of life alone. The general prejudice against the Negro is, to a certain extent, natural, and what any one can realize. If the European has a difficulty in appreciating the feeling which is exhibited by Americans against the African, in their general intercourse of daily life, few Americans can realize the feeling which is entertained toward the tented Gipsy. Should such a Gipsy be permitted to enter the dwelling of a native, the most he will let him come in contact with will be the chair he will give him to sit on, and the dish and spoon out of which he will feed him, all of which can again be cleaned. His guest will never weary his patience, owing to the embodiment of restlessness which characterizes his race; nor will his feelings ever be tried by his asking him for a bed, for what the herb commonly called catnip is to the animal somewhat corresponding to that word, a bundle of straw in an out-house is to the tented Gipsy.

INTRODUCTION.

The new era which the series of splendid works, called the Waverly Novels, created in literature, produced, among other effects, that of directing attention to that singular anomaly in civilization—the existence of a race of men scattered over the world, and known, wherever the English language is spoken, as Gipsies; a class as distinct, in some respects, from the people among whom they live, as the Jews at the present day. The first of the series in which their singular characters, habits, and modes of life were illustrated, was that of Guy Mannering; proving one of the few happy instances in which a work of fiction has been found to serve the end of specially stirring up the feelings of the human mind, in its various phases, toward a subject with which it has a common sympathy. The peasant and the farmer at once felt attracted by it, from the dread of personal danger which they had always entertained for the race, and the uncertainty under which they had lived, for the safety of their property from fire and robbery, and the desire which they had invariably shown to propitiate them by the payment of a species of blackmail, under the form of kind treatment, and a manner of hospitality when occasion called for it. The work at the same time struck a chord in the religious and humane sentiments of others, and the result, but a very tardily manifested one, was the springing up of associations for their reformation; with comparatively little success, however, for it was found, as a general thing, that while some of the race allowed their children, very indifferently, even precariously, to attend school, yet to cure them of their naturally wandering and other peculiar dispositions, was nearly as hopeless as the converting of the American Indians to some of the ways of civilized life. That general class was also interested, which consist of the more or less educated, moral, or refined, to whom anything exciting comes with relish. To the historical student, the subject was fraught with matter for curious investigation, owing to the race having been ignored, for a length of time, as being in no respect different from a class to be found in all countries; and, whatever their origin, as having had their nationality extinguished in that general process which has been found to level every distinction of race in our country. The antiquary and philologist, in their respective pursuits, found also a sphere which they were unlikely to leave unexplored, considering that they are often so untiring in their researches in such matters as sometimes to draw upon themselves a smile from the rest of mankind: and while the latter was thinking that he had exhausted the languages of his native land, and was contemplating others elsewhere, he struck accidentally upon a mine under his feet, and at once turned up a specimen of virgin ore; coming all the more acceptably to him, from those in possession of it keeping it as secret as if their existence depended on its being concealed from others around them. All, indeed, but especially those brought up in rural places, knew from childhood more or less of the Gipsies, and dreaded them by day or night, in frequented or in lonely places, knowing well that, if insulted, they would threaten vengeance, if they could not execute it then; which they in no way doubted, with the terror of doomed men.

Among others, I felt interested in the subject, from having been brought up in the pastoral district of Tweed-dale, the resort of many Gipsies, who were treated with great favour by the inhabitants, for many reasons, the most important of which were the desire of securing their good-will, for their own benefit, and the use which they were to them in selling them articles in request, and the various mechanical turns which they possessed; and often from the natural generosity of people so circumstanced. My curiosity was excited, and having various sources of information at command, I proceeded to write a few short articles for Blackwood's Magazine, which were well received, as the following letters from Mr. William Blackwood will show:

"I now send a proof of No. 2 Gipsy article. I hope you are pleased, and will return it with your corrections on Monday or Tuesday. We shall be glad to hear you are going on with the continuation, for I assure you your former article has been as popular as anything almost we ever had in the magazine."

Again,

"Your magazine was sent this morning by the coach, but I had not time to write you last night. Mr. Walter Scott is quite delighted with the Gipsies."

Again,

"I am this moment favoured with your interesting packet. Your Gipsies, from the slight glance I have given them, seem to be as amusing as ever."

And again,

"It was not in my power to get your number sent off. It is a very interesting one. You will be much pleased with Mr. Scott's little article on Buckhaven, in which he pays you some very just compliments."*

At the same time I was much encouraged, by the author of Guy Mannering, to prosecute my enquiries, by receiving several communications from him, and conversing with him at Abbotsford, on the subject.

* The following is the article alluded to: "The following enquiries are addressed to the author of the Gipsies in Fife, being suggested by the research and industry which he has displayed in collecting memorials of that vagrant race. They relate to a class of persons who, distinguished for honest industry in a laborious and dangerous calling, have only this in common with the Egyptian tribes, that they are not originally native of the country which they inhabit, and are supposed still to exhibit traces of a foreign origin. . . . . I mean the colony of fishermen in the village of Buckhaven, in Fife. . . . .

"I make no apology to your respectable correspondent for engaging him in so troublesome a research. The local antiquary, of all others, ought, in the zeal of his calling, to feel the force of what Spencer wrote and Burke quoted: 'Love esteems no office mean.'—'Entire affection scorneth nicer hands.' The curious collector who seeks for ancient reliques among the ruins of ancient Rome, often pays for permission to trench or dig over some particular piece of ground, in hopes to discover some remnant of antiquity. Sometimes he gets only his labour, and the ridicule of having wasted it, to pay for his pains; sometimes he finds but old bricks and shattered pot-sherds; but sometimes also his toil is rewarded by a valuable medal, cameo, bronze, or statue. And upon the same principle it is, by investigating and comparing popular customs, often trivial and foolish in themselves, that we often arrive at the means of establishing curious and material facts in history."

This extract is given for the benefit of the latter part of it, which applies admirably to the present subject; yet falls as much short of it as the interest in the history of an Egyptian mummy falls short of that of a living and universally scattered race, that appears a riddle to our comprehension.

I received a letter from Sir Walter, in which he says:

"This letter has been by me many weeks, waiting for a frank, and besides, our mutual friend, Mr. Laidlaw, under whose charge my agricultural operations are now proceeding in great style, gave me some hope of seeing you in this part of the country. I should like much to have asked you some questions about the Gipsies, and particularly that great mystery—their language. I cannot determine, in my own mind, whether it is likely to prove really a corrupt eastern dialect, or whether it has degenerated into mere jargon."

About the same time I received the following letter from Mr. William Laidlaw, the particular friend of Sir Walter Scott, and manager of his estate at Abbotsford, as mentioned in the foregoing letter; the author of "Lucy's Flittin," and a contributor to Blackwood:

"I was very seriously disappointed at not seeing you when you were in this (part of the) country, and so was no less a person than the mighty minstrel himself. He charged me to let him know whenever you arrived, for he was very anxious to see you. What would it be to you to take the coach, and three days before you, and again see your father and mother, come here on an evening, and call on Mr. Scott next day? We would then get you full information upon the science of defence in all its departments. Quarterstaff is now little practised; but it was a sort of legerdemain way of fighting that I never had *muckle broo of*, although I know somewhat of the method. It was a most unfortunate and stupid trick of the man to blow you up with your kittle acquaintances. I hope they will forgive and forget. I am very much interested about the language (Gipsy). Mr. Scott has repeatedly said, that whatever you hear or see, you should *never let on to naebody*, no doubt excepting himself. Be sure and come well provided with specimens of the vocables, as he says he might perhaps have it in his power to assist you in your enquiries."

Shortly after this, Sir Walter wrote me as follows:

"The inclosed letter has long been written. I only now send it to show that I have not been ungrateful, though late in expressing my thanks. The progress you have been able to make in the Gipsy language is most extremely interesting. My acquaintance with most European languages, and with slang words and expressions, enables me to say positively, that the Gipsy words you have collected have no reference to either, with the exception of three or four.* I have little doubt, from the sound and appearance, that they are Oriental, probably Hindostanee. When I go to Edinburgh, I shall endeavour to find a copy of Grellmann, to compare the language of the German Gipsies with that of the Scottish tribes. As you have already done so much, I pray you to proceed in your enquiries, but by no means to make anything public, as it might spread a premature alarm, and obstruct your future enquiries. It would be important to get the same words from different individuals; and in order to verify the collection, I would recommend you to set down the names of the persons by whom they were communicated. It would be important to know whether they have a real language, with the usual parts of speech, or whether they have a collection of nouns, combined by our own language. I suspect the former to be the case, from the specimens I have had. I should like much to see the article you proposed for the magazine. I am not squeamish about delicacies, where knowledge is to be sifted out and acquired. I like Ebony's† idea of a history of the Gipsies very much, and I wish you would undertake it. I gave all my scraps to the magazine at its commencement, but I think myself entitled to say that you are welcome to the use of them, should you choose to incorporate them into such a work. Do not be in too great a hurry, but get as many materials as you can."‡

And again as follows:

"An authentic list of Gipsy words, as used in Scotland, especially if in such numbers as may afford any reasonable

* I sent him a specimen of forty-six words. [Many words used in Scotland, in every-day life, are evidently derived from the Gipsy, owing, doubtless, to the singularity of the people who have used them, or the happy peculiarity of circumstances under which they have been uttered; the original cause of such passing current in a language, no less than that degree of personal authority which sometimes occasions them to be adopted. *Randy*, a disreputable word for a bold, scolding, and not over nicely worded woman, is evidently derived from the Gipsy *raunie*, the chief of a tribe of viragos; so that the exceptions spoken of are as likely to have been derived from the Gipsy as *vice versa*.—Ed.]

† The name by which Mr. Blackwood was known in the celebrated Chaldee manuscript, published in his magazine.

‡ Previous to this, Mr. Blackwood wrote me as follows: "I received your packet some days ago, and immediately gave it to the editor. He

or probable conjecture as to the structure of the language, is a desideratum in Scottish literature which would be very acceptable to the philologist, as well as an addition to general history. I am not aware that any such exists, though there is a German publication on the subject, which it would be very necessary to consult.* That the language exists, I have no doubt, though I should rather think the number to which it is known is somewhat exaggerated. I need not point out to you the difference between the *cant* language, or *slang*, used by thieves or flash men in general, and the peculiar dialect said to be spoken by the Gipsies.† The difference ought to be very carefully noticed, to ascertain what sort of language they exactly talk; whether it is an original tongue, having its own mode of construction, or a speech made up of cant expressions, having an English or Scotch ground-work, and only patched up so as to be unintelligible to the common hearer. There is nothing else occurs to me by which I can be of service to your enquiry. My own opinion leads me to think that the Gipsies have a distinct and proper language, but I do not consider it is extensive enough to form any settled conclusion. If there occur any facts which I can be supposed to know, on which you desire information, I will be willing to give them, in illustration of so curious an enquiry. I have found them, in general, civil and amenable to reason; I must, nevertheless, add that they are vindictive, and that, as the knowledge of their language is the secret which their habits and ignorance make them tenacious of, I think your researches, unless conducted with great prudence, may possibly expose you to personal danger. For the same reason, you ought to complete all the information you can collect, before alarming them by a premature publication, as, after you

desires me to say that your No. 5, though very curious, would not answer, from the nature of the details, to be printed in the magazine. In a regular history of the Gipsies, they would, of course, find a place." This was what suggested the idea of the present work.

* Grellmann. I am not aware that he ever compared the words I sent him with those in this publication, as he wrote he would do, in the previous letter quoted.

† Throughout the whole of his works there does not appear, I believe, a single word of the proper Scottish Gipsy; although slang and cant expressions are to be found in considerable numbers. [Some of these are of Gipsy extraction.—Ed.]

have published, there will be great obstructions to future communications on the subject."

From what has been said, it will be seen that the following investigation has had quite a different object than a description of the manners and habits of the common vagrants of the country; for no possible entertainment could have been derived from such an undignified undertaking. And yet many of our youth, although otherwise well informed, have never made this distinction; owing, no doubt, to the encreased attention which those in power have, in late years, bestowed on the internal affairs of the country, and the unseen, but no less surely felt, pressure of the advancement of the general mass, and especially of the lower classes of the community, forcing many of these people into positions beyond the observation of those unacquainted with their language and traits of character. When it is, therefore, considered, that the body treated of, is originally an exotic, comprising, I am satisfied, no less than five thousand souls in Scotland,* speaking an original and peculiar language, which is mysteriously used among themselves with great secrecy, and differing so widely from the ordinary natives of the soil, it may well claim some little portion of public attention. A further importance attaches to the subject, when it is considered that a proportionate number is to be found in the other divisions of the British Isles, and large hordes in all parts of Europe, and more or less in every other part of the world; in all places speaking the same language, with only a slight difference in dialect, and manifesting the same peculiarities. In using the language of Dr. Bright, it may be said, that the circumstance is the most singular phenomenon in the history of man; much more striking, indeed, than that of the Jews. For the Jews have been favoured with the most splendid antecedents; a common parentage; a common history; a special and exclusive revelation; a deeply rooted religious prejudice, and antipathy; a common persecution; and whatever might appear necessary to preserve their identity in the world, excepting an isolated territorial and political existence.† The Gipsies,

* There cannot be less than 100,000 Gipsies in Scotland. See Disquisition on the Gipsies.—Ed.

† The following is a description of the Jews, throughout the world, as given by them, in their letters to Voltaire: "A Jew in London, bears as

on the other hand, have had none of these advantages. But it is certain that the leaders of their bands, in addition to their piteous representations, must have had something striking about them, to recommend them to the favourable notice which they seem to have met with, at the hands of some of the sovereigns of Europe, when they made their appearance there, and spread over its surface. Still, their assumptions might, and in all probability did, rest merely upon an amount of general superiority of character, of a particular kind, without even the first elements of education, which in that age would amount to something; a leading feature of character which their chiefs have ever since maintained; and yet, although everything has been left by them to tradition, the Gipsies speak their language much better than the Jews.

Gipsies and Jews have many things in common. They are both strangers and sojourners, in a sense, wherever they are to be found; "dwelling in tents," the one literally, the other figuratively. They have each undergone many bloody persecutions; the one for his stubborn blindness to the advent of the Messiah, the other for being a heathen, and worse than a heathen—for being nothing at all, but linked with the evil one, in all manner of witchcraft and sin. Each race has had many crimes brought against it; the Gipsy, those of a positive, and the Jew, those of a constructive and arbitrary nature. But in these respects they differ: the Jew has been known and famed for doing almost anything for money; and the Gipsy for the mere gratification of his most innate nature—that of appropriating to himself, when he needs it, that which is claimed by any out of the circle of his consanguinity. The one's soul is given to accumulating, and, if it is in his power, he becomes rich; the other more commonly aims at securing what meets his ordinary wants, and, perhaps, some little thing additional;

little resemblance to a Jew at Constantinople, as this last resembles a Chinese Mandarin! A Portuguese Jew, of Bordeaux, and a German Jew, of Metz, appear two beings of a different nature! It is, therefore, impossible to speak of the manners of the Jews in general, without entering into a very long detail, and into particular distinctions. The Jew is a chamellon, that assumes all the colours of the different climates he inhabits, of the different people he frequents, and of the different governments under which he lives."

These words are much more applicable to the Gipsy tribe, in consequence of their drawing into their body the blood of other people.—Ed.

or, if he prove otherwise, he liberally spends what he acquires. The Gipsy is humane to a stranger, when he has been rightly appealed to; but when that circumstance is wanting, he will never hesitate to rob him, unless when he stands indebted to him, or, it may be, his immediate relations, for previous acts of kindness. To indulge his hatred towards an enemy, a Jew will oppress him, if he is his debtor, "exacting his bond;" or if he is not his debtor, he will often endeavour to get him to become such, with the same motive; or it may be, if his enemy stands in need of accommodation, he will not supply his wants; at other times, if he is poor, he will ostentatiously make a display of his wealth, to spite him; and, in carrying out his vengeance, will sometimes display the malignity, barring, perhaps, the shedding of blood, of almost every other race combined. In such a case, a Gipsy will rob, burn, maltreat, maim, carry off a child, and sometimes murder, but not often the two last at the present day.* The two races are to be found side by side, in countries characterized by almost every degree of climate and stage of civilization, each displaying its peculiar type of feature, but differing in this respect, that the Gipsies readily adopt others into their tribe, at such a tender age as to secure an infallible attachment to their race and habits. This circumstance has produced, in many instances, a change in the colour of the hair and eyes of the descendants of those adopted. In some such cases, it requires an intimate knowledge of the body, to detect the peculiarity common to all, and especially in those who have conformed to the ways of the other inhabitants. In this they agree—that they despise and hate, and are despised and hated by, those among whom they live. But in this they differ—that the Jew entered Europe, as it were, singly and by stealth, pursuing pretty much the avocations he yet follows; but the Gipsies, in bands, and openly, although they were forced to betake themselves to places of retreat, and break up into smaller bands. It is true that the Jew was driven from his home eighteen centuries ago, and that it is not yet five since the Gipsy appeared in Europe. We know who the Jew is, and something of the providence and circumstances under which he suffers, and what future awaits him; but who is this sin-

* This, I need hardly say, is a description of what may be called a *wild* Gipsy.—Ed.

gular and unfortunate exile, whose origin and cause of banishment none can comprehend—who is this wandering Gipsy?

After the receipt of the second of Sir Walter Scott's letters, already alluded to, I discontinued the few short articles I had written for Blackwood, on the Fifeshire Gipsies; but I have incorporated the most interesting part of them into the work, forming, however, only a small part of the whole. Since it was written, I have seen Mr. Borrow on the Gipsies in Spain, and the short report of the Rev. Mr. Baird, to the Scottish Church Society; the latter printed in 1840, and the former in 1841. The *Gitanos* in Spain, and the *Tinklers* in Scotland, are, in almost every particular, the same people, while the Yetholm Gipsy words in Mr. Baird's report, and those collected by me, for the most part, between the years 1817 and 1831, are word for word the same.

In submitting this work to the public, I deem it necessary to say a word or two as to the authorities upon which the facts contained in it rest. My authorities for those under the head of Fife and Linlithgowshire Gipsies, were aged and creditable persons, who had been eye-witnesses to the greater part of the transactions; in some cases, the particulars were quite current in their time. The details under the head of Gipsies who frequented Tweed-dale, Ettrick Forest, Annandale, and the upper ward of Lanarkshire, were chiefly derived from the memories of some of my relatives, and other individuals of credit, who had many opportunities of observing the manners of these wanderers, in the South of Scotland, the greater number being confirmed by the Gipsies, on being interrogated. The particulars under the head of the ceremonies of marriage and divorce, and the sacrifice of horses, were related by Gipsies, and confirmed by other undoubted testimony, as will appear in detail. Almost every recent occurrence and matter relative to the present condition, employment, and number of the body, is the result of my own personal enquiries and observations, while the whole specimens of the language, and the facts immediately connected therewith, were written down, with my own hand, from the mouths of the Gipsies themselves, and confirmed, at intervals, by others. Indeed, my chief object has been to produce facts from an original source, in Scotland, as far as respects manners, customs, and language, for the purpose of ascertaining the origin of this mysterious race, and the country from which they have migrated; and the result, to my mind, is a complete confirmation of Grellmann, Hoyland, and Bright, that they are from Hindostan.

In writing the history of any barbarous race, if history it can be called, the field for our observation must necessarily be very limited. This may especially be said of a people like the Gipsies; for, having, as a people, neither literature, records, nor education,* all that can be drawn together of their history, from themselves, must be confined to that of the present, or of such time as the freshness of their tradition may suffice to illustrate; unless it be a few precarious notices of them, that may have been elicited from their having come, it may be, in violent contact with their civilized neighbours around them. In attempting such a work, in connection with so singular a people, the difficulties in the way of succeeding in it are extraordinarily great, as the reader may have perceived, from what has already been written, and as the "blowing up," alluded to in Mr. Laidlaw's letter, will illustrate, and which was as follows:

I had obtained some of the Gipsy language from a principal family of the tribe, on condition of not publishing names, or place of residence; and, at many miles' distance, I had also obtained some particulars relative to the customs and manners of the race, from a highly respectable farmer, in the south of Scotland. At his farm, the family alluded to always took up their quarters, in their periodical journeys through the country. The farmer, without ever thinking of the consequences, told them that I was collecting materials for a publication on the Tinklers, in Scotland, and that everything relative to their tribe would be given to the world. The aged chief of the family was thrown into the greatest distress, at the idea of the name and residence of himself and family being made public. I received a letter from the family, deeply lamenting that they had ever communicated a word to me relative to their language, and stating that the old man was like to break his heart, at his own imprudence, being in agony at the thought of his language being published to the world. I assured them, however, that they had no cause for fear, as I had never so much as mentioned their names to

* There are, comparatively speaking, few Gipsies in Scotland that have not some education, in common with the ordinary natives of the soil; but the same cannot be said of England.—Ed.

their friend, the farmer, and that I would strictly adhere to the promise I had given them. This was one of the many instances in which I was obstructed in my labours, for, however cautious I might personally be, others, who became in some way or other acquainted with my object, were, from inconsiderate meddling, the cause of many difficulties being thrown in my way, and the consequent loss of much interesting information. But for this unfortunate circumstance, I am sanguine, from the method I took in managing the Gipsies, I would have been able to collect songs, and sentences of their language, and much more information than what has been procured, at whatever value the reader may estimate that, for the Gipsies are always more or less in communication with each other, in their various divisions of the country, especially when threatened with anything deemed dangerous, which they circulate among themselves with astonishing celerity.

Professor Wilson, in a poetical notice of Blackwood's Magazine, writes:

> "Few things more sweetly vary civil life
> Than a barbarian, savage Tinkler tale;
> Our friend, who on the Gipsies writes in Fife,
> We verily believe promotes our sale."

And, in revising his works, in 1831, Sir Walter Scott, in a note to Quentin Durward, says, relative to the present work:

"It is natural to suppose, the band, (Gipsy), as it now exists, is much mingled with Europeans; but most of these have been brought up from childhood among them, and learned all their practices. . . . When they are in closest contact with the ordinary peasants around them, they still keep their language a mystery. There is little doubt, however, that it is a dialect of the Hindostanee, from the specimens produced by Grellmann, Hoyland, and others who have written on the subject. But the author, (continues Sir Walter,) has, besides their authority, personal occasion to know, that an individual, out of mere curiosity, and availing himself, with patience and assiduity, of such opportunities as offered, has made himself capable of conversing with any Gipsy whom he meets, or can, like the royal Hal, drink with any tinker, in his own language.* The astonishment

* Allowance must be made for the enthusiasm of the novelist.

excited among these vagrants, on finding a stranger participant of their mystery, occasions very ludicrous scenes. It is to be hoped this gentleman will publish the knowledge he possesses on so singular a topic. There are prudential reasons for postponing this disclosure at present, for, although much more reconciled to society since they have been less the objects of legal persecution, the Gipsies are still a ferocious and vindictive people."*

* Abbotsford, 1st Dec., 1831.

CHAPTER I.

CONTINENTAL GIPSIES.

Before giving an account of the Gipsies in Scotland, I shall, by way of introduction, briefly notice the periods of time at which they were observed in the different states on the continent of Europe, and point out the different periods at which their governments found it necessary to expel them from their respective territories. I shall also add a few facts illustrative of the manners of the continental tribes, for the purpose of showing that those in Scotland, England, and Ireland, are all branches of the same stock. I shall, likewise, add a few facts illustrative of the tribe who found their way into England. I am indebted for my information on the early history of the continental Gipsies, chiefly to the works of Grellmann, Hoyland and Bright.

It appears that none of these wanderers had been seen in Christendom before the year 1400.* But, in the beginning of the fifteenth century, this people first attracted notice, and, within a few years after their arrival, had spread themselves over the whole continent. The earliest mention which is made of them, was in the years 1414 and 1417, when they were observed in Germany. In 1418, they were found in Switzerland; in 1422, in Italy; in 1427, they are mentioned as being in the neighbourhood of Paris; and about the same time, in Spain.†

They seem to have received various appellations. In France, they were called *Bohemians;* in Holland, *Heydens*—heathens; in some parts of Germany, and in Sweden and Denmark, they were thought to be *Tartars;* but over Germany, in general, they were called *Zigeuners*, a word which means wanderers up and down. In Portugal, they received

* Sir Thomas Brown's vulgar errors. † Bright's travels in Hungary.

the name of *Siganos*; in Spain, *Gitanos*; and in Italy, *Cingari*. They were also called in Italy, Hungary, and Germany, *Tziganys*; and in Transylvania, *Cyganis*. Among the Turks, and other eastern nations, they were denominated *Tschingenes*; but the Moors and Arabians applied to them, perhaps, the most just appellation of any—*Charami*, robbers.*

"When they arrived at Paris, 17th August, 1427, nearly all of them had their ears bored, with one or two silver rings in each, which, they said, were esteemed ornaments in their country. The men were black, their hair curled; the women remarkably black, and all their faces scarred."† Dr. Hurd, in his account of the different religions of the world, says, that the hair of these men was "frizzled," and that some of the women were witches, and "had hair like a horse's tail." It is, I think, to be inferred from this passage, that the men had designedly curled their hair, and that the hair of the females was long and coarse—not the short, woolly hair of the African. I have, myself, seen English female Gipsies with hair as long, coarse, and thick as a black horse's tail.

"At the time of the first appearance of the Gipsies, no certain information seems to have been obtained as to the country from which they came. It is, however, supposed that they entered Europe in the south-east, probably through Transylvania. At first, they represented themselves as Egyptian pilgrims, and, under that character, obtained considerable respect during half a century; being favoured by different potentates with passports, and letters of security. Gradually, however, they really became, or were fancied, troublesome, and Italy, Sweden, Denmark and Germany, successively attempted their expulsion, in the sixteenth century."‡

With the exception of Hungary and Transylvania, it is believed that every state in Europe attempted either their expulsion or extermination; but, notwithstanding the dreadful severity of the numerous laws and edicts promulgated against them, they remained in every part of Europe, in defiance of every effort made by their respective governments to get rid of their unwelcome guests.

* Hoyland's historical survey of the Gipsies. † Ibid. ‡ Bright.

"German writers say that King Ferdinand of Spain, who esteemed it a good work to expatriate useful and profitable subjects—Jews, and even Moorish families—could much less be guilty of an impropriety, in laying hands on the mischievous progeny of Gipsies. The edict for their extermination was published in the year 1492. But, instead of passing the boundaries, they only slunk into hiding places, and shortly after appeared in as great numbers as before. The Emperor, Charles V, persecuted them afresh; as did Philip II. Since that time, they nestled in again, and were threatened with another storm, but it blew over without taking effect.

"In France, Francis I passed an edict for their expulsion, and at the assembly of the states of Orleans, in 1561, all governors of cities received orders to drive them out with fire and sword. Nevertheless, in process of time, they collected again, and encreased to such a degree that, in 1612, a new order came out for their extermination. In the year 1572, they were compelled to retire from the territories of Milan and Parma; and, at a period somewhat earlier, they were chased beyond the Venetian jurisdiction.

"They were not allowed the privilege of remaining in Denmark, as the code of Danish law specifies: 'The Tartar Gipsies, who wander about everywhere, doing great damage to the people, by their lies, thefts and witchcraft, shall be taken into custody by every magistrate.' Sweden was not more favourable, having attacked them at three different times. A very sharp order for their expulsion came out in 1662. The diet of 1723 published a second; and that of 1727 repeated the foregoing, with additional severity.

"They were excluded from the Netherlands, under the pain of death, by Charles V, and afterwards, by the United States, in 1582. But the greatest number of sentences of exile have been pronounced against them in Germany. The beginning was made under Maximilian I, at the Augsburg Diet, in 1500; and the same business occupied the attention of the Diet in 1530, 1544, 1548, and 1551; and was also again enforced, in the improved police regulations of Frankfort, in 1577."* The Germans entertained the notion that the Gipsies were spies for the Turks. They were not allowed to pass through, remain, or trade within the Empire. They were ordered to quit entirely the German dominions, by a

* Hoyland.

certain day, and whoever injured them, after that period, was considered to have committed no crime.

"But a general extermination never did happen, for the law banishing them passed in one state before it was thought of in the next, or when a like order had long become obsolete, and sunk into oblivion. These undesirable guests were, therefore, merely compelled to shift their quarters to an adjoining state, where they remained till the government began to clear them away, upon which the fugitives either retired whence they came, or went on progressively to a third place—thus making a continual circle."*

That almost the whole of Christendom had been so provoked by the conduct of the Gipsies as to have attempted their expulsion, or rather their extermination, merely because they were jugglers, fortune-tellers, astrologers, warlocks, witches and impostors, is a thing not for a moment to be supposed. I am inclined to believe that the true cause of the promulgation of the excessively sanguinary laws and edicts, for the extermination of the whole Gipsy nation in Europe, must be looked for in much more serious crimes than those mentioned; and that these greater offences can be no other than theft and robbery, and living upon the inhabitants of the countries through which they travelled, at free quarters, or what we, in Scotland, call sorning.† But, on the other hand, I am convinced that the Gipsies have committed few murders on individuals *out* of their own tribe. As far as our authorities go, the general character of these people seems to have been the same, wherever they have made their appearance on the face of the earth; and the chief and leading feature of that extraordinary character appears to me to have been, in general, an hereditary propensity to theft and robbery, in men, women and children.

In whatever country we find the Gipsies, their manners, habits, and cast of features are uniformly the same. Their occupations are in every respect the same. They were, on

* Grellmann.

† Dr. Hurd says, at page 785, "our over credulous ancestors vainly imagined that those Gipsies or Bohemians were so many spies for the Turks; and that, in order to expiate the crimes which they had committed in their own country, they were condemned to steal from and rob the Christians."

[Living at free quarters by force, or masterful begging, or "sorning," is surely a trifling, though troublesome, offence for the original condition of a wandering tribe, which has so progressed as, at the present day, to fill some of the first positions in Scotland.—ED.]

the continent, horse-dealers, innkeepers, workers in iron, musicians, astrologers, jugglers, and fortune-tellers by palmistry. They are also accused of cheating, lying, and witchcraft, and, in general, charged with being thieves and robbers. They roam up and down the country, without any fixed habitations, living in tents, and hawking small trifles of merchandise for the use of the people among whom they travel. The whole race were great frequenters of fairs. They seldom formed matrimonial alliances out of their own tribe.* It will be seen, in another part of this work, that the language of the continental Gipsies is the same as that of those in Scotland, England and Ireland. As to the religious opinions of the continental Gipsies, they appear to have had none at all. It is said they were "worse than heathens." "It is, in reality," says Twiss, "almost absurd to talk of the religion of this set of people, whose moral characters are so depraved as to make it evident they believe in nothing capable of being a check to their passions." "Indeed," adds Hoyland, "it is asserted that no Gipsy has any idea of submission to any fixed profession of faith." It appears to me that, to secure to themselves protection from the different governments, they only conformed outwardly to the customs and religion of the country in which they happened to reside at the time.

Cantemir, according to Grellmann, says that the Gipsies are dispersed all over Moldavia, where every baron has several families subject to him. In Wallachia and the Sclavonian countries they are quite as numerous. In Wallachia and Moldavia they are divided into two classes—the princely and boyardish. The former, according to Sulzer, amount to many thousands; but that is trifling in comparison with the latter, as there is not a single Boyard in Wallachia who has not at least three or four of them for slaves; the rich have often some hundreds under their command.† Grell-

* Hoyland.

† In the narrative of the Scottish Church Mission of Enquiry to the Jews, in 1839, are to be found the following remarks relative to the Gipsies of Wallachia:

"They are almost all slaves, bought and sold at pleasure. One was lately sold for 200 piastres, but the general price is 500. Perhaps £3 is the average price, and the female Gipsies are sold much cheaper. The sale is generally carried on by private bargain. The men are the best mechanics in the country; so that smiths and masons are taken from this class. The women are considered the best cooks, and therefore almost

mann divides those in Transylvania into four classes: 1st, city Gipsies, who are the most civilized of all, and maintain themselves by music, smith-work, selling old clothes, horse-dealing, &c.; 2d. gold-washers; 3d. tent Gipsies; and 4th. Egyptian Gipsies. These last are more filthy, and more addicted to stealing than any of the others. Those who are gold-washers, in Transylvania and the Banat, have no intercourse with others of their nation; nor do they like to be called Gipsies. They sift gold sand in summer, and in winter make trays and troughs, which they sell in an honest way. They seldom beg, and more rarely steal. Dr. Clarke says of the Wallachian Gipsies, that they are not an idle race; they ought rather to be described as a laborious race; and the majority honestly endeavour to earn a livelihood.

every wealthy family has a Gipsy cook. Their appearance is similar to that of the Gipsies in other countries; being all dark, with fine black eyes, and long black hair. They have a language peculiar to themselves, and though they seem to have no system of religion, yet are very superstitious in observing lucky and unlucky days. They are all fond of music, both vocal and instrumental, and excel in it. There is a class of them called the Turkish Gipsies, who have purchased their freedom from government; but these are few in number, and all from Turkey. Of these latter, there are twelve families in Galata. The men are employed as horse-dealers, and the women in making bags, sacks, and such articles. In winter, they live in town, almost under ground; but in summer, they pitch their tents in the open air, for, though still within the bounds of the town, they would not live in their winter houses during summer."

That these Gipsies should be in a state of slavery is, perhaps, a more marked exception to their race than the Indians in Spanish America were to those found in the territories colonized by the Anglo-Saxons. The Empress Maria Theresa could make nothing of the Gipsies in Hungary, where they are said to be almost as little looked after as the wolves of the forest so that the slavery of the Gipsies in Wallachia must be of a very nominal or mild nature, or the subjects of it must be far in excess of the demand, if £3 is the average price of a good smith or mason, and less for a good female cook. These Wallachian Gipsies evidently prefer a master whose property they will consider as their own, and whose protection will relieve them from the interference and oppression of others. A slavery that is not absolute or oppressive must gratify the vanity of the owner, and be easily borne by a race that is semi-civilized and despised by others around it.

Since the conclusion of the Russian war, the manumission of the Gipsies of the Principalities was debated and carried by a majority of something like thirteen against eleven; but I am not aware of its having been put in force. They are said to have been greatly attached to the late Sultan—calling him the "good father," for the interest he took in them. As spies, they rendered his generals efficient services, while contending with the Russians on the Danube.—ED.

"Bessarabia, all Turkey, Bulgaria, Greece, and Romania swarm with Gipsies; even in Constantinople they are innumerable. In Romania, a large tract of Mount Hæmus, which they inhabit, has acquired from them the name of *Tschenghe Valken*—Gipsy Mountain. This district extends from the city of Aydos quite to Phillippopolis, and contains more Gipsies than any other province in the Turkish empire.

"They were universally to be found in Italy, insomuch that even Sicily and Sardinia were not free. But they were most numerous in the dominions of the Church; probably because there was the worst police, with much superstition. By the former, they were left undisturbed; and the latter enticed them to deceive the ignorant, as it afforded them an opportunity of obtaining a plentiful contribution by their fortune-telling and enchanted amulets. There was a general law throughout Italy, that no Gipsy should remain more than two nights in any one place. By this regulation, it is true, no place retained its guests long; but no sooner was one gone than another came in his room: it was a continual circle, and quite as convenient to them as a perfect toleration would have been. Italy rather suffered than benefited by this law; as, by keeping these people in constant motion, they would do more mischief there, than in places where they were permitted to remain stationary.

"In Poland and Lithuania, as well as in Courland, there are an amazing number of Gipsies. A person may live many years in Upper Saxony, or in the districts of Hanover and Brunswick, without seeing a single Gipsy. When one happens to stray into a village or town, he occasions as much disturbance as if the black gentleman with his cloven foot appeared; he frightens children from their play, and draws the attention of the older people, till the police get hold of him, and make him again invisible. In some of the provinces of the Rhine, a Gipsy is a very common sight. Some years ago, there were such numbers of them in the Duchy of Wurtemberg, that they were seen lying about everywhere; but the government ordered departments of soldiers to drive them from their holes and lurking-places throughout the country, and then transported the congregated swarm, in the same manner as they were treated by the Duke of Deuxponts. In France, before the Revolution, there were but few Gipsies, for the obvious reason that every Gipsy who could be apprehended fell a sacrifice to the police."*

As regards the Gipsies of Spain, Dr. Bright remarks: That the disposition of the Gitano is more inclined to a fixed residence than that of the Gipsy of other countries, is beyond doubt. The generality are the settled inhabitants of considerable towns, and, although the occupations of some necessarily lead them to a more vagrant life, the proportion is small who do not consider some hovel in a suburb as a home. 'Money is in the city—not in the country,' is a saying frequently in their mouths. In the vilest quarters of every large town of the southern provinces, there are Gitanos living together, sometimes occupying whole barriers. But Seville is, perhaps, the spot in which the largest proportion is found. Their principal occupation is the manufacture and sale of articles of iron. Their quarters may always be traced by the ring of the hammer and anvil, and many amass considerable wealth. An inferior class have the exclusive trade in second-hand articles, which they sell at the doors of their dwellings, or at benches at the entrance of towns, or by the sides of frequented walks. A still inferior order wander about, mending pots, and selling tongs and other trifling articles. In Cadiz, they monopolize the trade of butchering, and frequently amass wealth. Others, again, exclusively fill the office of Matador of the Bull Plaza, while the Terceros are for the most part of the same race. Others are employed as dressers of mules and asses; some as figure-dancers, and many as performers in the theatre. Some gain a livelihood by their musical talents. Dancing, singing, music and fortune-telling are the only objects of general pursuit for the females. Sometimes they dance in the inferior theatres, and sing and dance in the streets. Palmistry is one of their most productive avocations. In Seville, a few make and sell an inferior kind of mat. Besides these, there is a class of Gipsies in Spain who lead a vagrant life

* Grellmann.—I would suppose that these severe edicts of the French would drive the Gipsies to adopt the costume and manners of the other inhabitants. In this way they would disappear from the public eye. The officers of justice would of course direct their attention to what would be understood to be Gipsies—that is tented Gipsies, or those who professed the ways of Gipsies, such as fortune-telling. I have met with a French Gipsy in the streets of New York, engaged as a dealer in candy.—Ed.

throughout—residing chiefly in the woods and mountains, and known as mountaineers. These rarely visit towns, and live by fraud and pillage. There are also others who wander about the country—such as tinkers, dancers, singers, and jobbers in asses and mules.

Bishop Pococke, prior to 1745, mentions having met with Gipsies in the northern part of Syria, where he found them in great numbers, passing for Mahommedans, living in tents or caravans, dealing in milch cows, when near towns, manufacturing coarse carpets, and having a much better character than their relations in Hungary or England. By the census of the Crimea, in 1793, the population was set down at 157,125, of which 3,225 were Gipsies. Bishop Heber states that the Persian Gipsies are of much better caste, and much richer than those of India, Russia or England. In India, he says, the Gipsies are the same tall, fine-limbed, bony, slender people, with the same large, black, brilliant eyes, lowering forehead, and long hair, curled at the extremities, which are to be met with on a common in England. He mentions, in his journal of travels through Bengal, having met with a Gipsy camp on the Ganges. The women and children followed him, begging, and had no clothes on them, except a coarse kind of veil, thrown back from the shoulders, and a ragged cloth, wrapped round their waists, like a petticoat. One of the women was very pretty, and the forms of all the three were such as a sculptor would have been glad to take as his models.

Besides those in Europe, it is stated by Grellmann that the Gipsies are also scattered over Asia, and are to be found in the centre of Africa. In Europe alone, he supposes (in 1782), their number will amount to between seven and eight hundred thousand. So numerous did they become in France, that the king, in 1545, sixteen years before they were expelled from that kingdom, entertained an idea of embodying four thousand of them, to act as pioneers in taking Boulogne, then in possession of England. It is impossible to ascertain, at the present day, how many Gipsies might be even in a parish; but, taking in the whole world, there must be an immense number in existence.

About the time the Gipsies first appeared in Europe, their chiefs, under the titles of dukes, earls, lords, counts, and knights of Little Egypt, rode up and down the country on horseback, dressed in gay apparel, and attended by a train of ragged and miserable inferiors, having, also, hawks and hounds in their retinue. It appears to me, that the excessive vanity of these chiefs had induced them, in imitation of the customs of civilized society, to assume these high-sounding European titles of honour. I have not observed, on record, any form of government, laws or customs, by which the internal affairs of the tribe, on the Continent, were regulated. On these important points, if I am not mistaken, all the authors, with the exception of Grellmann, who have written on the Gipsies, are silent. Grellmann says of the Hungarian Gipsies: "They still continue the custom among themselves of dignifying certain persons, whom they make heads over them, and call by the exalted Sclavonian title of Waywode. To choose their Waywode, the Gipsies take the opportunity, when a great number of them are assembled in one place, commonly in the open field. The elected person is lifted up three times, amidst the loudest acclamation, and confirmed in his dignity by presents. His wife undergoes the same ceremony. When this solemnity is performed, they separate with great conceit, imagining themselves people of more consequence than electors returning from the choice of an emperor. Every one who is of a family descended from a former Waywode is eligible; but those who are best clothed, not very poor, of large stature, and about the middle age, have generally the preference. The particular distinguishing mark of dignity is a large whip, hanging over the shoulder. His outward deportment, his walk and air, also plainly show his head to be filled with notions of authority." According to the same authority, the Waywode of the Gipsies in Courland is distinguished from the principals of the hordes in other countries, being not only much respected by his own people, but even by the Courland nobility. He is esteemed a man of high rank, and is frequently to be met with at entertainments, and card parties, in the first families, where he is always a welcome guest. His dress is uncommonly rich, in comparison with others of his tribe; generally silk in summer, and constantly velvet in winter.

As a specimen of the manners and ferocious disposition of the German Gipsies, so late as the year 1726, I shall here transcribe a few extracts from an article published in Blackwood's Magazine, for January, 1818. This interesting article is partly an abridged translation, or rather the substance, of a German work on the Gipsies, entitled "A Circumstantial Account of the Famous Egyptian Band of Thieves, and Robbers, and Murderers, whose Leaders were executed at Giessen, by Cord, and Sword, and Wheel, on the 14th and 15th November, 1726, &c." It is edited by Dr. John Benjamin Wiessenburch, an assessor of the criminal tribunal by which these malefactors were condemned, and published at Frankfort and Leipsic, in the year 1727. The translator of this work is Sir Walter Scott, who obligingly offered me the use of his "scraps" on this subject. The following are the details in his own words:

"A curious preliminary dissertation records some facts respecting the German Gipsies, which are not uninteresting.

"From the authorities collected by Wiessenburch, it appears that these wanderers first appeared in Germany during the reign of Sigismund. The exact year has been disputed; but it is generally placed betwixt 1416 and 1420. They appeared in various bands, under chiefs, to whom they acknowledged obedience, and who assumed the titles of dukes and earls. These leaders originally affected a certain degree of consequence, travelling well equipped, and on horseback, and bringing hawks and hounds in their retinue. Like John Faw, 'Lord of Little Egypt,' they sometimes succeeded in imposing upon the Germans the belief in their very apocryphal dignity, which they assumed during their lives, and recorded upon their tombs, as appears from three epitaphs, quoted by Dr. Wiessenburch. One is in a convent at Steinbach, and records that on St. Sebastians' eve, 1445, 'died the Lord Pannel, Duke of Little Egypt, and Baron of Hirschhorn, in the same land.' A monumental inscription at Bautmer, records the death of the 'Noble Earl Peter, of Lesser Egypt, in 1453;' and a third, at Pferz, as late as 1498, announces the death of the 'high-born, Lord John, Earl of Little Egypt, to whose soul God be gracious and merciful.'

"In describing the state of the German Gipsies, in 1726, the author whom we are quoting gives the leading features proper to those in other countries. Their disposition to wandering, to idleness, to theft, to polygamy, or rather promiscuous licence, are all commemorated; nor are the women's pretentions to fortune-telling, and their practice of stealing children, omitted. Instead of travelling in very large bands, as at their first arrival, they are described as forming small parties, in which the females are far more numerous than the men, and which are each under command of a leader, chosen rather from reputation than by right of birth. The men, unless when engaged in robbery or theft, lead a life of absolute idleness, and are supported by what the women can procure by begging, stealing or telling fortunes. These resources are so scanty that they often suffer the most severe extremities of hunger and cold. Some of the Gipsies executed at Giessen pretended that they had not eaten a morsel of bread for four days before they were apprehended; yet are they so much attached to freedom, and licence of this wandering life, that, notwithstanding its miseries, it has not only been found impossible to reclaim the native Gipsies, who claim it by inheritance, but even those who, not born in that state, have associated themselves with their bands, and become so wedded to it, as to prefer it to all others.*

"As an exception, Wiessenburch mentions some gangs, where the men, as in Scotland, exercise the profession of travelling smiths, or tinkers, or deal in pottery, or practise as musicians. Finally, he notices that in Hungary the gangs assumed their names from the countries which they chiefly traversed, as the band of Upper Saxony, of Brandenburg, and so forth. They resented, to extremity, any attempt on the part of other Gipsies to intrude on their province; and such interference often led to battles, in which they shot each other with as little remorse as they would have done to dogs.† By these acts of cruelty to each other, they became gradually familiarized with blood, as well as with arms, to which another cause contributed, in the beginning of the 18th century.

"In former times, these outcasts were not permitted to

* The natives here alluded to were evidently Germans, married to Gipsy women, or Germans brought up from infancy with the Gipsies, or mixed Gipsies, taking after Germans in point of appearance.—Ed.

† This is the only continental writer, that I am aware of, who mentions the circumstance of the Gipsies having districts to themselves, from which others of their race were excluded. This author also speaks of the German Gipsies stealing children. John Bunyan admits the same practice in England, when he compares his feelings, as a sinner, to those of a child carried off by Gipsies. He gives the Gipsy *women* credit for this practice.—Ed.

bear arms in the service of any Christian power, but the long wars of Louis XIV had abolished this point of delicacy; and both in the French army, and those of the confederates, the stoutest and boldest of the Gipsies were occasionally enlisted, by choice or compulsion. These men generally tired soon of the rigour of military discipline, and escaping from their regiments, on the first opportunity, went back to their forests, with some knowledge of arms, and habits bolder and more ferocious than those of their predecessors. Such deserters soon become leaders among the tribes, whose enterprises became, in proportion, more audacious and desperate.

"In Germany, as in most other kingdoms of Europe, severe laws had been directed against this vagabond people, and the Landgraves of Hesse had not been behind-hand in such denunciations. They were, on their arrest, branded as vagabonds, punished with stripes, and banished from the circle; and, in case of their return, were put to death without mercy. These measures only served to make them desperate. Their bands became more strong and more open in their depredations. They often marched as strong as fifty or a hundred armed men; bade defiance to the ordinary police, and plundered the villages in open day; wounded and slew the peasants, who endeavoured to protect their property; and skirmished, in some instances successfully, with parties of soldiers and militia, dispatched against them. Their chiefs, on these occasions, were John La Fortune, a determined villain, otherwise named Hemperla; another called the Great Gallant; his brother, Antony Alexander, called the Little Gallant; and others, entitled Lorries, Lampert, Gabriel, &c. Their ferocity may be judged of from the following instances:

"On the 10th October, 1724, a land-lieutenant, or officer of police, named Emerander, set off with two assistants to disperse a band of Gipsies who had appeared near Hirzenhayn, in the territory of Stolberg. He seized on two or three stragglers whom he found in the village, and whom, females as well as males, he seems to have treated with much severity. Some, however, escaped to a large band which lay in an adjacent forest, who, under command of the Great Gallant, Hemperla, Antony Alexander, and others, immediately put themselves in motion to rescue their comrades, and avenge themselves of Emerander. The land-lieutenant had the courage to ride out to meet them, with his two attendants, at the passage of a bridge, where he fired his pistol at the advancing gang, and called out 'charge,' as if he had been at the head of a party of cavalry. The Gipsies, however, aware, from the report of the fugitives, how weakly the officer was accompanied, continued to advance to the end of the bridge, and ten or twelve, dropping each on one knee, gave fire on Emerander, who was then obliged to turn his horse and ride off, leaving his two assistants to the mercy of the banditti. One of these men, called Hempel, was instantly beaten down, and suffered, especially at the hands of the Gipsy women, much cruel and abominable outrage. After stripping him of every rag of his clothes, they were about to murder the wretch outright; but at the earnest instance of the landlord of the inn, they contented themselves with beating him dreadfully, and imposing on him an oath that he never more would persecute any Gipsy, or save any *fleshman*, (dealer in human flesh,) for so they called the officers of justice or police.*

"The other assistant of Emerander made his escape. But the principal was not so fortunate. When the Gipsies had wrought their wicked pleasure on Hempel, they compelled the landlord of the little inn to bring them a flagon of brandy, in which they mingled a charge of gunpowder and three pinches of salt; and each, partaking of this singular beverage, took a solemn oath that they would stand by each other until they had cut thongs, as they expressed it, out of the fleshman's hide. The Great Gallant at the same time distributed to them, out of a little box, billets, which each was directed to swallow, and which were supposed to render them invulnerable.

"Thus inflamed and encouraged, the whole route, amounting to fifty well armed men, besides women armed with clubs and axes, set off with horrid screams to a neighbour-

* Great allowance ought to be made for the conduct of these Gipsies. Even at the present day, a Gipsy, in many parts of Germany, is not allowed to enter a town; nor will the inhabitants permit him to live in the street in which they dwell. He has therefore to go somewhere, and live in some way or other. In speaking of the Gipsies, people never take these circumstances into account. The Gipsies alluded to in the text seem to have been very cruelly treated, in the first place, by the authorities.—Ed.

ing hamlet, called Glazbutte, in which the object of their resentment sought refuge. They took military possession of the streets, posting sentinels to prevent interruption or attack from the alarmed inhabitants. Their leaders then presented themselves before the inn, and demanded that Emerander should be delivered up to them. When the innkeeper endeavoured to elude their demand, they forced their way into the house, and finding the unhappy object of pursuit concealed in a garret, Hemperla and others fired their muskets at him, then tore his clothes from his body, and precipitated him down the staircase, where he was dispatched with many wounds.

"Meanwhile, the inhabitants of the village began to take to arms; and one of them attempted to ring the alarm-bell, but was prevented by an armed Gipsy, stationed for that purpose. At length their bloody work being ended, the Gipsies assembled and retreated out of the town, with shouts of triumph, exclaiming that the fleshman was slain, displaying their spoils and hands stained with blood, and headed by the Great Gallant, riding on the horse of the murdered officer.

"I shall select from the volume another instance of this peoples' cruelty still more detestable, since even vengeance or hostility could not be alleged for its stimulating cause, as in the foregoing narrative. A country clergyman, named Heinsius, the pastor of a village called Dorsdorff, who had the misfortune to be accounted a man of some wealth, was the subject of this tragedy.

"Hemperla, already mentioned, with a band of ten Gipsies, and a villain named Esper George, who had joined himself with them, though not of their nation by birth, beset the house of the unfortunate minister, with a resolution to break in and possess themselves of his money; and if interrupted by the peasants, to fire upon them, and repel force by force. With this desperate intention, they surrounded the parsonage-house at midnight; and their leader, Hemperla, having cut a hole through the cover of the sink or gutter, endeavoured to creep into the house through that passage, holding in his hand a lighted torch made of straw. The daughter of the parson chanced, however, to be up, and in the kitchen, at this late hour, by which fortunate circumstance she escaped the fate of her father and mother. When the Gipsy saw there was a person in the kitchen, he drew himself back out of the gutter, and ordered his gang to force the door, regarding the noise which accompanied this violence as little as if the place had been situated in a wilderness, instead of a populous hamlet. Others of the gang were posted at the windows of the house, to prevent the escape of the inmates. Nevertheless, the young woman, already mentioned, let herself down from a window which had escaped their notice, and ran to seek assistance for her parents.

"In the meanwhile the Gipsies had burst open the outward door of the house, with a beam of wood which chanced to be lying in the court-yard. They next forced the door of the sitting apartment, and were met by the poor clergyman, who prayed them at least to spare his life and that of his wife. But he spoke to men who knew no mercy; Hemperla struck him on the breast with a torch; and receiving the blow as a signal for death, the poor man staggered back to the table, and sinking in a chair, leaned his head on his hand, and expected the mortal blow. In this posture Hemperla shot him dead with a pistol. The wife of the clergyman endeavoured to fly, on witnessing the murder of her husband, but was dragged back, and slain by a pistol-shot, fired either by Easper George, or by a Gipsy called Christian. By a crime so dreadful those murderers only gained four silver cups, fourteen silver spoons, some trifling articles of apparel, and about twenty-two florins in money. They might have made more important booty, but the sentinel, whom they left on the outside, now intimated to them that the hamlet was alarmed, and that it was time to retire, which they did accordingly, undisturbed and in safety.

"The Gipsies committed many enormities similar to those above detailed, and arrived at such a pitch of audacity as even to threaten the person of the Landgrave himself; an enormity at which Dr. Wiessenburch, who never introduces the name or titles of that prince without printing them in letters of at least an inch long, expresses becoming horror. This was too much to be endured. Strong detachments of troops and militia scoured the country in different directions, and searched the woods and caverns which served the banditti for places of retreat. These measures were for some time attended with little effect. The Gipsies had the advantages of a perfect knowledge of the country and excellent intelligence. They baffled the efforts of the officers detached against them, and, on one or two occasions, even engaged them with advantage. And when some females, unable to follow the retreat of the men, were made prisoners on such an occasion, the leaders caused it to be intimated to the authorities at Giessen that if their women were not set at liberty, they would murder and rob on the high roads, and plunder and burn the country. This state of warfare lasted from 1718 until 1726, during which period the subjects of the Landgrave suffered the utmost hardships, as no man was secure against nocturnal surprise of his property and person.

"At length, in the end of 1725, a heavy and continued storm of snow compelled the Gipsy hordes to abandon the woods which had long served them as a refuge, and to approach more near to the dwellings of men. As their movements could be traced and observed, the land-lieutenant, Krocker, who had been an assistant to the murdered Emerander, received intelligence of a band of Gipsies having appeared in the district of Sohnsassenheim, at a village called Fauerbach. Being aided by a party of soldiers and volunteers, he had the luck to secure the whole gang, being twelve men and women. Among these was the notorious Hemperla, who was dragged by the heels from an oven in which he was attempting to conceal himself. Others were taken in the same manner, and imprisoned at Giessen, with a view to their trial.

"Numerous acts of theft, and robbery, and murder were laid to the charge of these unfortunate wretches; and, according to the existing laws of the empire, they were interrogated under torture. They were first tormented by means of thumb-screws, which they did not seem greatly to regard; the Spanish boots, or 'leg-vices,' were next applied, and seldom failed to extort confession. Hemperla alone set both means at defiance, which induced the judges to believe he was possessed of some spell against these agonies. Having in vain searched his body for the supposed charm, they caused his hair to be cut off; on which he himself observed that, had they not done so, he could have stood the torture for some time longer. As it was, his resolution gave way, and he made, under the second application of the Spanish boots, a full confession, not only of the murders of which he was accused, but of various other crimes. While he was in this agony, the judges had the cruelty to introduce his mother, a noted Gipsy woman, called the crone, into the torture-chamber; who shrieked fearfully, and tore her face with her nails, on perceiving the condition of her son, and still more on hearing him acknowledge his guilt.

"Evidence of the guilt of the other prisoners was also obtained from their confessions, with or without torture, and from the testimony of witnesses examined by the fiscal. Sentence was finally passed on them, condemning four Gipsies, among whom were Hemperla and the Little Gallant, to be broken on the wheel, nine others to be hanged, and thirteen, of whom the greater part were women, to be beheaded. They underwent their doom with great firmness, upon the 14th and 15th November, 1726.

"The volume contains . . . . . . some rude prints, representing the murders committed by the Gipsies, and the manner of their execution. There are also two prints representing the portraits of the principal criminals, in which, though the execution be indifferent, the Gipsy features may be clearly traced."

Leaving this view of the character of the continental Gipsies, we may take the following as illustrative of one of its brighter aspects. So late as the time of the celebrated Baron Trenck, it would appear that Germany was still infested with prodigiously large bands of Gipsies. In a forest near Ginnen, to which he had fled, to conceal himself from the pursuit of his persecutors, the Baron says: "Here we fell in with a gang of Gipsies, (or rather banditti,) amounting to four hundred men, who dragged me to their camp. They were mostly French and Prussian deserters, and, thinking me their equal, would force me to become one of their band. But venturing to tell my story to their leader, he presented me with a crown, gave us a small portion of bread and meat, and suffered us to depart in peace, after having been four-and-twenty hours in their company."*

I shall conclude the notices of the continental Gipsies by some extracts from an article published in a French periodical work, for September, 1802, on the Gipsies of the Pyrenees; who resemble, in many points, the inferior class of our Scottish Tinklers, about the beginning of the French war, more, perhaps, than those of any other country in Europe.

* Life of Baron Trenck, translated by Thomas Holcroft, Vol. I., page 122.

"There exists, in the department of the Eastern Pyrenees, a people distinct from the rest of the inhabitants, of a foreign origin, and without any settled habits. It seems to have fixed its residence there for a considerable time. It changes its situation, multiplies there, and never connects itself by marriage with the other inhabitants. This people are called Gitanos, a Spanish word which signifies Egyptians. There are many Gitanos in Catalonia, who have similar habits to the above-mentioned, but who are very strictly watched. They have all the vices of those Egyptians, or Bohemians, who formerly used to wander over the world, telling fortunes, and living at the expense of superstition and credulity. These Gitanos, less idle and less wanderers than their predecessors, are afraid of publicly professing the art of fortune-tellers; but their manner of life is scarcely different.

"They scatter themselves among villages, and lonesome farms, where they steal fruit, poultry, and often even cattle; in short, everything that is portable. They are almost always abroad, incessantly watching an opportunity to practise their thievery; they hide themselves with much dexterity from the search of the police. Their women, in particular, have an uncommon dexterity in pilfering. When they enter a shop, they are watched with the utmost care; but with every precaution they are not free from their rapines. They excel, above all, in hiding the pieces of silver which are given in exchange for gold, which they never fail to offer in payment, and they are so well hidden that they are often obliged to be undressed before restitution can be obtained.

"The Gitanos affect, externally, a great attachment to the Catholic religion; and if one was to judge from the number of reliques they carry about with them, one would believe them exceedingly devout; but all who have well observed them assure us they are as ignorant as hypocritical, and that they practise secretly a religion of their own. It is not rare to see their women, who have been lately brought to bed, have their children baptized several times, in different places, in order to obtain money from persons at their ease, whom they choose for godfathers. Everything announces among them that moral degradation which must necessarily attach to a miserable, insulated caste, as strangers to society, which only suffers it through an excess of contempt.

"The Gitanos are disgustingly filthy, and almost all covered with rags. They have neither tables, chairs, nor beds, but sit and eat on the ground. They are crowded in huts, pell-mell, in straw; and their neglect of the decorum of society, so dangerous to morals, must have the most melancholy consequences on wretched vagabonds, abandoned to themselves. They consequently are accused of giving themselves up to every disorder of the most infamous debauchery, and to respect neither the ties of blood nor the protecting laws of the virtues of families.

"They feed on rotten poultry and fish, dogs and stinking cats, which they seek for with avidity; and when this resource fails them, they live on the entrails of animals, or other aliments of the lowest price. They leave their meat but a very few minutes on the fire, and the place where they cook it exhales an infectious smell.

"They speak the Catalonian dialect, but they have, besides, a language to themselves, unintelligible to the natives of the country, from whom they are very careful to hide the knowledge of it.

"The Gitanos are tanned like the mulattoes, of a size above mediocrity, well formed, active, robust, supporting all the changes of seasons, and sleeping in the open fields, whenever their interest requires it. Their features are irregular, and show them to belong to a transplanted race. They have the mouth very wide, thick lips, and high cheek-bones.

"As the distrust they inspire causes them to be carefully watched, it is not always possible for them to live by stealing: they then have recourse to industry, and a trifling trade, which seems to have been abandoned to them; they show animals, and attend the fairs and markets, to sell or exchange mules and asses, which they know how to procure at a cheap rate. They are commonly cast-off animals, which they have the art to dress up, and they are satisfied, in appearance, with a moderate profit, which, however, is always more than is supposed, because they feed these animals at the expense of the farmers. They ramble all night, in order to steal fodder; and whatever precautions may have been taken against them, it is not possible to be always guarded against their address.

"Happily the Gitanos are not murderers. It would, without doubt, be important to examine if it is to the natural goodness of their disposition, to their frugality, and the few wants they feel in their state of half savage, that is to be attributed the sentiment that repels them from great crimes, or if this disposition arises from their habitual state of alarm, or from that want of courage which must be a necessary consequence of the infamy in which they are plunged.*

* *Annals de Statistique, No. III, page* 31-37.—What the writer of this article says of the aversion which the Gipsies have to the shedding of human blood, *not of their own fraternity,* appears to have been universal among the tribe; but, on the other hand, they seem to have had little or no hesitation in putting to death *those of their own tribe.* This writer also says, that the Gipsies of the Pyrenees have a religion of their own, which they practise *secretly,* without mentioning what this secret religion is. It is probable that his remark is applicable to the sacrifice of horses, as described in chapter viii.

CHAPTER II.

ENGLISH GIPSIES.

THE first arrival of the Gipsies in England appears to have been about the year 1512,* but this does not seem to be quite certain. It is probable they may have arrived there at an earlier period. The author from which the fact is derived published his work in 1612, and states, generally, that "this kind of people, about a hundred years ago, began to gather an head, about the southern parts. And this, I am informed and can gather, was their beginning: Certain Egyptians, banished their country, (belike not for their good condition,) arrived here in England; who, for quaint tricks and devices, not known here at that time among us, were esteemed, and held in great admiration; insomuch that many of our English loiterers joined with them, and in time learned their crafty cozening.

"The speech which they used was the right Egyptian language, with whom our Englishmen conversing at least learned their language. These people, continuing about the country, and practising their cozening art, purchased themselves great credit among the country people, and got much by palmistry and telling of fortunes; insomuch that they pitifully cozened poor country girls both of money, silver spoons, and the best of their apparel, or any goods they could make."†

From this author it is collected they had a leader of the name of Giles Hather, who was termed their king; and a woman of the name of Calot was called queen. These, riding through the country on horseback, and in strange attire, had a pretty train after them.‡

* Hoyland.

† A quarto work by S. R., published to detect and expose the art of juggling and legerdemain, in 1612.

‡ Hoyland.

It appears, from this account, that the Gipsies had been observed on the continent about a hundred years before they visited England. According to Dr. Bright, they seemed to have roamed up and down the continent of Europe, without molestation, for about half a century, before their true character was perfectly known. If 1512 was really the year in which these people first set foot in England, it would seem that the English government had not been so easily nor so long imposed on as the kings of Scotland, and the authorities of Europe generally. For we find that, within about the space of ten years from this period, they are, by the 10th chapter of the 22d Henry VIII, denominated "an outlandish people, calling themselves Egyptians, using no craft nor feat of merchandise, who have come into this realm, and gone from shire to shire, and place to place, in great company; and used great subtlety and crafty means to deceive the people—bearing them in hand that they, by palmistry, could tell men's and women's fortunes; and so, many times, by craft and subtlety, have deceived the people for their money; and also have committed many heinous felonies and robberies." As far back as the year 1549, they had become very troublesome in England, for, on the 22d June of that year, according to Burnet's History of the Reformation, "there was privy search made through all Sussex for all vagabonds, Gipsies, conspirators, prophesiers, players, and such like."

The Gipsies in England still continued to commit numberless thefts and robberies, in defiance of the existing statutes; so that each succeeding law enacted against them became severer than the one which preceded it. The following is an extract from the 27th Henry VIII: "Whereas, certain outlandish people, who do not profess any craft or trade whereby to maintain themselves, but go about in great numbers, from place to place, using insidious means to impose on his majesty's subjects, making them believe that they understand the art of foretelling to men and women their good and evil fortunes, by looking in their hands, whereby they frequently defraud people of their money; likewise are guilty of thefts and highway robberies: It is hereby ordered that the said vagrants, commonly called Egyptians, in case as thieves and rascals . . . . and on the importation of any such Egyptians, he, the importer, shall forfeit forty pounds for every trespass." So much had the conduct of the Gipsies exasperated the government of Queen Elizabeth, that it was enacted, during her reign, that "If any person, being fourteen years, whether natural born subject or stranger, who had been seen in the fellowship of such persons, or disguised like them, and remain with them one month at once, or at several times, it should be felony without benefit of clergy."* It would thus appear that, when the Gipsies first arrived in England, they had not kept their language a secret, as is now the case; for some of the Englishmen of that period had acquired it by associating with them.†

In carrying out the foregoing extraordinary enactments, the public was at the expense of exporting the Gipsies to the continent; and it may reasonably be assumed that great numbers of these unhappy people were executed under these sanguinary laws. A few years before the restoration of Charles II, thirteen Gipsies were executed "at one Suffolk assize." This appears to have been the last instance of inflicting the penalty of death on these unfortunate people in England, merely because they were Gipsies.‡ But although these laws of blood are now repealed, the English Gipsies are liable, at the present day, to be proceeded against under the Vagrant Act; as these statutes declare all those persons "pretending to be Gipsies, or wandering in the habit and form of Egyptians, shall be deemed rogues and vagabonds."

In the reign of Queen Elizabeth it was thought England contained above 10,000 Gipsies; and Mr. Hoyland, in his historical survey of these people, supposes that there are 18,000 of the race in Britain at the present day. A member of Parliament, it is reported, stated, in the House of Commons, that there were not less than 36,000 Gipsies in Great Britain. I am inclined to believe that the statement of the latter will be nearest the truth; as I am convinced that the greater part of all those persons who traverse England with earthenware, in carts and waggons, are a superior class of Gipsies. Indeed, a Scottish Gipsy informed me,

* English acts of Parliament.

† This does not appear to be necessarily the case. These Englishmen may have married Gipsies, become Gipsies by adoption, and so learned the language, as happens at the present day.—Ed.

‡ Hoyland.

that almost all those people are actually Gipsies. Now Mr. Hoyland takes none of these potters into his account, when he estimates the Gipsy population at only 18,000 souls. Besides, Gipsies have informed me that Ireland contains a great many of the tribe; many of whom are now finding their way into Scotland.*

I am inclined to think that the greater part of the English Gipsies live more apart from the other inhabitants of the country, reside more in tents, and exhibit a great deal more of their pristine manners, than their brethren do in Scotland.†

The English Gipsies also travel in Scotland, with earthenware in carts and waggons. A body of them, to the number of six tents, with sixteen horses, encamped, on one occasion, on the farm of Kingledoors, near the source of the Tweed. They remained on the ground from Saturday night till about ten o'clock on Monday morning, before they struck their tents and waggons.

At St. Boswell's fair I once inspected a horde of English Gipsies, encamped at the side of a hedge, on the Jedburgh road as it enters St. Boswell's Green. Their name was Blewett, from the neighbourhood of Darlington. The chief possessed two tents, two large carts laden with earthenware, four horses and mules, and five large dogs. He was attended by two old females and ten young children. One of the women was the mother of fourteen, and the other the mother of fifteen, children. This chief and the two females were the most swarthy and barbarous looking people I ever saw. They had, however, two beautiful children with them,

* The number of the British Gipsies mentioned here is greatly understated. See Disquisition on the Gipsies.—Ed.

† In no part of the world is the Gipsy life more in accordance with the general idea that the Gipsy is like Cain—a wanderer on the face of the earth—than in England; for there, the covered cart and the little tent are the houses of the Gipsy; and he seldom remains more than three days in the same place. So conducive is the climate of England to beauty, that nowhere else is the appearance of the race so prepossessing as in that country. Their complexion is dark, but not disagreeably so; their faces are oval, their features regular, their foreheads rather low, and their hands and feet small. The men are taller than the English peasantry, and far more active. They all speak the English language with fluency, and in their gait and demeanour are easy and graceful; in both respects standing in striking contrast with the peasantry, who, in speech, are slow and uncouth, and, in manner, dogged and brutal.—*Borrow.*—Ed.

about five years of age, with light flaxen hair, and very fair complexions. The old Gipsy woman said they were twins; but they might have been stolen from different parents, for all that, as there was nothing about them that had the slightest resemblance to any one of the horde that claimed them. Apparently much care was taken of them, as they were very cleanly and neatly kept.*

This Gipsy potter was a thick-set, stout man, above the middle size. He was dressed in an old dark-blue frock coat, with a profusion of black, greasy hair, which covered the upper part of his broad shoulders. He wore a high-crowned, narrow-brimmed, old hat, with a lock of his black hair hanging down before each ear, in the same manner as the Spanish Gipsies are described by Swinburn. He also wore a pair of old full-topped boots, pressed half way down his legs, and wrinkled about his ankles, like buskins. His visage was remarkably dark and gloomy. He walked up and down the market alone, without speaking to any one, with a peculiar air of independence about him, as he twirled in his hand, in the Gipsy manner, by way of amusement, a strong bludgeon, about three feet long, which he held by the centre. I happened to be speaking to a surgeon in the fair, at the time the Gipsy passed me, when I observed to him that that strange-looking man was a Gipsy; at which the surgeon only laughed, and said he did not believe any such thing. To satisfy him, I followed the Gipsy, at a little distance, till he led me straight to his tents at the Jedburgh road already mentioned.

This Gipsy band had none of their wares unpacked, nor were they selling anything in the market. They were cooking a lamb's head and pluck, in a pan suspended from a triangle of rods of iron, while beside it lay an abundance of small potatoes, in a wooden dish. The females wore black Gipsy bonnets. The visage of the oldest one was remarkably long, her chin resting on her breast. These three old Gipsies were, altogether, so dark, grim, and outlandish-looking, that they had little or no appearance of being natives of Britain. On enquiring if they were Gipsies,

* It does not follow, from what our author says about these two children, that they were stolen. I have seen some of the children of English Gipsies as fair as any Saxon. It sometimes happens that the flaxen hair of a Gipsy child will change into raven black before he reaches manhood.—Ed.

and could speak the language, the oldest female gave me the following answer: "We are potters, and strangers in this land. The people are civil unto us. I say, God bless the people; God bless them all." She spoke these words in a decided, emphatic, and solemn tone, as if she believed herself possessed of the power to curse or bless at pleasure. On turning my back, to leave them, I observed them burst out a laughing; making merry, as I supposed, at the idea of having deceived me as to the tribe to which they belonged.

The following anecdote will give some idea of the manner of life of the Gipsies in England.

A man, whom I knew, happened to lose his way, one dark night, in Cambridgeshire. After wandering up and down for some time, he observed a light, at a considerable distance from him, within the skirts of a wood, and, being overjoyed at the discovery, he directed his course toward it; but, before reaching the fire, he was surprised at hearing a man, a little way in advance, call out to him, in a loud voice, "Peace or not peace?" The benighted traveller, glad at hearing the sound of a human voice, immediately answered, "Peace; I am a poor Scotchman, and have lost my way in the dark." "You can come forward then," rejoined the sentinel. When the Scotchman advanced, he found a family of Gipsies, with only one tent; but, on being conducted further into the wood, he was introduced to a great company of Gipsies. They were busily employed in roasting several whole sheep —turning their carcasses before large fires, on long wooden poles, instead of iron spits. The racks on which the spits turned were also made of wood, driven into the ground, cross-ways, like the letter X. The Gipsies were exceedingly kind to the stranger, causing him to partake of the victuals which they had prepared for their feast. He remained with them the whole night, eating and drinking, and dancing with his merry entertainers, as if he had been one of themselves. When day dawned, the Scotchman counted twelve tents within a short distance of each other. On examining his position, he found himself a long way out of his road; but a party of the Gipsies voluntarily offered their services, and went with him for several miles, and, with great kindness, conducted him to the road from which he had wandered.

The crimes of some of the English Gipsies have greatly exceeded those of the Scottish, such as the latter have been.

The following details of the history of an English Gipsy family are taken from a report on the prisons in Northumberland. The writer of this report does not appear to have been aware, however, of the family in question being Gipsies, speaking an Oriental language, and that, according to the custom of their tribe, a dexterous theft or robbery is one of the most meritorious actions they can perform.

"*Crime in Families. William Winters' Family.*

"William himself, and one of his sons, were hanged together for murder. Another son committed an offence for which he was sent to the hulks, and, soon after his release, was concerned in a murder, for which he was hanged. Three of the daughters were convicted of various offences, and the mother was a woman of notorious bad character. The family was a terror to the neighbourhood, and, according to report, had been so for generations. The father, with a woman with whom he cohabited, (himself a married man,) was hanged for house-breaking. His first wife was a woman of very bad character, and his second wife was transported. One of the sons, a notorious thief, and two of the daughters, were hanged for murder. Mr. Blake believes that the only member of the family that turned out well was a girl, who was taken from the father when he was in prison, previous to execution, and brought up apart from her brothers and sisters. The grandfather was once in a lunatic asylum, as a madman. The father had a quarrel with one of his sons, about the sale of some property, and shot him dead. The mother co-habited with another man, and was one morning found dead, with her throat cut. One of the sons, (not already spoken of,) had a bastard child by one of his cousins, herself of weak intellect, and, being under suspicion of having destroyed the child, was arrested. While in prison, however, and before the trial came on, he destroyed himself by cutting his throat."

This family, I believe, are the Winters noticed by Sir Walter Scott, in Blackwood's Magazine, as follows:

"A gang (of Gipsies), of the name of Winters, long inhabited the wastes of Northumberland, and committed many crimes; among others, a murder upon a poor woman, with singular atrocity, for which one of them was hung in chains, near Tonpitt, in Reedsdale. The mortal reliques having decayed, the lord of the manor has replaced them by a wooden effigy, and still maintains the gibbet. The remnant of this gang came to Scotland, about fifteen years ago, and assumed the Roxburghshire name of Wintirip, as they found their own something odious. They settled at a cottage within about four miles of Earlston, and became great plagues to the country, until they were secured, after a tight battle, tried before the circuit court at Jedburgh, and banished back to their native country of England. The dalesmen of Reedwater showed great reluctance to receive these returned emigrants. After the Sunday service at a little chapel near Otterbourne, one of the squires rose, and, addressing the congregation, told them they would be accounted no longer Reedsdale men, but Reedsdale women, if they permitted this marked and atrocious family to enter their district. The people answered that they would not permit them to come that way; and the proscribed family, hearing of the unanimous resolution to oppose their passage, went more southernly, by the heads of the Tyne, and I never heard more of them, but I have little doubt they are all hanged.*

* It is but just to say that this family of Winters is, or at least was, the worst kind of English Gipsies. Their name is a by-word among the race in England. When they say, "It's a winter morning," they wish to express something very bad. It is difficult to get them to admit that the Winters belong to the tribe.—Ed.

CHAPTER III.

SCOTTISH GIPSIES, DOWN TO THE YEAR 1715.

THAT the Gipsies were in Scotland in the year 1506 is certain, as appears by a letter of James IV, of Scotland, to the King of Denmark, in favour of Anthonius Gawino, Earl of Little Egypt, a Gipsy chief. But there is a tradition, recorded in Crawford's Peerage, that a company of Gipsies, or Saracens, were committing depredations in Scotland before the death of James II, which took place in 1460, being forty-six years after the Gipsies were first observed on the continent of Europe, and it is, therefore, probable that these wanderers were encamped on Scottish ground before the year 1460, above mentioned. As I am not aware of Saracens ever having set foot in Scotland, England, or Ireland, I am disposed to think, if there is any truth in this tradition, it alludes to the Gipsies.* The story relates to the estate and family of McLellan of Bombie, in Galloway, and is as follows:

In the reign of James II, the Barony of Bombie was again recovered by the McLellans, (as the tradition goes,) after this manner: In the same reign, says our author of small credit, (Sir George McKenzie, in his baronage M.S.,) it happened that a company of Saracens or Gipsies, from Ireland,†

* There is no reason to doubt that these were Gipsies. They were evidently a roving band, from some of the continental hordes, that had passed over into Scotland, to "prospect" and plunder. They would, very naturally, be called Saracens by the natives of Scotland, to whom any black people, at that time, would appear as Saracens. We may, therefore, assume that the Gipsies have been fully four hundred years in Scotland. I may mention, however, that Mediterranean corsairs occasionally landed and plundered on the British coast, to as late a period as the reign of Charles I.—ED.

† Almost all the Scottish Gipsies assert that their ancestors came by way of Ireland into Scotland.

[This is extremely likely. On the publication of the edict of Ferdinand

infested the county of Galloway, whereupon the king intimated a proclamation, bearing, that whoever should disperse them, and bring in their captain, dead or alive, should have the Barony of Bombie for his reward. It chanced that a brave young gentleman, the laird of Bombie's son, fortunated to kill the person for which the reward was promised, and he brought his head on the point of his sword to the king, and thereupon he was immediately seized in the Barony of Bombie; and to perpetuate the memory of that brave and remarkable action, he took for his crest a Moor's head, and 'Think on' for his motto.*

As armorial bearings were generally assumed to commemorate facts and deeds of arms, it is likely that the crest of the McLellans is the head of a *Gipsy* chief. In the reign of James II, alluded to, we find "away putting of *sorners*, (forcible obtruders,) fancied fools, vagabonds, out-liers, masterful beggars, *bairds*, (strolling rhymers,) and such like runners about," is more than once enforced by acts of parliament.†

But the earliest authentic notice which has yet been discovered of the first appearance of the Gipsies in Scotland, is the letter of James IV, to the King of Denmark, in 1506. At this period these vagrants represented themselves as Egyptian pilgrims, and so far imposed on our religious and melancholy monarch, as to procure from him a favourable recommendation to his uncle of Denmark, in behalf of one of these "Earls," and his "lamentable retinue." The following is a translation of this curious epistle:

"Most illustrious, &c.—Anthonius Gawino, Earl of Little Egypt, and the other afflicted and lamentable tribe of his retinue, whilst, through a desire of travelling, and, by command of the Pope,‡ (as he says,) pilgriming, over the Christian

of Spain, in 1492, some of the Spanish Gipsies would likely pass over to the south of Ireland, and thence find their way into Scotland, before 1506. Anthonius Gawino, above referred to, would almost seem to be a Spanish name. We may, therefore, very safely assume that the Gipsies of Scotland are of Spanish Gipsy descent.—Ed.

* Crawford's Peerage, page 238.

† Glendook's Scots' acts of parliament.

‡ Mr. Hoyland makes some very judicious remarks upon the capacity of the Gipsies, when they first appeared in Europe. He says: "The first of this people who came into Europe must have been persons of discernment and discrimination, to have adapted their deceptions so exactly to the genius and habits of the different people they visited, as to ensure success in all

world, according to their custom, had lately arrived on the frontiers of our kingdom, and implored us that we, out of humanity, would allow him to approach our limits without damage, and freely carry about all things, and the company he now has. He easily obtains what the hard fortune wretched men require. Thus he has sojourned here, (as we have been informed,) for several months, in peaceable and catholic manner. King and uncle, he now proposes a voyage to Denmark to thee. But, being about to cross the ocean, he hath requested our letters, in which we would inform your Highness of these, and at the same time commend the calamity of this tribe to your royal munificence. But we believe that the fates, manners, and race of the wandering Egyptians are better known to thee than us, because Egypt is nearer thy kingdom, and a greater number of such men sojourn in thy kingdom.—Most illustrious, &c."*

countries. The stratagem to which they had recourse, on entering France, evinces consummate artifice of plan, and not a little adroitness and dexterity in the execution. The specious appearance of submission to Papal authority, in the penance of wandering seven years, without lying in a bed, contained three distinct objects. They could not have devised an expedient more likely to recommend them to the favour of the ecclesiastics, or better concerted for taking advantage of the superstitious credulity of the people, and, at the same time, for securing to themselves the gratification of their own nomadic propensities. So complete was the deception they practised, that we find they wandered up and down France, under the eye of the magistracy, not for seven years only, but for more than a hundred years, without molestation."

Mr. Hoyland's remarks cover only half of the question, for, being "pilgrims," their chiefs must also assume very high titles, to give them consideration with the rulers of Europe—such as dukes, earls, lords, counts and knights. To carry out the character of pilgrims, the body would go very poorly clad; it would only be the chiefs who would be flashily accoutred. It is, therefore, by no means wonderful that the Gipsies should have succeeded so well, and so long, in obtaining an entrance, and a toleration, in every country of Europe.—Ed.

* Illustrissime, &c.—Anthonius Gawino, ex Parvo Egypto comes, et cætera ejus comitatus, gens afflicta et miseranda, dum Christianam orbem peregrinationes studio, Apostolicæ sedis, (ut refert) jussu, suorum more peregrinans, fines nostri regni dudum advenerat, atque in sortis suæ, et miseriarum hujus populi, refugium, nos pro humanitate imploraverat ut nostros limites sibi impune adire, res cunctas, et quam habet societatem libere circumagere liceret. Impetrat facile quæ postulat miserorum hominum dura fortuna. Ita aliquot menses bene et catholice, (sic accepimus,) hic versatus, ad te, Rex et avunculo, in Daciam transitum parat. Sed oceanum transmissurus nostras literas exoravit; quibus celsitudinem tuam horum certiorem redderemus, simul et calamitatem ejus gentis Regiæ tuæ munificentiæ commendaremus. Ceterum errabundæ Egypti fata, moresque, et genus, eo tibi quam nobis credimus notiora, quo Egyptus tuo regno

From 1506 to 1540, the 28th of the reign of James V, we find that the true character of the Gipsies had not reached the Scottish court; for, in 1540, the king of Scotland entered into a league or treaty with "John Faw, Lord and Earl of Little Egypt;" and a writ passed the Privy Seal, the same year, in favour of this Prince or *Rajah* of the Gipsies. As the public edicts in favour of this race are extremely rare, I trust a copy of this curious document, in this place, may not be unacceptable to the reader.*

"James, by the grace of God, King of Scots: To our sheriffs of Edinburgh, principal and within the constabulary of Haddington, Berwick, Roxburgh, &c., &c.; provosts, aldermen, and baillies of our burghs and cities of Edinburgh, &c., &c., greeting: Forasmuch as it is humbly meant and shown to us, by our loved John Faw, Lord and Earl of Little Egypt, that whereas he obtained our letter under our great seal, direct you all and sundry our said sheriffs, stewarts, baillies, provosts, aldermen, and baillies of burghs, and to all and sundry others having authority within our realm, to assist him in execution of justice upon his company and folk, conform to the laws of Egypt, and in punishing of all them that rebel against him: nevertheless, as we are informed, Sebastiane Lalow Egyptian, one of the said John's company, with his accomplices and partakers under written, that is to say, Anteane Donca, Satona Fingo, Nona Finco, Phillip Hatseyggaw, Towla Bailyow, Grasta Neyn, Goleyr Bailyow, Bernard Beige, Demen Matskalla (or Macskalla), Noffaw Lawlowr, Martyn Femine, rebels and conspirators against the said John Faw, and have removed them all utterly out of his company, and taken from him divers sums of money, jewels, clothes and other goods, to the quantity of a great sum of money; and on nowise will pass home with him, howbeit he has bidden and remained of long time upon them, and is bound and obliged to bring home with him all them of his company that are alive, and a testimony of them that are dead: and as the said John has the said

videlor, et major hujusmodi hominum frequentia tuo diversatur imperio. Illustrissime, &c.

* I have taken the liberty of translating the various extracts from the Scottish acts of parliament, quoted in this chapter, as the original language is not very intelligible to English or even Scottish readers. For doing this, I may be denounced as a Vandal by the ultra Scotch, for so treating such "rich old Doric," as the language of the period may be termed.—Ed.

Sebastiane's obligation, made in Dunfermline before our master household, that he and his company should remain with him, and on nowise depart from him, as the same bears: In contrary to the tenor of which, the said Sebastiane, by sinister and wrong information, false relation, circumvention of us, has purchased our writings, discharging him and the remnant of the persons above written, his accomplices and partakers of the said John's company, and with his goods taken by them from him; causes certain our lieges assist them and their opinions, and to fortify and take their part against the said John, their lord and master; so that he on nowise can apprehend nor get them, to have them home again within their own country, after the tenor of his said bond, to his heavy damage and *skaith* (hurt), and in great peril of losing his heritage, and expressly against justice: Our will is, therefore, and we charge you straightly and command that . . . . ye and every one of you within the bounds of your offices, command and charge all our lieges, that none of them take upon hand to reset, assist, fortify, supply, maintain, defend, or take part with the said Sebastiane and his accomplices above written, for no body's nor other way, against the said John Faw, their lord and master; but that they and ye, in likewise, take and lay hands upon them wherever they may be apprehended, and bring them to him, to be punished for their demerits, conform to his laws; and help and fortify him to punish and do justice upon them for their trespasses; and to that effect lend him your prisons, stocks, fetters, and all other things necessary thereto, as ye and each of you, and all other our lieges, will answer to us thereupon, and under all highest pain and charge that after may follow: So that the said John have no cause of complaint thereupon in time coming, nor to resort again to us to that effect, notwithstanding any our writings, sinisterly purchased or to be purchased, by the said Sebastiane on the contrary: And also charge all our lieges that none of them molest, vex, unquiet, or trouble the said John Faw and his company, in doing their lawful business, or otherwise, within our realm, and in their passing, remaining, or away-going forth of the same, under the pain above written: And such-like that ye command and charge all skippers, masters and mariners of all ships within our realm, at all ports and havens where the said John and his company shall happen to resort and come, to receive him and them therein, upon their expenses, for furthering of them forth of our realm to the parts beyond sea, as you and each of them such-like will answer to us thereupon, and under the pain aforesaid. Subscribed with our hand, and under our privy seal at Falkland, the fifteenth day of February, and of our reign the 28th year."*

* Ex. Registro Secreti Sigilli, Vol. XIV, fol. 59. Blackwood. Appendix to McLaurin's Criminal Trials.

This document may well be termed the most curious and important record of the early history of the Gipsy race in Europe; and it is well worthy of consideration. The meaning of it is simply this: John Faw had evidently been importuned by the Scottish Court, (at which he appears to have been a man of no small consequence,) to bring his so-called "pilgrimage," which he had undertaken "by command of the Pope," to an end, so far, at least, as remaining in Scotland was concerned. Being pressed upon the point, he evidently, as a last resource, formed a plan with Sebastiane Lalow, and the other "rebels," to leave him, and carry off, (as he said,) his property. To give the action an air of importance, and make it appear as a real rebellion, they brought the question into court. Then, John could turn round, and reply to the king: "May it please your majesty! I can't return to my own country. My company and folk have conspired, rebelled, robbed, and left me. I can't lay my hands upon them; I don't even know where to find them. I must take them home with me, or a testimony of them that are dead, under the great peril of losing my heritage, at the hands of my lord, the Duke of Egypt. However, if your majesty will help me to catch them, I will not be long in taking leave of *your* kingdom, with all my company. In the meantime, your majesty will be pleased to issue your commands to all the shipowners and mariners in the kingdom, to be ready, *when I gather together my folk* (!) to further our passage to Egypt, for which I will pay them handsomely." The whole business may be termed a piece of "thimble-rigging," to prolong their stay—that is, enable them to remain permanently—in the country. Our author, I think, is quite in error in supposing this to have been a real quarrel among the Gipsies. If it had been a real quarrel, the Gipsies would soon have settled the question among themselves, by their own laws; it would have been the last thing, under all the circumstances of the case, they would have thought of, to have brought it before the Scottish court. The Gipsies, according to Grellmann, assigned the following reason for prolonging their stay in Europe: "They endeavoured to prolong the term (of their pilgrimage) by asserting that their return home was prevented by soldiers, stationed to intercept them; and by wishing to have it believed that new parties of pilgrims were to leave their country every year, otherwise their land would be rendered totally barren."

The quarrel between the Faas and the Baillies, for the *Gipsy crown*, in after times, did not, in all probability, arise from this business, but most likely, as the English Gipsies believe, from some marriage between these families. The Scottish Gipsies, like the two Roses, have had, and for aught I know to the contrary, may have yet, two rival kings—Faa and Baillie, with their partisans—although the Faas, from the prominent position which they have always occupied in Scottish history, have been the only kings known to the Scottish public generally.

This curious league of John Faw with the Scottish king, who acknowledges the laws and customs of the Gipsies within his kingdom, was of very short duration. Like that of many other favourites of princes, the credit which the "Earl of Little Egypt" possessed at court was, the succeeding year, completely annihilated, and that with a vengeance, as will appear by the following order in council. The Gipsies, quarrelling among themselves, and publicly bringing their matters of dispute before the government, had, perhaps, contributed to produce an enquiry into the real character and conduct of these foreigners; verifying the ancient adage, that a house divided against itself cannot stand. But the immediate cause assigned for the sudden change of mind in the king, so unfortunate for the Gipsies, is handed down to us in the following tradition, current in Fife:

King James V, as he was travelling through part of his dominions, disguised under the character of the Gaberlunzie-man, or Guid-man of Ballangiegh, prosecuting, as was his custom, his low and vague amours, fell in with a band of Gipsies, in the midst of their carousals, in a cave, near Wemyss, in Fifeshire. His majesty heartily joined in their revels, but it was not long before a scuffle ensued, wherein the king was very roughly handled, being in danger of his life.* The Gipsies, perceiving at last that he was none of their people, and considering him a spy, treated him with great indignity. Among other humiliating insults, they compelled his royal majesty, as an humble servant of a Tinkler, to carry their budgets and wallets on his back, for several miles, until he was exhausted; and being unable to

In perusing this work, the reader will be pleased to take the above mentioned document as the starting point of the history of the Gipsies in Scotland; and consider the Gipsies of that time as the progenitors of all those at present in Scotland, including the great encrease of the body, by the mixture of the white blood that has been brought within their community. He will also be pleased to divest himself of the childish prejudices, acquired in the nursery and in general literature, against the name of Gipsy; and consider that there are people in Scotland, occupying some of the highest positions in life, who are Gipsies; not indeed Gipsies in point of purity of blood, but people who have Gipsy blood in their veins, and who hold themselves to be Gipsies, in the manner which I have, to a certain extent, explained in the Preface, and will more fully illustrate in my Disquisition on the Gipsies.—Ed.

* The Gipsies assert that, on this occasion, the king attempted to take liberties with one of their women: and that one of the male Gipsies "came crack over his head with a bottle."—Ed.

proceed a step further he sank under his load. He was then dismissed with scorn and contempt by the merciless Gipsies. Being exasperated at their cruel and contemptuous treatment of his sacred person, and having seen a fair specimen of their licentious manner of life, the king caused an order in council immediately to be issued, declaring that, if *three* Gipsies were found together, one of the three was instantly to be seized, and forthwith hanged or shot, by any one of his majesty's subjects that chose to put the order in execution.

This tradition is noticed by the Rev. Andrew Small, in his antiquities of Fife, in the following words. His book came into my hands after I had written down my account of the tradition.

"But, surely, this would be the last tinker that ever he would dub (a knight). If we may judge from what happened, one might imagine he, (James V,) would be heartily sick of them, (tinkers,) being taken prisoner by three of them, and compelled to stay with them several days, so that his nobles lost all trace of him, and being also forced, not only to lead their ass, but likewise to assist it in carrying part of the panniers! At length he got an opportunity, when they were bousing in a house at the east end of the village of Milnathort, where there is now a new meeting-house built, when he was left on the green with the ass. He contrived to write, some way, on a slip of paper, and gave a boy half-a-crown to run with it to Falkland, and give it to his nobles, intimating that the guid-man of Ballangiegh was in a state of captivity. After they got it, and knew where he was, they were not long in being with him, although it was fully ten miles they had to ride. Whenever he got assistance, he caused two of the tinkers, that were most harsh and severe to him, to be hanged immediately, and let the third one, that was most favourable to him, go free. They were hanged a little south-west of the village, at a place which, from the circumstance, is called the Gallow-hill to this day. The two skeletons were lately found after the division of the commonty that recently took place. He also, after this time, made a law, that whenever three tinkers, or Gipsies, were found going together, two of them should be hanged, and the third set at liberty."*

* Small's Roman Antiquities of Fife, pages 285 and 286. Small also records a song composed on James V dubbing a Tinker a knight.

The following order in council is, perhaps, the one to which this tradition alludes:

"Act of the lords of council respecting John Faw, &c., June 6, 1541. The which day anent the complaint given by John Faw and his brother, and Sebastiane Lalow, Egyptians, to the King's grace, ilk ane plenizeand . . . . upon other and divers faults and injuries; and that it is agreed among them to pass home, and have the same decided before the Duke of Egypt.* The lords of council, being advised with the points of the said complaints, and understanding perfectly the great thefts and *skaiths* (hurts) done by the said Egyptians upon our sovereign lord's lieges, wherever they come or resort, ordain letters to be directed to the provosts and baillies of Edinburgh, St. Johnstown (Perth), Dundee, Montrose, Aberdeen, St. Andrews, Elgin, Forres, and Inverness; and to the sheriffs of Edinburgh, Fife, Perth, Forfar, Kincardine, Aberdeen, Elgin and Forres, Banff, Cromarty, Inverness, and all other sheriffs, stewarts, provosts and baillies, where it happens the said Egyptians to resort.† To command and charge them, by open proclamation, at the market crosses of the head burghs of the sheriffdoms, to depart forth of this realm, with their wives, children, and companies, within xxx days after they be charged thereto, under the pain of death; notwithstanding any other letters or privileges granted to them by the king's grace, because his grace, with the advice of the lords, has discharged the same for the causes aforesaid: with certification that if they be found in this realm, the said xxx days being past, they shall be taken and put to death."‡

This sharp order in council seems to have been the first edict banishing the Gipsies as a whole people—men, women,

* It would seem that John Faw had become frightened at the mishap of one of his folk "coming crack over the king's head with a bottle," and that, to pacify his majesty, he had at once gone before him, and informed him that he had prevailed on his "rebellious subjects" to *pass home*, and have the matter in dispute decided by the *Duke of Egypt*. This would, so far, satisfy the king; but to make sure of getting rid of his troublesome visitors, he issued his commands to the various authorities to see that they really did leave the country.—Ed.

† It would appear, from the mention that is made here of the authorities of so many towns and counties, "where it happens the said Egyptians to resort," that the race was scattered over all Scotland at this time, and that it must have been numerous.—Ed.

‡ M. S. Act. Dom. Con. vol. 15, fol. 166.—*Blackwood's Magazine.*

and children—from Scotland. But the king, whom, according to tradition, they had personally so deeply offended, dying in the following year, (1542) a new reign brought new prospects to the denounced wanderers.* They seem to have had the address to recover their credit with the succeeding government; for, in 1553, the writ which passed the privy seal in 1540, forming a sort of league with "John Faw, Lord and Earl of Little Egypt," was renewed by Hamilton, Earl of Arran, then Regent during the minority of Queen Mary. McLaurin, in his criminal trials, when speaking of John Faw, gravely calls him "this peer." "There is a writ," says he, "of the same tenor in favour of this peer from Queen Mary, same record, 25 April, 1553; and 8 April, 1554, he gets remission for the slaughter of Ninian Small." In Blackwood's Magazine it is mentioned that "Andro Faw, Captain of the Egyptians,† and twelve of his gang specified by name, obtained a remission for the slaughter of Ninian Small, committed within the town of Linton, in the month of March last by past upon suddenly." This appears to be the slaughter to which McLaurin alludes. The following are the names of these thirteen Gipsies: "Andro Faw, captain of the Egyptians, George Faw, Robert Faw, and Anthony Faw, his sons, Johnne Faw, Andrew George Nichoah, George Sebastiane Colyne, George Colyne, Julie Colyne, Johnne Colyne, James Haw, Johnne Browne, and George Browne, Egyptians."

From the edict above mentioned, it is evident that the Gipsies in Scotland, at that time, were allowed to punish the criminal members of their own tribe, according to their own

* It is perfectly evident that the severe decree of James V against the Gipsies arose from the personal insult alluded to, owing to the circumstance of its falling to the ground after his death, and the Gipsies recovering their position with his successor. Apart from what the Gipsies themselves say on this subject, the ordinary tradition may be assumed to be well founded. If the Gipsies were spoken to on the subject of the insult offered to the king, they would naturally reply, that they did not know, from his having been dressed like a beggar, that it was the king; an excuse which the court, knowing his majesty's vagabond habits, would probably receive. But it is very likely that John Faw would declare that the guilty parties were those rebels whom he was desirous to catch, and take home with him to Egypt! This Gipsy king seems to have been a master of diplomacy.—Ed.

† The Gipsy chiefs were partial to the title of Captain; arising, I suppose, from their being leaders of large bands of young men employed in theft and robbery. [In Spain, such Gipsy chiefs, according to Mr. Borrow, assumed the name of Counts.—Ed.]

peculiar laws, customs and usages, without molestation. And it cannot be supposed that the ministers of three or four succeeding monarchs would have suffered their sovereigns to be so much imposed on, as to allow them to put their names to public documents, styling poor and miserable wretches, as we at the present day imagine them to have been, "Lords and Earls of Little Egypt." Judging from the accounts which tradition has handed down to us, of the gay and fashionable appearance of the principal Gipsies, as late as about the beginning of the eighteenth century, as will be seen in my account of the Tweed-dale bands, I am disposed to believe that Anthonius Gawino, in 1506, and John Faw, in 1540, would personally, as individuals, that is, as Gipsy Rajahs,* have a very respectable and imposing appearance in the eyes of the officers of the crown. And besides, John Faw appears to have been possessed of "divers sums of money, jewels, clothes and other goods, to the quantity of a great sum of money;" and it would seem that some of the officers of high rank in the household of our kings had fingered the cash of the Gipsy pilgrims. If there is any truth in the popular and uniform tradition that, in the seventeenth century, a Countess of Cassilis was seduced from her duty to her lord, and carried off by a Gipsy, of the name of John Faa, and his band, it cannot be imagined, that the seducer would be a poor, wretched, beggarly Tinkler, such as many of the tribe are at this day. If a handsome person, elegant apparel, a lively disposition, much mirth and glee, and a constant boasting of extraordinary prowess, would in any way contribute to make an impression on the heart of the frail countess, these qualities, I am disposed to think, would not be wanting in the "Gipsy Laddie." And, moreover, John Faw bore, on paper at least, as high a title as her husband, Lord Cassilis, from whom she absconded. It is said the individual who seduced the fair lady was a Sir John Faw, of Dunbar, her former sweetheart, and not a Gipsy; but tradition gives no account of a Sir John Faw, of Dunbar.† The Falls, merchants, at Dunbar, were descended from the Gipsy Faas of Yetholm.

* *Rajah*—The Scottish Gipsy word for a chief, governor, or prince.

† The author, (Mr. Finlay,) who claims a Sir John Faw, of Dunbar, to have been the person who carried off the Countess of Casillis, gives no authority, as a writer in Blackwood says, in support of his assertion. Nor does he account for a person of that name being any other than a Gipsy.

It is pretty clear that the Gipsies remained in Scotland, with little molestation, from 1506 till 1579—the year in which James VI took the government into his own hands, being a period of about seventy-three years, during which time these wanderers roamed up and down the kingdom, without receiving any check of consequence, excepting the short period—probably about one year—in which the severe order of James V remained in force, and which, in all probability, expired with the king.*

The civil and religious contests in which the nation had been long engaged, particularly during the reign of Queen Mary, produced numerous swarms of banditti, who committed outrages in every part of the country. The slighter depredations of the Gipsy bands, in the midst of the fierce and bloody quarrels of the different factions that generally prevailed throughout the kingdom, would attract but little attention, and the Gipsies would thereby escape the punishment which their actions merited. But the government being more firmly established, by the union of the different parties who distracted the country, and the king assuming the supreme authority, which all acknowledged, vigorous measures were adopted for suppressing the excess of strolling vagabonds of every description. In the very year the king was placed at the head of affairs, a law was passed, "For punishment of strong and idle beggars, and relief of the poor and impotent."

Against the Gipsies this sweeping statute is particularly directed, for they are named, and some of their practices pointed out, in the following passage: "And that it may be

Indeed, this is but an instance of the ignorance and prejudice of people generally in regard to the Gipsies. The tradition of the hero being a Gipsy, I have met with among the English Gipsies, who even gave me the name of the lady. John Faw, in all probability the king of the Gipsies, who carried off the countess, might reasonably be assumed to have been, in point of education, on a par with her, who, in that respect, would not, in all probability, rise above the most humble Scotch cow-milker at the present day, whatever her personal bearing might have been.—Ed.

* During these seventy-three years of peace, the Gipsies in Scotland must have multiplied prodigiously, and, in all probability, drawn much of the native blood into their body. Not being, at that time, a proscribed race, but, on the contrary, honoured by leagues and covenants with the king himself, the ignorant public generally would have few of those objections to intermarry with them, which they have had in subsequent times. The thieving habits of the Gipsies would prove no bar to such connections, as the Scottish people were accustomed to thieving of all kinds.—Ed.

known what manner of persons are meant to be strong and idle beggars and vagabonds, and worthy of the punishment before specified, it is declared that all idle persons going about the country of this realm, using subtle, crafty and unlawful plays—as jugglery, fast-and-loose, and such others, the idle people calling themselves Egyptians, or any other that fancy themselves to have knowledge of prophecy, charming, or other abused sciences, whereby they persuade the people that they can tell their weirds, deaths, and fortunes, and such other fantastical imaginations."* And the following is the mode prescribed for punishing the Gipsies, and the other offenders associated with them in this act of parliament: "That such as make themselves fools and are *bairds*, (strolling rhymers,) or other such like runners about, being apprehended, shall be put in the king's ward, or irons, so long as they have any goods of their own to live on, and if they have not whereupon to live of their own, that their ears be nailed to the tron or other tree, and cut off, and (themselves) banished the country; and if thereafter they be found again, that they be hanged."†

This statute was ratified and confirmed in the 12th parliament of James VI, cap. 147, 5th June, 1592, wherein the incorrigible Gipsies are again referred to: "And for the better trial of common *sorners* (forcible obtruders,) vagabonds, and masterful beggars, fancied fools, and counterfeit Egyptians, and to the effect that they may be still preserved till they be compelled to settle at some certain dwelling, or be expelled forth of the country, &c." The next law in which the Gipsies are mentioned, with other vagabonds, was passed in the 15th parliament of the same reign, 19th December, 1597, entitled, "Strong beggars, vagabonds, and Egyptians should be punished." The statute itself reads as follows: "Our sovereign lord and estates of parliament

* In this act of parliament are denounced, along with the Gipsies, "all minstrels, songsters, and tale-tellers, not avowed by special licence of some of the lords of parliament or great barons, or by the high burghs and cities, for their common minstrels." "All *vagabond scholars* (!) of the universities of St. Andrews, Glasgow, and Aberdeen, not licenced by the rector and dean of faculty *to ask alms*." It would seem, from this last extract, that the Scottish Universities granted diplomas to their students to beg! The Gipsies were associated or classed with good company at this time. But beggar students, or student-beggars, were common in other parts of Europe during that age.—Ed.

† Glendook's Scots Acts, James VI, 6th Par. cap. 74—20th Oct. 1579.

made before, against strong and idle beggars, vagabonds, and Egyptians," with this addition: "That strong beggars and their children be employed in common works, and their service mentioned in the said act of parliament, in the year of God, 1579, to be prorogate in during their life times, &c."*

All the foregoing laws were again ratified and enforced by another act, in the same reign, 15th November, 1600. The following extract will serve to give some explanation how these statutes were neglected, and seldom put in force: "And how the said acts have received little or no effect or execution, by the oversight and negligence of the persons who were nominated justices and commissioners, for putting of the said acts to full and due execution, so that the strong and idle beggars, being for the most part thieves, *bairds*, (strolling rhymers,) and counterfeit *limmers*, (scoundrels,) living most insolently and ungodly, without marriage or baptism, are suffered to *vaig* and wander throughout the whole country."† "But," says Baron Hume, "all ordinary means having proved insufficient to restrain so numerous and so sturdy a crew, the privy council at length, in June, 1603, were induced to venture on the more effectual expedient, (recommended by the example of some other realm,) of at once ordering the whole race to leave the kingdom by a certain day, and never to return under the pain of death.‡ A few years after, this proclamation was converted into per-

* By the above, and subsequent statutes, in the reign of James VI, "Coal and salt-masters might apprehend, and put to labour, all vagabonds and sturdy beggars." The truth is, these kidnapped individuals and their children were made slaves of to these masters. The colliers were emancipated only within these fifty years. It has been stated to me that some of the colliers in the Lothians are of Gipsy extraction. [Our author might have said *Gipsies;* for being "of Gipsy extraction," and "Gipsies," are expressions quite synonymous, notwithstanding the application by the public of the latter term to the more original kind of Gipsies only.—Ed.]

† If Fletcher of Saltoun be correct, when he states that, in his time, which was about the end of the 17th century, there were two hundred thousand people, (about one-fifth of the whole population,) begging from door to door in Scotland, it would be a task of no little difficulty, for those in power, to put in force the laws against the Gipsies, and vagabonds generally. The editor of Dr. Pennicuick's history of Tweed-dale, thinks Fletcher's is an over-charged picture. Some are of opinion that, when he made his statement, he included the greater part of the inhabitants of the Scottish Border, and also those in the north of Scotland; for, he said, the Highlands "was an inexhaustible source of beggars," and wished these banditti transplanted to the low country, and to people the Highlands from hence.

‡ The records in which this order is contained are lost.

petual law, by statute 1609, cap. 13, with this farther convenient, but very severe, provision toward the more effectual execution of the order, that it should be lawful to condemn and execute them to the death, upon proof made of the single fact 'that they are called, known, repute and holden Egyptians'!" As this is the only statute exclusively relating to, and denouncing, the Gipsies, I shall give it at length.

"13. Act anent the Egyptians. Our sovereign lord and estates of parliament ratify, approve, and perpetually confirm the act of secret council, made in the month of June or thereby, 1603 years, and proclamation following thereupon, commanding the vagabonds, *sorners* (forcible obtruders), and common thieves, commonly called Egyptians, to pass forth of this kingdom, and remain perpetually forth thereof, and never to return within the same, under pain of death; and that the same have force and execution after the first day of August next to come. After the which time, if any of the said vagabonds, called Egyptians, as well women as men, shall be found within this kingdom, or any part thereof, it shall be lawful to all his majesty's good subjects, or any one of them, to cause take, apprehend, imprison, and execute to death the said Egyptians, either men or women, as common, notorious, and condemned thieves, by one assize only to be tried, that they are called, known, repute and holden Egyptians: In the which cause, whosoever of the assize happens to *clenge* (exculpate) any of the aforesaid Egyptians pannelled, as said is, shall be pursued, handled and censured as committers of wilful error: And whoever shall, any time thereafter, reset, receive, supply, or entertain any of the said Egyptians, either men or women, shall lose their escheat, and be warded at the judge's will: And that the sheriffs and magistrates, in whose bounds they shall publicly and avowedly resort and remain, be called before the lords of his highness' secret council, and severely censured and punished for their negligence in execution of this act: Discharging all letters, protections, and warrants whatsoever, purchased by the said Egyptians, or any of them, from his majesty or lords of secret council, for their remaining within this realm, as surreptitiously and deceitfully obtained by their knowledge: Annulling also all warrants purchased, or hereafter to be purchased, by any subject of whatsoever rank within this kingdom, for their reset, entertaining, or doing any manner of favour to the said Egyptians, at any time after the said first day of August next to come, for now and ever."* In a subsequent enactment, in 1617, appointing justices of the peace and constables, the destruction of the proscribed Egyptians is particularly enjoined, in defining the different duties of the magistrates and their peace officers.†

But so little respected was the authority of the government, that in 1612, three years after the passing of the Gipsy act, his majesty was under the humiliating necessity of entering into a contract with the clan Scott, and their friends, by which the clan bound themselves "to give up all bands of friendship, kindness, oversight, maintenance or assurance, if any we have, with common thieves and broken clans, &c." It is certain there would be many bonds of the same nature with other turbulent clans throughout the kingdom. That Scotchmen of respectability and influence protected the Gipsies, and afforded them shelter on their lands, after the promulgation of the cruel statute of 1609, is manifest from the following passages, which I extract from Blackwood's Magazine, for 1817; the conductor of which seems to have been careful in examining the public records for the documents quoted by him; having been guided in his researches, I believe, by Sir Walter Scott.

"In February, 1615, we find a remission under the privy seal, granted to William Auchterlony, of Cayrine, for resetting of John Faw and his followers.‡ On the 14th July, 1616, the sheriff of Forfar is severely reprimanded for delaying to execute some Gipsies, who had been taken within his jurisdiction, and for troubling the council with petitions in their behalf. In November following appears a proclamation against Egyptians and their resetters. In December, 1619, we find another proclamation against resetters of them;

* Glendook's Scots Act. † Ib.

‡ The nature of this crime in Scotch law is fully explained in the following extract from the original, which also appears curious in other respects. The pardon is granted "pro receptione, supportatione, et detentione supra terra suas de Belmadie, et infra eius habitationis domum, aliaq. edificia eiusdem, *Joannis Fall, Ethiopis, lie Egiptian*, eiusq. uxoris, puerorum, servorum et associatorum; Necnon pro ministrando ipsis cibum, potum, pecunias, hospicium, aliaq. necessaria, quocunq. tempore vel occasione preterita, contra acta nostri Parliamenti vel secreti concilii, vel contra quecunq. leges, alia acta, aut constitutiones huius nostri regni Scotie in contrarium facta. Regist. secreti sigilli vol. lxxxiii, fol. 291, *Blackwood's Magazine*.—Ed.

in April, 1620, another proclamation of the same kind, and in July, 1620, a commission against resetters, all with very severe penalties. The nature of these acts will be better understood from the following extract from that of the 4th July, 1616, which also very well explains the way in which the Gipsies contrived to maintain their footing in the country, in defiance of all the efforts of the legislature to extirpate them." "It is of truth that the thieves and *limmers* (scoundrels), aforesaid, having for some short space after the said act of parliament, (1609,) . . . dispersed themselves in certain secret and obscure places of the country. . they were not known to wander abroad in troops and companies, according to their accustomed manner, yet, shortly thereafter, finding that the said act of parliament was neglected, and that no enquiry nor . . . was made for them, they began to take new breath and courage, and . . unite themselves in infamous companies and societies, under . . . . commanders, and continually since then have remained within the country, committing as well open and avowed *rieffis* (robberies) in all parts . . . . murders, . . . *pleine stouthe* (common theft,) and pickery, where they may not be mastered; and they do shamefully and mischievously abuse the simple and ignorant people, by telling fortunes, and using charms, and a number of juggling tricks and falseties, unworthy to be heard of in a country subject to religion, law, and justice; and they are encouraged to remain within the country, and to continue in their thievish and juggling tricks and falseties, not only through default of the execution of the said act of parliament, but, what is worse, that great numbers of his majesty's subjects, of whom some outwardly pretend to be famous and unspotted gentlemen, have given and give open and avowed protection, reset, supply and maintainance, upon their grounds and lands, to the said vagabonds, *sorners*, (forcible obtruders,) and condemned thieves and *limmers*, (scoundrels,) and suffer them to remain days, weeks, and months together thereupon, without controulment, and with connivance and oversight, &c." "So they do leave a foul, infamous, and ignominious spot upon them, their houses, and posterity, that they are patrons to thieves and *limmers*, (scoundrels,) &c.*

* The same state of things existed in Spain. Charles II, passed a law on the 12th June, 1695, the 16th article of which, as given by Mr. Borrow,

From their first arrival in the country till 1579, the Gipsies, as already mentioned, appear to have been treated as a separate people, observing their own laws and customs. In the year 1587, such was the state of society in Scotland, that laws were passed by James VI, compelling all the baronial proprietors of lands, chiefs and captains of clans, on the Borders and Highlands of Scotland, to find pledges and securities for the peaceable conduct of their retainers, tenants, clansmen, and other inhabitants of their respective estates and districts.* In the same parliament another act was passed, allowing vagabonds and broken and unpledged men to produce pledges and securities for their good conduct. The Gipsies, under these statutes, would remain unmolested, as they would readily find protection by becoming, nominally, clansmen, and assuming the surnames, of those chieftains and noblemen who were willing and able to afford them protection.† Indeed, the act allowing vagabonds to find sureties would include the Gipsy bands, for, about this

enacts: "And because we understand that the continnance of those who are called Gitanos has depended on the favour, protection, and assistance which they have experienced from persons of *different stations*, we do ordain that whosoever against whom shall be proved the fact of having, since the day of the publication hereof, favoured, received, or assisted the said Gitanos, in any manner whatever, whether *within their houses* or without, *provided he is a noble*, shall be subjected to the fine of *six thousand ducats*, ... and *if a plebeian*, to a *punishment of ten years in the galleys!* Such an enactment would surely prove that the Gipsies in Spain were *greatly* favoured by the Spanish people generally, even two centuries after they entered the country.

The causes to which may be attributed this toleration, even encouragement, of the Gipsies, are various. Among these may be mentioned a fear of consequences to person and property, tinkering, trafficking and amusement, and corruption on the part of those in power. But in the character of the Gipsies itself may be found a general cause for their escaping the effects of the laws passed against them, viz., *wheedling*. The term Gitano has been variously modified in the Spanish language, thus:

Gitano, *Gipsy, flatterer*; Gitanillo, *a little Gipsy*; Gitanismo, *the Gipsy tribe*; Gitanesco, *Gipsy-like*; Gitanear, *to flatter, entice*; Gitaneria, *wheedling, flattery*; Gitanamente, *in a sly, winning manner*; Gitanada, *blandishment, wheedling, flattery*.—ED.

* There were 17 clans on the Borders, and 34 clans in the Highlands, who appear to have had chiefs and captains over them. There were 22 baronial proprietors connected with the Borders, and 106 connected with the Highlands, named in a roll, who were likewise ordered to find pledges. —*Glendook's Scots Acts.*

† It sometimes happened, when an internal quarrel took place in a clan, portions of the tribe left their chief, and united themselves to another, whose name they assumed, and dropped their original one.

period, they seem to have been only classed with our own native vagabonds, moss-troopers, Border and Highland thieves, broken clans and masterless men. It appears by the act of 1609, that the Gipsies had even purchased their protection from the government. The inhabitants of Scotland being at this period still divided into clans, would greatly facilitate the escape of the Gipsies from the laws passed against them. The clans on the Borders and Highlands were in a state of almost constant warfare with one another; and frequently several of the clans were united in opposition to the regular government of the country, to whose mandates they paid little or no regard. The Gipsies had no settled residence, but roamed from place to place over the whole country; and when they found themselves in danger in one place, they had no more to do but remove into the district inhabited by a hostile clan, where they would immediately find protection. Besides, the Borderers and Highlanders, themselves plunderers and thieves, would not be very active in apprehending their brother thieves, the Gipsies. Even, according to Holinshed, "the poison of theft and robbery pervaded almost all classes of the Scottish community about this period."

The excessive severity of the sanguinary statute of 1609, and the unrelenting manner in which it was often carried into effect, were calculated to produce a great outward change on the Scottish Gipsies. Like stags selected from a herd of deer, and doomed to be hunted down by dogs, these wanderers were now singled out, and separated from the community, as objects to whom no mercy was to be shown.* The word Egyptian would never be allowed to escape their lips; not a syllable of their peculiar speech would be uttered, unless in the midst of their own tribe. It is also highly probable that every part of their dress by which their fraternity could be recognized, would be carefully discontinued. To deceive the public, they would also conform *externally* to some of the religious rites, ceremonies, observances, and

* The reader will see that the Gipsies, at this time, were not greater "vagabonds" than great numbers of native Scotch, if as great. But, being strangers in the country, sojourners according to their own accounts, the king would naturally enough banish them, as they seem always to have been saying that they were about leaving for "their own country." Their living in tents, a mode of life so different from that of the natives, would, of itself, make them obnoxious to the king personally.—Ed.

other customs of the natives of Scotland. I am further inclined to think that it would be about this period, and chiefly in consequence of these bloody enactments, the Gipsies would, in general, assume the ordinary christian and surnames common at that time in Scotland. And their usual sagacity pointed out to them the advantages arising from taking the cognomens of the most powerful families in the kingdom, whose influence would afford them ample protection, as adopted members of their respective clans. In support of my opinion of the origin of the surnames of the Gipsies of the present day, we find that the most prevailing names among them are those of the most influential of our noble families of Scotland; such as Stewart, Gordon, Douglas, Graham, Ruthven, Hamilton, Drummond, Kennedy, Cunningham, Montgomery, Kerr, Campbell, Maxwell, Johnstone, Ogilvie, McDonald, Robertson, Grant, Baillie, Shaw, Burnet, Brown, Keith, &c.* If, even at the present day, you enquire at the Gipsies respecting their descent, the greater part of them will tell you that they are sprung from a bastard son of this or that noble family, or other person of rank and influence, of their own surname.† This pretended connexion with families of high rank and power has saved some of the tribe from the gallows even in our own time. The names, however, of the two principal families, Faw, (now Faa,) and Bailyow, (now Baillie,) appear not to have been changed since the date of the order in council or league with James V, in the year 1540, as both of these names are inserted in that document.

Baron Hume, on the criminal law of Scotland, gives the

* The English Gipsies say that native names were assumed by their race in consequence of the proscription to which it was subjected. German Gipsies, on arrival in America, change, at least modify, their names. There are many of them who go under the names of Smith, Miller, and Waggoner. Jews frequently bear names common to the natives of the countries in which they are to be found, and sometimes, at the present day, assume Christian ones. I knew two German Jews, of the name of Cohen, who settled in Scotland. One of them, who was a priest, retained the original name; but the other, who was a watchmaker, assumed the name of Cowan, which, singularly enough, the priest said, was a corruption of Cohen.—Ed.

† It is stated by Paget, in his Travels in Hungary, that the Gipsies in that country have a profound regard for aristocracy; and that they invariably follow that class in the matter of religious opinions. Grellmann says as much in regard to the Gipsy's desire of getting hold of a distinguished old coat to put on his person.—Ed.

following account of some of the trials and executions of the Gipsies:

"The statute (1609) annuls at the same time all protection and warrants purchased by the Egyptians from his majesty's privy council, for their remaining within the realm; as also all privileges purchased by any person to reset, entertain, or do them any favour. It appears, indeed, from a paper in the appendix to McLaurin's Cases, that even the king's servants and great officers had not kept their hands entirely pure of this sort of treaty with the Egyptian chiefs, from whom some supply of money might in this way be occasionally obtained.

"The first Gipsies that were brought to trial on the statute, were four persons of the name of Faa, who, on the 31st July, 1611, were sentenced to be hanged. They had pleaded upon a special license from the privy council, to abide within the country; but this appearing to be clogged with a condition of finding surety for their appearance when called on, and their surety being actually at the horn, for failure to present themselves, they were held to have infringed the terms of their protection.

"The next trial was on the 19th and 24th July, 1616, in the case of other two Faas and a Baillie, (which seem to have been noted names among the Gipsies;) and here was started that plea which has since been repeated in almost every case, but has always been overruled, viz: that the act and proclamation were temporary ordinances, and applicable only to such Egyptians as were in the country at their date. These pannels, upon conviction, were ordered by the privy council to find caution to the extent of 1,000 merks, to leave Scotland and never to return; and having failed to comply with this injunction, they were in consequence condemned to die.

"In January, 1624, follows a still more severe example; no fewer than eight men, among whom Captain John Faa and other five of the name of Faa, being convicted, were doomed to death on the statute. Some days after, there were brought to trial Helen Faa, relict of Captain Faa, Lucretia Faa, and other women to the number of eleven; all of whom were in like manner convicted, and condemned to be drowned! But, in the end, their doom was commuted for banishment, (under pain of death,) to them and all their race. The sentence was, however, executed on the male convicts; and it appears that the terror of their fate had been of material service; as, for the space of more than 50 years from that time, there is no trial of an Egyptian."

But notwithstanding this statement of Baron Hume, of the Gipsy trials having ceased for half a century, we find, twelve years after 1624, the date of the above trials, the following order of the privy council: "Anent some Egyptians. At Edinburgh, 10th November, 1636. Forasmuch as Sir Arthur Douglas of Quhittinghame having lately taken and apprehended some of the vagabond and counterfeit thieves and *limmers*, (scoundrels,) called the Egyptians, he presented and delivered them to the sheriff principal of the sheriffdom of Edinburgh, within the constabulary of Haddington, where they have remained this month or thereby: and whereas the keeping of them longer, within the said tolbooth, is troublesome and burdensome to the town of Haddington, and fosters the said thieves in an opinion of impunity, to the encouraging of the rest of that infamous *byke* (hive) of lawless *limmers* (scoundrels) to continue in their thievish trade: Therefore the lords of secret council ordain the sheriff of Haddington, or his deputies, to pronounce doom and sentence of death against so many of these counterfeit thieves as are men, and against so many of the women as want children; ordaining the men to be hanged, and the women to be drowned; and that such of the women as have children, to be scourged through the burgh of Haddington, and burned in the cheek; and ordain and command the provost and baillies of Haddington to cause this doom be executed upon the said persons accordingly."*

"Towards the end of that century," continues Baron Hume, "the nuisance seems to have again become troublesome. On the 13th of December, 1698, John Baillie and six men more of the same name, along with the wife of one of them, were indicted as Egyptians, and also for sundry special misdeeds; and being convicted, (all but the woman,) they were ordered for execution. But in this case it is to be remarked, that the court had so far departed from the rigour of the statute as not to sustain a relevancy on the habit and repute of being an Egyptian of itself, but only 'along with one or other of the facts of picking and little

* Blackwood's Magazine.

thieving;' thus requiring some proof of actual guilt in aid of the fame. In the next trial, which was that of William Baillie, June 26th, 1699, a still further indulgence was introduced; for the interlocutor required a proof, not of *one* only, but of *several*, of the facts of 'picking or little thieving, or of several acts of beating and striking with invasive weapons.' He was only convicted as an Egyptian, and of *one* act of striking with an invasive weapon, and he escaped in consequence with his life.

"This lenient course of dealing with the Gipsies was not taken, however, from any opinion of it as a necessary thing, nor was there any purpose of prescribing it as a rule for other times, or for further cases of the kind where such an indulgence might seem improper, as appears from the interlocutor of relevancy in the case of John Kerr, and Helen Yorkston, and William Baillie and other seven; in both of which the simple fame and character of being an Egyptian is again found *separatum* relevant to infer the pain of death, (10th and 11th August, 1714.) Kerr and Yorkston had a verdict in their favour; Baillie and two of his associates were condemned to die; but as far as concerns Baillie, (for the others were executed,) his doom was afterwards mitigated into transportation, under pain of death in case of return.

"As early as the month of August, 1715, the same man, (as I understand it,) was again indicted, not only for being found in Britain, but for continuing his former practices and course of life. Notwithstanding this aggravation, the interlocutor is again framed on the indulgent plan, and only infers the pain of death, from the fame and character of being an Egyptian, joined with various acts of violence and sorning, to the number of three, that are stated in the libel. Though convicted nearly to the extent of the interlocutor, he again escaped with transportation.*

"Nor have I observed that the court, in any later case, have thought it necessary to proceed upon the repute alone, unavouched by evidence of, at least, one act of theft or violence; so that, upon the whole, according to the practice of later times, this sort of charge seems to be reduced nearly to the level of the charge of being habit and repute a thief at common law."

* This, and part of the preceding paragraph, will be quoted again, under the chapter of Tweed-dale and Clydesdale Gipsies.

It is noticed by Baron Hume that the Faas and the Baillies were noted names among the Gipsies. Indeed, the trials referred to by him are all of persons bearing these two surnames, except two individuals only. The truth is, the Faas and the Baillies were the two principal families among the Gipsies; giving, according to their customs, kings and queens to their countrymen in Scotland. They would be more bold, daring, and presumptuous in their conduct than the most part of their followers; and, being leaders of the banditti, government, in all probability, would fix upon them as the most proper objects for destruction, as the best and easiest method of overawing and dispersing the whole tribe in the country, by cutting off their chiefs. As I have already mentioned, these two principal clans of Faw and Bailyow appear to be the only Gipsy families in Scotland who have retained the original surnames of their ancestors, at least of those whose names are inserted in the treaty with James V, in 1540.

It will be seen, under the head Tweed-dale and Clydesdale Gipsies, that tradition has represented William Baillie, who was tried in 1714 and 1715, as a bastard son of the ancient family of Lamington, (his mother being a Gipsy). It appears to me that the Gipsy policy of joining themselves to some family of rank was, in Baillie's case, of very important service, not only to himself but to the whole tribe in Scotland.*

* From the time of arrival of the Gipsies in the country, in 1506, till 1611, the date of the first trials of the tribe, as given by Baron Hume, a period of 105 years had elapsed; during which time there had doubtless been five generations of Gipsies added to the population, as Scottish subjects; to put whom to death, on the mere ground of being Egyptians, was contrary to every principle of natural justice. The cruelty exercised upon them was quite in keeping with that of reducing to slavery the individuals, and their descendants, who constituted the colliers, coal-bearers, and salters referred to in the following interesting note, to be found in "My Schools and Schoolmasters," of Hugh Miller.

"The act for manumitting our Scotch colliers was passed in the year 1775, forty-nine years prior to the date of my acquaintance with the class of Niddry. But though it was only such colliers of the village as were in their fiftieth year when I knew them, (with, of course, all the older ones,) who had been born slaves, even its men of thirty had actually, though not nominally, come into the world in a state of bondage, in consequence of certain penalties attached to the emancipation act, of which the poor ignorant workers under ground were both too improvident and too little ingenious to keep clear. They were set free, however, by a second act passed in 1799. The language of both these acts, regarded as British ones of the latter half of the last century, and as bearing reference to British subjects

The extraordinary lenity shown to him by the court, after such repeated aggravation, cannot be accounted for in any other way than that great interest had been used in his behalf, in some quarter or other; and that, by creating a merciful precedent in his case, it was afterwards followed in the trial of all others of the race in Scotland.

living within the limits of the island, strikes with startling effect. 'Whereas,' says the preamble of the older act—that of 1775—'by the statute law of Scotland, as explained by the judges of the courts of law there, many colliers, and coal-bearers, and salters, are in a state of *slavery or bondage*, bound to the collieries or salt works, where they work *for life, transferable with the collieries or salt works*; and whereas, the emancipation,' &c., &c. A passage in the preamble of the act of 1799 is scarcely less striking: it declares that, notwithstanding the former act, 'many colliers and coal-bearers *still continue in a state of bondage*' in Scotland. The history of our Scotch colliers would be found a curious and instructive one. Their slavery seems not to have been derived from the ancient time of general serfship, but to have originated in comparatively modern acts of the Scottish Parliament, and in decisions of the Court of Session—in acts of Parliament in which the poor ignorant subterranean men of the country were, of course, wholly unrepresented, and in decisions of a court in which no agent of theirs ever made appearance in their behalf."

What is here said of a history of Scotch colliers being "curious and instructive," is applicable in an infinitely greater degree to that of the Gipsies.—Ed.

CHAPTER IV.

LINLITHGOWSHIRE GIPSIES.*

THE Gipsies who frequented the banks of the Forth, and the counties northward, appear to have been more daring than those who visited some other parts of Scotland.

Within these sixty years, a large horde, of very desperate character, resided on the banks of the Avon, near the burgh of Linlithgow. At first, they quartered higher up on the Stirling side of the stream, at a place called Walkmilton; but latterly they took up their abode in some old houses, on the Linlithgow side of the river, at or near the bridge of Linlithgow.

These Gipsies displayed much sagacity in carrying on their trade, by selecting the neighbourhood of Falkirk and Linlithgow for their headquarters, as this was, perhaps, the most advantageous position in all Scotland that a Gipsy band could occupy. This district was of itself very populous, and a very considerable trade and bustle then existed at the port of Bo'ness, in the vicinity. All the intercourse between Edinburgh and Glasgow passed a few miles to the south of their quarters. The traffic, by carts, between Glasgow and the west of Scotland, and the shipping at Carron-shore, Elphingston-Pow and Airth, on the Forth, before the canal was cut, was immense; all which traffic, as well as that between Fife and the western districts, passed a few miles north of

* This and the following three chapters are illustrative of the Gipsies, in their wild state, previous to their gradual settlement and civilization, and are applicable to the same class in every part of the world. Chapter VI, on the Gipsies of Tweed-dale, and Clydesdale, might have been taken the first in order, as descriptive of the tribe in its more primitive condition, but I have allowed it to remain where it stands. A description of the habits peculiar to the race will be found, more or less, in all of these chapters, where they can be consulted, for the better identification of the facts given.—ED.

their position. The road for travellers and cattle from the Highlands, by way of Stirling, crossed the above-mentioned roads, and led, through Falkirk and Linlithgow, to Edinburgh, the eastern and southern counties of Scotland, and England.

The principal surnames of this Gipsy band were McDonald, Jamieson, Wilson, Gordon and Lundie. Frequently the number that would assemble together would amount to upwards of thirty souls, and it was often observed that a great many females and children were seen loitering about their common place of residence. No protection was given by them to our native vagrants, nor were any of our common plunderers, vagabonds, or outlaws suffered to remain among them. When at home, or traversing the country, the trade and occupation of this band were exactly the same as those of their friends in other parts of Scotland, viz: making wool-cards, cast-iron soles for ploughs, smoothing-irons, horn spoons, and repairing articles in the tinker line. The old females told fortunes, while the women in general assisted their husbands in their work, by blowing the bellows, scraping and polishing the spoons with glass and charred wood, and otherwise completing their articles for sale. Many of the males dealt in horses, with which they frequented fairs —that great resort of the Gipsies; and these wanderers, in general, were considered excellent judges of horses. Numbers of them were fiddlers and pipers, and the tribe often amused themselves with feasting and dancing.*

Like their race generally, these Gipsies were extremely civil and obliging to their immediate neighbours, and those who lived nearest to their quarters, and had the most intercourse with them, in the ordinary affairs of life, were the least afraid of them.† But the farmers and others at a dis-

* It appears that, at this period, James Wilson, town-piper, and John Livingston, hangman, of Linlithgow, were both Gipsies. [Formerly the Gipsies were exclusively employed in Hungary and Transylvania as hangmen and executioners. *Grellmann.*—Ed.]

† This trait in the character of the Scottish Gipsies is well illustrated in the following anecdote, which appeared in Blackwood's Magazine. It was obtained by an individual who frequently heard the clergyman in question relate it.

"The late Mr. Leck, minister of Yetholm, happened to be riding home one evening from a visit in Northumberland, when, finding himself likely to be benighted, for sake of a near cut, he struck into a wild, solitary track, or drove-road, across the fields, by a place called the Staw. In one of the

tance, who frequented the markets at Falkirk, and other fairs in the neighbourhood, were always a plentiful harvest for the plundering Tinklers. Their plunderings on such occasions spread a general alarm over the country. But that good humour, mirth, and jocund disposition, peculiar to many of the males of the Gipsies, seldom failed to gain the good-will of those who deigned to converse with them with familiarity, or treated them with kindness. They even formed strong attachments to certain individuals of the community, and afforded them protection on all occasions, giving them tokens to present to others of their fraternity, while travelling under night. Notwithstanding the good disposition which they always showed under these circumstances, the fiery Tinklers often fell out among themselves, on dividing, at home, the booty which they had collected at fairs, and excited feelings of horror in the minds of their astonished neighbours, when they beheld the hurricanes of wrath and fury exhibited by both sexes, and all ages, in the heat of their battles.

The children of these Gipsies attended the principal school

derne places through which this path led him, there stood an old deserted shepherd's house, which, of course, was reputed to be haunted. The minister, though little apt to be alarmed by such reports, was, however, somewhat startled on observing, as he approached close to the cottage, a 'grim visage' staring out past a *window claith*, or sort of curtain, which had been fastened up to supply the place of a door, and also several 'dusky figures,' skulking among the bourtree-bushes that had once sheltered the shepherd's garden. Without leaving him any time for speculation, however, the knight of the curtain bolted forth upon him, and, seizing his horse by the bridle, demanded his money. Mr. Leck, though it was now dark, at once recognised the gruff voice, and the great, black, burly head of his next-door neighbour, *Gleid Neckit Will*, the Gipsy chief. 'Dear me, William,' said the minister, in his usual quiet manner, 'can this be you? ye're surely no serious wi' me? ye wadna sae far wrang your character for a good neighbour, for the bit trifle I ha'e to gi'e, William?'—'Lord saif us, Mr. Leck!' said Will, quitting the rein, and lifting his hat, with great respect, 'Whao wad hae thought o' meeting you out owre here-away? Ye needna gripe for ony siller to me—I wadna touch a plack o' your gear, nor a hair o' your head, for a' the gowd o' Tividale. I ken ye'll no do us an ill turn for this mistak—and I'll e'en see ye safe through the eirie Slaw—it's no reckoned a very *canny bit*, mair ways nor ane; but I wat ye'll no be feared for the *dead*, and I'll tak care o' the *living*.' Will accordingly gave his reverend friend a safe convoy through the haunted pass, and, notwithstanding this ugly mistake, continued ever after an inoffensive and obliging neighbour to the minister, who, on his part, observed a prudent and inviolable secrecy on the subject of this rencounter, during the life time of *Gleid Neckit Will*."

I understand this anecdote to apply to old Will Faa, mentioned in the Gipsies, under chapter VII.—ED.

at Linlithgow, and not an individual at the school dared to cast the slightest reflection on, or speak a disrespectful word of, either them or their parents, although their robberies were everywhere notorious, yet always conducted in so artful a manner that no direct evidence could ever be obtained of them. Such was the fear that the audacious conduct of these Gipsies inspired, that the magistrates of the royal burgh of Linlithgow stood in awe of them, and were deterred from discharging their magisterial duties, when any matter relative to their conduct came before their honours. The truth is, the magistrates would not interfere with them at all, but stood nearly on the same terms with them that a tribe of American Indians, who worshipped the devil—not from any respect which they had for his Satanic majesty, but from being in constant dread of his diabolical machinations. Not a justice of the peace gave the horde the least annoyance, but, on the contrary, allowed them to remain in peaceable possession of some old, uninhabited houses, to which they had no right whatever. Instead of endeavouring to repress the unlawful proceedings of the daring Tinklers, numbers of the most respectable individuals in Linlithgowshire deigned to play at golf and other games with the principal members of the body. The proficiency which the Gipsies displayed on such occasions was always a source of interest to the patrons and admirers of such games. At throwing the sledge-hammer, casting the putting-stone, and all other athletic exercises, not one was a match for these powerful Tinklers. They were also remarkably dexterous at handling the cudgel, at which they were constantly practising themselves.

The honourable magistrates, indeed, frequently admitted the presumptuous Tinklers to share a social bowl with them at their entertainments and dinner parties. Yet these friends and companions of the magistrates and gentlemen of Linlithgowshire were no other than the occasional tenants of kilns, or temporary occupiers of the ground floor of some ruinous, half-roofed houses, without furniture, saving a few blankets and some straw, to prevent their persons from resting upon the cold earth. But, nevertheless, these Gipsies made themselves of considerable importance, and possessed an influence over the minds of the community to an extent hardly to be credited at the present day. It was well known that the provost of Linlithgow, who was much exposed by riding at all times through the country, in the way of his business as a brewer, had himself received from the Gipsies assurance that he would not be molested by the band, and that he was, therefore, at all times, and on all occasions, perfectly safe from being plundered. Having in this manner rendered the local authorities entirely passive, or rather neutral, from fear and interest, the audacious Gipsies prosecuted their system of plunder and robbery to an alarming extent.

Notwithstanding the fear which these Gipsies inspired in the mind of the community, there were yet individuals of courage who would brave them, if circumstances rendered a meeting with them unavoidable. None, indeed, would dream of wantonly molesting them, but, if brought to the pinch, some would not shrink from encountering them, when acting under the influences of those feelings which call forth the latent courage of even the most timid and considerate of people. Such a rencounter resulted in the death of the chief of the Linlithgow band, of the name of McDonald, to whom the others of the tribe gave the title of captain.

In a dark night, a gentleman of the name of H——, an officer in the army, and a man of courage, while travelling on the high road, from the eastward to Stirlingshire, to visit, as was said, his sweetheart, had occasion to stop, for refreshment, at a public-house near the bridge of Linlithgow. The landlord advised him to go no further that night, owing to the road being "foul," meaning that the Tinklers had been seen lurking in the direction in which he was travelling. Foul or not foul, he would proceed; his particular engagement with the lady making him reluctant to break his promise, and turn back. He called for a gill of brandy, which he shared with the landlord, and deliberately loaded, in his presence, a brace of pistols which he carried about his person. His courage rose with the occasion, and he declared that whoever dared to molest him should not go unpunished. He then mounted his horse and rode forward. On arriving at a place called Sandy-ford-burn, a man, in the dark, sprang out from the side of the road, and, laying hold of the bridle of his horse, demanded his money. The horseman being on the alert, and quite prepared for such a demand, with his spirits, moreover, elevated by his dram of brandy, instantly replied by firing one of his pistols at the robber, who fell to the ground. He, however, held fast the bridle reins in his convulsive death grasp, and the horse, being urged forward, dragged him a short distance along the ground. Hardly had the shot been fired, ere a voice, close by, was heard to exclaim, "There goes our captain," while a confused cry of vengeance was uttered on all sides, against him by whom he had fallen. But the rider, clapping his spurs to his horse, instantly galloped forward, yet made a narrow escape, for several shots were fired at him, which were heard by the landlord of the public-house which he had just left.

The Gipsies, in this awkward predicament, carried the body of their chieftain home, and gave out to their neighbours, the country people, the following morning, (Sunday,) that he had died very suddenly of iliac passion. His lyke-wake was kept up in their usual manner, and great feastings and drinkings were held by them while his body lay uninterred. After several days of carousing, the remains of the robber were buried in the church-yard of Linlithgow.* His funeral was very respectable, having been attended by the magistrates of Linlithgow, and a number of the most genteel persons in the neighbourhood. The real cause of the sudden death of the Tinkler began to spread abroad, a short time after the burial, but no enquiry was made into the matter. The individual who had done the public a service, by taking off the chief of the banditti, mentioned the circumstance afterwards to his friends, and was afraid of the band for some time thereafter; although it was improbable that, in the dark, they were able to make out, or afterwards ascertain, the person who had made himself so obnoxious to them.

Notwithstanding this prompt and well-merited chastisement which the Gipsies received, in their leader being shot dead in his attempt at highway robbery, in the immediate vicinity of their ordinary place of rendezvous, they continued their depredations in their usual manner, but generally took care, as is their custom, to give no molestation to their

* Some of the Gipsies only put a paper cap on the head, and paper round the feet, of their dead; leaving all the body bare, excepting that they place upon the breast, opposite the heart, a circle made of red and blue ribbons, in form something like the shape of the variegated cockade, worn in the hats of newly-enlisted recruits in the army. [In England it was customary with the Gipsies, at one time, to burn the dead, but now they only burn the clothes, and some of the effects of the deceased.—Ed.

nearest neighbours. The deceased captain was succeeded, in the chieftainship of the tribe, by his son, Alexander McDonald, who also assumed the title of captain. This man trod in the footsteps of his father in every respect, and exercised his hereditary profession of theft and robbery, with an activity and audacity unequalled by any among his tribe in that part of Scotland. The very name of McDonald and his gang appalled the boldest hearts of those who ventured to travel under night with money in their pockets, in certain parts of the country. His band appears to have been very numerous, as among them some held the subordinate rank of lieutenants, as if they had been organized like a regular military company. James Jamieson, his brother-in-law, was also styled captain in this notorious band of Gipsies, who were connected with similar bands in England and Ireland.

McDonald and his brother-in-law, Jamieson, were considered remarkably stout, handsome, and fine-looking men. By constant training at all kinds of athletic exercises, they brought themselves to perform feats of bodily strength and agility which were almost incredible. They were often elegantly dressed in the finest clothes of the first fashion, with linen to correspond. At the same time they were perfect chameleons in respect to their appearance and apparel. McDonald was frequently observed in three or four different dresses in one market-day. At one time of the day, he was seen completely attired in the best of tartan, assuming the appearance and manners of a highland gentleman in full costume. At another time, he appeared ruffled at hands and breast, booted and spurred, on horseback, as if he had been a man of some consideration. He would again be seen in a ragged coat, with a budget and wallet on his back—a common travelling Tinkler. Both of these men often dealt in horses, and were themselves frequently mounted on the best of animals. The Arabians and Tartars are scarcely more partial to horses than the Gipsies.

The pranks and tricks played by McDonald were numerous, and many a story is yet remembered of his extraordinary exploits. He took great pains in training and learning some of his horses various evolutions and tricks. He had, at one time, a piebald horse so efficiently trained, and so completely under his management, that it, in some respects, assisted him in his depredations. By certain signals and motions, he could, when he found it necessary, make it clap close to the ground, like a hare in its furrow. It would crouch down in a hollow piece of ground, in a ditch, or at the side of a hedge, so as to hide itself, when McDonald's situation was like to expose him to detection. With the assistance of one of these well trained-horses, this man, on one occasion, saved his wife, Ann Jamieson, from prison, and perhaps from the gallows. Ann was apprehended near Dunfermline for some of her unlawful practices. As the officers of the law were conducting her to prison, McDonald rode up to the party, and requested permission to speak with their prisoner, which was readily granted, as, from McDonald's appearance, the officers supposed he had something to say to the woman. He then drew her aside, under the pretence of conversing with her in private, when, in an instant, Ann, with his assistance, sprang upon the horse, behind him, and bade good-bye to the messengers, who were amazed at the sudden and unexpected escape of their prisoner. Ann was a little, handsome woman, and was considered one of the most expert of the Scottish Gipsies at conducting a plundering at a fair; and was, on that account, much respected by her tribe.

McDonald and Jamieson, like others of the superior classes of Gipsies, gave tokens of protection to their particular friends of the community generally. The butchers of Linlithgow, when they went to the country, with money to buy cattle, frequently procured these assurances from the Gipsies. The shoemakers did likewise, when they had to go to distant markets with their shoes. Linlithgow appears even to have been under the special protection of these banditti. Mr. George Hart, and Mr. William Baird, two of the most respectable merchants of Bo'ness, who had been peddlers in their early years, scrupled not to say that, when travelling through the country, they were seldom without tokens from the Gipsies. But if the Gipsies were kind to those who kept on good terms with them, they, on the other hand, vindictively tormented their enemies. They would steal sheep, and put the blood and parts of the animal about the premises of those they hated, that they might be suspected of the theft, searched and affronted by the enquiries made about the stolen property.

When McDonald and Jamieson attacked individuals on the highway, or elsewhere, and were satisfied that they had little or no money, they were just as ready to supply their wants as to rob them. The idea of plundering the wealthy, and giving the booty to the poor, gives the Gipsies great satisfaction. The standard by which this people's conduct can be measured, must be sought for among the robber tribes of Tartary, Afghanistan, or Arabia. Many of our Scottish Gipsies have, indeed, been as ready to give a purse as take one; and it cannot be said that they have lacked in the display of a certain degree of honour peculiar to themselves, as the following well-authenticated fact will illustrate.*

A gentleman, whose name is not mentioned, while travelling, under night, between Falkirk and Linlithgow, fell in, on the road, with a man whom he did not know. During the conversation which ensued, he mentioned to the stranger that he was afraid of being attacked, for many a one, he observed, had been robbed on that road. He then urged that they should return, as the safest plan for them both. The stranger, however, replied that he had often travelled the road, yet had never been troubled by any one. After some further conversation, he put his hand into his pocket, and gave the traveller a knife, with which he was desired to proceed without fear.† The traveller now perfectly understood the relation that existed between them, and continued his journey with confidence; but he had not proceeded far ere he was accosted by a foot-pad, to whom he produced the knife. The pad looked at it carefully, said nothing, but passed on, without giving the traveller the slightest annoyance. It is needless to say that the mysterious stranger was no other than the notorious Captain McDonald. The traveller, by his fears and the nature of his conversation, had plainly informed McDonald of his being possessed of money —a considerable quantity of which he had, indeed, with him— and had the love of booty been the Gipsy's sole and con-

* Instances have occurred in which an Afghan has received a stranger with all the rights of hospitality, and afterwards, meeting him in the open country, has robbed him. The same person, it is supposed, who would plunder a cloak from a traveller who had one, would give a cloak to one who had none.—*Hugh Murray's Asia, vol. 2, page* 506.

† A pen-knife, a snuff-box, and a ring are some of the Gipsy pass-ports. It is what is marked upon them that protects the bearer from being disturbed by others of the tribe.

stant object, how easily could he, in this instance, have possessed himself of it. But the stranger had put himself, in a measure, under the protection of the robber, who disdained to take advantage of the confidence reposed in him.

Another instance of a Gipsy's honour, generosity, or caprice, or by whatever word the act may be expressed, occurred between McDonald and a farmer of the name of Campbell, and exhibits a singular cast of character, which has not been uncommon among the Scottish Gipsies. On this occasion, it would appear, the Gipsy had been influenced rather by a desire of enjoying the extraordinary surprise of the simple countryman, than of obtaining booty. The occurrence will also give some idea of the part which the cautious chiefs take in plundering at a fair. The particulars are derived from a Mr. David McRitchie, of whom I shall again make mention.

While Campbell was on his way to a market in Perth, he fell in with Captain McDonald. Being unacquainted with the character of his fellow-traveller, the unsuspecting man told him, among other things, that he had just as much money in his pocket as would purchase one horse, for his four-horse plough, having other three at home. McDonald heard all this with patience till he came to a solitary part of the road, when, all at once, he turned upon the astonished farmer, and demanded his money. The poor man, having no alternative, immediately produced his purse. But in parting, the robber desired him to call next day at a certain house in Perth, where he would find a person who might be of some service to him. Campbell promised to do as desired, and called at the house appointed, and great was his surprise, when, on being ushered into a room, he found himself face to face with the late robber, sitting with a large bowl of smoking toddy before him. The Gipsy, in a frank and hearty manner, invited his visitor to sit down and share his toddy with him; a request which he readily complied with, although bewildered with the idea of the probable fate of his purse, and the result of his personal adventure. He had scarcely got time, however, to swallow one glass, before he was relieved of his suspense, by the Gipsy returning him every farthing of the money he had robbed him of the day before. Being now pleased with his good fortune, and the Gipsy pressing him to drink, Campbell was in no hurry to be gone, his spirits having become elevated with his good cheer, and the confidence with which his host's conduct had inspired him. But his suspicions returned upon him, as he saw pocket-book after pocket-book brought in to his entertainer, during the time he was enjoying his hospitality. The Gipsy chief was, in fact, but following a very important branch of his calling, and was, on that day, doing a considerable business, having a number of youths ferreting for him in the market, and coming in and going out constantly.

But this crafty Gipsy, and his brother-in-law, Jamieson, were at last apprehended for house-breaking and robbery. Their trials took place at Edinburgh, on the 9th and 13th of August, 1770, and "the fame of being Egyptians" made part of the charge against them in the indictment; a charge well founded, as both of them spoke the "right Egyptian language." It was the last instance, I believe, that the fact of their being "called, known, repute, and holden Egyptians," made part of the indictment against any of the tribe in Scotland, under the sanguinary statute of James VI, chap. 13, passed in 1609. So cunning are the Gipsies, however, in committing crimes, that, in this instance, the criminals, it was understood, would have escaped justice, for want of sufficient proof, had not one of their own band, of the name of Jamieson, a youth of about twenty-two years of age, turned king's evidence against his associates. The two unhappy men were then found guilty by the jury, and condemned to die. They were ordered to be executed at Linlithgow bridge, near the very spot where their band had their principal rendezvous, with the apparent object of daunting their incorrigible race.

Immediately after the trial, a report was spread, and generally believed, that the Gipsies would attempt a rescue of the criminals on the way to execution, or even from under the gallows itself; and it was particularly mentioned that thirty stout and desperate members of the race had undertaken to set their chieftains free. Every precaution was therefore taken, by the authorities, to prevent any such attempt being made. A large proportion of the gentlemen and farmers of the shire of Linlithgow were requested, with what arms they could procure, to attend, on foot or horseback, the execution of the desperate Tinklers. Indeed, every third man of all the fencible men of the county was called upon to appear on the occasion; while a company of pensioners, with a commissioned officer at their head, and a strong body of the military, completed the force deemed necessary for the due execution of justice. Besides guarding against the possibility of a rescue on the part of the Gipsies, it was generally understood that the steps taken by the authorities, in bringing together so large a body of men, had in view the object of exhibiting to the people the ignominious death of two men who had not only been allowed to remain among them, but, in many instances, countenanced by some of the most respectable inhabitants of the county; and that not only in out-door amusements, but even in some of the special hospitalities of daily life, while in fact they were nothing but the leaders of a band of notorious thieves and robbers.

These precautions being completed, the condemned Gipsies were bound hand and foot, and conveyed, by the sheriff of Edinburgh and a company of the military, to the boat-house bridge, on the river Almond—the boundary of the two counties—and there handed over to the sheriff of Linlithgow; under whose guard they were carried to the jail of the town of Linlithgow, and securely bound in irons, to wait their execution on the morrow.* As night approached, fires were kindled at the door of the prison, and guards posted in the avenues leading to the building, while all the entrances to the town were guarded, and all ingress and egress prohibited, as if the burgh had been in a state of siege. So strictly were these orders put in force, that many of the inhabitants of Bo'ness, who had gone to Linlithgow, to view the bustle occasioned by the assemblage of so great a number of armed men, were forced to remain in the town over night; so alarmed were the authorities for the onset of the resolute Gipsies. It was soon perceived, by some sagacious individuals, that the fires would do more harm than good, as the light would show the prison, expose the sentinels, and guide the Gipsy bands. They were accordingly extinguished,

* "This morning, a little after nine o'clock, McDonald and Jamieson were transported from the Tolbooth here, (Edinburgh,) escorted by a party of the military, and attended by the sheriff-depute on horseback, with the officers of court, armed with broad-swords, amidst an innumerable crowd of spectators. They were securely pinioned to a cart, and are to be received by the sheriff-depute of Linlithgow, on the confines of this county, whither they are to be conveyed, in order to their execution to-morrow, near Linlithgow-bridge, pursuant to their sentence."—*Ruddiman's Weekly Magazine*, vol 9, page 384.

and the guards placed in such positions as would enable them, with the most advantage, to repel any attack that might be attempted: yet the enemy that caused all this alarm and precaution was nowhere visible.

On the following morning, McDonald's wife requested permission to visit her husband before being led to execution, with what particular object can only be conjectured; a favour which was readily granted her, in the company of a magistrate. On beholding the object of her affection, she became overwhelmed with grief; she threw her arms around his neck, and embraced him most tenderly; and after giving vent to her sorrow in sobs and tears, she tore herself from him, and, turning to the magistrate, exclaimed, with a bursting heart, "Is he not a pretty man? What a pity it is to hang him!"

Arrangements were then made to carry the prisoners to the place of execution, at the bridge of Linlithgow, which lay about a mile from the town. The armed force was drawn up at the town-cross, and those who carried muskets were ordered to load them with ball cartridge, and hold themselves ready, at the word of command, upon the least appearance of an attempt at rescue, to fire upon the aggressors. The whole scene presented such an alarming and warlike appearance, that the people of the town and surrounding country compared it to the bustle and military parade which took place, twenty-five years before, when the rebel army made its appearance in the neighbourhood. The judicious arrangements adopted by the officers of the crown had the desired effect; for not the slightest symptom of disturbance, not even a movement, was observed among the Gipsies, either on the night before, or on the morning of the execution. The formidable armed bands, ready to overwhelm the presumptuous Gipsies, clearly showed them that they had not the shadow of a chance for carrying out their intended rescue. All was peace and silence throughout the immense crowd surrounding the gallows, patiently waiting the appearance of the criminals. In due time the condemned made their appearance, in a cart, accompanied by Charles and James Jamieson, two youths, sitting beside their father and uncle, busily eating rolls, and, to all appearance, totally indifferent to the fate of their relatives, and the awful circumstances surrounding them.

On ascending the platform, Jamieson's demeanour was suitable to the circumstances in which he found himself placed; but McDonald appeared quite unconcerned. He was observed frequently to turn a quid of tobacco in his mouth, and squirt the juice of it around him; it was even evident, from his manner, that he expected to be delivered from the gallows by his tribe; and more especially as he had been frequently heard to say that the hemp was not grown that would hang him. He then began to look frequently and wistfully around him for the expected aid, yet none made its appearance; and his heart began to sink within him. Indeed, the overwhelming force then surrounding him rendered a deliverance impossible. Every hope having failed him, and seeing his end at hand, McDonald resigned himself, with great firmness, to his fate, and exclaimed: "I have neither friends on my right hand nor on my left; I see I now must die." Jamieson, who appeared from the first never to indulge in vain expectations of being rescued, exclaimed to his fellow-sufferer: "Sandie, Sandie! it is all over with us, and I told you so long ago." McDonald then turned to the executioner, whose name was John Livingston, and dropping into his hand something, supposed to be money, undauntedly said to him: "Now, John, don't bungle your job." Both of the unhappy men were then launched into eternity. Ever afterwards, the inhabitants of Linlithgow pestered the hangman, by calling to him: "Now, John, don't bungle your job. What was it the Tinkler gave you, John?"*

McDonald's wife had stood by, a quiet spectator, among the promiscuous crowd, of the melancholy scene displayed before her. But when she had witnessed the closing act of an eventful life—the heroism and fortitude which all she held as dear displayed in his last moments—and enjoyed the satisfaction which it had given her, nature, which the odium of her fellow-creatures, not of her blood, could not destroy, burst forth with genuine expression. The silence attending the awful tragedy was abruptly broken by the lamentable yells and heart-rending screams which she gave vent to, as

* "On Friday last, about three o'clock, McDonald and Jamieson were hanged, at the end of Linlithgow bridge. The latter appeared very penitent, but the former very little affected, and, as the saying is, *died hard*."—*Ruddiman's Weekly Magazine*, vol. 9, page 416.

she beheld her husband turned off the scaffold. Two gentlemen, who were present, informed me that she foamed at the mouth, and tore her hair out of her head, and was so completely frantic with grief and rage, that the spectators were afraid to go near her.

On the bodies being taken down from the scaffold, an attempt was made to restore them to life, by opening a vein, but without effect. It is said they were buried in the moor near Linlithgow, by the Gipsies, and that the magistrates of the town ordered them to be taken up, and interred in the east end of the church-yard of Linlithgow. However that may be, the bodies were buried in the church-yard of Linlithgow; but the populace, delivered from the terror with which these daring Gipsies inspired them, treated with ignominy the remains of those whom they dared scarcely look in the face when alive. They dug them out of the place of Christian sepulture, and interred them in a solitary field in the neighbourhood. A clump of trees, I believe, marks the spot, and the gloomy pine now waves, in the winds of heaven, over the silent and peaceful graves of the restless and lawless Gipsies.

McDonald, it would appear, was married, first of all, to a daughter of a Gipsy of the name of Eppie Lundie, with whom he lived unhappy, and was divorced from her over a horse sacrificed for the occasion, a ceremony which I will describe in another chapter.* He was more fortunate in his second matrimonial alliance, for, in Ann Jamieson, he found a wife after his own heart in every way. Previous to his own execution, she had witnessed the violent deaths of at least six of her own nearest relatives. But, if anything could have influenced, in the slightest degree, a reformation in her own character, it would have been the melancholy scene attending his miserable end; yet, we find it had not the slightest effect upon her after career, for she continued, to the last, to follow the practices of her race, as an anecdote told of her will show.

At the North Queensferry was a very respectable inn, kept by a Mr. McRitchie, which was much frequented and patron-

* This Eppie Lundie lived to the advanced age of a hundred years, and was a terror wherever she travelled. Without the least hesitation or scruple, she frequently stripped defenceless individuals of their wearing apparel, leaving them sometimes naked in the open fields.

ized by the Gipsies. On such occasions they did not visit the house in whole families or hordes, fluttering in rags, but as well-dressed individuals, arriving from different directions, as if by chance. In this house they were always treated with consideration and kindness, for other reasons than that of the liberal custom which they brought to it, and, as a natural consequence, the landlord and his family became great favourites with them. One of the members of the family, David McRitchie, my informant, happened one day to purchase a horse, at a fair in Dunfermline, but in feeling for his pocket-book, to pay for the animal, he found, to his surprise and grief, that book and money were gone. The person from whom he bought the horse commenced at once to abuse him as an impostor, for he not only would not believe his tale, but would not trust him for a moment. Under these distressing circumstances, he sought out Ann Jamieson, or Annie McDonald, after her husband's name, for he knew well enough where his money had gone to, and the sovereign influence which Ann exercised over her tribe. Being well acquainted with her, from having often met her in his father's house, he went up to her, and putting his hand gently on her shoulder, in a kind and familiar manner, and with a long face, told her of his misfortune, and begged her friendly assistance to help him out of the difficulty, laying much stress on the horse-dealer charging him with an attempt to impose on him. "Some o' my laddies will hae seen it, Davie; I'll enquire," was her immediate reply. She then took him to a public-house, called for brandy, saw him seated, and desired him to drink. Taking the marks of the pocket-book, she entered the fair, and, after various doublings and windings among the crowd, proceeded to her temporary depot of stolen goods. In about half an hour she returned, with the book and all its contents. The cash, bills, and papers which it contained, were in the same parts of the book in which the owner had placed them. This affair was transacted in as cool and business-like a manner as if Annie and her "laddies" had been following any of the honest callings in ordinary life. Indeed, no example, however severe, no punishment, however awful, seems to have had any beneficial effect upon the minds of these Gipsies, or their friends who frequented the surrounding parts of the country, for they continued to follow the ways of their race, in spite of the sanguinary laws of the country. A continuation of their history, up to a period, is little better than a melancholy narrative of a series of imprisonments, banishments, and executions.

Ann Jamieson's two nephews, Charles and James Jamieson, who rode alongside of their father and uncle to the place of their execution, eating rolls, as if nothing unusual was about to befall them, and who had witnessed their miserable end, in 1770, were themselves executed in 1786 for robbing the Kinross mail. It was their intention to have committed the deed upon the highway, for, the night before the robbery, their mother, Euphan Graham, to prevent detection, insisted upon the post-boy being put to death, to which bloody proposition her sons would not consent. It was then agreed that they should secure their prize in the stable yard of an inn in the town, where the post-boy usually stopped. The two highwaymen were traced to a small house near Stirling, in which they made a desperate resistance. One of them attempted to ascend the chimney, to effect his escape; but, failing in that, they attacked the officers, and tore at them with their teeth, after having struck furiously at them with a knife. But they were overpowered, and secured in irons. Two females were in their company at the time, on whom some of the money was found, most artfully concealed about their persons. So illiterate were these two men that, in crossing the Forth at Kincardine, they presented a twenty-pound note, to be changed, instead of a twenty-shilling one. According to Baron Hume, the trial of these two Gipsies took place on the 18th December, 1786. They were assisted in the robbery by other members of their band, including women and children. Their mother was said to have been transported for the part which she took in the affair; while another member of the gang was below the age at which criminals can be tried and punished in this country. The two brothers, before they committed the crime, measured themselves in a room in Kinross, kept by a Mary Barclay, and marked their heights on the wall. The one stood six feet two inches, and the other five feet four inches.*

* Perhaps the author intended to say, six feet two inches, and *six* feet four inches. Still, it might have been as stated in the MS.; for with Gipsies of mixed blood, the individual, if he takes after the Gipsy, is apt to be short and thick-set. The mixture of the two people produces a strong race of men.—Ed.

CHAPTER V.

FIFE AND STIRLINGSHIRE GIPSIES.

In this account of the Gipsies in Fife, the horde which at one period resided at the village of Lochgellie are frequently referred to. But it is proper to premise that this noted band were not the only Gipsies in Fife. This populous county contained, at one time, a great number of nomadic Gipsies. The Falkland hills and the Falkland fairs were greatly frequented by them;* and, not far from St. Andrews, some of the tribe had, within these fifty years, a small farm, containing about twenty acres of waste land, on which they had a small foundry, which the county people, on that account, called "Little Carron." As my materials for this chapter are chiefly derived from the Lochgellie band, and their immediate connexions in other districts not far from Fife, their manners and customs are, on that account, brought more under review.

The village of Lochgellie was, at one time, a favourite resort of the Gipsies. The grounds in its immediate vicinity are exactly of that character upon which they seem to have

* In Oliver and Boyd's Scottish Tourist, (1852), page 181, occurs the following passage: "A singular set of vagrants existed long in Falkland, called *Scrapies*, who had no other visible means of existence than a horse or a cow. Their ostensible employment was the carriage of commodities to the adjoining villages, and in the intervals of work they turned out their cattle to graze on the Lomond Hill. Their excursions at night were long and mysterious, for the pretended object of procuring coals, but they roamed with their little carts through the country-side, securing whatever they could lift, and plundering fields in autumn. Whenever any enquiry was addressed to a Falkland *Scrapie* as to the support of his horse, the ready answer was, 'Ou, he gangs up the (Lomond) Hill, ye ken.' This is now prevented; the Lomond is enclosed, and the *Scrapies* now manage their affairs on the road-sides."

The people mentioned in this extract are doubtless those to whom our author alludes. The reader will notice some resemblance between them and the tribe in the Pyrenees, as described at page 87.—Ed.

fixed their permanent, or rather winter's residence, in a great many parts of Scotland. By the statistical account of the parish of Auchterderran, Lochgellie was almost inaccessible for nearly six months in the year. The bleak and heathy morasses, and rushy wastes, with which the village is surrounded, have a gloomy and melancholy aspect. The scenery and face of the adjoining country are very similar to those in the neighbourhood of Biggar, in Lanarkshire, and Middleton, in Midlothian, which were also, at that time, Gipsy stations. A little to the south of the spot where the Linlithgow band, at one period, had their quarters, the country becomes moory, bleak, and barren. The village of Kirk-Yetholm, at present full of Gipsies, is also situated upon the confines of a wild, pastoral tract, among the Cheviot hills.* The Gipsies, in general, appear to have located themselves upon grounds of a flattish character, between the cultivated and uncultivated districts; having, on one side, a fertile and populous country, and, on the other, a heathy, boggy, and barren waste, into which they could retire in times of danger.†

In the statistical account of Auchterderran, just alluded to, is to be found the following notice of the Lochgellie Gipsies: "There are a few persons called *Tinkers* and *Horners*, half resident and half itinerant, who are feared and suspected by the community. Two of them were banished within these six years." This horde, at one time, consisted of four or five families of the names of Graham, Brown, Robertson, &c. The Jamiesons and Wilsons were also often seen at Lochgellie; but such were the numbers that were coming and going about the village, that it was difficult to say who were residenters, and who were not. Some of them had feus from the proprietor of the estate of Lochgellie. They were dreaded for their depredations, and were well known to the country people, all over the shires of Fife, Kinross, Perth, Forfar, Kincardine and Aberdeen, by the name of the "Lochgellie band." The chiefs of

* Yetholm lies in a valley which, surrounded on all sides by lofty mountains, seems completely sequestered from the rest of the world—alike inaccessible from without, and not to be left from within. The valley has, however, more than one outlet.—*Chambers' Gazetteer of Scotland.*—Ed.

† In Hungary, their houses, which are always small, and poor in appearance, are commonly situated in the outskirts of the village, and, if possible, in the neighbourhood of some thicket or rough land.—*Bright.*—Ed.

this band were the Grahams, at the head of which was old Charles Graham, an uncommonly stout and fine-looking man. He was banished the kingdom for his many crimes. Charlie had been often in courts of justice, and on one occasion, when he appeared for some crime or other, the judge, in a surly manner, demanded of him, what had brought him there?—"The auld thing again, my lord, but nae proof," was the Tinkler's immediate reply. Ann Brown, one of his wives, and the chief female of the band, was also sentenced to banishment for fourteen years; seven of which, however, she spent in the prison of Aberdeen. She remained altogether nine years at Botany Bay, married a Gipsy abroad, returned to Scotland, with more than a hundred pounds in cash, and now sells earthenware at St. Andrews.* Being asked why she left Botany Bay, while making so much money there, she said, "It was to let them see I could come back again."

Young Charlie Graham, son and successor, as chief, to old Charlie, was hanged at Perth, about thirty years ago, for horse-stealing. The anecdotes which are told of this singular man are numerous. When he was apprehended, a number of people assembled to look at him, as an object of wonder; it being considered a thing almost impossible to take him. His dog had discovered to the messengers the place of his concealment, having barked at them as they came near the spot. His feelings became irritated at the curiosity of the people, and he called out in great bitterness to the officers: "Let me free, and gie me a stick three feet lang, and I'll clear the knowe o' them." His feet and hands were so handsome and small, in proportion to the other parts of his athletic body, that neither irons nor hand-cuffs could be kept on his ankles or wrists; without injury to his person the gyves and manacles always slipped over his joints. He had a prepossessing countenance, an elegant figure, and much generosity of heart; and, notwithstanding all his tricks, was an extraordinary favourite with the public. Among the many tricks he played, it is related that he once, unobserved, in a grass park, converted a young colt into a gelding. He allowed the animal to remain for some time in the possession of the owner, and then stole it. He was immediately detected, and apprehended; but as the owner

* This woman is most probably dead, and the same may be said of some of the other characters mentioned in this and other chapters.—ED.

swore positively to the description of his horse, and Charlie's being a gelding, he got off clear. The man was amazed when he discovered the trick that had been played upon him, but when, where, and by whom done, he was entirely ignorant. Graham sold the animal to a third person, again stole it, and replaced it in the park of the original owner. He seemed to take great delight in stealing in this ingenious manner, trying how dexterously he could carry off the property of the astonished natives. He sometimes stole from wealthy individuals, and gave the booty to the indigent, although they were not Gipsies; and so accustomed were the people, in some places, to his bloodless robberies, that some only put their spurs to their horses, calling out, as they passed him: "Ah ha, Charlie lad, ye hae missed your mark to—night!" A widow, with a large family, at whose house he had frequently been quartered, was in great distress for want of money to pay her rent. Graham lent her the amount required; but as the factor was returning home with it in his pocket, Charlie robbed him, and, without loss of time, returned to the woman, and gave her a full discharge for the sum she had just borrowed from him.

He was asked, immediately before his execution, if he had ever performed any good action during his life, to recommend him to the mercy of his offended God. That of giving the widow and fatherless the money of which he immediately afterwards robbed the factor, was the only instance he adduced in his favour; thinking that thereby he had performed a virtuous deed. In the morning of the day on which he was to suffer, he sent a messenger to one of the magistrates, requesting a razor to take off his beard; at the same time, in a calm manner, desiring the person to tell the magistrate that, "unless his beard was shaven, he could appear before neither God nor man." A short time before he was taken out to the gallows, he was observed reclining very pensively and thoughtfully on a seat. All at once he started up, exclaiming, in a mournful tone of voice, "Oh, can ony o' ye read, sirs; will some o' ye read a psalm to me?" at the same time regretting much that he had not been taught to read. The fifty-first psalm was accordingly read to him, by a gentleman present, which soothed his feelings exceedingly, and gave him much ease and comfort. He was greatly agitated after ascending the platform—his knees knocking against each other; but just before he was cast off, his inveterate Gipsy feelings returned upon him with redoubled violence. He kicked from his feet both of his shoes, in sight of the spectators—to set at nought, as was supposed, some prophecy that he would die with them on; and addressed the assembled crowd in the following words: "I am this day to be married to the gallows-tree, by suffering in the manner of many of my ancestors; and I am extremely glad to see such a number of respectable people at my wedding." A number of the band attended his execution, and, when his body was returned to them, they all kissed it with great affection, and held the usual lyke-wake over it. His sweetheart, or widow, I am uncertain which, of the name of Wilson, his own cousin, put his corpse into hot lime, then buried it, and sat on his grave, in a state of intoxication, till it was rendered unfit for the use of the medical gentlemen; it having been reported that he was to be taken out of his grave for the purpose of dissection. This man boasted greatly, while under sentence of death, of never having spilled human blood by committing murder.

Hugh Graham, brother to Charlie, above-mentioned, was stabbed with a knife by his own cousin, John Young, in Aberdeenshire. These powerful Gipsies never fell in with each other but a wrestling bout took place. Young generally came off victorious, but Graham, although worsted, would neither quit Young nor acknowledge his inferiority of strength. Young frequently desired Graham to keep out of his way, as his obstinate disposition would prove fatal to one of them some time or other. They, however, met again, when a desperate struggle ensued. Graham was the aggressor; he drew his knife to stab Young, who wrested it out of his hand, and stabbing him in the upper part of the stomach, close to the breast, laid his opponent dead at his feet.* In this battle the Gipsy females, in their usual manner, took a conspicuous part, by assisting the combatants on either side.

* Young was chased for nearly thirty miles, by Highlanders, on foot, and General Gordon of Cairnfield, and others, on horseback; and, as he was frequently in view, the affair much resembled a fox-hunt. The hounds were most of them game-keepers—an active race of men; and so exhausted were they, before the Gipsy was caught, that they were seen lying by the springs, lapping water with their tongues, like dogs.—*Blackwood's Magazine.*—Ed.

Jenny Graham, sister of these Grahams, was kept by a gentleman as his mistress; but, although treated with affection, such was her attachment to her old wandering way of life, that she left her protector and his wealth, and rejoined her erratic associates in the gang. She was a remarkably handsome and good-looking woman, and, while she traversed the country, she frequently rode upon an ass, which was saddled and bridled. On these occasions, she was sometimes dressed in a blue riding-habit and a black beaver hat. It was generally supposed that the stolen articles of value belonging to the family were committed to the care of Jenny. Margaret Graham, another sister, is still living, and is a woman of uncommon bodily strength; so much so, that she is considered to be a good deal stronger than the generality of men. She was married to William Davidson, a Gipsy, at Wemyss. They have a large family, and sell earthenware through the country.

John Young, who stabbed his cousin, Hugh Graham, was one of seven sons, and though above five feet ten inches in height, his mother used to call him "the dwarf o' a' my bairns." He was condemned and hanged at Aberdeen for the murder. He wrote a good hand, and the country-people were far from being displeased with his society, while he was employed in repairing their pots and pans in the way of his calling. Sarah Graham, his mother, was of the highest Tinkler mettle. She lost a forefinger in a Gipsy fray. Peter Young, another son of Sarah's, was also hanged at Edinburgh, after breaking a number of prisons in which he was confined. He is spoken of as a singular man. Such was his generosity of character, that he always exerted himself to the utmost to set his fellow-prisoners free, although they happened not to be in the same apartment of the prison. The life of this man was published about the time of his execution. When any one asked old John Young where his sons were, his reply was, "They are all hanged." They were seven in number, and it was certainly a fearful end of a whole family. The following is an extract of a letter addressed to Mr. Blackwood, from Aberdeen, relative to Peter Young: "It is said, in your far-famed magazine, that Peter Young, brother to John Young, the Gipsy, likewise suffered at *Aberdeen*. It is true that he received sentence to die there, but the prison and all the irons the persons were able to load him with, somehow or other, were found insufficient to prevent him from making his escape. After he had repeatedly broken loose, and had been as often retaken, the magistrates at last resolved that he should be effectually secured; and, for that purpose, ordered a great iron chain to be provided, and Peter to be fast bound in it. As the jailer was making everything, as he thought, most secure, Peter, with a sigh, gazed on him, and said, 'Ay, ay, I winna come out now till I come out at the door;' making him believe that he would not be able to make his escape again, nor come out till the day fixed for his execution. But the great iron chain, bolts and bars, were all alike unable to withstand his skill and strength: he came out, within a few nights, at the 'door,' along with such of his fellow-prisoners as were inclined to avail themselves of the 'catch;' but he was afterwards taken, and conveyed to Edinburgh, and there made to suffer the penalty which his crimes deserved.—D. C."*

* Our author says that the Life of Peter Young was published. The following particulars, quoted in an account of the Gipsies, in the sixteenth volume of Chambers' Miscellany, are probably taken from that source:

"Peter was Captain of a band well known in the north of Scotland, where his exploits are told to this day. Possessed of great strength of body, and very uncommon abilities, he was a fine specimen of his race, though he retained all their lawless propensities. He was proud, passionate, revengeful, a great poacher, and an absolute despot, although a tolerably just one, over his gang, maintaining his authority with an oak stick, the principal sufferers from which were his numerous wives."—"He esteemed himself to be a very honourable man, and the keepers of the different public-houses in the country seem to have thought that, to a certain extent, he was so. He never asked for trust as long as he had a halfpenny in his pocket. At the different inns which he used to frequent, he was seldom or never denied anything. If he pledged his word that he would pay his bill the next time he came that way, he punctually performed his promise."

"Peter's work was that of a very miscellaneous nature. It comprehended the profession of a blacksmith, in all its varieties, a tin-smith, and brazier. His original business was to mend pots, pans, kettles, &c., of every description, and this he did with great neatness and ingenuity. Having an uncommon turn for mechanics, he at last cleaned and repaired clocks and watches. He could also engrave on wood or metal; so also could his brother John; but where they learned any of these arts I never heard. Peter was very handy about all sorts of carpenter work, and occasionally amused himself, when the fancy seized him, in executing some pieces of curious cabinet work that required neatness of hand. He was particularly famous in making fishing-rods, and in the art of fishing he was surpassed by few."

Immediately before *one* of the days fixed for his execution, he seized the

Charles Brown, one of the principal members of the Lochgellie band, was killed in a desperate fight at Raploch, near Stirling. A number of Gipsy boys, belonging to several gangs in the south, obtained a considerable quantity of plunder, at a fair in Perth, and had, in the division of the spoil, somehow or another, imposed on the Lochgellie tribe, and their associates. Charles Graham, already mentioned, and Charles Brown, went south in pursuit of the young depredators, for the purpose of compelling them to give up their ill-gotten booty to those to whom, by the Gipsy regulations, it of right belonged. After an arduous chase, the boys were overtaken near Stirling, when a furious battle immediately commenced. Both parties were armed with bludgeons. After having fought for a considerable time, with equal success on both sides, Graham, from some unknown cause, fled, leaving his near relation, Brown, to contend alone with the youths, in the best way he could. The boys now became the assailants, and began to press hard upon Brown, who defended himself long and manfully with his bludgeon, displaying much art in the use of his weapon, in warding off the lighter blows of his opponents, which came in upon him from all quarters. At length he was forced to give way, although very few of the blows reached his person. On retreating, with his front to his assailants, his foot struck upon an old feal dyke, when he fell to the ground. The enraged youths now sprang in upon him, like tigers, and, without showing him the least mercy, dispatched him on the spot, by literally beating out his brains with their bludgeons. Brown's coat was brought home to Lochgellie, by some of his wife's friends, with the collar and shoulders besmeared all over with blood and brains, with quantities of his hair sticking in the gore. It was preserved for some time in this shocking condition by his wife, and exhibited as a proof that her husband had not fled, as well as to

jailer, and, upon the threat of instant death, compelled him to lay on his back, as one dead, till he had set at liberty every one in the prison, himself being the last to leave the building. After travelling twenty-four miles, he went to sleep in the snow, and was apprehended by a company of sportsmen, whose dogs had made a dead set at him. On being taken to the gallows, one of the crowd cried: "Peter, deny you are the man!"—which he did, declaring that his name was John Anderson, and wondered what the people wanted with him. And there being none present who could identify him, although he was well known in Aberdeen, he managed to get off clear.—Ed.

arouse the clan to vengeance. My informant, a man about fifty years of age, with others, saw this dreadful relique of Brown, in the very state in which it is now described.

Alexander Brown, another member of the Lochgellie band, happened, on one occasion, to be in need of butcher meat, for his tribe. He had observed, grazing in a field, in the county of Linlithgow, a bullock that had, by some accident, lost about three-fourths of its tail. He procured a tail of a skin of the same colour as that of the animal, and, in an ingenious manner, made it fast to the remaining part of its tail. Disguised in this way, he drove off his booty; but after shipping the beast at the Queens-ferry, on his way to the north, a servant, who had been dispatched in quest of the depredator, overtook him as he was stepping into the boat. An altercation immediately commenced about the ox. The countryman said he could swear to the identity of the animal in Brown's possession, were it not for its long tail; and was proceeding to examine it narrowly, to satisfy himself on that particular, when the ready-witted Gipsy, ever fertile in expedients to extricate himself from difficulties, took his knife out of his pocket, and, in view of all present, cut off the tail above the juncture, drawing blood instantly; and, throwing it into the sea, called out to the pursuer, with some warmth: "Swear to the ox now, and be —— to ye." The countryman said not another word, but returned home, while the Tinkler proceeded on his journey with his prize.*

* Besides getting themselves out of scrapes in such an adroit manner, the Scotch Gipsies have been known to serve a friend, when innocently placed in a position of danger. It happened once that Billy Marshall, the Gipsy chief in Gallowayshire, attacked and robbed the laird of Bargally, and in the tussle lost his cap. A respectable farmer, passing by, some time afterwards, picked up the cap, and put it on his head. The laird, with his mind confused by the robbery and the darkness combined, accused the farmer of the crime; and it would have gone hard with him at the trial, had not Billy come to his rescue. He seized the cap, in the open court, and, putting it on his head, addressed the laird: "Look at me, sir, and tell me, by the oath you have sworn, am not I the man that robbed you?"—"By heaven! you are the very man."—"You see what sort of memory this gentleman has," exclaimed the Gipsy; "he swears to the bonnet, whatever features are under it. If you, yourself, my lord, will put it on your head, he will be willing to swear that your lordship was the person who robbed him." The farmer was unanimously acquitted.

Notwithstanding Billy's courage in "taking care of the *living*," an anecdote is related of his having been frightened almost out of his wits, under very ludicrous circumstances. He and his gang had long held possession of a cavern in Gallowayshire, where they usually deposited their plunder,

But this Gipsy was not always so fortunate as he was on this occasion. Being once apprehended near Dumblane, it was the intention of the messengers to carry him direct to Perth, but they were under the necessity of lodging him in the nearest prison for the night. Brown was no sooner in custody than he began to meditate his escape. He requested, as a favour, that the officers would sit up all night with him, in a public-house, instead of a prison, promising them as much meat and drink, for their indulgence and trouble, as they should desire. His request having been granted, four or five officers were placed in and about the room in which he was confined, as a guard on his person, being aware of the desperate character they had to deal with. He took care to ply them well with the bottle; and early next morning, before setting out, he desired one of them to put up the window a little, to cool the apartment. After walking several times across the room, the Gipsy, all at once, threw himself out of the window, which was a considerable height from the ground. The hue and cry was at his heels in an instant; and as some of the messengers were gaining on him, he boldly faced about, drew forth, from below his coat, a dagger, which he brandished in the air, and threatened death to the first who should approach him. He was, on this occasion, suffered to make his escape, as none had the courage to advance upon him.

When in full dress, Brown wore a hat richly ornamented and trimmed with beautiful gold lace, which was then fashionable among the first ranks in Scotland, particularly among the officers of the army. His coat was made of superfine cloth, of a light green colour, long in the tails, and having one row of buttons at the breast. His shirt, of the finest quality, was ruffled at hands and breast, with a black

and sometimes resided, secure from the officers of the law. Two Highland pipers, strangers to the country, happened to enter it, to rest themselves during the night. They perceived, at once, the character of its absent inhabitants; and they were not long within it, before they were alarmed by the voices of a numerous band advancing to its entrance. The pipers, expecting nothing but death from the ruthless Gipsies, had the presence of mind to strike up a pibroch, with tremendous fury; at the terrific reception of which—the yelling of the bag-pipes issuing from the bowels of the earth—Billy and his gang precipitately fled, as before a blast from the infernal regions, and never afterwards dared to visit their favourite haunt. The pipers, as might naturally be expected, carried off, in the morning, the spoils of the redoubted Gipsies.—*Sir Walter Scott*.—Ed.

stock and buckle round the neck. He also wore a pair of handsome boots, with silver-plated spurs, all in the fashion of the day. Below his garments he carried a large knife, and in the shaft or butt-end of his large whip, a small spear, or dagger, was concealed. His brother-in-law, Wilson, was frequently dressed in a similar garb, and both rode the best horses in the country. Having the appearance of gentlemen in their habits, and assuming the manners of such, which they imitated to a wonderful degree, few persons took these men for Gipsies. Like many of their race, they are represented as having been very handsome, tall, and stout-made men, with agreeable and manly countenances. Among the numerous thefts and robberies which they committed in their day, they were never known to have taken a sixpence from people of an inferior class, but, on the contrary, rather to have assisted the poor classes in their pecuniary matters, with a generous liberality, not at all to be looked for from men of their singular habits and manner of life. The following particulars are descriptive of the manner and style in which some of the Gipsies of rank, at one time, traversed this country.

Within these forty-five years, Mr. McRitchie, already alluded to, happened to be in a smithy, in the neighbourhood of Carlisle, getting the shoes of his riding-horse roughened on a frosty day, to enable him to proceed on his journey, when a gentleman called for a like purpose. The animal on which he was mounted was a handsome blood-horse, which was saddled and bridled in a superior manner. He was himself dressed in superfine clothes, with a riding-whip in his hand; was booted and spurred, with saddle-bags behind him; and had, altogether, man and horse, the equipment and appearance of a smart English mercantile traveller, riding in the way of his business. There being several horses in the smithy, he, in a haughty and consequential manner, enquired of the smith, very particularly, whose turn it was first; indicating a strong desire to be first served, although he was the last that had entered the smithy. This bold assurance made my acquaintance take a steady look at the intrusive stranger, whom he surveyed from head to foot. And what was his astonishment when he found the mighty gentleman to be no other than Sandie Brown, the Tinkler's son, from the neighbourhood of Crieff; whom he had often seen strolling through the country in a troop of Gipsies, and frequently in his father's house, at the North Queensferry. He could scarcely believe his eyes, so to prevent any disagreeable mistake, politely asked the "gentleman" if his name was not Brown; observing that he thought he had seen him somewhere before. The surprised Tinkler hesitated considerably at the unexpected question, and, after having put some queries on his part, answered that "he would not deny himself—his name was really Brown." He had, in all likelihood, been travelling under a borrowed name, a practice very common with the Gipsies. When he found himself detected, yet seeing no danger to be apprehended from the accidental meeting, he very shrewdly showed great marks of kindness to his acquaintance. Being now quite free from embarrassment, he, in a short time, began to display, as is the Gipsy custom, extraordinary feats of bodily strength, by twisting with his hands strong pieces of iron; taking bets regarding his power in these practices, with those who would wager with him. Before parting with my friend, Brown very kindly insisted upon treating him with a bottle of any kind of liquor he would choose to drink. At some sequestered station of his tribe, on his way home, the equestrian Tinkler would unmask himself—dispose of his horse, pack up his fine clothes, and assume his ragged coat, leathern apron, and budget—before he would venture among the people of the country, who were acquainted with his real character. Here we see a haughty, overbearing, highway robber, clothed in excellent apparel, and mounted on a good steed, metamorphose himself, in an instant, into a poor, wandering, beggarly, and pitiful Gipsy.

This Alexander Brown, and his brother-in-law, Wilson, carried on conjointly a considerable trade in horse-stealing between Scotland and England. The horses which were stolen in the South were brought to Scotland, and sold there; those stolen in Scotland were, on the other hand, disposed of in the South by English Gipsies. The crime of horse-stealing has brought a great many of these wanderers to an untimely end on the gallows. Brown was at last hanged at Edinburgh, to expiate the many crimes he had, from time to time, committed. It is said that his brother-in-law, Wilson, was hanged along with him on the same day, having been also guilty of a number of crimes. Brown was taken in a wood in Rannach, having been surprised and overpowered by a party of Highlanders, raised for the purpose of apprehending him, and dispersing his band, who lay in the wood in which he was captured. He thought to evade them by clapping close to the ground, like a wild animal. Upon being seized, a furious scuffle ensued; and during the violent tossing and struggling which took place, while they were securing this sturdy wanderer, he took hold of the bare thigh of one of the Highlanders, and bit it most cruelly. Martha, the mother of Brown, and the mother-in-law of Wilson, was apprehended in the act of stealing a pair of sheets while attending their execution.

Charles, by some called William, a brother of Alexander Brown, was run down by a party of the military and some messengers, near Dundee. He was carried to Perth, where he was tried, condemned and executed, to atone for the numerous crimes of which he was guilty. He was conveyed to Perth by water, in consequence of it being reported that the Gipsies of Fife, with the Grahams and Ogilvies at their head, were in motion to rescue him. He, also, was a man of great personal strength; and regretting, after being handcuffed, having allowed himself to be so easily taken, he, in wrath, drove the messengers before him with his feet, as if they had been children. While in the apartment of the prison called the condemned cell, or the cage, he freed himself from his irons, and by some means set on fire the damp straw on which he lay, with the design of making his escape in the confusion. Surprised at the building being on fire, and suspecting Brown to have been the cause of it, and that he was free from his chains, ramping like a lion in his den, no one, in the hurry, could be found with resolution enough to venture near him, till a sergeant of the forty-second regiment volunteered his services. Before he would face the Tinkler, however, he requested authority from the magistrates to defend himself with his broad-sword, and, in case the prisoner became desperate, to cut him down. This permission being obtained, the sergeant drew his sword, and, assisted by the jailer's daughter, unbarred the doors, till he came to the cage, whence the prison was being filled with smoke. As he advanced to the door, he asked with a loud voice, "Who is there?" "The devil," vociferated the Gipsy, through fire and smoke. "I am also a devil, and of the black-watch," thundered back the intrepid Highlander. The resolute reply of the soldier sounded like a death knell to the artful Tinkler—he knew his man—it daunted him completely; for, after some threats from the sergeant, he quietly allowed himself to be again loaded with irons, and thoroughly secured in his cell, whence he did not stir till the day of his execution.

Lizzy Brown, by some called Snippy, a member of the same family, was a tall, stout woman, with features far from being disagreeable. She lost her nose in a battle, fought in the shire of Angus. In this rencounter, the Gipsies fought among themselves with highland dirks, exhibiting all the fury of hostile tribes of Bedouin Arabs of the desert. When this woman found that her nose was struck off, by the sweep of a dirk, she put her hand to the wound, and, as if little had befallen her, called out, in the heat of the scuffle, to those nearest her: "But, in the middle o' the meantime, where is my nose?" Poor Lizzy's tall figure was conspicuous among the tribe, owing to the want of that ornamental part of her face.

The Grahams of Lochgellie, the Wilsons of Raploch, near Stirling, and the Jamiesons, noticed under the head of Linlithgowshire Gipsies, were all, by the female side, immediately descended from old Charles Stewart, a Gipsy chief, at one period of no small consequence among these hordes.* When I enquired if the Robertsons, who lived, at one time, at Menstry, were related to the Lochgellie band, the answer which I received was: "The Tinklers are a' sib"—meaning that they are all connected with one another by the ties of blood, and considered as one family. This is a most powerful bond of union among these desperate clans, which almost bids defiance to the breaking up of their strongly cemented society. Old Charles Stewart was described to me as a stout, good-looking man, with a fair complexion; and I was informed that he lived to a great age. He affirmed, wherever he went, that he was a descendant of the royal Stewarts of Scotland. His descendants still assert that they are sprung from the royal race of Scotland. In

* It is interesting to notice that the three criminals who gave occasion to the Porteous mob, in 1736, were named Stewart, Wilson and Robertson. They were doubtless Gipsies of the above mentioned clans. Their crimes and modes of escape were quite in keeping with the character of the Gipsies.—Ed.

support of this pretension, Stewart, in the year 1774, at a wedding, in the parish of Corstorphine, actually wore a large cocked hat, decorated with a beautiful plume of white feathers, in imitation of the white cockade of the Pretender. On this occasion, he wore a short coat, philabeg and purse, and tartan hose. He sometimes wore a piece of brass, as a star, on his left breast, with a cudgel in his hand. Such ridiculous attire corresponds exactly with the taste and ideas of a Gipsy.* These pretensions of Stewart are exactly of a piece with the usual Gipsy policy of making the people believe that they are descended from families of rank and influence in the country. At the same time, it cannot be denied that some of our Scottish kings, especially James V, the "Gaberlunzie-man,"† were far from being scrupulous or fastidious in their vague amours. As old Charles Stewart was, on one occasion, crossing the Forth, at Queensferry, chained to his son-in-law, Wilson, in charge of messengers, he, with considerable shame in his countenance, observed David McRitchie, whose father, as already mentioned, kept a first-rate inn at the north-side, and in which the Tinkler had frequently regaled himself with his merry companions. Stewart called McRitchie to him, and, taking five shillings out of his pocket, said to him, "Hae, Davie, there's five shillings to drink my health, man; I'll laugh at them

* Grellmann, in giving an account of the attire of the poorer kind of Hungarian Gipsies, says: We are not to suppose, however that they are indifferent about dress; on the contrary, they love fine clothes to an extravagant degree. Whenever an opportunity offers of acquiring a good coat, either by gift, purchase, or theft, the Gipsy immediately bestirs himself to become master of it. Possessed of the prize, he puts it on directly, without considering in the least whether it suits the rest of his apparel. If his dirty shirt had holes in it as big as a barn door, or his breeches so out of condition that any one might, at the first glance, perceive their antiquity; were he unprovided with shoes and stockings, or a covering for his head; none of these defects would prevent his strutting about in a laced coat, feeling himself of still greater consequence in case it happened to be a red one. They are particularly fond of clothes which have been worn by people of distinction, and will hardly ever deign to put on a boor's coat. They will rather go half naked, or wrap themselves up in a sack, than condescend to wear a foreign garb. Green is a favourite colour with the Gipsies, but scarlet is held in great esteem among them. It is the same with the Hungarian female Gipsies. In Spain, they hang all sorts of trumpery in their ears, and baubles around their necks.

Mr. Borrow says of the Spanish Gipsies, that there is nothing in the dress of either sex differing from that of the other inhabitants. The same may be said of the Scottish tribes, and even of those in England.—Ed.

† *Gaberlunzie-man*—The beggar-man with the ragged apparel.

a'." He did laugh at them all, for nothing could be proved against him, and he was immediately set at liberty. It was, as Charles Graham said—"The auld thing again, but nae proof."*

Another very singular Gipsy, of the name of Jamie Robertson, a near relation of the Lochgellie tribe, resided at Menstry, at the foot of the Ochil hills. James was an excellent musician, and was in great request at fairs and country weddings. Although characterized by a dissoluteness of manners, and professed roguery, this man, when trusted, was strictly honest. A decent man in the neighbourhood, of the name of Robert Gray, many a time lent him sums of money, to purchase large ox horns and other articles, in the east of Fife, which he always repaid on the very day he promised, with the greatest correctness and civility. The following anecdote will show the zeal with which he would resent an insult which he conceived to be offered to his friend: In one of his excursions through Fife, he happened to be lying on the ground, basking himself in the sun, while baiting his ass, on the roadside, when a countryman, an entire stranger to him, came past, singing, in lightness of heart, the song of "Auld Robin Gray," which, unfortunately for the man, Robertson had never heard before. On the unconscious stranger coming to the words "Auld Robin Gray was a kind man to me," the hot-blooded Gipsy started to his feet, and, with a volley of oaths, felled him with his bludgeon to the ground; repeating his blows in the most violent manner, and telling him, "Auld Robin Gray was a kind man to him indeed, but it was not for him to make a song on Robin for that." In short, he nearly put the inno-

* The unabashed hardihood of the Gipsies, in the face of suspicion, or even of open conviction, is not less characteristic than the facility with which they commit crimes, or their address in concealing them. A Gipsy of note, (known by the title of the "Earl of Hell,") was, about twenty years ago, tried for a theft of a considerable sum of money at a Dalkeith market. The proof seemed to the Judge fully sufficient, but the Jury rendered a verdict of "not proven." On dismissing the prisoner from the bar, the Judge informed him, in his own characteristic language, "That he had rubbit shouthers wi' the gallows that morning;" and warned him not again to appear there with a similar body of proof against him, as it seemed scarcely possible he should meet with another Jury who would construe it as favourably. His counsel tendered him a similar advice. The Gipsy, however, replied, to the great entertainment of all around, "That he was proven an innocent man, and that naebody had ony right to use siccan language to him."—*Blackwood's Magazine.*—Ed.

cent man to death, in the heat of his passion, for satirizing, as he thought, his friend in a scurrilous song. It was an invariable custom with Robertson, whenever he passed Robert Gray's house, even were it at the dead hour of night, to draw out his "bread winner," and give him a few of his best airs, in gratitude for his kindness.

Robertson's wife, a daughter of Martha, whose son and son-in-law, Brown and Wilson, were executed, as already mentioned, was sentenced to transportation to Botany Bay; but, owing to her advanced years, it was not thought worth the expense and trouble of sending her over seas, and she was set at liberty. Her grandson, Joyce Robertson, would also have been transported, if not hanged, but for the assistance of some of his clan rescuing him from Stirling jail. So coolly and deliberately did he go about his operations, in breaking out of the prison, that he took along with him his oatmeal bag, and a favourite bird, in a cage, with which he had amused himself during his solitary confinement. The following anecdote of this audacious Gipsy, which was told to me by an inhabitant of Stirling, who was well acquainted with the parties, is, I believe, unequalled in the history of robberies: While Robertson was lying in jail, an old man, for what purpose is not mentioned, went to the prison window, to speak to him through the iron staunchcons. Joyce, putting forth his hand, took hold of the unsuspecting man by the breast of his coat, and drew him close up to the iron bars of the window; then thrusting out his other hand, and pointing a glittering knife at his heart, threatened him with instant death, if he did not deliver him the money he had on him. The poor man, completely intimidated, handed into the prison all the money he had; but had it returned, on the jailer being informed of the extraordinary transaction.* After escaping from confinement, this Gipsy stole a watch from a house at Alva, but had hardly got it into his possession before he was discovered, and had the inhabitants of the village in pursuit of him. A man, of the name of Dawson, met him in his flight, and, astonished at seeing the crowd at his heels, enquired, impatiently, what was the matter.

* The "game" of such a Gipsy may be fitly compared to that of a sparrow-hawk. This bird has been known, while held in the hand, after being wounded, to seize, when presented to it, a sparrow with each claw, and a third with its beak.—Ed.

"They are all running after me, and you will soon run too," replied the Tinkler, without shortening his step. He took to Tullibody plantations, but was apprehended, and had the watch taken from him.

I will notice another principal Gipsy, closely connected by blood with the Fife bands, and of that rank that entitled him to issue tokens to the members of his tribe. The name of this chief was Charles Wilson, and his place of residence, at one time, was Raploch, close by Stirling castle, where he possessed some heritable property in houses. He was a stout, athletic, good-looking man, fully six feet in stature, and of a fair complexion; and was, in general, handsomely dressed, frequently displaying a gold watch, with many seals attached to its chain. In his appearance he was respectable, very polite in his manners, and had, altogether, little or nothing about him which, at first sight, or to the general public, indicated him to be a Gipsy. But, nevertheless, I was assured by one of the tribe, who was well acquainted with him, that he spoke the language, and observed all the customs, and followed the practices of the Gipsies.

He was a pretty extensive horse-dealer, having at times in his possession numbers of the best bred horses in the country. He most commonly bought and sold hunters, and such as were suitable for cavalry; and for some of his horses he received upwards of a hundred guineas apiece. In his dealings he always paid cash for his purchases, but accepted bills from his customers of respectability. Many a one purchased horses of him; and he was taken notice of by many respectable people in the neighbourhood; but the community in general looked upon him, and his people, with suspicion and fear, and were by no means fond of quarrelling with any of his vindictive fraternity. When any of his customers required a horse from him, and told him that the matter was left wholly to himself, as regards price, but to provide an animal suitable for the purpose required, no man in Scotland would act with greater honour than Charles Wilson. He would then fit his employer completely, and charge for the horse exactly what the price should be. To this manner of dealing he was very averse, and endeavoured to avoid it as much as possible. It is said he was never known to deceive any one in his transactions, when entire confidence was placed in him. But, on the other hand, when any tried to make a bargain with him, without any reference to himself, but trusting wholly to their own judgment, he would take three prices for his horses, if he could obtain them, and cheat them, if it was in his power. It is said his people stole horses in Ireland, and sent them to him, to dispose of in Scotland. On one occasion his gang stole and sold in Edinburgh, Stirling and Dumbarton a grey stallion, three different times in one week. Wilson himself was almost always mounted on a blood-horse of the highest mettle.

At one time, Charles Wilson travelled the country with a horse and cart, vending articles which his gang plundered from shops in Glasgow and other places. He had an associate who kept a regular shop, and when Wilson happened to be questioned about his merchandise, he always had fictitious bills of particulars, invoices and receipts, ready to show that the goods were lawfully purchased from his merchant, who was no other than his friend and associate. As Charles was chief of his tribe, he received the title of captain, to distinguish him from the meaner sort of his race. Like others of his rank among the Gipsies, he generally had a numerous gang of youths in fairs, plundering for him in all directions, among the heedless and unthinking crowd. But he always managed matters with such art and address that, however much he might be suspected, no evidence could ever be found to show that he acted a part in such transactions. It was well understood, however, that Charlie, as he was commonly called, divided the contents of many a purse with his band; all the plundered articles being in fact brought to him for distribution.

This chief, as I have already mentioned, issued tokens to the members of his own tribe; a part of the polity of the Gipsies which will be fully described in the following chapter. But, besides these regular Gipsy tokens, he, like many of his nation, gave tokens of protection to his particular friends of the community at large. The following is one instance, among many, of this curious practice among the Gipsies. I received the particulars from the individual himself who obtained the token or passport from Wilson. My informant, Mr. Buchanan, a retired officer of the Excise, chanced, in his youth, to be in a fair at Skirling, in Peeblesshire, when an acquaintance of his, of the name of John Smith, of Carnwath Mill, received, in a tent, fifty pounds for horses which he had sold in the market. Wilson, who was acquainted with both parties, was in the tent at the time, and saw the latter receive the money. On leaving the tent, Smith mentioned to his friend that he was afraid of being robbed in going home, as Wilson knew he had money in his possession. Mr. Buchanan, being well acquainted with Wilson, went to him in the fair, and told him the plain facts; that Smith and himself were to travel with money on their persons, and that they were apprehensive of being robbed of it, on their way home. The Gipsy, after hesitating for a moment, gave Buchanan a pen-knife, which he was to show to the first person who should offer to molest them; at the same time enjoining him to keep the affair quite private. After my informant and his friend had travelled a considerable distance on their way home, they observed, at a little distance before them, a number of Tinklers—men and women—fighting together on the side of the road. One of the females came forward to the travellers, and urged them vehemently to assist her husband, who, she said, was like to be murdered by others who had fallen upon him on the highway. My friend knew quite well that all the fighting was a farce, got up for the purpose of robbing him and his companion, the moment they interfered with the combatants in their feigned quarrel. Instead of giving the woman the assistance she asked, he privately and very quietly, as if he wished nobody to see it, showed her Wilson's knife in his hand, when she immediately exclaimed, "You are our friends," and called, at the same moment, to those engaged in the scuffle, in words to the same effect. Both the travellers now passed on, but, on looking behind them, they observed that the squabble had entirely ceased. The pen-knife was returned to Wilson the day following.

I may give, in this place, another instance of these tokens being granted by the Gipsies to their particular favourites of the community. The particulars were given to me by the individual with whom the incident occurred; and the Gipsy mentioned I have myself seen and spoken to: A—— A——, a small farmer, who resided in the west of Fife, happened to be at one of the Falkland fairs, where, in the evening, he fell in with old Andrew Steedman, a Gipsy horse-dealer from Lochgellie, with whom he was well acquainted.

They entered a public-house in Falkland to have a dram together, before leaving the fair, and after some conversation had passed, on various subjects, Steedman observed to his acquaintance that it would be late in the night before he could reach his home, and that he might be exposed to some danger on the road; but he would give him his snuff-box, to present and offer a snuff to the first person who should offer to molest him. My informant, possessed of the Gipsy's snuff-box, mounted his horse, and left his acquaintance and Falkland behind for his home. He had not proceeded far on his journey, before a man in the dark seized the bridle of his horse, and ordered him to stop; without, however, enforcing his command to surrender in that determined tone and manner common to highwaymen with those they intend to rob. The farmer at once recognized the robber to be no other than young Charles Graham, one of the Lochgellie Tinklers, whom he personally knew. Instead of delivering him his purse, he held out to him the snuff-box, as if nothing had happened, and, offering him a pinch, asked him if he was going to Lochgellie to-night. A sort of parley now ensued, the farmer feeling confident in the strength of his protection, and Graham confounded at being recognized by an acquaintance whom he was about to rob, and who, moreover, was in possession of a Gipsy token. At first a dry conversation ensued, similar to that between persons unacquainted with each other when they happen to meet; but Graham, recovering his self-possession, soon became very frank and kind, and insisted on the farmer accompanying him to a public-house on the road-side, where he would treat him to a dram. The farmer, a stout, athletic man, and no coward, complied with the Gipsy's invitation without hesitation. While drinking their liquor, Graham took up the snuff-box, and examined it all over very attentively, by the light of the candle, and returned it, without making a single remark, relative either to the untoward occurrence or the snuff-box itself. The farmer was equally silent as to what had taken place; but he could not help noticing the particular manner in which the Gipsy examined the token. They drank a hearty dram together, and parted the best of friends; the farmer for his home, and Graham, as he supposed, for the highway, to exercise his calling. Graham, about this period, resided in a house belonging to Steedman, in Lochgellie.

Instances occurred of individuals, who happened to be plundered, applying to Charles Wilson for his assistance to recover their property. The particulars of the following case are in the words of a friend who gave me the anecdote: "A boy, having received his hard-earned fee, at the end of a term, set out for Stirling to purchase some clothes for himself. On the road he was accosted by two men, who conversed with and accompanied him to Stirling. The lad proceeded accordingly to fit himself in a shop with a new suit, but, to his utter disappointment and grief, his small penny-fee was gone. The merchant questioned him about the road he had come, and whether he had been in company with any one on the way or otherwise. Upon the appearance of his companions being described, the shop-keeper suspected they might have picked his pocket unobserved. As a last resource, the boy was advised to call upon Charlie Wilson, and relate to him the particulars of his misfortune; which he accordingly did. Charles heard his story to the end, and desired him to call next day, when he might be able to give him some information relative to his loss. The young lad kept the appointment, and, to his great joy, the Tinkler chief paid him down every farthing of his lost money; but at the same time told him to ask no questions."

This Gipsey chief died within these thirty-five years in his own house, on the castle-hill at Stirling, whither he had removed from Raploch. It is stated that, for a considerable time before his death, he relinquished his former practices, and died in full communion with the church.* He was, about the latter end of his life, reduced to considerable poverty, and was under the necessity of betaking himself to his original occupation of making horn spoons for a subsistence. In the days of his prosperity, Charles was considered a very kind-hearted and generous man to the poor; and it seldom happened that poverty and distress were not relieved by him, when application was made to him by the needy. Although many of the more original kind of Gipsies have a respectable appearance, and may possess a little money, during the prime of life, yet the most of them, in their old age, are in a condition of poverty and misery.

* In the "Monthly Visitor," for February, 1856, will be found an account of the conversion of one of this Gipsy clan, of the name of Jeanie Wilson. The tract is very appropriately headed, "A lily among thorns."—Ed.

Charles Wilson had a family of very handsome daughters, one of whom was considered a perfect beauty. She did not travel the country, like the rest of her family, but remained at home, and acted as her father's housekeeper; and, when any of the tribe visited him, they always addressed her by the title of "my lady," (*raunie,*) and otherwise treated her with great respect. This beautiful girl was, about the year 1795, kept as a mistress by an adjutant of a Scotch regiment of fencible cavalry. She was frequently seen as handsomely and fashionably attired as the first females in Stirling; and some of the troopers were not displeased to see their adjutant's mistress equal in appearance to the highest dames in the town. But Wilson's daughters were all frequently dressed in a very superior manner, and could not have been taken for Gipsies.

To suit their purposes of deception, in practising their pilfering habits, the female Gipsies, as well as the males, often changed their wearing apparel. Some of them have been seen in four different dresses in one fair day, varying from the appearance of a sturdy female beggar to that of a young, flirting wench, fantastically dressed, and throwing herself, a perfect lure, in the way of the hearty, ranting, half-intoxicated, and merry young farmers, for the sole purpose of stripping them of their money.* The following is given as an instance of this sort of female deception:—On a fair-day, in the town of Kinross, a Brae-laird,† in the same county, fell in with a Gipsy harpy of the above character, of the name of Wilson, one of Charles' daughters, it was understood. She had a fine person, an agreeable and prepossessing countenance, was handsomely dressed, and was, altogether, what one would pronounce a pretty girl. Her charms made a very sudden and deep impression on the susceptible laird; and as it was an easy matter, in those times,

* An old woman, whom I found occupying the house of Charles Wilson, at Raploch, in 1846, informed me that she had seen his wife in *five* different dresses, in one market-day. She was, at the time, a servant in a *blacksmith's* family in Stirling, who were *great friends* of Charles Wilson; and every time Mrs. Wilson came into the smith's house, from her plundering in the market, this servant girl, then nine years old, *cleaned her shoes* for a fresh expedition in the crowd. When suspected, or even detected, in their practices, these female Gipsies, by such change of dress and character, easily escaped apprehension by the authorities.

† There are a number of small landed proprietors in the hilly parts of Kinross-shire; hence the appellation of Brae-laird.

to make up acquaintance at these large and promiscuous gatherings, the enamoured rustic soon found means to introduce himself to the stranger lady. He treated her in a gallant manner, and engaged to pay his respects to her at her place of residence. It happened, however, that a number of Tinklers were, that very evening, apprehended in the fair, for picking pockets, and a great many purses were found in their custody. Proclamation was made by the authorities, that all those who had lost their money should appear at a place named, and identify their property. The Brae-laird, among others, missed his pocket-book and purse, and accordingly went to enquire after them. His purse was produced to him; but greatly was he ashamed and mortified when the thief was also shown to him, lying in prison—the very person of his handsome and beautiful sweetheart, now metamorphosed into a common Tinkler wench. Whether he now provoked the ire of his dulcinea, by harsh treatment, is not mentioned; but the woman sent, as it were, a dagger to his heart, by calling out before all present: "Ay, laird, ye're no sae kind to me noo, lad, as when ye treated me wi' wine in the forenoon." The man, confounded at his exposure, was glad to get out of her presence, and, rather than bear the cutting taunts of the Gipsy, fled from the place of investigation, leaving his money behind him.*

It is almost needless to mention that the Stirlingshire Gipsies contributed their full proportion to the list of victims to the offended laws of the country. Although Charles Wilson, the chieftain of the horde, dexterously eluded justice himself, two of his brothers were executed within the memory of people still living. Another of his relatives, of the name of Gordon, also underwent the last penalty of the law, at Glasgow, where an acquaintance of mine saw him hanged. Wilson had a son who carried a box of jewelry through the country, and was suspected of having been concerned in robbing a bank, at, I believe, Dunkeld. Some of the descendants of this Stirlingshire tribe still roam up and down the kingdom, nearly in the old Gipsy manner; and several

* It is interesting to notice such rencounters between these pretty, genteel-looking Gipsies and the ordinary natives. The denouement, in this instance, might have been a marriage, and the plantation of a colony of Gipsies among the Braes of Kinross-shire. The same might have happened in the case of the other lady Wilson, with the adjutant at Stirling, or with one of his acquaintances.—Ed.

of them have their residence, when not on the tramp, in the town of Stirling.

The great distinguishing feature in the character of the Gipsies is an incurable propensity for theft and robbery, and taking openly and forcibly (sorning) whatever answers their purpose. A Gipsy, of about twenty-one years of age, stated to me that his forefathers considered it quite lawful, among themselves, to take from others, not of their own fraternity, any article they stood in need of. Casting his eyes around the inside of my house, he said: "For instance, were they to enter this room, they would carry off anything that could be of service to them, such as clothes, money, victuals, &c.:" "but," added he, "all this proceeded from ignorance; they are now quite changed in their manners." Another Gipsy, a man of about sixty years of age, informed me that the tribe have a complete and thorough hatred of the whole community, excepting those who shelter them, or treat them with kindness; and that a dexterous theft or robbery, committed on any of the natives among whom they travel, is looked upon as one of the most meritorious actions which a Gipsy can possibly perform.

But the Gipsies are by no means the only nation in the world that have considered theft reputable. In Sparta, under the celebrated law-giver Lycurgus, theft was also reputable. In Hugh Murray's account of an embassy from Portugal to the Emperor of Abyssinia, in 1620, we find the following curious passage relative to thieves in that part of the world: "As the embassy left the palace, a band of thieves carried off a number of valuable articles, while a servant who attempted to defend them was wounded in the leg. The ambassadors, enquiring the mode of obtaining redress for this outrage, were assured that these thieves formed a regular part of the court establishment, and that officers were appointed who levied a proportion of the articles stolen, for behoof his imperial majesty."* In another part of Africa, there is a horde of Moors who go by the name of the tribe of thieves. This wandering, vagabond horde do not blush at adopting this odious denomination. Their chief is called chief of the tribe of thieves.† In Hugh Murray's Asia, we have the following passage relative to the professed thieves in India.

* Vol. II., page 17.
† Golbery's Travels, translated by Francis Blagden. Vol. I., page 158.

'Nothing tends more to call in question the mildness of the Hindoo disposition than the vast scale of the practice of decoity. This term, though essentially synonymous with robbery, suggests, however, very different ideas. With us, robbers are daring and desperate outlaws, who hide themselves in the obscure corners of great cities, shunned and detested by all society. In India, they are regular and reputable persons, who have not only houses and families, but often landed property, and have much influence in the villages where they reside. This profession, like all others, is hereditary; and a father has been heard, from the gallows, carefully admonishing his son not to be deterred, by his fate, from following the calling of his ancestors. They are very devout, and have placed themselves under the patronage of the goddess Kali, revered in Bengal above all other deities, and who is supposed to look with peculiar favour on achievments such as theirs. They are even recognized by the old Hindoo laws, which contain enactments for the protection of stolen goods, upon a due share being given to the magistrate. They seldom, however, commit depredations in their own village, or even in that immediately adjoining, but seek a distant one, where they have no tie to the inhabitants. They are formed into bands, with military organization, so that when a chief dies, there is always another ready to succeed him. They calculate that they have ten chances to one of never being brought to justice."

The old Hindoo law alluded to in the above passage is, I presume, the following enactment in the Gentoo Code, translated by Nathaniel Brassey Halhed, page 146: "The mode of shares among robbers is this: If any thieves, by the command of the magistrate, and with his assistance, have committed depredations upon, and brought any booty from, another province, the magistrate shall receive a share of one-sixth of the whole; if they receive no command or assistance from the magistrate, they shall give the magistrate, in that case, one-tenth of his share; and of the remainder, their chief shall receive four shares: and whoso ever among them is perfect master of his occupation, shall receive three shares; also whichever of them is remarkably strong and stout, shall receive two shares; and the rest shall receive each one share. If any one of the community of thieves happens to be taken, and should be released from the Cutchery, (court of justice), upon payment of a sum of money, all the thieves shall make good that sum by equal shares."—"In the Gentoo code containing this law, there are many severe enactments against theft and robbery of every description; but these laws refer to domestic disturbers of their own countrymen, or violators of the first principles of society. The law which regulates these shares of robbers, refers only to such bold and hardy adventurers as sally forth to levy contributions in a foreign province."

Now our Gipsies are, in one point, exactly on a level with the adventurers here mentioned. They look upon themselves as being in a foreign land, and consider it fair game to rob, plunder, and cheat all and every one of the "strangers" among whom they travel. I am disposed to believe that there were also rules among the Gipsy bands for dividing their booty, something like the old Hindoo law alluded to.*

We find the following curious particulars mentioned of a tribe among the mountains in India, who are supposed to be the aborigines of Hindostan. They are called Kookies or Lunctas. "Next to personal valour, the accomplishment most esteemed in a warrior is superior address in stealing; and if a thief can convey, undiscovered, to his own house, his neighbour's property, it cannot afterwards be reclaimed; nor, if detected in the act, is he otherwise punished than by exposure to the ridicule of the Porah, and being obliged to restore what he may have laid hold of." "It is a great recommendation in obtaining a wife, when a Kookie can say that his house is full of stolen articles."† There are several other tribes in the world among whom theft and robbery are considered meritorious actions. It appears that among the Coords "no one is allowed to marry a wife till he has committed some great act of robbery or murder." In an account of Kamtschatka, it is mentioned that "among all these barbarous nations, excepting the Kamtschadales, theft

* What is said here is, of course, applicable to a class, only, of the Gipsies. Our author need not have gone so very far away from home, for instances of theft and robbery being, under certain circumstances, deemed honourable. Both were, at one time, followed in Scotland, when all practised

"The good old rule, the simple plan,
That they should take who have the power,
And they should keep who can."

See Disquisition on the Gipsies.—Ed.

† Asiatic Researches, vol. vii., pages 189 and 193.

is reputable, provided they do not steal in their own tribe, or if done with such art as to prevent discovery.: on the other hand, it is punished very severely if discovered; not for the theft, but for the want of address in the art of stealing. A Tschukotskoe girl cannot be married before she has shown her dexterity in this way."*

Halhed, in apologizing for the Hindoo magistrate participating in the plunder of banditti, which applies equally well to the Gipsies, remarks that, "unjust as this behaviour may appear in the eye of equity, it bears the most genuine stamp of antiquity, and corresponds entirely with the manners of the early Grecians, at or before the period of the Trojan war, and of the western nations before their emersion from barbarism; a practice still kept up among the piratic States of Barbary, to its fullest extent by sea, and probably among many hordes of Tartars and Arabian banditti by land." It is proper to mention that the Gipsies seldom or never steal from one another; at least, I never could find out an instance of a theft having been committed by a Gipsy on one of his own tribe.

It will be seen, from the following details, that the sanguinary laws which have been, from time to time, promulgated all over Europe against the Gipsies, were not enacted to put down fanciful crimes, as an author of the present day seems, in his travels, to insinuate. To plunder the community with more safety to their persons, the Gipsies appear to have had a system of theft peculiar to themselves. Those of Lochgellie trained all their children to theft. Indeed, this has been the general practice with the tribe all over Scotland. Several individuals have mentioned to me that the Lochgellie band were exercised in the art of thieving under the most rigid discipline. They had various ways of making themselves expert thieves. They frequently practised themselves by picking the pockets of each other. Sometimes a pair of breeches were made fast to the end of a string, suspended from a high part of the tent, kiln, or outhouse in which they happened to be encamped. The children were set at work to try if they could, by sleight of hand, abstract money from the pockets of the breeches hanging in this position, without moving them. Sometimes they

* Dr. James Grieve's translation of a Russian account of Kamtschatka, page 323.

used bells in this discipline. The children who were most expert in abstracting the money in this manner, were rewarded with applause and presents; while, on the other hand, those who proved awkward, by ringing the bell, or moving the breeches, were severely chastised. After the youths were considered perfect in this branch of their profession, a purse, or other small object, was laid down in an exposed part of the tent or camp, in view of all the family. While the ordinary business of the Gipsies was going forward, the children again commenced their operations, by exerting their ingenuity and exercising their patience, in trying to carry off the purse without being perceived by any one present. If they were detected, they were again beaten; but if they succeeded unnoticed, they were caressed and liberally rewarded. As far as my information goes, this systematic training of the Gipsy youth was performed by the chief female of the bands. These women seem to have had great authority over their children. Ann Brown, of the Lochgellie tribe, could, by a single stamp of her foot, cause the children to crouch to the ground, like trembling dogs under the lash of an angry master. The Gipsies, from these constant trainings, became exceedingly dexterous at picking pockets. The following instance of their extraordinary address in these practices, will show the effects of their careful training, as well as exhibit the natural ingenuity which they will display in compassing their ends.

A principal male Gipsy, of a very respectable appearance, whose name it is unnecessary to mention, happened, on a market day, to be drinking in a public-house, with several farmers with whom he was well acquainted. The party observed, from the window, a countryman purchase something at a stand in the market, and, after paying for it, thrust his purse into his watch-pocket, in the band of his breeches. One of the company remarked that it would be a very difficult matter to rob the cautious man of his purse, without being detected. The Gipsy immediately offered to bet two bottles of wine that he would rob the man of his purse, in the open and public market, without being perceived by him. The bet was taken, and the Gipsy proceeded about the difficult and delicate business. Going up to the unsuspecting man, he requested, as a particular favour, if he would ease the stock about his neck, which buckled behind—an article of dress at that time in fashion. The countryman most readily agreed to oblige the stranger gentleman—as he supposed him to be. The Gipsy, now stooping down, to allow his stock to be adjusted, placed his head against the countryman's stomach, and, pressing it forward a little, he reached down one hand, under the pretence of adjusting his shoe, while the other was employed in extracting the farmer's purse. The purse was immediately brought into the company, and the cautious, unsuspecting countryman did not know of his loss, till he was sent for, and had his property returned to him.

The Gipsy youth, trained from infancy to plunder, in the manner described, were formed into companies or bands, with a captain at their head. These captains were generally the grown-up sons of the old chieftains, who, having been themselves leaders in their youth, endeavoured, in their old age, to support, outwardly, a pretty fair character, although under considerable suspicion. The captains were generally well dressed, and could not be taken for Gipsies. The youths varied in age from ten to thirty years. They travelled to fairs singly, or at least never above two together, while their captains almost always rode on horse-back, but never in company with any of their men.* The band consisted of a great number of individuals, and in a fair several of these companies would be present; each company acting independent of the others, for behoof of its own members and chief. Each chief, on such occasions, had his own head-quarters, to which his men repaired with their booty, as fast as they obtained it. Some of the chiefs, handsomely dressed, pretended to be busily employed in buying and selling horses, but were always ready to attend to the operations of their

* An old Gipsy told me that he had seen one of the principal chiefs, dressed like a gentleman, travelling in a post-chaise, for the purpose of attending fairs.

[Vidocq, of the French secret police, thus writes of the Hungarian Gipsies, visiting the west of Europe: Raising my eyes towards a crowd in front of a menagerie, I perceived one of the *false jockeys* taking the purse of a fat glazier, whom we saw the next moment seeking for it in his pocket; the *Bohemian* then entered a jeweller's shop, where were already two of the *pretended Zealand peasants*, and my companion assured me that he would not come out until he had pilfered some of the jewels that were shown to him. In every part of the fair where there was a crowd, I met some of the lodgers of the Duchess, (the inn kept by a Gipsy woman in which he had spent the previous night.)—Ed.]

tribe, employed in plundering in the market. The purses were brought to the horse-dealer by the members of his band, who, to prevent being discovered, pretended to be buying horses from him, while communicating with him relative to their peculiar vocation. When a detection was likely to take place, the chief mounted a good horse, and rode off to a distant part of the country, previously made known to his men, with the whole of the booty in his custody. To this place the band, when all was quiet, repaired, and received their share of the plunder. They could communicate information to one another by signs, to say nothing of their language, which frequently enabled them to get the start of their pursuers. Like the fox, the dog, and the *corbie*, they frequently concealed their stolen articles in the earth. Parties of them would frequently commence sham fights in markets, to facilitate the picking of the pockets of the people, while crowded together to witness the scuffles.

Many of the male Gipsies used a piece of strong leather, like a sailmaker's palm, having a short piece of sharp steel, like the point of a surgeon's lancet, where the sailmaker has his thimble. The long sleeves of their coats concealed the instrument, and when they wished to cut a purse out of an arm-pocket, they stretched out the arm, and ran it flatly and gently along the cloth of the coat, opposite the pocket of the individual they wished to plunder. The female Gipsies wore, upon their forefingers, rings of a peculiar construction, yet nothing unusual in their appearance, excepting their very large size. On closing the hand, the pressure upon a spring sent forth, through an aperture or slit in the ring, a piece of sharp steel, something like the manner in which a bee thrusts out and withdraws its sting. With these ingenious instruments the female Gipsies cut the outside of the pockets of their victims, exactly as a glazier runs his diamond over a sheet of glass. The opening once made by the back of the forefinger, the hand, following, was easily introduced into the pocket. In the midst of a crowded fair, the dexterous Gipsies, with their nimble fingers, armed with these invisible instruments, cut the pocket-books and purses of the honest farmers, as if they had been robbed by magic. So skillful were the wife and one of the sisters of Charles Wilson, in the art of thieving, that although the loss of the pocket-book was, in some instances, immediately discovered, nothing was ever found upon their persons by which their guilt could be established. No instrument appeared in their possession with which the clothes of the plundered individuals could have been cut, as no one dreamt that the rings on their fingers contained tools so admirably adapted for such purposes.

The Gipsy chiefs in Scotland appear, at one time, to have received a share of the plundered articles in the same manner as those of the same rank received from their inferiors in Hungary. Grellmann says: "Whenever a complaint is made that any of their people have been guilty of theft, the Waywode (chief) not only orders a general search to be made in every tent or hut, and returns the stolen goods to the owner, if they can be found; but he punishes the thief, in presence of the complainant, with his whip. He does not, however, punish the aggressor from any regard to justice, but rather to quiet the plaintiff, and at the same time to make his people more wary in their thefts, as well as more dexterous in concealing their prey. These very materially concern him, since, by every discovery that is made, his income suffers, as the whole profit of his office arises from his share of the articles that are stolen. Every time any one brings in a booty, he is obliged to give information to the Arch-gipsy of his successful enterprise, then render a just account of what and how much he has stolen, in order that the proper division may be made. This is the situation in which a Gipsy looks on himself as bound to give a fair and true detail, though, in every other instance, he does not hesitate to perjure himself."

A shrewd and active magistrate, in the west of Fife, knew our Scottish Gipsy depredators so well, that he caused them all to be apprehended as they entered the fairs held in the town in which he resided; and when the market, which lasted for several days, was over, the Gipsies were released from prison, with empty pockets and hungry bellies—most effectually baffled in their designs.

Great numbers of these Gipsy plunderers, at one time, crossed the Forth at the Queensferry, for the purpose of stealing and robbing at the fairs in the north of Scotland. They all travelled singly or in pairs. Very few persons knew whence they came, or with whom they were connected. They were, in general, well dressed, and could not have been taken for Gipsies. Every one put up at a public-house, at

North Queensferry, kept by a Mr. McRitchie, already mentioned, an inn well known in the neighbourhood for its good fare, and much frequented by all classes of society. In this house, on the morning after a fair in Dunfermline, when *their business* was all over, and themselves not alarmed by detection, or other scaring incidents, no fewer than fourteen of these plunderers have frequently been seen sitting at breakfast, with Captain Gordon, their commander, at their head. The landlord's son informed me that they ate and drank of the best in the house, and paid most handsomely for everything they called for. I believe they were among the best customers the landlord had. Gipsies, however, are by no means habitual drinkers, or tiplers; but when they do sit down, it is, in the phraseology of the sea, a complete *blow-out.* About this public-house, these Gipsies were perfectly inoffensive, and remarkably civil to all connected with it. They troubled or stole from none of the people about the inn, nor from those who lodged in the house, while they were within doors, or in the immediate neighbourhood. Anything could have been trusted with them on these occasions. At these meetings, the landlord's son frequently heard them talking in the Gipsy language. Gordon, at times, paid the reckoning for the whole, and transacted any other business with the landlord; but, when the Gipsy company was intermixed with females, which was commonly the case, each individual paid his own share of the bill incurred. It was sometimes the practice with the young bands to leave their reckoning to be paid by their chiefs, who were not present, but who, perhaps next day, came riding up, and paid the expenses incurred by their men. I am informed that two chiefs, of the names of Wilson and Brown, often paid the expenses of their bands in this way. When any of these principal Gipsies happened to remain in the public-house all night, they behaved very genteelly. They paid the chambermaid, boots, and waiter with more liberality than was the custom with mercantile travellers generally. Captain Gordon, just mentioned, assumed very considerable consequence at this place. Frequently he hired boats and visited the islands in the Forth, and adjacent coasts, like a gentleman of pleasure. On one occasion he paid no less than a guinea, with brandy and eatables *ad libitum*, to be rowed over to Inch-colm, a distance of four miles.

The female Gipsies from the south, on visiting their friends at Lochgellie, in the depth of winter, often hired horses at the North Queensferry, and rode, with no small pomp and pride, to the village. Sometimes two females would ride upon one horse. A very decent old man, of the name of Thomas Chalmers, a small farmer, informed me that he himself had rode to Lochgellie, with a female Gipsy behind him, accompanied by other two, mounted on another of his horses, riding with much spirit and glee by his side. Chalmers said that these women not only paid more than the common hire, but treated the owners of the horses with as much meat and drink as they could take. The male Gipsies also hired horses at this Ferry, with which they rode to markets in the north.

The young Gipsies, male and female, of whom I have spoken, appear to have been the flower of the different bands, collected and employed in a general plundering at the fairs in the north. So well did they pay their way at the village and passage alluded to, that the boatmen gave them the kindly name of "our frien's." These wanderers were all known at the village by the name of "Gillie Wheesels," or "Killie Wheesh," which, in the west of Fife, signified "the lads that take the purses." Old Thomas Chalmers informed me that he had frequently seen these sharks of boatmen shake these Gipsy thieves heartily by the hand, and, with a significant smile on their harsh, weather-beaten countenances, wish them a good market, as they landed them on the north side of the Forth, on their way to picking pockets at fairs.

As an incident in the lives of these Gipsies, I will give the following, which was witnessed by Chalmers: A Gillie of a Gipsy horse-couper stole a black colt, in the east of Fife, and carried it direct to a fair in Perth, where he exchanged it for a white horse, belonging to a Highlander wearing a green kilt. The Highlander, however, had not long put the colt into the stable, before word was brought to him that it was gone. Suspecting the Gipsy of the theft, the sturdy Gael proceeded in search of him, and receiving positive information of the fact, he pursued him, like a staunch hound on the warm foot of reynard, till he overtook him in a house on the north side of Kinross. The Gipsy was taking some refreshment in the same room with Chalmers, when the Highlander, in a storm of broken English, burst into their presence. The astute and polished Gipsy instantly sprang to his feet, and, throwing his arms around the foaming Celt, embraced and hugged him in the eastern manner, overpowering him with expressions of joy at seeing him again. This quite exasperated the mountaineer: almost suffocated with rage, he shook the Gipsy from his person, with the utmost disdain, and demanded the colt he had stolen from him. Notwithstanding the deceitful embraces and forced entreaties of the Gipsy, he was, with the assistance of a messenger, at the back of the Highlander, safely lodged in the jail of Cupar.

Considering the great aptitude which the Gipsies have always shown for working in metals, it is not surprising that they should have resorted to coining, among their many expedients for circumventing and plundering the "strangers" among whom they sojourn. The following instance will illustrate the singular audacity which they can display in this branch of their profession: As an honest countryman, of much simplicity of character, of the name of W—— O——, was journeying along the public road, a travelling Tinkler, whom he did not know, chanced to come up to him. After walking and conversing for some time, the courteous Gipsy, on arriving at a public-house, invited him to step in, and have a "tasting." They accordingly entered the house, and had no sooner finished one half *mutchken*, than the liberal wanderer called for another; but when the reckoning came to be thought of, the countryman was surprised when his friend the Tinkler declared that he had not a coin in his possession. Unfortunately, the honest man happened also to be without a farthing in his pocket, and how they were to get out of the house, without paying the landlord, whom neither of them knew, puzzled him not a little. While meditating over their dilemma, the Gipsy, with his eyes rolling about in every direction, as is their wont, espied a pewter basin under a bed in the room. This was all he required. Bolting the door of the apartment, he opened his budget, and, taking out a pair of large shears, cut a piece from the side of the basin, and, putting it into his crucible on the fire, in no time, with his coining instruments, threw off several half-crowns, resembling good, sterling money. If the simple countryman was troubled at not being able to pay his reckoning, he was now terrified at being locked up with a man busily engaged in coining base money from an article stolen in the very apartment in which he was confined. He expected, every moment, some one to burst the door open, and apprehend them, while the Tinkler had all his coining apparatus about him. His companion, however, was not in the least disturbed, but deliberately finished his coin in a superior manner, and cutting the remainder of the basin into pieces, packed it into his wallet. Unlocking the door, he rang the bell, and tendered one of his half-crowns to his host, to pay his score, which was accepted without a suspicion. The Tinkler then offered his fellow-traveller part of his remaining coin; but the unsophisticated man, far from touching one of them, was only too glad to rid himself of so dangerous an acquaintance. The Gipsy, on his part, marched off, with his spirits elevated with liquor, and his pockets replenished with money, smiling at the simplicity and terror of the countryman.

However numerous the crimes which the Gipsies have committed, or the murders they have perpetrated in their own tribe, yet, in justice to them, I must say that only two instances have come to my knowledge of their having put to death natives of Scotland who were not of their own fraternity. One of these instances was that of a man of the name of Adam Thomson, whom they murdered because he had encroached, it was said, upon one of their supposed privileges—that of gathering rags through the country. Amongst other acts of cruelty, they placed the poor man on a fire, in his own house. Two Gipsies were tried for the murder, but whether they were both executed, I do not know. The following particulars connected with this deed will show how exactly the Gipsies know the different routes and halting-places of each band, as they travel through the country. Indeed, I have been informed that the track which each horde is to take, the different stages, and the number of days they are to remain at each place, are all marked out and fixed upon in the spring, before they leave their winter residence. One of the Gipsies concerned in the murder of Thomson lay in prison, in one of the towns in the south of Scotland, for nearly twelve months, without having had any communication with his tribe. There was not sufficient evidence against him to justify his being brought to trial; nor would he give any information regarding the transaction.

At last he changed his mind, and told the authorities they would find the murderer at a certain spot in the Highlands, on a certain day and hour of that day; but if he could not be found there, they were to proceed to another place, at twenty miles' distance, where they would be sure to find him.

The murderer was found at the place, and on the day, mentioned by the Gipsy. But, on entering the house, the constables could not discover him, although they knew he had been within its walls a few minutes before they approached it. A fire having been kindled in the house, a noise was heard in the chimney, which attracted the notice of the constables; and, on examination, they found the object of their search; the heat and smoke having caused him to become restless in his place of concealment. He was secured, and some of the country-people were called upon to assist in carrying him to Edinburgh. The prisoner was bound into a cart with ropes, to prevent him making his escape; the party in charge of him being aware of the desperate character of the man. Nothing particular occurred on the road, until after they had passed the town of Linlithgow, when, to their astonishment, they found a woman in the pangs of labour, in the open field. She called upon them either to bring her a midwife, or take her to one; a claim that could not be resisted. She was accordingly put into the cart, beside the prisoner, and driven with all speed to a place where a midwife could be procured. On arriving opposite a dell, full of trees and bushes, about the west-end of Kirkliston, the guards were confounded at seeing their prisoner, all at once, spring out of the cart, and, darting into the cover, vanish in an instant. Pursuit was immediately given, and, in the excitement, the unfortunate woman was left to her fate. In searching for the Gipsy, they met a gentleman shooting in the neighbourhood, who had observed a man hide himself among the bushes. On going to the spot, they found the criminal, lying like a fox in his hole. The sportsman, presenting his gun, threatened to blow out his brains, if he did not come out, and deliver himself up to the constables. On returning with him to the cart, his captors, to their astonishment, found that the woman in labour had also vanished. It is needless to add that she was a Gipsy, who had feigned being in travail, and, while in the cart, had cut the ropes with which the prisoner was bound, to enable him to make his escape.

The female Gipsies have had recourse to many expedients in their impositions on the public. The following is an instance, of a singular nature, that took place a good many years ago. When it is considered that the Gipsies, in their native country,* would not be encumbered with much wearing-apparel, but would go about in a state little short of nudity, the extreme indecency of such an action will appear somewhat lessened. The inhabitants of Winchburgh and neighbourhood were one day greatly astonished at beholding a female, with a child in her arms, walking along the road, as naked as when she was born. She stated to the country-people that she had just been plundered, and stripped of every article of her wearing-apparel, by a band of Tinklers, to whom she pointed, lying in a field hard by. She submitted her piteous condition to the humanity of the inhabitants, and craved any sort of garment to cover her nakedness. The state in which she was found left not the slightest doubt on the minds of the spectators as to the truth of her representations. Almost every female in the neighbourhood ran with some description of clothing to the unfortunate woman; so that, in a short time, she was not only comfortably clad, but had many articles of dress to spare. Shortly after, she left the town, and proceeded on her journey. But some one, observing her motions more closely than the rest, was astonished at seeing her go straight to the very Tinklers who, she said, had stripped her. Her appearance among her band convulsed them all with laughter, at the dexterous trick she had played upon the simple inhabitants.

The following anecdote, related to me of one of the well-attired female Gipsies, belonging to the Stirling horde, will illustrate the gratitude which the Scottish Gipsies have, on all occasions, shown to those who have rendered them acts of kindness and attention: A person, belonging to Stirling, had rendered himself obnoxious to the Gipsies, by giving information relative to one of the gang, of the name of Hamilton, whom he had observed picking a man's pocket of forty pounds in a fair at Doune. Hamilton was apprehended

* It is pretty certain that the Gipsies came from a warm country, for they have no words for frost or snow, as will be seen in my enquiry into the history of their language.

immediately after committing the theft, but none of the money was found upon him. The informer, however, was marked out for destruction by the band, for his officious conduct; and they only waited a convenient opportunity to put their resolution into execution. Some time afterwards, the proscribed individual had occasion to go to a market at no great distance from Stirling, and while on his way to it, he observed, on the road before him, a female, in the attire of a lady, riding on horseback. On coming to a pond at the road-side, the horse suddenly made for the water, and threw down its head to drink. Not being prepared for the movement, the rider was thrown from her seat, with considerable violence, to the ground. The proscribed individual, observing the accident, ran forward to her assistance; but, being only slightly stunned, she was, with his help, safely placed in her seat again. She now thanked him for his kind and timely assistance, and informed him of the conspiracy that had been formed against him. She said it was particularly fortunate for him that such an accident had befallen her under the circumstances; for, in consequence of the information he had given about the pocket-picking at Doune, he was to have been way-laid and murdered; that very night having been fixed upon for carrying the resolution into effect. But, as he had shown her this kindness, she would endeavour to procure, from her people, a pardon for him, for the past. She then directed him to follow slowly, while she would proceed on, at a quick pace, and overtake some of her people, to whom she would relate her accident, and the circumstances attending it. She then informed him that if she waved her *hand*, upon his coming in sight of herself and her people, he was to retrace his steps homeward, there being then no mercy for him; but if she waved her *handkerchief*, he might advance without fear. To his heartfelt delight, on coming near the party, the signal of peace was given, when he immediately hastened forward to the spot. The band, who had been in deliberation upon his fate, informed him that the lady's intercession had prevailed with them to spare his life; and that now he might consider himself safe, provided he would take an oath, there and then, never again to give evidence against any of their people, or speak to any one about their practices, should he discover them. The person in question deemed it prudent, under all the circumstances of the case, to take the oath; after which, nothing to his hurt, in either purse or person, ever followed.* The lady, thus equipped, and possessed of so much influence, was the chief female of the Gipsy band, to whom all the booty obtained at the fair was brought, at the house where she put up at for the day. It would seem that she was determined to save her friend at all events; for, had her band not complied with her wishes, the waving of her hand—the signal for him to make his escape—would have defeated their intentions for that time.

When occurrences of so grave and imposing a nature as the above are taken into consideration, the fear and awe with which the Gipsies have inspired the community are not to be wondered at.

The Gipsies at Lochgellie had a dance peculiar to themselves, during the performance of which they sung a song, in the Gipsy language, which they called a "croon." A Gipsy informed me that it was exactly like the one old Charles Stewart, and other Gipsies, used to perform, and which I will describe. At the wedding near Corstorphine, which Charles Stewart attended, as already mentioned, there were five or six female Gipsies in his train. On such occa-

* Such interference with the Gipsies causes them much greater offence than if the informer was a principal in the transaction. To such people, their advice has always been: "Follow your nose, and let sleeping dogs lie." The following anecdote will illustrate the way in which they have revenged themselves, under circumstances different from the above:

Old Will, of Phaup, at the head of Ettrick, was wont to shelter them for many years. They asked nothing but house-room, and grass for their horses; and, though they sometimes remained for several days, he could have left every chest and press about the house open, with the certainty that nothing would be missing; for, he said, "he aye ken'd fu' weel that the tod wad keep his ain hole clean." But it happened that he found one of the gang, through the trick of a neighbouring farmer, feeding six horses on the best piece of grass on his farm, which he was keeping for winter fodder. A desperate combat followed, and the Gipsy was thrashed to his heart's content, and hunted out of the neighbourhood. A warfare of five years' duration ensued between Will and the Gipsies. They nearly ruined him, and, at the end of that period, he was glad to make up matters with his old friends, and shelter them as formerly. He said he could have held his own with them, had it not been for their warlockry; for nothing could he keep from them—they once found his purse, though he had made his wife bury it in the garden.—*Blackwood's Magazine*. It is the afterclap that keeps the people off the Gipsies, and secures for them a sort of toleration wherever they go.—ED.

sions he did not allow males to accompany him. At some distance from the people at the wedding, but within hearing of the music, the females formed themselves into a ring, with Charles in the centre. Here, in the midst of the circle, he danced and capered in the most antic and ludicrous manner, sweeping his cudgel around his body in all directions, and moving with much grace and agility. Sometimes he danced round the outside of the circle. The females danced and courtesied to him, as he faced about and bowed to them. When they happened to go wrong, he put them to rights by a movement of his cudgel; for it was by the cudgel that all the turns and figures of the dance were regulated. A twirl dismissed the females; a cut recalled them; a sweep made them squat on the ground; a twist again called them up, in an instant, to the dance. In short, Stewart distinctly spoke to his female dancers by means of his cudgel, commanding them to do whatever he pleased, without opening his mouth to one of them.

George Drummond, a Gipsy chief of an inferior gang in Fife, danced with his seraglio of females, amounting sometimes to half a dozen, in the same manner as Stewart, without the slightest variation, excepting that his gestures were, on some occasions, extremely lascivious. He threw himself into almost every attitude in which the human body can be placed, while his cudgel was flying about his person with great violence. All the movements of the dance were regulated by the measures of an indecent song, at the chorus of which the circular movements of Drummond's cudgel ceased; when one of the females faced about to him, and joined him with her voice, the gestures of both being exceedingly obscene. Drummond's appearance, while dancing, has been described to me, by a gentleman who has often seen him performing, as exactly like what is called a "jumping-jack"—that is, a human figure, cut out of wood or paste-board, with which children often amuse themselves, by regulating its ludicrous movements by means of strings attached to various parts of it.

Dr. Clark, in his account of his travels through Russia, gives a description of a Gipsy dance in Moscow, which is, in all respects, very similar to that performed by Stewart and Drummond. These travels came into my hands some time after I had taken notes of the Scottish Gipsy dance. Napkins appear to have been used by the Russian Gipsies, where sticks were employed by our Scottish tribes. No mention, however, is made, by Dr. Clark, whether the females, in the dance at Moscow, were guided by signs with the napkins, in the manner in which Stewart and Drummond, by their cudgels, directed their women in their dances. The eyes of the females were constantly fixed upon Stewart's cudgel. Dr. Clark is of opinion that the national dance in Russia, called the *barina*, is derived from the Gipsies; and thinks it probable that our common hornpipe is taken from these wanderers.*

George Drummond was, in rank, quite inferior to the Lochgellie band, who called him a "beggar Tinkler," and seemed to despise him. He always travelled with a number of females in his company. These he married after the custom of the Gipsies, and divorced some of them over the body of a horse, sacrificed for the occasion; a description of both of which ceremonies will be given in another chapter. He chastised his women with his cudgel, without mercy, causing the blood to flow at every blow, and frequently knocked them senseless to the ground; while he would call out to them, "What the deevil are ye fighting at—can ye no' 'gree? I'm sure there's no' sae mony o' ye!" although, perhaps, four would be engaged in the scuffle. Such was this man's impudence and audacity, that he sometimes carried off the flesh out of the kail-pots of the farmers; and so terrified were some of the inhabitants of Fife, at some of the Gipsy women who followed him, that, the moment they entered their doors, salt was thrown into the fire, to set at defiance the witchcraft which they believed they possessed. One female, called Dancing Tibby, was, in particular, an object of apprehension and suspicion. In Drummond's journeys through the country, when he came at night to a farmer's premises, where he intended to lodge, and found his place occupied by others of his gang, he, without hesitation, turned them out of their quarters, and

* If I am not mistaken, Col. Todd is of opinion that the Gipsies originally came from Cabool, in Afghanistan. I will here give a description of an Afghan dance, very like the Gipsy dance in Scotland. "The western Afghans are fond of a particular dance called *Attun*, or *Ghoomboor*, in which from fourteen to twenty people move, in strange attitudes, with shouting, clapping of hands, and snapping of fingers, in a circle, round a single person, who plays on an instrument in the centre.—*Fraser's Library.*

took possession of their warm beds himself; letting them shift for themselves as they best might. This man lived till he was ninety years of age, and was, from his youth, impressed with a belief that he would die in the house in which he was born; although he had travelled a great part of the continent, and, while in the army, had been in various engagements. He fell sick when at some distance from the place of his nativity, but he hired a conveyance, and drove with haste to die on his favourite spot. To this house he was allowed admittance, where he closed his earthly career, in about forty-eight hours after his arrival. Like others of his tribe, Drummond, at times, gave tokens of protection to some of his particular friends, outside of the circle of his own fraternity.

James Robertson, a Gipsy closely related to the Lochgellie band, of whom I have already made mention, frequently danced, with his wife and numerous sisters, in a particular fashion, changing and regulating the figures of the dance by means of a bonnet; being, I believe, the same dance which I have attempted to describe as performed by others of the tribe in Scotland. When his wife and sisters got intoxicated, which was often the case, it was a wild and extravagant scene to behold those light-footed damsels, with loose and flowing hair, dancing, with great spirit, on the grass, in the open field, while James was, with all his "might and main," like the devil playing to the witches, in "Tam o' Shanter," keeping the bacchanalians in fierce and animated music. When like to flag in his exertions to please them with his fiddle, they have been heard calling loudly to him, like Maggy Lawder to Rob the Ranter, "Play up, Jamie Robertson; if ever we do weel, it will be a wonder;" being totally regardless of all sense of decorum and decency.

The Gipsies in Fife followed the same occupations, in all respects, as those in other parts of Scotland, and were also dexterous at all athletic exercises. They were exceedingly fond of cock-fighting, and, when the season came round for that amusement, many a good cock was missing from the farm-yards. The Lochgellie band considered begging a disgrace to their tribe. At times they were handsomely dressed, wearing silver buckles in their shoes, gold rings on their fingers, and gold and silver brooches in the bosoms of their ruffled shirts. They killed, at Martinmass, fat cattle for their winter's provisions, and lived on the best victuals the country could produce. It is, I believe, the common practice, among inferior Scotch traders, for those who receive money to treat the payer, or return a trifle of the payment, called a luck-penny: but, in opposition to this practice, the Lochgellie Gipsies always treated those to whom they paid money for what they purchased of them. They occasionally attended the church, and sometimes got their children baptized; but when the clergyman refused them that privilege, they baptized them themselves. At their baptisms, they had great feastings and drinkings. Their favourite beverage, on such occasions, was oatmeal and whiskey, mixed. When intoxicated, they were sometimes very fond of arguing and expostulating with clergymen on points of morality. With regard to the internal government of the Lochgellie Gipsies, I can only find that they held consultations among themselves, relative to their affairs, and that the females had votes as well as the males, but that old Charles Graham had the casting vote; while, in his absence, his wife, Ann Brown, managed their concerns.

There is a strict division of property among the Gipsies; community of goods having no place among them. The heads of each family, although travelling in one band, manufacture and vend their own articles of merchandise, for the support of their own families. The following particulars are illustrative of this fact among the Gipsies:—A farmer in Fife, who would never allow them to kindle fires in his out-houses, had a band of them, of about twenty-five persons, quartered one night on his farm. Next morning, the chief female borrowed from the family a large copper caldron, used for the purposes of the dairy, with which she had requested permission to cook the breakfast of the horde upon the kitchen fire. This having been granted, each family produced a small linen bag, (not the beggar's wallet,) made of coarse materials, containing oatmeal; of which at least four were brought into the apartment. The female who prepared the repast went regularly over the bags, taking out the meal in proportion to the members of the families to which they respectively belonged, and repeated her visits in this manner till the porridge was ready to be served up.

I shall conclude my account of the Gipsies in Fife by mentioning the curious fact that, within these sixty years, a gentleman of considerable landed property, between the Forth and the Tay, abandoned his relatives, and travelled over the kingdom in the society of the Gipsies. He married one of the tribe, of the name of Ogilvie, who had two daughters to him. Sometimes he quartered, it is said, upon his own estate, disguised, of course, among the gang, to the great annoyance of his relatives, who were horrified at the idea of his becoming a Tinkler, and alarmed at the claims which he occasionally made upon the estate. His daughters travel the country, at the present day, as common Gipsies.

CHAPTER VI.

TWEED-DALE AND CLYDESDALE GIPSIES.

The county of Peebles, or Tweed-dale, appears to have been more frequented by the Gipsies than, perhaps, any other part of Scotland. So far back as the time of Henry Lord Darnley, when the Gipsies were countenanced by the government, we find, according to Buchanan, that this county was a favourite resort of banditti; so much so, that when Darnley took up his residence in Peebles, for the purpose of shunning the company of his wife, Queen Mary, he "found the place so cold, so infested with thieves, and so destitute of provisions, that he was driven from it, to avoid being fleeced and starved by rogues and beggars." In the poems of Dr. Pennecuik, as well as in his history of Peebles-shire, published in the year 1715, the Gipsy bands are frequently taken notice of. But, notwithstanding the attachment which the tribe had for the romantic glens of Tweed-dale, no evidence exists of their ever having had a permanent habitation within the shire. They appear to have resorted to that pastoral district during only the months of spring, summer and autumn. Their partiality for this part of Scotland may be attributed to three reasons.

The first reason is, Tweed-dale was part of the district in which, if not the first, at least the second, Gipsy family in Scotland claimed, at one time, a right to travel, as its own peculiar privilege. The chief of this family was called Baillie, who claimed kindred, in the bastard line, to one of the most ancient families in the kingdom, of the name of Baillie, once Balliol.* In consequence of this alleged connexion, this Gipsy family also claimed, as its right, to travel in the up-

* This claim appears doubtful, for there were Gipsies of the name of Baillie (Bailyow) as far back as 1540, as already mentioned. However, the particulars of the laird's intrigue with the beautiful Gipsy girl, are imprinted on the minds of the Gipsies of that name at the present day.

per ward of Lanarkshire, adjoining Tweed-dale, in which district the Scottish family alluded to possessed estates; and one of the principal places of the Gipsy rendezvous was an old ruin, among the hills, in the upper part of the parish of Lamington, or rather Wanel in those days.

The second reason is, that the surface of Tweed-dale is much adapted to the wandering disposition of the Gipsies. It is mountainous, but everywhere intersected by foot-paths and bridle-roads, affording an easy passage to the Gipsies, on foot or horseback. On its many hills are plenty of game; and its infinite number of beautiful streams, including about thirty-five miles of the highest part of the Tweed, abound with trout of the finest quality. The Gipsies, being fond of game, and much addicted to poaching and fishing, flocked to Tweed-dale and the adjoining upland districts of a similar character, comprehending some of the most remote and least frequented parts in the south of Scotland. All these districts being covered with vast flocks of sheep, many of which were frequently dying of various diseases, the Gipsies never wanted a plentiful supply of that sort of food from the families of the store-masters.*

And the third reason is, that, in the pastoral districts in the upper parts of the shires of Peebles, Selkirk, Dumfries, and Lanark, including all that mountainous tract of land in which the rivers Tweed, Annan and Clyde have their sources, the Gipsies were, in a great measure, secure from the officers of the law, and enjoyed their favourite amusements without molestation or hindrance.

Before, and long after, the year 1745, the male branches of the Baillies traversed Scotland, mounted on the best hor-

* The Gipsies were not spared of *brazy*, of which they were fond. I have known natives of Tweed-dale and Ettrick Forest, who preferred *brazy* to the best meat *killed by the hand of man*. It has a particular *sharp* relish, which made them so fond of it.

[Brazy is the flesh of sheep which have died of a certain disease. When the Gipsies are taunted with eating what some call carrion, they very wittily reply: "The flesh of a beast which God kills must be better than that of one killed by the hand of man." Such flesh, "killed by the hand of God," is often killed in this manner: They will administer to swine a drug affecting the brain only, which will cause speedy death; when they will call and obtain the carcass, without suspicion, and feast on the flesh, which has been in no way injured.—*Borrow*. They will also stuff wool down a sheep's throat, and direct the farmer's attention to it when near its last gasp, and obtain the carcass after being skinned.—Ed.]

ses to be found in the country; themselves dressed in long coats, made of the finest scarlet and green cloth, ruffled at hands and breast, booted and spurred; with cocked hats on their heads, pistols in their belts, and broad-swords by their sides: and at the heels of their horses followed greyhounds, and other dogs of the chase, for their amusement. Some of them assumed the manners and characters of gentlemen, which they supported with wonderful art and propriety. The females attended fairs in the attire of ladies, riding on ponies, with side-saddles, in the best style. On these occasions, the children were left in charge of their servants, perhaps in an old out-house or hut, in some wild, sequestered glen, in Tweed-dale or Clydesdale.

The greater part of the tenantry were kind to the Gipsies, and many encouraged them to frequent their premises. Tweed-dale being the favourite resort of the principal horde, they generally abstained from injuring the property of the greater part of the inhabitants. Indeed, I have been informed, by eye-witnesses, that several of the farmers in Tweed-dale and Clydesdale, at so late a period as about the year 1770, accepted of entertainments from the principal Gipsies, dining with them in the open fields, or in some old, unoccupied out-house, or kiln. Their repast, on such occasions, was composed of the best viands the country could produce. On one occasion, a band dined on the green-sward, near Douglass-mill, when the Gipsies drank their wine, after dinner, as if they had been the best in the land. Some of the landed proprietors, however, introduced clauses in their leases prohibiting their tenants from harbouring the Gipsies; and the Laird of Dolphington is mentioned as one. The tribe, on hearing of the restriction, expressed great indignation at the Laird's conduct in adopting so effectual a method of banishing them from the district. But so strong were the attachments which some of the Gipsies displayed towards the inhabitants, that the chief of the Ruthvens actually wept like a child, whenever the misfortunes of the ancient family of Murray, of Philliphaugh, were mentioned to him.

In giving an account of the Gipsies who frequented Tweed-dale, and the country adjacent, I have thought it proper to mention particularly the family of Baillie; for this family produced kings and queens, or, in their language, *baurie rajahs* and *baurie raunies*, to the Scottish Gipsies. At one period they seem to have exercised a sort of sovereign authority in the tribe, over almost the whole of Scotland; and, according to the ordinary practice of writing history of a great deal more importance, they should, as the chief family of a tribe, be particularly noticed.

The quarrels of the Gipsies frequently broke out in an instant, and almost without a visible cause. A farmer's wife, with whom I was acquainted, was one day sitting in the midst of a band of them, at work in an old out-house, enquiring the news of the country of them, when, in an instant, a shower of horns and hammers, open knives, files, and fiery peats, were flying through the house, at one another's heads. The good-wife took to her heels immediately, to get out of the fray. Some of their conflicts were terrible in the extreme. Dr. Pennecuik, in his history of Peebles-shire, already referred to, gives an account of a sanguinary struggle that took place on his estate of Romanno, in Tweeddale. The following are the particulars in his own words:

"Upon the 1st of October, 1677, there happened at Romanno, on the very spot where now the dove-cot is built, a remarkable polymachy betwixt two clans of Gipsies, the Fawes and the Shawes, who had come from Haddington fair, and were going to Harestanes, to meet two other clans of these rogues, the Baillies and Browns, with a resolution to fight them. They fell out, at Romanno, among themselves, about dividing the spoil they had got at Haddington, and fought it manfully. Of the Fawes, there were four brethren and a brother's son; of the Shawes, the father with three sons; and several women on both sides. Old Sandie Fawe, a bold and proper fellow,* with his wife, then with child, were both killed dead upon the place; and his brother George very dangerously wounded. In February, 1678, old Robin Shawe, the Gipsy, and his three sons, were hanged at the Grass-market, for the above-mentioned murder, committed at Romanno; and John Fawe was hanged, the Wednesday following, for another murder. Sir Archibald Primrose was justice general at the time, and Sir George McKenzie king's advocate." Contrasting the obstinate

* It is interesting to notice that the Doctor calls this Gipsy a "bold and proper fellow." He was, in all probability, a fine specimen of physical manhood.—Ed.

ferocity of the Gipsy with the harmless and innocent nature of the dove, Dr. Pennecuik erected on the spot a dove-cot; and, to commemorate the battle, placed upon the lintel of the door the following inscription:

"A. D. 1683.
The field of Gipsie blood, which here you see,
A shelter for the harmless dove shall be."

This Gipsy battle is also noticed by Lord Fountainhall, in the following extract from his MS., now in the Advocate's Library:—"Sixth February, 1678.—Four Egyptians, of the name of Shaw, were this day hanged—the father and three sons—for the slaughter committed by them on the Faws, (another tribe of these vagabonds, worse than the mendicants validi, mentioned in the code,) in a drunken squabble, made by them in a rendezvous they had at Romanno, with a design to unite their forces against the clans of Browns and Baillezies (Baillies), that were come over from Ireland,* to chase them back again, that they might not share in their labours; but, in their ramble, they discovered and committed the foresaid murder; and sundry of them, of both sides, were apprehended."—"The four being thrown into a hole dug for them in the Greyfriars churchyard, with their clothes on, the next morning the body of the youngest of the three sons, (who was scarce sixteen,) was missed. Some thought that, being last thrown over the ladder, and first cut down, and in full vigour, and not much earth placed upon him, and lying uppermost, and so not so ready to smother, the fermentation of the blood, and heat of the bodies under him, might cause him to rebound, and throw off the earth, and recover ere the morning, and steal away. Which, if true, he deserved his life, though the magistrates deserved a reprimand. But others, more probably, thought his body was stolen away by some chirurgeon, or his servant, to make an anatomical dissection on."

About a century after this conflict, we find the nature of the Gipsies still unchanged. The following details of one

* The Scottish Gipsies, as I have already said, have a tradition that their ancestors came into Scotland by way of Ireland.

[The allusion to that circumstance by the Gipsies, on this occasion, was evidently to throw dust into the eyes of the Scottish authorities, by whom the whole tribe in Scotland were proscribed.—Ed.]

of their general engagements will serve as a specimen of the obstinate and desperate manner in which, to a late period, they fought among themselves. The battle took place at the bridge of Hawick, in the spring of the year 1772, or 1773. The particulars are derived from the late Mr. Robert Laidlaw, Tenant of Fanash, a gentleman of respectability, who was an eye-witness to the scene of action. It was understood that this battle originated in some encroachments of the one tribe upon the district assigned to the other; a principal source of quarrels among these wanderers. And it was agreed to, by the contending parties, that they were to fight out their dispute the first time they should meet, which, as just said, happened at Hawick.

On the one side, in this battle, was the celebrated Alexander Kennedy, a handsome and athletic man, and head of his tribe. Next to him, in consideration, was little Wull Ruthven, Kennedy's father-in-law. This man was known, all over the country, by the extraordinary title of the Earl of Hell;* and, although he was above five feet ten inches in height, he got the appellation of Little Wull, to distinguish him from Muckle William Ruthven, who was a man of uncommon stature and personal strength.† The earl's son was also in the fray. These were the chief men in Kennedy's band. Jean Ruthven, Kennedy's wife, was also present; with a great number of inferior members of the clan, males as well as females, of all ages, down to mere children. The opposite band consisted of old Rob Tait, the chieftain of his horde, Jacob Tait, young Rob Tait, and three of old Rob Tait's sons-in-law. These individuals, with Jean Gordon, old Tait's wife, and a numerous train of youths of both sexes and various ages, composed the adherents of old Robert Tait. These adverse tribes were all closely connected with one another by the ties of blood. The Kennedys and Ruthvens were from the ancient burgh of Lochmaben.

* This seems a favourite title among the Tinklers. One, of the name of Young, bears it at the present time. But the Gipsies are not singular in these terrible titles. In the late Burmese war, we find his Burmese majesty creating one of his generals "King of Hell, Prince of Darkness."—See *Constable's Miscellany.*

† A friend, in writing me, says: "I still think I see him, (Muckle Wull,) bruising the charred peat over the flame of his furnace, with hands equal to two pair of hands of the modern day; while his withered and hairy shackle-bones were more like the postern joints of a sorrel cart-horse than anything else."

The whole of the Gipses in the field, females as well as males, were armed with bludgeons, excepting some of the Taits, who carried cutlasses, and pieces of iron hoops, notched and serrated on either side, like a saw, and fixed to the end of sticks. The boldest of the tribe were in front of their respective bands, with their children and the other members of their clan in the rear, forming a long train behind them. In this order both parties boldly advanced, with their weapons uplifted above their heads. Both sides fought with extraordinary fury and obstinacy. Sometimes the one band gave way, and sometimes the other; but both, again and again, returned to the combat with fresh ardour. Not a word was spoken during the struggle; nothing was heard but the rattling of the cudgels and the strokes of the cutlasses. After a long and doubtful contest, Jean Ruthven, big with child at the time, at last received, among many other blows, a dreadful wound with a cutlass. She was cut to the bone, above and below the breast, particularly on one side. It was said the slashes were so large and deep that one of her breasts was nearly severed from her body, and that the motions of her lungs, while she breathed, were observed through the aperture between her ribs. But, notwithstanding her dreadful condition, she would neither quit the field nor yield, but continued to assist her husband as long as she was able. Her father, the Earl of Hell, was also shockingly wounded; the flesh being literally cut from the bone of one of his legs, and, in the words of my informant, "hanging down over his ankles, like beef steaks." The earl left the field to get his wounds dressed; but observing his daughter, Kennedy's wife, so dangerously wounded, he lost heart, and, with others of his party, fled, leaving Kennedy alone, to defend himself against the whole of the clan of Tait.

Having now all the Taits, young and old, male and female, to contend with, Kennedy, like an experienced warrior, took advantage of the local situation of the place. Posting himself on the narrow bridge of Hawick, he defended himself in the defile, with his bludgeon, against the whole of his infuriated enemies. His handsome person, his undaunted bravery, his extraordinary dexterity in handling his weapon, and his desperate situation, (for it was evident to all that the Taits thirsted for his blood, and were determined to despatch him on the spot,) excited a general and lively interest in his favour, among the inhabitants of the town, who were present, and had witnessed the conflict with amazement and horror. In one dash to the front, and with one powerful sweep of his cudgel, he disarmed two of the Taits, and cutting a third to the skull, felled him to the ground. He sometimes daringly advanced upon his assailants, and drove the whole band before him, pell-mell. When he broke one cudgel on his enemies, by his powerful arm, the town's people were ready to hand him another. Still, the vindictive Taits rallied, and renewed the charge with unabated vigour; and every one present expected that Kennedy would fall a sacrifice to their desperate fury. A party of messengers and constables at last arrived to his relief, when the Taits were all apprehended, and imprisoned; but, as none of the Gipsies were actually slain in the fray, they were soon set at liberty.*

In this battle, it was said that every Gipsy, except Alexander Kennedy, the brave chief, was severely wounded; and that the ground on which they fought was wet with blood. Jean Gordon, however, stole, unobserved, from her band, and, taking a circuitous road, came behind Kennedy, and struck him on the head with her cudgel. What astonished the inhabitants of Hawick the most of all, was the fierce and stubborn disposition of the Gipsy females. It was remarked that, when they were knocked down senseless to the ground, they rose again, with redoubled vigour and energy, to the combat. This unconquerable obstinacy and courage of their females is held in high estimation by the

* This Gipsy battle is alluded to by Sir Walter Scott, in a postcript to a letter to Captain Adam Ferguson, 16th April, 1819.

"By the by, old Kennedy the tinker swam for his life at Jedburgh, and was only, by the sophisticated and timed evidence of a seceding doctor, who differed from all his brethren, saved from a well-deserved gibbet. He goes to botanize for fourteen years. Pray tell this to the Duke (of Buccleuch,) for he was an old soldier of the Duke, and the Duke's old soldier. Six of his brethren were, I am told, in the court, and kith and kin without end. I am sorry so many of the clan are left. The cause of the quarrel with the murdered man, was an old feud between two Gipsy clans, the Kennedys and Irvings, which, about forty years since, gave rise to a desperate quarrel and battle at Hawick-green, in which the grandfather of both Kennedy and the man whom he murdered were engaged."—*Lockhart's Life of Sir Walter Scott.* Alexander Kennedy was tried for murdering Irving, at Yarrowford.

[This Gipsy fray at Hawick, is known among the English Gipsies as "the Battle of the Bridge."—Ed.

tribe. I once heard a Gipsy sing a song, which celebrated one of their battles; and, in it, the brave and determined manner in which the girls bore the blows of the cudgel over their heads was particularly applauded.

The battle at Hawick was not decisive to either party. The hostile bands, a short time afterwards, came in contact, in Ettrick Forest, at a place, on the water of Teema, called Deephope. They did not, however, engage here; but the females on both sides, at some distance from one another, with a stream between them, scolded and cursed, and, clapping their hands, urged the males again to fight. The men, however, more cautious, only observed a sullen and gloomy silence at this meeting. Probably both parties, from experience, were unwilling to renew the fight, being aware of the consequences which would follow, should they again close in battle. The two clans then separated, each taking different roads, but both keeping possession of the disputed district. In the course of a few days, they again met in Eskdale moor, when a second desperate conflict ensued. The Taits were here completely routed, and driven from the district, in which they had attempted to travel by force.

The country-people were horrified at the sight of the wounded Tinklers, after these sanguinary engagements. Several of them, lame and exhausted, in consequence of the severity of their numerous wounds, were, by the assistance of their tribe, carried through the country on the backs of asses; so much were they cut up in their persons. Some of them, it was said, were slain outright, and never more heard of. Jean Ruthven, however, who was so dreadfully slashed, recovered from her wounds, to the surprise of all who had seen her mangled body, which was sewed in different parts by her clan. These battles were talked of for thirty miles around the country. I have heard old people speak of them, with fear and wonder at the fierce, unyielding disposition of the willful and vindictive Tinklers.*

* Grellmann, on the Hungarian Gipsies, says: "They are loquacious and quarrelsome in the highest degree. In the public markets, and before ale-houses, where they are surrounded by spectators, they bawl, spit at each other, catch up sticks and cudgels, vapour and brandish them over their heads, throw dust and dirt; now run from each other, then back again, with furious gestures and threats. The women scream, drag their husbands by force from the scene of action; these break from them again, and return to it. The children, too, howl piteously." But I am at a loss

We have already seen that the female Gipsies are nearly as expert at handling the cudgel, and fully as fierce and unyielding in their quarrels and conflicts, as the males of their race. The following particulars relative to a Gipsy scuffle, derived from an eye-witness, will illustrate how a Gipsy woman, of the name of Rebecca Keith, displayed no little dexterity in the effective use which she made of her bludgeon.

Two gangs of Gipsies, of different tribes, had taken up their quarters, on a Saturday, the one at the town of Dumblane, the other at a farm-steading on the estate of Cromlix, in the neighbourhood. On the Sunday following, the Dumblane horde paid a visit to the others, at their country quarters. The place set apart for their accommodation was an old kiln, of which they had possession, where they were feasted with abundance of savoury viands, and regaled with mountain dew, in copious libations, of quality fit for a prince. The country squad were of the Keith fraternity, and their queen, or head personage, at the time, was Rebecca Keith, past the middle age, but of gigantic stature, and great muscular power. In the course of their carousal, a quarrel ensued between the two gangs, and a fierce battle followed. The Keiths were the weaker party, but Becca, as she was called by the country-people, performed prodigies of valour, against fearful odds, with only the aid of her strong, hard-worn shoe, which she wielded with the dexterity and effect of an experienced cudgelist. She appeared, however, unable much longer to contend against her too numerous opponents. Being a great favourite with all, especially with the inmates of the farm which was the scene of encounter, two young boys—the informant and the herd-callant—who witnessed the engagement, and whose sympathy was altogether on the side of the valourous Becca, exchanged a hurried and whispering remark to each other that, "if she had the *soople* of a flail, they thought she would do gude wark." No sooner said than done. The herd-boy went off at once to the barn, cut the thongs asunder, and returned, in a twinkling, with

to understand the object of such an affray, as given by this author, on any other theory than that of collecting crowds, in the places mentioned, to enable them the more easily to pick pockets. For Grellmann adds: "After a short time, without any persons interfering, when they have cried and make a noise till they are tired, and without either party having received any personal injury, the affair terminates, and they separate with as much ostentation as if they had performed the most heroic feat."—Ed.

the soople below his jacket, concealing it from view, with the cunning of a thief. Edging up to Becca, and uncovering the end of the weapon, it was seized upon by her with avidity. She flourished it in the air, and plied it with such effect, about the ears of her adversaries, that they were speedily driven off the field, with "sarks full of sore bones." In this furious manner would the friendly meetings of the Gipsies frequently terminate.*

So formidable were the numbers of the nomadic Gipsies, at one time, and so alarming their desperate and sanguinary battles, in the upper parts of Tweed-dale and Clydesdale, that the fencible men in their neighbourhood, (the *country-side* was the expression,) had sometimes to turn out to quell and disperse them. A clergyman was, on one occasion, under the necessity of dismissing his congregation, in the middle of divine service, that they might quell one of these furious Gipsy tumults, in the immediate vicinity of the church.†

* It is astonishing how trifling a circumstance will sometimes set such Gipsies by the ears. In England, they will frequently "cast up" the history of their respective families on such occasions. "What was your father, I would like to know? He hadn't even an ass to carry his traps, and was a rogue at that, you ——— Gipsy. *My* father was an honest man.' "'*Honest* man?'—" Yes, honest man, and that's more than you can say of your kin." The other, having more of "the blood," will taunt his acquaintance with some such expression as "Gorgio like," (like the white.)—" And what are you, you black trash? Will blood put money in your pocket? Blood, indeed! I'm a better Gipsy than you are, in spite of the black devil that every one sees in your face!" Then the fray commences.

When Gipsies take up their quarters on the premises of country people, a very effectual way of sometimes getting rid of them is to stir up discord among them. For when it comes to "hammers and tongs," "tongs and hammers," they will scatter, uttering howls of vengeance, on some more appropriate occasion, against their most intimate friends, who have just incurred their wrath, yet who will be seen "cheek by jowl" with them, perhaps, the next day, or even before the sun has gone down upon them; so easily are they sometimes irritated, and so easily reconciled.—ED.

† A writer in Blackwood's Magazine mentions that the Gipsies, late in the seventeenth century, broke into the house of Penniculk, when the greater part of the family were at church. Sir John Clerk, the proprietor, barricaded himself in his own apartment, where he sustained a sort of siege—firing from the windows upon the robbers, who fired upon him in return. One of them, while straying through the house in quest of booty, happened to ascend the stairs of a very narrow turret, but, slipping his foot, caught hold of the rope of the alarm bell, the ringing of which startled the congregation assembled in the parish church. They instantly came to the rescue of the Laird, and succeeded, it is said, in apprehending some of the Gipsies,

About the year 1770, the mother of the Baillies received some personal injury, or rather insult, at a fair at Biggar, from a gardener of the name of John Cree. The insult was instantly resented by the Gipsies; but Cree was luckily protected by his friends. In contempt and defiance of the whole multitude in the market, four of the Baillies—Matthew, James, William, and John—all brothers, appeared on horse-back, dressed in scarlet, and armed with broad-swords, and, parading through the crowd, threatened to be avenged of the gardener, and those who had assisted him. Burning with revenge, they threw off their coats, rolled up the sleeves of their shirts to the shoulder, like butchers when at work, and, with their naked and brawny arms, and glittering swords in their clenched hands, furiously rode up and down the fair, threatening death to all who should oppose them. Their bare arms, naked weapons, and resolute looks, showed that they were prepared to slaughter their enemies without mercy. No one dared to interfere with them, till the minister of the parish appeased their rage, and persuaded them to deliver up their swords. It was found absolutely necessary, however, to keep a watch upon the gardener's house, for six months after the occurrence, to protect him and his family from the vengeance of the vindictive Gipsies.

To bring into view and illustrate the character and practices of our Scottish Gipsies, I will transcribe the following details, in the original words, from a MS. which I received from the late Mr. Blackwood, as a contribution towards a history of the Gipsies. Mr. Blackwood did not say who the writer of the paper was, but some one mentioned to me that he was a clergyman. I am satisfied that the statements it contains are true, and that the William Baillie therein mentioned was, in his day and generation, well known, over the greater part of Scotland, as chief of his tribe within the kingdom. He was the grandfather of the four Gipsies who, as just mentioned, set at defiance the whole multitude at Biggar fair. It will be seen, by this MS., that while the principal Gipsies, with their subordinates, were plundering the public, in all directions, they sometimes performed acts of gratitude and great kindness to their favourites of the community among whom they travelled. In it will also be

who were executed. There is a written account of this daring assault kept in the records of the family.—ED

exhibited the cool and business-like manner in which they delivered back stolen purses, when circumstances rendered such restoration necessary.

"There was formerly a gang of Gipsies, or pick-pockets, who used to frequent the fairs in Dumfries-shire, headed by a William Baillie, or Will Baillie, as the country-people were accustomed to call him, of whom the old men used to tell many stories.

"Before any considerable fair, if the gang were at a distance from the place where it was to be held, whoever of them were appointed to go, went singly, or, at most, never above two travelled together. A day or so after, Mr. Baillie himself followed, mounted like a nobleman; and, as journeys, in those days, were almost all performed on horseback, he sometimes rode, for many miles, with gentlemen of the first respectability in the country. And, as he could discourse readily and fluently on almost any topic, he was often taken to be some country gentleman of property, as his dress and manners seemed to indicate.

"Once, in a very crowded fair at Dumfries, an honest farmer, from the parish of Hatton, in Annandale, had his pocket picked of a considerable sum, in gold, with which he was going to buy cattle. On discovering his loss, he immediately went and got a purse like the one he had lost, into which he put a good number of small stones, and, going into a crowded part of the fair, he kept a watchful eye on his pocket, and, in a little while, he caught a fellow in the very act of picking it. The farmer, who was a stout, athletic man, did not wish to make any noise, as he knew a more ready way of recovering his money; but whispered to the fellow, while he still kept fast hold of him, to come out of the throng a little, as he wanted to speak to him. There he told him that he had lost his money, and that, if he would get it to him again, he would let him go; if not, he would have him put in jail immediately. The pick-pocket desired him to come along with him, and he would see what could be done, the farmer still keeping close to him, lest he should escape. They entered an obscure house, in an unfrequented close, where they found Mr. Baillie sitting. The farmer told his tale, concluding with a promise that, as the loss of the money would hurt him very much, he would, if he could get it back again, make no more ado about it. On which, Mr. Baillie went to a concealment in the wall, and brought out the very purse the farmer had lost, with the contents untouched, which he returned to the farmer, who received it with much gratitude.

"The farmer, after doing his business in the fair, got a little intoxicated in the evening; on which he thought he would call on Mr. Baillie, and give him a treat, for his kindness in restoring his purse; but on entering the house, the woman who kept it, a poor widow, fell on him and abused him sadly, asking him what he had done to cause Mr. Stewart, by which name she knew Mr. Baillie, to leave her house; and saying she had lost the best friend that ever she had, for always when he stayed a day or two in her house, (which he used to do twice a year,) he gave her as much as paid her half-year's rent; but after he, (the farmer,) called that day, Mr. Stewart, she said, left her house, telling her he could not stay with her any longer; but before he went, she said, he had given her what was to pay her half-year's rent, a resource, she lamented, she would lose in future. About two years afterwards, the farmer again had the curiosity to call on her, and ask her if her lodger had ever returned. She said he never had, but that, ever since, a stranger had called regularly, and given her money to pay her rent.

"In the parish of Kirkmichael, about eight miles from Dumfries, lived a widow who occupied a small farm. As she had a number of young children, and no man to assist her, she fell behind in paying her rent, and at last got a summons of removal. She had a kiln that stood at a considerable distance from the other houses, which was much frequented by Baillie's people, when they came that way; and she gave them, at all times, peaceable possession, as she had no person to contend with them, or put them away, and she herself did not wish to differ with them. They, on the other hand, never molested anything she had. One evening, a number of them arrived rather late, and went into the kiln, as usual; after which, one come into the house, to ask a few peats, to make a fire. She gave the peats, saying she believed they would soon have to shift their quarters, as she herself was warned to flit, and she did not know if the next tenant would allow them such quiet possession, and she did not know what would become of herself and her helpless family. Nothing more was said, but, after having put her children to bed, as she was sitting by the fire, in a disconsolate manner, she heard a gentle tap at the door. On opening it, a genteel, well-dressed man entered, who told her he just wished to speak with her for a few minutes, and, sitting down, said he had heard she was warned to remove, and asked how much she was behind. She told him exactly. On which, rising hastily, he slipt a purse into her hand, and went out before she could say a single word.

"The widow, however, kept the farm, paid off all old debts, and brought up her family decently; but still, it grieved her that she did not know who was her benefactor. She never told any person till about ten years afterwards, when she told a friend who came to see her, when she was rather poorly in health. After hearing the story, he asked her what sort of a man he was who gave her the money. She said their interview was so short, and it was so long past, that she could recollect little of him, but only remembered well that he had the scar of a cut across his nose. On which, her friend immediately exclaimed, 'Then Will Baillie was the man.'

"Before the year 1740, the roads were bad through all the country. Carts were not then in use, and all the merchants' goods were conveyed in packs, on horseback. Among others, the farmers on the water of Ae, in Dumfries-shire, were almost all pack-carriers. As there was little improvement of land then, they had little to do at home, and so they made their rents mostly by carrying. Among others, there was an uncle of my father, whose name was Robert McVitie, who used to be a great carrier. This man, once, in returning from Edinburgh, stopt at Broughton, and in coming out of the stable, he met a man, who asked him if he knew him. Robert, after looking at him for a little, said: 'I think you are Mr. Baillie.'' He said, I am, and asked if Robert could lend him two guineas, and it should be faithfully repaid. As there were few people who wished to differ with Baillie, Robert told him he was welcome to two guineas, or more if he wanted it. He said that would just do; on which Robert gave them to him, and he put them into his pocket. Baillie then asked, if ever he was molested by any person, when he was travelling late with his packs. He said he never was, although he was sometimes a little afraid. Baillie then gave him a kind of brass token, about the size of a half-crown, with some marks upon it, which he desired him to carry in his purse, and it might be of use to him some time, as he was to show it, if any person offered to rob him. Baillie then mounted his horse and rode off.

"Some considerable time after this, as Robert was one evening travelling with his packs, between Elvanfoot and Moffat, two men came up to him, whom he thought very suspicious-looking fellows. As he was a stout man himself, and carried a good cudgel, he kept on the alert for a considerable way, lest they should take him by surprise. At last, one of them asked him if he was not afraid to travel alone, so late at night. He said he was under a necessity to be out late, sometimes, on his lawful business. But recollecting his token, he said a gentleman had once given him a piece of brass, to show, if ever any person troubled him. They desired him to show it, as it was moonlight. He gave it to them. On seeing it, they looked at one another, and then, whispering a few words, told him it was well for him he had the token, which they returned; and they left him directly.

"After a lapse of nearly two years, when he had almost forgotten his two guineas, as he was one morning loading his packs, at the door of a public-house, near Gretna-green, he felt some person touch him behind, and, on looking round, saw it was Mr. Baillie, who slipped something into his hand, wrapped in paper, and left him, without speaking a single word. On opening the paper, he found three guineas, which was his own money, and a guinea for interest.

"There was another gang of Gipsies that stayed mostly in Annandale, headed by a Jock Johnstone, as he was called in the country. These were counted a kind of lower caste than Baillie's people, who would have thought themselves degraded if they had associated with any of the Johnstone gang. Johnstone confined his travels mostly to Dumfries-shire; while Baillie went over all Scotland, and even made long excursions into England. Johnstone kept a great many women about him,* several of whom had children to him; and, in kilns and in barns, Johnstone always slept in the middle of the whole gang. Baillie sometimes told his

* A great many of the inferior Gipsy chiefs travelled with a number of women in their company; such as George Drummond, Doctor Duds, John Lundie, and others.

select friends that he had a wife, but never any of them could find out where she stayed; and as he used to disappear now and then, for a considerable time together, it was supposed he was with her. He never slept, in barn or kiln, with any of his people. Johnstone travelled all day in the midst of a crowd of women and children, mounted on asses. Baillie travelled always by himself, mounted on the best horse he could get for money.

"Some time in the year 1739, Johnstone, with a number of his women, came to the house of one Margaret Farish, an old woman who sold ale at Lonegate, six miles from Dumfries, on the Edinburgh road. After drinking for a long time, some of Jock's wives and the old woman quarrelled. On which he took up the pewter pint-stoup, with which she measured her ale, and, giving her two or three severe blows on the head, killed her on the spot. Next day he was apprehended near Lockerby, and brought into Dumfries' jail. He had a favourite tame jack-daw that he took with him in all his travels, and he desired it might be brought to stay with him in the jail, which was done. When the lords were coming into the circuit, as they passed the jail, the trumpeters gave a blast, on which the jack-daw gave a flutter against the iron bars of the window, and dropped down dead. When Jock saw that, he immediately exclaimed: "Lord have mercy on me, for I am gone." He was accordingly tried and condemned. When the day of execution came, he would not walk to the scaffold, and so they were forced to carry him. The executioner, being an old man, could not turn him over. Several of the constables refused to touch him. At last, one of the burgh officers turned him off; but the old people about Dumfries used to say that the officer never prospered any more after that day."*

* Dr. Alexander Carlyle, in a note to his autobiography, mentions having seen this Jock Johnstone hanged. The date given by him (1733), differs, however, from that mentioned above. According to him, Johnstone was but twenty years of age, but bold, and a great ringleader, and was condemned for robbery, and being accessory to a murder. The usual place of execution was a moor, adjoining the town; but, as it was strongly reported that the "thieves" were collecting from all quarters, to rescue the criminal from the gallows, the magistrates erected the scaffold in front of the prison, with a platform connecting, and surrounded it with about a hundred of the stoutest burgesses, armed with Lochaber axes. Jock made his appearance, surrounded by six officers. He was curly-haired, and fierce-looking, about five feet eight inches in height, and very strong of his size. At first he ap-

The extraordinary man Baillie, who is here so often mentioned, was well known in Tweed-dale and Clydesdale; and my great-grandfather, who knew him well, used to say that he was the handsomest, the best dressed, the best looking, and the best bred man he ever saw. As I have already mentioned, he generally rode one of the best horses the kingdom could produce; himself attired in the finest scarlet, with his greyhounds following him, as if he had been a man of the first rank. With the usual Gipsy policy, he represented himself as a bastard son of one of the Baillies of Lamington, his mother being a Gipsy. On this account, considerable attention was paid to him by the country-people; indeed, he was taken notice of by the first in the land. But, from his singular habits, his real character at last became well known. He acted the character of the gentleman, the robber, the sorner, and the tinker, whenever it answered his purpose. He was considered, in his time, the best swordsman in all Scotland. With this weapon in his hand, and his back at a wall, he set almost everything, saving fire-arms, at defiance. His sword is still preserved by his descendants, as a relic of their powerful ancestor. The stories that are told of this splendid Gipsy are numerous and interesting. I will relate only two well-authenticated anecdotes of this *baurie rajah*, this king of the Scottish Gipsies; who was, in all probability, a descendant of Towla Bailyow, who, with other Gipsies, rebelled against, and plundered, John Faw, "Lord and Earl of Little Egypt," in the reign of James V. The following transaction of his has some resemblance to a custom among the Arabians.

peared astonished, but, looking around awhile, proceeded with a bold step. Psalms and prayers being over, and the rope fastened about his neck, he was ordered to mount a short ladder, attached to the gallows, in order to be thrown off; when he immediately seized the rope, and pulled so violently at it as to be in danger of bringing down the gallows—causing much emotion among the crowd, and fear among the magistrates. Jock, becoming furious, like a wild beast, struggled and roared, and defied the six officers to bind him; and, recovering the use of his arms, became more formidable. The magistrates then with difficulty prevailed on by far the strongest man in Dumfries, for the honour of the town, to come on the scaffold. Putting aside the six officers, this man seized the criminal, with as little difficulty as a nurse handles her child, and in a few minutes bound him hand and foot; and quietly laying him down on his face, near the edge of the scaffold, retired. Jock, the moment he felt his grasp, found himself subdued, and, becoming calm, resigned himself to his fate.—*Carlyle's Autobiography.*—ED.

William, with his numerous horde, happened to fall in with a travelling packman, on a wild spot between Hawkshaw and Menzion, near the source of the Tweed. The packman was immediately commanded to halt, and lay his packs upon the ground. Baillie then unsheathed his broadsword, with which he was always armed, and, with the point of the weapon, drew, on the ground, a circle around the trembling packman and his wares. Within this circle no one of the tribe was allowed by him to enter but himself.* The poor man was now ordered to unbuckle his packs, and exhibit his merchandise to the Gipsies. Baillie, without the least ceremony, helped himself to some of the most valuable things in the pack, and gave a great many to the members of his band. The unfortunate merchant, well aware of the character of his customers, concluded himself a ruined man; and, in place of making any resistance, handed away his property to the Gipsies. But when they were satisfied, he was most agreeably surprised by Baillie taking out his purse, and paying him, on the spot, a great deal more than the value of every article he had taken for himself and given to his band. The delighted packman failed not to extol, wherever he went, the gentlemanly conduct and extraordinary liberality of "Captain Baillie"—a title by which he was known all over the country.

The perilous situations in which Baillie was often placed did not repress the merry jocularity and sarcastic wit which he, in common with many of his tribe, possessed. He sometimes almost bearded and insulted the judge while sitting on the bench. On one of these occasions, when he was in court, the judge, provoked at seeing him so often at the bar, observed to him that he would assuredly get his ears cut out of his head, if he did not mend his manners, and abandon his way of life. "That I defy you to do, my lord," replied the Tinkler. The judge, perceiving that his ears had already been "nailed to the tron, and cut off," and being displeased at the effrontery and levity of his conduct, told him

* Bruce, in his travels, when speaking of the protection afforded by the Arabs to shipwrecked Christians, on the coasts of the Red Sea, says:—"The Arabian, with his lance, draws a circle large enough to hold you and yours. He then strikes his lance in the sand, and bids you abide within the circle. You are thus as safe, on the desert coast of Arabia, as in a citadel; there is no example or exception to the contrary that has ever been known."—*Bruce's Travels in Abyssinia.*

that he was certainly a great villain. "I am not such a villain as your lordship," retorted Baillie. "What do you say?" rejoined the judge, in great surprise at the bold manner of the criminal. "I say," continued the Gipsy, "that I am not such a villain as your lordship——takes me to be." "William," quoth the judge, "put your words closer together, otherwise you shall have cause to repent of your insolence and audacity."*

Tradition states that William Baillie's conduct involved him in numerous scrapes. He was brought before the Justiciary Court, and had "his ears nailed to the tron, or other tree, and cut off, and banished the country," for his many crimes of "sorning, pickery, and little thieving." It also appears, from popular tradition, that he is the same William Baillie who is repeatedly noticed by Hume and McLaurin, in their remarks on the criminal law of Scotland.

In June, 1699, William Baillie, for being an Egyptian, and for forging and using a forged pass, was sentenced to be "hanged; but the privy council commuted his sentence to banishment, but under the express condition that, if ever he returned to this country, the former sentence should be executed against him." William entered into a bond with the privy council, under the penalty of 500 merks, to leave the kingdom, and to "suffer the pains of death, in case of contravention thereof."

This Gipsy chief paid little regard to the terrible conditions of his bond, in case of failure; for, on the 10th and 11th August, 1714, "Baillie," says Hume, "and two of his associates, were convicted and condemned to die; but as far as concerned Baillie, (for the others were executed,) his doom was afterwards mitigated into transportation, under pain of death in case of return." "The jury," says McLaurin, "brought in a special verdict as to the sorning,† but said nothing at

* It might be supposed that the pride of a Gipsy would have the good effect of rendering him cautious not to be guilty of such crimes as subject him to public shame. But here his levity of character is rendered conspicuous; for he never looks to the right or to the left in his transactions; and though his conceit and pride are somewhat humbled, during the time of punishment, and while the consequent pain lasts; these being over, he no longer remembers his disgrace, but entertains quite as good an opinion of himself as before.—*Grellmann on the Hungarian Gipsies.*—Ed.

† *Sorn*, (Scottish and Irish;) an arbitrary exaction, by which a chieftain lived at pleasure, in free quarters, among his tenants: also one who obtrudes himself upon another, for bed and board, is said to sorn.—*Bailey.*

all as to any other points; all they found proved was, that William, in March, 1713, had taken possession of a barn, without consent of the owner, and that, during his abode in it, there was corn taken out of the barn, and he went away without paying anything for his quarters, or for any corn during his abode, which was for several days; and that he was habit and repute an Egyptian, and did wear a pistol* and shable," (a kind of sabre.)

"As early as the month of August, 1715, the same man, as I understand it," says Baron Hume, "was again indicted, not only for being found in Britain, but for continuing his former practices and course of life. Notwithstanding this aggravation, the interlocutor is again framed on the indulgent plan; and only infers the pain of death from the fame and character of being an Egyptian, joined with various acts of violence and sorning, to the number of three that are stated in the libel. Though convicted nearly to the extent of the interlocutor, he again escaped with transportation."

Baillie's policy in representing himself as a bastard son of an ancient and honourable family had, as I have already observed, been of great service to him; and in no way would it be more so than in his various trials. It is almost certain, as in cases of more recent times, that great interest would be used to save a bastard branch of an honourable house from an ignominious death upon the scaffold, when his crimes amounted only to "sorning, pickery, and little thieving, and habit and repute an Egyptian."†

* A great many of the Scottish Gipsies, in former times, carried arms. One of the Baillies once left his budget in a house, by mistake. A person, whom I knew, had the curiosity to examine it; and he found it to contain a pair of excellent pistols, loaded and ready for action.

† What our author says of "the usual Gipsy policy of making the people believe that they are descended from families of rank and influence in the country," (page 154,) and that "the greater part of them will tell you that they are sprung from a bastard son of this or that noble family, or other person of rank and influence, of their own surname," (117,) is doubtless true as a rule; but there were as likely cases of what the Gipsies assert, and that Gipsy women, "in some instances, bore children to some of the 'unspotted gentlemen' mentioned by act of parliament as having so greatly protected and entertained the tribe," (114,) and that Baillie was one of them, (121 and 185.) If Baillie had been following the occupation, and bearing the reputation, of an ordinary native of Scotland, there would have been some chance "that great interest would be used to save a bastard branch of an honourable house from an ignominious death upon the scaffold," for almost any offence he had committed, but not for one who was guilty of "sorning, pickery, and little thieving, and habit and repute an

The descendants of William Baillie state that he was married to a woman of the name of Rachel Johnstone; and that he was killed, in a scuffle, by a Gipsy of the name of Pinkerton, in a quarrel among themselves. Baillie being quite superior in personal strength to Pinkerton, his wife took hold of him, for fear of his destroying his opponent, and, while he was in her arms, Pinkerton ran him through with his sword. Upon his death, his son, then a youth of thirteen years of age, took a solemn oath, on the spot, that he would never rest until the blood of his father should be avenged. And, true to his oath, his mother and himself followed the track of the murderer over Scotland, England, and Ireland, like staunch bloodhounds, and rested not, till Pinkerton was apprehended, tried, and executed.

The following particulars, relative to the slaughter of William Baillie, were published in Blackwood's Magazine, but apparently without any knowledge, on the part of the writer, of that individual's history, further than that he was a Gipsy.

"In a precognition, taken in March, 1725, by Sir James Stewart, of Coltness, and Captain Lockhart, of Kirkton, two of his majesty's justices of the peace for Lanarkshire, anent the murder of William Baillie, brazier,* commonly called Gipsy, the following evidence is adduced:—John Meikle, wright, declares, that, upon the twelfth of November last, he, being in the house of Thomas Riddle, in Newarthill, with some others, the deceased, William Baillie, James Kairns, and David Pinkerton, were in another room, drinking, where, after some high words, and a confused noise and squabble, the said three persons, above-named, went all out; and the declarant, knowing them to be three of those idle sorners that pass in the country under the name of Gipsies, in hopes they were gone off, rose, and went to the door, to take the air; where, to his surprise, he saw William Baillie standing,

Egyptian." There was doubtless a connexion, in *Gipsy* blood, between Baillie and his influential friends who saved him and his relatives so often from the gallows.—*See Baillies of Lamington and McLaurin's Criminal Trials, in the Index.*—Ed.

* On some of the tombstones of the Gipsies, the word "brazier" is added to their names. [Brazier is a favourite name with the Gipsies, and sounds better than tinker. Southey, in his Life of Bunyan, says: "It is stated, in a history of Bedfordshire, that he was bred to the business of a brazier, and worked, as a journeyman, at Bedford."—Ed.]

and Kairns and Pinkerton on horseback, with drawn swords in their hands, who both rushed upon the said William Baillie, and struck him with their swords; whereupon, the said William Baillie fell down, crying out he was gone; upon which, Kairns and Pinkerton rode off: That the declarant helped to carry the said William Baillie into the house, where, upon search, he was found to have a great cut or wound on his head, and a wound in his body, just below the slot of his breast: And declares, he, the said William Baillie, died some time after.

"Thomas Riddle, tenant and change-keeper in Newarthill, &c., declares, that the deceased, William Baillie, James Kairns, and David Pinkerton, all idle sorners, that are known in the country by the name of Gipsies, came to the declarant's, about sun-setting, where, after some stay, *and talking a jargon the declarant did not well understand*, they fell a squabbling, when the declarant was in another room, with some other company; upon the noise of which, the declarant ran in to them, where he found the said James Kairns lying above the said William Baillie, whose nose the said James Kairns had bitten with his teeth till it bled; upon which, the declarant and his wife threatened to raise the town upon them, and get a constable to carry them to prison; but Kairns and Pinkerton called for their horses, William Baillie saying he would not go with them: Declares that, after the said Kairns and Pinkerton had got their horses, and mounted, they ordered the declarant to bring a chopin of ale to the door to them, where William Baillie was standing, talking to them: That, when the declarant had filled about the ale, and left them, thinking they were going off, the declarant's wife went to the door, where Kairns struck at her with a drawn sword, to fright her in; upon which she ran in; and thereupon the declarant went to the door, where he found the said William Baillie, lying with the wounds upon him, mentioned in John Meikle's declaration."

By Hume's work on the criminal law, it appears that the trial of David Pinkerton, with others of his tribe, took place on the 22nd August, 1726, for "sorning and robbery;" but no mention is made of the murder of Baillie; yet it was Baillie's relatives that pursued Pinkerton to the gallows. Probably sufficient evidence could not then be adduced to substantiate the fact, being about twenty-one months after the murder was committed; and, besides, Baillie was himself dead in law, having either returned from banishment, or remained at large in the country, and so forfeited his life, when he was killed by Pinkerton, in 1724. The following is part of the interlocutor pronounced upon the indictment of the prisoners: "Find the said David Pinkerton, alias Maxwell, John Marshall, and Helen Baillie, alias Douglass, or any of them, their being habit and repute Egyptians, sorners or masterful beggars, in conjunction with said pannels, or any of them, their being, at the times and places libelled, guilty, art and part, of the fact of violence, theft, robbery, or attempts of robbery libelled, or any of the said facts relevant to infer the pain of death and confiscation of moveables."

William Baillie was succeeded, in the chieftainship, by his son Matthew, who married the celebrated Mary Yowston or Yorkston, and became the leader of a powerful horde of Gipsies in the south of Scotland. He frequently visited the farms of my grandfather, about the year 1770. It appears that his courtship had been after the Tartar manner; for he used to say that the toughest battle he ever fought was that of taking, by force, his bride, then a very young girl, from her mother, at the hamlet of Drummelzier.* This Matthew Baillie had, by Mary Yorkston, a son, who was also named Matthew, and who married Margaret Campbell, and had by her a family of remarkably handsome and pretty daughters. Of this principal Gipsy family, I can trace, distinctly, six generations in descent, and have myself seen the great-great-great-grand-children of the celebrated William Baillie. Some of his descendants still travel the country, in the manner of their ancestors, and at this moment speak the Gipsy language with fluency. Some of them, however, are little better than common beggars. There were, at one period, a captain and a quarter-master in the army, belonging to the Baillie clan; and another was a country surgeon.

Mary Yorkston, above mentioned, went under the appellations of "my lady," and "the duchess," and bore the title of queen, among her tribe. She presided at the celebration of

* The English Gipsies say that the old mode of getting a wife among the tribe was to *steal* her. The intended bride was nothing loth, still it was necessary to steal her, while the tribe were on the watch to detect and prevent it.—Ed.

their barbarous marriages, and assisted at their equally singular ceremonies of divorce. What the custom of this queen of the Gipsies was, when in full dress, in her youth, on gala days, cannot now be easily known; but the following is a description of her masculine figure, and *public* travelling apparel, when advanced in years. It was taken from the mouth of an aged and very respectable gentleman, the late Mr. David Stoddart, at Bankhead, near Queensferry, who had often seen her in his youth: She was fully six feet in stature, stout made in her person, with very strongly-marked and harsh features; and had, altogether, a very imposing aspect and manner. She wore a large black beaver-hat, tied down over her ears with a handkerchief, knotted below her chin, in the Gipsy fashion. Her upper garment was a dark-blue short cloak, somewhat after the Spanish fashion, made of substantial woollen cloth, approaching to superfine in quality. The greater part of her other apparel was made of dark-blue camlet cloth, with petticoats so short that they scarcely reached to the calves of her well-set legs. [Indeed, all the females among the Baillies wore petticoats of the same length.] Her stockings were of dark-blue worsted, flowered and ornamented at the ankles with scarlet thread; and in her shoes she displayed large, massy, silver buckles. The whole of her habiliments were very substantial, with not a rag or rent to be seen about her person. [She was sometimes dressed in a green gown, trimmed with red ribbons.] Her outer petticoat was folded up round her haunches, for a lap, with a large pocket dangling at each side; and below her cloak she carried, between her shoulders, a small flat pack, or pad, which contained her most valuable articles. About her person she generally kept a large clasp-knife, with a long, broad blade, resembling a dagger or carving-knife; and carried in her hand a long pole or pike-staff, that reached about a foot above her head.

It was a common practice, about the middle of last century, for old female Gipsies of authority to strip, without hesitation, defenceless individuals of their wearing-apparel when they met them in sequestered places. Mary Yorkston chanced, on one occasion, to meet a shepherd's wife, among the wild hills in the parish of Stobo, and stripped her of the whole of her clothes. The shepherd was horrified at beholding his wife approaching his house in a state of perfect nakedness. A Jean Gordon was once detected, by a shepherd, stripping a female of her wearing-apparel. He at once assisted the helpless woman; but Jean drew from below her garments a dagger, and threw it at him. Evading the blow, the shepherd closed in upon her, and struck her over the head with his staff, knocking her to the ground. Another Gipsy of the old fashion, of the name of Esther Grant, was also celebrated for the practice of stripping people of their clothing. The Arabian principle, expressed in these words, on meeting a stranger in the desert, "Undress thyself—my wife, (thy aunt,) is in want of a garment," is truly applicable to the disposition of the old female Gipsies.

Nothing was more common, in the counties of Peebles and Lanark, when the country-people lost their purses at fairs, than to have recourse to the chief Gipsy females, to get their property returned to them. Mary Yorkston, having a sovereign influence and power among her tribe, was often applied to, in such cases of distress, of which the following is a good specimen:—On one of these occasions, in a market in the South of Scotland, a farmer lost his purse, containing a considerable sum of money, which greatly perplexed and distressed him. He immediately went to Mary Yorkston, to try if she would exert her wonderful influence to recover his property. Being a favourite of Mary's, she, without the least hesitation, took him along with her to the place in the fair where her husband kept his temporary depôt, or rather his office, in which he exorcised his extraordinary calling during the continuance of the market. The presence of Mary was a sufficient assurance that all was right; and, upon the matter being explained, Matthew Baillie instantly produced, and spread out before the astonished farmer, from twenty to thirty purses, and desired him to pick out his own from amongst them. The countryman soon recognized his own, and grasped at it without ceremony. "Hold on," said Baillie, "let us count its contents first." The Gipsy chief, with the greatest coolness and deliberation, as if he had been an honest banker or money-changer, counted over the money in the purse, when not a farthing was found wanting. "There is your purse, sir," continued Baillie; "you see what it is, when honest people meet!"

The following incident, that occurred one night after a

fair, in a barn belonging to one of my relatives, will strikingly illustrate the character of the Gipsies in the matter of stealing purses:—A band of superior Gipsies were quartered in the barn, after several of them had attended the fair, in their usual manner. The principal female, whom I shall not name, had also been at the market; but the old chief had thought proper to remain at home, in the barn. My relative, as was sometimes his custom, chanced to take a turn about his premises that night, when it was pretty late. He heard the voice of a female weeping in the barn, and, being curious to know the cause of the disturbance among the Tinklers, stepped softly up, close to the back of the door, to listen to what they were doing, as the woman was crying bitterly. He was greatly astonished at hearing, and never could forget, the following expressions: "Oh, cruel man, to beat me in this way. I have had my hands in as good as twenty pockets, but the honest people had it not to themselves." The chieftain was, in fact, chastising his wife, in the presence of his family, for her want of diligence or success, in not obtaining enough of booty at the fair. And yet this individual bore, among the country-people, the character of an honest man.

Another story is told of Mary Yorkston and the Goodman of Coulter-park. It differs in its nature from the above anecdote, yet is very characteristic of the Gipsies. Mary and her band were lurking one night at a place in Clydesdale, called Roggingill. As a man on horseback approached the spot where they were concealed, some of the tribe immediately laid hold of the horse, and, without ceremony, commenced to plunder the rider. But Mary, stepping forth to superintend the operation, was astonished to find that the horseman was her particular friend, the Goodman of Coulter-park. She instantly exclaimed, with all her might: "It's Mr. Lindsay, the Gudeman o' Couter-park—let him gang—let him gang—God bless him, honest man!" It is needless to add that Mr. Lindsay had always given Mary and her horde the use of an out-house when they required it.

Mary Yorkston despised to ask what is properly understood to be alms. She sold horn spoons and other articles; and, when she made a bargain, she would take, almost by force, what she called her "boontith," which is a present of victuals, exclusive of the cash paid; a practice which I will explain further on in the chapter.

Matthew Baillie had, by Mary Yorkston, among other children, a son, named James Baillie, who, along with his brothers, as we have seen, threatened with destruction the people assembled in Biggar fair, in consequence of an affront offered to his mother by a gardener of that town. He was condemned, in 1771, to be hung, for the murder of his wife, by beating her with a horse-whip, and tumbling her over a steep; but he "obtained a pardon from the king, on condition that he transported himself beyond seas within a limited time, otherwise the pardon was to have no effect." Baillie, paying little regard to the serious conditions of this pardon, did not "transport himself beyond seas," but continued his former practices, as appears by the following extract from the Weekly Magazine of the 8th October, 1772:—"James Baillie, who was last summer condemned for the murder of a woman, and afterwards obtained his majesty's pardon, on condition of transporting himself to America, for life, was lately apprehended at Falkirk, on suspicion of robbery. On the 1st October he was brought to town, and committed to the Tolbooth, by a warrant of Lord Auchinleck. This warrant was granted upon the petition of the procurator fiscal of Stirling, in which he set forth that, as Baillie was a very daring fellow, and suspected of being concerned with a gang equally so with himself, there was great reason to apprehend a rescue might be attempted, by breaking the prison; and therefore praying that he might be removed to Edinburgh, where a scheme of that nature could not so easily be effected." On the 18th December, 1773, and 27th February, 1774, the "Lords, in terms of the said former sentence, decree and adjudge the said James Baillie to be hanged on the 30th March then next." He thus appears to have remained in prison from October, 1772, till March, 1774. "Soon after this sentence, he got another pardon," and was again discharged from prison, in order to his transporting himself; but he remained at home, and again relapsed into his former way of life. He was, some time afterwards, committed to Newcastle gaol, but made his escape. A short time after that, he was committed to Carlisle gaol, on suspicion of having stolen some plate. On the 4th December, 1776, three sheriff-officers set out from

Edinburgh, to bring him hither; but before they reached Carlisle, he had again broken prison and escaped.*

During one of the periods of Baillie's imprisonment, he escaped from jail, attired as a female; having been assisted by some of his tribe, residing in the Grass-market of Edinburgh. Tradition states that the then Mistress Baillie, of Lamington, and her family, used all their interest in obtaining these pardons for James Baillie; who, like his fathers before him, pretended to be a bastard relative of the family of Lamington, and thereby escaped the punishment of death. McLaurin justly remarks that "few cases have occurred in which there has been such an expenditure of mercy."†

I have already mentioned how handsomely the superior order of Gipsies dressed at the period of which we are speaking. The male head of the Ruthvens—a man six feet some inches in height—who, according to the newspapers of the day, lived to the advanced age of 115 years, when in full dress, in his youth, wore a white wig, a ruffled shirt, a blue Scottish bonnet, scarlet breeches and waistcoat, a long blue superfine coat, white stockings, with silver buckles in his shoes. Others wore silver brooches in their breasts, and gold rings on their fingers. The male Gipsies in Scotland were often dressed in green coats, black breeches, and leathern aprons. The females were very partial to green clothes. At the same time, the following anecdote will show how artful they were at all times, by means of dress and other equipments, to transform themselves, like actors on the stage, into various characters, whenever it suited their purposes.‡

My father, when a young lad, noticed a large band of

* Scot's Magazine, vol. xxxviii., page 676.

† McLaurin's Trials, page 655. [See note at page 205.—Ed.]

‡ It appears, from Vidocq's memoirs, that the Gipsies on the continent changed their apparel, so as they could not again be recognized: "At break of day everybody was on foot, and the general toilet was made. But for their (the Gipsies') prominent features, their raven-black tresses, and oily and tanned skins, I should scarcely have recognized my companions of the preceding evening. The men, clad in rich jockey Holland vests, with leathern sashes like those worn by the men of Poirey, and the women, covered with ornaments of gold and silver, assumed the costume of Zealand peasants; even the children, whom I had seen covered with rags, were neatly clothed, and had an entirely different appearance. All soon left the house, and took different directions, that they might not reach the market place together, where the country-people were assembled in crowds."—Vidocq had lodged all night in a ruinous house, with a band of Gipsies.

Gipsies taking up their quarters one night in an old out-house on a farm occupied by his father. The band had never been observed on the farm before, and seemed all to be strangers, with, altogether, a very ragged and miserable appearance. Next morning, a little after breakfast, as the band began to pack up their baggage, and load their asses, preparatory to proceeding on their journey, the youth, out of curiosity, went forward to see the horde decamp. Among other articles of luggage, he observed a large and heavy sack put upon one of the asses; and, as the Gipsies were fastening it upon the back of the animal, the mouth of it burst open, and the greater part of its contents fell upon the ground. He was not a little surprised when he beheld a great many excellent cocked hats, suits of fine green clothes, great-coats, &c., with several handsome saddles and bridles, tumble out of the bag. At this unexpected accident, the Gipsies were much disconcerted. By some strange expressions and odd manœuvres, they endeavoured to drive the boy from their presence, and otherwise engage his attention, to prevent him observing the singular furniture contained in the unlucky sack. By thus carrying along with them these superior articles, so unlike their ordinary wretched habiliments, the ingenious Gipsies had it always in their power to disguise themselves, whenever circumstances called for it. The following anecdote will, in some measure, illustrate the "gallant guise" in which these wanderers, at one time, rode through Scotland:

About the year 1768, early in the morning of the day of a fair, held annually at Peebles, in the month of May, two gentlemen were observed riding along the only road that led to my grandfather's farm. One of the servant girls was immediately told to put the parlour in order, to receive the strangers, as, from their respectable appearance, at a distance, it was supposed they were friends, coming to breakfast, before going to the market; a custom common enough in the country. This preparation, however, proved unnecessary, as the strangers rode rapidly past the dwelling-house, and alighted at the door of an old smearing-house, nearly roofless, situated near some alder trees, about three hundred yards further up a small mountain stream. In passing, they were observed to be neatly dressed in long green coats, cocked hats, riding-boots and spurs, armed with broad-swords, and mounted on handsome grey ponies, saddled and bridled; everthing, in short, in style, and of the best quality. The people about the farm were extremely curious to know who these handsomely-attired gentlemen could be, who, without taking the least notice of any one, dismounted at the wretched hovel of a sheep-smearing house, where nothing but a band of Tinklers were quartered. Their curiosity, however, was soon satisfied, and not a little mirth was excited, on it being ascertained that the gallant horsemen were none other than James and William Baillie, sons of old Matthew Baillie, who, with part of his tribe, were, at the moment, in the old house, making horn spoons. But greater was their surprise, when several of the female Gipsies set out, immediately afterwards, for the fair, attired in very superior dresses, with the air of ladies in the middle ranks of society.*

Besides the large hordes that traversed the south of Scotland, parties of twos and threes also passed through the country, apparently not at all connected, nor in communication, at the time, with the large bands. When a single Gipsy and his wife, or other female, were observed to take up their quarters by themselves, it was supposed they had either fallen out with their clan, or had the officers of the law in pursuit of them. Sometimes the chief would enquire of the country people, if such and such a one of their tribe had passed by, this or that day, lately. Under any circumstances, the presence of a female does not excite so much suspicion as a single male. In following their profession, as tinkers, the Gipsies seldom, or never, travel without a female in their company, and, I believe, they sometimes hire them to accompany them, to hawk their wares through the country. The tinker keeps himself snug in an out-house, at his work, while the female vends his articles of sale, and forages for him, in the adjoining country.

One of these straggling Gipsies, of the name of William Keith, was apprehended in an old smearing-house, on a farm occupied by my grandfather, in Tweed-dale. William had been concerned, with his brother Robert, in the murder of

* The females of this tribe also rode to the fairs at Moffat and Biggar, on horses, with side-saddles and bridles, the ladies themselves being very gaily dressed. The males wore scarlet cloaks, reaching to their knees, and resembling exactly the Spanish fashion of the present day.

one of their clan, of the name of Charles Anderson, at a small public-house among the Lammermoor hills, called Lourie's Den. Robert Keith and Anderson had fallen out, and had followed each other for some time, for the purpose of fighting out their quarrel. They at last met at Lourie's Den, when a terrible combat ensued. The two antagonists were brothers-in-law; Anderson being married to Keith's sister. Anderson proved an over-match for Keith; and William Keith, to save his brother, laid hold of Anderson; but Mage Greig, Robert's wife, handed her husband a knife, and called on him to despatch him, while unable to defend himself. Robert repeatedly struck with the knife, but it rebounded from the ribs of the unhappy man, without much effect. Impatient at the delay, Mage called out to him, "strike laigh, strike laigh in;" and, following her directions, he stabbed Anderson to the heart. The only remark made by any of the gang was this exclamation from one of them: "Gude faith, Rob, ye have done for him noo!" But William Keith was astonished when he found that Anderson was stabbed in his arms, as his interference was only to save the life of his brother from the overwhelming strength of Anderson. Robert Keith instantly fled, but was immediately pursued by people armed with pitchforks and muskets. He was apprehended in a braken-bush, in which he had concealed himself, and was executed at Jedburgh, on the 24th November, 1772.

Sir Walter Scott, and the Ettrick Shepherd, slightly notice this murder at Lourie's Den, in their communications to Blackwood's Magazine. One of the individuals who assisted at the apprehension of Keith was the father of Sir Walter Scott. The following notice of this bloody scene appeared in one of the periodical publications at the time it occurred: "By a letter from Lauder, we are informed of the following murder: On Wednesday se'night, three men, with a boy, supposed to be tinkers, put up at a little public-house near Soutra. From the after conduct of two of the men, it would appear that a difference had subsisted between them, before they came into the house, for they had drunk but very little when the quarrel was renewed with great vehemence, and, in the dispute, one of the fellows drew a knife, and stabbed the other in the body no less than seven different times, of which wounds he soon after expired. The gang then immediately made off; but upon the country-people being alarmed, the murderer himself and one of the women were apprehended.*

Long after this battle took place, James Bartram and Robert Brydon, messengers-at-arms in Peebles, were dispatched to apprehend William Keith, in the ruinous house already mentioned. As they entered the building, early in the morning, with cocked pistols in their hands, Keith, a powerful man, rose up, half naked, from his *shake-down*, and, holding out a pistol, dared them to advance. Bartram, the chief officer, with the utmost coolness and bravery, advanced close up to the muzzle of the Gipsy's pistol, and, clapping his own to the head of the desperate Tinkler, threatened him with instant death if he did not surrender. A Gipsy, who had informed against Keith, was with the officers, as their guide; but the moment he saw Keith's pistol, he artfully threw himself, upon his back, to the ground. He immediately rose to his feet, but, in great terror, sprang, like a greyhound, over a *fauld dyke*, to escape the shot which Keith threatened. The intrepid conduct of the officers completely daunted the Gipsy. He yielded, and allowed himself to be hand-cuffed, thinking that the messengers were strongly supported by the servants on the farm; for, on perceiving only the two officers, he became desperate, but he was now fast in irons. In great bitterness he exclaimed, "Had I not, on Saturday night, observed five stout men on Mr. Simson's turf-hill, ye wadna a' hae ta'en me." The five individuals were all remarkably strong men. It was on Monday morning the Gipsy was apprehended, and it would appear he had been reconnoitering on Saturday, before risking to take up his quarters, which he did without asking permission from any one. He imagined that the five turf-casters were ready to assist the officers in the execution of their duty, and that it would have been in vain for him to make any resistance. The frantic Gipsy now leaped and tossed about in the most violent manner imaginable. He struck with so much vigour, with his hands bound in irons, and kicked so powerfully with his feet, that it was with the greatest difficulty the officers could get him carried to the jail at Peebles. His wife came into the kitchen of the farm-house, weeping and wailing excessively; and on some of the servant-girls endeavouring to calm her grief, she, among

* Weekly Magazine, 10th September, 1772, page 354.

other bitter expressions, exclaimed, "Had a decent, honest man, like the master, informed, I would not have cared; but for a blackguard like ourselves to inform, is unsufferable." Keith was tried, condemned, and banished to the plantations, for the part he acted at the slaughter at Lourie's Den.

Here we have seen the melancholy fate of two, if not three, of the then *Gipsy constabulary force* in Peebles-shire; one murdered, another hanged, and the third banished. However strange it may appear at the present day, it is nevertheless true, that the magistrates of this county, about this period, (1772,) actually appointed and employed a number of the principal Gipsies as peace officers, constables, or country-keepers, as they were called, of whom I will speak again in another place.

The nomadic Gipsies in general, like the Baillies in particular, have gradually declined in appearance, till, at the present day, the greater part of them have become little better than beggars, when compared to what they were in former times. Among those who frequented the south of Scotland were to be found various grades of rank, as in all other communities of men. There were then wretched and ruffian-looking gangs, in whose company the superior Gipsies would not have been seen.

The reader will have observed the complete protection which William Baillie's token afforded Robert McVitie, when two men were about to rob him, while travelling with his packs, between Elvanfoot and Moffat. This system of tokens made part of the general internal polity of the Gipsies. These curious people stated to me that Scotland was at one time divided into districts, and that each district was assigned to a particular tribe. The chieftains of these tribes issued tokens to the members of their respective hordes, "when they scattered themselves over the face of the country." The token of a local chieftain protected its bearer only while within his own district. If found without this token, or detected travelling in a district for which the token was not issued, the individual was liable to be plundered, beaten, and driven back into his own proper territory, by those Gipsies on whose rights and privileges he had infringed. These tokens were, at certain periods, called in and renewed, to prevent any one from forging them. They were generally made of tin, with certain characters impresed upon them; and the token of each tribe had its own particular mark, and was well known to all the Gipsies in Scotland. But while these passes of the provincial chieftains were issued only for particular districts, a token of the Baillie family protected its bearer throughout the kingdom of Scotland; a fact which clearly proves the superiority of that ancient clan. Several Gipsies have assured me that "a token from a Baillie was good over all Scotland, and that kings and queens had come of that family." And an old Gipsy also declared to me that the tribes would get into utter confusion, were the country not divided into districts, under the regulations of tokens. It sometimes happened, as in the case of Robert McVitie and others, that the Gipsies gave passes or tokens to some of their particular favourites who were not of their own race.

This system of Gipsy polity establishes a curious fact, namely, the double division and occupation of the kingdom of Scotland; by ourselves as a civilized people, and by a barbarous community existing in our midst, each subject to its own customs, laws and government; and that, while the Gipsies were preying upon the vitals of the civilized society which harboured them, and were amenable to its laws, they were, at the same time, governed by the customs of their own fraternity.

The surnames most common among the old Tweed-dale bands of Gipsies were Baillie, Ruthven, Kennedy, Wilson, Keith, Anderson, Robertson, Stewart, Tait, Geddes, Grey, Wilkie and Halliday. The three principal clans were the Baillies, Ruthvens and Kennedys; but, as I have already mentioned, the tribe of Baillie were superior to all others, in point of authority as well as in external appearance.*

Besides the christian and surnames common to them in Scotland, the Gipsies have names in their own language;†

* According to Hoyland, the most common names among the English tented Gipsies are Smith, Cooper, Draper, Taylor, Boswell, Lee, Lovel, Loversedge, Allen, Mansfield, Glover, Williams, Carew, Martin, Stanley, Berkley, Plunket, and Corrie. Mr. Borrow says: "The clans Young and Smith, or Curraple, still haunt two of the eastern counties. The name Curraple is a favourite among the English Gipsies. It means a smith—a name very appropriate to a Gipsy. The root is *Curaw*, to strike, hammer, &c." Among the English and Scottish Gipsies in America, I have found a great variety of surnames.—ED.

† In the "Gipsies in Spain," Mr. Borrow says: "Every family in Eng-

and, while travelling through the country, assume new names every morning, before commencing the day's journey, and retain them till money is received, in one way or other, by each individual of the company; but if no money is received before twelve o'clock, they all, at noon-tide, resume their permanent Scottish names. They consider it unlucky to set out on a journey, in the morning, under their own proper names; and if they are, by any chance, called back, by any of their neighbours, they will not again stir from home for that day. The Gipsies also frequently change their British names when from home: in one part of the country they have one name, and in another part they appear under a different one, and so on.

I will now describe the appearance of the Gipsies in Tweed-dale during the generation immediately following the one in which we have considered them; and would make this remark, that this account applies to them of late years, with this exception, that the numbers in which the nomadic class are to be met with are greatly reduced, their condition greatly fallen, and the circumstances attending their reception, countenance and toleration, much modified, and in some instances totally changed.

Within the memories of my father and grandfather, which take in about the last hundred years, none of the Gipsies who traversed Tweed-dale carried tents with them for their accommodation. The whole of them occupied the kilns and out-houses in the country; and so thoroughly did they know the country, and where these were to be found, and the disposition of the owners of them, that they were never at a loss for shelter in their wanderings.

Some idea may be formed of the number of Gipsies who would sometimes be collected together, from the following extract from the Clydesdale Magazine, for May, 1818: "Mr. Steel, of Kilbucho Mill, bore a good name among 'tanderal gangerals.' His kiln was commodious, and some hardwood trees, which surrounded his house, bid defiance to the plough, and formed a fine pasture-sward for the cuddies, on a green of considerable extent. On a summer Saturday night, Mary came to the door, asking quarters, pretty

land has two names: one by which they are known to the Gentiles, and another which they use among themselves."—Ed.

late. She had only a single ass, and a little boy swung in the panniers. She got possession of the kiln, as usual, and the ass was sent to graze on the green; but Mary was only the avant-garde. Next morning, when the family rose, they counted no less than forty cuddies on the grass, and a man for each of them in the kiln, besides women and children." Considering the large families the Gipsies generally have, and allowing at this meeting two asses for carrying the infants and luggage of each family, there could not have been less than one hundred Gipsies on the spot.

My parents recollect the Gipsies, about the year 1775, traversing the county of Tweed-dale, and parts of the surrounding shires, in bands varying in numbers from ten to upwards of thirty in each horde. Sometimes ten or twelve horses and asses were attached to one large horde, for the purpose of carrying the children, baggage, &c. In the summer of 1784, forty Gipsies, in one band, requested permission of my father to occupy one of his out-houses. It was good-humouredly observed to them that, when such numbers of them came in one body, they should send their quartermaster in advance, to mark out their camp. The Gipsies only smiled at the remark. One half of them got the house requested; the other half occupied an old, ruinous mill, a mile distant. There were above seven of these large bands which frequented the farms of my relatives in Tweed-dale down to about the year 1790. A few years after this period, when a boy, I assisted to count from twenty-four to thirty Gipsies who took up their quarters in an old smearing-house on one of these farms. The children, and the young folks generally, were running about the old house like bees flying about a hive. Their horses, asses, dogs, cats, poultry, and tamed birds were numerous.

These bands did not repeat their visits above twice a year, but in many instances the principal families remained for three or four weeks at a time. From their manner and conduct generally, they seemed to think that they had a right to receive, from the family on whose grounds they halted, food gratis for twenty-four hours; for, at the end of that period, they almost always provided victuals for themselves, however long they might remain on the farm. The servants of my grandfather, when these large bands arrived, frequently put on the kitchen fire the large family *kail-pot*, of the capacity of thirty-two Scotch pints, or about sixteen gallons, to cook victuals for these wanderers.

The first announcement of the approach of a Gipsy band was the chief female, with, perhaps, a child on her back, and another walking at her feet. The chieftain himself, with his asses and baggage, which he seldom quits, is, perhaps, a mile and a half in the rear, baiting his beasts of burden, near the side of the road, waiting the return and report of his quarter-mistress. This chief female requests permission for her *gude-man* and *weary bairns* to take up their quarters for the night, in an old out-house. Knowing perfectly the disposition of the individual from whom she asks lodgings, she is seldom refused. A farmer's wife, whom I knew, on granting this indulgence to a female in advance of her band, added, by way of caution, "but ye must not steal anything from me, then." "We'll no' play ony tricks on you, mistress; but others will pay for that," was the Gipsy's reply.

Instead, however, of the chief couple and a child or two, the out-house, before night-fall, or next morning, will perhaps contain from twenty to thirty individuals of all ages and sexes. The different members of the horde are observed to arrive at head-quarters as single individuals, in twos, and in threes; some of the females with baskets on their arms, some of the males with fishing-rods in their hands, trout creels on their backs, and large dogs at their heels. The same rule is observed when the camp breaks up. The old chief and two or three of his family generally take the van. The other members of the band linger about the old house in which they have been quartered, for several days after the chiefs are gone; they, however, move off, in small parties of twos or as single individuals, on different days, till the whole horde gradually disappear. Above three grown-up Gipsies are seldom seen travelling together. In this manner have the Gipsies traversed the kingdom, concealing their numbers from public observation, and only appearing in large bands on the grounds of those individuals of the community who were not disposed to molest them. On such occasions, when the chief Gipsies continued encamped, they would be visited by small parties of their friends, arriving and departing almost daily.

Excepting that of sometimes allowing their asses to go, under night, into the barn-yard, as if it were by accident, to draw the stacks of corn, it is but fair and just to state, that I am not aware of a single Gipsy ever having injured the property of any of my relatives in Tweed-dale, although their opportunities were many and tempting. My ancestor's extensive business required him, almost daily, to travel, on horseback, over the greater part of the south of Scotland; and he was often under the necessity of exposing himself, by riding at night, yet he never received the slightest molestation, to his knowledge, from the Gipsies. They were as inoffensive and harmless as lambs to him, and to every one connected with his family. Whenever they beheld him, every head was uncovered, while they would exclaim, "There is Mr. Simson; God bless him, honest man!" And woe would have been to that man who would have dared to treat him badly, had these determined wanderers been present.

The Gipsies may be compared to the raven of the rock, as a complete emblem of their disposition. Allow the *corbie* shelter, and to build her nest in your cliffs and wastes, and she will not touch your property; but harass her, and destroy her brood, and she will immediately avenge herself upon your young lambs, with terrible fury.* Washings of clothes, of great value, were often left out in the fields, under night, and were as safe as if they had been within the dwelling-house, under lock and key, when the Gipsies happened to be quartered on the premises. If any of their children had dared to lay its hands upon the most trifling article, its parents would have given it a severe beating. On one occasion, when a Gipsy was beating one of his children, for some trifling offence it had committed, my relative observed to him that the boy had done no harm. "If he has not been in fault just now, sir, it will not be long till he be in one; so the beating he has got will not be thrown away on him," was the Tinkler's reply.

* It is known that the rock-raven, or *corbie*, seldom preys upon the flocks around her nest; but the moment she is deprived of her young, she will, to the utmost of her power, wreak her vengeance on the young lambs in her immediate neighbourhood. I have known the corbie, when bereaved of her brood, tear, with her beak, the very foggage from the earth, and toss it about; and before twenty-four hours elapsed, several lambs would fall a sacrifice to her fury. I have also observed that grouse, where the ground suits their breeding, are generally very plentiful close around the eyrie of the relentless falcon.

When the Gipsies took up their residence on the cold earthen floor of an old out-house, the males and females of the different families had always beds by themselves, made of straw and blankets, and called shake-downs. The younger branches also slept by themselves, in separate beds, the males apart from the females. When the band consisted of more families than one, each family occupied a separate part of the floor of the house, distinct from their neighbours; kindled a separate fire, at which they cooked their victuals; and made horn spoons and other articles for themselves, for sale in the way of their calling. They formed, as it were, a camp on the ground-floor of the ruinous house, in which would sometimes be observed five mothers of families, some of whom would be such before they were seventeen years of age. The principal Gipsies who, about this period, travelled Tweed-dale, were never known to have had more than one wife at a time, or to have put away their wives for trifling causes.

On such occasions, the chief and the grown-up males of the band seldom or never set foot within the door of the farm-house, but generally kept themselves quite aloof and retired; exposing themselves to observation as little as possible. They employed themselves in repairing broken china, utensils made of copper, brass and pewter, pots, pans and kettles, and white-iron articles generally; and in making horn spoons, smoothing-irons, and sole-clouts for ploughs. But working in horn is considered by them as their favourite and most ancient occupation. It would certainly be one of the first employments of man, at a very early stage of human society—that of converting the horns of animals for the use of the human race: and such has been the regard which the Gipsies have had for it, that every clan knows the spoons which are made by another. The females also assisted in polishing, and otherwise finishing, the spoons. However early the farm-servants rose to their ordinary employments, they always found the Tinklers at work.

A considerable portion of the time of the males was occupied in athletic amusements. They were constantly exercising themselves in leaping, cudgel-playing, throwing the hammer, casting the putting-stone, playing at golf, quoits, and other games; and while they were much given, on other occasions, to keep themselves from view, the extraordinary ambition which they all possessed, of beating every one they met with, at these exercises, brought them sometimes in contact with the men about the farm, master as well as servants. They were fond of getting the latter to engage with them, for the purpose of laughing at their inferiority in these healthy and manly amusements; but when any of the country-people chanced to beat them at these exercises, as was sometimes the case, they could not conceal their indignation at the affront. Their haughty scowl plainly told that they were ready to wipe out the insult in a different and more serious manner. Indeed, they were always much disposed to treat farm-servants with contempt, as quite their inferiors in the scale of society; and always boasted of their own high birth, and the antiquity of their family. They were extremely fond of the athletic amusement of "o'erending the tree," which was performed in this way: The end of a spar or beam, above six feet long, and of a considerable thickness and weight, is placed upon the upper part of the right foot, and held about the middle, in a perpendicular position, by the right hand. Standing upon the left foot, and raising the right a little from the ground, and drawing it as far back as possible, and then bringing the foot forward quickly to the front, the spar is thrown forward into the air, from off the foot, with great force. And he who "overends the tree" the greatest number of times in the air, before it reaches the ground, is considered the most expert, and the strongest man. A great many of these Gipsies had a saucy military gesture in their walk, and generally carried in their hands short, thick cudgels, about three feet in length. While they travelled, they generally unbuttoned the knees of their breeches, and rolled down the heads of their stockings, so as to leave the joints of their knees bare, and unincumbered by their clothes.

During the periods they occupied the out-houses of the farms, the owners of which were kind to them, the Gipsies were very orderly in their deportment, and temperate in the use of spirituous liquors, being seldom seen intoxicated; and were very courteous and polite to all the members of the family. Their behaviour was altogether very orderly, peaceable, quiet, and inoffensive. In gratitude for their free-quarters, they frequently made, from old metal, smoothing-irons for the mistress, and sole-clouts for the ploughs of the master, and spoons for the family, from the horns of rams, or other horns that happened to be about the house; for all of which they would take nothing. They, however, did not attend the church, while encamped on the premises; at the same time, they took especial care to give no molestation, or cause of offence, to any about the farm, on Sunday; being, indeed, seldom seen on that day out-side of the doors of the house in which they were quartered, saving an individual to look after their horses or asses, while grazing in the neighbouring fields. Their religious sentiments were confined entirely within their own breasts; and it was impossible to know what were their real opinions on the score of religion. However, within the last ten years, I enquired, very particularly, of an intelligent Gipsy, what religion his forefathers professed, and his answer was, that "the Gipsies had no religious sentiments at all; that they worshipped no sort of thing whatever."

Many practised music; and the violin and bag-pipes were the instruments they commonly used. This musical talent of the Gipsies delighted the country-people; it operated like a charm upon their feelings, and contributed much to procure the wanderers a night's quarters. Many of the families of the farmers looked forward to the expected visits of the merry Gipsies with pleasure, and regretted their departure. Some of the old women sold salves and drugs, while some of the males had pretensions to a little surgery. One of them, of the name of Campbell, well known by the title of Dr. Duds, traversed the south of Scotland, accompanied by a number of women. He prescribed, and sold medicines to the inhabitants; and several odd stories are told of the very unusual, but successful, cures performed by him.

As in arranging for, and taking up, their quarters, the principal female Gipsy almost always negotiates the transactions which the horde have with the farmer's family, during their abode on his premises. Indeed, the females are the most active, if not the principal, members of the tribe, in vending their articles of merchandise. The time at which, on such occasions, they present these for sale, is the day after their arrival on the farm, and immediately after the breakfast of the farmer's family is over. When there are more families than one in the band, but all of one horde, the chief female of the whole gets the first chance of selling her wares; but every head female of the respective families bargains for her own merchandise, for the behoof of her own family. When the farmer's family is in want of any of their articles, an extraordinary higgling and chaffering takes place in making the bargain. Besides money, the Gipsy woman insists upon having what she calls her "boontith"—that is, a present in victuals, as she is fond of bartering her articles for provisions. If the mistress of the house agrees, and goes to her larder or milk-house for the purpose of giving her this boontith, the Gipsy is sure to follow close at her heels. Admitted into the larder, the voracious Tinkler will have part of everything she sees—flesh, meal, butter, cheese, &c., &c. Her fiery and penetrating eye darts, with rapidity, from one object to another. She makes use of every argument she can think of to induce the farmer's wife to comply with her unreasonable demands. "I'm wi' bairn, mistress," she will say; "I'm greenin'; God bless ye, gie me a wee bit flesh to taste my mouth, if it should no' be the book o' a robin-red-breast."* If the farmer's wife still disregards her importunities, the Gipsy will, in the end, snatch up a piece of flesh, and put it into her lap, in a twinkling; for out of the larder she will not go, without something or other. The farmer's wife, ever on the alert, now takes hold of the *sorner*, to wrest the flesh from her clutches, when a serious personal struggle ensues. She will frequently be under the necessity of calling for the assistance of her servants, to thrust the intruder out of the apartment; but the cautious Gipsy takes care not to let matters go too far: she yields the contest, and, laughing heartily at the good-wife losing her temper, immediately assumes her ordinary polite manner. And notwithstanding all that has taken place, both parties generally part on good terms.

On one of these bargain-making occasions, as the wife of the farmer of Glencotha, in Tweed-dale, went to give a boontith to Mary Yorkston, the harpy thrust, unobserved, about four

* After recovery from child-birth, the Gipsy woman recommences her course of begging or stealing, with her child in her arms; and then she is more rapacious than at other times, taking whatever she can lay her hands upon. For she calculates upon escaping without a beating, by holding up her child to receive the blows aimed at her; which she knows will have the effect of making the aggrieved person desist, till she finds an opportunity of getting out of the way.—*Grellmann on the Hungarian Gipsies.*—Ed.

pounds weight of tallow into her lap. On the return of the good-wife, the tallow was missed. She charged Mary with the theft, but Mary, with much gravity of countenance, exclaimed: "God bless ye, mistress, I wad steal from mony a one before I wad steal from you." The good-wife, however, took hold of Mary, to search her person. A struggle ensued, when the tallow fell out of Mary's lap, on the kitchen-floor. At this exposure, in the very act of stealing, the Gipsy burst into a fit of laughter, exclaiming: "The Lord hae a care o' me, mistress; ye hae surely little to spare, whan ye winna let a body take a bit tauch for a candle, to light her to bed." At another time, this Gipsy gravely told the good-wife of Rachan-mill, that she must give her a pound of butter for her boontith, that time, as it would be the last she would ever give her. Astonished at the extraordinary saying, the good-wife demanded, with impatience, what she meant. "You will," rejoined the Gipsy, "be in eternity (by a certain day, which she named,) and I will never see you again; and this will be the last boontith you will ever give me." The good-wife of Rachan-mill, however, survived the terrible prediction for several years.*

The female Gipsies also derived considerable profits from their trade of fortune-telling. The art of telling fortunes was not, however, general among the Gipsies; it was only certain old females who pretended to be inspired with the

* The following facts will show what a Scottish Tinkler, at the present day, will sometimes do in the way of "sorning," or masterful begging.

One of the race paid a visit to the house of a country ale-wife, and, in a crowded shop, vaulted the counter, and applied his bottle to her whiskey-tap. Immediately a cry, with up-lifted hands, was raised for the police, but the prudent ale-wife treated the circumstance with indifference, and exclaimed: "Hout, tout, tout! *let* the deil tak' a wee drappie."

On another occasion, a Gipsy woman entered a country public-house, leaving her partner at a short distance from the door. Espying a drawn bottle of porter, lying on a table, in a room in which were two females sitting, she, without the least ceremony, filled a glass, and drank it off; but before she could decant another, the other Gipsy, feeling sure of the luck of his mate, from her being admitted into the premises, immediately proceeded to share it with her. But he had hardly drank off the remainder of the porter, ere a son of the mistress of the house made his appearance, and demanded what was wanted. "Want—*want?*" replied the Gipsy, with a leering eye towards the empty bottle; "we want nothing—we've got all that we want!" On being ordered to "walk out of that," they left, with a smile of satisfaction playing on their weather-beaten countenances.

Such displays of Gipsy impudence sometimes call forth only a hearty laugh from the people affected by them.—Ed.

gift of prophecy. The method which they adopted to get at the information which often enabled them to tell, if not fortunes, at least the history, and condition of mind, of individuals, with great accuracy, was somewhat this:

The inferior Gipsies generally attended our large country "penny-weddings," in former times, both as musicians and for the purpose of receiving the fragments of the entertainments. At the wedding in the parish of Corstorphine, to which I have alluded, under the chapter of Fife and Stirlingshire Gipsies, Charles Stewart entered into familiar conversation with individuals present; joking with them about their sweet-hearts, and love-matters generally; telling them he had noticed such a one at such a place; and observing to another that he had seen him at such a fair, and so on. He always enquired about their masters, and places of abode, with other particulars relative to their various connections and circumstances in life. Here, the Gipsy character displays itself; here, we see Stewart, while he seems a mere merry-andrew, to the heedless, merry-making people at these weddings, actually reading, with deep sagacity, their characters and dispositions; and ascertaining the places of residence, and connexions, of many of the individuals of the country through which he travelled. In this manner, by continually roaming up and down the kingdom, now as individuals in disguise, at other times in bands—not passing a house in their route—observing everything taking place in partial assemblies, at large weddings, and general gatherings of the people at fairs—scanning, with the eye of a hawk, both males and females, for the purpose of robbing them—did the Gipsies, with their great knowledge of human character, become thoroughly acquainted with particular incidents concerning many individuals of the population. Hence proceed, in a great measure, the warlockry and fortune-telling abilities of the shrewd and sagacious Gipsies.

Or, suppose an old Gipsy female, who traverses the kingdom, has a relative a lady's maid in a family of rank, and another a musician in a band, playing to the first classes of society, in public or private assemblies, the travelling *spae-wife* would not be without materials for carrying on her trade of fortune-telling. The observant handmaid, and the acute, penetrating fiddler would, of course, communicate to their wandering relative every incident and circumstance that came under their notice, which would, at an after and suitable period, enable the cunning fortune-teller to astonish some of the parties who had been at these meetings, when in another part of the country, remote in time, and distant in place, from the spot where the occurrences happened.

In order that they might not lessen the importance and value of their art, these Gipsies pretended they could tell no one's fortune for anything less than silver, or articles of wearing-apparel, or other things of value. Besides telling fortunes by palmistry,* they foretold destinies by divination of the cup, their method of doing which appears to be nearly the same as that practised among the ancient Assyrians, Chaldeans, and Egyptians, perhaps, about the time of Joseph. The Gipsy method was, and I may say is, this: The divining cup, which is made of tin, or pewter, and about three inches in diameter, was filled with water, and sometimes with spirits. Into the cup a certain quantity of a melted substance, resembling tin, was dropped from a crucible, which immediately formed itself, in the liquid, into curious figures, resembling frost-work, seen on windows in winter. The compound was then emptied into a trencher, and from the arrangements or constructions of the figures, the destiny of the enquiring individual was predicted.† While per-

* The Kamtschadales, says Dr. Grieve, in his translation of a Russian account of Kamtschatka, pretend to chiromancy, and tell a man's good or bad fortune by the lines of his hand; but the rules which they follow are kept a great secret. *Page* 206.

† Julius Serenus, says Stackhouse, tells us, that the method among the Assyrians, Chaldeans, and Egyptians was to fill the cup with water, then throw into it thin plates of gold and silver, together with some precious stones, whereon were engraven certain characters, and, after that, the person who came to consult the oracle used certain forms of incantation, and, so calling upon the devil, were wont to receive their answer several ways: sometimes by particular sounds; sometimes by the characters which were in the cup rising upon the surface of the water, and by their arrangement forming the answer; and many times by the visible appearance of the persons themselves, about whom the oracle was consulted. Cornelius Agrippa (De Occult. Philos. LI, c. 57,) tells us, likewise, that the manner of some was to pour melted wax into the cup wherein was water; which wax would range itself in order, and so form answers, according to the questions proposed.—*Saurin's Dissertation*, 38, *and Hudegger's His. patriar. exercit.* 20.

Fortune-telling is punishable by the 9th Geo. II, chap. 5th. In June, 1806, a woman, of the name of Maxwell, commonly called the Galloway sorceress, was tried for this offence, by a jury, before the Stewart of Kirkcudbright, and was sentenced to imprisonment and the pillory.—*Burnet on Criminal Law, page* 173.

forming the ceremony, the Gipsies muttered, in their own language, certain incantations, totally unintelligible to the spectator. The following fact, however, will, more particularly, show the manner in which these Gipsy sorceresses imposed on the credulous.

A relative of mine had several servant-girls who would, one day, have their fortunes told. The old Gipsy took them, one at a time, into an apartment of the house, and locked the door after her. My relative, feeling a curiosity in the matter, observed their operations, and overheard their conversation, through a chink in the partition of the room. A bottle of whiskey, and a wine glass, were produced by the girl, and the sorceress filled the glass, nearly full, with the spirits. Into the liquor she dropped part of the white of a raw egg, and taking out of her pocket something like chalk, scraped part of it into the mixture. Certain figures now appeared in the glass, and, muttering some jargon, unintelligible to the girl, she held it up between her eyes and the window. "There is your sweetheart now—look at him—do you not see him?" exclaimed the Gipsy to the trembling girl; and, after telling her a number of events which were to befall her, in her journey through life, she held out the glass, and told her to "cast that in her mouth"—"Me drink that? The Lord forbid that I should drink a drap o't." "E'ens ye like, my woman; I can tak' it mysel," quoth the Gipsy, and, suiting the action to the word, "cast" the whiskey, eggs and chalk* down her throat, in an instant. Knowing well that the idea of swallowing the glass in which their future husbands were seen, and their own fortunes told, in so mysterious a manner, would make the girls shudder, the cunning Gipsy gave each of them, in succession, the order to drink, and, the moment they refused, threw the contents of the "divining cup" into her own mouth. In this manner did the Gipsy procure, at one time, no less than four glasses of ardent spirits, and sixpence from each of the credulous girls.

The country-girls, however, never could stand out the operations of telling fortunes by the method of turning a corn-riddle, with scissors attached, in a solitary out-house.

* It is not unlikely that the "something like chalk," here mentioned, was nothing but a nutmeg, with which, and the eggs and whiskey, the Gipsy would make, what is called, "egg-nogg."—Ed.

Whenever the Gipsy commenced her work, and, with her mysterious mutterings, called out: "Turn riddle—turn—shears and all," the terrified girls fled to the house, impressed with the belief that the devil himself would appear to them, on the spot.

The Gipsies in Tweed-dale were never in want of the best of provisions, having always an abundance of fish, flesh, and fowl. At the stages at which they halted, in their progress through the country, it was observed that the principal families, at one time, ate as good victuals, and drank as good liquors, as any of the inhabitants of the country. A lady of respectability informed me of her having seen, in her youth, a band dine on the green-sward, near Douglass-mill, in Lanarkshire, when, as I have already mentioned, the Gipsies handed about their wine, after dinner, as if they had been as good a family as any in the land. Those in Fifeshire, as we have already seen, were in the habit of purchasing and killing fat cattle, for their winter's provisions. In a communication to Blackwood's Magazine, to which I will again allude, the illustrious author of the Waverley Novels mentions that his father was, in some respects, forced to accept a dinner from a party of Gipsies, carousing on a moor, on the Scottish Border. The feast consisted of "all the varieties of game, poultry, pigs, and so forth." And, according to the same communication, it would appear that they were in the practice of stewing game and all kinds of poultry into soup, which is considered very rich and savoury, and is now termed "Pottage a la Meg Merrilies de Derncleugh;" a name derived from the singular character in the celebrated novel of Guy Mannering.

But the ancient method of cooking practised among the Scottish Gipsies, and which, in all probability, they brought with them, when they arrived in Europe, upwards of four hundred years ago, is, if I am not mistaken, new to the world, never having as yet, that I am aware of, been described.* It is very curious, and extremely primitive, and appears to be of the highest antiquity. It is admirably adapted to the wants of a rude and barbarous people, travelling over a wild and thinly-inhabited country, in which cooking utensils could not be procured, or conveniently carried with them.

* I published the greater part of the Gipsy method of cooking, in the Fife Herald, of the 18th April, 1833.

My facts are from the Gipsies themselves, and are corroborated by people, not of the tribe, who have witnessed some of their cooking operations.

The Gipsies, on such occasions, make use of neither pot, pan, spit, nor oven, in cooking fowls. They twist a strong rope of straw, which they wind very tightly around the fowl, just as it is killed, with the whole of its feathers on, and its entrails untouched. It is then covered with hot peat ashes, and a slow fire is kept up around and about the ashes, till the fowl is sufficiently done. When taken out from beneath the fire, it is stripped of its hull, or shell, of half-burned straw-rope and feathers, and presents a very fine appearance. Those who have tasted poultry, cooked by the Gipsies, in this manner, say that it is very palatable and good. In this invisible way, these ingenious people could cook stolen poultry, at the very moment, and in the very place, that a search was going on for the pilfered article.

The art of cooking butcher-meat among the Gipsies, is similar to that of making ready fowls, except that linen and clay are substituted for feathers and straw. The piece of flesh to be cooked is first carefully wrapped up in a covering of cloth or linen rags, and covered over with well wrought clay, and either frequently turned before a strong fire, or covered over with hot ashes, till it is roasted, or rather stewed. The covering or crust, of the shape of the article enclosed, and hard with the fire, is broken, and the meat separated from its inner covering of burned rags, which, with the juice of the meat, are reduced to a thick sauce or gravy. Sometimes a little vinegar is poured upon the meat. The tribe are high in their praise of flesh cooked in this manner, declaring that it has a particularly fine flavour. These singular people, I am informed, also boiled the flesh of sheep in the skins of the animals, like the Scottish soldiers in their wars with the English nation, when their camp-kettles were nothing but the hides of the oxen, suspended from poles, driven into the ground.

The only mode of cooking butcher-meat, bearing any resemblance to that of the Gipsies, is practised by some of the tribes of South America, who wrap flesh in *leaves*, and, covering it over with clay, cook it like the Gipsies. Some of the Indians of North America roast deer of a small size in their skins, among hot ashes. An individual of great respectability, who had tasted venison cooked in this fashion, said that it was extremely juicy, and finely flavoured. In the Sandwich Islands, pigs are baked on hot stones in pits, or in the leaves of the bread-fruit tree, on hot stones, covered over with earth, during the operation of cooking. It is probable that the Gipsy art of cooking would be amongst the first modes of making ready animal food, in the first stage of human society, in Asia—the cradle of the human race.* Substitute the leaves of trees for linen rags, and what method of cooking can be more primitive than that of our Scottish Gipsies?

The Gipsy method of smelting iron, for sole-clout for ploughs, and smoothing-irons, is also simple, rude, and primitive.† The tribe erect, on the open field, a small circle, built of stone, turf, and clay, for a furnace, of about three feet in height, and eighteen inches in diameter, and plastered, closely round on the outside, up to the top, with mortar made of clay. The circle is deepened by part of the earth being scooped out from the inside. It is then filled with coal or charred peat; and the iron to be smelted is placed in small pieces upon the top. Below the fuel an aperture is left open, on one side, for admitting a large iron ladle, lined inside with clay. The materials in the furnace are powerfully heated, by the blasts of a large hand-bellows, (generally wrought by females,) admitted at a small hole, a little from the ground. When the metal comes to a state of

* Pouqueville considers the Gipsies contemporary of the first societies. *Paris*, 1830.

† According to Grellmann, working in iron is the most usual occupation of the Gipsies. In Hungary it is so common, as to have given rise to the proverb, "So many Gipsies, so many smiths." The same may be said of those in Transylvania, Wallachia, and Moldavia, and all Turkey in Europe; at least, Gipsies following that occupation are very numerous in those countries.

This occupation seems to have been a favourite one with them, from the most distant period. Uladislaus, King of Hungary, in the year 1496, ordered: "That every officer and subject, of whatever rank or condition, do allow Thomas Polgar, leader of twenty-five tents of wandering Gipsies, free residence everywhere, and on no account to molest either him or his people, because they prepared musket balls and other military stores, for the Bishop Sigismund, at Fünf-kirchen." In the year 1565, when Mustapa, Turkish Regent of Bosnia, besieged Crupa, the Turks having expended their powder and cannon-balls, the Gipsies were employed to make the latter, part of iron, the rest of stone, cased with lead.

fusion, it finds its way down to the ladle, and, after being skimmed of its cinders, is poured into the different sand moulds ready to receive it.

Observe the Gipsies at whatever employment you may, there always appear sparks of genius. We cannot, indeed, help wondering, when we consider the skill they display in preparing and bringing their work to perfection, from the scarcity of proper tools and materials.—*Grellmann on the Hungarian Gipsies.*—Ed.

CHAPTER VII.

BORDER GIPSIES.

It would be an unpardonable omission were I to overlook the descendants of John Faw, "Lord and Earl of Little Egypt," in this history of the Gipsies in Scotland. But to enter into details relative to many of the members of this ancient clan, would be merely a repetition of actions, similar in character to those already related of some of the other bands in Scotland.

It would appear that the district in which the Faw tribe commonly travelled, comprehended East Lothian, Berwickshire and Roxburghshire; and that Northumberland was also part of their walk. I can find no traces of Gipsies, of that surname, having, in families, traversed the midland or western parts of the south of Scotland, for nearly the last seventy years; and almost all the few ancient public documents relative to this clan seem to imply that they occupied the counties above mentioned.

I am inclined to believe that the Faws and the Baillies, the two principal Gipsy clans in Scotland, had frequently lived in a state of hostility with one another. These two tribes quarrelled in the reign of James V, when they brought their dispute before the king in council; and from the renewal of the order in council, in the reign of Queen Mary, it appears their animosities had then existed. In the year 1677, the Faws and the Shaws, as already noticed, advanced into Tweed-dale, to fight the Baillies and the Browns, as mentioned by Dr. Pennecuik, in his history of Tweed-dale. At the present day, the Baillies consider themselves quite superior in rank to the Faas; and, on the other hand, the Faas and their friends speak with great bitterness and contempt of the Baillies, calling them "a parcel of thieves and vagabonds."*

* This long standing feud between the Baillies and the Faas is notorious.

In Ruddiman's Weekly Magazine, of the 4th August, 1774, the following notice is taken of this tribe, which shows the fear which persons of respectability entertained for them: "The descendants of this Lord of Little Egypt continued to travel about in Scotland till the beginning of this century, mostly about the southern Border; and I am most credibly informed that one, Henry Faa, was received, and ate at the tables of people in public office, and that men of considerable fortune paid him a gratuity, called blackmail, in order to have their goods protected from thieves."

One of the Faas rose to great eminence in the mercantile world, and was connected by marriage with Scotch families of the rank of baronets. This family was the highly respectable one of Fall, now extinct, general merchants in Dunbar, who were originally members of the Gipsy family at Yetholm. So far back as about the year 1670, one of the baillies of Dunbar was of the surname of Faa, spelled exactly as the Gipsy name, as appears by the Rev. J. Blackadder's Memoirs. On the 18th of May, 1734, Captain James Fall, of Dunbar, was elected member of parliament for the Dunbar district of burghs. On the 28th of May, 1741, Captain Fall was again elected member for the same burghs; but, there being a double return, Sir Hew Dalrymple ousted him. The family of Fall gave Dunbar provosts and baillies, and ruled the political interests of that burgh for many years. When hearty over their cups, they often mentioned their origin; and, to perpetuate the memory of their descent from the family of Faa, at Yetholm, the late Mrs. Fall, of Dunbar, whose husband was provost of the town, had the whole family, with their asses, &c., &c., as they took their departure from Yetholm, represented, by herself, in needle-work, or tapestry.* The particulars, or details, of this family group

In paying a visit to a family of English Gipsies in the United States, the head of the family said to me: "You must really excuse us to-day. It's the Faas and Baillies over again: it will be all I can do to keep them from coming to blows." The noise inside of the house was frightful. There had been a "difficulty" between two families in consequence of some gossip about one of the parties before marriage, which the families were sifting to the bottom.

The Faas and their partisans, on reading this work, will not overwell relish the prominence given to the Baillie clan.—Ed.

* "He will be pleased to learn that there is, in the house of Provost Whyte, of Kirkaldy, a piece of needle-work, or tapestry, on which is depicted, by the hands of Mrs. Fall, the principal events in the life of the founder of her

were derived from her husband, who had the facts from his grandfather, one of the individuals represented in the piece. A respectable aged gentleman, yet living in Dunbar, has often seen this family piece of the Falls, and had its details pointed out and explained to him by Mrs. Fall herself.*

The mercantile house of the Falls, at Dunbar, was so extensive as to have many connexions in the ports of the Baltic and Mediterranean, and supported so high a character that several of the best families in Scotland sent their sons to it, to be initiated in the mysteries of commerce. Amongst others who were bred merchants by the Falls, were Sir Francis Kinloch, and two sons of Sir John Anstruther. It appears that the Falls were most honourable men in all their transactions; and that the cause of the ruin of their eminent firm was the failure of some considerable mercantile houses who were deeply indebted to them.

One of the Misses Fall was married to Sir John Anstruther, of Elie, baronet. It appears that this alliance with the family of Fall was not relished by the friends of Sir John, of his own class in society. The consequence was that Lady Anstruther was not so much respected, and did not receive those attentions from her neighbours, to which

family, from the day the Gipsey child came to Dunbar in its mother's creel, until the same Gipsey child had become, by its own honourable exertions, the head of the first mercantile establishment then existing in Scotland." [This seems to be an extract from a letter. The authority has been omitted in the MS.—Ed.]

* "There are," says a correspondent, "several gentlemen in this town and neighbourhood who have heard declare, that the Falls themselves had often acknowledged to them their descent from the Gipsey Faas. I am told by an old Berwickshire gentleman, who had the account from his mother, that the Falls, on their departure from Yetholm, stopped some little time at a country village-hamlet called Hume, in Berwickshire, where they had some female relations; and after a few days spent there, they set out for Dunbar, taking their female friends along with them.

"Latterly, the late Robert and Charles Fall, who were cousins, kept separate establishments. Robert possessed the dwelling-house now occupied by Lord Lauderdale; and Charles possessed one at the shore, (now the custom-house,) built on the spot where some old houses formerly stood, and was called 'Lousy Law.' It was in these old cot-houses that the Falls first took up their residence on coming to Dunbar. It appears the mother of the first of the Falls who came to Dunbar was a woman of much spirit and great activity. Old William Faa, the chief of the Gipsies at Yetholm, when in Lothian, never failed to visit the Dunbar family, as his relations. The Dunbar Falls were connected, by marriage, with the Anstruthers, Footies, of Balgonie, Coutts, now bankers, and with Collector Whyte, of the customs, at Kirkaldy, and Collector Melville, of the customs, at Dunbar."

her rank, as Sir John's wife, gave her a title. The tradition of her Gipsy descent was fresh in the memories of those in the vicinity of her residence; and she frequently got no other name, or title, when spoken of, than "Jenny Faa." She was, however, a woman of great spirit and activity. Her likeness was taken, and, I believe, is still preserved by the family of Anstruther.*

At a contested election, for a member of parliament, for the burghs in the east of Fife, in which Sir John was a candidate, his opponents thought to annoy him, and his active lady, by reference to the Gipsy origin of the latter. Whenever Lady Anstruther entered the burghs, during the canvass, the streets resounded with the old song of the "Gipsy Laddie." A female stepped up to her ladyship, and expressed her sorrow at the rabble singing the song in her presence. "Oh, never mind them," replied Lady Anstruther; "they are only repeating what they hear from their parents."† The following is the song alluded to:

JOHNNY FAA, THE GIPSY LADDIE.

The Gipsies came to my Lord Cassillis' yett,
And oh! but they sang bonnie;
They sang sae sweet, and sae complete,
That down came our fair ladie.

She came tripping down the stair,
And all her maids before her;
As soon as they saw her weel-far'd face
They coost their glamourie owre her.

* I beg the reader to take particular notice of this circumstance. A Scotch rabble is the lowest and meanest of all rabbles, at such work as this. In their eyes, it was unpardonable that Lady Anstruther, or "Jenny Faa," should have been of Gipsy origin; but it would have horrified them, had they known the meaning of her ladyship "being of Gipsy origin," and that she doubtless "chattered Gipsy," like others of her tribe.—Ed.

† Speaking of a gentleman in his autobiography, Dr. Alexander Carlyle, in 1744, says: "He had the celebrated Jenny Fall, (afterwards Lady Anstruther,) a coquette and a beauty, for months together in the house with him; and as his person and manners drew the marked attention of the ladies, he derived considerable improvement from the constant intercourse with this young lady and her companions, for she was lively and clever, no less than beautiful."—Ed.

She gave to them the good wheat bread,
  And they gave her the ginger;
But she gave them a far better thing,
  The gold ring off her finger.

"Will ye go wi' me, my hinny and my heart,
  Will ye go wi' me, my dearie;
And I will swear, by the staff of my spear,
  That thy lord shall nae mair come near thee."

"Gar take from me my silk manteel,
  And bring to me a plaidie;
For I will travel the world owre,
  Along with the Gipsy laddie.

"I could sail the seas with my Jockie Faa,
  I could sail the seas with my dearie;
I could sail the seas with my Jockie Faa,
  And with pleasure could drown with my dearie."

They wandered high, they wandered low,
  They wandered late and early,
Until they came to an old tenant's barn,
  And by this time she was weary.

"Last night I lay in a weel-made bed,
  And my noble lord beside me;
And now I must lie in an old tenant's barn,
  And the black crew glowring owre me."

"O hold your tongue, my hinny and my heart,
  O hold your tongue, my dearie;
For I will swear by the moon and the stars
  That thy lord shall nae mair come near thee."

They wandered high, they wandered low,
  They wandered late and early,
Until they came to that wan water,
  And by this time she was weary.

"Aften I have rode that wan water,
  And my Lord Cassilis beside me;
And now I must set in my white feet, and wade,
  And carry the Gipsy laddie."

By-and-by came home this noble lord,
  And asking for his ladie;
The one did cry, the other did reply,
  "She is gone with the Gipsy laddie."

"Go, saddle me the black," he says,
"The brown rides never so speedie;
And I will neither eat nor drink
Till I bring home my ladie."

He wandered high, he wandered low,
He wandered late and early,
Until he came to that wan water,
And there he spied his ladie.

"O wilt thou go home, my hinny and my heart,
O wilt thou go home, my dearie;
And I will close thee in a close room
Where no man shall come near thee."

"I will not go home, my hinny and heart,
I will not come, my dearie;
If I have brewn good beer, I will drink of the same;
And my lord shall nae mair come near me.

"But I will swear by the moon and the stars,
And the sun that shines sae clearly,
That I am as free of the Gipsy gang
As the hour my mother did bear me."

They were fifteen valiant men,
Black, but very bonny,
And they all lost their lives for one,
The Earl of Cassilis' ladie.

Tradition states that John Faa, the leader of a band of Gipsies, seizing the opportunity of the Earl of Cassilis' absence, on a deputation to the Assembly of divines at Westminster, in 1643, to ratify the solemn league and covenant, carried off the lady. The Earl was considered a sullen and ill-tempered man, and perhaps not a very agreeable companion to his lady.*

Before proceeding to give an account of the modern Gipsies on the Scottish Border, I shall transcribe an interesting note which Sir Walter Scott gave to the public, in explaining the origin of that singular character Meg Merrilies, in the novel Guy Mannering. The illustrious author kindly offered me the "scraps" which he had already given to Blackwood's Magazine, to incorporate them, if I chose, in my history of the Gipsies; but I prefer giving them in his own words.

"My father," says Sir Walter, "remembered Jean Gor-

* See page 108.

don of Yetholm, who had a great sway among her tribe. She was quite a Meg Merrilies, and possessed the savage virtue of fidelity in the same perfection. Having been hospitably received at the farm-house of Lochside, near Yetholm, she had carefully abstained from committing any depredations on the farmer's property. But her sons, (nine in number,) had not, it seems, the same delicacy, and stole a brood-sow from their kind entertainer. Jean was so much mortified at this ungrateful conduct, and so much ashamed of it, that she absented herself from Lochside for several years. At length, in consequence of some temporary pecuniary necessity, the good-man of Lochside was obliged to go to Newcastle, to get some money to pay his rent. Returning through the mountains of Cheviot, he was benighted, and lost his way. A light, glimmering through the window of a large waste-barn, which had survived the farm-house to which it had once belonged, guided him to a place of shelter; and when he knocked at the door, it was opened by Jean Gordon. Her very remarkable figure, for she was nearly six feet high, and her equally remarkable features and dress, rendered it impossible to mistake her for a moment; and to meet with such a character, in so solitary a place, and probably at no great distance from her clan, was a terrible surprise to the poor man, whose rent, (to lose which would have been ruin to him,) was about his person. Jean set up a loud shout of joyful recognition. 'Eh, sirs! the winsome gude-man of Lochside! Light down, light down; for ye manna gang farther the night, and a friend's house sae near!' The farmer was obliged to dismount, and accept of the Gipsy's offer of supper and a bed. There was plenty of meat in the barn, however it might be come by, and preparations were going on for a plentiful supper, which the farmer, to the great encrease of his anxiety, observed was calculated for ten or twelve guests of the same description, no doubt, with his landlady. Jean left him in no doubt on the subject. She brought up the story of the stolen sow, and noticed how much pain and vexation it had given her. Like other philosophers, she remarked that the world grows worse daily, and, like other parents, that the bairns got out of her guiding, and neglected the old Gipsy regulations which commanded them to respect, in their depredations, the property of their benefactors. The end of all this was an enquiry what money the farmer had about him, and an urgent request that he would make her his purse-keeper, as the bairns, as she called her sons, would be soon home. The poor farmer made a virtue of necessity, told his story, and surrendered his gold to Jean's custody. She made him put a few shillings in his pocket; observing it would excite suspicion should he be found travelling altogether penniless. This arrangement being made, the farmer lay down on a sort of *shake-down*, as the Scotch call it, upon some straw; but, as is easily to be believed, slept not. About midnight the gang returned with various articles of plunder, and talked over their exploits, in language which made the farmer tremble. They were not long in discovering their guest, and demanded of Jean whom she had got there. 'E'en the winsome gude-man of Lochside, poor boy,' replied Jean; 'he's been at Newcastle, seeking siller to pay his rent, honest man, but deil-be-licket he's been able to gather in; and sae he's gaun e'en hame wi' a toom purse and a sair heart.' 'That may be, Jean,' replied one of the banditti, but we maun ripe his pouches a bit, and see if it be true or no.' Jean set up her throat in exclamation against this breach of hospitality, but without producing any change of their determination. The farmer soon heard their stifled whispers and light steps by his bed-side, and understood they were rummaging his clothes. When they found the money which the prudence of Jean Gordon had made him retain, they held a consultation if they should take it or not; but the smallness of the booty, and the vehemence of Jean's remonstrances, determined them on the negative. They caroused, and went to rest. So soon as day dawned, Jean roused her guest, produced his horse, which she had accommodated behind the *hallan*, and guided him for some miles, till he was on the high-road to Lochside. She then restored his whole property, nor could his earnest entreaties prevail on her to accept so much as a single guinea.

"I have heard the old people at Jedburgh say that all Jean's sons were condemned to die there on the same day. It is said the jury were equally divided, but that a friend of justice, who had slept during the whole discussion, waked suddenly, and gave his vote for condemnation, in the emphatic words: 'Hang them a'.' Jean was present, and only said, 'The Lord help the innocent in a day like this.'

Her own death was accompanied with circumstances of brutal outrage, of which poor Jean was, in many respects, wholly undeserving. Jean had, among other demerits, or merits, as you may choose to rank it, that of being a staunch Jacobite. She chanced to be at Carlisle, upon a fair or market day, soon after the year 1746, where she gave vent to her political partiality, to the great offence of the rabble in that city. Being zealous in their loyalty when there was no danger, in proportion to the tameness with which they had surrendered to the Highlanders, in 1745, they inflicted upon poor Jean Gordon no slighter penalty than that of ducking her to death in the Eden. It was an operation of some time, for Jean was a stout woman, and, struggling with her murderers, often got her head above water; and, while she had voice left, continued to exclaim, at such intervals, 'Charlie yet! Charlie yet!'

"When a child, and among the scenes which she frequented, I have often heard these stories, and cried piteously for poor Jean Gordon.

"Before quitting the Border Gipsies, I may mention that my grandfather, riding over Charter-house moor, then a very extensive common, fell suddenly among a large band of them, who were carousing in a hollow of the moor, surrounded by bushes. They instantly seized on his horse's bridle, with many shouts of welcome, exclaiming, (for he was well known to most of them,) that they had often dined at his expense, and he must now stay, and share their good-cheer. My ancestor was a little alarmed, for, like the good man of Lochside, he had more money about his person than he cared to venture with into such society. However, being a bold, lively man, he entered into the humour of the thing, and sate down to the feast, which consisted of all the different varieties of game, poultry, pigs, and so forth, that could be collected by a wide and indiscriminate system of plunder. The feast was a very merry one, but my relative got a hint, from some of the elder Gipsies, to retire just when 'The mirth and fun grew fast and furious;' and, mounting his horse, accordingly, he took French leave of his entertainers, but without experiencing the least breach of hospitality. I believe Jean Gordon was at the festival.

"The principal settlements of the Gipsies, in my time,

have been the two villages of Easter and Wester Gordon, and what is called Kirk-Yetholm,

> Making good the proverb odd,
> Near the church and far from God."

In giving an account of the modern Gipsies on the Scottish Border, I shall transcribe, at full length, the faithful and interesting report of Baillie Smith, of Kelso, which was published in Hoyland's "Historical Survey of the Gipsies."

"A considerable time," says Mr. Smith, "having elapsed since I had an opportunity or occasion to attend to the situation of the colony of Gipsies in our neighbourhood, I was obliged to delay my answer to your enquiries, until I could obtain more information respecting their present numbers.

"The great bar to the benevolent intentions of improving their situation, will be the impossibility to convince them that there either is, or can be, a mode of life preferable, or even equal, to their own.

"A strong spirit of independence, or what they would distinguish by the name of liberty, runs through the whole tribe. It is, no doubt, a very licentious liberty, but entirely to their taste. Some kind of honour peculiar to themselves seems to prevail in their community. They reckon it a disgrace to steal near their homes, or even at a distance, if detected. I must always except that petty theft of feeding their *shelties* and asses, on the farmer's grass and corn, which they will do, whether at home or abroad.

"When avowedly trusted, even in money matters, they never deceived me, nor forfeited their promise. I am sorry to say, however, that when checked in their licentious appropriations, &c., they are very much addicted both to threaten and to execute revenge.

"Having so far premised with respect to their general conduct and character, I shall proceed to answer, as far as I am able, the four queries subjoined to the circular which you sent me; and then subjoin, in notes, some instances of their conduct in particular cases, which may perhaps elucidate their general disposition and character.

"*Query* 1*st.* What number of Gipsies in the county?

"*Answer.* I know of none except the colony of Yetholm, and one family who lately removed from that place to Kelso.

Yetholm consists of two towns, or large villages, called Town-Yetholm and Kirk-Yetholm. The first is in the estate of Mr. Wauchope, of Niddry; the latter in that of the Marquis of Tweed-dale. The number of the Gipsy colony at present in Kirk-Yetholm amounts to, at least, 109 men, women and children; and perhaps two or three may have escaped notice. They marry early in life; in general have many children; and their number seems to be encreasing.

"*Query 2d.* In what do the men and women mostly employ themselves?

"*Answer.* I have known the colony between forty and fifty years. At my first remembrance of them, they were called the *Tinklers* (Tinkers) of Yetholm, from the males being chiefly then employed in mending pots and other culinary utensils, especially in their peregrinations through the hilly and less frequented parts of the country. Sometimes they were called *Horners*, from their occupation in making and selling horn-spoons, called *cutties*. Now, their common appellation is that of *Muggers*, or, what pleases them better, *Potters*. They purchase, at a cheap rate, the cast or faulty articles from the different manufacturers of earthenware, which they carry for sale all over the country; consisting of groups of six, ten, and sometimes twelve or fourteen persons, male and female, young and old, provided with a horse and cart, to transport the pottery, besides shelties and asses, to carry the youngest of the children, and such baggage as they find necessary. A few of the colony also employ themselves, occasionally, in making besoms, foot-basses, &c., from heath, broom, and bent, and sell them at Kelso and the neighbouring towns. After all, their employment can be considered little better than an apology for idleness and vagrancy. I do not see that the women are otherwise employed than attending the young children, and assisting to sell the pottery when carried through the country.

"They are, in general, great adepts in hunting, shooting and fishing; in which last they use the net and spear, as well as the rod; and often supply themselves with a hearty meal by their dexterity. They have no notion of being limited in their field sports, either in time, place, or mode of destruction. In the country, they sleep in barns and byres, or other out-houses; and when they cannot find that accommodation, they take the canvas covering from the pottery cart and squat below it like a covey of partridges in the snow.

"*Query 3d.* Have they any settled abode in winter, and where?

"*Answer.* Their residence, with the exception of a single family, who, some years ago, came to Kelso, is at Kirk-Yetholm, and chiefly confined to one row of houses, or street, of that town, which goes by the name of the *Tinkler Row.* Most of them have leases of their possessions, granted for a term of nineteen times nineteen years, for payment of a small sum yearly, something of the nature of a quit-rent. There is no tradition in the neighbourhood concerning the time when the Gipsies first took up their residence at that place, nor whence they came. Most of their leases, I believe, were granted by the family of the Bennets, of Grubit, the last of whom was Sir David Bennet, who died about sixty years ago. The late Mr. Nisbet, of Dirlton, then succeeded to the estate, comprehending the baronies of Kirk-Yetholm and Grubit. He died about the year 1783; and long after, the property was acquired by the late Lord Tweed-dale's trustees. During the latter part of the life of the late Mr. Nisbet, he was less frequently at his estate in Roxburghshire than formerly. He was a great favourite of the Gipsies, and was in use to call them his body-guards, and often gave them money, &c.

"On the other hand, both the late and present Mr. Wauchope were of opinion that the example of these people had a bad effect upon the morals and industry of the neighbourhood; and seeing no prospect of their removal, and as little of their reformation, considered it as a duty to the public to prevent the evil encreasing; and never would consent to any of the colony taking up their residence in *Town*-Yetholm.

"They mostly remain at home during winter, but as soon as the weather becomes tolerably mild, in spring, most of them, men, women and children, set out on their peregrinations over the country; and live in a state of vagrancy, until driven into their habitations by the approach of winter.

"Seeming to pride themselves as a separate tribe, they very seldom intermarry out of the colony; and, in rare instances, when that happens, the Gipsy, whether male or female, by influence and example, always induces the stranger husband, or wife, to adopt the manners of the colony; so that no improvement is ever obtained in that way. The progeny of such alliances have almost universally the tawny complexion, and fine black eyes, of the Gipsy parent, whether father or mother. So strongly remarkable is the Gipsy cast of countenance, that even a description of them to a stranger, who has had no opportunity of formerly seeing them, will enable him to know them whenever he meets them. Some individuals, but very rarely, separate from the colony altogether; and when they do so, early in life, and go to a distance, such as London, or even Edinburgh, their acquaintances in the country get favourable accounts of them. A few betake themselves to regular and constant employments at home, but soon tire, and return to their old way of life.

"When any of them, especially a leader, or man of influence, dies, they have full meetings, not only of the colony, but of the Gipsies from a distance; and those meetings, or *late-wakes*, are by no means conducted with sobriety or decency.

"*Query 4th.* Are any of their children taught to read, and what portion of them? With any anecdotes respecting their customs and conduct.

"*Answer.* Education being obtained at a cheaper rate, the Gipsies, in general, give their male children as good a one as is bestowed on those of the labouring people, and farm servants, in the neighbourhood; such as reading, writing, and the first principles of arithmetic. They all apply to the clergyman of the parish for baptism to their children; and a strong, superstitious notion universally prevails with them, that it is unlucky to have an unchristened child in the house. Only a very few ever attend divine service, and those as seldom as they can, just to prevent being refused as sponsors at their children's baptism.

"They are, in general, active and lively, particularly when engaged in field sports, or in such temporary pursuits as are agreeable to their habits and dispositions; but are destitute of the perseverance necessary for a settled occupation, or even for finishing what a moderate degree of continued labour would enable them to accomplish in a few weeks.

"I remember that, about 45 years ago, being then apprenticed to a writer, who was in use to receive the rents and the small duties of Kirk-Yetholm, he sent me there with a list of names, and a statement of what was due, recommending me to apply to the landlord of the public-house, in the village, for any information or assistance which I might need.

"After waiting a long time, and receiving payment from most of the feuers, or rentalers, I observed to him, that none of the persons of the names of Faa, Young Blythe, Fluckie, &c., who stood at the bottom of the list, for small sums, had come to meet me, according to the notice given by the baron-officer, and proposed sending to inform them that they were detaining me, and to request their immediate attendance.

"The landlord with a grave face, enquired whether my master had desired me to ask money from those men. I said, not particularly; but they stood on the list. 'So I see,' said the landlord; 'but had your master been here himself, he did not dare to ask money from them, either as rent or feu duty. He knows that it is as good as if it were in his pocket. They will pay when their own time comes, but do not like to pay at a set time, with the rest of the barony, and still less to be craved.'

"I accordingly returned without their money, and reported progress. I found that the landlord was right: my master said, with a smile, that it was unnecessary to send to them, after the previous notice from the baron-officer; it was enough if I had received the money, if offered. Their rent and feu duty was brought to the office in a few weeks. I need scarcely add that those persons all belonged to the tribe.

"Another instance of their licentious, independent spirit occurs to me. The family of Niddry always gave a decent annual remuneration to a baron-baillie, for the purpose of keeping good order within the barony of Town-Yetholm. The person whom I remember first in possession of that office was an old man, called Doctor Walker, from his being also the village surgeon; and from him I had the following anecdote:

"Between Yetholm and the Border farms, in Northumberland, there were formerly, as in most Border situations, some uncultivated lands, called the Plea-lands, or Debatable-lands, the pasturage of which was generally eaten up by the sorners and vagabonds, on both sides of the marches. Many years ago, Lord Tankerville and some others of the English Borderers made their request to Sir David Bennet, and the late Mr. Wauchope, of Niddry, that they would accompany them at a riding of the Plea-lands, who readily complied with their request. They were induced to this, as they understood that the Gipsies had taken offence, on the supposition that they might be circumscribed in the pasturage for their shelties and asses, which they had held a long time, partly by stealth, and partly by violence.

"Both threats and entreaties were employed to keep them away; and, at last, Sir David obtained a promise from some of the heads of the gang, that none of them should show their faces on the occasion. They, however, got upon the hills, at a little distance, whence they could see everything that passed. At first they were very quiet. But when they saw the English court-book spread out, on a cushion, before the clerk, and apparently him taking in a line of direction, interfering with what they considered to be their privileged ground, it was with great difficulty that the most moderate of them could restrain the rest from running down and taking vengeance, even in sight of their own lord of the manor.

"They only abstained for a short time; and no sooner had Sir David and the other gentlemen taken leave of each other, in the most polite and friendly manner, as Border chiefs were wont to do, since Border feuds ceased, and had departed to a sufficient distance, than the clan, armed with bludgeons, pitchforks, and such other hostile weapons as they could find, rushed down in a body, and before the chiefs, on either side had reached their home, there was neither English tenant, horse, cow nor sheep left upon the premises.

"Meeting at Kelso, with Mr. Walter Scott, whose discriminating habits and just observations I had occasion to know, from his youth, and, at the same time, seeing one of my Yetholm friends in the horse-market, I said to Mr. Scott, 'Try to get before that man with the long drab coat, look at him on your return, and tell me whether you ever saw him, and what you think of him.' He was as good as to indulge me; and, rejoining me, he said, without hesitation: 'I never saw the man that I know of; but he is one of the Gipsies of Yetholm, that you told me of, several years ago.' I need scarcely say that he was perfectly correct.

"When first I knew anything about the colony, old Will Faa was king, or leader; and had held the sovereignty for many years. The descendants of Faa now take the name of Fall, from the Messrs. Fall, of Dunbar, who, they pride themselves in saying, are of the same stock and lineage. When old Will Faa was upwards of eighty years of age, he called on me, at Kelso, on his way to Edinburgh, telling me that he was going to see the laird, the late Mr. Nisbet, of Dirlton, as he understood that he was very unwell; and he himself being now old, and not so stout as he had been, he wished to see him once more before he died. He set out by the nearest road, which was by no means his common practice. Next market-day, some of the farmers informed me that they had been in Edinburgh, and seen Will Faa, upon the bridge, (the south bridge was not then built;) that he was tossing about his old brown hat, and huzzaing, with great vociferation, that he had seen the laird before he died. Indeed, Will himself had no time to lose; for, having set his face homewards, by the way of the sea-coast, to vary his route, as is the general custom of the gang, he only got the length of Coldingham, when he was taken ill and died.

"His death being notified to his friends at Yetholm, they and their acquaintances at Berwick, Spittal, Horncliff, &c., met to pay the last honours to their old leader. His obsequies were continued three successive days and nights, and afterwards repeated at Yetholm, whither he was brought. I cannot say that the funeral rites were celebrated with decency and sobriety, for that was by no means the case. This happened in the year 1783, or 1784, and the late Mr. Nisbet did not long survive."*

In addition to the above graphic report of Baillie Smith, I will now give a few details from a MS., given to me by Mr. Blackwood, towards the elucidation of the history of the Gipsies. This MS. bears the initials of A. W., and appears to have been written by a gentleman who had ample opportunities of observing the manners of the Border Gipsies.

* When Mr. Hoyland commenced making enquiries into the condition of the Gipsies, he addressed circulars to the sheriffs, for information. No less than thirteen Scotch sheriffs reported, "No Gipsies within the county." A report of this kind was nearly as good as would be that of a cockney, as to their being no *foxes* in the country; because, while riding through it, on the stage, he did not *see* any! Baillie Smith's report, although graphic, is superficial. He states that the Gipsies "marry early in life, and in general have many children;" yet "that their number *seems* to be encreasing."—ED.

"I am a native of Yetholm parish, and a residenter in it, with a little exception, for upwards of fifty years. I well remember Kirk-Yetholm, when the Faas and Youngs alone had a footing in it.* The Taits came next, and latterly, at various periods, the Douglasses, Blyths, Montgomerys, &c. Old William Faa, (with whom I was well acquainted, and saw him married to his third wife,†) constantly claimed kindred with the Falls of Dunbar; and persisted, to the last, that he himself was the male descendant, in a direct line, from the Earl of Little Egypt. For many years before his death, Mr. Nisbet of Dirlton, (the then laird of Kirk-Yetholm,) gave him the charge of his house, at Marlfield, and all its furniture, although he resided six miles distant from it. The key of the principal door was regularly delivered to him, at the laird's departure. I remember a sale of wood at Cherry-trees, belonging to the late Sheriff Murray. William Faa was a purchaser at the roup, and the sheriff proclaimed aloud to the clerk, that he would be Mr. Faa's cautioner. All the Tinklers in the village, and even strangers resorting thither, considered William Faa as the head and leader of the whole. His corpse was es-

* The tribe of Young have preserved the following tradition respecting their first settlement in Yetholm: At a siege of the city of Namur, (date unknown,) the laird of Kirk-Yetholm, of the ancient family of Bennets, of Grubit and Marlfield, in attempting to mount a breach, at the head of his company, was struck to the ground, and all his followers killed, or put to flight, except a Gipsy, the ancestor of the Youngs, who resolutely defended his master till he recovered his feet, and then, springing past him upon the rampart, seized a flag which he put into his leader's hand. The besieged were struck with panic—the assailants rushed again to the breach—Namur was taken, and Captain Bennet had the glory of the capture. On returning to Scotland, the laird, out of gratitude to his faithful follower, settled him and his family, (who had formerly been travelling tinkers and heckle-makers,) in Kirk-Yetholm; and conferred upon them, and the Faas, a feu of their cottages, for the space of nineteen times nineteen years; which they still hold from the Marquis of Tweed-dale, the present proprietor of the estate.—*Blackwood's Magazine.*—Ed.

† On solemn occasions, Will Faa assumed, in his way, all the stately deportment of sovereignty. He had twenty-four children, and at each of their christenings he appeared, dressed in his original wedding-robes. These christenings were celebrated with no small parade. Twelve young handmaidens were always present, as part of the family retinue, and for the purpose of waiting on the numerous guests, who assembled to witness the ceremony, or partake of the subsequent festivities. Besides Will's Gipsy associates, several of the neighbouring farmers and lairds, with whom he was on terms of friendly intercourse, (among others, the Murrays, of Cherry-trees,) used to attend these christenings.—*Blackwood's Magazine.*—Ed.

corted betwixt Coldstream and Yetholm by above three hundred asses.

"He was succeeded by his eldest son William, one of the cleverest fellows upon the Border. For agility of person, and dexterity in every athletic exercise, he had rarely met with a competitor. He had a younger brother impressed, when almost a boy. He deserted from his ship, in India; enlisted as a soldier, and, by dint of merit, acquired a commission in a regular regiment of foot, and died a lieutenant, within these thirty years, at London. He was an officer under Governor Wall, at Goree, when he committed the crime for which he suffered, twenty years after, in England.

"It was the present William Faa that the 'Earl of Hell' contended with; not for sovereignty, but to revenge some ancient animosity.* His lordship lives at New Coldstream, and was the only person in Berwickshire that durst encounter, in single combat, the renowned Bully-More. Young fought three successive battles with Faa, and one desperate engagement with More, midway between Dunse and Coldstream; and was defeated in all of them. He is a younger son of William Young, of Yetholm, the cotemporary chieftain of old William Faa. It was still a younger brother that migrated to Kelso, where he supported a good character till he died. Charles Young, the eldest brother, is still alive, and chief of the name. The following anecdote of him will serve to establish his activity.

"Mr. Walker, of Thirkstane, the only residing heritor in Yetholm parish, missed a valuable mare, upon a Sunday morning. After many fruitless enquiries, at the adjacent kirks and neighbourhood, he dispatched a servant for Charles, in the evening. He privately communicated to him his loss, and added, that he was fully persuaded he could be the means of recovering the mare. Charles boldly answered, 'If she was betwixt the Tyne and the Forth, she should be restored.' On the Thursday after, at sunrise, the mare was found standing at the stable door, much jaded, and very warm.

"When the Kirk-Yetholm families differed among them-

* This is in contradiction to the assertion, in Blackwood's Magazine, that, on the death of his father, a sort of civil war broke out among the Yetholm Gipsies; and that the usurper of the regal office was dispossessed, after a battle, by the subjects who adhered to the legitimate heir.—Ed.

selves, and terrible conflicts at times they had, this same Mr. Walker was often chosen sole arbitrator, to decide their differences. He has often been locked up in their houses for twenty-four hours together, but carefully concealed their secrets.*

"The Yetholm Tinklers keep up an intercourse with their friends at Horncliff, Spittal, Rothbury, Hexam, and Harbottle. They go frequently to Newcastle, and even to Staffordshire, for earthenware, and the whole family embark in every expedition.

"I was at school with most of the present generation of Tinklers. I mean the males; for, to speak truth, I never heard of a female Gipsy being educated at all.

"None of this colony have been either impeached or tried for a crime for fifty years past. Two Tinklers have been executed at Jedburgh, in my remembrance, named Keith and Clark, for murder and horse-stealing. They were strangers, from a distance."

When I visited Yetholm, I fell in with a gentleman who resided at that time in Town-Yetholm. I chanced to mention to him that I was sure all the Gipsies had a method of their own in handling the cudgel, but he would not believe it. At my request, he took me into some of their houses, and, observing an old, rusty sword lying upon the joists of an apartment in which we were sitting, I took it down, and, under pretence of handling it, in their fashion, gave some of the guards of the Hungarian sword-exercise. An old Gipsy, of the name of Blyth, shook his head, and observed: "Ay,

* There would appear to be something remarkable in the position which this Mr. Walker held with the Gipsies. I know, from the best of authority, that most of the people living in and about Yetholm are Gipsies, settled or unsettled, civilized or uncivilized, educated or uneducated; and of one in particular, who went under the title of "Lord Mayor of Yetholm." He is now dead. The above mentioned Mr. Walker was probably a relation of Dr. Walker, mentioned by Baillie Smith, as the baron-baillie of Yetholm. I notice in Blackwood's Magazine, that one William Walker, a Gipsy, in company with various Yetholm Gipsies, was indicted at Jedburgh, in 1714, for fire-raising, but was acquitted. The Walkers alluded to in the text are very probably of the same family, settled, and raised in the world. As I have just said, most of the people in and about Yetholm are Gipsies. Gipsydom has even eaten its way in among the population round about Yetholm. The Rev. Mr. Baird, in conducting the Scottish Church Mission among the *travelling* Gipsies, hailing from Yetholm, doubtless encountered many of them *incog.* But all this will be better understood by the reader after he peruses the Disquisition on the Gipsies.—ED.

that is an art easily carried about with you; it may be of service to you some day." My friend was then convinced of his mistake.

William Faa, when I was in his house, showed me the mark of a stroke of a sword on his right wrist, by which he had nearly lost his hand. With others of his clan, he had been engaged in a smuggling speculation, on the coast of Northumberland, when they were overtaken by a party of dragoons, one of whom singled out and attempted to take Faa prisoner. William was armed with a stick only, but, with his stick in his dexterous hand, he, for a long time, set the dragoon, with all his arms, at defiance. The horseman, now galloping round and round him, attempting to capture him, became exasperated at the resistance of a man on foot, armed with a cudgel only, and struck with such vigour that the cudgel became shattered, and cut in pieces, till nothing but a few inches of it remained. Still holding up the stump, to meet the stroke of his antagonist's sword, William was cut to the bone, and compelled to yield himself a prisoner. A person, present at the scuffle, informed me that the only remark the brave Tinkler made to the dragoon was, "Yo've spoiled a good fiddler."

William Faa, the lineal descendant of John Faw, "Lord and Earl of Little Egypt," when I saw him, appeared about sixty years of age, and was tall and genteel-looking, with grey hair, and dark eyes. He is the individual who fought the three battles with Young, between Dunse and Coldstream. The following notice of his death I have extracted from the "Scotsman" newspaper, of the 20th October, 1847:

"A LAMENT FOR WILL FAA,

"THE DECEASED KING OF LITTLE EGYPT.

"The daisy has faded, the yellow leaf drops;
The cold sky looks grey o'er the shrivelled tree-tops;
And many around us, since Summer's glad birth,
Have dropt, like the old leaves, into the cold earth.
And one worth remembering hath gone to the home
Where the king and the kaiser must both at last come,
The King of the Gipsies—the last of a name*
Which in Scotland's old story is rung on by fame.
The cold clod ne'er pressed down a manlier breast
Than that of the old man now gone to his rest.

* Will Faa had a brother, a house-carpenter, in New York, who survived

"It is meet we remember him; never again
Will such foot as old Will's kick a ball o'er the plain,
Or such hand as his, warm with the warmth of the soul,
Bid us welcome to Yetholm, to bicker and bowl.
Oh, the voice that could make the air tremble and ring
With the great-hearted gladness becoming a king,
Is silent, is silent; oh, wail for the day
When Death took the Border King, brave Willie Faa.

"No dark Jeddart prison e'er closed upon him,
The last lord of Egypt ne'er wore gyve on limb.
Though his grey locks were crownless, the light of his eye
Was kingly—his bearing majestic and high.
Though his hand held no sceptre, the stranger can tell
That the full bowl of welcome became it as well;
The fisher or rambler, by river or brae,
Ne'er from old Willie's hallan went empty away.

"In the old house of Yetholm we've sat at the board,
The guest, highly honoured, of Egypt's old lord,
And mark'd his eye glisten as oft as he told
Of his feats on the Border, his prowess of old.
It is meet, when that dark eye in death hath grown dim,
That we sing a last strain in remembrance of him.
The fame of the Gipsy hath faded away
With the breath from the brave heart of gallant Will Faa."

him a few years. He was considered a fine old man by those who knew him. He left a family in an humble, but respectable, way of doing. The Scottish Gipsy throne was occupied by another family of Gipsies, in consequence of this family being "forth of Scotland." There are a great many Faas, under one name or other, scattered over the world.—Ed

CHAPTER VIII.

MARRIAGE AND DIVORCE CEREMONIES.

The Gipsies in Scotland are all married at a very early age. I do not recollect ever having seen or heard of them, male or female, being unmarried, after they were twenty years old. There are few instances of bastard children among them; indeed, they declare that their children are all born in wedlock.* I know, however, of one instance to the contrary; and of the Gipsy being dreadfully punished for seducing a young girl of his own tribe.

The brother of the female, who was pregnant, took upon himself the task of chastising the offender. With a knife in his hand, and at the dead hour of night, he went to the house of the seducer. The first thing he did was deliberately to sharpen his knife upon the stone posts of the door of the man's house; and then, in a gentle manner, tap at the door, to bring out his victim. The unsuspecting man came to the door, in his shirt, to see what was wanted; but the salutation he received was the knife thrust into his body, and the stabs repeated several times. The avenger of his sister's wrongs fled for a short while; the wounded Tinkler recovered, and, to repair the injury he had done, made the girl his wife. The occurrence took place in Mid-Lothian, about twenty years ago. The name of the woman was Baillie, and her husband, Tait.

* There is one word in the Gipsy language to which is attached more importance than to any otherthing whatever—*Lácha*—the corporeal chastity of woman; the loss of which she is, from childhood, taught to dread. To ensure its preservation, the mother will have occasion to the *Dicló*—a kind of drapery which she ties around the daughter; and which is never removed, but continually inspected, till the day of marriage; but not for fear of the "stranger" or the "white blood." A girl is generally betrothed at fourteen, and never married till two years afterward. Betrothal is invariable. But the parties are never permitted, previous to marriage, to have any intimate associations together.—*Borrow on the Spanish Gipsies.*—Ed.

I have not been able to discover any peculiarity in the manner of Gipsy courtships, except that a man, above sixty years of age, affirmed to me that it was the universal custom, among the tribe, not to give away in marriage the younger daughter before the elder. In order to have this information confirmed, I enquired of a female, herself one of eleven sisters,* if this custom really existed among her people. She was, at first, averse, evidently from fear, to answer my question directly, and even wished to conceal her descent. But, at last, seeing nothing to apprehend from speaking more freely, she said such was once the custom; and that it had been the cause of many unhappy marriages. She said she had often heard the old people speaking about the law of not allowing the younger sister to be married before the elder. She, however, would not admit of the existence of the custom at the present day, but appeared quite well ac-

* A GIPSY MULTIPLICATION TABLE.

Births of Children.	Marriages.	Births of Grand-children.	1												
1822, Oct. 1.	1842	1843, Jul.	1	2											
1824, Jan. 1.	1844	1844, Oct.	1	1	3										
1825, Apl. 1.	1845	1846, Jan.	1	1	1	4									
1826, Jul. 1.	1846	1847, Ap.	1	1	1	1	5								
1827, Oct. 1.	1847	1848, Jul.	1	1	1	1	1	6							
1829, Jan. 1.	1849	1849, Oct.	1	1	1	1	1	1	7						
1830, Apl. 1.	1850	1851, Jan.	1	1	1	1	1	1	1	8					
1831, Jul. 1.	1851	1852, Ap.	1	1	1	1	1	1	1	1	9				
1832, Oct. 1.	1852	1853, Jul.	1	1	1	1	1	1	1	1	1	10			
1834, Jan. 1.	1854	1854, Oct.	1	1	1	1	1	1	1	1	1	1	11		
1835, Apl. 1.	1855	1856, Jan.	1	1	1	1	1	1	1	1	1	1	1	12	
1836, Jul. 1.	1856			..	..	..	..	..	..	..	..	..	..	..	Total.
12			11	10	9	8	7	6	5	4	3	2	1	0	78

The above table will give a general idea of the natural encrease of the Gipsies. The reader can make what allowances he pleases, for ages at time of marriage, intervals between births, twins, deaths, or numbers of children born. By this table, the Gipsy, by marrying at twenty years of age, would, when 54 years old, have a "following" of no less than 78 souls. "There is one of the divine laws," said I to a Gipsy, "which the Gipsies obey more than any other people." "What is that?" replied he, with great gravity. "The command to 'Be fruitful, and multiply, and replenish (but not subdue) the earth.'" Even five generations can be obtained from the male, and six from the female Gipsy, in a century, counting from first-

quainted with it, and could have informed me fully of it, had she been disposed to speak on the subject.

The exact parallel to this custom is to be found in the Gentoo code of laws, translated by Halhed; wherein it is made criminal for "a man to marry while his elder brother remains unmarried; or when a man marries his daughter to such a person; or where a man gives the younger sister in marriage while the elder sister remains unmarried."* The learned translator of the code considers this custom of the Gentoos of the remotest antiquity, and compares it with that passage in the Book of Genesis, where Laban excuses himself to Jacob for having substituted Leah for Rachel, in these words, "It must not be so done in our country, to give the younger before the first-born."

The nuptial ceremony of the Gipsies is undoubtedly of the highest antiquity, and would, probably, be one of the first marriage ceremonies observed by mankind, in the very first stages of human society. When we consider the extraordinary length of time the Gipsies have preserved their speech, as a secret among themselves, in the midst of civilized society, all over Europe, while their persons were proscribed and hunted down in every country, like beasts of the chase, we are not at all surprised at their retaining some of their ancient customs; for these, as distinguished from their language, are of easy preservation, under any circumstances in which they may have been placed. That may much more be said of this ceremony, as there would be an occasion for its almost daily observance. It was wrapped up with their very existence—the choice of their wives, and the love of their offspring—the most important and interesting transactions of their lives; and would, on that account, be one of the longest observed, the least easily forgotten, of their ancient usages.

The nuptial rites of the Scottish Gipsies are, perhaps, unequalled in the history of marriages. At least, I have neither seen nor heard of any marriage ceremony that has the slightest resemblance to it, except the extraordinary benediction which our countryman, Mungo Park, received from the bride at the Moorish wedding in Ali's camp, at Benown; and that of a certain custom practised by the Mandingoes,

born to first-born. The reader will notice how large are the Gipsy families incidentally mentioned by our author.—ED.

* Major Archer says that this law is still in force.

at Kamalia, in Africa, also mentioned by Park.* This custom with the Mandingoes and the Gipsies is nearly the same as that observed by the ancient Hebrews, in the days of Moses, mentioned in the Book of Deuteronomy. When we have the manners and customs of every savage tribe hitherto discovered, including even the Hottentots and Abyssinians, described, in grave publications, by adventurous travellers, I can see no reason why there should not be preserved, and exhibited for the inspection of the public, the manners and customs of a barbarous race that have lived so long at our own doors—one more interesting, in some respects, than any yet discovered; and more particularly as marriage is a very important, indeed the most important, institution among the inhabitants of any country, whether civilized or in a state of barbarism. How much would not our antiquarians now value authenticated specimens of the language, manners, and customs of the ancient Picktish nation that once inhabited Scotland!

In describing the marriage ceremony of the Scottish Gipsies, it is scarcely possible to clothe the curious facts in language fit to be perused by every reader. But I must adopt the sentiment of Sir Walter Scott, as given in the Introduction, and "not be squeamish about delicacies, where knowledge is to be sifted out and acquired."†

A marriage cup, or bowl, made out of solid wood, and of a capacity to contain about two Scotch pints, or about one gallon, is made use of at the ceremony. After the wedding-party is assembled, and everything prepared for the occa-

* "I was soon tired," says Park, "and had retired into my tent. When I was sitting, almost asleep, an old woman entered with a wooden bowl in her hand, and signified that she had brought me a present from the bride. Before I could recover from the surprise which this message created, the woman discharged the contents of the bowl full in my face. Finding that it was the same sort of holy water with which, among the Hottentots, a priest is said to sprinkle a new-married couple, I began to suspect that the lady was actuated by mischief or malice; but she gave me seriously to understand that it was a nuptial benediction from the bride's own person; and which, on such occasions, is always received by the young unmarried Moors, as a mark of distinguished favour. This being the case, I wiped my face, and sent my acknowledgment to the lady.—*Park's Travels, pages* 205 *and* 206.

† Whatever prudes and snobs may think of this chapter, I believe that the sensible and intelligent reader will agree with me in saying, that the marriage and divorce ceremonies of the Gipsies are historical gems of the most antique and purest water.—ED.

sion, the priest takes the bowl and gives it to the bride, who passes urine into it; it is then handed, for a similar purpose, to the bridegroom. After this, the priest takes a quantity of earth from the ground, and throws it into the bowl, adding sometimes a quantity of brandy to the mixture. He then stirs the whole together, with a spoon made of a ram's horn, and sometimes with a large ram's horn itself, which he wears suspended from his neck by a string. He then presents the bowl, with its contents, first to the bride, and then to the bridegroom; calling at the same time upon each to separate the mixture in the bowl, if they can. The young couple are then ordered to join hands over the bowl containing the earth, urine, and spirits; when the priest, in an audible voice, and in the Gipsy language, pronounces the parties to be husband and wife; and as none can separate the mixture in the bowl, so they, in their persons, cannot be separated till death dissolves their union.

As soon as that part of the ceremony is performed, the couple undress, and repair to their nuptial couch. After remaining there for a considerable time, some of the most confidential relatives of the married couple are admitted to the apartment, as witnesses to the virginity of the bride; certain tokens being produced to the examining friends, at this stage of the ceremony. If all the parties concerned are satisfied, the bride receives a handsome present from the friends, as a mark of their respect for her remaining chaste till the hour of her marriage. This present is, in some instances, a box of a particular construction.*

* On their return from church, the bride is seated at one extremity of a room, with the unmarried girls by her; the bridegroom on the right, and the father and mother, or those who perform their office, on the left. The male part of the company stand in the corners, singing, and playing on the guitar. About one o'clock, the oldest matron, accompanied by others advanced in years, conducts the bride into the bed-room, which, according to the custom of Spain, is usually a small chamber, without a window, opening into the general apartment. *Tunc vetula, manu suâ sponsæ naturalibus admotâ, membranam, valvæ ori oppositam unguibus scindit et cruorem à plagâ fusum linteolo excipit.* The Gitanos without make a loud noise with their whistles, and the girls, striking the door, sing the following couplets, or some other like them:

"Abre viñó la puerta Snr. Joaquin
Que le voy á viñó á poner un pañuelito
En las manos que tienen que llorar
Toditas las callis."

The bride then returns from the chamber, accompanied by the matrons,

These matters being settled on the spot, the wedded pair rise from the marriage-bed, again dress themselves in their finest apparel, and again join the wedding-party. The joy and happiness on all sides is now excessive. There is nothing to be heard or seen but fiddling and piping, dancing, feasting and drinking, which are kept up, with the utmost spirit and hilarity imaginable, for many hours together.*

and the new-married couple are placed upon a table, where the bride dances, *et coram astantibus linteolum, intemerati pudoris indicium explicat;* whilst the company, throwing down their presents of sweetmeats, &c., dance and cry, "Viva la honra."—*Bright, on the Spanish Gipsy marriage.*

Before the marriage festival begins, four matrons—relations of the contracting parties—are appointed to scrutinize the bride; in which a handkerchief, of the finest French cambric, takes a leading part. Should she prove frail, she will likely be made away with, in a way that will leave no trace behind. In carrying out some marriage festivals, a procession will take place, led by some vile-looking fellow, bearing, on the end of a long pole, the *dicté* and unspotted handkerchief; followed by the betrothed and their nearest friends, and a rabble of Gipsies, shouting and firing, and barking of dogs. On arriving at the church, the pole, with its triumphant colours, is stuck into the ground, with a loud huzza; while the train defile, on either side, into the church. On returning home, the same takes place. Then follows the most ludicrous and wasteful kind of revelling, which often leaves the bridegroom a beggar for life.—*Borrow, on the Spanish Gipsy marriage.*—ED.

* The part of the marriage ceremony of the Gipsies which relates to the chastity of the bride has a great resemblance to a part of the nuptial rites of the Russians, and the Christians of St. John, in Mesopotamia and Chaldea. Dr. Hurd says: "When a new-married couple in Russia retire to the nuptial bed, an old domestic servant stands sentinel at the chamber-door. Some travellers tell us that this old servant, as soon as it is proper, attends nearer the bedside, to be informed of what happens. Upon the husband's declaration of his success and satisfaction, the kettle-drums and trumpets proclaim the joyful news." Among the Christians of St. John, as soon as the marriage is consummated, "both parties wait upon the bishop, and the husband deposes before him that he found his wife a virgin; and then the bishop marries them, puts several rings on their fingers, and baptizes them again. . . . . A marriage with one who is discovered to have lost her honour beforehand but very seldom, if ever, holds good."

When speaking of the marriages of the Mandingoes, at Kamalia, about 500 miles in the interior of Africa, Park says: "The new-married couple are always disturbed toward morning by the women, who assemble to inspect the nuptial sheet, (according to the manners of the ancient Hebrews, as recorded in Scripture,) and dance around it. This ceremony is thought indispensably necessary, nor is the marriage considered valid without it." *Park's Travels, page* 399.

By the laws of Menu, the Hindoo could reject his bride, if he found her not a virgin.—*Sir William Jones.*

[The reader will observe that the marriage ceremony of the Gipsies, though barbarous, is very figurative and emphatic, and certainly moral enough. To show that the Gipsies, as a people, have not been addicted

The nuptial mixture is carefully bottled up, and the bottle marked with the Roman character, M. In this state, it is buried in the earth, or kept in their houses or tents, and is carefully preserved, as evidence of the marriage of the parties. When it is buried in the fields, the husband and wife to whom it belongs frequently repair to the spot, and look at it, for the purpose of keeping them in remembrance of their nuptial vows. Small quantities of the compound are also given to individuals of the tribe, to be used for certain rare purposes, such, perhaps, as pieces of the bride's cake are used for dreaming-bread, among the natives of Scotland, at the present day.

What is meant by employing earth, water, spirits, and, of course, air, in this ceremony, cannot be conjectured; unless these ingredients may have some reference to the four elements of nature—fire, air, earth, and water. That of using a ram's horn, in performing the nuptial rites, has also its meaning, could information be obtained concerning that part of the ceremony.

This marriage ceremony is observed by the Gipsies in Scotland at the present day. A man, of the name of James Robertson, and a girl, of the name of Margaret Graham, were married, at Lochgellie, exactly in the manner described. Besides the testimony of the Gipsies themselves, it is a popular tradition, wherever these people have resided in Scotland, that they were all married by mixing of earth and urine together in a wooden bowl. I know of a girl, of about sixteen years of age, having been married in the Gipsy fashion, in a kiln, at Appindull, in Perthshire. A Gipsy informed me that he was at a wedding of a couple on a moor near Lochgellie, and that they were married in the ancient

to the most barbarous customs, in regard to marriage, I note the following very singular form of the Scottish Highlanders, which, according to Skene, continued in use *until a very late period.* "This custom was termed *hand-fasting,* and consisted in a species of contract between two chiefs, by which it was agreed that the heir of one should live with the daughter of the other, as her husband, for twelve months and a day. If, in that time, the lady became a mother, or proved to be with child, the marriage became good in law, even although no priest had performed the marriage in due form; but should there not have occurred any appearance of issue, the contract was considered at an end, and each party was at liberty to marry, or *hand-fast, with any other.*" Which fact shows that Highland chiefs, at one time, would have annulled any, or all, of the laws of God, whenever it would have served their purposes.—ED.]

Gipsy manner described. Shortly after this, a pair were married near Stirling, after the custom of their ancestors. In this instance, a screen, made of an old blanket, was put up in the open field, to prevent the parties seeing each other, while furnishing the bowl with what was necessary to lawfully constitute their marriage.* The last-named Gipsy further stated to me, that when two young folks of the tribe agree to be married, the father of the bridegroom sleeps with the bride's mother, for three or four nights immediately previous to the celebration of the marriage.

Having endeavoured to describe the ancient nuptial ceremony of the Scottish Gipsies, I have considered it proper to give some account of an individual who acted as priest on such occasions. The name of a famous celebrator of Gipsy marriages, in Fifeshire, was Peter Robertson, well known, towards the latter end of his days, by the name of Blind Pate. Peter was a tall, lean, dark man, and wore a large cocked hat, of the olden fashion, with a long staff in his hand. By all accounts, he must have been a hundred years of age when he died. He was frequently seen at the head of from twenty to forty Gipsies, and often travelled in the midst of a crowd of women. Whenever a marriage was determined on, among the Lochgellie horde, or their immediate connexions, Peter was immediately sent for, however far distant he happened to be at the time from the parties requiring his assistance, to join them in wedlock: for he was the oldest member of the tribe at the time, and head of the Tinklers in the district, and, as the oldest member, it was his prerogative to officiate, as priest, on such occasions. A friend, who obligingly sent me some anecdotes of this Gipsy priest, communicated to me the following facts regarding him:

"At the wedding of a favourite Brae-laird, in the shire of Kinross, Peter Robertson appeared at the head of a numer-

* On reading the above ceremony to an intelligent native of Fife, he said he had himself heard a Gipsy, of the name of Thomas Ogilvie, say that the Tinklers were married in the way mentioned. On one occasion, when a couple of respectable individuals were married, in the usual Scottish Presbyterian manner, at Elie, in Fife, Ogilvie, Gipsy-like, laughed at such a wedding ceremony, as being, in his estimation, no way binding on the parties. He at the same time observed that, if they would come to him, he would marry them in the Tinkler manner, which would make it a difficult matter to separate them again.

ous band of Tinklers, attended by twenty-four asses. He was always chief and spokesman for the band. At the wedding of a William Low, a multerer, at Kinross, Peter, for the last time, was seen, with upwards of twenty-three asses in his retinue. He had certain immunities and privileges allowed him by his tribe. For one thing, he had the sole profits arising from the sale of keel, used in marking sheep, in the neighbouring upland districts; and one of the asses belonging to the band was always laden with this article alone. Peter was also notorious as a physician, and administered to his favourites medicines of his own preparation, and numbers of extraordinary cures were ascribed to his superior skill. He was possessed of a number of wise sayings, a great many of which are still current in the country. Peter Robertson was, altogether, a very shrewd and sensible man, and no acts of theft were ever laid to his charge, that I know of. He had, however, in his band, several females who told fortunes. The ceremony of marriage which he performed was the same you mentioned to me. The whole contents of the bowl were stirred about with a large ram's horn, which was suspended from a string round his neck, as a badge, I suppose, of his priestly office.* He attended all the fairs and weddings for many miles round. The Braes of Kinross were his favourite haunt; so much so that, in making his settlement, and portioning his children, he allowed them all districts, in the country round

* Two ram's horns and two spoons, crossed, are sculptured on the tombstone of William Marshall, a Gipsy chief, who, according to a writer in Blackwood's Magazine, died at the age of 120 years, and whose remains are deposited in the church-yard of Kirkcudbright.

A horn is the hieroglyphic of authority, power, and dignity, and is a metaphor often made use of in the Scriptures. The Jews held ram's horns in great veneration, on account, it is thought, of that animal having been caught in a bush by the horns, and used as a substitute, when Isaac was about to be sacrificed by his father; or, perhaps, on account of this animal being first used in sacrifice. So much were ram's horns esteemed by the Israelites, that their Priests and Levites used them as trumpets, particularly at the taking of Jericho. The modern Jews, when they confess their sins, in our month of September, announce the ceremony by blowing a ram's horn, the sound of which, they say, drives away the Devil. In ancient Egypt, and other parts of Africa, Jupiter Ammon was worshipped under the figure of a ram, and to this deity one of these animals was sacrificed annually. A ram seems to have been an emblem of power in the East, from the remotest ages. It would, therefore, appear that the practice of the Gipsy priest "wearing a ram's horn, suspended from a string, around his neck," must be derived from the highest antiquity.

about, to travel in; but he reserved the Braes of Kinross as his own pendicle, and hence our favourite toast in the shire of Kinross, 'The lasses of Blind Pate's Pendicle.' Besides the Braes of Kinross, this Gipsy, in his sweeping verbal testament, reserved the town of Dunfermline, also, to himself, 'because,' said he, 'Dunfermline was in cash, what Lochleven was in water—it never ran dry.'" A great deal of booty was obtained by the Tinklers, at the large and long-continued fairs which were frequently held in this populous manufacturing town, in the olden times.

This Gipsy priest was uncommonly fond of a bottle of good ale. Like many other celebrators of marriages, he derived considerable emoluments from his office. A Gipsy informed me that Robertson, on these occasions, always received presents, such as a pair of candlesticks, or basins and platters, made of pewter, and such like articles. The disobedient and refractory members of his clan were chastised by him at all times, on the spot, by the blows of his cudgel, without regard to age or sex, or manner of striking. When any serious scuffle arose among his people, in which he was like to meet with resistance, he would, with vehemence, call to his particular friends, "Set my back to the wa';" and, being thus defended in the rear, he, with his cudgel, made his assailants in front smart for their rebellion. Although he could not see, his daughter would give him the word of command. She would call to him, "Strike down"—"Strike laigh" (low)—"Strike amawn" (athwart,)—"Strike haunch-ways,"—"Strike shoulder-ways," &c. In these, we see nearly all the cuts or strokes of the Hungarian sword-exercise. As I have frequently mentioned, all the Gipsies were regularly trained to a peculiar method of their own in handling the cudgel, in their battles. I am inclined to think that part of the Hungarian sword-exercise, at present practised in our cavalry, is founded upon the Gipsy manner of attack and defence, including even the direct thrust to the front, which the Gipsies perform with the cudgel.

Notwithstanding all that has been said of the licentious manners of the Scottish Gipsies, I am convinced that the slightest infidelity, on the part of their wives, would be punished with the utmost severity. I am assured that nothing can put a Gipsy into so complete a rage as to impute incontinence to his wife. In India, the Gipsy men "are extremely jealous of their wives, who are kept in strict subservance, and are in danger of corporeal punishment, or absolute dismissal, if they happen to displease them."* The Gipsies are complete Tartars in matters of this kind.†

But in the best-regulated society—in the most virtuous of families—the sundering of the marriage-tie is often unavoidable, even under the most heinous of circumstances. And it is not to be expected that the Gipsies should be exempted from the lot common to humanity, under whatever circumstances it may be placed. The separation of husband and wife is, with them, a very serious and melancholy affair—an event greatly to be lamented, while the ceremony is attended with much grief and mourning, blood having to be shed, and life taken, on the occasion.

It would be a conclusion naturally to be drawn from the circumstance of the Gipsies having so singular a marriage ceremony, that they should have its concomitant in as singular a ceremony of divorce. The first recourse to which a savage would naturally resort, in giving vent to his indignation, and obtaining satisfaction for the infidelity of the female, (assuming that savages are always susceptible of such a feeling,) would be to despatch her on the spot. But the principle of expiation, in the person of a dumb creature, for offences committed against the Deity, has, from the very creation of the world, been so universal among mankind, that it would not be wondered at if it should have been applied for the atonement of offences committed against each other, and nowhere so much so as in the East—the land of figure and allegory. The practice obtains with the Gipsies in the matter of divorce, for they lay upon the head of that noble animal, the horse, the sins of their offending sister, and generally let her go free. But, it may be asked, how has this sacrifice of the horse never been mentioned in Scotland before? The same question applies equally well to their language, and marriage ceremony, yet we know that both of these exist at the present day. The fact is, the Gipsies have hitherto been so completely despised, and held in such thorough contempt, that few ever thought of, or would

* Edinburgh Encyclopædia, vol. x.

† Mr. Borrow bears very positive testimony to the *personal* virtue of Gipsy females. I have heard natives of Hungary speak lightly of them in that respect; but I conclude that they alluded to exceptions to the general rule among the race.—Ed.

venture to make enquiries of them relative to, their ancient customs and manners; and that, when any of their ceremonies were actually observed by the people at large, they were looked upon as the mere frolics, the unmeaning and extravagant practices, of a race of beggarly thieves and vagabonds, unworthy of the slightest attention or credit.* In whatever country the Gipsies have appeared, they have always been remarkable for an extraordinary attachment to the horse. The use which they make of this animal, in sacrifice, will sufficiently account, in one way at least, for this peculiar feature in their character. Many of the horses which have been stolen by them, since their arrival in Europe, I am convinced, have been used in parting with their wives, an important religious ceremony—or at least a custom—which they would long remember and practise.†

It is the general opinion, founded chiefly upon the affinity of language, that this singular people migrated from Hindostan. None of the authors on the Gipsies, however, that I am aware of, have, in their researches, been able to discover, among the tribe, any customs of a religious nature, by which their religious notions and ceremonies, at the time they entered Europe, could be ascertained. Indeed, the learned and industrious Grellmann expressly states that the Gipsies did not bring any particular religion with them, from their native country, by which they could be distinguished from other people. The Gipsy sacrifice of the horse, at parting with their wives, however, appears to be a remnant of the great Hindoo religious sacrifice of the *Aswamedha*, or *Assummeed Jugg*, observed by all the four principal castes in India, enumerated in the Gentoo code of laws, translated from the Persian copy, by Nathaniel Brassey Halhed, and is proof, besides the similarity of language,

* What our author says, relative to the sacrifice of the horse, by the Gipsies, not being known to the people of Scotland at large, is equally applicable to the entire subject of the tribe. And we see here how admirably the passions—in this case, the prejudice and incredulity—of mankind are calculated to blind them to facts, perhaps to facts the most obvious and incontestible. What is stated of the Gipsies in this work, generally, should be no matter of wonder; the real wonder, if wonder there should be, is that it should not have been known to the world before.—Ed.

† Grellmann says, of the Hungarian Gipsies, "The greatest luxury to them is when they can procure a roast of cattle that have died of any distemper, whether it be sheep, pig, cow, or other beast, *a horse only excepted*."—Ed.

that the Gipsies are from Hindostan. Before the Gentoo code of laws came into my hands, I was inclined to believe that this ceremony of sacrificing horses might be a Tartar custom, as the ancient Pagan tribes of Tartary also sacrificed horses, on certain occasions; and my conjectures were countenanced by the Gipsy and Tartar ceremonies being somewhat similar in their details. Indeed, in Sweden and Denmark, and in some parts of Germany, the Gipsies, as I have already stated, obtained the name of Tartars. "They were not allowed the privilege of remaining unmolested in Denmark, as the code of Danish laws specifies: The Tartar Gipsies, who wander about everywhere, doing great damage to the people, by their lies, thefts, and witchcraft, shall be taken into custody by every magistrate." And it also appears, according to Grellmann, that the Gipsies sometimes called themselves Tartars. If it was observed, on the continent, that they sacrificed horses, a custom very common at one time among the Tartars, their supposed Tartar origin would appear to have had some foundation. The Tartar princes seem to have ratified and confirmed their military leagues by sacrificing horses and drinking of a running stream; and we find our Scottish Gipsies dissolving their matrimonial alliances by the solemn sacrifice of the same animal, while some Gipsies state that horses were also, at one time, sacrificed at their marriage ceremonies. At these sacrifices of the Scottish Gipsies, no Deity—no invisible agency—appears, as far as I am informed, to have been invoked by the sacrificers.

I have alluded to this custom of the Tartars, more particularly, to show that the Gipsies are not the only people who have sacrificed horses. The ancient Hindoos, as already stated, sacrificed horses. The Greeks did the same to Neptune; the ancient Scandinavians to their god, Assa-Thor, the representative of the sun; and the Persians, likewise, to the sun.* But I am inclined to believe that the Gipsy sacrifice of the horse is the remains of the great *Assummeed Jugg* of the Hindoos, observed by tribes of greater antiquity than

* It appears that the Jews, when they lapsed into the grossest idolatry, dedicated horses to the sun. "And he (Josiah) took away the horses that the kings of Judah had given to the sun, at the entering in of the house of the Lord, by the chamber of Nathan-melech, the chamberlain, which was in the suburbs, and burnt the chariots of the sun with fire" II Kings, xxiii. 11.

the modern nations of India, as appears by the Gentoo code of laws already referred to.

The sacrificing of horses is a curious as well as a leading and important fact in the history of the Gipsies, and, as far as I know, is new to the world. I shall, in establishing its existence among the Scottish Gipsies, produce my authorities with my details.

In the first place, it was, and I believe it still is, a general tradition, over almost all Scotland, that, when the Tinklers parted from their wives, the act of separation took place over the carcass of a dead horse. In respect to McDonald's case, alluded to under the head of Linlithgowshire Gipsies, my informant, Mr. Alexander Ramsay, late an officer of the Excise, a very respectable man, who died in 1819, at the age of 74 years, stated to me that he saw McDonald and his wife separated over the body of a dead horse, on a moor, at Shieldhill, near Falkirk, either in the year 1758 or 1760, he was uncertain which. The horse was laying stretched out on the heath. The parties took hold of each other by the hand, and, commencing at the head of the dead animal, walked—the husband on one side, and the wife on the other—till they came to the tail, when, without speaking a word to each other, they parted, in opposite directions, as if proceeding on a journey. Mr. Ramsay said he never could forget the violent swing which McDonald gave his wife at parting. The time of the day was a little after day-break. My informant, at the time, was going, with others, to Shieldhill for coals, and happened to be passing over a piece of rising ground, when they came close upon the Gipsies, in a hollow, quite unexpectedly to both parties.

Another aged man of credibility, of the name of James Wilson, at North Queensferry, also informed me that it was within his own knowledge, that a Gipsy, of the name of John Lundie, divorced four wives over dead horses, in the manner described. Wilson further mentioned that, when Gipsies were once regularly separated over a dead horse, they could never again be united in wedlock; and that, unless they were divorced in this manner, all the children which the female might have, subsequently to any other mode of separation, the husband was obliged to support. In fact, the transaction was not legal, according to the Gipsy usages, without the horse. The facts of Lundie, and another Gipsy, of the name of Drummond, having divorced many wives over dead horses, have been confirmed to me by several aged individuals who knew them personally. One intelligent gentleman, Mr. Richard Baird, informed me that, in his youth, he actually saw John Lundie separated from one of his wives over a dead horse, in the parish of Carriden, near Bo'ness. My father, who died in 1837, at the age of nearly 83 years, also stated that it was quite current, in Tweed-dale, that Mary Yorkstone, wife of Matthew Baillie, the Gipsy chief, parted married couples of her tribe over dead horses.

About ten years after receiving the above information, Malcolm's Anecdotes of the Manners and Customs of London came into my hands; wherein I found the following quotations, from a work published in 1674, describing the different classes of impostors at that period in England: "Patricos," says this old author, "are strolling priests; every hedge is their parish, and every wandering rogue their parishioner. The service, he saith, is the marrying of couples, without the Gospels or Book of Common Prayer; the solemnity whereof is this: The parties to be married find out a dead horse, or other beast; standing, one on the one side, and the other on the other, the Patrico bids them live together till death part them; so, shaking hands, the wedding is ended." Now the parties here described seem to have been no other than Gipsies. But it also appears that the ceremony alluded to is that of dissolving a marriage, and not that of celebrating it. It is proper, however, to mention, as I have already done, that horses, at one time, were sacrificed at their marriages, as well as at their divorces.

Feeling now quite satisfied that Gipsies were, at one time, actually separated over the bodies of dead horses, and horses only, (for I could find no other animal named but horses,) I proceeded to have the fact confirmed by the direct testimony of the people themselves. And whether these horses were sacrificed expressly for such purposes, or whether the rites were performed over horses accidentally found dead, I could not discover till the year 1828. It occurred to me that the using of dead horses, in separating man and wife, was a remnant of some ancient ceremony, which induced me to persevere in my enquiries, for the purpose of ascertaining, if not the origin, at least the particulars, of so extraordinary a custom. In the year mentioned, and in the year following, I examined a Gipsy on the subject; a man of about sixty years of age, who, a few years before, had given me a specimen of his language. He said that he himself had witnessed the sacrifices and ceremonies attending the separation of husband and wife. From this man I received the following curious particulars relative to the sacrifice of horses and ceremony of divorce; which I think may be depended on, as I was very careful in observing that his statements, taken down at four different times, agreed with each other.

When the parties can no longer live together as husband and wife, and a separation for ever is finally determined on, a horse, without blemish, and in no manner of way lame, is led forth to the spot for performing the ceremony of divorce. The hour at which the rites must be performed is, if possible, twelve o'clock at noon, "when the sun is at his height."* The Gipsies present cast lots for the individual who is to sacrifice the animal, and whom they call the priest, for the time. The priest, with a long pole or staff in his hand,† walks round and round the animal several times; repeating the names of all the persons in whose possession it has been, and extolling and expatiating on the rare qualities of so useful an animal. It is now let loose, and driven from their presence, to do whatever it pleases. The horse, perfect and free, is put in the room of the woman who is to be divorced;

* This Gipsy mentioned one particular instance of having seen a couple separated in this way, on a wild moor, near Huntly, about the year 1805. He particularly stated that a horse found dead would not do for a separation, but that one must be killed for the express purpose; and that "the sun must be at his height" before the horse could be properly sacrificed. From the fact of Ramsay stumbling upon the Gipsies "a little before day-break," it would seem that circumstances had compelled them to change the time, or adjourn the completion, of the sacrifice; or that the extreme wildness of the victim had prevented its being caught, and so led to the "violent swing which McDonald gave his wife at parting." And it might be that Ramsay had come upon them when McDonald and his wife were performing the last part of the ceremony, or had caused them to finish it abruptly; as the old Gipsy stated that not only are none but Gipsies allowed to be present on such occasions, but that the greatest secrecy is observed, to prevent discovery by those who are not of the tribe.

† It appears all the Gipsies, male as well as female, who perform ceremonies for their tribe, carry long staffs. In the Institutes of Menu, page 23, it is written: "The staff of a priest must be of such length as to reach his hair; that of a soldier to reach his forehead; and that of a merchant to reach the nose."

and by its different movements is the degree of her guilt ascertained. Some of the Gipsies now set off in pursuit of it, and endeavour to catch it. If it is wild and intractable, kicks, leaps dykes and ditches, scampers about, and will not allow itself to be easily taken hold of, the crimes and guilt of the woman are looked upon as numerous and heinous. If the horse is tame and docile, when it is pursued, and suffers itself to be taken without much trouble, and without exhibiting many capers, the guilt of the woman is not considered so deep and aggravated; and it is then sacrificed in her stead. But if it is extremely wild and vicious, and cannot be taken without infinite trouble, her crimes are considered exceedingly wicked and atrocious; and my informant said instances occurred in which both horse and woman were sacrificed at the same time; the death of the horse, alone, being then considered insufficient to atone for her excessive guilt. The individuals who catch the horse bring it before the priest. They repeat to him all the faults and tricks it had committed; laying the whole of the crimes of which the woman is supposed to have been guilty to its charge; and upbraiding and scolding the dumb creature, in an angry manner, for its conduct. They bring, as it were, an accusation against it, and plead for its condemnation. When this part of the trial is finished, the priest takes a large knife and thrusts it into the heart of the horse; and its blood is allowed to flow upon the ground till life is extinct. The dead animal is now stretched out upon the ground. The husband then takes his stand on one side of it, and the wife on the other; and, holding each other by the hand, repeat certain appropriate sentences in the Gipsy language. They then quit hold of each other, and walk three times round the body of the horse, contrariwise, passing and crossing each other, at certain points, as they proceed in opposite directions. At certain parts of the animal, (the *corners* of the horse, was the Gipsy's expression,) such as the hind and fore feet, the shoulders and haunches, the head and tail, the parties halt, and face each other; and again repeat sentences, in their own speech, at each time they halt. The two last stops they make, in their circuit round the sacrifice, are at the head and tail. At the head, they again face each other, and speak; and lastly, at the tail, they again confront each other, utter some more Gipsy expressions, shake hands, and finally part, the one going north, the other south, never again to be united in this life.* Immediately after the separation takes place, the woman receives a token, which is made of cast-iron, about an inch and a half square, with a mark upon it resembling the Roman character, T. After the marriage has been dissolved, and the woman dismissed from the sacrifice, the heart of the horse is taken out and roasted with fire, then sprinkled with vinegar, or brandy, and eaten by the husband and his friends then present; the female not being allowed to join in this part of the ceremony. The body of the horse, skin and everything about it, except the heart, is buried on the spot; and years after the ceremony has taken place, the husband and his friends visit the grave of the animal, to see whether it has been disturbed. At these visits, they walk round about the grave, with much grief and mourning.

The husband may take another wife whenever he pleases, but the female is never permitted to marry again.† The token, or rather bill of divorce, which she receives, must never be from about her person. If she loses it, or attempts to pass herself off as a woman never before married, she becomes liable to the punishment of death. In the event of her breaking this law, a council of the chiefs is held upon her conduct, and her fate is decided by a majority of the members; and, if she is to suffer death, her sentence must be confirmed by the king, or principal leader. The culprit is then tied to a stake, with an iron chain, and there cudgelled to death. The executioners do not extinguish life at one beating, but leave the unhappy woman for a little while, and return to her, and at last complete their work by despatching her on the spot.

I have been informed of an instance of a Gipsy falling out with his wife, and, in the heat of his passion, shooting his own horse dead on the spot with his pistol, and forthwith

* That I might distinctly understand the Gipsy, when he described the manner of crossing and wheeling round the corners of the horse, a common sitting-chair was placed on its side between us, which represented the animal lying on the ground.

† Bright, on the Spanish Gipsies, says: "Widows never marry again, and are distinguished by mourning-veils, and black shoes made like those of a man; no slight mortification, in a country where the females are so remarkable for the beauty of their feet." It is most likely that *divorced female Gipsies* are confounded here with *widows*.—Ed.

performing the ceremony of divorce over the animal, without allowing himself a moment's time for reflection on the subject. Some of the country-people observed the transaction, and were horrified at so extraordinary a proceeding. It was considered by them as merely a mad frolic of an enraged Tinkler. It took place many years ago, in a wild, sequestered spot between Galloway and Ayrshire.

This sacrifice of the horse is also observed by the Gipsies of the Russian Empire. In the year 1830, a Russian gentleman of observation and intelligence, proprietor of estates on the banks of the Don, stated to me that the Gipsies in the neighbourhood of Moscow, and on the Don, several hundred versts from the sea of Asoph, sacrificed horses, and ate part of their flesh, in the performance of some very ancient ceremony of idolatry. They sacrifice them under night, in the woods, as the practice is prohibited by the Russian Government. The police are often detecting the Gipsies in these sacrifices, and the ceremony is kept as secret as possible. My informant could not go into the particulars of the Gipsy sacrifice in Russia; but there is little doubt that it is the same which the tribe performed in Scotland. In Russia, the Gipsies, like those in this country, have a language peculiar to themselves, which they retain as a secret among their own fraternity.

As regards the sacrificing of horses by the Gipsies of Scotland, at the present day, all that I can say is that I do not know of its taking place; nor has it been denied to me. The only conclusion to which I can come, in regard to the question, is that it is in the highest degree probable that, like their language and ceremony of marriage, it is still practised when it can be done. In carrying out this ceremony, there is an obstacle to be overcome which does not lay in the way of that of marriage, and it is this: Where are many of the Tinklers to find a horse, over which they can obtain a divorce? The difficulty with them is as great as it is with the people of England, who must, at a frightful expense, go to no less than the House of Lords to obtain an act to separate legally from their unfaithful partners.* The Gipsies, besides being generally unable or unwilling to bear the expense of what will procure them a release in their own way, find it a difficult matter, in these days, to steal, carry off,

* This difficulty has been removed by recent legislation.—Ed.

and dispose of such a bulky article as a horse, in the sacrifice of which they will find a new wife. I am not aware how they get quit of this solemn and serious difficulty, beyond this, that a Gipsy, a native of Yetholm, informed me that some of his brethren in that colony knock down their *asses*, for the purpose of parting with their wives, at the present day.*

As the code of the ancient laws of Hindostan is not in the hands of every one, I shall here transcribe from the work the account of the Gentoo Institution of the *Aswamedha* or the *Assummeed Jugg*,† that the reader may compare it with the Gipsy sacrifice of horses; for which, owing to its length, I must crave his indulgence. It is under the chapter of evidence, and is as follows:

"An *Assummeed Jugg* is when a person, having commenced a Jugg, writes various articles upon a scroll of paper on a horse's neck, and dismisses the horse, sending, along with the horse, a stout and valiant person, equipped with the best necessaries and accoutrements, to accompany the horse day and night, whithersoever he shall choose to go; and if any creature, either man, genius or dragon, should seize the horse, that man opposes such attempt, and, having gained the victory, upon a battle, again gives the horse his freedom. If any one in this world, or in heaven, or beneath the earth, would seize this horse, and the horse of himself comes to the house of the celebrator of the *Jugg*, upon killing that horse, he must throw the flesh of him upon the fire of the *Juk*, and utter the prayers of his Deity; such a *Jugg* is called a *Jugg Assummeed*, and the merit of it, as a religious work, is infinite." *Page* 127.

In another part of the same chapter of the Hindoo code of laws, are the following particulars relative to horses, which show the great respect in which these animals were held among the ancient natives of Hindostan. "In an affair concerning a horse: if any person gives false evidence, his guilt is as great as the guilt of murdering one hundred persons." *Page* 128. In the Asiatic Researches, the sacrifice

* "An ass is sometimes sacrificed by religious mendicants, as an atonement for some fault by which they had forfeited their rank as devotees."—*Account of the Hindoos.*

† Jugg, in Hindostance, is a word which signifies a religious ceremony; hence the well-known temple Juggernaut.

of the horse is frequently noticed; and in Sir William Jones' Institutes of Menu, chapter viii., page 202, it is said: "A false witness, in the case of a horse, kills, or incurs the guilt of killing, one hundred kinsmen." "The *Aswamedha*, or sacrifice of the horse: Considerable difficulties usually attend that ceremony; for the consecrated horse was to be set at liberty for a certain time, and followed at a distance by the owner, or his champion, who was usually one of his near kinsmen; and if any person should attempt to stop it in its rambles, a battle must inevitably ensue; besides, as the performer of an hundred *Aswamedhas* became equal to the god of the firmaments." (*Asiatic Researches, vol.* iii., *page* 216.) "The inauguration of *Indra*, (the Indian God of the firmaments,) it appears, was performed by sacrificing an hundred horses. It is imagined that this celebration becomes a cause of obtaining great power and universal monarchy; and many of the kings in ancient India performed this sacrifice at their inauguration, similar to that of Indra's." "These monarchs were consecrated by these great sacrifices, with a view to become universal conquerors." (*Asiatic Researches.*) It appears, by the Hindoo mythology, that *Indra* was at one time a mere mortal, but by sacrificing an hundred horses, he became sovereign of the firmament; and that should any Indian monarch succeed in immolating an hundred horses, he would displace *Indra*.

The above are literal and simple facts, which took place in performing the sacrifice; but the following is the explanation of the mystic signification contained in the ceremony.

"The *Assummeed Jugg* does not merely consist in the performance of that ceremony which is open to the inspection of the world, namely, in bringing a horse, and sacrificing him; but *Assummeed* is to be taken in a mystic signification, as implying that the sacrificer must look upon himself to be typified in that horse, such as he shall be described; because the religious duty of the *Assummeed Jugg* comprehends all those other religious duties, to the performance of which all the wise and holy direct all their actions; and by which all the sincere professors of every different faith aim at perfection. The mystic signification thereof is as follows: The head of that unblemished horse is the symbol of the morning; his eyes are the sun; his breath the wind; his wide-opening mouth is the *Bishwâner*, or that innate warmth which invigorates all the world; his body typifies one entire year; his back, paradise; his belly, the plains; his hoof, this earth; his sides, the four quarters of the heavens; the bones thereof, the intermediate spaces between the four quarters; the rest of his limbs represent all distinct matter; the places where those limbs meet, or his joints, imply the months, and halves of the months, which are called *Pèchè* (or fortnights); his feet signify night and day; and night and day are of four kinds; first, the night and day of Brihma; second, the night and day of angels; third, the night and day of the world of the spirits of deceased ancestors; fourth, the night and day of mortals. These four kinds are typified in his four feet. The rest of his bones are the constellations of the fixed stars, which are the twenty-eight stages of the moon's course, called the lunar year; his flesh is the clouds; his food the sand; his tendons the rivers; his spleen and liver the mountains; the hair of his body the vegetables, and his long hair the trees. The fore part of his body typifies the first half of the day, and the hinder part the latter half; his yawning is the flash of the lightning, and his turning himself is the thunder of the cloud; his urine represents the rain; and his mental reflection is his only speech.

"The golden vessels, which are prepared before the horse is let loose, are the light of the day; and the place where these vessels are kept is a type of the ocean of the East; the silver vessels, which are prepared after the horse is let loose, are the light of the night; and the place where those vessels are kept is a type of the ocean of the West. These two sorts of vessels are always before and after the horse. The Arabian horse, which, on account of his swiftness, is called *Hy*, is the performer of the journeys of angels; the *Tājee*, which is of the race of Persian horses, is the performer of the journeys of the *Kundherps* (or the good spirits); the *Wāzbā*, which is of the race of the deformed *Tājee* horses, is the performer of the journeys of *Jins* (or demons); and the *Ashoo*, which is of the race of Turkish horses, is the performer of the journeys of mankind. This one horse which performs these several services, on account of his four different sorts of riders, obtains the four different appellations. The place where this horse remains is the great ocean, which signifies the great spirit of *Perm-atmā*, or the universal soul, which proceeds also from that *Perm-atmā*, and is comprehended in the same *Perm-atmā*.

"The intent of this sacrifice is, that a man should consider himself to be in the place of that horse, and look upon all these articles as typified in himself; and conceiving the *Atmā* (or divine soul) to be an ocean, should let all thought of self be absorbed in that *Atmā*." *Page* 19.

Mr. Halhed, the translator, justly observes: "This is the very acme and enthusiasm of allegory, and wonderfully displays the picturesque powers of fancy in an Asiatic genius; yet, unnatural as the account there stands, it is seriously credited by the Hindoos of all denominations." On the other hand, he thinks there is a great resemblance between this very ancient Hindoo ceremony and the sacrifice of the scape-goat, in the Bible, described in the 21st and 22d verses of the 16th chapter of Leviticus, viz.: "And Aaron shall lay both his hands upon the head of the live goat, and confess over him all the iniquities of the children of Israel, and all their transgressions, in all their sins, putting them upon the head of the goat; and shall send him away, by the hand of a fit man, into the wilderness: and the goat shall bear upon him all their iniquities into a land not inhabited; and he shall let go the goat into the wilderness." *Page* 17. In the same manner, all the iniquities of the sacrificer, in the Gentoo ceremony, are laid upon the horse, which is let loose, and attended by a stout and valiant person. The same is done in the Gipsy sacrifice, as typifying the woman to be divorced.

The resemblance between the Gipsy and the Hindoo sacrifice is close and striking in their general bearings. The Hindoo sacrificer is typified in the horse, and his sins are ascertained and described by the motions or movements of the animal; for if the horse is very docile and tame, and of its own accord comes to the Hindoo celebrator of the sacrifice, his merits are then infinite, and extremely acceptable to the Deity worshipped. In the Gipsy sacrifice, if the horse is in like manner quiet, and easily caught, the woman, whom it represents, is then comparatively innocent. In India, part of the *flesh* of the horse was eaten: among the Gipsies, the *heart* is eaten. The Hindoos sacrificed their *enemies*, by substituting for them a *buffalo*, &c.: the Gipsies sacrifice their *unfaithful wives*, by the substitute of a *horse*. In the

Hindoo sacrifice, particular parts of the horse allegorically represent certain parts of the earth : at certain parts of the horse, (the *corners*, as the Gipsies call them,) the Gipsies, in their circuit round the animal, halt, and utter particular sentences in their own language, as if these parts were of more importance, and had more influence, than the other parts. And it is probable that, in these sentences, some invisible agency was addressed and invoked by the Gipsies.

As the *Aswamedha*, or sacrifice of the horse, was the most important of all the religious ceremonies of every caste of Hindoos, in ancient India, so it would be the last to be forgotten by the wandering Gipsies. And as both sacrificed at twelve o'clock, noon, I am inclined to believe that both offered their sacrifice to the sun, the animating soul of universal nature. As already stated, the Gipsies, while travelling, assume new names every morning before setting out ; but when noon-tide arrives, they resume their permanent English ones. This custom is practised daily, and has undoubtedly also some reference to the sun. By the account of the Gipsy already mentioned, the horse must, if possible, be killed at noon. According to Southey, in his curse of Kehamah, the sacrifice of the horse in India was performed at the same time. Colonel Tod, in his history of India, says : "The sacrifice of the horse is the most imposing, and the earliest, heathenish rite on record, and was dedicated to the sun, anciently, in India." According to the same author, the horse in India must be milk-white, with particular marks upon it. The Gipsy's horse to be sacrificed must be sound, and without blemish ; but no particular colour is mentioned. According to Halhed, the horse sacrificed in India was also without blemish.

I have, perhaps, been too minute and tedious in describing these rites and ceremonies of the Gentoos ; but the singular fact that our Scottish Tinklers yet—at least till very lately—retained the important fragments of the ancient mythology of the Pagan tribes of Hindostan, is offered as an apology to the curious reader for the trouble of perusing the details. I shall only add, that there appears to be nearly as great a resemblance between the sacrifices of the Gipsies and the ancient Hindoos, as there is affinity between modern Hindostanee and the language of the Gipsies in Scotland, at the present day, as will be seen in the following chapter.

CHAPTER IX.

LANGUAGE.

THE Scottish Gipsies appear to be extremely tenacious of retaining their language, as their principal secret, among themselves, and seem, from what I have read on the subject, to be much less communicative, on this and other matters relative to their history, than those of England and other countries. On speaking to them of their speech, they exhibit an extraordinary degree of fear, caution, reluctance, distrust, and suspicion; and, rather than give any information on the subject, will submit to any self-denial. It has been so well retained among themselves, that I believe it is scarcely credited, even by individuals of the greatest intelligence, that it exists at all, at the present day, but as slang, used by common thieves, house-breakers and beggars, and by those denominated flash and family men.*

* Before considering this trait in the character of the Scottish Gipsies, it may interest the reader to know that the same peculiarity obtains among those on the continent.

Of the Hungarian Gipsies, Grellmann writes: "It will be recollected, from the first, how great a secret they make of their language, and how suspicious they appear when any person wishes to learn a few words of it. Even if the Gipsy is not perverse, he is very inattentive, and is consequently likely to answer some other rather than the true Gipsy word."

Of the Hungarian Gipsies, Bright says: "No one, who has not had experience, can conceive the difficulty of gaining intelligible information, from people so rude, upon the subject of their language. If you ask for a word, they give you a whole sentence; and on asking a second time, they give the sentence a totally different turn, or introduce some figure altogether new. Thus it was with our Gipsy, who, at length, tired of our questions, prayed most piteously to be released; which we granted him, only on condition of his returning in the evening."

Of the Spanish Gipsies, Mr. Borrow writes: "It is only by listening attentively to the speech of the Gitanos, whilst discoursing among themselves, that an acquaintance with their dialect can be formed, and by seizing upon all unknown words, as they fall in succession from their lips. Nothing can be more useless and hopeless than the attempt to obtain possession

Among the causes contributing to this state of things among the Scottish Gipsies, and what are called Tinklers or Tinkers, for they are the same people, may be mentioned the following: The traditional accounts of the numerous imprisonments, banishments, and executions, which many of the race underwent, for merely being "by habit and repute Gipsies," under the severe laws passed against them, are still fresh in the memories of the present generation. They still entertain the idea that they are a persecuted race, and liable, if known to be Gipsies, to all the penalties of the statutes framed for the extirpation of the whole people. But, apart from this view of the question, it may be asked, how is it that the Gipsies in Scotland are more reserved, (they are generally altogether silent,) in respect to themselves, than their brethren in other countries seem to be? It may be answered, that our Scottish tribes

of their vocabulary, by enquiring of them how particular objects and ideas are styled in the same; for, with the exception of the names of the most common things, they are totally incapable, as a Spanish writer has observed, of yielding the required information; owing to their great ignorance, the shortness of their memories, or, rather, the state of bewilderment to which their minds are brought by any question which tends to bring their reasoning faculties into action; though, not unfrequently, the very words which have been in vain required of them will, a minute subsequently, proceed inadvertently from their mouths."

What has been said by the two last-named writers is very wide of the mark; Grellmann, however, hits it exactly. The Gipsies have excellent memories. It is all they have to depend on. If they had not good memories, how could they, at the present day, speak a word of their language at all? The difficulty in question is down-right shuffling, and not a want of memory on the part of the Gipsy. The present chapter will throw some light on the subject. Even Mr. Borrow himself gives an ample refutation to his sweeping account of the Spanish Gipsies, in regard to their language; for, in another part of his work, he says: "I recited the Apostles' Creed to the Gipsies, sentence by sentence, which they translated as I proceeded. They exhibited the greatest eagerness and interest in their unwonted occupation, and frequently broke into loud disputes as to the best rendering, many being offered at the same time. I then read the translation aloud, whereupon they raised a shout of exultation, and appeared not a little proud of the composition." On this occasion, Mr. Borrow evidently had the Gipsies in the right humour—that is, off their guard, excited, and much interested in the subject. He says, in another place: "The language they speak among themselves, and they are particularly anxious to keep others in ignorance of it." As a general thing, they seem to have been bored by people much above them in the scale of society; with whom, their natural politeness, and expectations of money or other benefits, would naturally lead them to do anything than give them that which it is inborn in their nature to keep to themselves.—Ed.

are, in general, much more civilized, their bands more broken up, and the individuals more mixed with, and scattered through, the general population of the country, than the Gipsies of other nations; and it therefore appears to me that the more their blood gets mixed with that of the ordinary natives, and the more they approach to civilization, the more determinedly will they conceal every particular relative to their tribe, to prevent their neighbours ascertaining their origin and nationality. The slightest taunting allusion to the forefathers of half-civilized Scottish Tinklers kindles up in their breasts a storm of wrath and fury: for they are extremely sensitive to the feeling which is entertained toward their tribe by the other inhabitants of the country.* "I have," said one of them to me, "wrought all my life in a shop with fellow-tradesmen, and not one of them ever discovered that I knew a single Gipsy word." A Gipsy woman also informed me that herself and sister had nearly lost their lives, on account of their language. The following are the particulars: The two sisters chanced to be in a public-house near Alloa, when a number of colliers, belonging to the coal-works at Sauchie, were present. The one sister, in a low tone of voice, and in the Gipsy language, desired the other, among other things, to make ready some broth for their repast. The colliers took hold of the two Gipsy words, *shaucha* and *blawkie*, which signify broth and pot; thinking the Tinkler women were calling them *Sauchie Blackies*, in derision and contempt of their dark, subterraneous calling. The consequence was, that the savage colliers attacked the innocent Tinklers, calling out that they would "grind them to powder," for calling them *Sauchie Blackies*. But the determined Gipsies would rather perish than explain the meaning of the words in English, to appease the enraged colliers; "for," said they, "it would have exposed our tribe, and made ourselves odious to the world." The two defenceless females might have been murdered by their brutal assailants, had not the master of the house fortunately come to their assistance. The poor Gipsies felt the effects

* This opinion is confirmed by the fact that the Gipsies whom the Rev. Mr. Crabbe has civilized will not now be seen among the others of the tribe, at his annual festival, at Southampton. We have already seen, under the head of Continental Gipsies, that "those who are gold-washers in Transylvania and the Banat have no intercourse with others of their nation; nor do they like to be called Gipsies."

of the beating they had received, for many months thereafter; and my informant had not recovered from her bruises at the time she mentioned the circumstances to me.*

They are also anxious to retain their language, as a secret among themselves, for the use which it is to them in conducting business in markets or other places of public resort. But they are very chary of the manner in which they employ it on such occasions. Besides this, they display all the pride and vanity in possessing the language which is common with linguists generally. The determined and uniform principle laid down by them, to avoid all communications with "strangers" on the subject, and their resolution to keep it a secret within their own tribe, will be strikingly illustrated by the following facts.

For seven years, a woman, of the name of Baillie, about fifty years of age, and the mother of a family, called regularly at my house, twice a year, while on her peregrinations through the country, selling spoons and other articles made from horn. Every time I saw her, I endeavoured to prevail upon her to give me some of her secret speech, as I was certain she was acquainted with the Gipsy tongue. But, not to alarm her by calling it by that name, I always said to her, in a jocular manner, that it was the *mason* word I wished her to teach me. She, however, as regularly and firmly declared that she knew of no such language among the Tinklers. I always treated her kindly, and desired her to continue her visits. I gave her, each time she called, a glass of spirits, a piece of flesh, and such articles; and generally purchased some trifle from her, for which I intentionally paid her more than its value. She so far yielded to my importunities, that, for the last three years she called, she went the length of saying that she would tell me "something" the next time she came back. But when she returned, she guardedly evaded all my questions, by constantly repeating nearly the same answer, such as, "I will speak to you the next time I come back, sir." After having been put off for *seven* years in this manner, I was determined to put her

* On the whole, however, our Scottish peasantry, in some districts, do not greatly despise the Tinklers; at least not to the same extent as the inhabitants of some other countries seem to do. When not involved in quarrels with the Gipsies, our country people, with the exception of a considerable portion of the land-owners, were, and are even yet, rather fond of the *superior* families of the *nomadic* class of these people, than otherwise.

to the usual test, should she never enter my door again, and, as she was walking out of the gate of my garden, I called to her, in the Gipsy language, "*Jaw vree, managie!*"—(go away, woman.) She immediately turned round, and, laughing, replied, "I will *jaw* with you when I come back, *gaugie*"—(I will go or speak with you, when I come back, man.) She returned, as usual, in December following. I again requested her to give me some of her words, assuring her that she would be in no danger from me on that account. I further told her it was of no use to conceal her speech from me, having, the last time she was in my house, shown her that I was acquainted with it. After considerable hesitation and reluctance, she consented; but then, she said, she would not allow any one in the house to hear her speak to me but my wife. I took her at once into my parlour, and, on being desired, she, without the least hesitation or embarrassment, took the seat next the fire. Observing the door of the room a little open, she desired it to be shut, in case of her being overheard, again mentioning that she had no objections to my wife being present, and gravely observing that "husbands and wives were one, and should know all one another's secrets." She stated that the public would look upon her with horror and contempt, were it known she could speak the Gipsy language. She was extremely civil and intelligent, yet placed me upon a familiar equality with herself, when she found I knew of the existence of her speech, and could repeat some of the words of it. Her nature, to appearance, seemed changed. Her bold and fiery disposition was softened and subdued. She was very frank and polite; retained her self-possession, and spoke with great propriety.* The words which I got on this occasion will be found in another part of the chapter.

In corroboration of this principle of concealment observed by the Scottish Gipsies, relative to their language, I may give a fact which will show how artful they are in avoiding any allusion to it. One evening, as a band of *potters*, with a cart of earthenware, were travelling on the high-road, in a wild glen in the south of Scotland, a brother of mine over-

* Their (the female's) speech is as fluent, and their eyes as unabashed, in the presence of royalty, as before those from whom they have nothing to hope or fear; the result of which is, that most minds quail before them.—*Borrow on the Spanish Gipsies.*—Ed.

heard them, male and female, conversing in a language, a word of which he did not understand. As the road was very bad, and the night dark, one of the females of the band was a few yards in advance of the cart, acting as a guide to the horde. Every now and then, among other unintelligible expressions, she called out "*Shan drom.*" My brother's curiosity was excited by hearing the potters conversing in this manner, and, next morning, he went to where they lodged, in an out-house on the farm, and enquired of the female what she was saying on the road, the night before, and what she meant by "*Shan drom.*" The woman appeared confused at the unexpected question; but in a short time recovered her self-possession, and artfully replied that they were talking *Latin (!)* and that "*Shan drom,*" in Latin, signified "bad road." But the truth is, "*Shan drom*" is the Gipsy expression for bad road, as will by and by be seen.

Besides the difficulties mentioned in the way of getting any of their language from them, there is a general one that arises from the suspicious, unsettled, restless, fickle and volatile nature by which they are characterized. It is a rare thing to get them to speak consecutively for more than a few minutes on any subject, thus precluding the possibility, in most instances, of taking advantage of any favourable humour in which they may be found, in the matter of their general history—leaving alone the formal and serious procedure necessary to be followed in regard to their language. If this favourable turn in their disposition is allowed to pass, it is rarely anything of that nature can be got from them at that meeting; and it is extremely likely that, at any after interviews, they will entirely evade the matter so much desired.

With these remarks, I will now proceed to state the method I adopted to get at the Gipsy language.

Short vocabularies of the language of the *Tschengenes* of Turkey, the *Cyganis* of Hungary, the *Zigeuners* of Germany, the *Gitanos* of Spain, and the *Gipsies* of England, have, at different periods, since 1783, issued from the press, in this country and in Germany; but I am not aware of any specimens of our Scottish *Tinkler* or Gipsy language having as yet been submitted to the public. Some of the former I committed to memory, and used, intermixed with English words, in questions I would put to the Scottish Gipsies. In this way, one word would lead to another. I would address them in a confident and familiar manner, as if I were one of themselves, and knew exactly who they were, and all about them. I would, for instance, ask them: Have you a *grye* (horse)? How many *chauvies* (children) have you? Where is your *gaugie* (husband)? Do you sell *roys* (spoons)? Being taken completely by surprise, they would give me at once a true answer. For, being the first, as far as I know, to apply the language of the Gipsies of the continent to our own tribes, they could naturally have no hesitation in replying to my questions; although they would wonder what kind of a Gipsy I could possibly be—dressed, as I was, in black, with black neck-cloth, and no display of linen, save a ruffled breast, thick-soled shoes and gaiters. The consequence was, I became a character of interest to many of the Gipsies to be found in a circuit of many miles; and great wonder was excited in their untutored minds, leading to a desire to see, and know something of, the *Riah Nawken*, or the gentleman Gipsy. On such occasions, I would treat them as I would land a fish—give them hook and line enough. But the circumstance was to them something incomprehensible, for, although Gipsies are very ready-witted, and possess great natural resources, in thieving, and playing tricks of every kind, and great tact in getting out of difficulties of that nature—which, with them, are matters of instinct, training, and practice—their whole mind being bent, and exclusively employed, in that direction, it was almost impossible for them to form any intelligible opinion as to my true character, provided I was any way discreet in disguising my real position among them. As little chance was there of any of themselves informing the others of what assistance they had inadvertently been to me, in getting at their language. Some of them might have an idea that one of their race had, in their own way of thinking, peached, turned traitor to their blood, and let the cat out of the bag. At times, if they happened to see me approach them, so as to have an opportunity to scrutinize me—which they are much given to, with people generally—they would not be so easily disconcerted at any question put to them in their language; but the result would be either direct replies, or the most ludicrous scenes of surprise and terror imaginable, which, to be enjoyed, were only to be seen, but could not be described, although the sequel will in some measure illustrate them. At other times, if I addressed a Gipsy in his own language, and spoke to him in a kind and familiar manner, as if I had been soothing a wild and unmanageable horse, before mounting him, he would either very awkwardly pretend not to understand what I meant, or, with a downcast and guilty look, and subdued voice, immediately answer my Gipsy words in English. But if I put the words to him in an abrupt, hasty, or threatening manner, he would either take to his heels, or turn upon me, like a tiger, and pour out upon me a torrent of abusive language. The following instances will show the manner in which my use of their language was sometimes appreciated by the female Gipsies.

When I spoke in a sharp manner to some of the old women, on the high-road, by way of testing them, they would quicken their paces, look over their shoulders, and call out, in much bitterness of spirit, "You are no gentleman, sir, otherwise you would not insult us in that way." On one occasion, I observed a woman with her son, who appeared about twelve years of age, lingering near a house at which they had no business, and I desired her, rather sharply, to leave the place, telling her that I was afraid her *chauvie* was a *chor*—(that her son was a thief). I used these two words merely to see what effect they would have upon her, as I did not really think she was a Gipsy. She instantly flew into a dreadful passion, telling me that I had been among thieves and robbers myself, otherwise I could not speak to her in such words as these. She threatened to go to Edinburgh, to inform the police that I was the head and captain of a band of thieves,* and that she would have me immediately apprehended as such. Four sailors who were present with me were astonished at the sudden wrath and insolence of the woman, as they could not perceive any provocation she had received from me—being ignorant of the meaning of the words *chauvie* and *chor*, which I applied to her boy.

One day I fell in by chance, on a lonely part of the old public road, on the hills within half a mile of the village of North Queensferry, with a woman of about twenty-seven years of age, and the mother, as she said, of seven children.

* This woman evidently mistook our author for a Gipsy *gent*, such as he is described at page 169.—Ed.

She had light hair, blue eyes, and a fair complexion. The youngest of her children appeared to be about nine months old, and the eldest about ten years. The mother was dressed in a brown cloak, and the group had altogether a very squalid appearance. In the most lamentable tone of voice, she informed me that her husband had set off with another woman, and left her and her seven children to starve; and that he had been lately employed at a paper-mill in Mid-Lothian. She sometimes appeared almost to choke with grief, but, nevertheless, I observed no tears in her eyes. She often repeated, in a sort of hypocritical and canting manner, "The Lord has been very kind to me, and will still protect me and my helpless babes. Last night we all slept in the open fields, and gathered peas and beans from the stubble for our suppers." She certainly seemed to be in very indigent circumstances; but that her husband had abandoned her, I did not credit. However, I gave her a few half-pence, for which she thanked me very civilly. From her extravagant behaviour, and a peculiar wildness in her looks, it occurred to me that she belonged to the lowest caste of Gipsies, although her appearance did not indicate it; that her grief was, for the most part, feigned, and that the story of her husband having abandoned her was got up merely to excite pity, for the purpose of procuring a little money for the subsistence of her band. I now put a number of questions to her, relative to many individuals whom I knew were Gipsies of a superior class, taking care not to call them by that name, in case of alarming her. I spoke to her as if I had been quite intimate with all the persons I was enquiring about. She gave me satisfactory answers to almost every question, and seemed well acquainted with every individual I named. She now appeared quite calm and collected, and answered me very gravely. But she said that some of the men I mentioned were rogues, and that their wives played many clever tricks. On mentioning the tricks of the wives, I noticed a smile come over her countenance. I observed to her that they were not faultless, but that they were often blamed for crimes of which they were not guilty. Upon perceiving that I took their part, which I did on purpose, to hear what she would say, she gradually changed her mind, and came over to my opinion. She said that they were exceedingly good-hearted people, and that some of them had frequently paid a night's lodging for herself and family. I now ventured to put a question to her, half in Gipsy and half in English. After a short pause and hesitation, she signified that she understood what I said. I then asked one or two questions in Gipsy words only. A Gipsy, with crockery-ware in a basket, happened to pass us at the very moment I was speaking to her; and to show her the knowledge I had of her speech and people, I said, "There is a *nawken*"—(there is a Gipsy.) She, in a very civil and polite manner, immediately replied, "Sir, I hope you will not take it ill, when I use the freedom of saying that you must have been among the people you are enquiring about, otherwise you could not speak to me in that way." To show her that I did not despise her for understanding my Gipsy words, I gave her a few pence more, and spoke kindly to her. She then became quite cheerful and frank, as if we had been old acquaintances. Instead of trying to impose upon me, by tales of grief and woe, and feigned piety, she appeared happy and contented, her whole conduct indicating that it was useless to play off her tricks upon me, as she was now sensible that I knew exactly what she was, and yet did not treat her contemptuously. She said her husband's name was Wilson, and her own Jackson, (the names of two Gipsy tribes;) that she could tell fortunes, and was acquainted with the *Irish* words I spoke, being afraid to call them by their right name. She further stated that every one of the people I was enquiring about spoke in the same language.

About half an hour after I parted with her, on the road, I met her in the village of North Queensferry, while I was walking with a friend. I then put a question to her in Gipsy words, in the presence of this third party, who knew not what she was, to see how she would conduct herself in public. She seemed surprised at my question, as if she did not understand a word of it—to prevent it being discovered to others of the community that she was a Gipsy. But she publicly praised me highly, for having given her something to help her poor children; and, with her trumped-up story at her tongue's end, proceeded on her travels.

These poor people were much alarmed when I let them see that I knew they were Gipsies. They thought I was despising them, and treating them with contempt; or they were afraid of being apprehended under the old sanguinary laws, condemning the whole unfortunate race to death; for the Gipsies, as I have already said, still believe that those bloody statutes are in full force against them at the present day.

I was advised by Sir Walter Scott, as mentioned in the Introduction, to "get the same words from different individuals; and, to verify the collection, to set down the names of the persons by whom they were communicated;" which I have done. For this reason, the words now furnished will appear as the confessions of so many individuals, rather than a vocabulary drawn up in the manner in which such is usually done; and which will be more satisfactory to the general reader, as well as the philologist, than if I had presented the words by themselves, without any positive or circumstantial evidence of their genuineness. To the general reader, as distinguished from the philologist, the anecdotes connected with the collection may prove interesting, if the words themselves have no attraction for him; while they will satisfy the latter, as far as they go, as to the existence of a language which has almost always been denied, yet which is known, at the present day, to a greater number of the population of the country than could at first have been imagined; this part of it having been drawn from a variety of individuals, at different and widely-separated times and places. On this account, I hope that the minuteness of the details of the present enquiry may not appear tedious, but, on the contrary, interesting, to my readers generally; inasmuch as the present collection is the first, as far as I know, of the Scottish Gipsy language that has ever been made; although the people themselves have lived amongst us for three hundred and fifty years, and talked it every hour of the day, but hardly ever in the hearing of the other inhabitants, excepting, occasionally, a word of it now and then, to disguise their discourse from those around them; which, on being questioned, they have always passed off for *cant*, to prevent the law taking hold of them, and punishing them for being Gipsies. These details will also show that our Scottish Tinklers, or Gipsies, are sprung from the common stock from which are descended those that are to be found in the other parts of Europe, as well as those that are scattered over the world generally; what secrecy they observe in all matters relative to their affairs; what an extraordinary degree of reluctance and fear they evince in answering questions tending to develop their history; and, consequently, how difficult it is to learn anything satisfactory about them.*

I fell in one day, on the public road, with an old woman and her two daughters, of the name of Ross, selling horn spoons, made by Andrew Stewart, a Tinkler at Bo'ness. I repeated to the woman, in the shape of questions, some of the Gipsy words presented in these pages. She at first affected, though very awkwardly, not to understand what I said, but in a few minutes, with some embarrassment in her manner, acknowledged that she knew the speech, and gave me the English of the following words:

Gaugie, man.	*Grye*, horse.
Managie, woman.	*Grye-femler*, horse-dealer.
Chauvies, children.	*Roys*, spoons.

I observed to this woman, that I saw no harm in speaking this language openly and publicly. "None in the least, sir," was her reply.

Two girls, of the name of Jamieson, came one day begging to my door. They appeared to be sisters, of about eight and seventeen years of age, and were pretty decently clothed. Both had light-blue eyes, light-yellow, or rather flaxen, hair, and fair complexions. To ascertain whether they were Tinklers or not, I put some Gipsy words to the eldest girl. She immediately hung down her head, as if she had been detected in a crime, and, pretending not to understand what was said, left the house; but, after proceeding about twelve paces, she took courage, turned round, and, with a smile upon an agreeable countenance, called back, "There are eleven of us, sir." I had enquired of her how many children there were of her family. I called both the girls back to my house, and ordered them some victuals, for which they were extremely grateful, and seemed much pleased that they were kindly treated. After I had dis-

* It would be well for the reader to consider what *a Gipsy* is, irrespective of the *language which he speaks*; for the *race* comes *before* the *speech* which it uses. That will be done fully in my Disquisition on the Gipsies. The language, considered in itself, however interesting it may be, is a secondary consideration; it may ultimately disappear, while the people who now speak it will remain.—Ed.

covered they were Gipsies, I wormed out of them the following words:

Gaugie, man.	*Grye*, horse.
Managie, woman.	*Jucal*, dog.
Chauvies, children.	

When I enquired of the eldest girl the English of *Jucal*, she did not, at first, catch the sound of the word; but her little sister looked up in her face, and said to her, "Don't you hear? That is dog. It is dog he means." The other then added, with a downcast look, and a melancholy tone of voice, "You gentlemen understand all languages now-a-days."

At another time, four or five children were loitering about, and diverting themselves, before the door of a house, near Inverkeithing. The youngest appeared about five, and the eldest about thirteen years of age. One of the boys, of the name of McDonald, stepped forward, and asked some money from me in charity. From his importunate manner of begging, I suspected the children were Gipsies, although their appearance did not indicate them to be of that race. After some questions put to them about their parents and their occupations, they gave me the English of the following words:

Gaugie, man.	*Aizel*, ass.
Chauvies, children.	*Lowa*, silver.
Riah, gentleman.	*Chor*, thief.
Grye, horse.	*Staurdie*, prison.
Jucal, dog.	*Bing*, the devil.

A gentleman, an acquaintance of mine, was in my presence while the children were answering my words; and as the subject of their language was new to him, I made some remarks to him in their hearing, relative to their tribe, which greatly displeased them. One of the boys called out to me, with much bitterness of expression, "You are a Gipsy yourself, sir, or you never could have got these words."

Some years since, a female, of the name of Ruthven, was in the habit of calling at a farm occupied by one of my brothers. My mother, being interested about the Gipsies, began, on one occasion, to question this female Tinkler, relative to her tribe, and, among other things, asked if she was a Gipsy. "Yes," replied Ruthven, "I am a Gipsy, and a desperate, murdering race we are. I will let you hear me speak our language, but what the better will you be of that?" She accordingly uttered a few sentences, and then said, "Now, are you any the wiser of what you have heard? But that infant," pointing to her child of about five years of age, "understands every word I speak." "I know," continued the Tinkler, "that the public are trying to find out the secrets of the Gipsies, but it is in vain." This woman further stated that her tribe would be exceedingly displeased, were it known that any of their fraternity taught their language to "strangers."* She also mentioned that the Gipsies believe that the laws which were enacted for their extirpation were yet in full force against them. I may mention, however, that she could put confidence in the family in whose house she made these confessions.

On another occasion, a female, with three or four children, the eldest of whom was not above ten years of age, came up to me while speaking to an innkeeper, on a public pier on the banks of the Forth. She stated to us that her property had been burned to the ground, and her family reduced to beggary, and solicited charity of us both. After receiving a few half-pence from the innkeeper, she continued her importunities with an unusual impertinence, and hung upon me for a contribution. Her barefaced conduct displeased me. I thought I would put her to the test, and try if she was not a Gipsy. Deepening the tone of my voice, I called out to her, in an angry manner, "*Sallah, jaw drom*"—("Curse you, take the road.") The woman instantly wheeled about, uttered not another word, but set off, with precipitation; and so alarmed were her children, that they took hold of her clothes, to hasten and pull her out of my presence; calling to her, at the same time, "Mother, mother, come away." Mine host, the innkeeper, was amazed at the effectual manner in which I silenced and dismissed the importunate and troublesome beggars. He was anxious that I

* The Gipsies are always afraid to say what they would do in such cases. Perhaps they don't know, but have only a general impression that the individual would "catch it;" or there may be some old law on the subject. What Ruthven said of her's being a desperate race is true enough, and murderous too, among themselves as distinguished from the inhabitants generally. Her remark was evidently part of that *frightening* policy which keeps the natives from molesting the tribe. See page 44.—Ed.

should teach him the unknown words that had so terrified the poor Gipsies; with the design, it appeared to me, of frightening others, should they molest him with their begging. Had I not proved this family by the language, it was impossible for any one to perceive that the group were Gipsies.

In prosecuting my enquiries into the existence of the Gipsy language, I paid a visit to Lochgellie, once the residence of four or five families of Gipsies, as already mentioned, and procured an interview with young Andrew Steedman, a member of the tribe. At first, he appeared much alarmed, and seemed to think I had a design to do him harm. His fears, however, were in a short while calmed; and, after much reluctance, he gave me the following words and expressions, with the corresponding English significations. Like a true Gipsy, the first expression which he uttered, as if it came the readiest to him, was, "*Choar a chauvie*"—("rob that person,") which he pronounced with a smile on his countenance.

Gaugie, man.
Gourie, man.
Managie, woman.
Chauvie, a person of either sex.
Chauvies, children.
Been gaugie, gentleman.
Been gourie, gentleman.
Rajah, a chief, governor.
Baurie rajah, the king.
Greham, horse.
Grye, horse.
Scefer, ass.
Jucal, dog.
Mufler, cat.
Sloof, sheep.
Bashanie, cock.
Caunie, hen.
Borlan, sun.
Mang, moon.
Gaff, fire.
Garlan, ship.
Beefie, spoon.
Keechan, knife.
Chowrie, knife.
Scaf, hat.
Mass, flesh.
Mass, hand.
Bar, money.
Lowie, coin or money.
Roug, silver.
Neel, shilling.
Deek, to listen.
Chee, tongue.
Chee chee, hold your tongue.
Chor, thief.
Choar, to steal.
Quad, prison.
Moolie, death.
Moolie, I'll kill you.
Bing, the devil.
Bing feck, devil take you.
Bing feck eelreelee, devil take your soul.
Choar a chauvie, rob that person.

Choar a gaugie, steal from that man.
Cheeteromanie, a dram of whiskey.
Glowie a lowa, pay him the money.

The first expression which the Gipsies use in saluting one another, when they first meet, anywhere, is "*Auteenie, auteenie.*" Steedman, however, did not give me the English of this salutation. He stated to me that, at the present day, the Gipsies in Scotland, when by themselves, transact their business in their own language, and hold all their ordinary conversations in the same speech. In the course of a few minutes, Steedman's fears returned upon him. He appeared to regret what he had done. He now said he had forgotten the language, and referred me to his father, old Andrew Steedman, who, he said, would give me every information I might require. I imprudently sent him out, to bring the old man to me; for, when both returned, all further communication, with regard to their speech, was at an end. Both were now dead silent on the subject, denied all knowledge of the Gipsy language, and were evidently under great alarm. The old man would not face me at all; and when I went to him, he appeared to be shaking and trembling, while he stood at the head of his horses, in his own stable. Young Steedman entreated me to tell no one that he had given me any words, as the Tinklers, he said, would be exceedingly displeased with him for doing so. This man, however, by being kindly treated, and seeing no intention of doing him any harm, became, at an after period, communicative on various subjects relative to the Gipsies.

The following are the words which I obtained during an hour's interrogation of the woman that baffled me for seven years, and of whom I have said something already:

Gaugie, man.
Chauvie, child.
Mort, wife.
Shan mort, bad wife.
Blawkie, pot.
Roys, spoons.
Snypers, shears.
Fluff, tobacco-pipe.
Baurie mort, good wife.
Nais mort, grandmother.
Nais gaugie, grandfather.
Been riah, gentleman.
Been raunie, gentlewoman.
Dill, servant-maid.
Loudnie, whore.
Chor, thief.
Gawvers, pickpockets.
Nawkens, Tinklers.
Rachlin, hanged man.
Klistie, soldier.

Pawnie-col, sailor.
Femmel, hand.
Yak, eye.
Sherro, head.
Mooie, mouth.
Chatters, teeth.
Rat, blood.
Rat, night.
Moolie, death, to die, kill.
Shucha, coat.
Teeyakas, shoes.
Gawd, shirt.
Olivers, stockings.
Wiper, napkin,
Coories, blankets.
Grye, horse.
Aizel, ass.
Jucal, dog.
Routler, cow.
Bakra, sheep.
Kair, house.
Blinker, window.
Kep, bed.
Fluffan, tobacco.
Lowie, money.
Roug, silver.
Leel, bank notes.
Casties, trees.
Quad, prison.
Harro, sword.
Chourie, bayonet-knife.
Mass, meat, flesh.
Guffie, swine's flesh.
Flatrins, fish.
Habben, bread.
Blaw, meal.
Neddies, potatoes.
Thood, milk.
Smout, butter.
Chizcazin, cheese.
Bobies, peas.
Pooklie, pot-barley.
Shaucha, broth.
Geeve, corn, wheat, grain.
Faizim, hay.
Stramel, straw.
Paunie, water.
Yak, coal.
Mouds, peats.
Shan drom, bad road.
Beenlightment, daylight.
Jaw vree, go away.
Aucheer mangan, hold your tongue.
Bing lee ma, devil miss me.
Ruffie feck ma, devil take me.
Ruffie lee ma, devil miss me.

I observed to this woman that her language would, in course of time, be lost. She replied, with great seriousness, "It will never be forgotten, sir; it is in our hearts, and as long as a single Tinkler exists, it will be remembered." I further enquired of her, how many of her tribe were in Scotland. Her answer was, "There are several thousand; and there are many respectable shop-keepers and householders in Scotland that are Gipsies." I requested of this woman the Gipsy word for God.* She said they had no

* Pouqueville, in his travels, says that the Gipsies in the Levant have no words in their language to express either God or the soul. Of ten words of the Greek Gipsy, given by him, five of them are in use in Scotland.—*Paris*, 1820.

[The Gipsy for God, according to Grellmann, is *Deus, Dewel, Dewol, Devla.*]—ED.

corresponding word for God in their speech; adding, that she thought "it as well, as it prevented them having their Maker's name often unnecessarily and sinfully in their mouths." She acknowledged the justice, and highly approved of the punishment of death for murder; but she condemned, most bitterly, the law that took away the lives of human beings for stealing. She dwelt on the advantages which her secret speech gave her tribe in transacting business in markets. She said that she was descended from the first Gipsy family in Scotland. I was satisfied that she was sprung from the second, if not the first, family. I could make out, with tolerable certainty, the links of her descent for four generations of Gipsies. I have already described the splendid style in which her ancestors travelled in Tweeddale. Her mother, above eighty years of age, also called at my house. Both were fortune-tellers. It was evident, from this woman's manner, that she knew much she would not communicate. Like the Gipsy chief, in presence of Dr. Bright, at Csurgo, in Hungary, she, in a short time, became impatient; and, apparently, when a certain hour arrived, she insisted upon being allowed to depart. She would not submit to be questioned any longer.

Owing to the nature of my enquiries, and more particularly the fears of the tribe, I could seldom venture to question the Gipsies regarding their speech, or their ancient customs, with any hope of receiving satisfactory answers, when a third party was present. The following, however, is an instance to the contrary; and the facts witnessed by the gentleman who was with me at the time, are, besides the testimony of the Gipsies themselves, convincing proofs that these people, at the present day, in Scotland, can converse among themselves, on any ordinary subject, in their own language, without making use of a single word of the English tongue.*

In May, 1829, while near the manse of Inverkeithing, my friend and I accidentally fell in, on the high road, with four children, the youngest of whom appeared to be about four,

* Had a German listened a whole day to a Gipsy conversation, he would not have understood a single expression.—*Grellmann.*

The dialect of the English Gipsies, though mixed with English, is tolerably pure, from the fact of its being intelligible to the race in the centre of Russia.—*Borrow.*—ED.

and the eldest about thirteen, years of age. They were accompanied by a woman, about twenty years old, who had the appearance of being married, but not the mother of any of the children with her. Not one of the whole party could have been taken for a Gipsy, but all had the exact appearance of being the family of some indigent tradesman or labourer. Excepting the woman, whose hair was dark, all of the company had hair of a light colour, some of them inclining to yellow, with fair complexions. In not one of their countenances could be seen those features by which many pretend the Gipsies can, at all times, be distinguished from the rest of the community. The manner, however, in which the woman, at first, addressed me, created in my mind a suspicion that she was one of the tribe. In order to ascertain the fact, I put a question to her in Gipsy, in such a manner that it might appear to her that I was quite certain she was one of the fraternity. She immediately smiled at my question, held down her head, cast her eyes to the ground, then appeared as if she had been detected in something wrong, and pretended not to understand what I said. One of the children, however, being thrown entirely off his guard, immediately said to her, "You know quite well what he says." The woman, recovering from her surprise and confusion, and being assured she had nothing to fear from me, now answered my question. She also replied to every other interrogation I put to her, without showing the least fear or hesitation. After I had repeated a few words more, and a sentence in the Gipsy tongue, one of the boys exclaimed, "He has good cant!" and then addressed me entirely in the Gipsy language. (All the Gipsies, as I have already mentioned, call their language *cant*, for the purpose of concealing their tribe.) The whole party seemed extremely happy that I was acquainted with their speech. The woman put several questions to me, in return, some of which were wholly in her own peculiar tongue. She asked my name, place of residence, and whether I was a *nawken*—that is a Gipsy. She further enquired whether my friend was also a *nawken;* adding, with a smile, that she was sure I was a *tramper*. The children sometimes conversed among themselves wholly in their own language; and, when I could not understand the woman, as she requested, in her own speech, to know my name, &c., one of them instantly interpreted the sentence into English for me. One of the oldest boys, however, thinking I was only pretending to be ignorant of their speech, observed, in English, to his companions, "I am sure he is a tramper, and can speak as good cant as any of us." To keep up the character, my friend told them that I had been a tramper in my youth, but that I had now nearly lost the language. On hearing this, the woman, with great earnestness, exclaimed, "God bless the gentleman!" In order to confirm their belief that I was one of their tribe, I bade the woman good-day in her own tongue, and parted with them. She informed me, on leaving, that she resided at Banff, but that her husband was then at Perth.

During the short interview which I had with these Gipsies, I collected the following words:

Gaugie, man.
Riah, gentleman.
Raunie, lady.
Vast, hand.
Sonnakie, gold.
Sonnakie vanister, gold ring.
Roug, silver.
Lowie, money.
Grye, horse.
Aizel, ass.
Jucal, dog.
Matchka, cat.
Baurie, great.
Vile, village.
Baurie vile, large village.
Nawken, Gipsy.
Davies, day.
Beenship davies, Nawken, good-day, Gipsy.
Pen yer naam? what is your name?
Shucha, coat.
Calshes, breeches.
Gogle, hat.
Coories, blankets.
Roys, spoons.
Skews, platters.
Habben kairer, baker of bread.

The method I adopted with them, as I have already hinted, was to ask them the English of the words I gave them in Gipsy, so that the answers I got were confirmations of the same words collected from other individuals, and which I drew from memory for the occasion. Had I attempted to write down any of their sentences, it would have instantly shut the door to all further conversation on the subject, and, in all probability, the Gipsies would have taken to their heels, muttering imprecations against me for having insulted them. Of this I was satisfied, that had I really been acquainted with their speech, these Gipsy children could have kept up a regular and connected conversation with me, with the greatest fluency, and without their sentences being intermixed with any English or Scotch words whatever, a fact which has been repeatedly stated to me by the Gipsies.

In confirmation of these facts, I shall transcribe a letter addressed to me by the gentleman who was present on the occasion.*

INVERKEITHING, 25*th May*, 1820.

"MY DEAR SIR:

"Agreeably to your desire, I have looked over that part of your manuscript of the Scottish Gipsies which details the particulars of a short and accidental interview which we had with a woman and four children, whom we met near Inverkeithing Manse, on the 22d inst., and who turned out to be Gipsies. I have no hesitation in averring that your statements, to my knowledge, are substantially correct—being present during the whole conversation which took place with the individuals mentioned. It was the first time I ever heard the Gipsy language spoken, and it appeared quite evident that those Gipsies could converse, in a regular and connected manner, on any subject, without making use of a single English word; and which particularly appeared from the questions which they put to you, as well as from the conversation which they had among themselves, in their own peculiar speech: and that, otherwise, the woman and children had not, in the colour of their hair, complexion, and general appearance, any resemblance to those people whom I always considered to be Gipsies. I am, &c.,

"JAMES H. COBBAN,

Deputy Compt. of Customs, Inverkeithing.

"MR. WALTER SIMSON,

Supt. of Quarantine, Inverkeithing."†

I have already mentioned having succeeded in obtaining

* This letter is interesting to the extent that it illustrates the amount of knowledge possessed by the Scottish community, generally, regarding the subject of the Gipsies.—ED.

† Sir Walter Scott was disposed to think that our Gipsy population was rather exaggerated at five thousand souls; but when families such as the above-mentioned are taken into account—leaving alone those who may be classed as settled Gipsies—I am convinced that their number is not over-estimated.

[Not being in possession of sufficient information on the subject of the Gipsies, the opinion of Sir Walter Scott, on the point in question, amounted to nothing. See the Index, for Sir Walter Scott's ideas of the Scottish Gipsy population.—ED.]

a few words of Gipsy, from two sisters, of the name of Jamieson, who came begging to my door. I had reason to suppose they would acquaint their relatives of having been questioned in their own speech, and would greatly exaggerate my knowledge of it; for I always observed that the individuals with whom I conversed were at first impressed with a belief that I knew much more of it than I really did.

During the following summer, a brother and a cousin of these girls called at my house, selling baskets. The one was about twenty-one, the other fifteen, years of age. I happened to be from home, but one of my family, suspecting them to be Gipsies, invited them into the house, and mentioned to them, (although very incorrectly,) that I understood every word of their speech. "So I saw," replied the eldest lad, "for when he passed us on the road, some time ago, I called, in our language, to my neighbour, to come out of the way, and he understood what I said, for he immediately turned round, and looked at us." I, however, knew nothing of the circumstance; I did not even recollect having seen them pass me. It is likely, however, I had been examining their appearance, and it is as likely they had been trying if I understood their speech. At all events, they appeared to have known me, while I was entirely ignorant of who they were, and to have had their curiosity excited, on account, as I imagined, of their relatives having told them I was acquainted with their language. This occurrence produced a wonderful effect upon the two lads, for they appeared pleased to think I could speak their language. At this moment, one of my daughters, about seven years of age, repeated, in their hearing, the Gipsy word for pot, having picked it up from hearing me mention it. The young Tinklers now thought they were in the midst of a Gipsy family, and seemed quite happy. "But are you really a *nawken?*" I asked the eldest of them. "Yes, sir," he replied; "and to show you I am no impostor, I will give you the names of everything in your house;" which, in the presence of my family, he did, to the extent I asked of him. "My speech," he continued, "is not the cant of packmen, nor the slang of common thieves."

But Gipsy-hunting is like deer-stalking. In prosecuting it, it is necessary to know the animal, its habits, and the locality in which it is to be found. I saw the unfavourable

turn approaching: the Gipsies' time was up; their patience was exhausted. I dropped the subject, and ordered them some refreshment. On their taking leave of me, I said to them, "Do you intend coming round this part of the country again?" (I need not have asked them such a question as that.) "That we do, sir; and we will not fail to come and see you again." They thus left me, with the strong impression on their minds, that I was a *nawken*, like themselves, but a *riah*—a gentleman Gipsy. I waited patiently for their return, which would happen in due season, on their half-yearly *tramp*. Everything looked so favourably, circumstances had contributed so fortunately, to the end which I had so much at heart, that I looked upon the information to be drawn from these poor Tinkler lads, with as much solicitude and avarice as one would who had discovered a treasure hid in his field.

This species of Gipsy-hunting, I believe, I had exclusively to myself. I had none of the difficulties to contend with, which would be implied in the field of it having been gone over by others before me. That kind of Gipsy-hunting which implied imprisonment, banishment, and hanging, was a thing of which the Gipsies had had sad experience; if not in their own persons, at least in that which the traditions of their tribe had so carefully handed down to them. Besides this, the experience of the daily life of the members of their tribe afforded an excellent school of training, for acquiring a host of expedients for escaping every danger and difficulty to which their habits exposed them. But so thoroughly had they preserved their secrets, and especially the grand one—their language—that they came to their wits' end how to understand, and how to act in, the new sphere of danger into which they were now thrown, or even to comprehend its nature. Such was the advantage which education and enlightenment had given their civilized neighbour over them. How could *they* imagine that the commencement of my knowledge of their language had been drawn from *books?* What did some of them know of *books*, beyond, perhaps, a youth sent to school, where, owing to his restless and unsettled good-for-nothingness, he would advance little beyond his alphabet?* For we know that some Gip-

* In speaking of the more original kind of Gipsy, Grellmann says: "No Gipsy has ever signalized himself in literature, notwithstanding many of

sies are so intensely vain as to send a child to school, merely to brag before their civilized neighbours that their children have been educated. How could *they* comprehend that *their* language had found, or could find, its way into *books?* The thing to them was impossible; the idea of it could not, by any exertion of their own, even enter into their imagination. The danger to arise from such a quarter was altogether beyond their capacity of comprehension. Knowing, however, that there was danger of some singular nature surrounding them, yet being unable to comprehend it, they flickered about it, like moths about a candle; till at last they did come to comprehend, if not its origin, or extent, at least its tendency, and the consequences to which it would lead.

According to promise, the eldest of the Gipsy boys called at my house, in about six months, accompanied by his sister. He was selling white-iron ware, for he was a tin-smith by occupation. Without entering into any preliminary conversation, for the purpose of smoothing the way for more direct questions, I took him into my parlour, and at once enquired if he *could* speak the Tinkler language? He applied to my question the construction that I doubted if he could, and the consequences which that would imply, and answered firmly, "Yes, sir; I have been bred in that line all my life." "Will you allow me," said I, "to write down your words?" "O yes, sir; you are welcome to as many as you please." "Have you names for everything, and can you converse on any subject, in that language?" "Yes, sir; we can converse, and have a name for everything, in our own speech." I now commenced to "make hay while the sun shone," as the phrase runs; for I knew that I could have only about an hour with the Gipsy,

them have partaken of the instruction to be obtained at public schools. Their volatile disposition and unsteadiness will not allow them to complete anything which requires perseverance or application. In the midst of his career of learning, the recollection of his origin seizes him; he desires to return to what he thinks a more happy manner of life; this solicitude encreases; he gives up all at once, turns back again, and consigns over his knowledge to oblivion."

There are too many circumstances surrounding such a Gipsy to remind him of his origin, and arrest him in his career of learning: for his race never having been tolerated—that is, no position ever having been assigned it, he feels as if he were a vagabond, if known or openly avowed to the public as a member of the tribe. And this, in itself, is sufficient to discourage such a Gipsy in every effort towards improvement.—Ed.

at the most. The following, then, are the words and sentences which I took down, on this occasion :

Slaps, tea.
Moozies, porridge.
Mass, flesh.
Shaucha, broth.
Mumlie, candle.
Stramel, straw.
Parnie, wheat.
Duff, smoke.
Yak, fire.
Wuther, door.
Glue, window.
Kair, house.
Shucha, coat.
Shuch-hamie, waistcoat.
Castie, stick.
Coories, blankets.
Eegees, bed-clothes.
Wautheriz, bed.
Suchira, sixpence.
Sye-boord, sixpence.
Chinda, shilling.
Chinda ochindies, twelve shillings.
Trin chindies, three shillings.
Baurie, grand, great, good.
Shan, bad.
Davies-pagrin, daybreak.
Baurie davies, good day.
Shan davies, bad day.
Paunie davies, wet day.
Sheelra davies, frosty or cold day.
Sneepa davies, snowy or white day.
Baurie forest, the chief city.
Baurie paunie, the sea, ocean, grand water.
Bing, the devil.
Ruffie, the devil.
Feck, take.
Chauvies wautheriz, the children's bed-clothes.
Sherro, head.
Carlie, neck.
Lears, ears.
Chatters, teeth,
Yak, eye.
Nak, nose.
Mooie, mouth.
Vast, hand.
Jaur, leg.
Nek, knee.
Peerie, foot.
Bar, stone.
Drom, the earth.
Cang-geerie, church.
Sonnakie, gold.
Sonnakie vanister, gold ring.
Callo, black.
Callo gaugie, black man.
Leehgh callo, blue.
Sneepa, white, snow.
Sheelra, cold, frost.
Lon, salt.
Lon paunie, the sea, salt water.
Rat, night.
Rat, blood.
Habben kairer, baker of bread.
Aizel, ass.
Gournie, cow.
Jucal, dog.
Paupeenie, goose.
Caunie, hen.
Boord, penny.
Curdie, half-penny.
Lee, miss.
Ruffie feck ma, devil take me.
Ruffie lee ma, devil miss me.
Feck a bar and mar the gaugie, lift a stone and fell the man.
Chee, chee, silence, hold your tongue.
Aurie, come here.
Jaw vree, go away.

Jaw wree wautheris, go away to your bed.
Baish doun, sit down.
Baish doun bettiment, sit down on the chair.
Howie been baishen? how are you?
Riah, gentleman.
Raunie, gentlewoman.
Baurie riah, king.
Baurie raunie, queen.
Praw, son.
Prawl, daughter.
Yaggers, colliers.
Nawken, Tinkler, Gipsy.
Cam, the moon.
Quad, prison.
Staurdie, prison.
Yaik, one.
Duie, two.
Trin, three.
Tor, four.
Fo, five.
Shaigh, six.
Naivairn, seven.
Naigh, eight.
Line, nine.
Nay, ten.

This young man sang part of two Gipsy songs to me, in English; and then, at my request, he turned one of them into the Gipsy language, intermingled a little, however, with English words; occasioned, perhaps, by the difficulty in translating it. The subject of one of the songs was that of celebrating a robbery, committed upon a Lord Shandos; and the subject of the other was a description of a Gipsy battle. The courage with which the females stood the rattle of the cudgels upon their heads was much lauded in the song. Like the Gipsy woman with whom I had no less than seven years' trouble ere getting any of her speech, this Gipsy lad became, in about an hour's time, very restless, and impatient to be gone. The true state of things, in this instance, dawned upon his mind. He now became much alarmed, and would neither allow me to write down his songs, nor stop to give me any more of his words and sentences. His terror was only exceeded by his mortification; and, on parting with me, he said that, had he, at first, been aware I was unacquainted with his speech, he would not have given me a word of it.

As far as I can judge, from the few and short specimens which I have myself heard, and had reported to me, the subjects of the songs of the Scottish Gipsies, (I mean those composed by themselves,) are chiefly their plunderings, their robberies, and their sufferings. The numerous and deadly conflicts which they had among themselves, also, afforded them themes for the exercise of their muse. My father, in his youth, often heard them singing songs, wholly in their own language. They appear to have been very fond of our ancient Border marauding songs, which celebrate the daring exploits of the lawless freebooters on the frontiers of Scotland and England. They were constantly singing these compositions among themselves. The song composed on Hughie Græme, the horse-stealer, published in the second volume of Sir Walter Scott's Border Minstrelsy, was a great favourite with the Tinklers. As this song is completely to the taste of a Gipsy, I will insert it in this place, as affording a good specimen of that description of song in the singing of which they take great delight. It will also serve to show the peculiar cast of mind of the Gipsies.

HUGHIE THE GRÆME.

Gude Lord Scroope's to the hunting gane,
He has ridden o'er moss and muir;
And he has grippit Hughie the Græme,
For stealing o' the Bishop's mare.

"Now, good Lord Scroope, this may not be!
Here hangs a broadsword by my side;
And if that thou canst conquer me,
The matter it may soon be tryed."

"I ne'er was afraid of a traitor-thief;
Although thy name be Hughie the Græme,
I'll make thee repent thee of thy deeds,
If God but grant me life and time."

"Then do your worst now, good Lord Scroope,
And deal your blows as hard as you can!
It shall be tried, within an hour,
Which of us two is the better man."

But as they were dealing their blows so free,
And both so bloody at the time,
Over the moss came ten yeomen so tall,
All for to take brave Hughie the Græme.

Then they hae grippit Hughie the Græme,
And brought him up through Carlisle town;
The lasses and lads stood on the walls,
Crying, "Hughie the Græme, thou'se ne'er gae down."

Then hae they chosen a jury of men,
The best that were in Carlisle town;
And twelve of them cried out at once,
"Hughie the Græme, thou must gae down."

Then up bespak him gude Lord Hume,
As he sat by the judge's knee,—
"Twenty white owsen, my gude lord,
If you'll grant Hughie the Græme to me."

"O no, O no, my gude Lord Hume!
For sooth and sae it manna be;
For, were there but three Græmes of the name,
They suld be hanged a' for me."

'Twas up and spake the gude Lady Hume,
As she sat by the judge's knee,—
"A peck of white pennies, my gude lord judge,
If you'll grant Hughie the Græme to me."

"O no, O no, my gude Lady Hume!
For sooth and so it must na be;
Were he but the one Græme of the name,
He suld be hanged high for me."

"If I be guilty," said Hughie the Græme,
"Of me my friends shall have small talk;"
And he has louped fifteen feet and three,
Though his hands they were tied behind his back.

He looked over his left shoulder,
And for to see what he might see;
There was he aware of his auld father,
Came tearing his hair most piteouslie.

"O! hald your tongue, my father," he says,
"And see that ye dinna weep for me!
For they may ravish me o' my life,
But they canna banish me fro Heavin hie.

"Fare ye weel, fair Maggie, my wife!
The last time we came ower the muir,
'Twas thou bereft me of my life,
And wi' the Bishop thou play'd the whore.

"Here, Johnie Armstrang, take thou my sword,
That is made o' the metal sae fine;
And when thou comest to the English side,
Remember the death of Hughie the Græme."*

* On mentioning to Sir Walter Scott, when at Abbotsford, that the Gipsies were very partial to Hughie the Græme, he caused his oldest daughter, afterwards Mrs. Lockhart, to sing this ancient Border song, which she readily did, accompanying her voice with the harp. We were, at the time, in the room which contained his old armour and other antiquities; to which place he had asked me, after tea, to hear his daughter play on the harp.

I will now give the testimony of the Gipsy chief from whom I received the "blowing up" alluded to, by Mr. Laidlaw, in the Introduction to the work.*

One of the greatest fairs in Scotland is held, annually, on the 18th day of July, at St. Boswell's Green, in Roxburghshire. I paid a visit to this fair, for the purpose of taking a view of the Gipsies. An acquaintance, whom I met at the fair, observed to me, that he was sure if any one could give me information regarding the Tinklers, it would be old ——, the horner, at ——. To ensure a kind reception from the Gipsies, it was agreed upon, between us, that I should introduce myself by mentioning who my ancestors were, on whose numerous farms, (sixteen, rented by my grandfather, in 1781,†) their forefathers had received many a night's quarters, in their out-houses. We soon found out the old chieftain, sitting in a tent, in the midst of about a dozen of his tribe, all nearly related to him. The moment I made myself known to them, the whole of the old persons immediately expressed their gratitude for the humane treatment they, and their forefathers, had received at the farms of my relatives. They were extremely glad to see me; and "God bless you," was repeated by several of the old females. "Ay," said they, "those days are gone. Christian charity has now left the land. We know the people are growing more hard and uncharitable every year." I found the old man shrewd, sensible, and intelligent; far beyond what could have been expected from a person of his caste and station in life. He, besides, possessed all that merriness and jocularity which I

She sang Hughie the Græme, in a plain, simple, unaffected manner, exactly in the style in which I have heard the humble country-girls singing the same song, in the south of Scotland. Sir Walter was much interested about the Gipsies; and when I repeated to him a short sentence in their speech, he, with great feeling, exclaimed, "Poor things! do you hear that?" This was the first time, I believe, that he ever heard a Scottish Gipsy word pronounced. It appeared to me that the mind of the great magician was not wholly divested of the fear that the Gipsies might, in some way or other, injure his young plantations.

* See pages 58 and 65.—Ed.

† These sixteen farms embraced about 25,000 acres of mountainous land, and maintained 13,000 sheep, 100 goats, 250 cattle, 50 horses, 20 draught-oxen, and 60 dogs; 29 shepherds, 28 other servants, and 15 cotters, making, with their families, 228 souls, supported by my ancestor's property, as that of a Scotch gentleman-farmer. On the farms mentioned, which lay in Mid-Lothian, Tweed-dale, and Selkirkshire, the Gipsies were allowed to remain as long as they pleased; and no loss was ever sustained by the indulgence.

have often observed among a number of the males of his race. After some conversation with this chief, who appeared about eighty years of age, I enquired if his people, who, in large bands, about sixty years ago, traversed the south of Scotland, had not an ancient language, peculiar to themselves. He hesitated a little, and then readily replied, that the Tinklers had no language of their own, except a few cant words. I observed to him that he knew better—that the Tinklers had, beyond dispute, a language of their own; and that I had some knowledge of its existence at the present day. He, however, declared that they had no such language, and that I was wrongly informed. In the hearing of all the Gipsies in the tent, I repeated to him four or five Gipsy words and expressions. At this he appeared amazed; and on my adding some particulars relative to some of the ancestors of the tribe then present, enumerating, I think, three generations of their clan, one of the old females exclaimed, "Preserve me, he kens a' about us!" The old chief immediately took hold of my right hand, below the table, with a grasp as if he were going to shake it; and, in a low and subdued tone of voice, so as none might hear but myself, requested me to say not another word in the place where we were sitting, but to call on him, at the town of ——, and he would converse with me on that subject. I considered it imprudent to put any more questions to him relative to his speech, on this occasion, and agreed to meet him at the place he appointed.

Several persons in the tent, (it being one of the public booths in the market,) who were not Gipsies, were equally surprised, when they observed an understanding immediately take place between me and the Tinklers, by means of a few words, the meaning of which they could not comprehend. A farmer, from the south of Scotland, who was present in the tent, and had that morning given the Tinklers a lamb to eat, met me, some days after, on the banks of the Yarrow. He shook his head, and observed, with a smile, "Yon was queer-looking wark wi' the Tinklers."

As I was anxious to penetrate to his secret speech, I resolved to keep the appointment with the Gipsy, whatever might be the result of our meeting, and I therefore proceeded to the town which he mentioned, eleven days after I had seen him at the fair. On enquiring of the landlord of the principal inn, at which I put up my horse, where the house of ——, the Tinkler, was situated in the town, he appeared surprised, and eyed me all over. He told me the street, but said he would not accompany me to the house, thinking that I wished him to go with me. It was evident that the landlord, whom I never saw before, considered himself in bad company, in spite of my black clothes, black neck-cloth, and ruffles aforesaid, and was determined not to be seen on the street, either with me or the Tinkler. I told him I by no means wished him to accompany me, but only to tell me in what part of the town the Tinkler's house was to be found.

On entering the house, I found the old chief sitting, without his coat, with an old night-cap on his head, a leathern apron around his waist, and all covered with dust or soot, employed in making spoons from horn. After conversing with him for a short time, I reminded him of the ancient language with which he was acquainted. He assumed a grave countenance, and said the Tinklers had no such language, adding, at the same time, that I should not trouble myself about such matters. He stoutly denied all knowledge of the Tinkler language, and said no such tongue existed in Scotland, except a few cant words. I persisted in asserting that they were actually in possession of a secret language, and again tried him with a few of my words; but to no purpose. All my efforts produced no effect upon his obstinacy. At this stage of my interview, I durst not mention the word Gipsy, as they are exceedingly alarmed at being known as Gipsies. I now signified that he had forfeited his promise, given me at the fair, and rose to leave him. At this remark, I heard a man burst out a-laughing, behind a partition that ran across the apartment in which we were sitting. The old man likewise started to his feet, and, with both his sooty hands, took hold of the breast of my coat, on either side, and, in this attitude, examined me closely, scanning me all over from head to foot. After satisfying himself, he said, "Now, give me a hold of your hand—farewell—I will know you when I see you again." I bade him good-day, and left the house.*

* I am convinced the Gipsies have a method of communicating with one another by their hands and fingers, and it is likely this man tried me, in that way, both at the fair and in his own house. I know a man who has seen the Gipsies communicating their thoughts to each other in this way.

" Bargains among the Indians are conducted in the most profound silence,

I had now no hope of obtaining any information from this man, regarding his peculiar language. I had scarcely, however, proceeded a hundred yards down the street, from the house, when I was overtaken by a young female, who requested me to return, to speak with her father. I immediately complied. On reaching the door, with the girl, we met one of the old man's sons, who said that he had overheard what passed between his father and me, in the house. He assured me that his father *was ashamed to give me his language;* but that, if I would promise not to publish their names, or place of residence, he would himself give me some of their speech, if his father still persevered in his refusal. I accordingly agreed not to make public the names, and place of residence, of the family. I again entered the little factory of horn spoons. Matters were now, to all appearance, quite changed. The old man was very cheerful, and seemed full of mirth. "Come away," said he; "what is this you are asking after? I would advise you to go to Mr. Stewart, at Hawick, and he will tell you everything about our language." "Father," said the son, who had resumed his place behind the partition before mentioned, "you know that Mr. Stewart will give our speech to nobody." The old chief again hesitated and considered, but, being urged by his son and myself, he, at last, said, "Come away, then; I will tell you whatever you think proper to ask me. I gave you my oath, at the fair, to do so. Get out your paper, pen and ink, and begin." He gave me no other oath, at the fair, than his

and by merely touching each other's hands. If the seller takes the whole hand, it implies a thousand rupees or pagodas; five fingers import five hundred; one finger, one hundred; half a finger, fifty; a single joint only ten. In this manner, they will often, in a crowded room, conclude the most important transactions, without the company suspecting that anything whatever was doing."—*Historical Account of Travels in Asia, by Hugh Murray.*

"*Method of the English selling their cargoes, at Jedda, to the Turks:* Two Indian brokers come into the room to settle the price, one on the part of the Indian captain, the other on that of the buyer or Turk. They are neither Mahommedans nor Christians, but have credit with both. They sit down on the carpet, and take an Indian shawl, which they carry on their shoulders like a napkin, and spread it over their hands. They talk, in the meantime, indifferent conversation, of the arrival of ships from India, or of the news of the day, as if they were employed in no serious business whatever. After about twenty minutes spent in handling each other's fingers, below the shawl, the bargain is concluded, say for nine ships, without one word ever having been spoken on the subject, or pen or ink used in any shape whatever."—*Bruce's Travels.*

doing any manner of favour to the said Egyptians, at any time after the said first day of August next to come, for now and ever."* In a subsequent enactment, in 1617, appointing justices of the peace and constables, the destruction of the proscribed Egyptians is particularly enjoined, in defining the different duties of the magistrates and their peace officers.†

But so little respected was the authority of the government, that in 1612, three years after the passing of the Gipsy act, his majesty was under the humiliating necessity of entering into a contract with the clan Scott, and their friends, by which the clan bound themselves "to give up all bands of friendship, kindness, oversight, maintenance or assurance, if any we have, with common thieves and broken clans, &c." It is certain there would be many bonds of the same nature with other turbulent clans throughout the kingdom. That Scotchmen of respectability and influence protected the Gipsies, and afforded them shelter on their lands, after the promulgation of the cruel statute of 1609, is manifest from the following passages, which I extract from Blackwood's Magazine, for 1817; the conductor of which seems to have been careful in examining the public records for the documents quoted by him; having been guided in his researches, I believe, by Sir Walter Scott.

"In February, 1615, we find a remission under the privy seal, granted to William Auchterlony, of Cayrine, for resetting of John Faw and his followers.‡ On the 14th July, 1616, the sheriff of Forfar is severely reprimanded for delaying to execute some Gipsies, who had been taken within his jurisdiction, and for troubling the council with petitions in their behalf. In November following appears a proclamation against Egyptians and their resetters. In December, 1619, we find another proclamation against resetters of them;

* Glendook's Scots Act. † Ib.

‡ The nature of this crime in Scotch law is fully explained in the following extract from the original, which also appears curious in other respects. The pardon is granted "pro receptione, supportatione, et detentione supra terra suas de Belmadie, et infra eius habitationis domum, aliaq. edificia eiusdem, *Joannis Fall, Ethiopis, lie Egiptian*, eiusq. uxoris, puerorum, servorum et associatorum; Necnon pro ministrando ipsis cibum, potum, pecunias, hospicium, aliaq. necessaria, quocunq. tempore vel occasione preterita, contra acta nostri Parliamenti vel secreti concilii, vel contra quecunq. leges, alia acta, aut constitutiones huius nostri regni Scotiæ in contrarium facta. Regist. secreti sigilli vol. lxxxiii, fol. 291, *Blackwood's Magazine*.—Ed.

in April, 1620, another proclamation of the same kind, and in July, 1620, a commission against resetters, all with very severe penalties. The nature of these acts will be better understood from the following extract from that of the 4th July, 1616, which also very well explains the way in which the Gipsies contrived to maintain their footing in the country, in defiance of all the efforts of the legislature to extirpate them." "It is of truth that the thieves and *limmers* (scoundrels), aforesaid, having for some short space after the said act of parliament, (1609,) . . . dispersed themselves in certain secret and obscure places of the country. . they were not known to wander abroad in troops and companies, according to their accustomed manner, yet, shortly thereafter, finding that the said act of parliament was neglected, and that no enquiry nor . . . was made for them, they began to take new breath and courage, and . . unite themselves in infamous companies and societies, under . . . . commanders, and continually since then have remained within the country, committing as well open and avowed *rieffis* (robberies) in all parts . . . . murders, . . . *pleine stouthe* (common theft,) and pickery, where they may not be mastered; and they do shamefully and mischievously abuse the simple and ignorant people, by telling fortunes, and using charms, and a number of juggling tricks and falseties, unworthy to be heard of in a country subject to religion, law, and justice; and they are encouraged to remain within the country, and to continue in their thievish and juggling tricks and falseties, not only through default of the execution of the said act of parliament, but, what is worse, that great numbers of his majesty's subjects, of whom some outwardly pretend to be famous and unspotted gentlemen, have given and give open and avowed protection, reset, supply and maintainance, upon their grounds and lands, to the said vagabonds, *sorners*, (forcible obtruders,) and condemned thieves and *limmers*, (scoundrels,) and suffer them to remain days, weeks, and months together thereupon, without controulment, and with connivance and oversight, &c." "So they do leave a foul, infamous, and ignominious spot upon them, their houses, and posterity, that they are patrons to thieves and *limmers*, (scoundrels,) &c.*

* The same state of things existed in Spain. Charles II, passed a law on the 12th June, 1695, the 16th article of which, as given by Mr. Borrow,

From their first arrival in the country till 1579, the Gipsies, as already mentioned, appear to have been treated as a separate people, observing their own laws and customs. In the year 1587, such was the state of society in Scotland, that laws were passed by James VI, compelling all the baronial proprietors of lands, chiefs and captains of clans, on the Borders and Highlands of Scotland, to find pledges and securities for the peaceable conduct of their retainers, tenants, clansmen, and other inhabitants of their respective estates and districts.* In the same parliament another act was passed, allowing vagabonds and broken and unpledged men to produce pledges and securities for their good conduct. The Gipsies, under these statutes, would remain unmolested, as they would readily find protection by becoming, nominally, clansmen, and assuming the surnames, of those chieftains and noblemen who were willing and able to afford them protection.† Indeed, the act allowing vagabonds to find sureties would include the Gipsy bands, for, about this

enacts: "And because we understand that the continuance of those who are called Gitanos has depended on the favour, protection, and assistance which they have experienced from persons of *different stations*, we do ordain that whosoever against whom shall be proved the fact of having, since the day of the publication hereof, favoured, received, or assisted the said Gitanos, in any manner whatever, whether *within their houses* or without, *provided he is a noble*, shall be subjected to the fine of *six thousand ducats*, ... and *if a plebeian*, to a *punishment of ten years in the galleys!* Such an enactment would surely prove that the Gipsies in Spain were *greatly* favoured by the Spanish people generally, even two centuries after they entered the country.

The causes to which may be attributed this toleration, even encouragement, of the Gipsies, are various. Among these may be mentioned a fear of consequences to person and property, tinkering, trafficking and amusement, and corruption on the part of those in power. But in the character of the Gipsies itself may be found a general cause for their escaping the effects of the laws passed against them, viz., *wheedling*. The term Gitano has been variously modified in the Spanish language, thus:

Gitano, *Gipsy, flatterer*; Gitanillo, *a little Gipsy*; Gitanismo, *the Gipsy tribe*; Gitanesco, *Gipsy-like*; Gitanear, *to flatter, entice*; Gitaneria, *wheedling, flattery*; Gitanamente, *in a sly, winning manner*; Gitanada, *blandishment, wheedling, flattery*.—Ed.

* There were 17 clans on the Borders, and 34 clans in the Highlands, who appear to have had chiefs and captains over them. There were 22 baronial proprietors connected with the Borders, and 108 connected with the Highlands, named in a roll, who were likewise ordered to find pledges. —*Glendook's Scots Acts.*

† It sometimes happened, when an internal quarrel took place in a clan, portions of the tribe left their chief, and united themselves to another, whose name they assumed, and dropped their original one.

period, they seem to have been only classed with our own native vagabonds, moss-troopers, Border and Highland thieves, broken clans and masterless men. It appears by the act of 1609, that the Gipsies had even purchased their protection from the government. The inhabitants of Scotland being at this period still divided into clans, would greatly facilitate the escape of the Gipsies from the laws passed against them. The clans on the Borders and Highlands were in a state of almost constant warfare with one another; and frequently several of the clans were united in opposition to the regular government of the country, to whose mandates they paid little or no regard. The Gipsies had no settled residence, but roamed from place to place over the whole country; and when they found themselves in danger in one place, they had no more to do but remove into the district inhabited by a hostile clan, where they would immediately find protection. Besides, the Borderers and Highlanders, themselves plunderers and thieves, would not be very active in apprehending their brother thieves, the Gipsies. Even, according to Holinshed, "the poison of theft and robbery pervaded almost all classes of the Scottish community about this period."

The excessive severity of the sanguinary statute of 1609, and the unrelenting manner in which it was often carried into effect, were calculated to produce a great outward change on the Scottish Gipsies. Like stags selected from a herd of deer, and doomed to be hunted down by dogs, these wanderers were now singled out, and separated from the community, as objects to whom no mercy was to be shown.* The word Egyptian would never be allowed to escape their lips; not a syllable of their peculiar speech would be uttered, unless in the midst of their own tribe. It is also highly probable that every part of their dress by which their fraternity could be recognized, would be carefully discontinued. To deceive the public, they would also conform *externally* to some of the religious rites, ceremonies, observances, and

* The reader will see that the Gipsies, at this time, were not greater "vagabonds" than great numbers of native Scotch, if as great. But, being strangers in the country, sojourners according to their own accounts, the king would naturally enough banish them, as they seem always to have been saying that they were about leaving for "their own country." Their living in tents, a mode of life so different from that of the natives, would, of itself, make them obnoxious to the king personally.—Ed.

other customs of the natives of Scotland. I am further inclined to think that it would be about this period, and chiefly in consequence of these bloody enactments, the Gipsies would, in general, assume the ordinary christian and surnames common at that time in Scotland. And their usual sagacity pointed out to them the advantages arising from taking the cognomens of the most powerful families in the kingdom, whose influence would afford them ample protection, as adopted members of their respective clans. In support of my opinion of the origin of the surnames of the Gipsies of the present day, we find that the most prevailing names among them are those of the most influential of our noble families of Scotland; such as Stewart, Gordon, Douglas, Graham, Ruthven, Hamilton, Drummond, Kennedy, Cunningham, Montgomery, Kerr, Campbell, Maxwell, Johnstone, Ogilvie, McDonald, Robertson, Grant, Baillie, Shaw, Burnet, Brown, Keith, &c.* If, even at the present day, you enquire at the Gipsies respecting their descent, the greater part of them will tell you that they are sprung from a bastard son of this or that noble family, or other person of rank and influence, of their own surname.† This pretended connexion with families of high rank and power has saved some of the tribe from the gallows even in our own time. The names, however, of the two principal families, Faw, (now Faa,) and Bailyow, (now Baillie,) appear not to have been changed since the date of the order in council or league with James V, in the year 1540, as both of these names are inserted in that document.

Baron Hume, on the criminal law of Scotland, gives the

* The English Gipsies say that native names were assumed by their race in consequence of the proscription to which it was subjected. German Gipsies, on arrival in America, change, at least modify, their names. There are many of them who go under the names of Smith, Miller, and Waggoner. Jews frequently bear names common to the natives of the countries in which they are to be found, and sometimes, at the present day, assume Christian ones. I knew two German Jews, of the name of Cohen, who settled in Scotland. One of them, who was a priest, retained the original name; but the other, who was a watchmaker, assumed the name of Cowan, which, singularly enough, the priest said, was a corruption of Cohen.—Ed.

† It is stated by Paget, in his Travels in Hungary, that the Gipsies in that country have a profound regard for aristocracy; and that they invariably follow that class in the matter of religious opinions. Grellmann says as much in regard to the Gipsy's desire of getting hold of a distinguished old coat to put on his person.—Ed.

following account of some of the trials and executions of the Gipsies:

"The statute (1609) annuls at the same time all protection and warrants purchased by the Egyptians from his majesty's privy council, for their remaining within the realm; as also all privileges purchased by any person to reset, entertain, or do them any favour. It appears, indeed, from a paper in the appendix to McLaurin's Cases, that even the king's servants and great officers had not kept their hands entirely pure of this sort of treaty with the Egyptian chiefs, from whom some supply of money might in this way be occasionally obtained.

"The first Gipsies that were brought to trial on the statute, were four persons of the name of Faa, who, on the 31st July, 1611, were sentenced to be hanged. They had pleaded upon a special license from the privy council, to abide within the country; but this appearing to be clogged with a condition of finding surety for their appearance when called on, and their surety being actually at the horn, for failure to present themselves, they were held to have infringed the terms of their protection.

"The next trial was on the 19th and 24th July, 1616, in the case of other two Faas and a Baillie, (which seem to have been noted names among the Gipsies;) and here was started that plea which has since been repeated in almost every case, but has always been overruled, viz: that the act and proclamation were temporary ordinances, and applicable only to such Egyptians as were in the country at their date. These pannels, upon conviction, were ordered by the privy council to find caution to the extent of 1,000 merks, to leave Scotland and never to return; and having failed to comply with this injunction, they were in consequence condemned to die.

"In January, 1624, follows a still more severe example; no fewer than eight men, among whom Captain John Faa and other five of the name of Faa, being convicted, were doomed to death on the statute. Some days after, there were brought to trial Helen Faa, relict of Captain Faa, Lucretia Faa, and other women to the number of eleven; all of whom were in like manner convicted, and condemned to be drowned! But, in the end, their doom was commuted for banishment, (under pain of death,) to them and all their race. The sentence was, however, executed on the male convicts; and it appears that the terror of their fate had been of material service; as, for the space of more than 50 years from that time, there is no trial of an Egyptian."

But notwithstanding this statement of Baron Hume, of the Gipsy trials having ceased for half a century, we find, twelve years after 1624, the date of the above trials, the following order of the privy council: "Anent some Egyptians. At Edinburgh, 10th November, 1636. Forasmuch as Sir Arthur Douglas of Quhittinghame having lately taken and apprehended some of the vagabond and counterfeit thieves and *limmers*, (scoundrels,) called the Egyptians, he presented and delivered them to the sheriff principal of the sheriffdom of Edinburgh, within the constabulary of Haddington, where they have remained this month or thereby: and whereas the keeping of them longer, within the said tolbooth, is troublesome and burdensome to the town of Haddington, and fosters the said thieves in an opinion of impunity, to the encouraging of the rest of that infamous *byke* (hive) of lawless *limmers* (scoundrels) to continue in their thievish trade: Therefore the lords of secret council ordain the sheriff of Haddington, or his deputies, to pronounce doom and sentence of death against so many of these counterfeit thieves as are men, and against so many of the women as want children; ordaining the men to be hanged, and the women to be drowned; and that such of the women as have children, to be scourged through the burgh of Haddington, and burned in the cheek; and ordain and command the provost and baillies of Haddington to cause this doom be executed upon the said persons accordingly."*

"Towards the end of that century," continues Baron Hume, "the nuisance seems to have again become troublesome. On the 13th of December, 1698, John Baillie and six men more of the same name, along with the wife of one of them, were indicted as Egyptians, and also for sundry special misdeeds; and being convicted, (all but the woman,) they were ordered for execution. But in this case it is to be remarked, that the court had so far departed from the rigour of the statute as not to sustain a relevancy on the habit and repute of being an Egyptian of itself, but only 'along with one or other of the facts of picking and little

* Blackwood's Magazine.

thieving;' thus requiring some proof of actual guilt in aid of the fame. In the next trial, which was that of William Baillie, June 26th, 1699, a still further indulgence was introduced; for the interlocutor required a proof, not of *one* only, but of *several*, of the facts of 'picking or little thieving, or of several acts of beating and striking with invasive weapons.' He was only convicted as an Egyptian, and of *one* act of striking with an invasive weapon, and he escaped in consequence with his life.

"This lenient course of dealing with the Gipsies was not taken, however, from any opinion of it as a necessary thing, nor was there any purpose of prescribing it as a rule for other times, or for further cases of the kind where such an indulgence might seem improper, as appears from the interlocutor of relevancy in the case of John Kerr, and Helen Yorkston, and William Baillie and other seven; in both of which the simple fame and character of being an Egyptian is again found *separatum* relevant to infer the pain of death, (10th and 11th August, 1714.) Kerr and Yorkston had a verdict in their favour; Baillie and two of his associates were condemned to die; but as far as concerns Baillie, (for the others were executed,) his doom was afterwards mitigated into transportation, under pain of death in case of return.

"As early as the month of August, 1715, the same man, (as I understand it,) was again indicted, not only for being found in Britain, but for continuing his former practices and course of life. Notwithstanding this aggravation, the interlocutor is again framed on the indulgent plan, and only infers the pain of death, from the fame and character of being an Egyptian, joined with various acts of violence and sorning, to the number of three, that are stated in the libel. Though convicted nearly to the extent of the interlocutor, he again escaped with transportation.*

"Nor have I observed that the court, in any later case, have thought it necessary to proceed upon the repute alone, unavouched by evidence of, at least, one act of theft or violence; so that, upon the whole, according to the practice of later times, this sort of charge seems to be reduced nearly to the level of the charge of being habit and repute a thief at common law."

* This, and part of the preceding paragraph, will be quoted again, under the chapter of Tweed-dale and Clydesdale Gipsies.

The surprised thimble-men were instantly silent. They spoke not a word, but looked at one another. Only, one of them whispered to his companions, "He is not to be meddled with." They immediately took up their board, thimbles and all, and left the place, apparently in considerable alarm, some taking one direction and some another. The female in question was also surprised at seeing their insolent conduct repressed, in a moment, by a single expression. "But, sir," said she, "what was that you said to them, for they seem afraid?" I was myself afraid to say another word to them, and took care they did not see me go to my dwelling-house.*

One of the favourite, and permanent, fields of operation of these thimblers is on the Queensferry road, from where it is

chee" was, in Hindostanee, an expression of reproof, corresponding exactly with our "Fie, shame!" "Oh fie, shame!"

* About four years after this occurrence, I was invited to dine at the house of a friend, with whose wife I was not acquainted. On being introduced to her, I was rather surprised at the repeated hard looks which she took at me. At last she said, "I think I have seen you before. Were you never engaged with a band of thimble-men, near Newhaven?" I said I was, some years ago. "Do you recollect," continued she, "of a female taking you by the arm, and urging you to leave them?" I said, "Perfectly." "Well, then, I am the female; and I yet recollect your words were *Chee, chee.*" She mentioned the circumstance to her husband at the time; but he always said to her that I must have been only one of the blackguards themselves, deceiving her. He would not listen to her when she described me as not at all like a thimble-rigger, but always answered her, "I tell ye, woman, the man you spoke to was nothing but one of these villains."

The thimble-riggers who molested Mr. Rose, ship-builder, so much, also answered my Gipsy words distinctly; and, ever afterwards, took off their hats to me, as I passed them playing at their game.

[The thimble-men here alluded to took up their quarters immediately to the west of Leith Fort, where the road takes a turn, at a right angle, a little in front of Mr. Rose's house, and there takes a similar turn towards the west: the best position for carrying on the thimble game. So exasperated was this gentleman, when, by every means in his power, he failed to dislodge them, that he sent some of the men from his yard, to erect, on the spot, a pole, which he covered with sheet-iron, to prevent its being cut down; and placed on the top of it a board, having this upon it, "Beware of thimble-riggers and chain-droppers," with a hand pointing directly below. This had no effect, however, for the "knights of the thimble" pursued their game right under it. A gentleman, in passing one day, directed their attention to the board, but the only reply he got was, "Hah! that's nothing. Where can you find a shop without a sign? and where 's the other person that gets a sign from the public for nothing?"

Thimble-rigging is peculiarly a Gipsy game. In Great Britain, the Gipsies nearly monopolize it; and it would be singular if some of the American thimblers were not Gipsies.—ED.]

intersected by the street leading from the back of Leith Fort, on the east, to the new road leading from Granton pier, on the west. This part of the Queensferry road is intersected by about half-a-dozen cross-roads, all leading from the landing and shipping places at the piers of Granton, Trinity, and Newhaven. These cross-roads are cut by three roads running nearly parallel to each other, viz., the road along the sea-beach, Trinity road, and the Queensferry road. A great portion of the passengers, by the many steamboats, pass along all these different roads, to and from Edinburgh. On all of these roads, between the water of Leith and the Forth, the thimble-riggers station themselves, as single individuals, or in numbers, as it may answer their purpose. In fact, this part of the country between the sea and Edinburgh, is so much chequered by roads crossing each other, that it may be compared to the meshes of a spider's web, and the thimblers as so many spiders, watching to pounce upon their prey. The moment one of these sentinels observes a stranger appear, signals are made to his confederates, when their organized plan of operations for entrapping the unwary person is immediately put in execution. Strangers, unacquainted with the locality, are greatly bewildered among all the cross-roads mentioned, and have considerable difficulty in threading their way to the city. One of the gang will then step forward, and, pretending to be a stranger himself, will enquire of the others the road to such and such a place. Frequently the unsuspecting and bewildered individual will enquire of the thimbler for some street or place in Edinburgh. The decoy and the victim now walk in company, and converse familiarly together on various topics; the thimbler offers snuff to his friend, and makes himself as agreeable as he can; while one of the gang, at a distance in front, drops a watch, chain, or other piece of mock jewelry, or commences playing at the thimble-board. The decoy is sure to lead his dupe exactly to the spot where the trap is laid, and where he will probably be plundered. One of these entrapments terminated in the death of its subject. A working man, having risked his half-year's wages at the thimble-board, of course lost every farthing of the money; and took the loss so much to heart as, in a fit of despondency, to drown himself in the water of Leith.

In the beginning of 1842, I fell in with six of these thimble-riggers and chain-droppers, on Newhaven road, on their way to Edinburgh. I was anxious to discover the nature of their conversation, and kept as close to them as I could, without exciting their suspicion. Like that of most people brought up in one particular line of life, their conversation related wholly to their own trade—that of swindling, theft, and robbery. I overheard them speaking of "bloody swells," and of dividing their booty. One of them was desired by the others to look after a certain steamboat, expected to arrive, and to get a bill to ascertain its movements exactly. He said he would "require three men to take care of that boat"; meaning, as I understood him, that all these men were necessary for laying his snares, and executing his designs upon the unsuspecting passengers, as they landed from the vessel, and were on their way to their destinations. The manager of the steamboat company could not have consulted with his subordinates, about their lawful affairs, with more care and deliberation, or in a more cool, business-like way, than were these villains in contriving plans for plundering the public. On their approach to Pilrig street, the band separated into pairs; some taking the north, and some the south, side of Leith walk, for Edinburgh, where they vanished in the crowd. Their language was fearful, every expression being accompanied by a terrible oath.

On another occasion, I fell in with another band of these vagabond thimble-men, on the Dalkeith road, near Craigmiller Castle. I asked the fellow with the thimbles, "Is that *gaugie a nawken?*" pointing to one of the gang who had just left him. The question, in plain English, was, "Is that man a Gipsy?" The thimbler flew at once into a great passion, and bawled out, "Ask himself, sir." He then fell upon me, and a gentleman who was with me, in most abusive language, applying to us the most insulting epithets he could think of. It was evident to my friend that the thimble-man perfectly understood my Gipsy question. So enraged was he, that we were afraid he would follow us, and do us some harm. My friend did not consider himself safe till he was in the middle of Edinburgh, for many a look did he cast behind him, to see whether the Gipsy was not in pursuit of us.*

* There is a Gipsy belonging to one of these bands, known by the sobriquet of the "winged duck," from having lost an arm, of whom I have

The Gipsies in Scotland consider themselves to be of the same stock as those in England and Ireland, for they are all acquainted with the same speech. They afford assistance to one another, whenever they happen to meet. The following

often heard our author speak. He is what may be called the captain of the company. A description of him, and his way of life, may be interesting, inasmuch as it illustrates a class of Scottish Gipsies at the present day.

About the year 1853, three young gentlemen, from the town of Leith, had occasion to take a stroll over Arthur's Seat, a hill that overhangs Edinburgh, on the east side of the city. In climbing the hill, they observed, a little way before them, a man toiling up the ascent, whom they did not notice till they came close upon him, and who had evidently been laying off on the side of the path, and entered it as they approached it. He appears about sixty years of age, is well dressed, and carries a fine cane, which he keeps pressing into the ground, to help him up the hill. Just as they make up to him, he abruptly stops, and turns round, so as almost to touch them. "Hech, how! I'm blown, I'm blown; I'm fairly done up. Young gentlemen, you have the advantage of me; I'm getting old, and it is hard for me to climb the hill." (Blown, done up, indeed! The fellow has stamina enough to outclimb any of them for years yet.) An agreeable conversation ensues, such as at once gains for him the confidence of the youths. He appears to them so mild, so bland, so fatherly, so worthy of respect, in short, a "nice old cove," who is evidently enjoying his *otium cum dignitate* in his old age, in some cottage near by, upon a pension, an annuity, or a moderate competency of some sort. During the conversation, he manages to ascertain that his young friends have not been on the hill for some time—that one of them, indeed, has never been there before. All at once he exclaims, "Ah! what can this be? Let us go and see." Upon which they step forward to look at a person like a mechanic playing at the thimbles. Placing his arm around the neck of one of the young men, he begins to moralize: "Pray, young gentlemen, don't bet, (they had not shown the least symptoms of doing that;) it's wrong to bet; it's a thing I never do; I would advise you not to do it. This is a rascally thimbler; he'll cheat, he'll rob you." At this time there are three playing at the board, winning and losing money rapidly. The "old cove" becomes impatient to be gone, and motions so as to imply, "Boys, let us go, let us go." Moving a few steps forward, he halts to admire the scenery, (but casts a leering eye in the direction of the board.) "Ah! there's another goose gone to be plucked; let us see what luck he meets with."

Now thimble-rigging is the game, of all others, by which the uninitiated can be duped. They see the pea put under one of the thimbles, (nutshells they are, indeed;) there seems to be no doubt of that. The thimbles are then so gently moved, that any one can follow them. The pea is not afterwards tampered with—that is evident. All, then, that remains to be done, is to lift the thimble under which the pea is, and secure your prize. But the thimble-man, with his long nail, and nimble finger, has secured the pea under his nail, or, with the crook of his little finger, thrust it into the palm of his hand, while he pretended to cover it with the thimble. An accomplice, to make doubly sure of the pea being under the thimble, lifts it, and shows a pea, which he, by sleight of hand, drops, and, while pretending to cover it, as nimbly takes it up again.

facts will at least show that the Scottish and Irish Gipsies are one and the same people.

In the county of Fife, I once fell in with an Irish family, to appearance in great poverty and distress, resting themselves on the side of the public road. A shelty

Betting and playing go on as before. The player makes some fine hauls,[1] but loses a game. He swears that foul play has been used. An altercation follows. The man at the board gets excited, and to show that he really is honourable in his playing, exclaims, "Well, sir, there's your money again; try another game if you have a mind." "Now that is really honest, and no mistake about it," remarks the "old cove." Then the thimbler averts his head, to speak to a person behind him, and the "old cove" slyly lifts a thimble and shows the pea, and whispers very confidentially to his friends, "Now, young gentlemen, you can safely bet a few shillings on that." They shake their heads, however, for they know too much about thimbling. The "old cove" now gets fidgetty, and, managing to edge a little away from the board, commences, in a subdued tone, to speak, in a strange gibberish, to another bystander; but, forgetting himself, drops a word rather louder than the others, on which, as he turns round and catches the eyes of his young friends, he coughs and hems. On hearing the gibberish, a fear steals over the young men, on finding themselves surrounded by a band of desperadoes, in so solitary a place, and they make haste to be off. But the "old cove," to quiet their suspicions, accompanies them to a convenient spot, where he leaves them, to go to his home, by a side-path that soon leads him out of sight. On separating, he looks around him at the scenery, now lets fall his stick, now picks up something, that he may, with less suspicion, watch the movements of his escaped victims. They feel a singular relief in getting rid of his company, and, with tact, dog him over the hill, till they see him go back to the thimblers. They then think over their adventure, and the strange jargon they have heard, and unanimously exclaim, "Wasn't he a slippery old serpent, after all!"

On this occasion, there were no less than fourteen of these fellows present, some of them stationed here, some there, while they kept artfully moving around and about the hill, so as not to appear connected, but frequently approached the board, to contribute to and watch their luck. They personated various characters. One of them played the country lout, whose dress, gait, gape, and stare were inimitable. On the slightest symptom of danger manifesting itself, they would, by the movement of a hat, scatter, and vanish in an instant.

Among the people generally, a mystery attaches to these and other thimble-men. No one seems to know any thing about them—who they are or where they come from—and yet they are seen flitting everywhere through the country; but hardly ever two days together in one dress. But the mystery is solved by their being Gipsies. They are dangerous fellows to meddle with; yet they seem to prefer thimbling, chain-dropping, card-playing, pocket-picking, in fairs and thoroughfares, and pigeon-plucking in every form, to robbery on the high-way, after the manner of their ancestors.

Thimble-rigging, according to Sir J. Gardner Wilkinson, was practised in ancient Egypt. He calls it "thimble-rig, or the game of cups, under which a ball was put, while the opposite party guessed under which of four it was concealed."—Ed.

and an ass were grazing hard by. The ass they used in carrying a woman, who, they said, was a hundred and one years of age. She was shrunk and withered to a skeleton, or rather, I should say, to a bundle of bones; and her chin almost rested on her knees, and her body was nearly doubled by age. On interrogating the head of the family, I found that his name was Hugh White, and that he was an Irishman, and a son of the old woman who was with him. I put some Gipsy words to him, to ascertain whether or not he was one of the tribe. He pretended not to understand what I said; but his daughter, of about six years of age, replied, "But I understand what he says." I then called out sharply to him, "*Jaw vree*"—("Go away," or "get out of the way.") "As soon as I can," was his answer. On leaving him, I again called, "*Beenship-davies*"—("Good-day.") "Good-day, sir; God bless you," was his immediate reply.

I happened, at another time, to be in the court-house of one of the burghs north of the Forth, when two Irishmen, of the names of O'Reilly and McEwan, were at the bar for having been found drunk, and fighting within the town. They were sentenced by the magistrates to three days' imprisonment, and to be "banished the town," for their riotous conduct. The men had the Irish accent, and had certainly been born and brought up in Ireland; but their habiliments and general appearance did not correspond exactly with the ordinary dress and manners of common Irish peasants, although their features were in all respects Hibernian. When the magistrates questioned them in respect to their conduct, the prisoners looked very grave, and said, "Sure, and it plase your honours, our quarrel was nothing but whiskey, and sure we are the best friends in the world;" and seemed very penitent. But when the magistrates were not looking at them, they were smiling to each other, and keeping up a communication in pantomime. Suspecting them to be Irish Gipsies, I addressed the wife of McEwan as follows: "For what is the *riah* (magistrate) going to put your *gaugie* (man) in *staurdie*, (prison)?" "Only for a little whiskey, sir," was her immediate reply. She gave me, on the spot, the English of the following words; adding, at the same time, that I had got the *Gipsy* language, but that her's was only the *English cant*. She was afraid to acknowledge that she was a Gipsy, as such a confession might, in her opinion, have proved prejudicial to her husband, in the situation in which he was placed.

Gaugie, man.	*Yaka*, eyes.
Managie, woman.	*Grye*, horse.
Chauvies, children.	*Roys*, spoons.
Riah, magistrate.	*Skews*, platters.
Chor, thief.	*Mashlam*, metal.

I observed the woman instantly communicate to her husband the conversation she had with me. She immediately returned to me, and, after questioning me as to my name, occupation, and place of residence, very earnestly entreated me to save her *gaugie* from the *staurdie*. I asked her, how many *chauvies* she had? "Twelve, sir." Were any of them *chors?* "None, sir." Two of her *chauvies* were in her hand, weeping bitterly. The woman was in great distress, and when she heard the sound of her own language, she thought she saw a friend. I informed one of the magistrates, whom I knew, that the prisoners were Gipsies; and proposed to him to mitigate the punishment of the woman's husband, on condition of his giving me a specimen of his secret speech. But the reply of the man of authority was, "The scoundrel shall lie in prison till the last hour of his sentence." The "scoundrel," however, did not remain in durance so long. While the jailer was securing him in prison, the determined Tinkler, with the utmost coolness and indifference, asked him, which part of the jail would be the easiest for him to break through. The jailer told him that, if he attempted to escape, the watchman, stationed in the churchyard, close to the prison, would shoot him. On visiting the prison next morning, the turnkey found that the Gipsy had undone the locks of the doors, and fled during the night. O'Reilly, the other Gipsy, remained, in a separate cell, the whole period of his sentence. When the officers were completing the other part of his punishment—"banishing him from the town"—the regardless, light-hearted Irish Tinkler went capering along the streets, with his coat off, brandishing, and sweeping, and twirling his shillalah, in the Gipsy fashion. Meeting, in this excited state, his late judge, the Tinkler, with the utmost contempt and derision, called out to him, "Plase your honour! won't you now take a fight with me, for the sake of friendship?" This worthy Irish Gipsy represented himself as the head Tinkler in Perth, and the first of the second class of boxers.

On another occasion, I observed a horde of Gipsies on the high street of Inverkeithing, employed in making spoons from horn. I spoke to one of the young married men, partly in Scottish Gipsy words, when he immediately answered me in English. He said they were all natives of Ireland. They had, male and female, the Irish accent completely. I invited this man to accompany me to a public-house, that I might obtain from him a specimen of his Irish Gipsy language. The town-clerk being in my company at the time, I asked him to go with me, to hear what passed; but he refused, evidently because he considered that the company of a Gipsy would contaminate and degrade him. I treated the Tinkler with a glass of spirits, and obtained from him the following words:

Yaik, one.
Duie, two.
Trin, three.
Punch, five.
Saus, six.
Luften, eight.
Sonnakie, gold.
Roug, silver.
Vanister, ring.
Rat, night.
Cham, the moon.
Borlan, the sun.
Yak, fire.
Chowrie, knife.
Bar, stone.
Shuha, coat.
Roy, spoon.
Chauvie, child.
Gaugie, man.
Mort and kinshen, wife and child.
Klistie, soldier.
Ruffie lee ma, devil miss me.
Nasher, deserter.
Daw-douglars, hand-cuffs.
Staurdie, prison.
Lodie, lodgings.
Vile, town.
Yak, eye.
Deekers, eyes.
Shir, head.
Test, head.
Nuk, nose.
Mooie, mouth.
Meffemel, hand.
Grye, horse,
Aizel, ass.
Dugal, dog.
Bakra, sheep.
Ruffie, devil.
Bing, devil.
Feck, take.
Ruffie feck ma, devil take me.
Nawken, Tinkler,
Baurie-dews, Nawken, good-day, Tinkler.

This man conducted himself very politely, his behaviour being very correct and becoming; and he seemed much pleased at being noticed, and kindly treated. At first, he spoke wholly in the Gipsy language, thinking that I was as well acquainted with it as himself. But when he found that I knew only a few words of it, he, like all his tribe, stopped in his communications, and, in this instance, began to quiz and laugh at my ignorance. On returning to the street, I repeated some of the words to one of the females. She laughed, and, with much good humour, said, "You will put me out, by speaking to me in that language."

These facts prove that the Irish Gipsies have the same language as those in Scotland. The English Gipsy is substantially the same. There are a great many Irish Gipsies travelling in Scotland, of whom I will again speak, in the following chapter. They are not easily distinguished from common Irish peasants, except that they are generally employed in some sort of traffic, such as hawking earthen-ware, trinkets, and various other trifles, through the country.

It may interest the reader to know how the idea originated that the Gipsies, at all events their speech, came, or was thought to have come, from Hindostan. According to Grellmann, it was in this way:

"The following is an article to be found in the Vienna Gazette, from a Captain Szekely, who was thinking of searching for (the origin of) the Gipsies, and their language, in the East Indies: In the year 1763, on the 6th of November, a printer, whose name was Stephen Pap Szathmar Nemethi, came to see me. Talking upon various subjects, we at last fell upon that of the Gipsies; and my guest related to me the following anecdote, from the mouth of a preacher of the Reformed Church, Stephen Vali, at Almasch. When the said Vali studied at the University of Leyden, he was intimately acquainted with some young Malabars, of whom three are obliged constantly to study there; nor can they return home till relieved by three others. Having observed that their native language bore a great affinity to that spoken by the Gipsies, he availed himself of the opportunity to note down from themselves upwards of one thousand words, together with their significations. After Vali was returned from the University, he informed himself of the Raber Gipsies, concerning the meaning of his Malabar words, which they explained without trouble or hesitation."*

None of the Scottish Gipsy words have as yet, I believe, been collated with the Hindostanee, the supposed mother tongue of the Gipsies.† I showed my list to a gentleman lately from India, who, at first sight, pointed out, from among several hundred words and sentences scattered through these pages, about thirty-nine which very closely resembled Hindostanee. But in ascertaining the origin of the Gipsies, the traveller, Dr. Bright, thinks it would be desirable to procure some of the speech of the lowest classes in India, and compare it with the Gipsy, as spoken in Europe; for the purpose of showing, more correctly, the affinity of the two languages. He supposes, as I understand him, that the terms used by the despised and unlettered Gipsies would probably resemble more closely the vulgar idiom of the lowest castes in India, than the Hindostanee spoken by the higher ranks, or that which is to be found in books. The following facts show that Dr. Bright's conjectures are not far from the truth.

I had occasion at one time to be on board of a vessel lying in the harbour of Limekilns, Fifeshire, where I observed a black man, acting as cook, of the name of John Lobbs, about twenty-five years of age, and a native of Bombay, who could neither read nor write any language whatever. He stated that he was now a Christian, and had been baptized by the name of John. He had been absent from India three years, as cabin boy, in several British vessels, and spoke English well. He appeared to be of a low caste in his native land, but sharpened by his contact with Europeans. Recollecting Dr. Bright's hint, it occurred to

* "The opinion, that the Gipsies came originally from India, seems to have been very early entertained, although it was again soon forgotten, or silently relinquished. Hieronymus Forolivienale, in the nineteenth volume of Muratori, says, that on the 7th day of August, A. D. 1422, 200 of the Cingari came to his native town, and remained there two days, on their way to Rome, and that some of them said that they came from India, '*et ut audiri aliqui dicebant quod erant de Indiâ;*' and the account which Munster gives of what he gathered from one of the Cingari, in 1524, seems to prove that an impression existed amongst them of their having come from that country."—*Bright.*—Ed.

† Mr. Baird's Missionary Report contained a collation of the Scottish Gipsy with Hindostanee, but that appeared considerably after what our author has said was written.—Ed.

me that this Hindoo's vulgar dialect might resemble the language of our Scottish Gipsies. I repeated to him about one hundred and eighty Gipsy words and expressions. The greater part were familiar to his ear, but many of them that meant one thing in Gipsy, had quite a different signification in his speech. I shall, however, give the following Gipsy words, with the corresponding words of Lobb's language, and the English opposite.*

SCOTTISH GIPSY.	JOHN LOBBS' HINDOSTANEE.	ENGLISH.
Baurie, great, grand, rich.	*Bura*,	Grand, good, great, rich.
Been, great, grand, rich.	*Beenie*,	Grand, good, great, rich.
Callo,	*Kala*,	Black.
Lon,	*Loon*,	Salt.
Gourie, a man.	*Gowra*,	White man.
Gaugie, a man.	*Gaugie*, or *Fraugie*,	Rich man.
Mort, a wife.	*Murgia*,	Dead wife.
Chavo,	*Chokna*,	A boy, a son.
Praw,	*Praw*,	Son.
Prawl,	*Prawl*,	Daughter.
Nais-gaugie, grandfather.	*Nais gaugie*,	Old man.
Nais-mort, grandmother.	*Nais mort*,	Old woman.
Riah,	*Riah*,	A chief, a gentleman.
Rajah, a chief, governor.	*Rajah*,	A chief, a lord.
Raunie, lady, wife of a gentleman.	*Raunie*,	The wife of a prince.
Been riah,	*Beenie riah*,	The king.
Been raunie,	*Beenie raunie*,	The queen.
Been gourie,	*Beenie gourie*,	A gentleman.
Bauree rajah,	*Bura rajah*,	The king.

* Meeting a Bengalee at Peebles, begging money to pay his passage back to India, I repeated to him, from memory, a few of the Gipsy words I had collected a week before. After listening attentively, he answered that it was the Moor's language I had got, and gave me the English of *pannie*, water, and *davies*, day. I took the first opportunity of mentioning this interview to the Gipsies, observing it was the general opinion that their forefathers came from India. They, however, persisted in their own tradition, that they were a tribe of Ethiopians, which is believed by all the Scottish Gipsies. [See pages 113 and 315.—Ed.]

SCOTTISH GIPSY.	JOHN LOBBS' HINDOSTANEE.	ENGLISH.
Baurie raunie,	*Bura raunie*,	The queen.
Baurie forest,	*Bura frost, bura malook*,	Great town.
Baurie paunie,	*Bura paunie*,	The sea, the great water.
Lon paunie,	*Loon paunie*,	Salt water, the ocean.
Grye,	*Ghora*,	Horse.
Prancie, a horse.	*Prawncie*,	A gentleman's carriage.
Gournie,	*Goroo*,	A cow.
Backra,	*Buckra*,	A sheep.
Sherro,	*Sir*,	Head.
Yak,	*Aukh*,	Eye.
Yaka,	*Aukha*,	Eyes.
Nak,	*Nak*,	Nose.
Mooie,	*Mooih*,	Mouth.
Chee,	*Jeebh*,	The tongue.
Chee chee,	*Choopra*,	Hold your tongue.
Femmel, hand.	*Fingal*,	Ends of the fingers.
Vast,	*Wast*,	The hand.
Peerie,	*Peir*,	The foot.
Gave,	*Gaw*,	Village.
Kair,	*Gur*,	A house.
Wautheriz,	*Waudrie*,	A bed.
Outhrie, a window.	*Outrie, Durvaja*,	A door.
Eegees, bed clothes.	*Eegees*,	Bed curtains.
Shuch-hamie,	*Shuamie*,	A waistcoat.
Jair-dah,	*Jairda*,	Woman's apron.
Gawd,	*Dowglaw*,	A man's shirt.
Teeyakas,	*Teeyaka*,	Shoes.
Scaf, a hat.	*Scaf*, a small piece of cloth tied around the head, like a fillet.	
Skews,	*Skows*,	Platters, jugs.
Chowrie,	*Choree*,	Knife.
Harro,	*Dhoro*,	Sword.
Sauster, iron.	*Sauspoon*,	Iron pot-lid, iron.
Mass,	*Mass*,	Flesh.
Thood,	*Doodh*,	Milk.
Chizcazin, cheese.	*Chizcaizim*,	Cheese-knife.
Blaw, meal.	*Blaw*,	Indian corn.
Flatrin,	*Flatrin*,	Fish of any kind.
Shaucha, broth.	*Shoorwa*,	Soup.
Molzie,	*Mool*,	Wine.

SCOTTISH GIPSY.	JOHN LOBB' HINDOSTANEE.	ENGLISH.
Romanie, whiskey.	*Rominie*,	Spirits, liquor.
Mumlie, a candle.	*Membootie*,	Candles.
Fluffan,	*Floofan*,	Smoking tobacco.
Yak,	*Ag*,	Fire.
Paunie,	*Paunie*,	Water.
Casties,	*Cashtes*,	Fruit trees.
Bar,	*Dunbar*,	A stone.
Sonnakie,	*Sona*,	Gold.
Roug,	*Roopa*,	Silver.
Chinda, silver.	*Chindee*,	Silver, tin.
Geeve,	*Guing*,	Wheat.
Mang,	*Chan*, *Jung*,	The moon.
Bumie,	*Boomie*,	To drink.
Mar,	*Marna*,	To strike.
Rauge,	*Rawd*,	Mad.
Choar,	*Chorna*,	To steal.
Chor,	*Chor*,	Thief.
Humff,	*Huff*,	Give me.
Moolie, death, to die, dead.	*Moola*,	Dead.
Quad,	*Quid*,	Prison.
Staurdie, prison.	*Staurdee*,	A prison, to confine, hold.
Jaw vree,	*Jowa*,	Go away.
Auvie,	*Aow*,	Coming, come here.
Davies,	*Din*,	Day.
Rat,	*Raut*,	Night.
Pagrin,	*Pawgrin*,	To break.
Davies-pagrin,	*Dawis-pawgrin*,	Day-break, the morning.
Klistie, a soldier.	*Kleestie*,	Black soldier, Sepoy.
Nash, deserter.	*Natch*,	To run away.
Loudnie,	*Loonie*,	A bad woman.*

My informant understood, he said, two of the dialects of Hindostan, the one called the Hindoo, and the other the Moors' language. The former, he said, the English in

* A lady who resided seventeen years in India, already alluded to, mentioned to me that the pronunciation of the Hindoos is broad, like that of the Scotch, particularly where the letter *a* occurs; and that the Scotch learn Hindostanee sooner, and more correctly, than the natives of other countries. For this reason, I am inclined to think that the Scottish Gipsy will have a greater resemblance to Hindostanee than the Gipsy of some other countries.

India generally spoke, but understood little of the latter; and that he himself did not know a word of the language of the Brahmins. When he failed to produce, in the Moors' language, the word corresponding to the Gipsy one, he frequently found it in what he called the Hindoo speech. The greater part of the Gipsy words, as I have already mentioned, were familiar to his ear; but many of them that signified one thing in his speech, meant quite another in Gipsy. For example, the word *Graunagie*, in Gipsy, signifies a *barn*; with Lobbs, it meant *an old rich man*. *Coories*, bed clothes or blankets, signified, in Lobb's dialect, *ornaments for the ears*. *Dill*, a servant maid, according to Lobbs, was a *church*. *Shan davies*, a bad day, was the Hindostanee for *holiday*. *Managie*, a woman, signifies the *name of a person*, such as John or James. *Chavo*, a son, meant a *female child*; and *Pooklie*, hulled barley, *anything fine*. The two Gipsy words *Callo* and *Rat* are black and night; but, according to Lobbs, *Callorat* is simply anything dark.*

To confirm my collection of Scottish Gipsy words, I will collate some of those which I sent to Sir Walter Scott, for examination but not for publication, with those to be found in Mr. Baird's report, a publication which I first saw in 1842.

SCOTTISH GIPSY.	YETHOLM GIPSY.	ENGLISH.
Gaugie,	*Gadgé*,	Man.
Managie,	*Manishee*,	Woman.
Mort,		Wife.
Chavo, (*chauvies*, children,)	*Shavies*, children,	Son.

* In the report of the Fourteenth Gipsies' Festival, held at Southampton, under the superintendence of the Rev. James Crabb, the Gipsies' friend, on the 25th December, 1841, is the following statement:

"The above gentleman, (the Rev. J. West, one of the speakers at the festival,) with the Rev. Mr. Crabb, and two elderly Gipsies, who speak the Gipsy language, called, the following morning, on a lady who had long resided in India, and speaks the Hindostanee language; and it was clear that many of the Rommany (Gipsy) words were pure Hindostanee, and other words strongly resembled that language."—*Hampshire Advertiser, 1st January*, 1842.

This statement, made some years subsequent to the period at which I took down the words from Lobbs and the Gipsies in Scotland, is nearly in my own words, and proves that my opinion, as to the close affinity between Hindostanee and the Scottish Gipsy language, is correct.

SCOTTISH GIPSY.	YETHOLM GIPSY.	ENGLISH.
Praw,	*Gouré*, a boy,	Son.
Prawl,	*Racklé*, a girl,	Daughter.
Riah,	*Rai*, a gentleman,	A chief.
Rajah,		Governor.
Baurie,	*Baré*,	Good.
Sherro,	*Shero*,	Head.
Yak,	*Yack*,	Eye.
Yaka,		Eyes.
Nak,	*Nak*,	Nose.
Mooie,	*Moi*,	Mouth.
Vast,	*Vastie*,	Hand.
Grye,	*Grâi*,	Horse.
Bashanie,	*Basné*,	Cock.
Caunie,	*Kanné*,	Hen.
Drom,	*Drone*,	Road.
Gave,	*Gaave*,	Village.
Graunagie,		Barn.
Graunsie,	*Gransé*,	Barn.
Kair,	*Keir*,	House.
Outhrie,		Window.
Yag,	*Yag*,	Fire.
Thood,	*Thud*,	Milk.
Mass,	*Mass*,	Flesh.
Peerie, (or *blawkie*,)	*Blakie*,	Pot.
Paunie,	*Pawné*,	Water.
Paurie,		Water.
Molzie,	*Mul*,	Wine.
Roy,	*Roy*,	Spoon.
Nab,		Horn.
Chorie,		Knife.
Chowrie,	*Chouré*,	Knife.
Shuha,	*Shohé*,	Coat.
Scaf, (or *gogle*,)	*Gogel*,	Hat.
Harro,		Sword.
Beerie,		Ship.
Bumie,	*Peevan*, drinking,	To drink.
Choar,		To steal.
Chor,	*Tschor*,	Thief.
Staurdie,	*Stardé*, a jail,	Prison.
Moolie,	*Moulian*, dying,	Death.
Moolie,	*Moulé*, to kill,	I'll kill you.
Bing,	*Bing*,	The devil.

The following Scottish Gipsy words appear to have some relation to the Sanscrit:

SCOTTISH GIPSY.	SANSCRIT.	ENGLISH.
Yag,	*Agnish*,	Fire.
Paurie,	*Varni*,	Water.
Custies,	*Cashth*,	Wood.
Duff,	*Dhupah*,	Smoke.
Sneepa,	*Sweta*,	White.
Callo,	*Cala*,	Black.
Sherro,	*Sira*,	The head.
Rajah,	*Rajah*,	Lord.
Vast,	*Hastah*,	The hand.
Praw,	*Putra*,	Son.
Gave, or *Gau*,	*Gramam*,	A village.
Mar,	*Mar*,	To strike.
Loudnie,	*Lodha*, loved,	A whore.

In order to show the relationship of the language of the Gipsies in Scotland, England, Germany, Hungary, Spain, and Turkey, and the affinity between it and the Persian, Hindostanee, Sanscrit, Pali, and Kawi, I append a table containing the first ten numerals in all these tongues:

TABLE OF THE FIRST TEN NUMERALS IN VARIOUS GIPSY DIALECTS, COMPARED WITH THOSE IN OTHER ORIENTAL LANGUAGES.

English.	Scottish Gipsy.	English Gipsy.	German Gipsy.	Hungarian Gipsy	Hungarian Gipsy	Turkish Gipsy.	Spanish Gipsy.	Persian.	Vulgar Hindostanee.	Sanscrit.	Sanscrit.	Pali.	Kawi.
	W. S.	Hoyland.	Grellmann.	Bright.	Borrow.	Hoyl'd.	Borrow.	Borrow.	John Lobbs	Polocz.	Borrow.	Polocz.	Polocz.
One	Yaik	Aick	Ick, Ek	Jeg	Jek	Yeck	Yeque	Ek	Yek	Eka	Ega	Ekka	Eka
Two	Dule	Dooce	Duj, Duj	Dui	Dui	Duy	Dui	Du	Doh	Dui	Dwaya	Di	Dui
Three	Trin	Trin	Trin, Tri	Tri	Trin	Trin	Trin	So	Tin	Tri	Treya	Tri	Tri
Four	Tor	Shtar, Staur	Schtar, Star	Stah	Schtar	Shtar	Estar	Chohar	Char	Chatur	Tschatvar	Chatwa	Chatur
Five	Pauch, Fo	Panji	Pantsch, Panach	Panach	Panach	Panch	Pansche	Panach	Pannah	Pancha	Pantscha	Pancha	Pancha
Six	Shaigh	Shove	Tschowe, Schow, Sof	Schof	Tschov	Shove	Joh, Zoi	Schesche	Shaish	Shat	Schasda	Che	Sat
Seven	Naivalrn*	Hoftan	Efta	Epta	Efta	Efta	Hefta	Heft	Saut	Sapta	Sapta	Sap	Sapta
Eight	Naigh, Luften	....	Ochto	Opto	Ochto	Okto	Otor	Hescht	Aut	Ashta	Aschta	At-tha	Asta
Nine	Line	Henya	Enja, Eija	Ennia	Enija	Enia	Enmia	Nu	Nong	Nava	Nava	Nawa	Nawa
Ten	Nay	Desh	Desch, Des	Desh	Desch	Desh	Deque	De	Dest	Dasa	Dascha	Thotsa	Dasa

* The four last of these numerals, in the Scottish Gipsy language, differ very considerably from the corresponding ones in the Table. I leave the matter to be settled by philologists.

That the Gipsy language, in Scotland, is intermixed with cant, or slang, and other words, is certain, as will appear by the specimens I have exhibited.* I am inclined to believe, however, that were the cant and slang used by our flash men and others carefully examined, much of it would turn out to be corrupted Hindostanee, picked up from the Gipsies. I have, after considerable trouble, produced, and, I may venture to say, faithfully recorded, the raw materials as I found them: to separate the other words from the original and genuine Gipsy, is a task I leave to the learned philologist. I shall only observe, that the way in which the Gipsy language has been corrupted is this: That whenever the Gipsies find words not understood by the people among whom they travel, they commit such to memory, and use them in their conversation, for the purpose of concealment. In the Lowlands of Scotland, for example, they make use of Gaelic,† Welsh, Irish, and French words. These picked-up words and terms have, in the end, become part of their own peculiar tongue; yet some of the Gipsies are able to point out a number of these foreign words, as distinguished from their own. In this manner do the Gipsies carry along with them part of the language of every country through which they pass.‡

* It is remarkable, considering how much the habits and occupations of the Gipsies bring them in contact with beggars, thieves, and other bad and disorderly characters, how few of the slang words used by such persons have been adopted by them.—*Rev. Mr. Baird's Missionary Report to the Scottish Church*, 1840.—Ed.

† Of the Highland Gipsies, I had the following account from a person of observation, and highly worthy of credit: There are many settled in Kintyre, who travel through the Highlands and Lowlands annually. They certainly speak, among themselves, a language totally distinct from either Gaelic or Lowland Scotch.—*Blackwood's Magazine*.—Ed.

‡ "There is reason for supposing that the Gipsies had been wandering in the remote regions of Sclavonia, for a considerable time previous to entering Bohemia—the first civilized country of Europe in which they made their appearance; as their language abounds with words of Sclavonic origin, which could not have been adopted in a hasty passage through a wild and half populated country."—*Borrow.*

That the Gipsies were, in some way, drawn together, at a very remote age, and became amalgamated, so as to form a race, can hardly admit of a doubt. But it is an opinion that has no reasonable foundation which supposes that they suddenly took their departure from India, and travelled together, till they entered and spread over Europe. They may, as I have conjectured in the Introduction, have separated into bands, and passed into countries in Asia, as they have done in Europe; and existed in Asia, and Africa, long before they appeared in Europe. For this reason, their language ought to vary in different countries; and it would be enough to

In concluding my account of the Scottish Gipsy language, I may observe, that I think few who have perused my details will hesitate for a moment in pronouncing that the people have migrated from Hindostan. Many convincing proofs of the origin of the race have been adduced by Grellmann, Hoyland, and Bright; and I think that my researches, made in Scotland alone, have confirmed the statements of these respectable authors.

The question which now remains to be solved is this: From what tribe or nation at present in, or originally from, Hindostan are the Gipsies descended? That they have been a robber or predatory nation, from principle as well as practice, I am convinced little doubt can be entertained. Even yet, the greater the art and address displayed in committing a dexterous theft or robbery, the higher is the merit of such an action esteemed among their fraternity. I am also convinced that this general, or national, propensity to plunder has been the chief cause of the Gipsies concealing their origin, language, customs, and religious observances, at the time they entered the territories of civilized nations, and up to this time. The intelligent old Gipsy, whose acquaintance I made at St. Boswell's, distinctly told me, that his tribe were originally a nation of thieves and robbers; and it is quite natural to suppose that, when they found theft and robbery punished with such severity, in civilized society, everything relating to them would be kept a profound secret.

The tribe in India whose customs, manners, and habits have the greatest resemblance to those of the Gipsies, are the *Nuts*, or *Bazegurs;* an account of which is to be found in the 7th volume of the Asiatic Researches, page 451. In Blackwood's Magazine we find the following paragraph relative to these Nuts, or Bazegurs, which induces a belief that these people are a branch of the Gipsy nation, and a tribe of the highest antiquity. They are even supposed to be the wild, aboriginal inhabitants of India.

identify them as the same race, were the substance of their language, and their customs, or even their cast of mind, the same. In speaking of the Hungarian Gipsies, Grellmann says, that their speech contains words from the Turkish, Sclavonian, Greek, Latin, Wallachian, Hungarian, and German; but that it would not be absurd to pronounce that there remain more, or at least different, Gipsy words among those residing in one country than another.—Ed.

"A lady of rank, who has resided some time in India, lately informed me that the Gipsies are to be found there, in the same way as in England, and practise the same arts of posture-making and tumbling, fortune-telling, stealing, and so forth. The Indian Gipsies are called Nuts, or Bazegurs, and they are believed by many to be the remains of an aboriginal race, prior even to the Hindoos, and who have never adopted the worship of Bramah. They are entirely different from the Parias, who are Hindoos that have lost caste, and so become degraded."

The Nuts, or Bazegurs, under the name of Decoits or Dukyts, are, it seems, guilty of frequently sacrificing victims to the goddess Calie, under circumstances of horror and atrocity scarcely credible. Now the old Gipsy, who gave me the particulars relative to the Gipsy sacrifice of the horse, stated that sometimes both woman and horse were sacrificed, when the woman, by the action of the horse, was found to have greatly offended.

In the ordinances of Menu, the Nuts, or Bazegurs, are called *Nata.* Now, our Scottish Gipsies, at this moment, call themselves *Nawkens*, a word not very dissimilar in sound to *Nata.* When I have spoken to them, in their own words, I have been asked, "Are you a *nawken?*" a word to which they attach the meaning of a *wanderer*, or *traveller*—one who can do any sort of work for himself that may be required in the world.

CHAPTER X.

PRESENT CONDITION AND NUMBER OF THE GIPSIES IN SCOTLAND.

EVERY author who has written on the subject of the Gipsies has, I believe, represented them as all having remarkably dark hair, black eyes, and swarthy complexions. This notion has been carried to such an extent, that Hume, on the criminal laws of Scotland, thinks the black eyes should make part of the evidence in proving an individual to be of the Gipsy race. The Gipsies, in Scotland, of the last century, were of all complexions, varying from light flaxen hair, and blue eyes, and corresponding complexions, to hair of raven black, dark eyes, and swarthy countenances. Many of them had deep-red and light-yellow hair, with very fair complexions. I am convinced that one-half of the Gipsies in Scotland, at the present day, have blue eyes, instead of black ones. According to the statistical account of the parish of Borthwick, Mid-Lothian, (1839,) the Baillies, Wilsons, and Taits, at Middleton, the descendants of the old Tweed-dale Gipsies, are described as, "in general, of a colour rather cadaverous, or of a darkish pale; their cheekbones high; their eyes small, and light coloured; their hair of a dingy white or red colour, and wiry; and their skin, drier and of a tougher texture than that of the people of this country." This question of colour has been illustrated in my enquiry into the history of the Gipsy language; for the language is the only satisfactory thing by which to test a Gipsy, let his colour be what it may.

In other countries, besides Scotland, the Gipsies are not all of one uniform swarthy hue. A Russian gentleman stated to me that many of the Gipsies in Finland have light hair, and fair complexions. I am also informed there are Gipsies in Arabia with fair hair.

Among many other mal-practices, the Gipsies have, in all countries, been accused of stealing children; but what became of these kidnapped infants, no one appears to have given any account, that I am aware of. To satisfy myself on this trait of their character, I enquired of a Gipsy the reasons which induced his tribe to steal children. He candidly acknowledged the practice, and said that the stolen children were adopted as members of the tribe, and instructed in the language, and all the mysteries of the body. They became, he said, equally hardy, clever, and expert in all the practices of the fraternity. The male Gipsies were very fond of marrying the stolen females. Some of the kidnapped children were made servants, or, rather, a sort of slaves, to the tribe. They considered that the occasional introduction of another race into their own, and mixing the Gipsy blood, in that manner, invigorated and strengthened their race. In this manner would the Gipsies alter the complexion of their race, by the introduction of foreign blood among them.*

* An objection is perhaps started, that these incorporated individuals are not Gipsies. They have been brought into the body at such an age as to leave no trace of past recollections, leaving alone past associations. There was no occasion for such children being either "squalling infants," or of such an age as was likely to lead them to "betray the Gipsies," as Mr. Borrow supposes would be the case, when he says that Gipsies have never stolen children, to bring them up as Gipsies. How are they to discover their origin, when so many of the body around them have the same colour of hair and complexion? If the idea has ever entered into their imaginations, it has led to a greater antipathy towards their own race, and attachment to the tribe, from the special education which they have received to those ends. So far as the matter of blood is concerned, they are not what may be physiologically called Gipsies; and, by being married to Gipsies, they become doubly attached to the body. What has been said of children introduced among the Gipsies, in the way described, applies with infinitely greater force to those born of one of such parents.

Suppose, for instance, that the Spanish race was originally of an exclusively *dark* hair and complexion: should we therefore say that a *fair* Spaniard, at the present day, was no Spaniard? Or that the Turks of Constantinople, on account of the mixture of their blood, were not Turks? In the same manner are Gipsies with white blood in their veins Gipsies. They may be half-breed, but it would be improper to call them half-caste, Gipsies. But what are full-blood Gipsies, to commence with? The idea itself is intangible; for, by adopting, more or less, wherever they have been, others into their body, during their singular history, a pure Gipsy, like the pure Gipsy language, is doubtless nowhere to be found.

An English Gipsy acquaintance, of perfect European appearance, who, for love of race and language, may be termed "a Gipsy of the Gipsies," admitted that he was only one-eighth Gipsy; his father, a full-blood white,

Before going into details to show the condition in which the Gipsies are at the present day, I will consider, shortly, the causes which have contributed to the change that has come over their outward circumstances, and driven so many of them, as it were, "to cover," in consequence of the unfortunate times on which they had fallen; a state of things which, however unfortunate to them, in their peculiar way of thinking, has been of so much benefit to civilization, and society at large.

About the commencement of the American war of independence, in 1775, the Gipsies, in Scotland, occupied a very singular position in society. Instead of being the proscribed, and, as they thought, persecuted, members of the community, many of them then became the *preservers* of the peace and good order of the country. The country, as appears by the periodical publications of the day, was, about this time, greatly pestered by rogues and vagabonds. The Gipsies had art enough to get a number of their chiefs appointed constables, peace-officers, and *country-keepers*, in several counties in Scotland. These public officers were to clear the country of all idle vagrants, vagabonds, and disturbers of the peace. This was, sure enough, a very extraordinary employment for the Gipsies. The situation of country-keeper was, of all others, the office in society the most com-

having married a quadroon Gipsy. He spoke Gipsy with great fluency. He married a seven-eighths Gipsy. Were his descendants to marry what are supposed to be pure Gipsies, the result would be as follows: The first generation, (his children,) would be one-half Gipsy; the second, three-fourths; the third, seven-eighths; the fourth, fifteen-sixteenths; the fifth, thirty-one thirty-seconds; and the sixth, sixty-three sixty-fourths. If this were to go on *ad infinitum*, the issue would always lack the one part to make the full blood. But the Gipsies do not calculate their vulgar fractions so closely as that; the division of the blood doubtless bothers them, so that they "lump" the question. What has been said, is breeding *up*. Sometimes they breed *down*, and sometimes *across*. Mixing the blood, in this way, is quite a peculiarity among the English Gipsies. I asked my friend, if he was sure his wife was a pure Gipsy. He said she was considered such, (I have put her down at seven-eighths,) but that one of her forefathers was a fair-haired French Gipsy. According to a well-admitted principle in physiology, a fair-haired Gipsy, of almost full blood, is by no means so *rara avis in terris* as a white crow. Some of the children of my acquaintance took after himself, and had blue eyes; and others after the mother, and had black ones. But the English Gipsies, (the tented ones at least,) are much purer, in point of blood, than their brethren in Scotland. Many of the Irish Gipsies have very red hair—fiery and shaggy in the extreme. Indeed, they seem to be pretty much all of a fairish kind.—Ed.

pletely to their liking. It gave them authority over every rogue in the country, and they certainly followed out their instructions to the very letter. They hunted down, with the utmost vigilance, every delinquent who was not of their tribe; but, on the other hand, they took especial care to protect every individual of their own fraternity, excepting those that were obnoxious to themselves. When it agreed with their inclinations, these Gipsy country-keepers sometimes caused stolen property to be returned to the owners, as if it had been done by magic. It is needless to observe that they were themselves the very chiefs of the depredators, but had generally the dexterity never to be seen in the transactions.*

A Gipsy country-keeper was at the height of his vanity and glory, when he got an unfortunate individual of the community into his clutches. In the presence of his captive, he would draw his sword, flourish it in the air, and swear a terrible oath, that he would, at a blow, cut the head from his body, if he made the least attempt at escape.

The public services of the Gipsies were in a short time discontinued, as their conduct only made matters a great deal worse. A friend of mine† saw those Gipsy constables, for Peebles-shire, sworn into office, at the town of Peebles, when they were first appointed. He said he never saw such a set of gloomy, strange-looking fellows, in his life; and expressed his surprise at the conduct of the county magistrates, for employing such banditti as conservators of the public peace. The most extraordinary circumstance attending their appointment, he said, was, that not one of them had a permanent residence within the county.

During the American war, however, the tide of fortune again completely turned against the Gipsies. The Government was in need of soldiers and sailors; the Gipsies were a proscribed race; their peculiar habits were continually

* The following extract from the Fife Herald, for the 18th June, 1829, will give the reader an idea of a Scotch "country-keeper," at the time alluded to: "A Gipsy chief, of the name of Pat. Gillespie, was keeper for, the county of Fife. He rode on horse-back, armed with a sword and pistols attended by four men, on foot, carrying staves and batons. He appears to have been a sort of travelling justice of the peace. The practice seems to have been general. About the commencement of the late French war, a man, of the name of Robert Scott, (Rob the Laird,) was keeper for the counties of Peebles, Selkirk, and Roxburgh."

† The late Mr. Charles Alexander, tenant of Happrew.

involving them in serious scrapes and difficulties; the consequence was, that the Tinklers were apprehended all over the country, and forced into our fleets and armies then serving in America. All the aged persons of intelligence with whom I have conversed on this subject, agree in representing that the kidnapping system at that period was the means of greatly breaking up and dispersing the Gipsy bands in Scotland. From this blow these unruly vagrants have never recovered their former position in the country.*

The war in America had been concluded only a few years before that with France broke out. Our army and navy were, of necessity, again augmented to an extent beyond precedent. It was not difficult to find pretences for renewing the chase of the Gipsies, and apprehending them, under the name of vagrants and disorderly persons. They were again compelled to enlist into our regiments, and embark on board our ships of war, as sailors and marines. An individual stated to me that, about the commencement of this war, he had seen English Gipsies sent, in scores at a time, on board of men-of-war, in the Downs.

But, rather than be forced into a service so much against their inclinations, numerous instances occurred of Gipsies voluntarily mutilating themselves. In the very custody of press-gangs, and other hardened kidnappers, the determined Gipsies have, with hatchets, razors, and other sharp instruments, struck from their hands a thumb, or finger or two, to render them unfit for a military life. Several instances have come to my knowledge of these resolute acts of the Scottish Gipsies. I have myself seen several of the tribe without fingers; and, on enquiry, I found that they themselves had struck them from their hands, in consequence of their aversion to become soldiers and sailors. One man, of the name of Graham, during the last war, laid his hand upon a block of wood, and, in a twinkling, struck, with a hatchet, his thumb from one of his hands. Another, of the name of Gordon, struck two of his fingers from one of his hands

* We may very readily believe that almost all of the Gipsies would desert the army, on landing in America, and marry Gipsy women in the colonies, or bring others out from home, or marry with common natives, or return home. Indeed, native-born American Gipsies say that many of the British Gipsies voluntarily accepted the bounty, and a passage to the colonies, during the war of the Revolution, and deserted the army on landing. This would lead to a migration of the tribe generally to America.—Ed.

with a razor. Such, indeed, was the aversion which the whole Gipsy race had to a military life, that even mothers sometimes mutilated their infants, by cutting off certain fingers, to render them, when they became men, entirely incapable of serving in either the army or navy.*

Such causes as these, taken in connection with the improved

* "When Paris was garrisoned by the allied troops, in the year 1815, I was walking with a British officer, near a post held by the Prussian troops. He happened, at the time, to smoke a cigar, and was about, while passing the sentinel, to take it out of his mouth, in compliance with a general regulation to that effect; when, greatly to the astonishment of the passengers, the soldier addressed him in these words; 'Rauchen Sie immer fort; verdamt sey der Preussische Dienst;' that is: 'Smoke away; may the Prussian service be d——d.' Upon looking closer at the man, he seemed plainly to be a *Zigeuner*, or Gipsy, who took this method of expressing his detestation of the duty imposed on him. When the risk he ran, by doing so, is considered, it will be found to argue a deep degree of dislike which could make him commit himself so unwarily. If he had been overheard by a sergeant or corporal, the *prugel* would have been the slightest instrument of punishment employed."—*Sir Walter Scott: Note to Quentin Durward.*

Mutilation was also very common among the English Gipsies, during the French war. Strange as it may appear, the same took place among them, at the commencement of the late Russian war; from which we may conclude, that they had suffered severely during the previous war, or they would not have resorted to so extreme a measure for escaping military duty, when a press-gang was not even thought of. An English Gipsy, at the latter time, laid two of his fingers on a block of wood, and, handing his broom-knife to his neighbour, said, "Now, take off these fingers, or I'll take off your head with this other hand!"

During the French war, Gipsies again and again, accepted the bounty for recruits, but took "French leave" of the service. The idea is finely illustrated in Burns' "Jolly Beggars:"

"Tune—*Clout the caudron.*

"My bonny lass, I work in brass,
A Tinkler is my station:
I've travell'd round all Christian ground,
In this my occupation.
I've ta'en the gold, an' been enroll'd
In many a noble squadron:
But vain they search'd when off I march'd
To go and clout the caudron."

Poosie Nancie and her reputed daughter, Racer Jess, were very probably Gipsies, who kept a poor "Tinkler Howff" at Mauchline.

Gipsies sometimes voluntarily join the navy, as musicians. Here their vanity will have a field for conspicuous display; for a good fifer, on board of a man-of-war, in accompanying certain work with his music, is equal to the services of ten men. There were some Gipsy musicians in the fleet at Sebastopol. But, generally speaking, Gipsies are like cats—not very fond of the water.—Ed.

internal administration of the country, and the progression of the age, have cast a complexion over the outward aspect of the bulk of the Scottish Gipsy race, entirely different from what it was before they came into existence.

Many of the Gipsies now keep shops of earthen-ware, china, and crystal. Some of them, I am informed on the best authority, have from one to eight thousand pounds invested in this line of business.* I am disposed to think that few of these shops were established prior to the commencement of the French war; as I find that several of their owners travelled the country in their early years. Perhaps the fear of being apprehended as vagrants, and compelled to enter the army or navy, forced some of the better sort to settle in towns.† Like their tribe in other countries, numbers of our Scottish Gipsies deal in horses; others keep public-houses; and some of them, as innkeepers, will, in heritable and moveable property, possess, perhaps, two or three thousand pounds. These innkeepers and stone-ware merchants are scarcely to be distinguished as Gipsies; yet they all retain the language, and converse in it, among themselves. The females, as is their custom, are particularly active in managing the affairs of their respective concerns.

Many of them have betaken themselves to some of the regular occupations of the country, such as coopers, shoemakers, and plumbers; some are masons—an occupation to which they seem to have a partiality. Some of them are members of masons' lodges. There are many of them itinerant bell-hangers, and umbrella-menders. Among them there are tin-smiths, braziers, and cutlers, in great numbers; and the tribe also furnish a proportion of chimney-sweeps. I recollect of a Gipsy, who travelled the country, selling

* Mr. Borrow mentions having observed, at a fair in Spain, a family of Gipsies, richly dressed, after the fashion of their nation. They had come a distance of upwards of a hundred leagues. Some merchants, to whom he was recommended, informed him, that they had a credit on their house, to the amount of twenty thousand dollars.—Ed.

† In his enquiry into the present condition of the Gipsies, our author has apparently confined his remarks exclusively to the body in its present wandering state, and such part of it as left the tent subsequently to the commencement of the French war. In the Disquisition on the Gipsies, the subject will be fully reviewed, from the date of arrival of the race in the country.—Ed.

earthen-ware, becoming, in the end, a master-sweep. Several were, and I believe are, constables; and I am inclined to think that the police establishments, in large as well as small towns, contain some of the fraternity.* Individuals of the female Gipsies are employed as servants, in the families of respectable persons, in town and country. Some of them have been ladies' maids, and even house-keepers, to clergymen and farmers.† I heard of one, in a very respectable family, who was constantly boasting of her ancient and high descent; her father being a Baillie, and her mother a Faa—the two principal families in Scotland. Some of those persons who sell gingerbread at fairs, or what the country-people call *rowly-powly-men*, are also of the Gipsy race. Almost all these individuals hawking earthen-ware through the country, with carts, and a large proportion of those hawking japan and white-iron goods, are Gipsies.

Some of the itinerant venders of inferior sorts of jewelry, part of which they also manufacture, and carry about in boxes on their shoulders, are of the tribe; and some of them even carry these articles in small, handsome, light-made carts. I had frequently observed, in my neighbour-

* This is quite common. An English mixed Gipsy spontaneously informed me that he had been a constable in L——, and that he had a cousin who was lately a *runner* in the police establishment of M——. Among other motives for the Gipsies joining the police is the following: that such is their dislike for the people among whom they live, owing to the prejudice which is entertained against them, that nothing gives them greater satisfaction than being the instruments of affronting and punishing their hereditary enemies. Besides this, the lounging and idle kind of life, coupled with the activity, of a constable, is pretty much to their natural disposition. An intelligent mixed Gipsy is calculated to make a first-rate constable and thief-catcher. Of course, he will not be very hard on those of his own race who come in his way.—Ed.

† Our author frequently spoke of a dissenting Scottish clergyman having been married to a Gipsy, but was not aware, as far as I know, of the circumstances under which the marriage took place. The clergyman was not, in all probability, aware that he was taking a Gipsy to his bosom; and as little did the public generally; but it was well known to the initiated that both her father and mother had cut and divided many a purse. The unquestionable character and standing of the father, and the prudent conduct of the mother, protected the children. One of the daughters married another dissenting clergyman, which fairly disarmed those not of the Gipsy race of any prejudice towards the grand-children. The issue of these marriages would pass into Gipsydom, as explained in the Disquisition on the Gipsies.—Ed.

hood, a very smart-looking and well-dressed man, who, with his wife and family, and a servant to take care of his children, travelled the country, in a neat, light cart, selling jewelry. All the family were well dressed. I was curious to know the origin of this man, and, upon enquiring of one of the tribe, but of a different clan, I found that he was a Gipsy, of the name of Robertson, descended from the old *horners* who traversed the kingdom, about half a century ago. He still retained the speech, peculiar dance, and manner of handling the cudgel, the practices and roguish tricks of his ancestors. I believe he also practised chain-dropping. To show the line of life which some of the descendants of the old style of Gipsies are now pursuing, in Scotland, I will give the following anecdote, which I witnessed, relative to this Gipsy jeweller.

I happened to be conversing, about twenty years ago, with four or five individuals, on a public quay in Fifeshire, when a smart, well-dressed sailor, apparently of the rank of a mate, obtruded himself on our company. He said he was "a sailor, and had spent all his money in a frolic, as many thoughtless sailors had done;" and, pulling out a watch, he continued, "he would give his gold watch for a mere trifle, to supply his immediate wants." One of the company at once thought he was an impostor, and told him his watch was not gold at all, and worth very little money. "Not worth much money!" he exclaimed; "why, I paid not less than ten francs for it, in France, the other day!" At this assertion, all present burst out a laughing at the impostor's ignorance in exposing his own trick. "Why, friend," said a ship-master, who was one of the company, "a franc is only worth tenpence; so you have paid just eight and fourpence for this valuable watch of yours. Do not attempt to cheat us in this manner." At finding himself so completely exposed, the villain became furious, and stepping close up to the ship-master, with abusive language, *chucked* him under the chin, to provoke him to fight. I at once perceived that the feigned sailor was a professional boxer and cudgelist, and entreated the ship-master not to touch him, notwithstanding his insolence. The "sailor," now disappointed on all hands, brandished his bludgeon, and retreated backwards, dancing in the Gipsy manner, and twirling his weapon before him, till he got his back to a wall. Here he set all at defiance, with a design that some one should strike at him, that he might avenge the affront he had received. But he was allowed to go away without interruption. This man was, in short, Robertson, the Gipsy travelling jeweller, disguised as a sailor, and a well-known prize-fighter.

Almost all those cheats called thimble-riggers, who infest thoroughfares, highways and byways, are also Gipsies, of a superior class. I have tried them by the language, and found they understood it, as has been seen in my account of the Gipsy language.

I need scarcely say, that all those females who travel the country in families, selling articles made from horn, while the males practise the mysteries of the tinker, are that portion of the Gipsies who adhere more strictly to their ancient customs and manner of life. Some of the principal families of these nomadic horner bands have yet districts on which none others of the tribe dare encroach. This division of the Gipsies are, by superficial observers, considered the only Gipsies in existence in Scotland; which is a great mistake. The author of Guy Mannering, himself, seems to have had this class of Gipsies, only, in view, when he says, "There are not now above five hundred of the tribe in Scotland." Those who deal in earthen-ware, and work at the tinsmith business, call these horners Gipsies; and nothing can give greater offence to these Gipsy potters and smiths than to ask them if they ever *made horn spoons;* for, by asking them this question, you indirectly call them Gipsies, an appellation that alarms them exceedingly.*

Since the termination of the long-protracted French war, the Gipsies have, to some extent, resumed their ancient manners; and many of them are to be seen encamped in the open fields. There are six tents to be observed at present, for one during the war. To substantiate what I have said of the numbers and manners of the nomadic Gipsies since

* It is only within these forty years that spoon-making from horn became a regular trade. It would seem the Gipsies had a monopoly of the business; for I am informed that the first man in Scotland who served a regular apprenticeship to it was alive, in Glasgow, in 1836. [There is nothing in this remark to imply that the manufacturing of spoons, and other articles, from horn, may not be monopolized by the Gipsies yet, whatever the way in which it may be carried on.—ED.]

the peace, I will give the two following paragraphs, taken from the Caledonian Mercury newspaper:

"*Tinklers and vagabonds:* The country has been much infested, of late years, by wandering hordes of vagabonds, who, under pretence of following the serviceable calling of tinkers, assume the name and appearance of such, merely to extort contributions of victuals, and other articles of value, from the country-people, particularly in lonely districts. The evil has encreased rapidly of late, and calls loudly for redress upon those in whose charge the police of the country districts is placed. They generally travel in bands, varying in number from ten to thirty; and wherever they pitch their camp, the neighbours are certain of suffering loss of cattle or poultry, unless they submit to pay a species of black-mail, to save themselves from heavier and more irregular contributions. These bands possess all the vices peculiar to the regular Gipsies, without any of the extenuating qualities which distinguish these foreign tribes. Unlike the latter, they do not settle in one place sufficiently long to attach themselves to the soil, or to particular families; and seem possessed of no industrious habits, but those of plunder, knavery, and riot. The chief headquarters of the hordes are at the caves of Auchmithie, on the east coast of Forfarshire; from which, to the wilds of Argyleshire, seems to be the usual route of their bands; small detachments being sent off, at intermediate places, to extend the scene of their plunder. Their numbers have been calculated by one who lives on the direct line of their passage, through the braes of Perthshire, and who has had frequent opportunities for observation; and he estimates them at several hundred."—*22d August*, 1829.

"A horde of Gipsies and vagabonds encamped, last week, in a quarry, on the back of the hill opposite Cherry-bank. Their number amounted to about thirty. The inhabitants in that quarter became alarmed; and Provost Ross, whose mansion is in the vicinity of the new settlers, ordered out a strong posse of officers from Perth, to dislodge them; which they effected. The country is now kept in continual terror by these vagabonds, and it will really be imperative on the landed proprietors to adopt some decided measure for the suppression of this growing evil."—*3d October*, 1829.*

* From the numerous enquiries I have made, I am fully satisfied that the

A gentleman informed me that, in the same year, he counted, in Aberdeenshire, thirty-five men, women, and children, in one band, with six asses and two carts, for carrying their luggage and articles of merchandise. Another individual stated to me, that upwards of three hundred of the Gipsies attended the funeral of one of their old females, who died near the bridge of Earn. So late as 1841, the sheriff of East Lothian addressed a representation to the justices of the peace of Mid-Lothian, recommending a new law for the suppression of the numerous Gipsy tents in the Lothians. I have, myself, during a walk of two hours, counted, in Edinburgh and its suburbs, upwards of fifty of these vagrants, strolling about.*

When I visited St. Boswell's, I felt convinced, as mentioned in the last chapter, that there were upwards of three hundred Gipsies in the fair held at that place. Part of them formed their carts, laden with earthen-ware, into two lines, leaving a space between them, like a street. In the rear of the carts were a few small tents, in which were Gipsies, sleeping in the midst of the noise and bustle of the market; and numbers of children, horses, asses, and dogs, hanging around them. There were also kettles, suspended from triangles, in which victuals were cooking; and many of the Gipsies enjoyed a warm meal, while others at the market had to content themselves with a cold repast. In the midst of the throng of this large and crowded fair, I noticed, without the least discomposure on their part, some of the male Gipsies changing their dirty, greasy-looking shirts for clean ones,

greater part of the vagrants mentioned in these notices are Gipsies; at least most of them speak the Gipsy language. [It matters not whether the people mentioned are wholly or only partly of Gipsy blood; it is sufficient if they have been reared as Gipsies. There are enough of the tribe in the country to follow the kind of life mentioned, to the extent the people can afford to submit to, without having their prerogatives infringed upon by ordinary natives. Where will we find any of the latter, who would betake themselves to the tent, and follow such a mode of life? Besides, the Gipsies, with their organization, would not tolerate it; and far less would they allow any common natives, of the lowest class, to travel in their company.—Ed.]

* Owing to such causes as these, many of the Gipsies have been again driven into their holes. It is amusing to notice the tricks which some of them resort to, in evading the letter of the Vagrant Act. They generally encamp on the borders of two counties, which they will cross—passing over into the other—to avoid being taken up: for county officers have no jurisdiction over them, beyond the boundaries of their respective shires.—Ed.

leaving no covering on their tawny persons, but their breeches; and some of the old females, with bare shoulders and breasts, combing their dark locks, like black horses' tails, mixed with grey. "Ae whow! look at that," exclaimed a countryman to his companion; and, without waiting for his friend's reply, he gravely added: "Everything after its kind." The Gipsies were, in short, dressing themselves for the fair, in the midst of the crowd, regardless of everything passing around them.

On my return from the English Border, I passed over the field where the fair had been held, two days before, and found, to my surprise, the Gipsies occupying their original encampment. They, alone, were in possession of St. Boswell's Green. I counted twenty-four carts, thirty horses, twenty asses, and about thirty dogs; and I thought there were upwards of a hundred men, women, and children, on the spot. The horses were, in general, complete rosinantes—as lean, worn-out, wretched-looking animals, as possibly could be imagined. The field trampled almost to mortar, by the multitude of horses, cattle, and sheep, and human beings, at the fair; the lean, jaded and lame horses, braying asses, and surly-looking dogs; the groups of miserable furniture, ragged children, and gloomy-looking parents; a fire, here and there, smoking before as many miserable tents—when contrasted with the gaily-dressed multitude, of both sexes, on the spot, two days before—presented a scene unequalled for its wretched, squalid and desolate appearance. Any one desirous of viewing an Asiatic encampment, in Scotland, should visit St. Boswell's Green, a day or two after the fair.*

The following may be said to be about the condition in which the present race of Scottish *tinkering* Gipsies are to

* St. Boswell's fair "is the resort of many salesmen of goods, and, in particular, of *tinkers*. Bands of these very peculiar people, the direct descendants of the original Gipsies, who so much annoyed the country in the fifteenth century, haunt the fair, for the disposal of earthen-ware, horn spoons, and tin culinary utensils. They possess, in general, horses and carts, and they form their temporary camp by each *whomling* his cart upside down, and forming a lodgement with straw and bedding beneath. Cooking is performed outside the *craal*, in Gipsy fashion. There could not, perhaps, be witnessed, at the present day, in Britain, a more amusing and interesting scene, illustrative of a rude period, than is here annually exhibited."—*Chambers' Gazetteer of Scotland.* [This writer is in error as to the Gipsies annoying the country in the *fifteenth* century: that occurred during the three following centuries.—Ed.]

be found: I visited, at one time, a horde of Gipsy tinsmiths, bivouacked by the side of a small streamlet, about half a mile from the town of Inverkeithing. It consisted of three married couples, the heads of as many families, one grown-up, unmarried female, and six half-clad children below six years of age. Including the more grown-up members, scattered about in the neighbourhood, begging victuals, there must have been above twenty souls belonging to this band. The tinsmiths had two horses and one ass, for carrying their luggage, and several dogs. They remained, during three cold and frosty nights, encamped in the open fields, with no tents or covering, for twenty individuals, but two pairs of old blankets.* Some of the youngest children, however, were pretty comfortably lodged at night. The band had several boxes, or rather old chests, each about four feet long, two broad, and two deep, in which they carried their white-iron plates, working tools, and some of their infants, on the backs of their horses. In these chests the children passed the night, the lids being raised a little, to prevent suffocation. The stock of working tools, for each family, consisted of two or three files, as many small hammers, a pair of bellows, a wooden mallet, a pair of pincers, a pair of large shears, a crucible, a soldering-iron or two, and a small anvil, of a long shape, which was stuck into the ground.

The females as well as the males of this horde of Gipsies were busily employed in manufacturing white-iron into household utensils, and the clink of their hammers was

* The Gipsies' supreme luxury is to lie, day and night, so near the fire as to be in danger of burning. At the same time, they can bear to travel in the severest cold, bare-headed, with no other covering than a torn shirt, or some old rags carelessly thrown over them, without fear of catching cold, cough, or any other disorder. They are a people blessed with an iron constitution. Neither wet nor dry weather, heat nor cold, let the extremes follow each other ever so close, seems to have any effect upon them. —*Grellmann on the Hungarian Gipsies.*

Their power of resisting cold is truly wonderful, as it is not uncommon to find them encamped, in the midst of the snow, in light canvas tents, when the temperature is 25 or 30 degrees below freezing point, according to Raumer.—*Borrow on the Russian Gipsies.*

It is no uncommon thing to see a poor Scottish Gipsy wrap himself and wife in a thin, torn blanket, and pass the night, in the cold of December, in the open air, by the wayside. On rising up in the morning, they will shake themselves in their rags, as birds of prey, in coming off their perch, do their feathers; make for the nearest public-house, with, perhaps, their last copper, for a gill; and, like the ravens, go in search of a breakfast, wherever and whenever Providence may send it to them.—ED.

heard from daybreak till dark.* The males formed the plates into the shapes of the different utensils required, and the females soldered and otherwise completed them, while the younger branches of the families presented them for sale in the neighbourhood. The breakfast of the band consisted of potatoes and herrings, which the females and children had collected in the immediate neighbourhood by begging. I noticed that each family ate their meals by themselves, wrought at their calling by themselves, and sold their goods for themselves. The name of the chief of the gang was Williamson, who said he travelled in the counties of Fife and Perth. When I turned to leave them, they heaped upon me the most fulsome praises, and so loud, that I might distinctly hear them, exactly in the manner as those in Spain, mentioned by Dr. Bright.

I have, for many months running, counted above twenty Gipsies depart out of the town of Inverkeithing, about ten o'clock in the forenoon, every day, on their way to various parts of the country; and I have been informed that from twenty to thirty vagrants lodged in this small burgh nightly. Some of the bakers declared that the persons who were the worst to please with hot rolls for breakfast, were the beggars, or rather Gipsies, who frequented the place. On one occasion, I observed twelve females, without a single male among them, decamp out of the town, all travelling in and around a cart, drawn by a shagged pony. The whole party were neatly attired, some of the young girls having trowsers, with frills about their ankles; and very few would have taken them for Gipsies. A large proportion of those miserable-looking females, who are accompanied by a number of ragged children, and scatter themselves through the streets, and beg from door to door, are Gipsies. I do not recollect, distressing as the times ever have been, of having seen reduced Scotch tradesmen *begging in families.* I remember once seeing a man with a white apron wrapped around his waist, his coat off, an infant in his arms, and

* Some of the itinerant Gipsies, doubtless, use their trades, in a great measure, as a cover for living by means such as society deems very objectionable. Many of them work hard while they are at it, as in the above instance, when "the clink of their hammers was heard from daybreak till dark;" and as has been said of those in Tweed-dale—"however early the farm servants rose to their ordinary employments, they always found the Tinklers at work."—Ed.

two others at his feet, accompanied by a dark-looking fellow of about twenty, singing through the town mentioned. They represented themselves as broken-down tradesmen, and had the appearance of having just left their looms, to sing for bread; and many half-pence they received. Suspecting them to be impostors, I observed their motions, and soon saw them join other vagrants, outside of the town, among whom were females. The poor tradesmen were now dressed in very substantial drab surtouts. They were nothing but a family of Tinklers. They were proceeding, with great speed, to the next town, to practise their impositions on the inhabitants; and I learned that they had, in this manner, traversed several counties in Scotland. At a subsequent period, I fell in with another family, consisting of five children and their parents, driving an ass and its colt, near the South Queensferry. Upon the back of the ass were two stone-hammers, and two reaping-hooks, placed in such a manner as any one, in passing, might observe them. I enquired where they had been. "We have been in England, sir, seeking work, but could find none." Few would have taken them for anything but country labourers; but the truth was, they were a family of Gipsies, of the well-known name of Marshall, from about Stranraer. Their implements of industry, so conspicuously exhibited on the back of their ass, was all deception.

It is only about twenty-five years since the Irish Gipsies, in bands, made their appearance in Scotland. Many severe conflicts they had with our Scottish tribes, before they obtained a footing in the country. But there is a new swarm of Irish Gipsies at present scattered, in bands, over Scotland, all acquainted with the Gipsy language. They are a set of the most wretched creatures on the face of the earth. A horde of them, consisting of several families, encamped, at one time, at Port Edgar, on the banks of the Forth, near South Queensferry. They had three small tents, two horses, and four asses, and trafficked in an inferior sort of earthenware. On the outside of one of the tents, in the open air, with nothing but the canopy of heaven above her, and the greensward beneath her, one of the females, like the deer in the forest, brought forth a child, without either the infant or mother receiving the slightest injury.* The woman.

* I know another instance of a Gipsy having a child in the open fields.

however, was attended by a midwife from Queensferry, who said that these Irish Gipsies were so completely covered with filth and vermin, that she durst not enter one of their tents, to assist the female in labour. Several individuals were attracted to the spot, by the novelty of such an occurrence, in so unusual a place as the open fields. Immediately after the child was born, it was handed about to every one of the band, that they might look at the "young donkey," as they called it. In about two days after the accouchement, the horde proceeded on their journey, as if nothing had happened.*

It took place among the rushes on Stanhope-haugh, on the banks of the Tweed. In the forenoon, she was delivered of her child, without the assistance of a midwife, and in the afternoon the hardy Gipsy resumed her journey. The infant was a daughter, named Mary Baillie.

[When a Gipsy woman is confined, it is either in a miserable hut or in the open air, but always easily and fortunately. True Gipsy-like, for want of some vessel, a hole is dug in the ground, which is filled with cold water, and the new-born child is washed in it.—*Grellmann, on the Hungarian Gipsies.* We may readily believe that a child coming into the world under the circumstances mentioned, would have some of the peculiarities of a wild duck. Mr. Hoyland says that "on the first introduction of a Gipsy child to school, he flew like a bird against the sides of its cage; but by a steady care, and the influence of the example of the other children, he soon became settled, and fell into the ranks." It pleases the Gipsies to know that their ancestors came into the world "like the deer in the forest," and, when put to school, "flew like a bird against the sides of its cage."—ED.]

* This invasion of Scotland by Irish Gipsies has, of late years, greatly altered the condition of the nomadic Scottish tribes; for this reason, that as Scotland, no less than any other country, can support only a certain number of such people who "live on the road," so many of the Scottish Gipsies have been forced to betake themselves to other modes of making a living. To such an extent has this been the case, that Gipsies, speaking the Scottish dialect, are in some districts comparatively rarely to be met with, where they were formerly numerous. The same cause may even lead to the extinction of the Scottish Gipsies as wanderers; but as the descendants of the Irish Gipsies will acquire the Scottish vernacular in the second generation, (a remarkably short period among the Gipsies,) what will then pass for Scottish Gipsies will be Irish by descent. The Irish Gipsies are allowed, by their English brethren, to speak good Gipsy, but with a broad and vulgar accent; so that the language in Scotland will have a still better chance of being preserved.

England has likewise been invaded by these Irish swarms. The English Gipsies complain bitterly of them. "They have no law among them," they say; "they have fairly destroyed Scotland as a country to travel in; if they get a loan of anything from the country-people, to wrap themselves in, in the barn, at night, they will decamp with it in the morning. They have brought a disgrace upon the very name of Gipsy, in Scotland, and are heartily disliked by both English and Scotch." "There is a family of Irish Gipsies living across the road there, whom I would not be seen speaking

But there are Irish Gipsies of a class much superior to the above, in Scotland. In 1836, a very respectable and wealthy master-tradesman informed me that the whole of the individuals employed in his manufactory, in Edinburgh, were Irish Gipsies.*

The Gipsies do not appear to have been altogether free from the crime of destroying their offspring, when, by infirmities, they could not be carried along with them in their wanderings, and thereby became an encumbrance to them. It has, indeed, been often noticed that few, or no, deformed or sickly individuals are to be found among them.† The following appears to be an instance of something like the practice in question. A family of Gipsies were in the habit of calling periodically, in their peregrinations over the country, at the house of a lady in Argyleshire. They frequently brought with them a daughter, who was ailing of some lingering disorder. The lady noticed the sickly child, and often spoke kindly to her parents about her condition. On one occasion, when the family arrived on her premises, she missed the child, and enquired what had become of her, and whether she had recovered. The father said his daughter was "a poor sickly thing, not worth carrying about with them," and that he had "made away with her." Whether any notice was taken of this murder, by the authorities, is

to," said a superior English Gipsy; "I hate a Jew, and I dislike an Irish Gipsy." But English and Scottish Gipsies pull well together; and are on very friendly terms in America, and frequently visit each other. The English sympathize with the Scottish, under the wrongs they have experienced at the hands of the Irish, as well as on account of the persecutions they experienced in Scotland, so long after such had ceased in England.

Twenty-five years ago, there were many Gipsies to be found between Londonderry and Belfast, following the style of life described under the chapter of Tweed-dale and Clydesdale Gipsies. Their names were Docherty, McCurdy, McCloskey, McGuire, McKay, Holmes, Dinsmore, Morrow, Allan, Stewart, Lindsay, Cochrane, and Williamson. Some of these seem to have migrated from Scotland and the North of England.—Ed.

* In England, some of the Irish Gipsies send their children to learn trades. There are many of such Irish mechanic Gipsies in America. A short time ago, a company of them landed in New York, and proceeded on to Chicago. Their occupations, among others, were those of hatters and tailors.—Ed.

† They are neither overgrown giants nor diminutive dwarfs; and their limbs are formed in the justest proportions. Large bellies are as uncommon among them as humpbacks, blindness, or other corporeal defects.—*Grellmann on the Hungarian Gipsies.*—Ed.

not mentioned. The Gipsies, however, are generally noted for a remarkable attachment to their children.*

Several authors have brought a general charge of cowardice against the Gipsies, in some of the countries of Europe; but I never saw or heard of any grounds for bringing such a charge against the Scottish Gipsies. On the contrary, I always considered our Tinklers the very reverse of cowards. Heron, in his journey through part of Scotland, before the year 1793, when speaking of the Gipsies in general, says: "They make excellent soldiers, whenever the habit of military discipline can be sufficiently impressed upon them." Several of our Scottish Gipsies have even enjoyed commissions, as has already been noticed.† But the

* The *Ross-shire Advertiser*, for April, 1842, says: "Gipsy Recklessness.—Last week, two Gipsy women, who were begging through the country, each with a child on her back, having got intoxicated, took up their lodgings, for the night, in an old sawpit, in the parish of Logie-Easter. It is supposed that they forgot to take the children off their backs, when going to rest; for, in the morning, they were found to be both dead, having been smothered by their miserable mothers lying upon them through the night. One of the women, upon awakening in the morning, called to the other, "that her baby was dead," to which the reply was, "that it could not be helped." Having dug a hole, they procured some straw, rolled up the children in it, put them in the hole, and then filled it up with the earth."

† Though Gipsies everywhere, they differ, in some respects, in the various countries which they inhabit. For example, an English Gipsy, of pugilistic tendencies, will, in a vapouring way, engage to *thrash* a dozen of his Hungarian brethren. The following is the substance of what Grellmann says on this feature of their character:

Sulzer says a Gipsy requires to have been a long time in the army before he can meet an enemy's balls with decent soldiers' resolution. They have often been employed in military expeditions, but never as regular soldiers. In the thirty years' war, the Swedes had a body of them in the army; and the Danes had three companies of them at the siege of Hamburg, in 1686. They were chiefly employed in flying parties, to burn, plunder, or lay waste the enemy's country.

In two Hungarian regiments, nearly every eighth man is a Gipsy. In order to prevent either them (!) or any others from remembering their descent, it is ordered, by the Government, that as soon as a Gipsy joins the regiment, he is no longer to be called by that appellation. Here he is placed promiscuously with other men. But whether he would be adequate to a soldier's station—unmixed with strangers, in the company of his equals only—is very doubtful. He has every outward essential for a soldier, yet his innate properties, his levity, and want of foresight, render him incompatible for the services of one, as an instance may illustrate. Francis von Perenyi, who commanded at the siege of Nagy Ida, being short of men, was obliged to have recourse to the Gipsies, of whom he collected a thousand. These he stationed behind the entrenchments, while he reserved his own men to garrison the citadel. The Gipsies sup

military is not a life to their taste, as we have already seen; for, rather than enter it, they will submit to even personal mutilation. There is even danger in employing them in our regiments at the seat of war; as I am convinced that, if there are any Gipsies in the ranks of the enemy, an improper intercourse will exist between them in both armies. During the last rebellion in Ireland, the Gipsy soldiers in our regiments kept up an intimate and friendly correspondence with their brethren among the Irish rebels.*

The Scottish Gipsies have ever been distinguished for their gratitude to those who treated them with civility and kindness, during their progress through the country. The

ported the attack with so much resolution, and returned the fire of the enemy with such alacrity, that the assailants—little suspecting who were the defendants—were compelled to retreat. But the Gipsies, elated with victory, immediately crept out of their holes, and cried after them, "Go, and be hanged, you rascals! and thank God that we had no more powder and shot, or we would have played the devil with you!" "What!" they exclaimed, bearing in mind the proverb, "You can drive fifty Gipsies before you with a wet rag," "What! are *you* the heroes?" and, so saying, the beleaguers immediately wheeled about, and, sword in hand, drove the black crew back to their works, entered them along with them, and in a few minutes totally routed them.—Ed.

* A Gipsy possesses all the properties requisite to render him a fit agent to be employed in traitorous undertakings. Being necessitous, he is easily corrupted; and his misconceived ambition and pride persuade him that he thus becomes a person of consequence. He is, at the same time, too inconsiderate to reflect on danger; and, artful to the greatest degree, he works his way under the most difficult circumstances. Gipsies have not only served much in the capacity of spies, but their garb and manner of life have been assumed by military and other men for the same purpose.—*Grellmann on the Hungarian Gipsies.*

Mr. Borrow gives a very interesting description of a meeting of two Gipsies, in a battle between the French and Spaniards, in the Peninsula, in Bonaparte's time. In the midst of a desperate battle—when everything was in confusion—sword to sword and bayonet to bayonet—a French soldier singled out one of the enemy, and, after a severe personal contest, got his knee on his breast, and was about to run his bayonet through him. His cap at this moment fell off, when his intended victim, catching his eye, cried, "*Zincali, Zincali!*" at which the other shuddered, relaxed his grasp, smote his forehead, and wept. He produced his flask, and poured wine into his brother Gipsy's mouth; and they both sat down on a knoll, while all were fighting around. "Let the dogs fight, and tear each other's throats, till they are all destroyed: what matters it to us? They are not of our blood, and shall that be shed for them?"

What our author says of there being danger in employing Gipsies in time of war has little or no foundation; for the associations between those in the opposite ranks would be merely those of interest, friendship, assistance, and scenes like the one depicted by Mr. Borrow. The objection to Gipsies, on such occasions, is as applicable to Jews and Freemasons.—Ed.

particulars of the following instance of a Gipsy's gratitude are derived from a respectable farmer, to whom one of the tribe offered assistance in his pecuniary distress. I was well acquainted with both of them. The occurrence, which took place only about ten years ago, will show that gratitude is still a prominent feature in the character of the Scottish Gipsy.

The farmer became embarrassed in his circumstances, in the spring of the year, when an ill-natured creditor, for a small sum, put him in jail, with a design to extort payment of the debt from his relatives. The farmer had always allowed a Gipsy chief, of the name of ——, with his family, to take up his quarters on his premises, whenever the horde came to the neighbourhood. The Gipsy's horse received the same provender as the farmer's horses, and himself and family the same victuals as the farmer's servants. So sure was the Gipsy of his lodgings, that he seldom needed to ask permission to stay all night on the farm, when he arrived. On learning that the farmer was in jail, he immediately went to see him. When he called, the jailer laughed at him, and, for long, would not intimate to the farmer that he wished to see him. With tears in his eyes, the Gipsy then told him he "would be into the jail, and see the honest man, whether he would or not." At last, an hour was fixed when he would be allowed to enter the prison. When the time arrived, the Gipsy made his appearance, with a quantity of liquor in his hand, for his friend the farmer. "Weel, man," said he to the turnkey, "is this your hour, now?" being displeased at the delay which had taken place. The jailer again said to him that he was surely joking, and still refused him admittance. "Joking, man?" exclaimed the Gipsy, with the tears again glistening in his dark eyes, "I am not joking, for into this prison I shall be; and if it is not by the door, it shall be by another way." Observing the determined Gipsy quite serious, the jailer at last allowed him to see the object of his search. The moment he saw the farmer, he took hold of both his hands, and, immediately throwing his arms around him, burst into tears, and was for some time so overcome by grief, that he could not give utterance to his feelings. Recovering himself, he enquired if it was the laird that had put him in prison; but on being told it was a writer, one of his creditors, the Gipsy exclaimed,

"They are a d——d crew, thae writers,* and the lairds are little better." With much feeling, he now said to his friend, "Your father, honest man, was aye good to my horse, and your mother, poor body, was aye kind to me, when I came to the farm. I was aye treated like one of their own household, and I can never forget their kindness. Many a night's quarters I received from them, when others would not suffer me to approach their doors." The grateful Gipsy now offered the farmer fifty pounds, to relieve him from prison. "We are," said he, "not so poor as folk think we are;" and, putting his hand into his pocket, he added, "Here is part of the money, which you will accept; and if fifty pounds will not do, I will sell all that I have in the world, horses and all, to get you out of this place." "Oh, my bonnie man," continued the Gipsy, "had I you in my camp, at the back of the dyke, I would be a happy man. You would be far better there than in this hole." The farmer thanked him for his kind offer, but declined to accept it. "We are," resumed the Gipsy, "looked upon as savages, but we have our feelings, like other people, and never forget our friends and benefactors. Kind, indeed, have your relatives been to me, and all I have in this world is at your service." When the Gipsy found that his offer was not accepted, he insisted that the farmer would allow him to supply him, from time to time, with pocket money, in case he should, during his confinement, be in want of the necessaries of life. Before leaving the prison, the farmer asked the Gipsy to take a cup of tea with him; but long the Gipsy modestly refused to eat with him, saying, "I am a black thief-looking deevil, to sit down and eat in your company; but I will do it, this day, for your sake, since you ask it of me." The Gipsy's wife, with all her family, also insisted upon being allowed to see the farmer in prison.†

* A *writer* in Scotland corresponds with an *attorney* in England. It is interesting to notice the opinion which the Gipsy entertained of the writers. Possibly he had been a good deal worried by them, in connection with the conduct of some of his folk.—Ed.

† There is something singularly inconsistent in the mind of the Gipsies. They pride themselves, to an extraordinary degree, in their race and language; at the same time, they are extremely sensitive to the prejudice that exists against them. "We feel," say they, "that every other creature despises us, and would crush us out of existence, if it could be done. No doubt, there are things which many of the Gipsies do not hold to be a shame, that others do; but, on the other hand, they hold some things to

This interview took place in presence of several persons, who were surprised at the gratitude and manner of the determined Gipsy. It is proper to mention that he is considered a very honest man, and is a protection to the property of the country-people, wherever he is quartered. He sells earthen-ware, through the country, and has, sometimes, several horses in his possession, more for pleasure than profit, some of which the farmers graze for nothing, as he is a great favourite with those who are intimately acquainted with him. He is about fifty years of age, about six feet in height, is spare made, has small black eyes, and a swarthy complexion. He is styled King of the Gipsies, but the country-people call him "Terrible," for a by-name. It was said his mother was a witch, and many of the simple, ignorant people, in the country, actually believed she was one. That

be a shame which others do not. They have many good points. They are kind to their own people, and will feed and clothe them, if it is in their power; and they will not molest others who treat them civilly. They are somewhat like the wild American Indians: they even go so far as to despise their own people who will willingly conform to the ways of the people among whom they live, even to putting their heads under a roof. But, alas! a hard necessity renders it unavoidable; a necessity of two kinds—that of making a living under the circumstances in which they find themselves placed, and the impossibility of enforcing their laws among themselves. Let them do what they may, live as they may, believe what they may, they are looked upon as everything that is bad. Yet they are a people, an ancient and mysterious people, that have been scattered by the will of Providence over the whole earth."

It is to escape this dreadful prejudice that all Gipsies, excepting those who avowedly live and profess themselves Gipsies, will hide their race, if they can, and particularly so, in the case of those who fairly leave the tent, conform to the ordinary ways of society, and engage in any of its various callings. While being conveyed by the son of an English Gipsy, whose family I had been visiting, at their house, where I had heard them freely speak of themselves as Gipsies, and converse in Gipsy, I said, in quite a pleasant tone, "Ah, my little man, and you are a young Gipsy?—Eh, what's the matter?" "I don't wish to be known to the people as a Gipsy." His father, on another occasion, said, "We are not ashamed to say to a friend that we are Gipsies; but my children don't like people to be crying after them, 'Look at the Gipsies!'" And yet this family, like all Gipsies, were strongly attached to their race and language. It was pitiful to think that there was so much reason for them to make such a complaint. On one occasion, I was asked, "If you would not deem it presumptuous, might we ask you to take a bite with us?" "Eat with you? Why not?" I replied. "What will your people think, if they knew that you had been eating with us? You will lose caste." This was said in a serious manner, but slightly tinged with irony. Bless me, I thought, are all our Scottish Gipsies, of high and low degree, afraid that the ordinary natives would not even eat with them, if they knew them to be Gipsies!—Ed.

her son believed she possessed supernatural power, will appear from the following fact: As some one was lamenting the hard case of the farmer remaining in prison, the Gipsy gravely said, "Had my mother been able to go to the jail, to see the honest man, she possessed the power to set him free."

That numbers of our Gipsies attend the church, and publicly profess Christianity, and get their children baptized, is certain; and that many of the male heads of principal families have the appearance and reputation of great honesty of character, is also certain. Yet their wives and other members of their families are, in general, little better than professed thieves; and are secretly countenanced and encouraged in their practices by many of those very chief males, who designedly keep up an outward show of integrity, for the purpose of deception, and of affording their plundering friends protection. When the head of the family is believed to be an honest man, it excites a feeling of sympathy for his tribe on his account, and it enables him to step forward, with more freedom, to protect his kindred, when they happen to get into scrapes. I am convinced, could the fact be ascertained, that many of the offenders who are daily brought before our courts of justice are Gipsies, though their external appearance does not indicate them to be of that race.

With regard to the education of our Scottish Gipsies, I am convinced that very few of them receive any education at all; except some of those among the superior classes, who have property in houses, and permanent residences. A Gipsy, of some property, who gave one of her sons a good education, declared that the young man was entirely spoiled.* It appears, however, that the males of the Yetholm colony received such an education as is commonly given to the working classes; but it is supposed there is scarcely such a thing as a female Gipsy who has been educated. There are, however, instances to the contrary; and I know one

* It is well to notice the fact, that by giving a Gipsy child a good education, it became "entirely spoiled." It would be well if we could "spoil" all the Gipsies. A thoroughly-spoiled Gipsy makes a very good man, but leaves him a Gipsy notwithstanding. A "thorough Gipsy" has two meanings; one strongly attached to the tribe, and its *original habits*, or one without these original habits. There are a good many "spoiled" Gipsies, male and female, in Scotland.—Ed.

female at least, who can handle her pen with some dexterity.*

As to their religious sentiments, I am inclined to think that the greater part of the Scottish Gipsies are quite indifferent on the subject. Numbers of them certainly attend church, occasionally, when at home, in their winter quarters; but not one of them will enter its door when travelling through the country.† On Sundays, while resting themselves by the side of the public roads, the females employ themselves in washing and sewing their apparel, without any regard for that sacred day. It appears to me that a large proportion of them comply with our customs and forms of worship, more for the purpose of concealing their tribe and practices, than from any serious belief in the doctrines of Christianity. I recollect, however, of once conversing with an aged man who professed much apparent zeal in religious matters; and I mind well that he stoutly maintained, in opposition to Calvin's ideas on the subject of free grace, that everything depended upon our own works. "By my works in this life," said he, "I must stand, or fall, in the world to come." This very man acknowledged to me that the Gipsies were a tribe of thieves. But almost all the Gipsies, when the subject of religion is mentioned to them, affect to be very pious; speak of the goodness of God to them,

* The education and acquirements of the Spanish Gipsies, according to Mr. Borrow, are, on the whole, not inferior to those of the lower classes of the Spaniards; some of the young *men* being able to read and write in a manner by no means contemptible; but such never occurs among the females. Neglecting females, in the matter of education, is quite in keeping with the Oriental origin of the Gipsies. The same feature is observable among the Jews; and the Talmud bears heavily upon Jewish women. Every Jew says, in his morning prayer, "Blessed art thou, O Lord, our God, King of the Universe, who hast not made me a woman!" And the woman returns thanks for having been "created according to God's will." —ED.

† The ostensible reason which the Gipsy gives for not attending church, when travelling, is to prevent himself being ridiculed by the people. If he enters a place of worship, he makes the old people stare, and frightens the children. On returning from church, a child will exclaim, "Mother, mother, there was a Tinkler at the kirk, to-day."—"A what? a *Tinkler* at the kirk? What could have possessed *him* to go there?"

Gipsies are extremely sensitive to the feeling in question. A short time ago, one of them entered ——, in the State of ——, with a "shears to grind," having a small bell attached. Some bar-room gentry assembled around him, and saluted him with, "Oh, oh, a Gipsy in a new rig!" So keenly did he feel the insult, that he at once left the village.—ED.

with much apparent sincerity; lament the want of education; and reprobate, in strong terms, every act of immorality. This, I am sorry to say, is, in general, all hypocrisy and deception. There is not a better test, in a general way, for discovering who are Gipsies, than the expression of "God bless you," which is constantly in the mouth of every female.*

With regard to the general politics of the Scottish Gipsies, if they entertain any political sentiments at all, I am convinced they are monarchical; and that, were any revolutionary convulsion to loosen the bonds of society, and separate the lower from the higher classes, they would take to the side of the superior portion of the community. They have, at all times, heartily despised the peasantry, and been disposed to treat menials with great contempt, though, at the very moment, they were begging at the doors of their masters. In the few instances which have come to my knowledge, of Scottish Gipsies forming matrimonial connex-

* According to Grellmann, the Gipsies did not bring any particular religion with them from their own country, but have regulated it according to those of the countries in which they have lived. They suffer themselves to be baptized among Christians, and circumcised among Mahommedans. They are Greeks with Greeks, Catholics with Catholics, Protestants with Protestants, and as inconstant in their creed as their place of residence. They suffer their children to be several times baptized. To-day, they receive the sacrament as a Lutheran; next Sunday, as a Catholic; and, perhaps before the end of the week, in the Reformed Church. The greater part of them do not go so far as this, but live without any religion at all, and worse than heathens. So thoroughly indifferent are they in this respect, as to have given rise to the adage, "The Gipsy's church was built of bacon, and the dogs ate it." So perfectly convinced are the Turks of the insincerity of the Gipsy in matters of religion, that, although a Jew, by becoming a Mahommedan, is freed from the payment of the poll-tax, a Gipsy—at least in the neighbourhood of Constantinople—is not, even although his ancestors, for centuries, had been Mahommedans, or he himself should actually have made a pilgrimage to Mecca. His only privilege is to wear a white turban, which is denied to unbelieving Jews and Gipsies.

Mr. Borrow says, that when the female Gipsies, who sing in the choirs of Moscow, were questioned, in their own language, about their externally professing the Greek religion, they laughed, and said it was only to please the Russians.

The same author mentions an instance in which he preached to them; taking, for his text, the situation of the Hebrews in Egypt, and drawing a comparison between it and theirs in Spain. Warming with his subject, he spoke of the power of God in preserving both, as a distinct people, in the world, to this day. On concluding, he looked around to see what impression he had made upon them, but the only response he got from them all was—a squint of the eye!—Ed.

ions with individuals of the community, those individuals were not of the working or lower classes of society.*

I believe there are Gipsies, in more or less numbers, in almost every town in Scotland, permanent as well as periodical residenters. In many of the villages there are also Gipsy inhabitants. In Mid-Lothian there are great numbers of them, who have houses, in which they reside permanently, but a portion of them travel in other districts, during the summer season. I have been at no ordinary pains and trouble in making enquiries regarding the number of the Gipsies, and the result of my numerous investigations induces me to believe that there are about five thousand of them in Scotland, at the present day. Indeed, some of the Gipsies themselves entertain the same opinion, and they must certainly be allowed to have some idea of the number of their own fraternity.†

It appears to me that the civilization and improvement of the body, generally, would be a work of great difficulty. I would be apt to give nearly the same answer which a Hungarian nobleman gave to Dr. Bright, when that traveller asked him if he could not devise a plan for bettering the condition of the race in Hungary. The nobleman said he knew of no manner of improving the Gipsies.‡ The best plan yet proposed for improving the race appears to be

* What our author says of the politics of the Gipsies is rather more applicable to their ideas of their social position. Being a small body in comparison with the general population of the country, they entertain a very exclusive and, consequently, a very aristocratic idea of themselves, whatever others may think of them; and therefore scorn the prejudice of the very lowest order of the common natives.—Ed.

† Before the reformation of our criminal law, many of the male Gipsies perished on the gallows, but now, the greatest punishment they meet with is banishment, or a short imprisonment, for "sorning, pickery, and little thieving." Few of them are now "married to the gallows tree," in the manner of Graham, as described under the head of Fifeshire Gipsies. Owing to their, (the more original kind especially,) all marrying very young, and having very large families, their number cannot fail to encrease, under the present laws, in a ratio far beyond that of our own population. Instead of there being only 5,000 Gipsies in Scotland, there are, as I have already said, nearer 100,000, for reasons to be given in my Disquisition on the Gipsies. —Ed.

‡ Speaking of the attempted civilization of the Gipsies, by the Empress Maria Theresa, Grellmann says, "A boy, (for you must leave the old stock alone,) would frequently seem in the most promising train to civilization; on a sudden, his wild nature would appear, a relapse follow, and he become a perfect Gipsy again."

the one suggested by the Rev. James Crabb, of Southampton, and the Rev. John Baird, of Yetholm.* One of the first

"*Curate*—Could you not, by degrees, bring yourself to a more settled mode of life?

"*Gipsy*.—I would not tell you a lie, sir; I really think I could not, having been brought up to it from a child."—*Hoyland on the English Gipsies.*

The restless desire which the more original kind of Gipsies, and those more recently from the tent, have for moving about, is generally gratified in some way or other. The poorer class will send their wives and young ones to the "grass," in company with the nomadic portion, or to the streets in towns. In either case, they have no great occasion to feel uneasy about their support; for she would be a poor wife indeed, if she could not forage for herself and "weary bairns." Among other things, she can hire herself to assist in disposing of the wares made by another Gipsy. Her husband will then work at his calling, or go on the *tramp*, like some of our ordinary mechanics.

The feeling which mankind in general have for the sweets of the country, and the longing which so many of us have to end our days in the midst of them, amounts almost to a mania with these Gipsies. Frequently will Gipsies, in England, after spending the best part of their lives in a settled occupation, again take to the tent; while others of them, on arrival in America, will buy themselves places, and live on them till seized with the travelling epidemic, communicated by a roving company of their tribe accidentally arriving in their neighbourhood. Some of the more recently settled class of Gipsies, whose occupations do not easily admit of their enjoying the pleasure of a country or travelling life, show a great partiality to their wandering brethren, however poor, with whom they are on terms of intimacy, and especially if they happen to be related. Their children, from hearing their parents speak of the "good old times"—the "golden age" of the Gipsies—when they could wander hither and thither, with little molestation, and live, in a measure, at free-quarters, wherever they went, grow impatient under the restraint which society has thrown around them; and vent their feelings in abusing that same society, and all the members thereof. They envy the lot of these "country cousins." Meetings of that kind render these Gipsies, (old as well as young,) irritable, discontented, and gloomy: they feel like "birds in a cage," as a Gipsy expressed it. Not unfrequently will a young town Gipsy travel in the company of these country relatives, dressed *a la Tinklaire*, as a relief to the discontentment which a restrained and pent-up life creates within him. At other times, his parents will know nothing of his movements, beyond his coming home to "roost" at night.

The nomadic class take to winter-quarters in some village, towards the close of the year, and fret themselves all day long, till, on the return of spring, they can say, "To your tents, O Gipsies!" There is as little direct relation existing between the tent and the long-settled Gipsies, as there is between it and ordinary Scotch people. But there is that tribal or national association connected with it, that is inseparable from the feelings of a Gipsy, however high may be the position in life to which he may have risen.—ED.

* The Fourteenth Annual Festival of the Rev. James Crabb's Association, for civilizing and teaching the principles of Christianity to the Gipsies in England, was held on the 25th December, 1841. At that time, twenty

steps, however, should be a complete publicity to their language, if that was possible; and encouragement held out to them to speak it openly, without fear or reproach. Their secret speech is a strong bond of union among them, and forms, as it were, a wall of separation between them and the other inhabitants of the country.

Many of the Gipsies, following the various occupations enumerated, are not now to be distinguished from others of the community, except by the most minute observation; yet they appear a distinct and separate people; seldom contracting marriage out of their own tribe.* A tradesman of Gipsy blood will sooner give his hand to a lady's maid of his own race, than marry the highest female in the land; while the Gipsy lady's maid will take a Gipsy shoemaker, in preference to any one out of her tribe. A Gipsy woman will far rather prefer, in marriage, a man of her own blood who has escaped the gallows, to the most industrious and best-behaved tradesman in the kingdom. Like the Jews, almost all those in good circumstances marry among themselves, and, I believe, employ their poorer brethren as servants. I have known Gipsies most solemnly declare, that

Gipsy youths were attending his school. He was very sanguine of ultimately ameliorating the condition of the British Gipsies.

At Yetholm, in the same year, after the Rev. John Baird's school had been in existence about two years, there were about forty Gipsy children receiving instruction. When they were educated, they were hired as servants to families, or bound apprentices to different trades.

[I will offer some remarks on the improvement of the Gipsies, in the Disquisition on the Gipsies.—Ed.]

* It is a difficult matter to tell some of the settled Scottish Gipsies. In searching for them, some regard must be had to the employment of the individual, his associations, and his isolation from the community generally, beyond what is necessary in following his calling and out-door relations, as contrasted with his hospitality to strangers from a distance; a close scrutiny of the habits of himself and his numerous motley visitors; the rough-and-tumble way in which he sometimes lives; his attachment to animals, such as horses, asses, dogs, cats, birds, or pets of any kind: these, and other relative circumstances, go a great way to enable one to pounce upon some of them. But the use of their language, and the effect it has upon them, (barring their responding to it,) is, at the present stage of their history, the only satisfactory test. Scottish Gipsy families will generally be found to be all dark in their appearance, or all very fair or reddish, or partly very fair, and partly very dark, and sometimes dark or fair nondescript. Many of the residentary class of mechanic Gipsies are difficult of detection; so are the better classes, generally, if it is long since their ancestors left the tent.—Ed.

no consideration would induce them to marry out of their own tribe; and I am informed, and convinced, that almost every one of them marries in that way. One of them stated to me that, let them be in whatever situation of life they may, they all "stick to each other."

A DISQUISITION ON THE PAST, PRESENT, AND FUTURE OF GIPSYDOM.

"There is nothing hid that shall not be revealed."

In giving an account of the Gipsies, the subject would be very incomplete, were not something said about the manner in which they have drawn into their body the blood of other people, and the way in which the race is perpetuated; and a description given of their present condition, and future prospects, particularly as our author has overlooked some important points connected with their history, which I will endeavour to furnish. One of these important points is, that he has confined his description of the present generation of settled Gipsies to the descendants of those who left the tent subsequently to the commencement of the French war, to the exclusion of those who settled long anterior to that time. It is also necessary to treat the subject abstractly—to throw it into principles, to give the philosophy of it—to ensure the better understanding, and perpetuate the knowledge of it, amid the shifting objects that present themselves to the eye of the world, and even of the people described.

Gipsydom may, in a word, be said to be literally a sealed book, a *terra incognita*, to mankind in general. The Gipsies arrived in Europe a strange race; strange in their origin, appearance, habits and disposition. Supposing that their habits had never led them to interfere with the property of others, or obtain money by any objectionable way, but that they had confined their calling to tinkering, making and selling wares, trading, and such like, they would, in all probability, still have remained a caste in the community, with a strong feeling of sympathy for those living in other countries, in consequence of the singularity of their origin and development, as distinguished from those of the other inhabitants, their language, and that degree of prejudice which most nations have for foreigners settling among them, and particularly so in the case of a people so different in their appearance and mode of life as were the Gipsies from those among whom they settled. That may especially be said of tented Gipsies, and even of those who, from time to time, would be forced to leave the tent, and settle in towns, or live as *tramps*, as distinguished from tented Gipsies. The simple idea of their origin and descent, tribe and language, transmitted from generation to generation, being so different from those of the people among whom they lived, was, in itself, perfectly sufficient to retain them members of Gipsydom, although, in cases of intermarriages with the natives, the mixed breeds might have gone over to the white race, and been lost to the general body. But in most of such cases that would hardly have taken place; for between the two races, the difference of feeling, were it only a slight jealousy, would have led the smaller and more exclusive and bigoted to bring the issue of such intermarriages within its influence. In Great Britain, the Gipsies are entitled, in one respect at least, to be called Englishmen, Scotchmen, or Irishmen; for their general ideas as men, as distinguished from their being Gipsies, and their language, indicate them, at once, to be such, nearly as much as the common natives of these countries. A half or mixed breed might more especially be termed or pass for a native; so that, by clinging to the Gipsies, and hiding his Gipsy descent and affiliation from the native race, he would lose nothing of the outward character of an ordinary inhabitant; while any benefit arising from his being a Gipsy would, at the same time, be enjoyed by him.

But the subject assumes a totally different aspect when, instead of a slight jealousy existing between the two races, the difference in feeling is such as if a gulf had been placed between them. The effect of a marriage between a white and a Gipsy, especially if he or she is known to be a Gipsy, is such, that the white instinctively withdraws from any connexion with his own race, and casts his lot with the Gipsies. The children born of such unions become ultra Gipsies. A very fine illustration of this principle of half-breed ultra Gipsyism is given by Mr. Borrow, in his "Gipsies in Spain," in the case of an officer in the Spanish army adopting a young female Gipsy child, whose parents had been executed, and educating and marrying her. A son of this marriage, who rose to be a captain in the service of Donna Isabel, hated the white race so intensely, as, when a child, to tell his father that he wished he (his father) was dead. At whose door must the cause of such a feeling be laid? One would naturally suppose that the child would have left, perhaps despised, his mother's people, and clung to those whom the world deemed respectable. But the case was different. Suppose the mother had not been prompted by some of her own race, while growing up, and the son, in his turn, not prompted by the mother, all that was necessary to stir up his hatred toward the white race was simply to know who he was, as I will illustrate.*

Suppose that a great iron-master should fancy a Cinderella, living by scraping pieces of iron from the refuse of his furnaces, educate her, and marry her, as great iron-masters have done. Being both of the same race, a complete amalgamation would take place at once: perhaps the wife was the best person of the two. Silly people might sneer at such a marriage; but if no objection attached to the personal character of the woman, she might be received into society at once, and admired by some, and envied by others, particularly if she had no "low relations" living near her. She might even boast of having been a Cinderella, if it happened to be well known; in which case she might be deemed free of pride, and consequently a very sensible, amiable woman, and worthy of every admiration.

But who ever heard of such a thing taking place with a Gipsy? Suppose a Gipsy elevated to such a position as that

* This Spanish Gipsy is reported by Mr. Borrow to have said: "She, however, remembered her blood, and hated my father, and taught me to hate him likewise. When a boy, I used to stroll about the plain, that I might not see my father; and my father would follow me, and beg me to look upon him, and would ask me what I wanted; and I would reply, 'Father, the only thing I want is to see you dead!'"

This is certainly an extreme instance of the result of the prejudice against the Gipsy race; and no opinion can be formed upon it, without knowing some of the circumstances connected with the feelings of the father, or his relations, toward the mother and the Gipsy race generally. This Gipsy woman seems to have been well brought up by her protector and husband for she *taught her child Gipsy from a MS.*, and procured a teacher to instruct him in Latin. There are many reflections to be drawn from the circumstances connected with this Spanish Gipsy family, but they do not seem to have occurred to Mr. Borrow

spoken of; she would not, she dare not, mention her descent to any one not of her own race, and far less would she give an *exposé* of Gipsydom; for she instinctively perceives, or at least believes, that, such is the prejudice against her race, people would avoid her as something horridly frightful, although she might be the finest woman in the world. Who ever heard of a civilized Gipsy, before Mr. Borrow mentioned those having attained to such an eminent position in society at Moscow? Are there none such elsewhere than in Moscow? There are many in Scotland. It is this unfortunate prejudice against the name that forces all our Gipsies, the moment they leave the tent, (which they almost invariably do with their blood diluted with the white,) to hide from the public their being Gipsies; for they are morbidly sensitive of the odium which attaches to the name and race being applied to them. It is quite time enough to discover the great secret of Nature, when it is unavoidable to enter

> "The undiscovered country from whose bourne
> No traveller returns."

As little disposition is manifested by these Gipsies to "show their hands:" the uncertainty of such an experiment makes the very idea dreadful to them. Hence it is that the constant aim of settled Gipsies is to hide the fact of their being Gipsies from other people.

It is a very common idea that Gipsies do not mix their blood with that of other people. Now, what is the fact? I may, indeed, venture to assert, that there is not a full-blooded Gipsy in Scotland;* and, most positively, that in England, where the race is held to be so pure, all that can be said of *some* families is, that they have not been crossed, *as far as is known;* but that, with these exceptions, the body is much mixed: "dreadfully mixed" is the Gipsies' description, as, in many instances, my own eyes have witnessed. This brings me to an issue with a writer in the Edinburgh Review, who, in October, 1841, when reviewing the "Gipsies in Spain," by Mr. Borrow, says, "Their descent is purity itself; no mixture of European blood has con-

* It is claimed, by some Scottish Gipsies, that there are full-blood Gipsies at Yetholm, but I do not believe it. This, I may venture to say, that there can be no certainty, but, on the contrary, great doubt, on the subject. But, after all, what is a pure Gipsy? Was the race pure when it entered Scotland, or even Europe? The idea is perfectly arbitrary.

taminated theirs. . . . . . They, (the stranger and Gipsy,) may live together; the European vagrant is often to be found in the tents of the Gipsies; they may join in the fellowship of sport, the pursuit of plunder, the management of their low trades, but they can never fraternize." A writer in Blackwood's Magazine, on the same occasion, says, "Their care to preserve the purity of their race might, in itself, have confuted the unfounded charge, so often brought against them, of stealing children, and bringing them up as Gipsies." More unfounded ideas than those put forth by these two writers are scarcely possible to be imagined.*

This mixture of "the blood" is notorious. Many a full or nearly full-blood Gipsy will say that Gipsies do not mix their blood with that of the stranger. In such a case he only shuffles; for he whispers to himself two words, in his own language, which contradict what he says; which words I forget, but they mean "I belie it;" that is, he belies what he has just said. Besides, it lets the Gipsies down in their imagination, and, they think, in the imagination of others, to allow that the blood of their race is mixed. It is also a secret which they would rather hide from the world.† I am intimate with English Gipsy families, in none of whom is full blood; the most that can be said of them is, that they range from nearly full, say from seven-eighths, down to one-eighth, and perhaps less. Suppose that a fair-haired common native marries a full-blood Gipsy: the issue of such an union will show some of the children, in point of external

* It would be interesting to know where these writers got such ideas about the purity of the Gipsy blood. It certainly was not from Mr. Borrow's account of the Gipsies in Spain, whatever they may have inferred from that work.

† An instance of this kind of shuffling is given by Mr. Borrow, in the tenth chapter of the "Romany Rye," in the person of Ursula, a full or nearly full-blood Gipsy. She confines the crossing of the blood to such instances as when a Gipsy dies and leaves his children to be provided for by "*gorgios*, trampers, and basket-makers, who live in caravans;" but she says, "I hate to talk of the matter." When Mr. Borrow asked her, if a Gipsy woman, unless compelled by hard necessity, would have anything to do with a *gorgio*, she replied, "We are not over-fond of *gorgios*, and we hate basket-makers and folks that live in caravans." Here she makes a very important distinction between *gorgios*, (native English,) and *basket-makers and folks that live in caravans*, (mixed Gipsies.) She does not deny that a Gipsy woman will intermarry with a native under certain circumstances. A pretty-pure Gipsy, when angry, will very readily call a mixed Gipsy a *gorgio*, or, indeed, by any other name.

appearance, perfectly European, like the father, and others, Gipsies, like the mother. If two such European-like Gipsies marry, some of their children will take after the Gipsy, and be pretty, even very, dark, and others after the white race. In crossing a second time with full white blood, the issue will take still more after the white race. Still, the Gipsy cannot be crossed altogether out; he will come up, but of course in a modified form. Should the white blood be of a dark complexion and hair, and have no tendency, from its ancestry, to turn to fair, in its descent, then the issue between it and the Gipsy will always be dusky. I have seen all this, and had it fully explained by the Gipsies themselves.

The result of this mixture of the Gipsy and European blood is founded, not only on the ordinary principles of physiology, but on common sense itself; for why should not such issue take after the European, in preference to the Gipsy? If a residence in Europe of 450 years has had no effect upon the appearance of what may be termed pure Gipsies, (a point which, at least, is questionable,) the length of time, the effects of climate, and the influence of mind, should, at least, predispose it to merge, by mixture, into something bearing a resemblance to the ordinary European; which, by a continued crossing, it does. Indeed, it soon disappears to the common eye: to a stranger it is not observable, unless the mixture happens to be met with in a tent, or under such circumstances as one expects to meet with Gipsies. In paying a visit to an English Gipsy family, I was invited to call again, on such a day, when I would meet with some Welsh Gipsies. The principal Welsh Gipsy I found to be a very quiet man, with fair hair, and quite like an ordinary Englishman; who was admitted by his English brethren to "speak deep Gipsy." He had just arrived from Wales, where he had been employed in an iron work. Unless I am misinformed, the issue of a fair-haired European and an ordinary Hindoo woman, in India, sometimes shows the same result as I have stated of the Gipsies; but it ought to be much more so in the case of the Gipsy in Europe, on account of the race having been so long acclimated there. Indeed, it is generally believed, that the population of Europe contains a large part of Asiatic blood, from that continent having at one time been overrun by Asiatics, who mixed their blood with an indigenous race which they met with there.

Of the mixed Spanish Gipsy, to whom I have alluded, Mr. Borrow says, that "he had *flaxen hair;* his eyes small, and, like ferrets, red and fiery; and his complexion like a brick, or dull red, chequered with spots of purple." This description, with, perhaps, the exception of the red eyes, and spots of purple, is quite in keeping with that of many of the mixed Gipsies. The race seems even to have given a preference to fair or red hair, in the case of such children and grown-up natives as they have adopted into their body. I have met with a young Spaniard from Corunna, who is so much acquainted with the Gipsies in Spain, that I took him to be a mixed Gipsy himself; and he says that mixtures among the Spanish Gipsies are very common; the white man, in such cases, always casting his lot with the Gipsies. None of the French, German, or Hungarian Gipsies whom I have met with in America are full blood, or anything like it; but I am told there are such, and very black too, as the English Gipsies assert. Indeed, considering how "dreadfully mixed" the Gipsies are in Great Britain and Ireland, I cannot but conclude that they are more or less so all over the world.*

The blood once mixed, there is nothing to prevent a little more being added, and a little more, and so on. There are English Gipsy girls who have gone to work in factories in the Eastern States, and picked up husbands among the ordinary youths of these establishments. And what difference does it make? Is not the game in the Gipsy woman's own hands? Will she not bring up her children Gipsies, initiate them in all the mysteries of Gipsydom, and teach them the language? There is another married to an American farmer "down east." All that she has to do is simply to "tell her wonderful story," as the Gipsies express it.

* Grellmann evidently alludes to Gipsies of mixed blood, when he writes in the following manner: "Experience shows that the dark colour of the Gipsies, which is continued from generation to generation, is more the effect of education and manner of life than descent. Among those who profess music in Hungary, or serve in the Imperial army, where they have learned to pay more attention to order and cleanliness, there are many to be found whose extraction is not at all discernible in their colour." For my part, I cannot say that such language is applicable to full-blood Gipsies. Still, the change from tented to settled and tidy Gipsydom is apt to show its effects in modifying the complexion of such Gipsies, and to a much greater degree in their descendants.

Jonathan must think that he has caged a queer kind of a bird in the English Gipsy woman. But will he say to his friends, or neighbours, that his wife is a Gipsy? Will the children tell that their mother, and, consequently, they themselves are Gipsies? No, indeed. Jonathan, however, will find her a very active, managing woman, who will always be a-stirring, and will not allow her "old man" to kindle the fires of a morning, milk his cows, or clean his boots, and, as far as she is concerned, will bring him lots of *chabos*.

Gipsies, however, do not like such marriages; still they take place. They are more apt to occur when they have attained to that degree of security in a community where no one knows them to be Gipsies, or when they have settled in a neighbourhood to which they had come strangers. The parents exercise more constraint over their sons than daughters; they cannot bear the idea of a son taking a strange woman for a wife; for a strange woman is a snare unto the Gipsies. If a Scottish Gipsy lad shows a hankering after a stranger lass, the mother will soon "cut his comb," by asking him, "What would she say if she knew you to be a loon of a Gipsy? Take such or such a one (Gipsies) for a wife, if you want one." But it is different with the girls. If a Gipsy lass is determined to have the stranger for a husband, she has only to say, "Never mind, mother; it makes no earthly difference; I'll turn that fellow round my little finger; I'll take care of the children when I get them." I do not know how the settled Scottish Gipsies broach the subject of being Gipsies to the stranger son-in-law when he is introduced among them. I can imagine the girl, during the courtship, saying to herself, with reference to her intended, "I'll lead you captive, my pretty fellow!" And captive she does lead him, in more senses than one. Perhaps the subject is not broached to him till after she has borne him children; or, if he is any way soft, the mother, with a leering eye, will say to him at once, "Ah ha, lad, ye're among Gipsies now!" In such a case, the young man will be perfectly bewildered to know what it all means, so utterly ignorant is he about Gipsies; when, however, he comes to learn all about it, it will be *mum* with him, as if his wife's friends had *burked* him, or some "old Gipsy" had come along, and sworn him in on the point of a drawn dirk. It may be that the Gipsy never mentions the subject to her husband at all, for fear he should "take her life;" she can, at all events, trust her secret with her children.

Why should there be any hard feelings towards a Gipsy for "taking in and barking" a native in this way? She does not propose—she only disposes of herself. She has no business to tell the other that she is a Gipsy. She does not consider herself a worse woman than he is a man, but, on the contrary, a better. She would rather prefer a *chabo*, but, somehow or other, she sacrifices her feelings, and takes the *gorgio*, "for better or worse." Or there may be considerable advantages to be derived from the connexion, so that she spreads her snares to secure them. Being a Gipsy, she has the whip-hand of the husband, for no consideration will induce him to divulge to any one the fact that his wife is a Gipsy—should she have told him; in which case she has such a hold upon him, as to have "turned him round her little finger" most effectualy. "Married a Gipsy! it's no' possible!" "Ay, it is possible. There!" she will say, chattering her words, and, with her fingers, showing him the signs. He soon gets reconciled to the "better or worse" which *he* has taken to his bosom, as well as to her "folk," and becomes strongly attached to them. The least thing that the Gipsy can then do is to tell her "wonderful story" to her children. It is not teaching them any damnable creed; it is only telling them who they are; so that they may acknowledge herself, her people, her blood, and the blood of the children themselves.

And how does the Gipsy woman bring up her children in regard to her own race? She tells them her "wonderful story"—informs them who they are, and of the dreadful prejudice that exists against them, simply for being Gipsies. She then tells them about Pharaoh and Joseph in Egypt, terming her people, "Pharaoh's folk." In short, she dazzles the imagination of the children, from the moment they can comprehend the simplest idea. Then she teaches them her words, or language, as the "real Egyptian," and frightens and bewilders the youthful mind by telling them that they are subject to be hanged if they are known to be Gipsies, or to speak these words, or will be looked upon as wild beasts by those around them. She then informs the children how long the Gipsies have been in the country; how they lived in tents; how they were persecuted, banished, and hanged, merely for being Gipsies. She then tells them of her people being in every part of the world, whom they can recognize by the language and signs which she is teaching them; and that her race will everywhere be ready to shed their blood for them. She then dilates upon the benefits that arise from being a Gipsy—benefits negative as well as positive; for should they ever be set upon—garroted, for example—all that they will have to do will be to cry out some such expression as "*Biené raté, calo chabo,*" (good-night, Gipsy, or black fellow,) when, if there is a Gipsy near them, he will protect them. The children will be fondled by her relatives, handed about and hugged as "little ducks of Gipsies." The granny, while sitting at the fireside, like a witch, performs no small part in the education of the children, making them fairly dance with excitement. In this manner do the children of Gipsies have the Gipsy soul literally breathed into them.*

In such a way—what with the supreme influence which the mother has exercised over the mind of the child from its very infancy; the manner in which its imagination has been dazzled; and the dreadful prejudice towards the Gipsies, which they all apply, directly or indirectly, to themselves—does the Gipsy adhere to his race. When he comes to be a youth, he naturally enough endeavours to find his way to a tent, to have a look at the "old thing." He does not, however, think much of it as a reality; but it presents something very poetical and imaginative to his mind, when he contemplates it as the state from which his mysterious forefathers have sprung.† It makes very little difference, in the

* Mr. Offor, editor of a late edition of Bunyan's works, writes, in "Notes and Queries," thus: "I have avoided much intercourse with this class, fearing the fate of Mr. Hoyland, who, being a Quaker, was shot by one of Cupid's darts from a black-eyed Gipsy girl; *and J. S. may do well to be cautious.*" Mr. Offor is not far wrong. A Gipsy girl can sometimes fascinate a "white fellow," as a snake can a bird—make him flutter, and particularly so, should the "little Gipsy" be met with in some such dress as black silks and a white polka. This much can be said of Gipsy women, which cannot be said of all women, that they know their places, and are not apt to usurp the rights of the *rajahs*; they will even "work the nails off their fingers" to make them feel comfortable.

I should conclude, from what Mr. Offor says, that the Quaker married the Gipsy girl. If children were born of the union, they will be Gipsy-Quakers, or Quaker-Gipsies, whichever expression we choose to adopt.

† I have picked up quite a number of Scottish Gipsies of respectable character, from their having gone in their youth, to look at the "old thing."

case to which I have alluded, whether the father be a Gipsy or not; the children all go with the mother, for they inherit the blood through her. What with the blood, the education, the words, and the signs, they are simply Gipsies, and will be such, as long as they retain a consciousness of who they are, and any peculiarities exclusively Gipsy. As it sometimes happens that the father, only, is a Gipsy, the attachment may not be so strong, on the part of the children, as if the blood had come through the mother; still, it likewise attaches them to the body. A great deal of jealousy is shown by the Gipsies, when a son marries a strange woman. A greater ado is not made by some Catholics, to bring up their children Catholics, under such circumstances, than is exhibited by Gipsies for their children knowing their secret—that is, the "wonderful story;" which has the effect of leading them, in their turn, to marry with Gipsies. The race is very jealous of "the blood" being lost; or that their "wonderful story" should become known to those who are not Gipsies.

There are people who cannot imagine how a man can be a Gipsy and have fair hair. They think that, from his having fair hair, he cannot have the same feelings of what they imagine to be a true Gipsy, that is, a black-haired one. One naturally asks, what effect can the matter of colour of *hair* have upon the *mind* of a member of any community or clan, whether the hair be black, brown, red, fair, or white, or the person have no hair at all? Let us imagine a Gipsy with fair hair. How long is it since the white blood was introduced among his ancestors? Perhaps three hundred and fifty years. The race of which he comes has been, more or less, mixing and crossing ever since, but always retaining the issue within its own community. Is he fair-haired? Then he may be half a Gipsy; he may be three-fourths Gipsy, and perhaps even more. At the present day,

it is the most natural thing in the world for them to do. What is it to look back to the time of James V., in 1540, when John Faw was lord-paramount over the Gipsies in Scotland? Imagine, then, the natural curiosity of a young Gipsy, brought up in a town, to look at something like the original condition of his ancestors. Such a Gipsy will leave Edinburgh, for example, and travel over the south of Scotland, "casting his sign," as he passes through the villages, in every one of which he will find Gipsies. Some of these villages are almost entirely occupied by Gipsies. James Hogg is reported, in Blackwood's Magazine, to say, that Lochmaben is "stocked" with them.

the "points" of such a Gipsy are altogether arbitrary; some profess to know their points, but it is a thing altogether uncertain. All that they know and adhere to is, that they are Gipsies, and nothing else. In this manner are the British Gipsies, (with the exception of some English families, about whom there is no certainty,) members of the Gipsy community, or nation, as such—each having some of the blood; and not Gipsies of an ideal purity of race. What they know is, that their parents and relatives are Gipsies; that Gipsies separate them from the eternity that is past; and, consequently, that they are Gipsies. They, indeed, accept their descent, blood, and nationality as instinctively as they accept the very sex which God has given them. Which of the two knows most of Gipsydom—the fair-haired or black? Almost invariably the fair.*

We naturally ask, what effect has this difference in appearance upon two such members of one family—the one with European, the other with Gipsy, features and colour? and the answer is this: The first will hide the fact of his being a Gipsy from strangers; indeed, he is ashamed to let it be known that he is a Gipsy; and he is afraid that people, not knowing how it came about, would laugh at him. "What!" they would ask, "*you* a Gipsy? The idea is absurd." Besides, it facilitates his getting on in the world, to prevent it being known that he is a Gipsy. The other member cannot deny that he is a Gipsy, because any one can see it. Such are the Gipsies who are more apt to cling to the tent, or the more original ways of the old stock. They are very proud

* Among the English Gipsies, fair-haired ones are looked upon by the purer sort, or even by those taking after the Gipsy, as "small potatoes." The consequence is, they have to make up for their want of blood, by smartness, knowledge of the language, or something that will go to balance the deficiency of blood. They generally lay claim to the *intellect*, while they yield the *blood* to the others. A full or nearly full-blood young English Gipsy looks upon herself with all the pride of a little duchess, while in the company of young male mixed Gipsies. A mixed Gipsy may reasonably be assumed to be more intelligent than one of the old stock, were it only for this reason, that the mixture softens down the natural conceit and bigotry of the Gipsy; while, as regards his personal appearance, it puts him in a more improvable position. Still, a full-blood Gipsy looks up to a mixed Gipsy, if he is anything of a superior man, and freely acknowledges the blood. Indeed, the two kinds will readily marry, if circumstances bring them together. To a couple of such Gipsies I said: "What difference does it make, if the person *has the blood, and has his heart in the right place?*" "That's the idea; that's exactly the idea," they both replied.

of their appearance; but it is a pride accompanied with disadvantages, and even pain. For, after all, the beauty and pleasure in being a Gipsy is to have the other cast of features and colour; he has as much of the blood and language as the other, while he can go into any kind of company—a sort of Jack-the-Giant-Killer in his invisible coat. The nearer the Gipsy comes to the original colour of his race, the less chance is there of improving him. He knows what he is like; and well does he know the feeling that people entertain for him. In fact, he feels that there is no use in being anything but what people call a Gipsy. But it is different with those of European countenance and colour, or when these have been modified or diluted by a mixture of white blood. They can, then, enter upon any sphere of employment to which they have a mind, and their personal advantages and outward circumstances will admit of.*

Let us now consider the destiny of such European-like Gipsies. Suppose a female of this description marries a native in settled life, which both of them follow. She brings the children up as Gipsies, in the way described. The children are apt to become ultra Gipsies. If they, in their turn, marry natives, they do the same with their children; so that, if the same system were always followed, they would continue Gipseis forever. For all that is necessary to perpetuate the tribe, is simply for the Gipsies to know who they are, and the prejudice that exists toward the race of which they are a part; to say nothing of the innate associations connected with their origin and descent. Such a phenomenon may be fitly compared to the action of an auger; with this difference, that the auger may lose its edge, but the Gipsy will drill his way through generations of the ordinary natives, and, at the end, come out as sharp as ever; all the circumstances attending the two races being exactly the same at the end as at the beginning. In this way, let their blood be mixed as it may, let even their blood-relationship outside of their body be what it may, the Gipsies still remain, in their private associations, a distinct people, into whatever

* To thoroughly understand how a Gipsy, with fair hair and blue eyes, can be as much a Gipsy as one with black, may be termed "passing the *pons asinorum* of the Gipsy question." Once over the bridge, and there are no difficulties to be encountered on the journey, unless it be to understand that a Gipsy can be a Gipsy without living in a tent or being a rogue.

sphere of human action they may enter; although, in point of blood, appearance, occupation, character, and religion, they may have drifted the breadth of a hemisphere from the stakes and tent of the original Gipsy.

There can surely be no great difficulty in comprehending so simple an idea as this. Here we have a foreign race introduced amongst us, which has been proscribed, legally as well as socially. To escape the effects of this double proscription, the people have hidden the fact of their belonging to the race, although they have clung to it with an ardour worthy of universal admiration. The proscription is toward the name and race as such, that is, the blood; and is not general, but absolute; none having ever been received into society as Gipsies. For this reason, every Gipsy, every one who has Gipsy blood in his veins, applies the proscription to himself. On the other hand, he has his own descent—the Gipsy descent; and, as I have already said, he has naturally as little desire to wish a different descent, as he has to have a different sex. As Finns do not wish to have been born Englishmen, or Englishmen Finns, so Gipsies are perfectly satisfied with their descent, nay, extremely proud of it. They would not change it, if they could, for any consideration. When Gipsies, therefore, marry natives, they do not only willingly bring up their children as Gipsies, but by every moral influence they are forced to do it, and cling to each other. In this way has the race been absolutely cut off from that of the ordinary natives; all intercourse between the two, unless on the part of the *bush* Gipsy, in the way of dealings, having been of a clandestine nature, on the side of the Gipsy, or, in other words, *incog.* How melancholy it is to think that such a state of things exists in the British Islands!

The Gipsy, born of a Gipsy mother and a native father, does, therefore, most naturally, and, I may say, invariably, follow the Gipsy connexion; the simplest impulse of manhood compels him to do it. Being born, or becoming a member of settled society, he joins in the ordinary amusements or occupations of his fellow-creatures of both races; which he does the more readily when he feels conscious of the incognito which he bears. But he has been brought up from his mother's knee a Gipsy; he knows nothing else; his associations with his relatives have been Gipsy; and he has in his veins that which the white damns, and, he doubts not, would damn in him, were he to know of it. He has, moreover, the words and signs of the Gipsy race; he is brought in contact with the Gipsy race; he perceives that his feelings are reciprocated by them, and that both have the same reserve and timidity for "outsiders." He does not reason abstractly what he is *not*, but instinctively holds that he is "one of them;" that he has in his mind, his heart, and his blood, that which the common native has not, and which makes him a *chabo*, that is, a Gipsy.

The mother, in the case mentioned, is certainly not a full-blood Gipsy, nor anything like it; she does not know her real "points;" all that she knows is, that she is a "Gipsy:" so that, if the youth's father is an ordinary native, the youth holds himself to be a half-and-half, nominally, though he does not know what he really is, as regards blood. Imagine, then, that he takes such a half-and-half Gipsy for a wife, and that both tell their children that they are "Gipsies:" the children, perhaps, knowing nothing of the real origin of their parents, take up the "wonderful story," and hand it down to their children, initiating them, in their turn, in the "mysteries." These children never doubt that *they* are "Gipsies," although *their* Gipsyism may, as I have already said, have "drifted the breadth of a hemisphere from the stakes and tent of the original Gipsy." In this manner is Gipsydom kept alive, by its turning round and round in a perpetual circle. And in this manner does it happen, that a native finds his own children Gipsies, from having, in seeking for a wife, stumbled upon an Egyptian woman. Gipsydom is, therefore, the aggregate of Gipsies, wherever, or under whatever circumstances, they are to be found. It is, in two respects, an absolute question; absolute as to blood, and absolute as to those teachings, feelings, and associations, that, by a moral necessity, accompany the possession of the blood.

This brings me to an issue with Mr. Borrow. Speaking of the destination of the Spanish Gipsies, he says: "If the Gitanos are abandoned to themselves, by which we mean, no arbitrary laws are again enacted for their extinction, the sect will eventually cease to be, and its members become confounded with the residue of the population." I can well understand that such procedure, on the part of the Spanish

Government, was calculated to soften the ferocious disposition of the Gipsies; but did it bring them a point nearer to an amalgamation with the people than before? Mr. Borrow continues: "The position which they occupy is the lowest. . . . . The outcast of the prison and the *presidio*, who calls himself Spaniard, would feel insulted by being termed Gitano, and would thank God that he is not." He continues: "It is, of course, by intermarriage, alone, that the two races will ever commingle; and before that event is brought about, much modification must take place amongst the Gitanos, in their manners, in their habits, in their affections and their dislikes, and perhaps *even in their physical peculiarities*, (yet 'no washing,' as Mr. Borrow approvingly quotes, 'will turn the Gipsy white') much must be forgotten on both sides, and everything is forgotten in course of time." So great, indeed, was the prejudice against the Gipsies, that the law of Charles III, in 1783, forbade the people calling them Gitanos, under the penalty of being punished for *slander!* because, his majesty said: "I declare that those who go by the name of Gitanos are not so by origin or nature; nor do they proceed from any infected root (!)" What regard would the native Spaniards pay to the injunction, that they would be punished for "slander," for calling the Gipsies *Gitanos*, in place of *Spaniards?* We may well believe that such a law would be a dead letter in Spain; where, according to Mr. Borrow, "justice has invariably been a mockery; a thing to be bought and sold, terrible only to the feeble and innocent, and an instrument of cruelty and avarice."

Mr. Borrow leaves the question where he found it. Even remove the prejudice that exists against the Gipsies, as regards their colour, habits, and history; what then? Would they, as a people, cease to be? Would they amalgamate with the natives, *so as to be lost?* Assuredly not. They may mix their blood, but they preserve their mental identity in the world; even although, in point of physical appearance, habits, manners, occupation, character, and creed, they might "become confounded with the residue of the population." In that respect, they are the most exclusive people of almost any to be found in the world. We have only to consider what Freemasonry is, and we can form an idea of what Gipsyism is, in one of its aspects. It rests upon the broadest of all bases—flesh and blood, a common and mysterious origin, a common language, a common history, a common persecution, and a common odium, in every part of the world. Remove the prejudice against the Gipsies, make it as respectable to be Gipsies, as the world, with its ignorance of many of the race, deem it desreputable; what then? Some of them might come out with their "tents and encampments," and banners and mottoes: the "cuddy and the creel, the hammer and tongs, the tent and the tin kettle", forever. People need not sneer at the "cuddy and the creel." The idea conveys a world of poetry to the mind of a Gipsy. Mrs. Fall, of Dunbar, thought it so poetical, that she had it, as we have seen, worked in tapestry; and it is doubtless carefully preserved, as an heir-loom, among her collateral descendants.*

Mr. Borrow speaks of the Gipsies "declining" in Spain. Ask a Scotchman about the Scottish Gipsies, and he will answer: "The Scotch Gipsies have pretty much died out." "Died out?" I ask; "that is impossible; for who are more prolific than Gipsies?" "Oh, then, they have become settled,

* There is a considerable resemblance between Gipsyism, in its harmless aspect, and Freemasonry; with this difference, that the former is a general, while the latter is a special, society; that is to say, the Gipsies have the language, or some of the words, and the signs, peculiar to the whole race, which each individual or class will use for different purposes. The race does not necessarily, and does not in fact, have intercourse with every other member of it; in that respect, they resemble any ordinary community of men. Masonry, as my reader may be aware, is a society of what may be termed "a mixed multitude of good-fellows, who are all pledged to befriend and help each other." The radical elements of Masonry may be termed a "rope of sand," which the vows of the Order work into the most closely and strongly formed coil of any to be found in the world. But it is altogether of an artificial nature; while Gipsyism is natural—something that, when separated from objectionable habits, one might almost call divine; for it is founded upon a question of race—a question of blood. The cement of a creed is weak, in comparison with that which binds the Gipsies together; for a people, like an individual, may have one creed to-day, and another to-morrow; it may be continually travelling round the circle of every form of faith; but blood, under certain circumstances, is absolute and immutable.

There are many Gipsies Freemasons; indeed, they are the very people to push their way into a Mason's lodge; for they have secrets of their own, and are naturally anxious to pry into those of others, by which they may be benefited. I was told of a Gipsy who died lately, the Master of a Masons' Lodge. A friend, a Mason, told me, the other day, of his having entered a house in Yetholm, where were five Gipsies, all of whom responded to his Masonic signs. Masons should therefore interest themselves in, and befriend, the Gipsies.

and civilized." "And *ceased to be Gipsies?*" I continue. "Exactly so," he replies. What idea can be more ridiculous than that of saying, that if a Gipsy leaves the tent, settles in a town, and attends church, he ceases to be a Gipsy; and that, if he takes to the tent again, he becomes a Gipsy again? What has a man's occupation, habits, or character, to do with his clan, tribe, or nationality? Does education, does religion, remove from his mind a knowledge of who he is, or change his blood? Are not our own Borderers and Highlanders as much Borderers and Highlanders as ever they were? Are not Spanish Gipsies still Spanish Gipsies, although a change may have come over the characters and circumstances of some of them? It would be absurd to deny it.*

Mr. Borrow has not sufficiently examined into Spanish Gipsyism to pass a reliable opinion upon it. He says: "One thing is certain, in the history of the Gitanos; that the sect flourished and encreased, so long as the law recommended and enjoined measures the most harsh and severe for its suppression. . . . . The caste of the Gitanos still exists, but is neither so extensive, nor so formidable, as a century ago, when the law, in denouncing Gitanismo, pro-

* The principle, or rather fact, here involved, simple as it is in itself, is evidently very difficult of comprehension by the native Scottish mind. Any person understands perfectly well how a Highlander, at the present day, is still a Highlander, notwithstanding the great change that has come over the character of his race. But our Scottish *literati* seem to have been altogether at sea, in comprehending the same principle as applicable to the Gipsies. They might naturally have asked themselves, whether *Gipsies* could have procreated *Jews;* and, if not Jews, how they could have procreated *gorgios*, (as English Gipsies term natives.) A writer in Blackwood's Magazine says, in reference to Billy Marshall, a Gipsy chief, to whom allusion has already been made: "Who were his descendants I cannot tell; I am sure he could not do it himself, if he were living. It is known that they were prodigiously numerous; I dare say numberless." And yet this writer gravely says that "the *race* is in some risk of becoming extinct(!)" Another writer in Blackwood says: "Their numbers may perhaps have since been diminished, in particular States, by *the progress of civilization* (!)" We would naturally pronounce any person crazy who would maintain that there were no Highlanders in Scotland, owing to their having "changed their habits." We could, with as much reason, say the same of those who will maintain this opinion in regard to the Gipsies. There has been a great deal of what is called genius expended upon the Gipsies, but wonderfully little common sense.

As the Jews, during their pilgrimage in the Wilderness, were protected from their enemies by a cloud, so have the Gipsies, in their encrease and development, been shielded from theirs, by a mist of ignorance, which, it would seem, requires no little trouble to dispel.

posed to the Gitanos the alternatives of death for persisting in their profession, or slavery for abandoning it." These are very singular alternatives. The latter is certainly not to be found in any of the Spanish laws quoted by Mr. Borrow. I am at a loss to perceive the point of his reasoning. There can be no difficulty in believing that Gipsies would rather *encrease* in a state of peace, than if they were hunted from place to place, like wild beasts; and consequently, having renounced their former mode of life, they would, in Mr. Borrow's own words, "cease to play a distinct part in the history of Spain, and the *law* would no longer speak of them as a distinct people." And the same might, to a certain extent, be said of the Spanish *people*. Mr. Borrow again says: "That the Gitanos are not so numerous as in former times, witness those *barrios*, in various towns, still denominated *Gitanerias*, but from whence the Gitanos have disappeared, even like the Moors from the *Morerias*." But Mr. Borrow himself, in the same work, gives a good reason for the disappearance of the Gipsies from these *Gitanerias*; for he says: "The *Gitanerias* were soon considered as public nuisances, on which account the Gitanos were forbidden to live together in particular parts of the town, to hold meetings, and even to intermarry with each other." If the disappearance of the Gipsies from Spain was like that of the Moors, it would appear that they had left, or been expelled from, the country; a theory which Mr. Borrow does not advance. The Gipsies, to a certain extent, may have left these barriers, or been expelled from them, and settled, as tradesmen, mechanics, and what not, in other parts of the same or other towns; so as to be in a position the more able to get on in the world. Still, many of them are in the colonies. In Cuba there are many, as soldiers and musicians, dealers in mules and red pepper, which businesses they almost monopolize, and jobbers and dealers in various wares; and doubtless there are some of them innkeepers, and others following other occupations. In Mexico there are not a few. I know of a Gitano who has a fine wholesale and retail cigar store in Virginia.*

* In Olmstead's "Journey in the Seaboard Slave States" it is stated, that in Alexandria, Louisiana, when under the Spanish rule, there were "French and Spanish, *Egyptians* and Indians, Mulattoes and Negroes." This author reports a conversation which he had with a planter, by which it appears

Mr. Borrow concludes, in regard to the Spanish Gipsies, thus: "We have already expressed our belief that the caste has diminished of latter years; whether this diminution was the result of one or many causes combined; of a *partial change of habits*, of pestilence or sickness, of war or famine, or of a *freer intercourse with the Spanish population*, we have no means of determining, and shall abstain from offering conjectures on the subject." In this way does he leave the question just where he found it. Is there any reason to doubt that Gipsydom is essentially the same in Spain as in Great Britain; or that its future will be guided by any other principles than those which regulate that of the British Gipsies? Indeed, I am astonished that Mr. Borrow should advance the idea that Gipsies should *decrease* by "changing their habits;" they might not *encrease so fast*, in a settled life, as when more exposed to the air, and not molested by the Spanish Government. I am no less astonished that he should think they would decrease by "a freer intercourse with the Spanish population;" when, in fact, such mixtures are well known to go with the Gipsies; the mixture being, in the estimation of the British Gipsies, calculated to strengthen and invigorate the race itself. Had Mr. Borrow kept in mind the case of the half-blood Gipsy captain, he could have had no difficulty in learning what became of mixed Gipsies.*

that these Egyptians came from "some of the Northern Islands;" that they spoke a language among themselves, but could talk French and Spanish too; that they were black, but not very black, and as good citizens as any, and passed for white folk. The planter believed they married mostly with mulattoes, and that a good many of the mulattoes had Egyptian blood in them too. He believed these Egyptians had disappeared since the State became part of the Union. Mr. Olmstead remarks: "The Egyptians were probably Spanish Gipsies, though I have never heard of any of them being in America in any other way."

* Mr. Borrow surely cannot mean that a Gipsy ceases to be a Gipsy, when he settles down, and "turns over a new leaf;" and that this "change of habits" changes his descent, blood, appearance, language and nationality! What, then, does he mean, when he says, that the Spanish Gipsies have decreased by "a partial change of habits?"

And does an infusion of Spanish blood, implied in a "freer intercourse with the Spanish population," lead to the Gipsy element being wiped out; or does it lead to the Spanish feeling being lost in Gipsydom? Which is the element to be operated upon—the Spanish or the Gipsy? Which is the *leaven?* The Spanish element is the *passive*, the Gipsy the *active*. As a question of philosophy, the most simple of comprehension, and, above all, as a matter of fact, the foreign element introduced, *in detail*, into the *body*

It doubtless holds in Spain, as in Great Britain, that as the Gipsy enters into settled life, and engages in a respectable calling, he hides his descent, and even mixes his blood with that of the country, and becomes ashamed of the name before the public; but is as much, at heart, a Gipsy, as any others of his race. And this theory is borne out by Mr. Borrow himself, when he speaks of "the unwillingness of the Spanish Gipsies to utter, when speaking of themselves, the detested expression Gitano; a word which seldom escapes their mouths." We might therefore conclude, that the Spanish Gipsies, with the exception of the more original and bigoted stock, would *hide their nationality* from the common Spaniards, and so escape their notice. It is not at all likely that the half-pay Gipsy captain would mention to the public that he was a Gipsy, although he admitted it to Mr. Borrow, under the peculiar circumstances in which he met him. My Spanish acquaintance informs me that the Gitanos, generally, hide their nationality from the rest of the world.

Such a case is evidently told by Mr. Borrow, in the vagabond Gipsy, Antonio, at Badajoz, who termed a rich Gipsy, living in the same town, a hog, because he evidently would not countenance him. Antonio may possibly have been kicked out of his house, in attempting to enter it. He accused him of having married a Spaniard, and of fain attempting to pass himself for a Spaniard. As regards the wife, she might have been a Gipsy with very little of "the blood" in her veins; or a Spaniard, reared by Gipsies; or an ordinary Spanish maiden, to whom the Gipsy would teach his language, as sometimes happens among the English Gipsies. His wishing to pass for a Spaniard had nothing to do with his being, but not wishing to be known as, a Gipsy. The same is done by almost all our Scottish Gipsies. In England, those who do not follow the tent—I mean the more mixed and better class—are even afraid of each other. "Afraid of what?" said I, to such an English Gipsy; "ashamed of being Gipsies?" "No, sir," (with great emphasis;) "not ashamed of being Gipsies, but of being *known*

of Gipsydom, goes with that body, and, in feeling, becomes incorporated with it, although, in physical appearance, it changes the Gipsy race, so that it becomes "confounded with the residue of the population," but remains Gipsy, as before. A Spanish Gipsy is a Spaniard as he stands, and it would be hard to say what we should ask him to do, to become more a Spaniard than he is already.

to other people as Gipsies." "A world of difference," I replied. What does the world hold to be a *Gipsy*, and what does it hold to be the *feelings of a man?* If we consider these two questions, we can have little difficulty in understanding the wish of such Gipsies to disguise themselves. It is in this way, and in the mixing of the blood, that this so-called "dying out of the Gipsies" is to be accounted for.*

It is singular that Mr. Borrow should attribute the change which has come over the Spanish Gipsies, so much to the law passed by Charles III. in 1783; and that he should characterize it as an enlightened, wise, and liberal law; distinguished by justice and clemency; and as being calculated to exert considerable influence over the destiny of the race; nay, as being the principal, if not the only, cause for the "decline" of it in Spain. It was headed: "Rules for *repressing* and *chastising* the vagrant mode of life, and other excesses, of those who are called Gitanos." Article II. forbids, under penalties, the Gipsies "using their *language*, dress, or vagrant kind of life, which they had hitherto followed." Article XI. prohibits them from "wandering about the roads and uninhabited places, even with the pretext of *visiting markets and fairs.*" Article IX. reads thus: "Those *who have abandoned the dress, name, language or jargon, associations and manners of Gitanos*, and shall have, moreover, chosen and established a domicile, but shall not have devoted themselves to any office or employment, though it be only that of day-labourer, shall be *proceeded against as common vagrants.*" Articles XVI. and XVII. enact, that "the children, and young people of both sexes, who are not above sixteen years of age, shall be separated from their parents, *who wander about and have no employment*, [which was forbidden by the law itself,] and shall be destined to learn something, or shall be placed out in hospices or houses of instruction." Article XX. *dooms to death, without remis-*

* Mr. Borrow mentions, in the twenty-second chapter of the "Bible in Spain," having met several cavalry soldiers from Granada, Gipsies *incog.* who were surprised at being discovered to be Gipsies. They had been impressed, but carried on a trade in horses, in league with the captain of their company. They said: "We have been to the wars, but not to fight; we left that to the Busné. We have kept together, and like true Caloré, have stood back to back. We have made money in the wars."

sion, Gipsies who, for the second time, relapse into their old habits.

I cannot agree with Mr. Borrow, when he says, that this law "differs in *character*" from any which had hitherto been enacted, in connection with the body in Spain, if I take those preceding it, as given by himself. The only difference between it and some of the previous laws is, that it allowed the Gipsy to be admitted to whatever office or employment *to which he might apply himself*, and likewise to any guilds or communities; but it prohibited him from settling in the capital, or any of the royal residences; and forbade him, *on pain of death*, to publicly profess what he was—that is, a Gipsy. With the trifling exceptions mentioned, the law of Charles III. was as foolish a one as ever was passed against the Gipsies. These very exceptions show what the letter, whatever the execution, of previous laws must have been. Nor can we form any opinion as to the effects the law in question had upon the Gipsies, unless we know how it was carried out. The law of the Empress Maria Theresa produced no effect upon the Gipsies in Hungary. "In Hungary," says Mr. Borrow, "two classes are free to do what they please—the nobility and the Gipsies—the one above the law, the other below it." And what did Mr. Borrow find the Gipsies in Hungary? In England, the last instances of condemnation, under the old sanguinary laws, happened a few years before the Restoration, although these were not repealed till 23d Geo. III., c. 54. The Gipsies in England can follow any employment, common to the ordinary natives, they please: and how has Mr. Borrow described them there? In Scotland, the tribe have been allowed to do nothing, not even acknowledge their existence, as Gipsies: and this work describes what they are in that country.

Instead of the law of Charles III. exercising any great beneficial influence over the character of the Spanish Gipsies, I would attribute the change in question to what Mr. Borrow himself says: "It must be remembered that during the last seventy years, a revolution has been progressing in Spain, slowly it is true; and such a revolution may have affected the Gitanos." The Spanish Gipsy proverb, "Money is to be found in the town, not in the country," has had its influence on bringing the race to settle in towns. And by residing in towns, and not being persecuted, they have, in Mr. Borrow's own words, "insensibly become more civilized than their ancestors, and their habits and manners less ferocious." The only good which the law of Charles III. seems to have done to the Spanish Gipsies was, as already said, to permit them to follow any occupation, and be admitted to any guilds, or communities, (barring the capital, and royal residences,) they pleased; but only on the condition, and that *on the pain of death*, that they *renounced every imaginable thing connected with their tribe;* which, we may reasonably assume, no Gipsy submitted to, however much in appearance he might have done so.

But it is doubtful if the law of Charles III. was anything but the one which it was customary for every Spanish monarch to issue against the tribe. Mr. Borrow says: "Perhaps there is no country in which more laws have been framed, having in view the suppression and extinction of the Gipsy name, race, and manner of life, than Spain. Every monarch, during a period of three hundred years, appears, at his accession to the throne, to have considered that one of his first and most imperative duties consisted in suppressing and checking the robberies, frauds, and other enormities of the Gitanos, with which the whole country seems to have resounded since the time of their first appearance." The fact of so many laws being passed against the Gipsies, is, to my mind, ample proof, as I shall afterwards explain, that few, if any, of them were put, to any extent, in force; and that the act in question, viewed in itself, as distinct from the laws previously in existence, was little more than a form. It contains a flourish of liberality, implied in the Gitanos being allowed to enter, if they pleased, any guilds, (which they were not likely to do,) or communities, (where they were doubtless already;) but it debars, (that is, expels,) them from the king's presence, at the capital or any of the royal residences. Moreover, it allowed the Gitano to be "admitted to whatever office or employment to which he might apply himself," (against which, there probably was, or should have been, no law in existence.) His majesty must also impose his pragmatical conceit upon his loyal subjects, by telling them, that "Gitanos are *not* Gitanos"—that they "do *not* proceed from any infected root;" and threaten them, that if they maintain the contrary, and call them Gitanos, he will have them punished for slander!

The Gipsies, after a residence of 350 years in the country, would have comparatively little notice taken of them, under this law, except when they made themselves really obnoxious, or gave an official an occasion to display his authority, or his zeal for the public service.* Whatever may have been the treatment which the Gipsies experienced at the hands of the *civil* authorities, the *church* does not seem to have disturbed, and far less distressed, them. Mr. Borrow represents a priest of Cordova, formerly an Inquisitor, saying to him: "I am not aware of one case of a Gitano having been tried or punished by the Inquisition. The Inquisition always looked upon them with too much contempt, to give itself the slightest trouble concerning them; for, as no danger, either to the State or to the Church of Rome, could proceed from the Gitanos, it was a matter of perfect indifference to the holy office whether they lived without religion or not. The holy office has always reserved its anger for people very different; the Gitano having, at all times, been *Gente barrata y despreciable.*"

Should the Spanish Gipsies not now assist each other, to the extent they did when banditti, under the special proscription of the Government, it would be absurd to say that they were therefore not as much Gipsies as ever they were. The change in this respect arose, to some extent, from the toleration extended to them, as a people and as individuals, whether by the law, or society in general. Such Gipsies as Mr. Borrow seems to have associated with, in Spain, were not likely to be very reliable authority on the questions at issue; for he has described them as "being endowed with a kind of instinct, (in lieu of reason,) which assists them to a very limited extent, and no further."

Might it not be in Spain as in Great Britain? Even in England, those that pass for Gipsies are few in number, compared to the mixed Gipsies, following various occupations; for a large part of the Gipsy blood in England has, as it were, been spread over a large surface of the white. In Scotland it is almost altogether so. There seems consider-

* It would seem that the law in Spain, in regard to the Gipsies, stands pretty much where it did—that is, the people are, in a sense, tolerated, but that the use of their language is prohibited, as may be gathered from an incident mentioned in the ninth chapter of the "Bible in Spain," by Mr. Borrow.

able reason for believing that Gipsydom is, perhaps, as much mixed in Spain as in Great Britain, although Mr. Borrow has taken no notice of it. We have seen, (page 92.) how severe an enactment was passed by Queen Elizabeth, against "any person, whether natural born or *stranger*, to be seen in the fellowship of the Gipsies, or disguised like them." In the law of Ferdinand and Isabella, the first passed against the Gipsies, in Spain, a class of people is mentioned, in conjunction with them, but distinguished from them, by the name of "foreign tinkers." Philip III., at Belan, in Portugal, in 1619, commands all Gipsies to quit the kingdom within six months. "Those who should wish to remain are to establish themselves in cities, and are not to be allowed to use the dress, name, and language, in order, that forasmuch as they are not such by nation, (!) this name, and manner of life, may be for evermore confounded and forgotten(!)" Philip IV., on the 8th May, 1633, declares "that they are not Gipsies by origin or nature, but have adopted this form of life (!)" This idea of "Gitanos *not* being Gitanos, and not proceeding from any infected root," was not original with Charles III., in 1783; his proclamation having been in formal keeping with previous ones, whether of his own country, or, as in Scotland, in 1603, "recommended by the example of some other realm," (page 111.) There had evidently been a great curiosity to know who some of the "not Gipsies by origin and nature," (evidently judging from their appearance,) could be; for Philip IV. enacts, "that they shall, within two months, leave the quarters where now they *live with the denomination of Gitanos*, and that they shall *separate from each other*, and *mingle with the other inhabitants*: that the ministers of justice are to observe, *with particular diligence*, whether they *hold communication with each other*, or *marry among themselves*."

The "foreign tinkers" mentioned in the Act of Ferdinand and Isabella, and the individuals distinguished from the Gipsies in that of Queen Elizabeth, were doubtless *mixed* Gipsies; whose relationship with the Gipsies proper, and isolation from the common natives, are very distinctly pointed out in the above extract from the law of Philip IV. Mr. Borrow expresses a great difficulty to understand who these people could be, *if not Gipsies*. How easy it is to get quit of the difficulty, by concluding that they were Gipsies whose blood, perhaps for the most part, was native; and who had been brought into the body in the manner explained in the Preface to this work, and more fully illustrated in this Disquisition. If Mr. Borrow found in Spain a half-pay captain, in the service of Donna Isabel, with *flaxen* hair, a *thorough Gipsy*, who spoke Gipsy and Latin, with great fluency, and his cousin, Jara, in all probability another Gipsy, what difficulty can there be in believing that the "foreign tinkers," or tinkers of any kind, now to be met with in Spain, are, like the same class in Great Britain and Ireland, Gipsies of mixed blood? Indeed, the young Spaniard, to whom I have alluded, informs me that the Gipsies in Spain are very much mixed. Mr. Borrow himself admits that the Gipsy blood in Spain has been mixed; for, in speaking of the old Gipsy counts, he says: "It was the counts who determined what individuals were to be admitted into the fellowship and privileges of the Gitanos. . . . . . They (the Gipsies) were not to teach the language to any but those who, by birth or *inauguration*, belonged to that sect." And he gives a case in point, in the bookseller of Logrono, who was married to the only daughter of a Gitano count; upon whose death, the daughter and son-in-law succeeded to the authority which he had exercised in the tribe. If the Gipsies in Spain were not mixed in point of blood, why should they have taken Mr. Borrow for a Gipsy, as he said they did? The persecutions to which the race in Spain were subjected were calculated to lead to a mixture of the blood, as in Scotland, for the reasons given in the Preface; but, perhaps, not to the same extent; as the Spanish Acts seem to have given the tribe an opportunity of escape, under the condition of settling, &c., &c., which would probably be complied with, nominally, for the time being; while the face of part of the country would afford a refuge till the storm had blown over. (See pages 71 and 114.)

It is very likely that the following people, described by Paget, in his travels in Central Europe, are mixed Gipsies. He says: "In almost every part of the Austrian dominions are to be found a kind of wandering tinkers, wire-workers, and menders of crockery, whose language appears to be that of the Sclaves, who travel about, and, at certain seasons, return to their own settlements, where the women and children remain during their absence." The wandering

Rothwelsh, perhaps the same mentioned by Paget, may be mixed Gipsies. In the Encyclopædia Britannica they are spoken of as "a vagabond people, in the south of Germany, who have sometimes been confounded with the Gipsies." The *appearance* of such persons has nothing to do with their being, or not being, members of Gipsydom.*

I will now consider the present condition of the Scottish Gipsies. But, to commence with, what is the native capacity of a Gipsy? It is good. Take a common tinkering Gipsy, without a particle of education, and compare him with a common native, without a particle of education, and the tinker, in point of smartness, is worth, perhaps, a dozen of the other. If not a learned, he is at least a travelled, Athenian, considerably rubbed up by his intercourse with the world. This is the proper way by which to judge of the capacity of a Gipsy. It will differ somewhat according to the countries and circumstances in which he is found. Grellmann, about the year 1780, says, of evidently the more original kind of Hungarian Gipsies: "Imagine a people of childish thoughts, whose minds are filled with raw, undigested conceptions, guided more by sense than reason, and using understanding and reflection only so far as they promote the gratification of any particular appetite; and you have a perfect sketch of the general character of the Gipsies." "They are lively, uncommonly loquacious, fickle to an extreme; consequently, inconstant in their pursuits." Bischoff, in speaking of the German Gipsies, in 1827, says: "They have a good understanding, an excellent memory, are quick of comprehension, lively and talkative." Mr. Borrow, in evident allusion to the very lowest, and most ignorant, class of the Spanish Gipsies, says: "They seem to hunt for their bread, as if they were not of the human, but rather of the animal, species, and, in lieu of reason, were endowed with a kind of instinct, which assists them to a very limited extent, and no further." I admit that this class of Gipsies *may* have as little intellect as there is in an ant-catcher's nose, but the remark can apply to them exclusively.

Without taking into account any opinion expressed by other writers on the Gipsies, Mr. Borrow says: "Should it

* Paget says these tinkers leave their women and children at home when on their travels. That is not customary with the tribe, although it may be their habit in the Austrian dominions.

be urged that certain individuals have found them very different from what they are represented in these volumes, ('The Gipsies in Spain,') he would frankly say that he yields no credit to the presumed fact." And he refers his readers to his Spanish-Gipsy vocabulary for the words *hoax* and *hocus*, as a reason for such an opinion! He himself gives descriptions of quite a different caste. For example, he speaks of a rich Gipsy appearing in a fair, at Leon, in Spain, with a twenty thousand dollar credit in his pocket. And of another Gipsy, a native of Constantinople, who had visited the most remote and remarkable portions of the world, "passing over it like a cloud;" and who spoke several dialects of the Malay, and understood the original language of Java. This Gipsy, he says, dealt in precious stones and poisons; and that there is scarcely a bey or satrap in Persia, or Turkey, whom he has not supplied with both. In Moscow, he says, "There are not a few who inhabit stately houses, go abroad in elegant equipages, and are behind the higher orders of the Russians, neither in appearance nor mental acquirements." From these specimens, one might naturally conclude that there was some room for discrimination among different classes of Gipsies, instead of rating them as having the intellect of ant-catchers.

When the Gipsies appeared in Scotland, the natives themselves, as I have already said, were nearly wholly uneducated. Many of the Gipsies, then, and long afterwards, being smart, presumptuous, overbearing, audacious fellows, seem to have assumed great importance, and been looked upon as no small people by the authorities and the inhabitants of the country. In every country in which they have settled, they seem to have instinctively and very readily appreciated the ways and spirit of the people, while, at the same time, they preserved what belonged particularly to themselves—their Gipsyism. Gipsydom being, in its very essence, a "working in among other people," "a people within a people," it followed, that marriages between adopted Gipsies, and even Gipsies themselves, and the ordinary natives, would be encouraged, were it only to contribute to their existence in the country. The issue of such marriages, go where they might, would become centres of little Gipsy circles, which, in their turn, would throw off members that would become the centres of other little Gipsy circles; the leaven of Gipsydom leavening into a lump everything that proceeded out of itself. To such an extent has this been followed, that, at the present day, the Scottish Gipsies—at least the generality of them—have every outward characteristic of Scotchmen. But the secret of being Gipsies, which they carry in their bosoms, makes them appear a little queer to others; they have a something about them that makes them look somewhat odd to the other Scotchman, who is not "one of them," although he does not know the cause of it.

Upon, or shortly after, their arrival, they seem to have divided the country among themselves; each tribe exercising its rights over its own territory, to the exclusion of others, just as a native lord would have done against other natives; with a system of passes, regulated by councils of local or provincial chieftains, and a king over all. The Scottish Gipsies, from the very first, seem to have been thoroughly versed in their vocation, from having had about a hundred years' experience, in some other part of Europe, before they settled in Scotland; although stragglers of their race evidently had made their appearance in the country many years before. What might have been the number of Gipsies then in Scotland, it is impossible to conjecture; it must have been considerable, if we judge from what is said in Wraxall's History of France, vol. 2, page 32, when, in reference to the Act of Queen Elizabeth, in 1563, he states, that, in her reign, the Gipsies throughout England were supposed to exceed ten thousand. The employments of the original Gipsies, within their respective districts, seem to have been what is described under the head of Tweed-dale and Clydesdale Gipsies; that is, tinkering, making spoons and other wares, petty trading, telling fortunes, living as much as possible at free-quarters, dealing in horses, and visiting fairs. It is extremely likely that those who travelled Tweed-dale, for example, always averaged about the same number, down to the time of the American Revolution, (except in times of civil commotion, when they would have the country pretty much to themselves,) and were confined to such of the families of the respective tribes, or the members of these families, in whom the right was hereditary. The consequence seems to have been, that perhaps the younger members of the family had to betake themselves to towns and villages, and engage in whatever they could possibly turn their hands to. Some would, of course, take to the highway, and kindred fields of industry. Admitting that the circumstances attending the Gipsies in Scotland, at that time, and subsequently, were the same, as regards the manner of making a living, which attend those in England, at the present day, (with this difference, that they could more easily roam at large then than now,) and we can have no difficulty in coming to a conclusion how the surplus of the tented Gipsy population was disposed of. Among the English Gipsies of to-day, taking year with year, and tent with tent, there is, yearly, a continual moving out of the tent; a kind of Gipsy crop is annually gathered from tented Gipsydom; and some of these gradually find themselves drawn into almost every kind of mechanical or manual labour, even to working in coal-mines and iron-works; others become peddlers, itinerant auctioneers, and *tramps* of almost every imaginable kind; not to speak of those who visit fairs, in various capacities, or engage in various settled traffic.

Put a Gipsy to any occupation you like, and he shows a capability and handiness that is astonishing, if he can only muster up steadiness in his new vocation. But it is difficult to break him off the tent; he will return, and lounge, for weeks together, about that of his father, or some other relative. But get him fairly out of the tent, married, and, in a degree, settled to some occupation, in a town where there are not too many of his own race in close proximity to him, but where he gets mixed up, in his daily avocation, with the common natives, and he sooner or later falls into the ranks. Still, his intimate associations are always with Gipsies; for his ardent attachment to his people, and a corresponding resentment of the prejudice that exists against it, keep him aloof from any intimate intercourse with the ordinary inhabitants; his associations with them hardly ever extending beyond the commons or the public-house. If he experiences an attack from his old habits, he will take to the tramp, from town to town, working at his mechanical occupation; leaving his wife and children at home. But it is not long before he returns. His children, having been born and reared in a town, become habituated to a settled life, like other people.

There is a vast amount of ambition about every Gipsy, which is displayed. among the humble classes, in all kinds of athletic exercises.* The same peculiarity is discernible among the educated Scottish Gipsies. Carrying about with them the secret of being Gipsies, which they assume would be a terrible imputation cast upon them by the ordinary natives, if they knew of it, they, as it were, fly up, like game-cocks, and show a disposition to surpass the others in one way or other; particularly as they consider themselves better than the common inhabitants. They must always be "cock of the company," master of ceremonies, or stand at the top of the tree, if possible. The reader may ask, how do they consider themselves better than the ordinary natives? And I answer, that, from having been so long in Scotland, they are Scotchmen, (as indeed they are, for the most part, in point of blood,) and consider themselves as good as the others—nay, smarter than others in the same sphere, which, generally speaking, they are; and, in addition to that, being Gipsies, a great deal better. They pique themselves on their descent, and on being in possession of secrets which are peculiarly and exclusively theirs, and which they imagine no other knows, or will ever know. They feel that they are part and parcel of those mysterious beings who are an enigma to others, no less than to themselves. Besides this vanity, which is peculiar to the Gipsy everywhere, the Scottish Gipsies have chimed in with all the native Scotch ideas of clanism, kith, kin, and consequence, as regards family, descent, and so forth; and applied them so peculiarly to themselves, as to render their opinion of their body as something of no small importance. Some of them, whose descent leads them more directly back to the tented stock, speak of their families having possessed this district or the other district of the country, as much, almost, as we would expect to hear from some native Scottish chieftain.

As regards the various phases of history through which many of the Scottish Gipsies have passed, we can only form an estimate from what has been observed in recent times. The further back, however, we go, the greater were their facilities to rise to a position in society; for this reason,

* "I was one of these verminous ones, one of these great sin-breeders; I infected all the youth of the town where I was born with all manner of youthful vanities. The neighbours counted me so; my practice proved me so: wherefore Christ Jesus took me first, and taking me first, the contagion was much allayed all the town over."—*Bunyan.*

that a very little education, joined to good natural talents, were all that was necessary, in a mixed Gipsy, to raise himself in the world, at the time to which I allude. He could leave the district in which, when a youth, he had travelled, with his parents; settle in a town where he was not personally known; commence some traffic, and, by his industry, gradually raise himself up, and acquire wealth. He would not lack a proper degree of innate manners, or personal dignity, to deport himself with propriety in any ordinary company into which he might enter. Even at the present day, in Scotland, a poor Gipsy will commence life with a wheelbarrow, then get a donkey-cart, and, in a few years, have a very respectable crockery-shop. I am intimate with an English mixed Gipsy family, the father of which commenced life as a basket-maker, was afterwards a constable, and now occasionally travels with the tent. His son is an M. D., for I have seen his diploma; and is a smart, intelligent fellow, and quite an adept at chemistry. To illustrate the change that has taken place among some of the Scottish Gipsies, within the last fifty years, I may mention that the grand-children of a prominent Gipsy, mentioned in chapter V., follow, at the present day the medical, the legal, and the mercantile professions. Such occurrences have been frequent in Scotland. There are the cases mentioned by our author; such as one of the Faas rising to such eminence in the mercantile world, at Dunbar; and another who rose to the rank of lieutenant in the East India Company's service; and the Baillie family, which furnished a captain and a quarter-master to the army, and a country surgeon. These are but instances of many others, if they were but known. Some may object, that these were not full-blood Gipsies. That, I readily admit. But the objection is more nominal than real. If a white were to proceed to the interior of the American continent, and cast his lot with a tribe of Indians, his children would, of course, be expected to be superior, in some respects, to the children of the native blood exclusively, owing to what the father might be supposed to teach them. But it is different in the case of a white marrying a Scottish Gipsy woman, born and reared in the same community with himself; for the white, in general cases, brings only his blood, which enables the children, if they take after himself, in appearance, to enter such places as the black Gipsies would not enter, or might not be allowed to enter. The white father, in such a case, might not even be so intelligent as the Gipsy mother. Be that as it may, the individuals to whom I have alluded were nothing but Gipsies; possibly they did not know when, or through whom, the white blood was introduced among them; they knew, at least, that they were Gipsies, and that the links which connected them with the past were substantially Gipsy links. Besides the Scottish Gipsies rising to respectable positions in life, by their own exertions, I can well believe that Gipsydom has been well brought up through the female line; especially at a time when females, and particularly country females, were rude and all but uneducated. Who more capable of doing that than the lady Baillies, of Tweed-dale, and the lady Wilsons, of Stirlingshire? Such Gipsy girls could "turn natives round their little fingers," and act, in a way, the lady at once; "turn over a new leaf," and "pin it down;" and conduct themselves with great propriety.

Upon a superior Scottish Gipsy settling in a town, and especially a small town, and wishing to appear respectable, he would naturally take a pew in the church, and attend public worship, were it only, as our author asserts, to hide the fact of his being a Gipsy. Because, among the Scotch, there is that prying inquisitiveness into their neighbours' affairs, that compels a person to be very circumspect, in all his actions, movements, and expressions, if he wishes to be thought anything of, at all. The habit of attending church would then become as regular, in the Gipsy's family, as in the families of the ordinary natives, and, in a great measure, proceed from as legitimate a motive. The family would be very polite, indeed, extra polite, to their neighbours. After they had lulled to sleep every suspicion of what they were, or, by their really good conduct, had, according to the popular idea, "ceased to be Gipsies," they would naturally encourage a formal acquaintance with respectable (and nothing but respectable,) people in the place. The Gipsy himself, a really good fellow at heart, honourable in his dealings, but fond of a bargain, when he could drive a bargain, and, moreover, a jovial fellow, would naturally make plenty of business and out-door friends, at least. Rising in circumstances and the public esteem, he makes up his mind that his children ought to be something better than himself, at all events; in short, that they ought not to be behind those of his respectable neighbours. Some of them he, therefore, educates for a liberal profession. The Gipsy himself becomes more and more ambitious: besides attending church, he must become an elder of the church; or it may be that the grace of God takes hold of him, and brings him into the fold. He and his wife conduct themselves with much propriety; but some of the boys are rather wild; the girls, however, behave well. Altogether, the whole family is very much thought of. Such is a Scottish Gipsy family, (the parents of which are now dead,) that I have in my mind at the present moment. No suspicion existed in regard to the father, but there was a breath of suspicion in regard to the mother. But what difference did that make? What knowledge had the public of the nature of Gipsydom?

Consider, then, that the process which I have attempted to describe has been going on, more or less, for at least the last three hundred and fifty years; and I may well ask, where might we *not* expect to meet with Gipsies, in Scotland, at the present day? And I reply, that we will meet with them in every sphere of Scottish life, not excepting, perhaps, the very highest. There are Gipsies among the very best Edinburgh families. I am well acquainted with Scotchmen, youths and men of middle age, of education and character, and who follow very respectable occupations, that are Gipsies, and who admit that they are Gipsies. But, apart from my own knowledge, I ask, is it not a fact, that, a few years ago, a pillar of the Scottish church, at Edinburgh, upon the occasion of founding a society for the reformation of the poor class of Scottish Gipsies, and frequently thereafter, said that he himself was a Gipsy? I ask, again, is not that a fact? It is a fact. And such a man! Such prayers! Such deep-toned, sonorous piety! Such candour! Such judgment! Such amiability of manners! How much respected! How worthy of respect! The good, the godly, the saintly doctor! When will we meet his like again?*

* "Grand was the repose of his lofty brow, dark eye, and aspect of soft and melancholy meaning. It was a face from which every evil and earthly passion seemed purged. A deep gravity lay upon his countenance, which had the solemnity, without the sternness, of one of our old reformers. You could almost fancy a halo completing its apostolic character."

This leads me to speak of a high-class Scottish Gipsy family—the Falls, who settled at Dunbar, as merchants, alluded to under the chapter on Border Gipsies.* Who can doubt that they were Gipsies to the last? How could they avoid being Gipsies? The Gipsies were their people; their blood was Gipsy blood. How could they get rid of their blood and descent? Could they throw either off, as they would an old coat? Could medical science rid them of either? Assuredly not. They admitted their descent, *over their cups.* But being *descendants of Gipsies*, and yet *not Gipsies*, is a contradiction in terms. The principles which regulate the descent of other Gipsy families applied equally to theirs. The fact that Mrs. Fall had the history of her people, in the act of leaving Yetholm, represented in tapestry, may be taken as but a straw that indicated how the wind blew. Was not old Will Faa, the Gipsy king, down to his death, at the end of the first American war, admitted to their hospitality as a relative? And do not the Scottish

* Burns alludes to this family, thus: "Passed through the most glorious corn country I ever saw, till I reached Dunbar, a neat little town. Dine with Provost Fall, an eminent merchant, and most respectable character, but indescribable, as he exhibits no marked traits. Mrs. Fall, a genius in painting; fully more clever in the fine arts and sciences than my friend Lady Wauchope, without her consummate assurance of her own abilities."—*Life of Burns, by Robert Chambers.*

The crest of the Falls, of Dunbar, was *three* boars' heads, couped; that of Baillie, of Lamington, is *one* boar's head, couped. In the Statistical Account of Scotland, (1835,) appears the following notice of this family: "A family, of the name of Fall, established themselves at Dunbar, and became, during the last century, the most extensive merchants in Scotland. They were long the chief magistrates of the burgh, and preferred the public good to their own profit. They have left no one to bear their name, *not even a stone to tell where they lie;* but they will long be remembered for their enterprise and public spirit." There is apparently a reason for "not even a stone being left to tell where they lie;" for in Hoyland's "Survey of the Gipsies" appeared the account of Baillie Smith, in which it is said: "The descendants of Faa now take the name of Fall, from the Messrs. Fall, of Dunbar, who, they pride themselves in saying, *are of the same stock and lineage;*" which seems to have frightened their connexions at being known to be Gipsies.

Let all that has been said of the Falls be considered as their monument and epitaph; so that their memories may be preserved as long as this work exists.

It would be interesting to know who the Captain Fall was, who visited Dunbar, with an American ship-of-war, during the time of Paul Jones. He might have been a descendant of a Gipsy, sent to the plantations, in the olden times. There are, as I have said before, a great many scions of Gipsy Faas, under one name or other, scattered over the world.

Gipsies, at the present day, claim them to have been Gipsies? Why might not the Falls glory in being Egyptians among themselves, but not to others? Were not their ancestors *kings*? "Wee kings," no doubt, but still kings; one of them being the "loved John Faw," of James V., whom all the tribe consider as a great man, (which, doubtless, he was, in that barbarous age,) and the principal of the thirteen patriarchs of Scottish Gipsydom. Was not a Gipsy king, (themselves being Gipsies,) an ancestor of far more respect, in their eyes, than the founder of a native family, in their neighbourhood; who, in the reign of Charles II., was a common country *snip*, and most likely commenced life with "whipping the cat" around the country, for fivepence a day, and victuals and clippings?*

The truth of the matter is, these Falls must have considered themselves a world better than other people, merely on account of their being Gipsies, as all Gipsies do, arising, in part, from that antagonistic spirit of opposition which the prejudice of their fellow-creatures is so much calculated to stir up in their minds. Saying, over their cups, that they were descended from the Faws, the historical Gipsy name in Scotland, did not divulge very much to the public. For what idea had the public of the *working of Gipsydom*—what idea of the Gipsy language? Did the public know of the existence of a Gipsy language in Scotland? In all probability, it generally did not. If the public heard a Tinkler use a strange word, all that it would think of it would be, that it was *cant*, confined to vagabonds strolling the country. Would it ever dream that what the vagabonds used was carefully preserved and spoken among the great Falls, of Dunbar, within the sanctity of their own dwellings, as it assuredly must have been? Would the public believe in such a thing, if even its own ears were made the witnesses to it? Was the love which the Falls had for their Yetholm connexion confined to a mere group of their ancestors worked in tapestry? Where was the Gipsy language, during all this time? Assuredly it was well preserved in their family. If it showed the least symptoms of falling off, how easily could the mothers bring into the family, as servants,

* *Whipping the cat*: Tailoring from house to house. The *cat* is *whipped* by females, as well as males, in America, in some parts of which the expression is current.

other Gipsies, who would teach it to the children! For, besides the dazzling hold which the Gipsy language takes of the mind of a Gipsy, as the language of those black, mysterious heroes from whom they are descended, the keeping of it up forms the foundation of that self-respect which a Gipsy has for himself, amidst the prejudice of the world; from which, at the bottom of his heart, whatever his position in life, or character, or associations, may be, he considers himself separated. I am decidedly of opinion that all the domestics about this Fall family were Gipsies of one caste, colour, condition, or what not.

Then, we are told that Miss Fall, who married Sir John Anstruther, of Elie, baronet, was looked down upon by her husband's friends, and received no other name than Jenny Fan; and that she was indirectly twitted with being a Gipsy, by the rabble, while attending an election in which Sir John was a candidate. What real satisfaction could Jenny, or any other Gipsy, have for ordinary natives of the country, when she was conscious of being what she was, and how she was spoken of, by her husband's relatives and the public generally? She would take comfort in telling her "wonderful story" to her children, (for I presume she would have children,) who would sympathize with her; and in conversing with such of her own race as were near her, were it only her trusty domestics. It is the Gipsy woman who feels the prejudice that exists towards her race the most acutely; for she has the rearing of the children, and broods more over the history of her people. As the needle turns to the pole, so does the mind of the Gipsy woman to Gipsydom.

We are likewise told that this eminent Gipsy family were connected, by marriage, with the Footies, of Balgonie; the Coutts, afterwards bankers; Collector Whyte, of Kirkaldy, and Collector Melville, of Dunbar. We may assume, as a mathematical certainty, that Gipsydom, in a refined form, is in existence in the descendants of these families, particularly in such of them as were connected with this Gipsy family by the female side.*

* Of the Gipsies at Moscow, the following is the substance of what Mr. Borrow says: "Those who have been accustomed to consider the Gipsy as a wandering outcast . . . . will be surprised to learn that, amongst the Gipsies of Moscow, there are not a few who inhabit stately houses, go abroad in elegant equipages, and are behind the higher order of

A person who has never considered this subject, or any other cognate to it, may imagine that a Gipsy reproaches himself with his own blood. Pshaw! Where will you find a man, or a tribe of men, under the heavens, that will do that? It is not in human nature to do it. All men venerate their ancestors, whoever they have been. A Gipsy is, to an extraordinary degree, proud of his blood. "I have very little of the blood, myself," said one of them, "but just come and see my wife!" But people may say that the ancestors of the Falls were thieves. And were not all the Borderers, in their way, the worst kind of thieves? They might not have stolen from their nearest relatives; but, with that exception, did they not steal from each other? Now, Gipsies never, or hardly ever, steal from each other. Were not all the Elliots and Armstrongs thieves of the first water? Were not the Scotts and the Kers thieves, long after the Gipsies entered Scotland? When the servants of Scott of Harden drove out his last cow, and said, "There goes Harden's cow," did not the old cow-stealer say, "It will soon be Harden's *kye*"—meaning, that he would set out on a cow-stealing expedition? In fact, he lived upon spoil. Was it not his lady's custom, on the last bullock being killed, to place on the table a dish, which, on being uncovered, was found to contain a pair of clean spurs—a hint, to her husband and his followers, that they must shift for their next meal? The descendants of these Scotts, and the Scottish public generally, look, with the utmost complacency and pride, upon the history of such families; yet would be very apt to make a great ado, if the ancestress of a Gipsy should, in such a predicament, have hung out a cock's tail at the mouth of her tent, as a hint to her "laddies" to look after

Russians neither in appearance nor mental acquirements. . . . . The sums obtained by the Gipsy females, by the exercise of their art (singing in the choirs of Moscow,) enable them to support their relatives in affluence and luxury. Some are married to Russians; and no one who has visited Russia can but be aware that a lovely and accomplished countess, of the noble and numerous family of Tolstoy is, by birth, a Zigana, and was originally one of the principal attractions of a Romany choir at Moscow."

This short notice appears unsatisfactory, considering, as Mr. Borrow says, that one of his principal motives for visiting Moscow was to hold communication with the Gipsies. It might have occurred to him to enquire what relation the children of such marriages would bear to Gipsydom generally; that is, would they be initiated in the mysteries, and taught the language, and hold themselves to be Gipsies? It is evident, however, that the Gipsy-drilling process is going on among the Russian nobility.

poultry. Common sense tells us, that, for one excuse to be offered for such conduct on the part of the *landed-gentry* of the country, a hundred can be found for the ancestor of a Gipsy—an unfortunate wanderer on the face of the earth, who was hunted about, like a wolf of the forest.*

And what shall we say of our Highland thieves? Highlanders may be more touchy on this point, for their ancestors were the last of the British race to give up that kind of life. Talk of the laws passed against the Gipsies! Various of our Scottish monarchs issued decrees against "the wicked thieves and limmers of the clans and surnames, inhabiting the Highlands and Isles," accusing "the chieftains principal of the branches worthy to be esteemed the very authors, fosterers, and maintainers, of the wicked deeds of the vagabonds of their clans and surnames." Indeed, the doweries of the chiefs' daughters were made up by a share of the booty collected on their expeditions. The Highlands were, at one time, little better than a nest of thieves; thieving from each other, and more particularly from their southern neighbours. It is notorious that robbery, in the Highlands, was "held to be a calling not merely innocent, but honourable;" and that a high-born Highland warrior was "much more becomingly employed, in plundering the lands of others, than in tilling his own." At stated times of the year, such as at Candlemas, regular bands of Highlanders, the sons of gentlemen and what not, proceeded south in quest of booty, as part of their winter's provisions. The Highlanders might even have been compared, at one time, to as many tribes of Afghans. Mr. Skene, the historian of the Highlands, and himself a Highlander, says that the Highlanders "believed that they *had a right* to plunder the people of the low country, *whenever it was in their power.*" We

* On his return with his gallant prey, he passed a very large hay-stack. It occurred to the provident laird that this would be extremely convenient to fodder his new stock of cattle; but, as no means of transporting it were obvious, he was fain to take leave of it, with the apostrophe, now become proverbial, "*By my saul, had ye but four feet, ye should not stand lang there.*" In short, as Froissart says of a similar class of feudal robbers, "Nothing came amiss to them that was not *too heavy* or *too hot.*" Sir Walter Scott speaks, in the most jocular manner, of an ancestress who had a *curious hand at pickling the beef which her husband stole;* and that there was not a stain upon his escutcheon, barring Border theft and high treason.—*Lockhart's Life of Sir Walter Scott.*

We should never forget that a "hawk's a hawk," whether it is a falcon or a mosquito hawk, which is the smallest of all hawks.

naturally ask, how did the Highlanders *acquire* this right of plunder? Were they ever proscribed? Were any of them hung, merely for being Highlanders? No. What plea, then, did the Highlanders set up, in justification of this wholesale robbery?—"They believed, *from tradition*, that the Lowlands, *in old times*, were the possessions of their ancestors." (*Skene.*) But that was no excuse for their plundering each other.*

The Gipsy's ordinary pilfering was confined to such petty things as "hens and peats at pleasure," "cutting a bit lamb's throat," and "a mouthfu' o' grass and a pickle corn, for the cuddy"—"things that a farmer body ne'er could miss." But your Highlanders did not content themselves with such "needles and pins;" they must have "horned cattle." If the coast was clear, they would table their drawn dirks, and commence their *spulzie*, by making their victims furnish them with what was necessary to fill their bellies; upon the strength of which, they would "lift" whatever they could carry and drive, or take its equivalent in black-mail.

What an effort is made by our McGregors, at the present day, to scrape up kin with this or the other bandit McGregor; and yet how apt the McGregor is to turn up his nose—just as Punch, only, could make him turn it up—if a Gipsy were to step out, and say, that he was a descendant, and could speak the language, of Will Baillie, mentioned under the head of Tweed-dale and Clydesdale Gipsies: a Gipsy, described by my ancestor, (and he could judge,) to have been "the handsomest, the best dressed, the best looking, and the best bred, man he ever saw; and the best

* Sir Walter Scott makes Fitz-James, in the "Lady of the Lake," say to Roderick Dhu:

"But then, thy chieftain's robber life!—
Winning mean prey by causeless strife,
Wrenching from ruined Lowland swain
His herds and harvests reared in vain—
Methinks a soul like thine should scorn
The spoils from such foul foray borne."

The Gael beheld him, grim the while,
And answered with disdainful smile,—

. . . .

'Where live the mountain chiefs, who hold
That plundering Lowland field and fold
Is aught but retribution true?
Seek other cause 'gainst Roderick Dhu!'"

swordsman in Scotland, for, with his weapon in his hand, and his back at a wall, he could set almost everything, saving fire-arms, at defiance; a man who could act the gentleman, the robber, the sorner, and the tinker, whenever it answered his purpose."* And yet, some of this man's descendants will doubtless be found among our medical doctors, and even the clergy. I recollect our author pointing out a clergyman of the Scottish Church, who, he was pretty sure, was "one of them." What name could have stood lower, at one time, than McGregor? Both by legal and social proscription, it was looked upon as vagabond; and doubtless the clan brought it, primarily and principally, upon themselves; but as for the rapine they practised upon their neighbours, and the helpless southerners, they were, at first, no worse, in that respect, than others of their nation. Are the McGregors sure that there are no Gipsies among them? There are plenty of Gipsies of, at least, the name of McGregor, known to both the Scottish and English Gipsies. What more likely than some of the McGregors, when "out," and leading their vagabond lives, getting mixed up with the better kind of mixed Gipsies? They were both leading a wild life, and it is not unlikely that some of the McGregors, of even no small consequence, might have been led captive by such Gipsy girls as the lady Baillies, of Tweed-dale. Let a Gipsy once be grafted upon a native family, and she rises with it; leavens the little circle of which she is the centre, and leaves it, and its descendants, for all time coming, Gipsies.

I now come to ask, what constitutes a Gipsy, at the present day? And common sense replies: the simple fact of knowing from whom he is descended, that is, who he is, in connection with having the Gipsy words and signs, although these are not absolutely necessary. It requires no argument to show that there is no tribe or nation but finds something that leads it to cling to its origin and descent, and not despise the blood that runs in its own veins, although it may despise the condition or conduct of some of its members. Where shall we find an exception to this rule? The Gipsy race is no exception to it. Civilize a Gipsy, and you make him a civilized Gipsy; educate him, and you make him an educated Gipsy; bring him up to any profession you like,

* See page 202.

Christianize him as much as you may, and he still remains a Gipsy; because he is of the Gipsy race, and all the influences of nature and revelation do not affect the questions of blood, tribe, and nationality. Take all the Gipsies that ever came out of the tent, or their descendants, including those brought into the body through the male and female line; and what are they now? Still Gipsies. They even pass into the other world Gipsies. "But they will forget that they are Gipsies," say, perhaps, some of my readers. Forget that they are Gipsies! Will we hear, some of these days, that Scotch people, themselves, will get up of a morning, toss about their night-caps, and forget that they are Scotch? We may then see the same happen with the Gipsies. What I have said, of the Gipsy always being a Gipsy, is self-evident; but it has a wide difference of meaning from that contained in the quotation given by Mr. Borrow, in which it is said: "For that which is unclean by nature thou canst entertain no hope; no washing will turn the Gipsy white."* But, taking the world all over, there will doubtless be Gipsies, in larger or smaller numbers, who will always be found following the original ways of their race.

What were the Hungarians, at one time, and what are they now? Pritchard says of them: "The Hungarians

* In expatiating on the subject of the Gipsy race always being the Gipsy race, I have had it remarked to me: "Suppose Gipsies should not mention to their children the fact of their being Gipsies." In that case, I replied, the children, especially if, for the most part, of white blood, would simply not be Gipsies; they would, of course, have some of "the blood," but they would not be Gipsies if they had no knowledge of the fact. But to suppose that Gipsies should not learn that they are Gipsies, on account of their parents not telling them of it, is to presume that they had no other relatives. Their being Gipsies is constantly talked of among themselves; so that, if Gipsy children should not hear their "wonderful story" from their parents, they would readily enough hear it from their other relatives. This is assuming, however, that the Gipsy mind can act otherwise than the Gipsy mind; which it cannot.

It sometimes happens, as the Gipsies separate into classes, like all other races or communities of men, that a great deal of jealousy is stirred up in the minds of the poorer members of the tribe, on account of their being shunned by the wealthier kind. They are then apt to say that the exclusive members have *left* the tribe; which, with them, is an undefined and confused idea, at the best, principally on account of their limited powers of reflection, and the subject never being alluded to by the others. This jealousy sometimes leads them to dog these straggling sheep, so that, as far as lies in their power, they will not allow them to leave, as they imagine, the Gipsy fold.

laid aside the habits of rude and savage hunters, far below the condition of the nomadic hordes, for the manners of civilized life. In the course of a thousand years, they have become a handsome people, of fine stature, regular European features, and have the complexion prevalent in that tract of Europe where they dwell." Now the Gipsies have been in Scotland at least three hundred and fifty years; and what with the mixture of native blood, (which, at least, helped to remove the prejudice against the man's appearance, and, consequently, gave him a larger and freer scope of action;) the hard laws of necessity, and the being tossed about by society, like pebbles on the seashore; the influences of civilization, education, and the grace of God itself; by such means as these, some of the Scottish Gipsies have risen to a respectable, even eminent, position in life. But some people may say: "These are not Gipsies; they have little of the blood in them." That is nothing. Ask themselves what they are, and, if they are at all candid, they will reply that they *are* Gipsies. "No doubt," they say, "we have fair, or red, or black, hair, (as the case may be;) we know nothing about that; but we know that we *are* Gipsies; that is all." There is as much difference between such a high-class Gipsy and a poor Gipsian, as there is between a Scottish judge and the judge's fourth cousin, who makes his living by clipping dogs' ears. The principle of progression, the passing through one phase of history into another, while the race maintains its identity, holds good with the Gipsies, as well as with any other people.

Take a Gipsy in his original state, and we can find nothing really *vulgar* about him. What is popularly understood to be Gipsy life may be considered low life, by people who do not overmuch discriminate in such matters; but view it after its kind, and it is not really low; for a Gipsy is naturally polite and well mannered. He does not consider himself as belonging to the same race as the native, and would rather be judged by a different standard. The life which he leads is not that of the lowest class of the country in which he dwells, but the primitive, original state of a people of great antiquity, proscribed by law and society; himself an enemy of, and an enemy to, all around him; with the population so prejudiced against him, that attempts to change his condition, consistently with his feelings as a man, are frequently rendered in vain: so that, on the ground of strict morals, or even administrative justice, the man can be said to be only half responsible. The subject, however, assumes quite a different aspect, when we consider a Gipsy of education and refinement, like the worthy clergyman mentioned, between whose condition and that of his tented ancestor an interval of, perhaps, two or three centuries has elapsed. We should then put him on the footing of any other race having a barbarous origin, and entertain no prejudice against him on account of the race to which he belongs. He is then to be judged as we judge Highland and Border Scots, for the whole three were at one time robbers; and all the three having welled up to respectable life together, they ought to be judged on their merits, individually, as men, and treated accordingly. And the Gipsy ought to be the most leniently dealt with, on the principle that the actions of his ancestors were far more excusable, and even less heinous, than those of the others. And as regards antiquity of descent, the Gipsy's infinitely surpasses the others, being probably no less than the shepherd kings, part of whose blood left Egypt, in the train of the Jews. I would place such a Gipsy on the footing of the Hungarian race; with this difference, that the Hungarians entered Europe in the ninth century, and became a people, occupying a territory; while the Gipsies appeared in the fifteenth century, and are now to be found, civilized and uncivilized, in almost every corner of the known world.

The admission of the good man alluded to casts a flood of light upon the history of the Scottish Gipsy race, shrouded as it is from the eye of the general population; but the information given by him was apt to fall flat upon the ear of the ordinary native, unless it was accompanied by some such exposition of the subject as is given in this work. Still, we can gather from it, where Gipsies are to be found, what *a* Scottish Gipsy is, and what the race is capable of; and what might be expected of it, if the prejudice of their fellow-creatures was withdrawn from the race, as distinguished from the various classes into which it may be divided, or, I should rather say, the personal conduct of each Gipsy individually. View the subject any way I may, I cannot resist coming to the conclusion that, under more favourable circumstances, it is difficult to say what the Gipsies might not attain to. But that would depend greatly upon the country in which they are to be found. Scotland has been peculiarly favourable for them, in some respects.

As regards the Scottish Gipsy population, at the present day, I can only adopt the language of the immortal Dominie Sampson, and say, that it must be "prodigious." If we consider the number that appear to have settled in Scotland, the length of time they have been in Scotland, the great amount of white blood that has, by one means or other, been brought into, and mixed up with, the body, and its great natural encrease; the feelings that attach them to their descent—feelings that originate, more properly, within themselves, and feelings that press upon them from without—the various occupations and positions in life in which they are to be found; we cannot set any limit to their number. Gipsies are just like other people; they have their own sets or circles of associates, out of which, as a thing that is almost invariable, they will hide, if not deny, themselves to others of their race, for reasons which have already been given. So almost invariable is this, at the present day, amongst Gipsies that are not tented Gipsies, that, should an English Gipsy come across a settlement of them in America —German Gipsies, for example—and cast his sign, and address them in their own speech, they will pretend not to know what he means, although he sees the Gipsy in their faces and about their dwellings. But should he meet with them away from their homes, and where they are not known, they would answer, and be cheek-by-jowl with him, in a moment. I have found, by personal experience, that the same holds with the French and other continental Gipsies in America.* It is particularly so with the Scottish Gipsies.

* I very abruptly addressed a French Gipsy, in the streets of New York, thus: "Vous êtes un *Romany chiel.*" "Oui, monsieur," was the reply which he, as abruptly, gave me. But, ever afterwards, he got cross, when I alluded to the subject. On one occasion, I gave him the sign, which he repeated, while he asked, with much tartness of manner, "What is that—what does it mean?" This was a roguish Gipsy, and was afterwards lodged in jail.

On one occasion, I met with a German cutler, in a place of business, in New York. I felt sure he was a Gipsy, although the world would not have taken him for one. Catching his eye, I commenced to look around the room, from those present to himself, as if there was to be something confidential between us, and then whispered to him, "*Callo chabo,*" (Gipsy, or black fellow;) and the effect was instantaneous. I afterwards visited his family, on

For these reasons, it seems to be beyond question that the number at which our author estimates them in Scotland, viz., 5,000, must be vastly below the real number. If I were to say 100,000, I do not think I would over-estimate them. The opinion of the Gipsies whom our author questioned was a guess, so far as it referred to the class to which they belonged, or with which they were acquainted; so that, if we take all kinds of Gipsies into account, it would be a very moderate estimate to set the Scottish Gipsies down at 100,000; and those in all the British Isles at 300,000. The number might be double what I have stated. The intelligent English Gipsies say that, in England, they are not only "dreadfully mixed," but extremely numerous. There is not a race of men on the face of the earth more prolific than tented Gipsies; in a word, tented Gipsydom, if I may hazard such an expression, is, comparatively speaking, like a rabbit warren. The rough and uncouth kind of settled Gipsies are likewise very prolific; but the higher classes, as a rule, are by no means so much so. To set down any specific number of Gipsies to be found in the British Isles, would be a thing too arbitrary to serve any purpose; I think sufficient data have been given to enable the intelligent reader to form an opinion for himself.*

a Sabbath evening, and took tea with them. They were from Wurtemberg, and appeared very decent people. The mother, a tall, swarthy, fine-looking intelligent young woman, said grace, which was repeated by the children, whom I found learning their Sabbath-school lessons. The family regularly attend church. A fair-haired German called, and went to church with the Gipsy himself. What with the appearance of everything about the house, and the fine, clean, and neatly-dressed family of children, I felt very much pleased with my visit.

French and German Gipsies are very shy, owing to the severity of the laws against their race.

* Fletcher, of Saltoun, speaks of there being constantly a hundred thousand people in Scotland, leading the life (as Sir Walter Scott describes it,) of "Gipsies, Jockies, or Cairds." Between the time alluded to and the date of John Faw's league with James V., a period of 140 years had elapsed; and 174 years from the date of arrival of the race in the country: so that, from the natural encrease of the body, and the large amount of white blood introduced into it, the greater part, if not the whole, of the people mentioned, were doubtless Gipsies. But these Gipsies, according to Sir Walter's opinion, "died out by a change of habits." How strange it is that the very first class Scottish minds should have so little understood the philosophy of origin, blood, and descent, and especially as they applied to the Gipsies! For Sir Walter says: "The progress of time, and encrease both of the means of life and the power of the laws, gradually reduced this dreadful evil within more narrow bounds. . . . . Their numbers are

That many Gipsies were banished to America, in colonial times, from England, Wales, Scotland, and Ireland, sometimes for merely being "by habit and repute Gipsies," is beyond dispute. "Your Welsh and Irish," said an English Gipsy, in the United States, "were so mean, when they banished a Gipsy to the Plantations, as to make him find his own passage; but the English always paid the Gipsy's passage for him." The Scotch seem also to have made the Gipsy find his own passage, and failing that, to have hanged him. It greatly interests the English Gipsies arriving in America, to know about the native American Gipsies. I have been frequently in the company of an English Gipsy, in America, whose great-grandfather was so banished; but he did not relish the subject being spoken of. Gipsies may be said to have been in America almost from the time of its settlement. We have already seen how many of them found their way there, during the Revolution, by being impressed as soldiers, and taken as volunteers, for the benefit of the

so greatly diminished, that, instead of one hundred thousand, as calculated by Fletcher, it would now, perhaps, be impossible to collect above five hundred throughout all Scotland (!)" It is perfectly evident that Sir Walter Scott, in common with many others, never realized the idea, in all its bearings, of what a Gipsy was; or he never could have imagined that those, only, were of the Gipsy race, who followed the tent.

It is very doubtful if Anthonius Gawino, and his tribe, departed, with their letter of introduction from James IV. to his uncle, the king of Denmark, in 1506. Having secured the favour of the king of Scots, by this recommendatory notice, he was more apt, by delaying his departure, to secure his position in the country. The circumstances attending the league with his successor, John Faw, show that the tribe had been long in the country; doubtless from as far back as 1506. From 1506 till 1579, with the exception of about one year, during the reign of James V., the tribe as I have already said, (page 109,) must have encreased prodigiously. The persecutions against the body extended over the reign of James VI., and part of that of Charles I.; for, according to Baron Hume, such was the terror which the executions inspired in the tribe, that, "for the space of more than 50 years from that time, (1624,) there is no trial of an Egyptian;" although our author shows that an execution of a band of them took place in 1636. But "towards the end of that century," continues Baron Hume, "the nuisance seems to have again become troublesome;" in other words, that from the reign of Charles I. to the accession of William and Mary, the time to which Fletcher's remark applies, the attention of all being taken up with the troubles of the times, the Gipsies had things pretty much their own way; but when peace was restored, they would be called to strict account.

For all these reasons, it may be said that the 100,000 people spoken of were doubtless Gipsies of various mixtures of blood; so that, at the present day, there ought to be a very large number of the tribe in Scotland. I

bounty and passage; and how they deserted on landing. Tented Gipsies have been seen about Baltimore for the last seventy years. In New England, a colony is known which has existed for about a hundred years, and has always been looked upon with a singular feeling of distrust and mystery by the inhabitants, who are the descendants of the early emigrants, and who did not suspect their origin till lately. These Gipsies have never associated, in the common sense of the word, with the other settlers, and, judging from their exterior, seem poor and miserable, whatever their circumstances may be. They follow pretty much the employment and modes of life of the same class in Europe; the most striking feature being, that the bulk of them leave the homestead for a length of time, scatter in different directions, and reunite, periodically, at their quarters, which are left in charge of some of the feeble members of the band.

It is not likely that many of the colonial Gipsies would take to the tent; for, arriving, for the most part, as individuals, separated from family relations, they were more apt to follow settled, semi-settled, or general itinerant occupations; and the more so, as the face of the country, and the thin and scattered settlements, would hardly admit of it. They were apt to squat on wild or unoccupied lands, in the neighbourhood of towns and settlements, like their brethren in Europe, when they took up their quarters on the borders of well-settled districts, with a wild country to fall back on, in times of danger or prosecution by the lawful authorities. Besides disposing of themselves, to some little extent, in this way, many of the Gipsies, banished, or going to the colonies of their own accord, would betake themselves to the various occupations common to the ordinary emigrants; the more especially as, when they arrived, they would find a field

admit that many of the Scottish Gipsies have been hanged, and many banished to the Plantations; but these would be in a small ratio to their number, and a still smaller to the natural encrease of the body. Suppose that such and such Gipsies were either hanged or banished; so young did they all marry, that, when they were hanged or banished, they might leave behind them families ranging from five to ten children. We may say, of the Scottish Gipsies generally, in days that are past, what a writer in Blackwood's Magazine, already alluded to, said of Billy Marshall: "Their descendants were prodigiously numerous; I dare say, numberless." Many of the Scottish Gipsies have migrated to England, as well as elsewhere. In Liverpool, there are many of them, following various mechanical occupations.

in which they were not known to be Gipsies; which would give them greater scope and confidence, and enable them to go anywhere, or enter upon any employment, where, not being known to be Gipsies, they would meet with no prejudice to contend with. Indeed, a new country, in which the people had, more or less, to be, in a sense, tinkers, that is, jacks-of-all-trades, and masters of none, was just the sphere of a handy Gipsy, who could "do a' most of things." They would turn to the tinkering, peddling, horse-dealing, tavern-keeping, and almost all the ordinary mechanical trades, and, among others, broom-making. Perhaps the foundation of the American broom manufacture was laid by the British Gipsies, by whom it may be partly carried on at the present day; a business they pretty much monopolize, in a rough way, in Great Britain. We will doubtless find, among the fraternity, some of those whittling, meddling Sam Slick peddlers, so often described: I have seen some of those itinerant venders of knife-sharpeners, and such "Yankee notions," with dark, glistening eyes, that would "pass for the article." Some of them would live by less legitimate business. I entertain no doubt, what from the general fitness of things, and the appearance of some of the men, that we will find some of the descendants of the old British mixed Gipsies members of the various establishments of Messrs. Peter Funks and Company,* of the city of New York, as well as elsewhere. And I entertain as little doubt that many of those American women who tell fortunes, and engage in those many curious bits of business that so often come up at trials, are descendants of the British plantation stock of Gipsies. But there are doubtless many of these Gipsies in respectable spheres of life. It would be extremely unreasonable to say that the descendants of the colonial Gipsies do not still exist as Gipsies, like their brethren in Great Britain, and other parts of the Old World. The English Gipsies in America entertain no doubt of it; the more especially as they have encountered such Gipsies, of at least two descents. I have myself met with such a Gipsy, following a decidedly respectable calling, whom I found as much one of the tribe, barring the original habits, as perhaps any one in Europe.

There are many Hungarian and German Gipsies in Amer-

* *Peter Funks & Co.:* Mock auctioneers of mock jewelry, &c., &c.

ica; some of them long settled in Pennsylvania and Maryland, where they own farms. Some of them leave their farms in charge of hired hands, during the summer, and proceed South with their tents. In the State of Pennsylvania, there is a settlement of them, on the J—— river, a little way above H——, where they have saw-mills. About the Alleghany Mountains, there are many of the tribe, following somewhat the original ways of the race. In the United States generally, there are many Gipsy peddlers, British as well as continental. There are a good many Gipsies in New York—English, Irish, and continental—some of whom keep tin, crockery, and basket stores; but these are all mixed Gipsies, and many of them of fair complexion. The tin-ware which they make is generally of a plain, coarse kind; so much so, that a Gipsy tin store is easily known. They frequently exhibit their tin-ware and baskets on the streets, and carry them about the city. Almost all, if not all, of those itinerant cutlers and tinkers, to be met with in New York, and other American cities, are Gipsies, principally German, Hungarian, and French. There are a good many Gipsy musicians in America. "What!" said I, to an English Gipsy, "those organ-grinders?" "Nothing so low as that. Gipsies don't *grind* their music, sir; they *make* it." But I found in his house, when occupied by other Gipsies, a *hurdy-gurdy* and tambourine; so that Gipsies sometimes *grind* music, as well as *make* it. I know of a Hungarian Gipsy who is leader of a Negro musical band, in the city of New York; his brother drives one of the Avenue cars. There are a number of Gipsy musicians in Baltimore, who play at parties, and on other occasions. Some of the fortune-telling Gipsy women about New York will make as much as forty dollars a week in that line of business. They generally live a little way out of the city, into which they ride, in the morning, to their places of business. I know of one, who resides in New Jersey, opposite New York, and who has a place in the city, to which ladies, that is, females of the highest classes, address their cards, for her to call upon them. When she gets a chance of a young fellow with his female friend, she "puts the screws on;" for she knows well that he dare not "back out;" so she frequently manages to squeeze five dollars out of him.

Many hundred, perhaps several thousand, of English

tented, and partly tented Gipsies, have arrived in America within the last ten years. They, for the most part, travel, and have travelled every State in the Union, east of the Rocky Mountains, as well as the British Provinces, as horse-dealers, peddlers, doctors, exhibitors, fortune-tellers, and *tramps* generally. Such English Gipsies, above all men in America, may, with the greatest propriety, say,

> "No pent-up Utica contracts our powers,
> But the whole boundless continent is ours."

The fortune-tellers, every time they set out on their peregrinations, choose a new route; for they say it is more difficult to go over the same ground in America, than it is in England. The horse-dealers say that Jonathan is a good judge of a horse; that sometimes they get the advantage of him, and sometimes he of them; but that his demand for a warranty sometimes bothers them a deal. "What then?" I asked. "Well, we give him a warranty; and should the beast *happen* to turn out wrong, let him catch us if he can!" It is really astonishing how sensibly these English Gipsies talk of American affairs generally; they are very discriminating in their remarks, and wonderfully observant of places and localities. They do not like the Negroes. In their society they drop the name of king, and adopt that of president. "Cunning fellows," said I, "to eschew the name of king, and look down upon Negroes. That will do, in America!"

I have found the above kind of Gipsies, in America, to be generally pretty well off; they all seem to flourish, and have plenty of money about them. The fortune-telling, horse-dealing, and peddling branches of them have a fine field for following their respective businesses. America, indeed, is a "great country" for the Gipsies; for it contains "no end" of chickens, to say nothing of ducks, geese, and turkeys, many of which are carried off by *varmint*, anyhow. There, they will find, for some time, many opportunities of gathering rich harvests, among what has been termed the shrewdest, but, in some things, the most gullible, of mortals, as an instance may illustrate. A Gipsy woman, known as such, drags, into the meshes of her necromancy, 'cute Jonathan; who, with an infinite reliance on his own smartness, to "try the skill of the critter," by her directions, ties up, in gold and paper, something like a thousand dollars, and, after she has passed her hands over it, and muttered a few cabalistic words, deposits it in his strong box. She sets a day, on which she calls, handles the "dimes," while muttering some more expressions, rather accidentally drops them, then returns them to the box, and sets another day when she will call, and add much to his wealth. She does not appear, however, on the day mentioned. Our simpleton gets first anxious, then excited, then suspicious, then examines his "pile," and finds it transformed into a lot of copper and old paper! For, in dropping the parcel, Meg does it adroitly about the folds of her dress, quickly substitutes another, exactly alike, and makes off with the fruits of her labour. Then comes the hue and cry, telegraphing, and dispatching of warrants everywhere. But why need he trouble himself? So, after a harder day's work than, perhaps, he ever underwent in his life, he returns home: but knowing the sympathy he will find there, he puts on his best face, and, to have the first word of it, (for he is not to be laughed at,) wipes his forehead, twitches his mouth, winks his eyes, and remarks: "Waal, I reckon I've been most darnedly sold, anyhow!" Such occurrences are very common among almost all classes of rural Americans. Sometimes it is to discover treasure on the individual's lands, or in the neighbourhood; sometimes a mine, and sometimes an Indian, a trapper, a pirate, or a revolutionary deposit. When the Gipsy escapes with her spoil, she frequently makes for her home, but where that is, no one knows. On being molested, while there, she produces friends, in fair standing, who *prove* an alibi; and, with the further assistance of a well-feed lawyer, defies all the requisitions, made by the governors of neighbouring States, for her delivery. At other times, she will *divide* with the inferior authorities, or surrender the whole of the plunder; for, to go to jail she will not, if she can help it.*

* If the real characters of those "lady fortune-tellers," who flourish so much in the large cities, and publicly profess to reveal all matters in "love and law, health and wealth, losses and crosses," were to be ascertained, many of them would, in all probability, be found to belong to a superior class of Gipsies. And this may much more be said of the more humble ones, who trust to the gossipping of a class—and that a respectable class of females, for the advertising of their calling. For a certainty, those are Gipsies who stroll about, telling fortunes for dimes, clothes, or old bottles. The advertising members form a very small part of the fraternity. The

In Virginia, the more original kind of Gipsies are very frequently to be met with. It is in the Slave States they are more apt to flourish in the olden form. The planters need not trouble themselves about their tampering with the Negroes, for they have no sympathy with them. Were it otherwise, they would soon be *mum*, on finding what the results would be to them. I have given some of them some useful hints on that score. The general disposition of the people, the want of *learning* among so many of them, the distances between dwellings, the small villages, the handy mechanical services of the Gipsies, the uncultivated tracts of land, the game of various kinds, and the climate, seem to point out some of the Slave States as an elysium for the Gipsies; unless the wealthier part of the inhabitants should use the poorer class as tools to drive them out of the country.*

There are a good many very respectable Scottish Gipsies in the United States; but I do not wish to be too minute in describing them. In Canada, I know of a doctor, a lawyer, and an editor, Scottish Gipsies. The fact of the matter is, that, owing to the mixture of the blood, the improvement, and perpetuation, and secrecy, of the race, there may be many, very many, Gipsies, in almost every place in the world, and other people not know of it: and it is not

extent to which such business is patronized, by Americans, of both sexes, and of almost all positions in society is such, that it is doubtful if the English reader would credit it, if it were put on record.

* When travelling on the stage, towards Lake Huron, in Canada, I was surprised at finding a Gipsy tent on the road-side, with a man sitting in front of it, engaged in the mysteries of the tinker. I met a camp of Gipsies on a vacant space, beside a clump of trees, in Hamilton, at the head of Lake Ontario, but I deferred visiting them till the following morning. When I returned to the spot, I found that the birds had flown. Feeling disappointed, I began to question a man who kept a toll-bar, immediately opposite to where their tents had been, as to their peculiarities generally; when he said: "They seemed droll kind o' folk—quite like ourselves—no way foreign: yet I could not understand a word they were saying among themselves." Shortly after this, a company of them entered a shop, in the same town, to buy tin, when I happened to be in it. I accosted one of the mothers of the company, in an abrupt but bland tone. "You're a' Nawkens (Gipsies) I see."—"Ou ay, we're Nawkens," was her immediate reply, accompanied by a smile on her weather-beaten countenance. "You'll aye speak the language?" I continued. "We'll ne'er forget that," she again replied. This seemed to be a company of Gipsies from the Scottish Border; for the woman spoke about the broadest Scotch I ever heard. They dressed well, and bore a good reputation in the neighbourhood.

likely that, at the present time, they will say that they are Gipsies. Indeed, the intelligent English travelling Gipsies say that there are an immense number of Gipsies, of all countries, colours, and occupations, in America.

There is even some resemblance between the formation of Gipsydom and that of the United States. The children of emigrants, it is well known, frequently prove the most ultra Americans. Instead of the original colonists, at the Declaration of Independence, imagine the commencement of Gipsydom as proceeding from the original stock of Gipsies. The addition to their number, from without, differs from that which takes place among Americans, in this way: that all such additions to Gipsydom are made in such a manner, that the new blood gets innoculated, as it were, with the old, or part of the old; so that it may be said of the whole body,

One drop of blood makes all Gipsydom akin.

The simple fact of a person having Gipsy blood in his veins, in addition to the rearing of a Gipsy parent, acts upon him like a shock of electricity; it makes him spring to his feet, and—"snap his teeth at other dogs!" A very important circumstance contributing to this state of things is the antipathy which mankind have for the very name of Gipsy, which, as I have already said, they all take to themselves; insomuch that the better class will not face it. They imagine that, socially speaking, they are among the damned, and they naturally cast their lot with the damned. Still, the antagonistic spirit which would naturally arise towards society, in the minds of such Gipsies, remains, in a measure, latent; for they feel confident in their incognito, while moving among their fellow-creatures; which circumstance robs it of its sting.

Let a Lowlander, in times that are past, but have cast up a Highlander's blood to him, and what would have been the consequences? "Her ainsel would have drawn her dirk, or whipped out her toasting-iron, and seen which *was* the prettiest man." Let the same have been done to a Scottish Gipsy, in comparatively recent times, and he would have taken his own peculiar revenge. See how the Baillies, as mentioned under the chapter of Tweed-dale and Clydesdale Gipsies, mounted on horseback, and with drawn swords in their hands, threatened death to all who opposed them, for an affront offered to their mother. Twit a respectable Gipsy with his blood, at the present day, and he would suffer in silence; for, by getting into a passion, he would let himself out. For this reason, it would be unmanly to hint it to him, in any tone of disparagement. The difference of feeling between the two races, at the present day, proceeds from positive ignorance on the part of the native towards the other; an ignorance in which the Gipsy would rather allow him to remain; for, let him turn himself in whatever direction he may, he imagines he sees, and perhaps does see, nothing but a dark mountain of prejudice existing between him and every other of his fellow-creatures. He would rather retain his incognito, and allow his race to go down to posterity shrouded in its present mystery. The history of the Gipsy race in Scotland, more, perhaps, than in any other country, shows, to the eye of the world, as few traces of its existence as would a fox, in passing over a ploughed field. The farmer might see the foot-prints of reynard, but how is he to find reynard himself? He must bring out the dogs and have a hunt for him. As an Indian of the prairie, while on the "war path," cunningly arranges the long grass into its natural position, as he passes through it, to prevent his enemy following him, so has the Scottish Gipsy, as he entered upon a settled life, destroyed, to the eye of the ordinary native, every trace of his being a Gipsy. Still, I cannot doubt but that he has misgivings that, some day, he will be called up to judgment, and that all about him will be exposed to the world.

What is it that troubles the educated Gipsies? Nothing but the word Gipsy; a word which, however sweet when used among themselves, conveys an ugly, blackguard, and vagabond meaning to other people. The poet asks, What is there in a name? and I reply, Everything, as regards the name Gipsy. For a respectable Scottish Gipsy to say to the public, that "his mother is a Gipsy," or, that "his wife is a Gipsy," or, that "he is a Gipsy;" such a Gipsy simply could not do it. These Gipsies will hardly ever use the word among themselves, except in very select circles; but they will say "he's one of us;" "he's from Yetholm;" "he's from the metropolis," (Yetholm being the metropolis of Scottish Gipsydom;) or, "he's a traveller." If the company is not over classical, they will say "he's from the black quarry," or, "he's been with the cuddies." Imagine a select party of educated Scottish Gipsies, all closely related. They will then chatter Gipsy over their tea; but if a person should drop in, one of the party, who is not acquainted with him, will nudge and whisper to another, "Is he one of the tribe?" or, "Is he one of us?" The better class of Scottish Gipsies are very exclusive in matters of this kind.

All things considered, in what other position could the Gipsy race, in Scotland especially, be, at the present day, than that described? How can we imagine a race of people to act otherwise than hide themselves, if they could, from the odium that attaches to the name of Gipsy? And what estimate should we place on that charity which would lead a person to denounce a Gipsy, should he deny himself to be a Gipsy?* As a race, what can they offer to society at large to receive them within its circle? They can offer little, as a race; but, if we consider them as individuals, we will find many of them whose education, character, and position in life, would warrant their admission into any ordinary society, and some of them into any society. Notwithstanding all that, none will answer up to the name of Gipsy. It necessarily follows, that the race must remain shrouded in its present mystery, unless some one, not of the race, should become acquainted with its history, and speak for it. In Scotland, the prejudice towards the name of Gipsy might be safely allowed to drop, were it only for this reason: that the race has got so much mixed up with the native blood, and even with good families of the country, as to be, in plain language, a jumble—a pretty kettle of fish, indeed. One's uncle, in seeking for a wife, might have stumbled over an Egyptian woman, and, either known or unknown to himself, had his children brought up bitter Gipsies; so that one's cousins may be Gipsies, for anything one knows. A man may have a colony of Gipsies in his own house, and know nothing about it! The Gipsies *died* out? Oh, no. They commenced in Scotland by wringing the neck of one's *chickens*, and now they sometimes

* Mixed Gipsies tell no lies, when they say that they are not Gipsies; for, physiologically speaking, they are not Gipsies, but only partly Gipsies, as regards blood. In every other way they are Gipsies, that is, *chabos*, *calos*, or *chals*.

. . . . ! But what is Gipsydom, after all, but a "working in among other people?"

In seeking for Gipsies among Scotch people, I know where to begin, but it puzzles me where to leave off. I would pay no regard to colour of hair or eyes, character, employment, position, or, indeed, any outward thing. The reader may say: "It must be a difficult matter to detect such mixed and educated Gipsies as those spoken of." It is not only difficult, but outwardly impossible. Such Gipsies cannot even tell each other, from their personal appearance; but they have signs, which they can use, if the others choose to respond to them. If I go into a company which I have reason to believe is a Gipsy one, and it know nothing of me, so far as my pursuit is concerned, I will bring the subject of the Gipsies up, in a very roundabout way, and mark the effect which the conversation makes, or the turn it takes. What I know of the subject, and of the ignorance of mankind generally in regard to it, enables me to say, in almost every instance, who they are, let them make any remark they like, look as they like, pretend what they like, wriggle about as they like, or keep dead silent. As I gradually glide into the subject, and expatiate upon the "greatness of the society," one remarks, "I know it;" upon the "respectability of some of its members," and another emphatically exclaims, "That's a fact;" and upon "its universality," and another bawls out, "That's so." Indeed, by finding the Gipsies, under such circumstances, completely off their guard, (for they do not doubt their secret being confined to themselves,) I can generally draw forth, in one way or other, as much moral certainty, barring their direct admission, as to their being Gipsies, as a dog, by putting his nose into a hole, can tell whether a rat is there, or not.

The principle of the transmutation of Gipsy blood into white, in appearance, is illustrated, in the ninth chapter of Mr. Borrow's "Bible in Spain," by its changing into almost pure black. A Gipsy soldier, in the Spanish army, killed his sergeant, for "calling him *calo*, (Gipsy,) and cursing him," and made his escape. His wife remained in the army, as a sutler, selling wine. Two years thereafter, a strange man came to her wine shop. "He was dressed like a Moor, (*corahano*,) and yet he did not look like one; he looked more like a black, and yet he was not a black, either, though he was almost black. And, as I looked upon him, I thought he looked something like the Errate, (Gipsies,) and he said to me, '*Zincali, chachipé,*' (the Gipsy salutation.) And then he whispered to me, in queer language, which I could scarcely understand, 'Your husband is waiting; come with me, my little sister, and I will take you to him.' About a league from the town, beneath a hill, we found four people, men and women, all very black, like the strange man; and we joined ourselves with them, and they all saluted me, and called me 'little sister.' And away we marched, for many days, amidst deserts and small villages. The men would cheat with mules and asses, and the women told baji. I often asked him (her husband) about the black men, and he told me that he believed them to be of the Errate." Her husband, then a soldier in the Moorish army, having been killed, this Gipsy woman married the black man, with whom she followed real Gipsy life. She said to him: "Sure I am amongst the Errate; . . . . and I often said that they were of the Errate; and then they would laugh, and say that it might be so, and that they were not Moors, (*corahai*,) but they could give no account of themselves." From this it would seem that, while preserving their identity, wherever they go, there are Gipsies who may not be known to the world, or to the tribe, in other continents, by the same name.*

* The people above-mentioned are doubtless Gipsies. According to Grellmann, the race is even to be found in the centre of Africa. Mollien, in his travels to the sources of the Senegal and Gambia, in 1818, says: "Scattered among the Joloffs, we find a people not unlike our Gipsies, and known by the name of Laaubés. Leading a roving life, and without fixed habitation, their only employment is the manufacture of wooden vessels, mortars, and bedsteads. They choose a well-wooded spot, fell some trees, form huts with the branches, and work up the trunks. For this privilege, they must pay a sort of tax to the prince in whose states they thus settle. In general, they are both ugly and slovenly.

"The women, notwithstanding their almost frightful faces, are covered with amber and coral beads, presents heaped on them by the Joloffs, from a notion that the favours, alone, of these women will be followed by those of fortune. Ugly or handsome, all the young Laaubé females are in request among the Negroes.

"The Laaubés have nothing of their own but their money, their tools, and their asses; the only animals on which they travel. In the woods, they make fires with the dung of the flocks. Ranged round the fires, the men and women pass their leisure time in smoking. The Laaubés have not those characteristic features and high stature which mark the Joloffs, and they seem to form a distinct race. They are exempted from all military

A word upon the universality of the Gipsies. English Gipsies, on arriving in America, feel quite taken aback, on coming across a tent or wigwam of Indians. "Didn't you feel," said I to some of them, "very like a dog when he comes across another dog, a stranger to him?" And, with a laugh, they said, "Exactly so." After looking awhile at the Indians, they will approach them, and "cast their sign, and salute them in Gipsy;" and if no response is made, they will pass on. They then come to learn who the Indians are. The same curiosity is excited among the Gipsies on meeting with the American farmer, on the banks of the Mississippi or Missouri; who, in travelling to market, in the summer, will, to save expenses, unyoke his horses, at mid-day or evening, at the edge of the forest, light his fire, and prepare his meal. What with the "kettle and tented wagon," the tall, lank, bony, and swarthy appearance of the farmer, the Gipsy will approach him, as he did the Indian; and pass on, when no response is made to his sign and salutation. Under such circumstances, the Gipsy would cast his sign, and give his salutation, whether on the banks of the Mississippi or the Ganges. Nay, a very respectable Scottish Gipsy boasted to me, that, by his signs alone, he could, push his way to the wall of China, and even through China itself. And there are doubtless Gipsies in China. Mr. Borrow says, that when he visited the tribe at Moscow, they supposed him to be one of their brothers, who, they said, were wandering about in Turkey, *China*, and other parts. It is very likely that Russian Gipsies have visited China, by the route taken by Russian traders, and met with Gipsies there.* But it tickles the Gipsy most, when it is insinuated, that if Sir John Franklin had been fortunate in his expedition, he would have found a Gipsy tinkering a kettle at the North Pole.

The particulars of a meeting between English and Ameri-

service. Each family has its chief, but, over all, there is a superior chief, who commands a whole tribe or nation. He collects the tribute, and communicates with such delegates of the king as receive the imposts: this serves to protect them from all vexation. The Laaubés are idolaters, speak the Poula language, and pretend to tell fortunes."

* Bell, in an account of his journey to Pekin, [1721,] says that upwards of sixty Gipsies had arrived at Tobolsky, on their way to China, but were stopped by the Vice-Governor, for want of passports. They had roamed, during the summer season, from Poland, in small parties, subsisting by selling trinkets, and telling fortunes.

can Gipsies are interesting. Some English Gipsies were endeavouring to sell some horses, in Annapolis, in the State of Maryland, to what had the appearance of being respectable American farmers; who, however, spoke to each other in the Gipsy language, dropping a word now and then, such as "this is a good one," and so on. The English Gipsies felt amazed, and at last said: "What is that you are saying? Why, you are Gipsies!" Upon this, the Americans wheeled about, and left the spot as fast as they could. Had the English Gipsies taken after the Gipsy in their appearance, they would not have caused such a consternation to their American brethren, who showed much of "the blood" in their countenances; but as, from their blood being much mixed, they did not look like Gipsies, they gave the others a terrible fright, on their being found out. The English Gipsies said they felt disgusted at the others not owning themselves up. But I told them they ought rather to have felt proud of the Americans speaking Gipsy, as it was the prejudice of the world that led them to hide their nationality. On making enquiry in the neighbourhood, they found that these American Gipsies had been settled there since, at least, the time of their grandfather, and that they bore an English name.

There are Scottish Gipsies in the United States, following respectable callings, who speak excellent Gipsy, according to the judgment of intelligent English Gipsies. The English Gipsies say the same of the Gipsy families in Scotland, with whom they are acquainted; but that some of their words vary from those spoken in England. There is, however, a rivalry between the English and Scottish Gipsies, as to whose pronunciation of the words is the correct one: in that respect, they somewhat resemble the English and Scottish Latinists. One intelligent Gipsy gave it as his opinion, that the word great, *baurie*, in Scotland, was softer than *boro*, in England, and preferable, indeed, the right pronunciation of the word. The German Gipsies are said, by their English brethren, to speak Gipsy backwards; from which I would conclude, that it follows the construction of the German language, which differs so materially, in that respect, from the English.* It is a thing well-nigh im-

* Mr. Borrow says, with reference to the Spanish Gipsy language: "Its grammatical peculiarities have disappeared, the entire language having

possible, to get a respectable Scottish Gipsy to own up to even a word of the Gipsy language. On meeting with a respectable—Scotchman, I will call him—in a company, lately, I was asked by him: "Are ye a' Tinklers?" "We're travellers," I replied. "But who is he?" he continued, pointing to my acquaintance. Going up to him, I whispered "His *dade* is a *baurie grye-femler*," (his father is a great horse-dealer;) and he made for the door, as if a bee had got into his ear. But he came back; oh, yes, he came back. There was a mysterious whispering of "pistols and coffee," at another time.

It is beyond doubt that the Gipsy language in Great Britain is broken, but not so broken as to consist of words only; it consists, rather, of expressions, or pieces, which are tacked together by native words—generally small words—which are lost to the ordinary ear, when used in conversation. In that respect, the use of Gipsy may be compared to the revolutions of a wheel: we know that the wheel has spokes, but, in its velocity, we cannot distinguish the colour or material of each individual spoke; it is only when it stands still that that can be done. In the same manner, when we come to examine into the British Gipsy language, we perceive its broken nature. But it still serves the purpose of a speech. Let any one sit among English Gipsies, in America, and hear them converse, and he cannot pick up an idea, and hardly a word which they say. "I have always thought Dutch bad enough," said an Irishman, who has often heard

been modified and subjected to the rules of Spanish grammar, with which it now coincides in syntax, in the conjugation of verbs, and in the declension of its nouns." We might have naturally expected that of the Gipsy language, in the course of four hundred years, from the people speaking it being so much scattered over the country, and coming so much in contact with the ordinary natives. But something different might be looked for, where the Gipsies have not been persecuted, but allowed to live together in a body, as in Hungary. Of the Hungarian Gipsy language, Mr. Borrow says, that in no part of the world is the Gipsy language better preserved than in Hungary; and that the roving bands of Gipsies from that country, who visit France and Italy, speak the pure Gipsy, with all its grammatical peculiarities. He estimates that the Spanish Gipsy language may consist of four or five thousand words; a sufficient number, one might suppose, to serve the purpose of everyday life. A late writer in the Dublin University Magazine estimates that five thousand words would serve the same purpose in the English language. Four thousand words is a very large language for the Gipsies of Spain to possess, in addition to the ordinary one of the country.

English Gipsies, in the State of New Jersey, speak among themselves; "but Gipsy is perfect gibble-gabble, like ducks and geese, for anything I can make of it." Some Gipsies can, of course, speak Gipsy much better than others. It is most unlikely that the Scottish Gipsies, with the head, the pride, and the tenacity of native Scotch, would be the first to forget the Gipsy language. The sentiments of the people themselves are very emphatic on that head. "It will never be forgotten, sir; it is in our hearts, and, as long as a single Tinkler exists, it will be remembered," (page 297.) "So long as there existed two Gipsies in Scotland, it would never be lost," (page 316.) The English Gipsies admit that the language is more easily preserved in a settled life, but more useful to travelling and out-door Gipsies; and that it is carefully kept up by both classes of Gipsies. This information agrees with our author's, in regard to the settled Scottish Gipsies. There is one very strong motive, among many, for the Gipsies keeping up their language, and that is, as I have already said, their self-respect. The best of them believe that it is altogether problematical how they would be received in society, were they to make an avowal of their being Gipsies, and lay bare the history of their race to the world. The prejudice that exists against the race, and against them, they imagine, were they known to be Gipsies, drives them back on that language which belongs exclusively to themselves; to say nothing of the dazzling hold which it takes of their imagination, as they arrive at years of reflection, and consider that the people speaking it have been transplanted from some other clime. The more intelligent the Gipsy, the more he thinks of his speech, and the more care he takes of it.

People often reprobate the dislike, I may say the hatred, which the more original Gipsy entertains for society; forgetting that society itself has had the greatest share in the origin of it. When the race entered Europe, they are not presumed to have had any hatred towards their fellow-creatures.* That hatred, doubtless, sprung from the severe

* I cannot agree with Mr. Borrow, when he says, that the Gipsies "travelled three thousand miles into Europe, *with hatred in their hearts towards the people among whom they settled.*" In none of the earliest laws passed against them, is anything said of their being other than thieves, cheats, &c., &c. They seem to have been too politic to commit murder;

reception, and universal persecution, which, owing to the singularity of their race and habits, they everywhere met with. The race then became born into that state of things. What would subsequent generations know of the origin of the feud? All that they knew was, that the law made them outlaws and outcasts; that they were subject, as Gipsies, to be hung, before they were born. Such a Gipsy might be compared to Pascal's man springing up out of an island: casting his eyes around him, he finds nothing but a legal and social proscription hanging over his head, in whatever direction he may turn. Whatever might be assumed to have been the original, innate disposition of a Gipsy, the circumstances attending him, from his birth to his death, were certainly not calculated to improve him, but to make him much worse than he might otherwise have been. The worst that can be said of the Scottish Gipsies, in times past, has been stated by our author. With all their faults, we find a vein of genuine nobility of character running through all their actions, which is the more worthy of notice, considering that they were at war with society, and society at war with them. Not the least important feature is that of gratitude for kind and hospitable treatment. In that respect, a true Scottish Gipsy has always been as true as steel; and that is saying a great deal in his favour. The instance given by our author, (pages 361–363,) is very touching, and to the point. I do not know how it may be, at the present day, in Scotland, where are to be found so many Irish Gipsies, of whom the Scottish and English Gipsies have not much good to say, notwithstanding the assistance they render each other when they meet, (page 324.) If the English farmers are questioned, I doubt not that a somewhat similar testimony will be borne to the English Gipsies, to this extent, at least, that, when civilly and hospitably treated, and per-

moreover, it appears to have been foreign to their disposition to do aught but obtain a living in the most cunning manner they could. There is no necessary connection between purloining one's property and hating one's person. As long as the Gipsies were not hardly dealt with, they could, naturally, have no actual hatred towards their fellow-creatures. Mr. Borrow attributes none of the spite and hatred of the race towards the community to the severity of the persecutions to which it was exposed, or to that hard feeling with which society has regarded it. These, and the example of the Spaniards, doubtless led the Gitanos to shed the blood of the ordinary natives.

sonally acquainted, they will respect the farmers' property, and even keep others off it. Indeed, both Scottish and English Gipsies call this "Gipsy law." It is certainly not the Scottish Gipsies, or, I may venture to say, the English Gipsies, to whom Mr. Borrow's words may be applied, when he says: "I have not expatiated on their gratitude towards good people, who treat them kindly, and take an interest in their welfare; for I believe, that, of all beings in the world, they are the least susceptible of such a feeling." Such a character may apply to the Spanish Gipsies for anything I know to the contrary; and the causes to which it may be attributed must be the influences which the Spanish character, and general deportment towards the tribe, have exercised over them. In speaking of the bloody and wolfish disposition which especially characterizes the Gitanos, Mr. Borrow says: "The cause to which this must be attributed, must be their residence in a country, unsound in every branch of its civil polity, where right has ever been in less esteem, and wrong in less disrepute, than in any other part of the world." Grellmann bears as poor testimony to the character of the Hungarian Gipsies, in the matter of gratitude, as Mr. Borrow does to the Spanish Gipsies, to whom I apprehend his remarks are intended to apply. But both of these authors give an opinion, unaccompanied by facts. Their opinion may be correct, however, so far as it is applicable to the class of Gipsies, or the individuals, to whom they refer. Gratitude is even a characteristic of the lower animals. "For every kind of beasts, and of birds, and of serpents, and of things in the sea, is tamed and hath been tamed of mankind," saith St. James; the means of attaining to which is frequently kindness. I doubt not that the same can be said of Gipsies anywhere; for surely we can expect to find as much gratitude in them as can be called forth from things that creep, fly, or swim in the sea. It is unreasonable, however, to look for much gratitude from such Gipsies as the two authors in question have evidently alluded to; for this reason: that it is a virtue rarely to be met with from those "to whom much has been given;" and, consequently, very little should be required of those to whom *nothing* has been given, in the estimation of their fellow-creatures. In doing a good turn to a Gipsy, it is not the act itself that calls forth, or perhaps merits, a return in gratitude; but it is the way in which it is done: for, while he is doubtless being benefited, he is, frequently, if not generally, as little sympathized with, personally, as if he were some loathsome creature to which something had been thrown.

As regards the improvement of the Gipsies, I would make the following suggestions: The facts and principles of the present work should be thoroughly canvassed and imprinted upon the public mind, and an effort made to bring, if possible, our high-class Gipsies to own themselves up to be Gipsies. The fact of these Gipsies being received into society, and respected, as Gipsies, (as it is with them, at present, as men,) could not fail to have a wonderful effect upon many of the humble, ignorant, or wild ones. They would perceive, at once, that the objections which the community had to them, proceeded, not from their being Gipsies, but from their habits, only. What is the feeling which Gipsies, who are known to be Gipsies, have for the public at large? The white race, as a race, is simply odious to them, for they know well the dreadful prejudice which it bears towards them. But let some of their own race, however mixed the blood might be, be respected as Gipsies, and it would, in a great measure, break down, at least in feeling, the wall of caste that separates them from the community at large. This is the first, the most important, step to be taken to improve the Gipsies, whatever may be the class to which they belong. Let the prejudice be removed, and it is impossible to say what might not follow. Before attempting to reform the Gipsies, we ought to reform, or, at least, inform, mankind in regard to them; and endeavour to reconcile the world to them, before we attempt to reconcile them to the world; and treat them as men, before we try to make them Christians. The *poor* Gipsies know well that there are many of their race occupying respectable positions in life; perhaps they do not know many, or even any, of them, personally, but they believe in it thoroughly. Still, they will deny it, at least hide it from strangers, for this reason, among others, that it is a state to which their children, or even they themselves, look forward, as ultimately awaiting them, in which they will manage to escape from the odium of their fellow-creatures, which clings to them in their present condition. The fact of the poor travelling Gipsies knowing of such respectable settled Gipsies, gives them a certain degree of respect in their own eyes, which leads them to repel any advance from the other race, let it come in almost whatever shape it may. The white race, as I have already said, is perfectly odious to them. This is exactly the position of the question. The more original kind of Gipsies feel that the prejudice which exists against the race to which they belong is such, that an intercourse cannot be maintained between them and the other inhabitants; or, if it does exist, it is of so clandestine a nature, that their appearance, and, it may be, their general habits, do not allow or lead them to indulge in it. I will make a few more remarks on this subject further on in this treatise.

What are the respectable, well-disposed Scottish Gipsies but Scotch people, after all? They are to be met with in almost every, if not every, sphere in which the ordinary Scot is to be found. The only difference between the two is, that, however mixed the blood of these Gipsies may be, their associations of descent and tribe go back to those black, mysterious heroes who entered Scotland, upwards of three hundred and fifty years ago; and that, with this descent, they have the words and signs of Gipsies. The possession of all these, with the knowledge of the feelings which the ordinary natives have for the very name of Gipsy, makes the only distinction between them and other Scotchmen. I do not say that the world would have any prejudice against these Gipsies, as Gipsies, still, they are morbidly sensitive that it would have such a feeling. The light of reason, of civilization, of religion, and the genius of Britons, forbid such an idea. What object more worthy of civilization, and of the age in which we live, than that such Gipsies would come forward, and, by their positions in society, their talents and characters, dispel the mystery and gloom that hang over the history of the Gipsy race!

But will these Gipsies do that? I have my misgivings. They may not do it now, but I am sanguine enough to think that it is an event that may take place at some future time. The subject must, in the meantime, be thoroughly investigated, and the mind of the public fully prepared for such a movement. The Gipsies themselves, to commence with, should furnish the public with information, anonymously, so far as they are personally concerned, or confidentially, through a person of standing, who can guarantee the trustworthiness of the Gipsy himself. I do not expect that they would give us any of the language; but they can furnish us with some idea of the position which the Gipsies occupy in the world, and throw a great deal of light upon the history of the race in Scotland, in, at least, comparatively recent times. In anticipation of such an occurrence, I would make this suggestion to them: that they must be very careful what they say, on account of the "court holding them interested witnesses;" and, whatever they may do, to deny nothing connected with the Gipsies. They certainly have kept their secret well; indeed, they have considered the subject, so far as the public is concerned, as dead and buried long ago. It is of no use, however, Gipsies; "murder will out;" the game is up; it is played out. I may say to you what the hunter said to the 'coon, or rather what the 'coon said to the hunter: "You may just as well come down the tree." Yes! come down the tree; you have been too long up; come down, and let us know all about you.*

Scottish Gipsies! I now appeal to you as men. Am I not right, in asserting, that there is nothing you hold more dear than your Egyptian descent, signs, and language? And nothing you more dread than such becoming known to your fellow-men around you? Do you not read, with the greatest interest, any and everything printed, which comes in your way, about the Gipsies, and say, that you thank God all that is a thousand miles away from you? Whence this incon-

* I accidentally got into conversation with an Irishman, in the city of New York, about secret societies, when he mentioned that he was a member of a great many such, indeed, "all of them," as he expressed it. I said there was one society of which he was not a member, when he began to enumerate them, and at last came to the Zincali. "What," said I, "are you a member of this society?" "Yes," said he; "the Zincali, or Gipsy." He then told me that there are many members of this society in the city of New York; not all members of it, under that name, but of its outposts, if I may so express it. The principal or arch-Gipsy for the city, he said, was a merchant, in —— street, who had in his possession a printed vocabulary, or dictionary, of the language, which was open only to the most thoroughly initiated. In the course of our conversation, it fell out that the native American Gipsy referred to at page 420 was one of the thoroughly initiated; which circumstance explained a question he had put to me, and which I evaded, by saying that I was not in the habit of telling tales out of school.

In Spain, as we have seen, a Gipsy taught her language to her son from a MS. I doubt not there are MS. if not printed, vocabularies of the Gipsy language among the tribe in Scotland, as well as in other countries.

sistency? Ah! I understand it well. Shall the prejudice of mankind towards the name of Gipsy drive you from the position which you occupy? Can it drive you from it? No, it cannot. The Gipsies, you know, are a people; a "mixed multitude," no doubt, but still a people. You know you are Gipsies, for your parents before you were Gipsies, and, consequently, that you cannot be anything but Gipsies. What effect, then, has the prejudice against the race upon you? Does it not sometimes appear to you as if, figuratively speaking, it would put a dagger into your hands against the rest of your species, should they discover that you belonged to the tribe? Or that it would lead you to immediately "take to your beds," or depart, bed and baggage, to parts unknown? But then, Gipsies, what can you do? The thought of it makes you feel as if you were sheep. Some of you may be bold enough to face a lion in the flesh; but who so bold as to own to the world that he is a Gipsy? There is just one of the higher class that I know of, and he was a noble specimen of a man, a credit to human nature itself. Although *you* might shrink from such a step, would you not like, and cannot you induce, *some one* to take it? Take my word for it, respectable Scottish Gipsies, the thing that frightens you is, after all, a bug-bear—a scare-crow. But, failing some of you "coming out," would you not rather that the world should now know that much of the history of the Gipsy race, as to show that it was no necessary disparagement in any of you to be a Gipsy? Would you not rather that a Gipsy *might* pass, anywhere, for a *gentleman*, as he *does* now, everywhere, for a *vagabond;* and that you and your children might, if they liked, show their true colours, than, as at present, go everywhere *incog*, and carry within them that secret which they are as afraid of being divulged to the world, as if you and all your kin were conspirators and murderers? The secret being out, the incognito of your race goes for nothing. Come then, Scottish Gipsy, make a clean breast of it, like a man. Which of you will exclaim,

> "Thus from the grave I'll rise, and save my love;
> Draw all your swords, and quick as lightning move!
> When I rush on, sure none will dare to stay;
> 'Tis love commands, and glory leads the way!"

Will none of you move? Ah! Gipsies, you are "great hens," and no wonder.

American Gipsies, descendants of the real old British stock! I make the same appeal to you. Let the world know how you are getting on, in this land of "liberty and equality;" and whether any of your race are senators, congressmen, and what not. I have heard of a Gipsy, a sheriff in the State of Pennsylvania; and I know of a Scottish Gipsy, who was lately returned a member of the Legislature of the State of New York.

The reader may ask: Is it possible that there is a race of men, residing in the British Isles, to be counted by its hundreds of thousands, occupying such a position as that described? And I reply, Alas! it is too true. Exeter Hall may hobnob with Negroes, Hottentots, and Bosjesmen—always with something or other from a distance; but what has it ever done for the Gipsies? Nothing! It will rail at the American prejudice towards the Negro, and entirely pass over a much superior race at its own door! The prejudice against the Negro proceeds from two causes—his appearance and the servitude in which he is, or has been, held. But there can be no prejudice against the Gipsy, on such grounds. It will not do to say that the prejudice is against the tented Gipsies, only; it is against the race, root and branch, as far as it is known. What is it but that which compels the Gipsy, on entering upon a settled life, to hide himself from the unearthly prejudice of his fellow-creatures? The Englishman, the Scotchman, and the Irishman may rail at the American for his peculiar prejudices; but the latter, if he can but capitalize the idea, has, in all conscience, much to throw back upon society in the mother country. Instead of a class of the British public spending so much of their time in an agitation against an institution thousands of miles away from home, and over which they have, and can expect to have, no control, they might direct their attention to an evil laying at their own doors—that social prejudice which is so much calculated to have a blasting influence upon the condition of so many of their fellow-subjects. It is beyond doubt that there cannot be less than a quarter of a million of Gipsies in the British Isles, who are living under a grinding despotism of caste; a despotism so absolute and odious, that the people upon whom it bears cannot, as in Scotland, were it almost to save their lives, even say who they are! Let the time and talents spent on the agitation in question be transferred, for a time, into some such channel as would be implied in a "British Anti-Gipsy-prejudice Association," and a great moral evil may disappear from the face of British society. In such a movement, there would be none of that direct or indirect interest to be encountered, which lies on the very threshold of slavery, in whatever part of the world it exists; nor would there be any occasion to appeal to people's pockets.* After the work mentioned has been accomplished, the British public might turn their attention to wrongs perpetrated in other climes. Americans, however, must not attempt to seek, in the British Gipsy-prejudice, an excuse for their excessive antipathy towards Negroes. I freely admit that the dislike of white men, generally, for the Negro, lies in something that is irremovable—something that is irrespective of character, or present or previous social condition. But it is not so with the Gipsy, for his race is, physically, among the finest that are to be found on the face of the earth. Americans ought also to consider that there are plenty of Gipsies among themselves, towards whom, however, there are none of those prejudices that spring from local tradition or association, but only such as proceed from literature, and that towards the tented Gipsy.

What is to be the future of the Gipsy race? A reply to this question will be found in the history of it during the past, as described; for it resolves itself into two very simple matters of fact. In the first place, we have a foreign race, deemed, by itself, to be, as indeed it is, universal, introduced into Scotland, for example, taken root there, spread, and flourished; a race that rests upon a basis the strongest imaginable. On the other hand, there is the prejudice of caste towards the name, which those bearing it escape, only, by assuming an incognito among their fellow-creatures. These two principles, acting upon beings possessing the feelings of men, will, of themselves, produce that state of things which will constitute the history of the Gipsies during all time coming, whatever may be the changes that may come

* Among the various means by which the name of Gipsy can be raised up, it may be mentioned, that beginning the word with a capital is one of no little importance. The almost invariable custom with writers, in that respect, has been as if they were describing rats and mice, instead of a race of men.

over their character and condition. They may, in course of time, lose their language, as some of them, to a great extent, have done already; but they will always retain a consciousness of being Gipsies. The language may be lost, but their signs will remain, as well as so much of their speech as will serve the purpose of pass-words. "There is something there," said an English Gipsy of intelligence, smiting his breast, "There is something there which a Gipsy cannot explain." And, said a Scottish Gipsy: "It will never be forgotten; as long as the world lasts, the Gipsies will be Gipsies." What idea can be more preposterous than that of saying, that a change of residence or occupation, or a little more or less of education or wealth, or a change of character or creed, can eradicate such feeling from the heart of a Gipsy; or that these circumstances can, by any human possibility, change his descent, his tribe, or the blood that is in his body? How can we imagine this race, arriving in Europe so lately as the fifteenth century, and in Scotland the century following, with an origin so distinct from the rest of the world, and so treated by the world, can possibly have lost a consciousness of nationality in its descent, in so short a time after arrival; or, that that can happen in the future, when there are so many circumstances surrounding it to keep alive a sense of its origin, and so much within it to preserve its identity in the history of the human family? Let the future history of the world be what it may, Gipsydom is immortal.*

In considering the question of the Gipsies being openly admitted, as a race, into the society of mankind, I ask, what possible reason could a British subject advance against such taking place with, at least, the better kind of Scottish Gipsies? Society, generally, would not be over-ready to lessen the distance between itself and the tented Gipsies, or those who live by means really objectionable; but it should have that much sense of justice, as to confine its peculiar feelings

* This sensation, in the minds of the Gipsies, of the perpetuity of their race, creates, in a great measure, its immortality. Paradoxical as it may appear, the way to preserve the existence of a people is to scatter it, provided, however, that it is a race thoroughly distinct from others, to commence with. When, by the force of circumstances, it has fairly settled down into the idea that it is a people, those living in one country become conscious of its existence in others; and hence arises the principal cause of the perpetuity of its existence as a scattered people.

to the ways of life of these individuals, and not keep them up against their children, when they follow different habits. If, for example, I should have made the acquaintance of some Scottish Gipsies, associated with them, and acquired a respect for them, (as has happened with me,) how could I take exceptions to them, on account of it afterwards leaking out that they were Gipsies? A sense of ordinary justice would forbid me doing so. I can see nothing objectionable in their conduct, as distinguished from that of other people; and as for their appearance, any person, on being asked to point out the Gipsy, would, so far as colour of hair and eyes goes, pitch upon many a common native, in preference to them. A sense of ordinary justice, as I have said, would disarm me of any prejudice against them; nay, it would urge me to think the more of them, on account of their being Gipsies. To the ordinary eye, they are nothing but Scotch people, and pass, everywhere, for such. There is a Scottish Gipsy in the United States, with whom I am acquainted —a liberal-minded man, and good company—who carries on a wholesale trade, in a respectable article of merchandise, and he said to me: "I will not deny it, nor am I ashamed to say it—*I come from Yetholm.*" And I replied: "Why should you be ashamed of it?"

It is this hereditary prejudice of centuries towards the name, that constitutes the main difficulty in the way of recognition of these Gipsies by the world generally. How long it may be since they or their ancestors left the tent, is a thing of no importance; personal character, education, and position in life, are the only things that should be considered. The Gipsies to whom I allude do not require to be reformed, unless in that sense in which all men stand in need of reformation: what is wanted is, that the world should raise up the name of Gipsy. And why should not that be done by the people of Great Britain, and Scotland especially, in whose mouths are continually these words: "God hath made of one blood all nations of men, for to dwell on all the face of the earth?" Will the British public spend its hundreds of thousands, annually, on every other creature under heaven, and refuse to countenance the Gipsy race? Will it squander its tens of thousands to convert, perhaps, on an average, one Jew, and refuse a kind word, nay, grudge a smile, towards that body, a member of which may be an official of that Missionary Society, or, it may be, the very chairman of it? I can conceive no liberal-minded Scotchman, possessing a feeling of true self-respect, entertaining a prejudice against such Gipsies. The only people in Scotland in whose mind such a prejudice might be supposed to exist, are those miserable old women around the neighbourhood of Stirling, who, under the influence of the old Highland feud, will look with the greatest contempt upon a person, if he but come from the north of the Ochils. I would class, with such old women, all of our Scotch people who would object to the Gipsies to whom I have alluded. A Scotchman should even have that much love of country, as to take hold of his own Gipsies, and "back them up" against those of other countries: and particularly should he do that, when the "Gipsies" might be his cousins, nay, his own children, for anything that he might know to the contrary. Scotch people should consider that the "Tinklers," whom they see going about, at the present day, are, if not the very lowest kind of Gipsies, at least those who follow the original ways of their race; and are greatly inferior, not only relatively, but actually, to many of those who have gone before them. They should also consider that Gipsies are a race, however mixed the blood may be; subject, as a race, to be governed, in their descent, by those laws which regulate the descent of all races; and that a Gipsy is as much a Gipsy in a house as in a tent, in a "but and a ben" as in a palace.

Wherever a Gipsy goes, he carries his inherent peculiarities with him; and the objection to him he considers to be to something inseparable from himself—that which he cannot escape; but the confidence which he has in his incognito neutralizes, as I have already said, the feelings which such a circumstance would naturally produce. But, to disarm him altogether of this feeling, all that is necessary is to state his case, and have it admitted by the "honourable of the earth;" so that his mind may be set at perfect rest on that point. He would, doubtless, still hide the fact of his being a Gipsy, but he would enjoy, in his retreat, that inward self-respect, among his fellow-creatures, which such an admission would give him; and which is so much calculated to raise the people, generally, in every moral attribute. It is, indeed, a melancholy thing, to contemplate this cloud which hangs over such a man, as he mixes with other people, in his daily calling; but to dispel it altogether, the Gipsy himself must, in the manner described, give us some information about his race. Apart from the sense of justice which is implied in admitting these Gipsies, as Gipsies, to a social equality with others, a motive of policy should lead us to take such a step; for it can augur no good to society to have the Gipsy race residing in its midst, under the cloud that hangs over it. Let us, by a liberal and enlightened policy, at least blunt the edge of that antipathy which many of the Gipsy race have, and most naturally have, to society at large.

In receiving a Gipsy, as a Gipsy, into society, there should be no kind of officious sympathy shown him, for he is too proud to submit to be made the object of it. Should he say that he is a Gipsy, the remark ought to be received as a mere matter of course, and little notice taken of it; just as if it made no difference to the other party whether he was a Gipsy or not. A little surprise would be allowable; but anything like condolence would be out of the question. And let the Gipsy himself, rather, talk upon the subject, than a desire be shown to ask him questions, unless his remarks should allow them, in a natural way, to be put to him. As to the course to be pursued by the Gipsy, should he feel disposed to own himself up, I would advise him to do it in an off-handed, hearty manner; to show not the least appearance that he had any misgivings about any one taking exceptions to him on that account. Should he act otherwise, that is, hesitate, and take to himself shamefacedness, in making the admission, it would, perhaps, have been better for him not to have committed himself at all: for, in such a matter, it may be said, that "he that doubteth is damned." The simple fact of a man, in Scotland, saying, after the appearance of this work there, that he is a Gipsy, if he is conscious of having the esteem of his neighbours, would probably add to his popularity among them; especially if they were men of good sense, and had before their eyes the expression of good-will of the organs of society towards the Gipsy race. Such an admission, on the part of a Gipsy, would presumptively prove, that he was a really candid and upright person; for few Scottish Gipsies, beyond those about Yetholm, would make such a confession. Having mentioned the subject, the Gipsy should allude to it, on every appropriate occasion, and boast of being in possession of those words and signs which the other is entirely ignorant of. He could well say: "What was Borrow to him, or he to Borrow; that, for his part, he could traverse the world over, and, in the centre of any continent, be received and feasted, by Gipsies, as a king." If but one respectable Scottish Gipsy could be prevailed upon to act in this way, what an effect might it not have upon raising up the name of this singular race! But there is a very serious difficulty to be encountered in the outset of such a proceeding, and it is this, that if a Gipsy owns himself up, he necessarily "lets out," perhaps, all his kith and kin; a regard for whom would, in all probability, keep him back. But there would be no such difficulty to be met with in the way of the Gipsy giving us information by writing. Let us, then, Gipsy, have some writing upon the Gipsies. It will serve no good purpose to keep such information back; the keeping of it back will not cast a doubt upon the facts and principles of the present work; for rest assured, Gipsy, that, upon its own merits, your secret is exploded. I would say this to you, young Scottish Gipsy; pay no regard to what that old Gipsy says, when he tells you, that "he is too old a bird to be caught with chaff in that way."

The history of the Gipsies is the history of a people (mixed, in point of blood, as it is,) which exists; not the history of a people, like the Aborigines of North America, which has ceased to exist, or is daily ceasing to exist.* It is the history of a people within a people, with whom we come in contact daily, although we may not be aware of it. Any person of ordinary intelligence can have little difficulty in comprehending the subject, shrouded as it is from the eye of the world. But should he have any such difficulty, it will be dispelled by his coming in contact with a Gipsy who has the courage to own himself up to be a Gipsy. It is no argument to maintain that the Gipsy race is not a race, because its blood is mixed with other people. That can be said of all the races of Western Europe, the English more especially; and, in a much greater degree, of that of the United States of America. Every Gipsy has part of the

* The fact of these Indians, and the aboriginal races found in the countries colonized by Europeans, disappearing so rapidly, prevents our regarding them with any great degree of interest. This circumstance detracts from that idea of dignity which the perpetuity and civilization of their race would inspire in the minds of others.

Gipsy blood, and more or less of the words and signs; which, taken in connection with the rearing of Gipsies, act upon his mind in such a manner, that he is penetrated with the simple idea that he is a Gipsy; and create that distinct feeling of nationality which the matters of territory, and sometimes dialect, government, and laws, do with most of other races. Take a Gipsy from any country in the world you may, and the feeling of his being a Gipsy comes as naturally to him as does the nationality of a Jew to a Jew; although we will naturally give him a more definite name, to distinguish him; such as an English, Welsh, Scotch, or Irish Gipsy, or by whatever country of which the Gipsy happens to be a native.

But I am afraid that what has been said is not sufficiently explanatory to enable some people to understand this subject. These people know what a Gipsy, in the popular sense, means; they have either seen him, and observed his general mode of life, or had the same described to them in books. This idea of a Gipsy has been impressed upon their minds almost from infancy. But it puzzles most people to form any idea of a Gipsy of a higher order; such a Gipsy, for example, as preaches the gospel, or argues the law: that seems, hitherto, to have been almost incomprehensible to them. They know intuitively what is meant by any particular people who occupy a territory—any country, tract of land, or isle. They also know what is meant by the existence of the Jews. For the subject is familiar to them from infancy; it is wrapt up in their early reading; it is associated with the knowledge and practice of their religion, and the attendance, on the part of the Jews, at a place of worship. They have likewise seen and conversed with the Jews, or others who have done either or both; or they are acquainted with them by the current remarks of the world. But a people resembling, in so many respects, the Jews, without having any territory, or form of creed, peculiar to itself, or any history, or any peculiar outward associations or residences, or any material difference in appearance, character, or occupation, is something that the general mind of mankind would seem never to have dreamt of, or to be almost capable of realizing to itself. We have already seen how a writer in Blackwood's Magazine gravely asserts, that, although "Billy Marshall left descendants numberless, the race, of which he was one, was in danger of becoming extinct;" when, in fact, it had only passed from its first stage of existence—the tent, into its second—tramping, without the tent; and after that, into its ultimate stage—a settled life. We have likewise seen how Sir Walter Scott imagines that the Scottish Gipsies have decreased, since the time of Fletcher, of Saltoun, about the year 1680, from 100,000 to 500, by "the progress of time, and encrease of the means of life, and the power of the laws." Mr. Borrow has not gone one step ahead of these writers; and, although I naturally enough excuse them, I am not inclined to let him go scot-free, since he has set himself forward so prominently as an authority on the Gipsy question.*

In explaining this subject, it is by no means necessary to "crack an egg" for the occasion. There is doubtless a "hitch," but it is a hitch so close under our very noses, that it has escaped the observation of the world. Still, the point can be readily enough realized by any one. Take, for example, the Walker family. Walker knows well enough who his father, grandfather, and so forth were; and holds himself to be a Walker. Is it not so with the Gipsies? What is it but a question of "folk?" A question more familiar to Scotch people than any other people. If one's ancestors were all Walkers, is not the present Walker still a Walker? If such or such a family was originally of the Gipsy race, is it not so still? How did Billy Marshall happen to be a Gipsy? Was he a Gipsy because he lived in a tent? or, did he live in a tent, like a Gipsy of the old stock? If Billy was a Gipsy, surely Billy's children must also have been Gipsies!

The error committed by writers, with reference to the so-called "dying-out" of the Gipsy race, arises from their not distinguishing between the questions of race, blood, descent and language, and a style of life, or character, or mode of making a living. Suppose that a native Scottish cobbler should leave his last, and take to peddling, as a packman,

* A writer in the Penny Cyclopædia illustrates this absurd idea, in very plain terms, when he says: "In England, the Gipsies have much diminished, of late years, in consequence of the enclosure of lands, and the laws against vagrants." Sir Walter Scott's idea of the Gipsies has been followed in a pictorial history of Scotland, lately issued from the Scottish press.

and ultimately settle again in a town, as a respectable tradesman. On quitting "the roads," he would cease to be a packman; nor could his children after him be called packmen, because the whole family were native Scotch from the first; following the pack having been only the occupation of the father, during part of his life. Should a company of American youths and maidens take to the swamp, cranberrying and gipsying, for a time, it could not be said that they had become Gipsies; for they were nothing but ordinary Americans. Should the society of Quakers dissolve into its original elements, it would just be English blood quakerized, returning to English blood before it was quakerized. But it is astonishing that intelligent men should conceive, and others retail, the ideas that have been expressed in regard to the destiny of the Gipsy race. What avails the lessons of history, or the daily experience of every family of the land, the common sense of mankind, or the instinct of a Hottentot, if no other idea of the fate of the Gipsy race can be given than that referred to? Upon the principle of the Gipsies "dying out," by settling, and changing their habits, it would appear that, when at home, in the winter, they were not Gipsies; but that they were Gipsies, when they resumed their habits, in the spring! On the same principle, it would appear, that, if every Gipsy in the world were to disappear from the roads and the fields, and drop his original habits, there would be no Gipsies in the world, at all! What idea can possibly be more ridiculous?*

It is better, however, to compare the Gipsy tribe in Scotland, at the present day, to an ordinary clan in the olden time; although the comparison falls far short of the idea.

* The following singular remarks appeared in a very late number of Chambers' Journal, on the subject of the Gipsies of the Danube: "As the wild cat, the otter, and the wolf, generally disappear before the advance of civilization, the wild races of mankind are, in like manner and degree, gradually coming to an end, and from the same causes (!) The waste lands get enclosed, the woods are cut down, the police becomes yearly more efficient, and the Pariahs vanish with their means of subsistence. [Where do they go to?] In England, there are, at most, 1,500 Gipsies (!) Before the end of the present century, they will probably be extinct over Western Europe (!)"

It is perfectly evident that the world, outside of Gipsydom, has to be initiated in the subject of the Gipsies, as in the first principles of a science, or as a child is instructed in its alphabet. And yet, the above-mentioned writer takes upon himself to chide Mr. Borrow, in the matter of the Gipsies.

We know perfectly well what it was to have been a member of this or that clan. Sir Walter Scott knew well that he was one of the Buccleuch clan, and a descendant of *Auld Beardie;* so that he could readily say that he was a Scott. Wherein, then, consists the difficulty in understanding what a Scottish Gipsy is? Is it not simply that he is "one of them;" a descendant of that foreign race of which we have such notice in the treaty of 1540, between James V. and John Faw, the then head of the Scottish Gipsy tribe? A Scottish Gipsy has the blood, the words, and the signs, of these men, and as naturally holds himself to be "one of them," as a native Scotchman holds himself to be one of his father's children. How, then, can a "change of habits" prevent a man from being his father's son? How could a "change of habits" make a McGregor anything but a McGregor? How could the effects of any just and liberal law towards the McGregors lead to the decrease, and final extinction, of the McGregors? Every man, every family, every clan, and every people, are continually "changing their habits," but still remain the same people. It would be a treat to have a treatise from Mr. Borrow upon the Gipsy race "dying out," by "changing its habits," or by the acts of any government, or by ideas of "gentility."

I have already alluded to a resemblance between the position of the Gipsy race, at the present day, and that of the English and American races. Does any one say that the English race is not a race? Or that the American is not a race? And yet the latter is a compost of everything that migrates from the Old World. But take some families, and we will find that they are almost pure English, in descent, and hold themselves to be actually such. But ask them if they are English, and they will readily answer: "*English?* No, siree!" The same principle holds still more with the Gipsy race. It is not a question of country against country, or government against government, separated by an ocean; but the difference proceeds from a prejudice, as broad and deep as the ocean, that exists between two races—the native, and that of such recent introduction—dwelling in the same community.

I have explained the effect which the mixing of native blood with Gipsy has upon the Gipsy race, showing that it only modifies its appearance, and facilitates its passing into settled and respectable life. I will now substantiate the principle from what is daily observed among the native race itself. Take any native family—one of the Scotts, for example. Let us commence with a family, tracing its origin to a Scott, in the year 1600, and imagine that, in its descent, every representative of the name married a wife of another family, or clan, having no Scotts' blood in her veins. In the seventh descent, there would be only one one-hundred and twenty-eighth part of the original Scott in the last representative of the family. Would not the last Scott be a Scott? The world recognizes him to be a Scott; he holds himself to be a Scott—"every inch a Scott;" and doubtless he is a Scott, as much as his ancestor who existed in the year 1600. What difficulty can there, therefore, be, in understanding how a man can be a Gipsy, whose blood is mixed, even "dreadfully mixed," as the English Gipsies express it? Gipsies are Gipsies, let their blood be mixed as much as it may; whether the introduction of the native blood may have come into the family through the male or the female line.

In the descent of a native family, in the instance given, the issue follows the name of the family. But, with the Gipsy race, the thing to be transmitted is not merely a question of family, but a race distinct from any particular family. If a Gipsy woman marries into a native family, the issue retains the family name of the husband, but passes into the Gipsy tribe; if a Gipsy man marries into a native family, the issue retains his name, in the general order of society, and likewise passes into the Gipsy tribe; so that such intermarriages, which almost invariably take place unknown to the native race, always leave the issue Gipsy. For the Gipsy element of society is like a troubled spirit, which has been despised, persecuted, and damned; cross it out, to appearance, as much as you may, it still retains its Gipsy identity. It then assumes the form of a disembodied spirit, that will enter into any kind of tabernacle, in the manner described, dispel every other kind of spirit, clean or unclean, as the case may be, and come up, under any garb, colour, character, occupation, or creed—Gipsy. It is perfectly possible, but not very probable, to find a Gipsy a Jew, in creed, and, for the most part, in point of blood, in the event of a Jew marrying a mixed Gipsy.

He might follow the creed of the Jewish parent, and be admitted into the synagogue; but, although outwardly recognised as a Jew, and having Jewish features, he would still be a *chabo;* for there are Gipsies of all creeds, and, like other people in the world, of no creed at all. But it is extremely disagreeable to a Gipsy to have such a subject mentioned in his hearing; for he heartily dislikes a Jew, and says that no one has any "chance" in dealing with him. A Gipsy likewise says, that the two races ought not to be mentioned in the same breath, or put on the same footing, which is very true; for reason tells us, that, strip the Gipsy of every idea connected with "taking bits o' things," and leading a wild life, and there should be no points of enmity between him and the ordinary native; certainly not that of creed, which exists between the Jew and the rest of the world, to which question I will by and by refer.

The subject of the Gipsies has hitherto been treated as a question of natural history, only, in the same manner as we would treat ant-bears. Writers have sat down beside them, and looked at them—little more than looked at them—described some of their habits, and reported their *chaff.* To get to the bottom of the subject, it is necessary to sound the mind of the Gipsy, lay open and dissect his heart, identify one's self with his feelings, and the bearings of his ideas, and construct, out of these, a system of mental science, based upon the mind of the Gipsy, and human nature generally. For it is the mind of the Gipsy that constitutes the Gipsy; that which, in reference to its singular origin and history, is, in itself, indestructible, imperishable and immortal.

Consider, then, this race, which is of such recent introduction upon the stage of the European world, of such a singular origin and history, and of such universal existence, with such a prejudice existing against it, and the merest impulse of reflection, apart from the facts of the case, will lead us to conclude, that, as it has settled, it has remained true to itself, in the various associations of life. In whatever position, or under whatever circumstances, it is to be found, it may be compared, in reference to its past history, to a chain, and the early Gipsies, to those who have charged it with electricity. However mixed, or however polished, the metal of the links may have since become, they have always served to convey the Gipsy fluid to every generation of the race. It is even unnecessary to enquire, particularly, how that has been accomplished, for it is self-evident that the process which has linked other races to their ancestry, has doubly linked the Gipsy race to theirs. Indeed, the idea of being Gipsies never can leave the Gipsy race. A Gipsy's life is like a continual conspiracy towards the rest of the world; he has always a secret upon his mind, and, from his childhood to his old age, he is so placed as if he were, in a negative sense, engaged in some gunpowder plot, or as if he had committed a crime, let his character be as good as it possibly may. Into whatever company he may enter, he naturally remarks to himself: "I wonder if there are any of us here." That is the position which the mixed and better kind of Gipsy occupies, generally and passively. Of course, there are some of the race who are always actually hatching some plot or other against the rest of the world. Take a Gipsy of the popular kind, who appears as such to the world, and there are two ideas constantly before him—that of the *Gorgio* and *Chabo:* they may slumber while he is in his house, or in his tent, or when he is asleep, or his mind is positively occupied with something; but let any one come near him, or him meet or accost any one, and he naturally remarks, to himself, that the person "is *not* one of us," or that he "*is* one of us." He knows well what the native may be thinking or saying of him, and he as naturally responds in his own mind. This circumstance of itself, this frightful prejudice against the individual, makes, or at least keeps, the Gipsy wild; it calls forth the passion of resentment, and produces a feeling of reckless abandon, that might otherwise leave him. To that is to be added the feeling, in the Gipsy's mind, of his race having been persecuted, for he knows little of the circumstances attending the origin of the laws passed against his tribe, and attributes them to persecution alone. He considers that he has a right to travel; that he has been deprived of rights to travel, which were granted to his tribe by the monarchs of past ages; and, moreover, that his ancestors—the "ancient wandering Egyptians"—always travelled. He feels perfectly independent of, and snaps his fingers at, everybody; and entertains a profound suspicion of any one who may approach him, inasmuch as he imagines that the stranger, however fair he may speak to him, has that feeling for him, as if he considered it pollution to touch him. But he is very civil and plausible when he is at home.

It is from such material that all kinds of settled Gipsies, at one time or other, have sprung. Such is the prejudice against the race, that, if they did not hide the fact of their being Gipsies from the ordinary natives, they would hardly have the "life of a dog" among them, because of their having sprung from a race which, in its original state, has been persecuted, and so much despised. By settling in life, and conforming with the ways of the rest of the community, they "cease to be Gipsies," in the estimation of the world; for the world imagines that, when the Gipsy conforms to its ways, there is an end of his being a Gipsy. Barring the "habits," such a Gipsy is as much a Gipsy as before, although he is one *incog*. The wonder is not that he and his descendants should be Gipsies; but the real wonder is, that they should not be Gipsies. Neither he nor his descendants have any choice in the matter. Does the settled Gipsy keep a crockery or tin establishment, or an inn, or follow any other occupation? Then his children cannot all follow the same calling; they must betake themselves to the various employments open to the community at large, and, their blood being mixed, they become lost to the general eye, amid the rest of the population. While this process is gradually going on, the Gipsy population which always remains in the tent—the hive from which the tribe swarms—attracts the attention of the public, and prevents it from thinking anything about the matter. In England, alone, we may safely assume that the tented Gipsy population, about the commencement of this century, must have encreased at least four-fold by this time, while, to the eye of the public, it would appear that "the Gipsies are gradually decreasing, so that, by and by, they will become extinct."

The world, generally, has never even thought about this subject. When I have spoken to people promiscuously in regard to it, they have replied: "We suppose that the Gipsies, as they have settled in life, have got lost among the general population:" than which nothing can be more unfounded, as a matter of fact, or ridiculous, as a matter of theory. Imagine a German family settling in Scotland. The feeling of being Germans becomes lost in the first generation, who do not, perhaps, speak a word of German.

There is no prejudice entertained for the family, but, on the contrary, much good-will and respect are shown it by its neighbours. The parents identify themselves with those surrounding them; the children, born in the country, become, or rather are, Scotch altogether; so that all that remains is the sense of a German extraction, which, but for the name of the family, would very soon be lost, or become a mere matter of tradition. In every other respect, the family, sooner or later, becomes lost amid the general population. In America, we daily see Germans getting mixed with, and lost among, Americans; but where is the evidence of such a process going on, or ever having taken place, in Great Britain, between the Gipsy and the native races? The prejudice which the ordinary natives have for the very name of Gipsy is sufficient proof that the Gipsy tribe has not been lost in any such manner. Still, it has not only got mixed, but "dreadfully mixed," with the native blood; but it has worked up the additional blood within itself, having thoroughly gipsyfied it. The original Gipsy blood may be compared to liquid in a vessel, into which native liquid has been put: the mixture has, as a natural consequence, lost, in a very great measure, its original colour; but, inasmuch as the most important element in the amalgamation has been *mind*, the result is, that, in its descent, it has remained, as before, Gipsy. Instead, therefore, of the Gipsies having become lost among the native population, a certain part of the native blood has been lost among them, greatly adding to the number of the body.

We cannot institute any comparison between the introduction of the Gipsies and the Huguenots, the last body of foreigners that entered Great Britain, relative to the destiny of the respective foreign elements. For the Huguenots were not a race, as distinguished from every other creature in the world, but a religious party, taking refuge among a people of cognate blood and language, and congenial religious feelings and faith; and were, to say the least of it, on a par, in every respect, with the ordinary natives, with nothing connected with them to prevent an amalgamation with the other inhabitants; but, on the contrary, having this characteristic, in common with the nations of Europe, that the place of birth constitutes the fact, and, taken in connection with the residence, creates the feelings of nationality and race. Many of my readers are, doubtless, conversant with the history of the Huguenots. Even in some parts of America, nothing is more common than for people to say that they are Huguenots, that is, of Huguenot descent, which is very commonly made the foundation of the connections and intimate associations of life. The peculiarity is frequently shown in the appearance of the individuals, and in such mental traits as spring from the contemplation of the Huguenots as an historical and religious party, even when the individual now follows the Catholic faith. But these people differ in no essential respect from the other inhabitants.

But how different is the position always occupied by the Gipsies! Well may they consider themselves "strangers in the land;" for by whom have they ever been acknowledged? They entered Scotland, for example, and have encreased, progressed, and developed, with so great a prejudice against them, and so separated in their feelings from others around them, as if none had almost existed in the country but themselves, while they were "dwelling in the midst of their brethren;" the native blood that has been incorporated with them having the appearance as if it had come from abroad. They, a people distinct from any other in the world, have sprung from the most primitive stage of human existence—the tent, and their knowledge of their race goes no further back than when it existed in other parts of the world, in the same condition, more or less, as themselves. They have been a migratory tribe, wherever they have appeared or settled, and have never ceased to be the same peculiar race, notwithstanding the changes which they have undergone; and have been at home wherever they have found themselves placed. The mere place of birth, or the circumstances under which the individual has been reared, has had no effect upon their special nationality, although, as citizens of particular countries, they have assimilated, in their general ideas, with others around them. And not only have they had a language peculiar to themselves, but signs as exclusively theirs as are those of Freemasons. For Gipsies stand to Gipsies as Freemasons to Freemasons; with this difference—that Masons are bound to respond to and help each other, while such associations, among the Gipsies, are optional with the individual, who, however, is persuaded that the same people, with these exclusive peculiarities, are to be met with in every part of the world. A Gipsy is, in his way, a Mason born, and, from his infancy, is taught to hide everything connected with his race, from those around him. He is his own *tyler*, and *tyles* his lips continually. Imagine, then, a person taught, from his infancy, to understand that he is a Gipsy; that his blood, (at least part of it,) is Gipsy; that he has been instructed in the language, and initiated in all the mysteries, of the Gipsies; that his relations and acquaintances in the tribe have undergone the same experience; that the utmost reserve towards those who are not Gipsies has been continually inculcated upon him, and as often practised before his eyes; and what must be the leading idea, in that person's mind, but that he is a Gipsy? His pedigree is Gipsy, his mind has been cast in a Gipsy mould, and he can no more "cease to be a Gipsy" than perform any other impossibility in nature. Thus it is that Gipsydom is not a work of man's hand, nor a creed, that is "revealed from faith to faith;" but a work which has been written by the hand of God upon the heart of a family of mankind, and is reflected from the mind of one generation to that of another. It enters into the feelings of the very existence of the man, and such is the prejudice against his race, on the part of the ordinary natives, that the better kind of Scottish Gispy feels that he, and more particularly she, would almost be "torn in pieces," if the public really knew all about them.

These facts will sufficiently illustrate how a people, "resembling, in so many respects, the Jews, without having any territory, or form of creed, peculiar to itself, or any history, or any peculiar outward associations or residences, or any material difference in appearance, character, or occupation," can be a people, living among other people, and yet be distinct from those among whom they live. The distinction consists in this people having *blood*, *language*, a *cast of mind*, and *signs*, peculiar to itself; the three first being the only elements which distinguish races; for religion is a secondary consideration; one religion being common to many distinct races. This principle, which is more commonly applied to people occupying different countries, is equally applicable to races, clans, families, or individuals, living within the boundary of a particular country, or dwelling in the same community. We can easily understand how two individuals can be two distinct individuals, notwithstanding their being members of the same family, and professing the same religion. We can still more easily understand the same of two families, and still more so of two septs or clans of the same general race. And, surely, there can be no difficulty in understanding that the Gipsy tribe, whatever may be its habits, is something different from any native tribe: for it has never yet found rest for the sole of its foot among the native race, although it has secured a shelter clandestinely; and of the extent, and especially of the nature, of its existence, the world may be said to be entirely ignorant. The position which the Gipsy race occupies in Scotland is that which it substantially occupies in every other country—unacknowledged, and, in a sense, damned, everywhere. There is, therefore, no wonder that it should remain a distinct family among mankind, cemented by its language and signs, and the knowledge of its universality. The phenomenon rests upon purely natural causes, and differs considerably from that of the existence of the Jews. For the Jews are, everywhere, acknowledged by the world, after a sort; they have neither language nor, as far as I know, signs peculiar to themselves, (although there are secret orders among them,) but possess the most ancient history, an original country, to which they, more or less, believe they will be restored, and a religion of divine origin, but utterly superseded by a new and better dispensation. Notwithstanding all that, the following remark, relative to the existence of the Jews, since the dispersion, may very safely be recalled: "The philosophical historian confesses that he has no place for it in all his generalizations, and refers it to the mysteries of Providence." For the history of the Gipsies bears a very great resemblance to it; and, inasmuch as that is not altogether "the device of men's hands," it must, also, be referred to Providence, for Providence has a hand in everything.

It is very true that the "philosophical historian has no place, in all his generalizations, for the phenomenon of the existence of the Jews, since the dispersion," for he has never investigated the subject inductively, and on its own merits. It is poor logic to assert that, because the American Indians are, to a great extent, and will soon be, extinct, therefore the existence of the Jews, to-day, is a miracle. And it would be nearly as poor logic to maintain the same of the Jews in connection with any of the ancient and extinct nations. There is no analogy between the history of the Jews, since the dispersion, and that of any other people, (excepting the Gipsies;) and, consequently, no comparison can be instituted between them.* Before asking how it is that the Jews exist to-day, it would be well to enquire by what possible process they could cease to be Jews. And by what human means the Jews, as a people, or even as individuals, will receive Christ as their Messiah, and thereby become Christian Jews. This idea of the Jews existing by a miracle has been carried to a very great length, as the following quotation, from an excellent writer, on the Evidences of Christianity, will show: "What is this," says he, "but a miracle? connected with the prophecy which it fulfills, it is a double miracle. Whether testimony can ever establish the credibility of a miracle is of no importance here. This one is obvious to every man's senses. All nations are its eye-witnesses. . . . . The laws of nature have been suspended in their case." This writer, in a spirit of gambling, stakes the whole question of revelation upon his own dogma; and, according to his hypothesis, loses it. The laws of nature would, indeed, have been suspended, in their case, and a miracle would, indeed, have been wrought, if the Jews had ceased to be Jews, or had become anything else than what they are to-day. Writers on the Christian Evidences should content themselves with maintaining that the Jews have fulfilled the prophecies, and will yet fulfill them, and assert nothing further of them.

The writer alluded to compares the history of the Jews, since the dispersion, to the following phenomenon: "A mighty river, having plunged, from a mountain height, into the depths of the ocean, and been separated into its component drops, and thus scattered to the ends of the world, and blown about, by all winds, during almost eighteen centuries, is still capable of being disunited from the waters of the ocean; its minutest drops, having never been assimilated to any other, are still distinct, unchanged, and ready to be gathered." Such language cannot be applied to the Jews; for the philosophy of their existence, to-day, is so very simple in its nature, as to have escaped the observation of man-

* I leave out of view various scattered nations in Asia.

kind. I will give it further on in this Disquisition. The language in question is somewhat applicable to the Gipsies, for they have become *worked into* all other nations, in regard to blood and language, and are "still distinct and unchanged," as to their being Gipsies, whatever their habits may be; and, although there is no occasion for them to be "gathered," they would yet, outwardly or inwardly, heartily respond to any call addressed to them.*

There is, as I have already said, no real outward difference between many settled and educated Scottish Gipsies and ordinary natives; for such Gipsies are as likely to have fair hair and blue eyes, as black. Their characters and occupations may be the same; they may have intimate associations together; may be engaged in business as partners; may even be cousins, nay, half-brothers. But let them, on separate occasions, enter a company of Gipsies, and the reception shown to them will mark the difference in the two individuals. The difference between two such Scotchmen, (for they really are both Scotch,) the reader may remark, makes the Gipsy only a Gipsy nominally, which, outwardly, he is; but he is still a Gipsy, although, in point of colour, character, or condition, not one of the old stock; for he has "the blood," and has been reared and instructed as a Gipsy. But such a Gipsy is not fond of entering a company of Gipsies, strangers to him, unless introduced by a friend in whom he has confidence, for he is afraid of being known to be a Gipsy. He is more apt to visit some of the more original kind of the race, where he is not known. On sitting down beside them, with a friendly air, they will be sure to treat him kindly, not knowing but that they may be entertaining a Gipsy unawares; for such original Gipsies, believing that "the blood" is to be found well up in life, feel very curious when they meet with such a person. If he "lets out" an idea in regard to the race, and expresses a kindly feeling towards "the blood," the suspicions of his friends are at once excited, so that, if he, in an equivocal manner, remarks that he is "*not* one of them," hesitates, stammers, and protests that he really is not one of them, they will as readily swear that he *is* one of them; for well does the blackguard

* It is interesting to hear the Gipsies speak of their race "taking of" this or the other race. Said an English Gipsy, to me, with reference to some Gipsies of whom we were speaking: "They take of the Arabians."

Gipsy, (as the world calls him,) know the delicacy of such settled and educated Gipsies in owning the blood. There is less suspicion shown, on such occasions, when the settled Gipsy is Scotch, and the *bush* Gipsy English; and particularly so should the occasion be in America; for, when they meet in America, away from the peculiar relations under which they have been reared, and where they can "breathe," as they express it, the respective classes are not so suspicious of each other.

Besides the difference just drawn between the Gipsy and ordinary native—that of recognizing and being recognized by another Gipsy—I may mention the following general distinction between them. The ordinary Scot knows that he is a Scot, and nothing more, unless it be something about his ancestors of two or three generations. But the Gipsy's idea of Scotland goes back to a certain time, indefinite to him, as it may be, beyond which his race had no existence in the country. Where his ancestors sojourned, immediately, or at any time, before they entered Scotland, he cannot tell; but this much he knows of them, that they are neither Scottish nor European, but that they came from the East. The fact of his blood being mixed exercises little or no influence over his feelings relative to his tribe, for, mixed as it may be, he knows that he is one of the tribe, and that the origin of his tribe is his origin. In a word, he knows that he has sprung from the tent. Substitute the word Scotch for Moor, as related of the black African Gipsies, at page 429, and he may say of himself and tribe: "We are not Scotch, but can give no account of ourselves." It is a little different, if the mixture of his blood is of such recent date as to connect him with native families; in that case, he has "various bloods" to contend for, should they be assailed; but his Gipsy blood, as a matter of course, takes precedence. By marrying into the tribe, the connection with such native families gradually drops out of the memory of his descendants, and leaves the sensation of tribe exclusively Gipsy. Imagine, then, that the Gipsy has been reared a Gipsy, in the way so frequently described, and that he "knows all about the Gipsies," while the ordinary native knows really nothing about them; and we have a general idea of what a Scottish Gipsy is, as distinguished from an ordinary Scotchman. If we admit that every native Scot knows who he is, we may readily assume that every Scottish Gipsy knows who *he* is. But, to place the point of difference in a more striking light, it may be remarked, that the native Scot will instinctively exclaim, that "the present work has no earthly relation either to him or his folk;" while the Scottish Gipsy will as instinctively exclaim: "It's us, there's no mistake about it;" and will doubtless accept it, in the main, with a high degree of satisfaction, as the history of his race, and give it to his children as such.

A respectable, indeed, any kind of, Scottish Gipsy does not contemplate his ancestors—the "Pilgrim Fathers," and "Pilgrim Mothers," too—as robbers, although he could do that with as much grace as any Highland or Border Scot, but as a singular people, who doubtless came from the Pyramids; and their language, as something about which he really does not know what to think; whether it is Egyptian, Sanscrit, or what it is. Still, he has part of it; he loves it; and no human power can tear it out of his heart. He knows that every intelligent being sticks to his own, and clings to his descent; and he considers it his highest pride to be an Egyptian—a descendant of those swarthy kings and queens, princes and princesses, priests and priestesses, and, of course, thieves and thievesses, that, like an apparition, found their way into, and, after wandering about, settled down in, Scotland. Indeed, he never knew anything else than that he was an Egyptian; for it is in his blood; and, what is more, it is in his heart, so that he cannot forget it, unless he should lose his faculties and become an idiot; and then he would be an Egyptian idiot. How like a Gipsy it was for Mrs. Fall, of Dunbar, to "work in tapestry the principal events in the life of the founder of her family, from the day the Gipsy child came to Dunbar, in its mother's creel, until the same Gipsy child had become, by its own honourable exertions, the head of the first merca..tile establishment then existing in Scotland."

The Scottish Gipsies, when their appearance has been modified by a mixture of the white blood, have possessed, in common with the Highlanders, the faculty of "getting out" of the original ways of their race, and becoming superior in character, notwithstanding the excessive prejudice that exists against the nation of which they hold themselves members. Except his strong partiality for his blood and tribe, language, and signs, such a Gipsy becomes, in his general disposition and ways, like any ordinary native. It is impossible that it should be otherwise. Whenever a Gipsy, then, forsakes his original habits, and conforms with the ways of the other inhabitants, he becomes, for all practical purposes, an ordinary citizen of the Gipsy clan. If he is a man of good natural abilities, the original wild ambition of his race acquires a new turn; and his capacity fits him for any occupation. Priding himself on being an Egyptian, a member of this world-wide community, he acquires, as he gains information, a spirit of liberality of sentiment; he reads history, and perceives that every family of mankind has not only been barbarous, but very barbarous, at one time; and, from such reflections, he comes to consider his own origin, and very readily becomes confirmed in his early, but indistinct, ideas of his people, that they really are somebody. Indeed, he considers himself not only as good, but better than other people. His being forced to assume an incognito, and "keep as quiet as pussy," chafes his proud spirit, but it does not render him gloomy, for his natural disposition is too buoyant for that. How, then, does such a Scottish Gipsy feel in regard to his ancestors? He feels exactly as Highlanders do, in regard to theirs, or, as the Scottish Borderers do, with reference to the "Border Ruffians," as I have heard a Gipsy term them. Indeed, the gallows of Perth and Stirling, Carlisle and Jedburgh, could tell some fine tales of many respectable Scottish people, in times that are past.

The children of such a Gipsy differ very much from those of the same race in their natural state, although they may have the same amount of blood, and the same eye. The eye of the former is subdued, for his passions, in regard to his race, have never been called forth; while the eye of the latter rolls about, as if he were conscious that every one he meets with is remarking of him, "There goes a vagabond of a Gipsy." Two fine specimens of the former kind of Gipsies attended the High School of Edinburgh, when I was at that institution. Hearing the family frequently spoken of at home, my attention was often taken up with the boys, without understanding what a Gipsy of *that* kind could mean; although I had a pretty good idea of the common Gipsy, or Tinkler, as he is generally called in Scotland. These two young Gipsies were what might be called sweet youths; modest and shy, among the other boys, as young tamed wild turkeys; very dark in colour, with an eye that could be caught in whatever way I might look at them. They now occupy very honourable positions in life. There were other Gipsies at the High School, at this time, but they were of the "brown sort." I have met, in the United States, with a Scottish Gipsy, taking greatly after the Gipsy, in his appearance; a man very gentlemanly in his manner and bearing, and as neat and trim as if he had "come out of a box." It is natural, indeed, to suppose that there must be a great difference, in many respects, between a wild, original Gipsy, and one of the tame and educated kind, whose descent is several, perhaps many, generations from the tent. In the houses of the former, things are generally found lying about, here-away, there-away, as if they were just going to be taken out and placed in the waggon, or on the ass's back.

It is certainly a singular position which is occupied, from generation to generation, and century to century, by our settled Scottish, as well as other, Gipsies, who are not known to the world as such, yet maintain a daily intercourse with others not of their own tribe. It resembles a state of semi-damnation, with a drawn sword hanging over their heads, ready to fall upon them at any moment. But the matter cannot be mended. They are Gipsies, by every physical and mental necessity, and they accommodate themselves to their circumstances as they best may. This much is certain, that they have the utmost confidence in their incognito, as regards their descent, personal feelings, and exclusively private associations. The word "Gipsy," to be applied to them by strangers, frightens them, in contemplation, far more than it does the children of the ordinary natives; for they imagine it a dreadful thing to be known to their neighbours as Gipsies. Still, they have never occupied any other position; they have been born in it, and reared in it; it has even been the nature of the race, from the very first, always to "work in the dark." In all probability, it has never occurred to them to imagine that it will ever be otherwise: nor do they evidently wish it; for they can see no possible way to have themselves acknowledged, by the world, as Gipsies. The very idea horrifies them. So far from letting the world know anything of them, as Gipsies, their constant care is to keep it in perpetual darkness on the subject. Of all men, these Gipsies may say:

> " . . . . rather bear those ills we have,
> Than fly to others we know not of."

Indeed, the only thing that worries such a Gipsy is the idea that the public should know all about *him*; otherwise, he feels a supreme satisfaction in being a Gipsy; as well as in having such a history of his race as I have informed him I proposed publishing, provided I do not in any way mix *him* up with it, or "let *him* out." By bringing up the body in the manner done in this work, by making a sweep of the whole tribe, the responsibility becomes spread over a large number of people; so that, should the Gipsy become, by any means, known, personally, to the world, he would have the satisfaction of knowing that he had others to keep him company; men occupying respectable positions in life, and respected, by the world at large, as individuals.

Here, then, we have one of the principal reasons for everything connected with the Gipsies being hidden from the rest of mankind. They have always been looked upon as arrant vagabonds, while they have looked upon their ancestors as illustrious and immortal heroes. How, then, are we to bridge over this gulf that separates them, in feeling, from the rest of the world? The natural reply is, that we should judge them, not by their condition and character in times that are past, but by what they are to-day.

That the Gipsies were a barbarous race when they entered Europe, in the beginning of the fifteenth century, is just what could have been expected of any Asiatic, migratory, tented horde, at a time when the inhabitants of Europe were little better than barbarous, themselves, and many of them absolutely so. To speak of the Highland clans, at that time, as being better than barbarous, would be out of the question; as to the Irish people, it would be difficult to say what they really were, at the same time. Even the Lowland Scotch, a hundred years after the arrival of the Gipsies in Europe, were, with some exceptions, divided into two classes—"beggars and rascals," as history tells us. Is it, therefore, unreasonable to say, that, in treating of the Gipsies of to-day, we should apply to them the same principles of judgment that have been applied to the ordinary natives? If we refer to the treaty between John Faw and James V., in 1540, we will very readily conclude that, three centuries ago, the leaders of the Gipsies were very superior men, in their way; cunning, astute, and slippery Oriental barbarians, with the experience of upwards of a century in European society generally; well up to the ways of the world, and the general ways of Church and State; and, in a sense, at home with kings, popes, cardinals, nobility, and gentry. That was the character of a superior Gipsy, in 1540. In 1840, we find the race represented by as fine a man as ever graced the Church of Scotland. "Grand was the repose of his lofty brow, dark eye, and aspect of soft and melancholy meaning. It was a face from which every evil and earthly passion seemed purged. A deep gravity lay upon his countenance, which had the solemnity, without the sternness, of one of our old reformers. You could almost fancy a halo completing its apostolic character." Some of the Scottish Gipsies of to-day could very readily exclaim:

"And, if thou said'st I am not peer
To any *one* in Scotland here,
Highland or Lowland, far or near,
Oh, Donald, thou hast lied!"

But it is impossible for any one to give an account of the Gipsies in Scotland, from the year 1506, down to the present time. This much, however, can be said of them, that they are as much Gipsies now as ever they were; that is, the Gipsies of to-day are the representatives of the race as it appeared in Scotland three centuries and a half ago, and hold themselves to be Gipsies now, as, indeed, they always will do.

Ever since the race entered Scotland, we may reasonably assume that it has been dropping out of the tent into settled life, in one form or other, and sometimes to a greater extent at one time than another. It never has been a nomadic race, in the proper sense of the word; for a nomad is one who possesses flocks and herds, with which he moves about from pasturage to pasturage, as he does in Asia to-day. Mr. Borrow says that there are Gipsies who follow this kind of life, in Russia; but that, doubtless, arises from the circumstances in which they have found themselves placed.* "I

* There is scarse a part of the habitable world where they are not to be found; their tents are alike pitched on the heaths of Brazil and the ridges of the Himalayan hills; and their language is heard at Moscow and Madrid, in the streets of London and Stamboul. They are found in all parts of

think," said an English Gipsy to me, "that we must take partly of the ancient Egyptians, and partly of the Arabs; from the Egyptians, owing to our settled ways, and from the Arabs, owing to our wandering habits." Upon entering Europe, they must have wandered about promiscuously, for some short time, before pitching upon territories, which they would divide among themselves, under their kings and chieftains. Here we find the proper sphere of the Gipsy, in his original state. In 1506, Anthonius Gawino is represented, by James IV., to his uncle, the king of Denmark, as having "sojourned in Scotland in peaceable and catholic manner:" and John Faw, by James V., in 1540, during his "pilgrimage," as "doing a lawful business;" which evidently had some meaning, as we find that seven pounds were paid to the Egyptians by the king's chamberlain. In 1496, the Gipsies made musket-balls for the king of Hungary; and, in 1565, cannon-balls for the Turks. In short, they were travelling smiths, or what has since been called tinkers, with a turn for any kind of ordinary mechanical employment, and particularly as regards working in metals; dealers in animals, petty traders, musicians, and fortune-tellers, with a wonderful knack for "transferring money from other people's pockets into their own;" living representatively, but apparently not wholly, in tents, and "helping themselves" to whatever they stood in need of.*

Speaking of the Gipsy chiefs mentioned in the act of James V., our author, as we have seen, very justly remarks: "It cannot be supposed that the ministers of three or four succeeding monarchs would have suffered their sovereigns to be so much imposed on, as to allow them to put their names

Russia, with the exception of the Government of St. Petersburg, from which they have been banished. In most of the provincial towns, they are to be found in a state of half civilization, supporting themselves by trafficking in horses, or by curing the disorders incidental to those animals. But the vast majority reject this manner of life, and traverse the country in bands, like the ancient Hamaxobioi; the immense grassy plains of Russia affording pasturage for their herds of cattle, on which, and the produce of the chase, they chiefly depend for subsistence.—*Borrow.*

* Considering what is popularly understood to be the natural disposition and capacity of the Gipsies, we would readily conclude that to turn innkeepers would be the most unlikely of all their employments; yet that is very common. Mahommed said, "If the mountain will not come to us, we will go to the mountain." The Gipsies say, "If we do not go to the people, the people must come to us;" and so they open their houses of entertainment.

to public documents styling poor and miserable wretches, as we at the present day imagine them to have been, 'Lords and Earls of Little Egypt.' . . . . . I am disposed to believe that Anthonius Gawino, in 1506, and John Faw, in 1540, would personally, as individuals, that is, as Gipsy rajahs, have a very respectable and imposing appearance, in the eyes of the officers of the crown." (Page 108.)* We have likewise seen how many laws were passed, by the Scots parliament, against "great numbers of his majesty's subjects, of whom some outwardly pretend to be famous and unspotted gentlemen," for encouraging and supporting the Gipsies; and, in the case of William Auchterlony, of Cayrine, for receiving into their houses, and feasting them, their wives, children, *servants*, and companies. All this took place more than a hundred years after the arrival of the Gipsies in Scotland, and seventy-six years after the date of the treaty between James V. and John Faw. We can very readily believe that the sagacity displayed by this chief and his folk, to evade the demand made upon them to leave the country, was likewise employed to secure their perpetual existence in it; for, from the first, their intention was evidently to possess it. Hence their original story of being pilgrims, which would prevent the authorities from disturbing them, but which had no effect upon Henry VIII., whom, of all the monarchs of Europe, they did not hoax. Grellmann mentions their having obtained passports from the Emperor Sigismund, and other princes, as well as from the king of France, and the Pope.

Entering Scotland with the firm determination to "possess" the country, the Gipsies would, from the very first, direct their attention towards its occupation, and draw into their body much of the native blood, in the way which I have already described. And there was certainly a large

* The following is a description of a superior Spanish Gipsy, in 1584, as quoted by Mr. Borrow, from the memoirs of a Spaniard, who had seen him: "At this time, they had a count, a fellow who spoke the Castilian idiom with as much purity as if he had been a native of Toledo. He was acquainted with all the ports of Spain, and all the difficult and broken ground of the provinces. He knew the exact strength of every city, and who were the principal people in each, and the exact amount of their property; there was nothing relative to the state, however secret, that he was not acquainted with; nor did he make a mystery of his knowledge, but publicly boasted of it."

floating population in the country, from which to draw it. It would little consist with the feelings of Highland or Lowland outlaws to exist without female society; nor was that female society easily to be found, apart from some kind of settled life; hence, in seeking for a home, which is inseparable from the society of a female, our native outlaw would very naturally and readily "haul up" with the Gipsy woman; for, being herself quite "at home," in her tent, she would present just the desideratum which the other was in quest of. For, although "Gipsies marry with Gipsies," it is only as a rule, the exceptions being many, and, in all probability, much more common, in the early stage of their European history. The present "dreadfully mixed" state of Gipsydom is a sufficient proof of this fact. The aversion, on the part of the Gipsy, to intermarry with the ordinary natives, proceeds, in the first place, from the feelings which the natives entertain for her race. Remove those feelings, and the Gipsies, as a body, would still marry among themselves; for their pride in their peculiar sept, and a natural jealousy of those outside of their mystic circle, would, alone, keep the world from penetrating their secrets, without its being extended to him who, by intermarriage, became "one of them." There is no other obstacle in the way of marriages between the two races, excepting the general one, on the part of the Gipsies, and which is inherent in them, to preserve themselves as a branch of a people to be found in every country. Admitting the general aversion, on the part of the Gipsies, to *marry* with natives, and we at once see the unlikelihood of their women *playing the wanton* with them. Still, it is very probable that they, in some instances, bore children to some of the "unspotted gentlemen," mentioned, by act of parliament, as having so greatly protected and entertained the tribe. Such illegitimate children would be put to good service by the Gipsy chiefs. By one means or other, there is no doubt but the Gipsies made a dead-set upon certain native families of influence. The capacity that could devise such a scheme for remaining in the country, as is contained in the act of 1540, and influence the courts of the regency, and of Queen Mary, to reinstate them in their old position, after the severe order of 1541, proclaiming banishment within thirty days, and death thereafter, even when the "lords understood, perfectly, the great thefts and *skaiths*, (damages,) done by the said Egyptians," could easily execute plans to secure a hold upon private families. If to all this we add the very nature of Gipsydom; how it always remains true to itself, as it gets mixed with the native blood; how it works its way up in the world; and how its members "stick to each other;" we can readily understand how the tribe acquired important and influential friends in high places. Do not speak of the attachment of the Jewess to her people: that of the Gipsy is greater. A Jewess passes current, anywhere, as a Jewess; but the Gipsy, as she gets dove-tailed into a native circle, and moves about in the world, does so clandestinely, for, as a Gipsy, she is *incog.;* so that her attachment remains, at heart, with her tribe, and is all the stronger, from the feelings that are peculiar to her singularly wild descent. I am very much inclined to think that Mrs. Baillie, of Lamington, mentioned under the head of Tweeddale and Clydesdale Gipsies, was a Gipsy; and the more so, from having learned, from two different sources, that the present Baillie, of ———, is a Gipsy. Considering that courts of justice have always stretched a point, to convict, and *execute,* Gipsies, it looks like something very singular, that William Baillie, a Gipsy, who was condemned to death, in 1714, should have had his sentence commuted to banishment, *and been allowed to go at large,* while others, condemned with him, were executed. And three times did he escape in that manner, till, at last, he was slain by one of his tribe. It also seems very singular, that James Baillie, another Gipsy, in 1772, should have been condemned for the murder of his wife, and, also, had his sentence commuted to banishment, and been allowed to go at large: and that twice, at least. Well might McLaurin remark: "Few cases have occurred in which there has been such an expenditure of mercy." And tradition states that "the then Mistress Baillie, of Lamington, and her family, used all their interest in obtaining these pardons for James Baillie." No doubt of it. But the reason for all this was, doubtless, different from that of "James Baillie, like his fathers before him, *pretending* that he was a bastard relative of the family of Lamington."

A somewhat similar case of pardoning Gipsies is related by a writer in Blackwood's Magazine, as having occurred towards the end of last century; the individual procuring the pardon being the excitable Duchess of Gordon, the same,

I presume, whom Burns' genius "fairly lifted off her feet." The following are the circumstances, as given by this writer: A Berwickshire farmer had been missing sheep, and lay in wait, one night, with a servant, for the depredators. They seized upon Tam Gordon, the captain of the Spittal Gipsies, and his son-in-law, Ananias Faa, in the very act of stealing the sheep; when the captain drew a knife, to defend himself. They were convicted and condemned for the crime; "but afterwards, to the great surprise of their Berwickshire neighbours, obtained a pardon, a piece of unmerited and ill-bestowed clemency, for which, it was generally understood, they were indebted to the interest of a noble northern family, of their own name. We recollect hearing a sort of ballad upon Tam's exploits, and his deliverance from the gallows, through the intercession of a celebrated duchess, but do not recollect any of the words."*

A transaction like this must strike the reader as something very remarkable. Sheep-stealing, at the time mentioned, was a capital offence, for which there was almost no pardon; and more especially in the case of people who were of notorious "habit and repute Gipsies," caught in the very act, which was aggravated by their drawing an "invasive weapon." Not only were they condemned, but we may readily assume that the "country-side" were crying, "Hang and bury the vagabonds;" and death seemed certain; when in steps the duchess, and snatches them both from the very teeth of the gallows. What guarantee have we that the duchess was not a Gipsy? It certainly was not likely that a Gipsy woman would step out of her tent, and seize a coronet; but what cannot we imagine to have taken place, in "the blood" working its way up, during the previous 250 years? What guarantee have we that Professor Wilson was not "taking a look at the old thing," when rambling with the Gipsies, in his youth? There are Gipsy families in Edinburgh, to-day, of as respectable standing, and of as good descent, as could be said of him, or many others who have distinguished themselves in the world.

We must not forget that, when the Gipsies entered Scotland, it was for better or for worse, just for what was to "turn up." Very soon after their arrival, the country

* I should suppose that this was Captain Gordon who behaved himself like a prince, at the North Queensferry. *See page* 172.

would become their country, as much as that of the ordinary natives; so that Scotland became their home, as much as if it had always been that of their race, except their retaining a tradition of their recent arrival from some part of the East, and a singular sense of being part and parcel of "the Egyptians that were scattered over the face of the earth;" neither of which the odious prejudice against "the blood" allowed them to forget; assuming that they were willing, and, moreover, that the cast of their minds allowed them, to do either. The idea which has been expressed by the world, generally, of the Gipsy tribe gradually assimilating with the native race, and ultimately "getting lost among it," applies to the principle at issue; for, as I have already said, it *has* got greatly lost, in point of appearance, and general deportment, among the ordinary natives, but has remained, heart and soul, Gipsy, as before. Even with the native race, we will find that the blood of the lowly is always getting mixed with that in the higher circles of life. We have the case of a girl going to service with a London brewer, then becoming his wife, then his widow, then employing a lawyer to manage her affairs, and afterwards marrying him, who, in his turn, became Earl of Clarendon, and father, by her, of the queen of James II. Towards the end of last, or beginning of the present, century, we hear of a poor actress, who commenced life in a provincial theatre, marrying one of the Coutts, the bankers, and dying Duchess of St. Albans. Such events have been of much more common occurrence in less elevated spheres of life; and the Gipsy race has had its share of them. For this reason, it is really impossible to say, who, among the Scotch, are, and who are not, of the Gipsy tribe; such a thorough mess has the "mixing of the blood" made of the Scottish population. Notwithstanding all that, there is a certain definite number of "Gipsies" in Scotland, known to God only; while each Gipsy is known in his or her conscience to belong to the tribe. This much is certain, that we need not consult the census returns for the number of the tribe in Scotland. However easy, or however difficult, it may be, to define what a Gipsy, in regard to external or internal circumstances, is, this much is certain, that the feeling in his mind as to his being a Gipsy, is as genuine and emphatic as is the feeling in the mind of a Jew being a Jew.

The circumstances connected with the perpetuation of the Gipsy and Jewish races greatly resemble each other. Both races are scattered over the face of the earth. The Jew has had a home; he has a strong attachment to it, and looks forward to enter it at some future day. The Gipsy may be said never to have had a home, but is at home everywhere. "What part of England did you come from?" said I to an English semi-tented Gipsy, in America. "What *part* of England did I come from, did you say? I come from *all over England!*" The Scottish race, as a race, is confined to people born in Scotland; for the children of expatriated Scots are not Scotchmen. And so it is with people of other countries. The mere birth upon the soil constitutes their race or nationality, although subsequent events, in early life, may modify the feelings, or draw them into a new channel, by a change of domicile, in infancy. But the Jew's nationality is everywhere; 'tis in his family, and his associations with others of his race. Make the acquaintance of the Jews, and you will find that each generation of them tell *their* "wonderful story" to the following generation, and the story is repeated to the following, and the following. The children of Jews are taught to know they are Jews, before they can even lisp. Soon do they know that much of the phenomenon of their race, as regards its origin, its history, and its universality, to draw the distinction between them and those around them who are not Jews. Soon do they learn how their race has been despised and persecuted, and imbibe the love which their parents have for it, and the resentment of the odium cast upon it by others. It has been so from the beginning of their history out of Palestine, and even while there. Were it only religion, considered in itself, that has kept the Jews together as a people, they might have got lost among the rest of mankind; for among the Jews there are to be found the rankest of infidels; even Jewish priests will say that, "it signifies not what a man's religion may be, if he is only sincere in it." Is it a feeling, or a knowledge, of religion that leads a Jewish child, almost the moment it can speak, to say that it is a Jew? It is simply the workings of the phenomena of race that account for this; the religion peculiar to Jews having been introduced among them centuries after their existence as a people. Being exclusively theirs in its very nature, they naturally follow it, as other people do theirs; but, although, from the nature of its origin, it presents infinitely greater claims upon their intelligent belief and obedience, they have yielded no greater submission to its spirit and morals, or even to its forms, than many other people have done to their religion, made up, as that has been, of the most fabulous superstition, on the principle, doubtless, that

> "The zealous crowds in ignorance adore,
> And still, the less they know, they fear the more."

The Jews being a people before they received the religion by which they are distinguished, it follows that the religion, in itself, occupies a position of secondary importance, although the profession of it acts and reacts upon the people, in keeping them separate from others. The most, then, that can be said of the religion of the Jews is, that, following in the wake of their history as a people, it is only one of the pillars by which the building is supported.* If enquiry is made of Jewish converts to Christianity, we will find that, notwithstanding their having separated from their brethren, on points of creed, they hold themselves as much Jews as before. But the conversions of Jews are,

> "Like angels' visits, few and far between."

In the case of individuals forsaking the Jewish, and joining the Christian, Church, that is, believing in the Messiah having come, instead of to come, it is natural, I may say inevitable, for them to hold themselves Jews. They have feelings which the world cannot understand. But beyond the nationality, physiognomy, and feelings of Jews, there are no points of difference, and there ought to be no grounds of offense, between them and the ordinary inhab-

* The only part of the religion of the Jews having an origin prior to the establishment of the Mosaic law was circumcision, which was termed the covenant made by God with Abraham and his seed. (Gen. xvii. 10–14.) The abolition of idols, and the worship of God alone, are presumed, although not expressed. The Jews lapsed into gross idolatry while in Egypt, but were not likely to neglect circumcision, as that was necessary to maintain a physical uniformity among the race, but did not enter into the wants, and hopes, and fears, inherent in the human breast, and stimulated by the daily exhibition of the phenomena of its existence. The second table of the moral law was, of course, written upon the hearts of the Jews, in common with those of the Gentiles. (Rom. ii. 14, 15.)

itants. While the points of antipathy between the Jew and Christian rest, not upon race, considered in itself, but mainly upon religion, and the relations proceeding from it, it has to be seen what is to be the feeling, on the part of the world, towards the Gipsy race; such part of it, at least, whose habits are unexceptionable. This is one of the questions which it is the object of this Disquisition to bring to an issue.

Substitute the language and signs of the Gipsies for the religion of the Jews, and we find that the rearing of the Gipsies is almost identical with that of the Jews; and in the same manner do they hold themselves to be Gipsies. But the one can be Gipsies, though ignorant of their language and signs, and the other, Jews, though ignorant of their religion; the mere sense of tribe and community being sufficient to constitute them members of their respective nationalities. The origin of the Gipsies is as distinct from that of the rest of the world, in three continents, at least, as is that of the Jews; and, laying aside the matter of religion, their history, so far as it is known to the world, is as different. If they have no religion peculiar to themselves, to assist in holding them together, like the Jews, they have that which is exclusively theirs—language and signs; about which there are no such occasions to quarrel, as in the affair of a religious creed. Indeed, the Gipsy race stands towards religions, as the Christian religion does towards races.

People are very apt to speak of the blood of the Jews being "purity itself;" than which nothing is more unfounded. If a person were asked, What is a pure Jew? he would feel puzzled to give an intelligent answer to the question. We know that Abraham and Sarah were the original parents of the Jewish race, but that much blood has been added to it, from other sources, ever since. Even four of the patriarchs, the third in descent from Abraham, were the sons of concubines, who were, doubtless, bought with money, from the stranger, (Gen. xvii. 12 and 13,) or the descendants of such, and were, in all probability, of as different a race from their mistresses, Leah and Rachel, as was the bondmaid, Hagar, the Egyptian, from her mistress, Sarah. Joseph married a daughter of the Egyptian priest of On, and Moses, a daughter of an Ethiopian priest of Midian. From a circumstance mentioned in the Exodus, it would appear that Egyptian blood, perhaps much of it, had been incorporated with that of the Jews, while in Egypt.* And much foreign blood seems to have been added to the body, between the Exodus and the Babylonian captivity, through the means of proselytes and captives, strange women and bondmaids, concubines and harlots. We read of Rahab, of Jericho, an innkeeper, or harlot, or both, marrying Salmon, one of the chief men in the tribe of Judah, and becoming the mother of Boaz, who married Ruth, a Moabitish woman, the daughter-in-law of Naomi, and grandmother of David, from whom Christ was lineally descended. Indeed, the Jews have always been receiving foreign blood into their body. We read of Timothy having been a Greek by the father's side, and a Jew by the mother's; and of his having been brought up a Jew. Such events are of frequent occurrence. There is no real bar to marriages between Jews and Christians, although circumstances render them difficult. The children of such marriages sometimes resemble the Jew, and sometimes the Christian; sometimes they cast their lot with the Jews, in the matter of religion, and sometimes with the Christians; but they generally follow the mother in that matter. Such, however, is the conceit which the Jew displays in regard to his race, that he is very reserved in speaking about this "mixing of the blood." I once addressed a string of questions to a Christian-Jew preacher, on this subject, but he declined answering them. I am intimate with a family the parents of which are half-blood Jews, all of whom belong to the Jewish connexion, and I

* It is an unnecessary stretch upon the belief in the Scriptures, to ask consent to the abstract proposition that the Jews, while in Egypt, encreased from seventy souls to "about six hundred thousand on foot that were men, besides children," at the time of the Exodus. Following a pastoral life, in a healthy and fertile country, and inspired with the prophecy delivered to Abraham, as to his numberless descendants, the whole bent of the mind of the Jews was to multiply their numbers; and polygamy and concubinage being characteristic of the people, there is no reason to doubt that the Jews encreased to the number stated. The original emigrants, doubtless, took with them large establishments of bondmen and bondwomen, and purchased others while in Egypt; and these being circumcised, according to the covenant made with Abraham, would sooner or later become, on that account alone, part of the nation; and much more so by such amalgamation as is set forth by Rachel and Leah giving their maids to Jacob to have children by them. Abraham was, at best, the representative head of the Jewish nation, composed, as that was originally, of elements drawn from the idolatrous tribes surrounding him and his descendants.

find that, notwithstanding the mixture of the blood, there is as little mental difference between them and the other Jews, as there is between Americans of six descents, by both sides of the house, and Americans whose descent, through one parent, goes as far back, while, through the other parent, it is from abroad. Purity of blood, as applicable to almost any race, and, among others, to the Jewish, is a figment. There are many Jews in the United States, and, doubtless, in other countries, who are not known to other people as Jews, either by their appearance or their attendance at the synagogue. As a general principle, no Jew will tell the world that he belongs to the race; he leaves that to be found out by other people. Sir J. Gardner Wilkinson says that the Jews of the East, to this day, often have red hair and blue eyes, and are quite unlike their brethren in Europe. He found the large nose at Jerusalem an invariable proof of mixture with a Western family. It is singular, however, how easy it is to detect the generality of Jews; the nose, the eyes, or the features, tell who they are, but not always so. What may be termed a "pure Jew," is when the person has no knowledge of any other blood being in his veins than Jewish blood; or when his feelings are entirely Jewish as to nationality, although his creed may not be very strongly Jewish.

I will now consider the relative positions which the Jews and Gipsies occupy towards the rest of mankind. I readily admit that, in their original and wild state, the Gipsies have not been of any use to the world, but, on the contrary, a great annoyance. Still, that cannot be said altogether; for the handy turn of the Gipsies in some of the primitive mechanical arts, and their dealing in various wares, have been, in a measure, useful to a certain part of the rural population; and themselves the sources of considerable amusement; but, taking everything into account, they have been decidedly annoying to the world generally. In their wild state, they have never been charged by any one with an outward contempt for religion, whatever their inward feelings may have been for it; but, on the contrary, as always having shown an apparent respect for it. No one has ever complained of the Gipsy scoffing at religion, or even for not yielding to its general truths; what has been said of him is, that he is, at heart, so heedless and volatile in his disposition, that everything in regard to religion passes in at the one ear, and goes out at the other. There are, doubtless, Gipsies who will be "unco godly," when they can make gain by it; but it more frequently happens that they will assume such an air, in the presence of a person of respectable appearance, to show him that they are really not the "horrible vagabonds" which, they never doubt, he holds them to be. They are then sure to overdo their part. As a general thing, they wish people to believe that "they are not savages, but have feelings like other people," as "Terrible" expressed it. This much is certain, that whenever the Gipsy settles, and acquires an incognito, we hear of little or nothing of the canting in question. As regards the question of religion, it is very fortunate for the Gipsy race that they brought no particular one with them; for, objectionable as they have been held to be, the feeling towards them would have been worse, if they had had a system of priestcraft and heathen idolatry among them. But this circumstance greatly worries a respectable Gipsy; he would much rather have it said that his ancestors had some sort of religion, than that they had none. It is generally understood that the Gipsies did not bring any particular religion with them; still, the ceremony of sacrificing horses at divorces, and, at one time, at marriages, has a strange and unaccountable significance.

Then, as regards the general ways of the Gipsies. If we consider them as those of a people who have emerged, or are emerging, from a state of barbarism, how trifling, how venial do they appear! Scotch people have suffered, in times past, far more at the hands of each other, than ever they knowingly did at the hands of the Gipsies. What was the nature of that system of black-mail which was levied by Highland gentlemen upon Southerners? Was it anything but robbery? So common, so unavoidable was the payment of black-mail, that the law had to wink at it, nay, regulate it. But after all, it was nothing but compounding for that which would otherwise have been stolen. It gave peace and security to the farmer, and a revenue to the Highland gentleman, whom it placed in the position of a nominal protector, but actually prevented from being a robber, in law or morals; for, let the payment of the black-mail but have been refused, and, perhaps the next day, the Southerner would have been ruined; so that the Highland gentleman would have obtained his rights, under any circumstances. For Highland people, by a process of reasoning peculiar to a people in a barbarous state, held, as we have seen, that they had a right to rob the Lowlanders, whenever it was in their power, and that two hundred years after the Gipsies entered Scotland.

Scottish Gipsies are British subjects, as much as either Highland or Lowland Scots; their being of foreign origin does not alter the case; and they are entitled to have that justice meted out to them that has been accorded to the ordinary natives. They are not a heaven-born race, but they certainly found their way into the country, as if they had dropped into it out of the clouds. As a race, they have that much mystery, originality, and antiquity about them, and that inextinguishable sensation of being a branch of the same tribe everywhere, that ought to cover a multitude of failings connected with their past history. Indeed, what we do know of their earliest history is not nearly so barbarous as that of our own; for we must contemplate our own ancestors, at one time, as painted and skin-clad barbarians. What we do know, for certainty, of the earliest history of the Scottish Gipsies, is contained, more particularly, in the Act of 1540; and we would naturally say, that, for a people in a barbarous state, such is the dignity and majesty, with all the roguishness, displayed in the conduct of the Gipsies of that period, one could hardly have a better, certainly not a more romantic, descent; provided the person whose descent it is is to be found amid the ranks of Scots, with talents, a character, and a position equal to those of others around him. For this reason, it must be said of the race, that whenever it shakes itself clear of objectionable habits, and follows any kind of ordinary industry, the cause of every prejudice against it is gone, or ought to disappear; for then, as I have already said, the Gipsies became ordinary citizens, of the Gipsy clan. It then follows, that in passing a fair judgment upon the Gipsy race, we ought to establish a principle of progression, and set our minds upon the best specimens of it, as well as the worst, and not judge of it, solely, from the poorest, the most ignorant, or the most barbarous part of it.*

* Tacitus gives the following glowing account of the destruction of the Druids, in the island of Anglesey: "On the opposite shore stood the Brit-

What shall we say further of the relative positions which the Jews and Gipsies occupy towards the rest of the world? In the first place, the Jews entered Europe a civilized, and the Gipsies a barbarous, people; so that, in instituting any comparison between them, we should select Gipsies occupying positions in life similar to those of the Jews. The settled Scottish Gipsy, we find, appears to the eye of the world as a Scotchman, and nothing more. It is the weak position which the Gipsy race occupies in the world, as it enters upon a settled life, and engages in steady pursuits, that compels it to assume an incognito; for it has nothing to appeal to, as regards the past; no history, except it be acts of legislation passed against the race. In looking into a Dictionary or a Cyclopædia, the Gipsy finds his race described as vagabonds, always as vagabonds; and he may be said never to have heard a good word spoken of it, during the whole of his life. Hence he and his descendants "keep as quiet as pussy," and pass from the observation of the world. Besides this, there is no prominent feature connected with his race, to bring it before the world, such as there is with the Jewish, viz., history, church, and literature. A history, the Gipsy, as we see, doubtless has; but anything connected with him, pertaining to the church or literature, he holds as a member of ordinary society. Still, it would not be incorrect to speak of Gipsy literature, as the work of a Gipsy, acquired from the sources common to other men; as we would say of the Jews, relative to the literature which they produce under similar circum-

ous, closely embodied, and prepared for action. Women were seen rushing through the ranks in wild disorder; their apparel funereal; their hair loose to the wind, in their hands flaming torches, and their whole appearance resembling the frantic rage of the Furies. The Druids were ranged in order, with hands uplifted, invoking the gods, and pouring forth horrible imprecations. The novelty of the sight struck the Romans with awe and terror. They stood in stupid amazement, as if their limbs were benumbed, riveted to one spot, a mark for the enemy. The exhortation of the general diffused new vigour through the ranks, and the men, by mutual reproaches, inflamed each other to deeds of valour. They felt the disgrace of yielding to a troop of women, and a band of fanatic priests; they advanced their standards, and rushed on to the attack with impetuous fury. The Britons perished in the flames which they themselves had kindled. The island fell, and a garrison was established to retain it in subjection. *The religious groves, dedicated to superstition and barbarous rites, were levelled to the ground. In those recesses, the natives imbrued their altars with the blood of their prisoners, and, in the entrails of men, explored the will of the gods.*"—*Murphy's Translation.*

stances. As to the Gipsy to whom I have alluded, it may be said that it is none of our business whether he is a Gipsy or not; there is certainly no prejudice against him as an individual, and there can be none as a Gipsy, except such as people may of their own accord conceive for him. Many of the Scottish Gipsies whom I have met with are civil enough, sensible enough, decent enough, and liberal and honourable enough in their conduct; decidedly well bred for their positions in life, and rather foolish and reckless with their means, than misers; and, generally speaking, what are called "good fellows." It is no business of mine to ask them, how long it is since their ancestors left the tent, or, indeed, if they even know when that occurred; and still less, if they know when any of them ever did anything that was contrary to law. Still, one feels a little irksome in such a Gipsy's company, until the Gipsy question has been fairly brought before the world, and the point settled, that a Gipsy may be a gentleman, and that no disparagement is necessarily connected with the name, considered in itself. Such Scottish Gipsies as I have mentioned are decidedly smart, and, Yankee-like, more adaptable in turning their hands to various employments, than the common natives; and are a fair credit to the country they come from, and absolutely a greater than many of the native Scotch that are to be met with in the New World. Let the name of Gipsy be as much respected, in Scotland, as it is now despised, and the community would stare to see the civilized Gipsies make their appearance; they would come buzzing out, like bees, emerging even from places where a person, not in the secret, never would have dreamt of.

If we consider, in a fair and philosophical manner, the origin of these people, we will find many excuses for the position which their ancestors have occupied. They were a tribe of men wandering upon the face of the earth, over which they have spread, as one wave follows and urges on another. Those that appeared in Europe seem to have been impelled, in their migration, by the same irresistible impulse; to say nothing of the circumstances connected with their coming in contact with the people whose territories they had invaded. No one generation could be responsible for the position in which it found itself placed. In the case of John Faw and his company, we find that, being on the face of the earth, they had to go somewhere, and invent some sort of excuse, to secure a toleration; and the world was bound to yield them a subsistence, of some kind, and in some way obtained. As a wandering, barbarous, tented tribe, with habits peculiar to itself, and inseparable from its very nature, great allowance ought to be made for the time necessary for its gradual absorption into settled society. That could only be the result of generations, even if the race had not been treated so harshly as it has been, or had such a prejudice displayed against it. The difficulties which a Gipsy has to encounter in leaving the tent are great, for he has been born in that state, and been reared in it. To leave his tent forever, and settle in a town, is a greater trial to the innate feelings of his nature, than would be the change from highly polished metropolitan life to a state of solitude, in a society away from everything that had hitherto made existence bearable. But the Gipsy will very readily leave his tent, temporarily, to visit a town, if it is to make money. It is astonishing how strong the circumstances are which bind him to his tent; even his pride and prejudices in being a "wandering Egyptian," will, if it is possible to live by the tent, bind him to it. Then, there is the prejudice of the world—the objection to receive him into any community, and his children into any school—that commonly prevails, and which compels him to *steal* into settled life. It has always been so with the Gipsy race. Gipsies brought up in the tent have the same difficulties to encounter in leaving it to-day, that others had centuries ago. But, notwithstanding all that, they are always keeping moving out of the tent, and becoming settled and civilized.

Tented Gipsies will naturally "take bits o' things;" many of them would think one simple if he thought they would not do it; some of them would even be insulted if he said they did not do it. After they leave the tent, and commence "tramping," they (I do not say all of them) will still "take bits o' things." From this stage of their history, they keep gradually dropping into unexceptionable habits; and particularly so if they receive education. But we can very readily believe that, independent of every circumstance, there will be Gipsies who, in a great measure, always will be rogues. The law of necessity exercises a great influence over the destiny of the Gipsy race; their natural encrease is such, that, as they progress and develop, they are always pushing others out of the sphere which those further advanced occupy; so that it would not pay for all Gipsies to be rogues. There is, therefore, no alternative left to the Gipsy but to earn his bread like other men. If every Gipsy actually "helped himself" to whatever he stood in need of, it could hardly be said that the ordinary inhabitants would have anything that they could really call their own. Notwithstanding the manner how the Gipsies progress, or the origin from which they spring, it is quite sufficient for me to hold the race in respect, when I find them personally worthy of it.

As a Scotchman, as a citizen of the world, whether should my sympathies lay more with the Gipsies than with the Jews? With the Gipsies, unquestionably. For, a race, emerging from a state of barbarism, and struggling upwards to civilization, surrounded by so many difficulties, as is the Gipsy, is entitled to a world of charity and encouragement. Of the Jews, who, though blessed with the most exalted privileges, yet allowed themselves to be reduced to their present fallen and degraded estate, it may be said: "Ephraim is joined to his idols; let him alone." The Gipsies are, and have always been, a rising people, although the world may be said to have known little of them hitherto. The Gipsy, as he emerges from his wild state, makes ample amends for his original offensiveness, by hiding everything relative to his being a Gipsy from his neighbours around him. In approaching one of this class, we should be careful not to express that prejudice for him as a Gipsy, which we might have for him as a man; for it is natural enough to feel a dislike for many people whom we meet with, and which, if the people were Gipsies, we might insensibly allow to fall upon them, on account of tribe alone; so difficult is it to shake one's self clear of the prejudice of caste towards the Gipsy name. The Gipsy has naturally a happy disposition, which circumstances cannot destroy, however much they may be calculated to sour it. In their original state, they are, what Grellmann says of them, "always merry and blithe;" not apt to be surly dogs, unless made such; and are capable of considerable attachment, when treated civilly and kindly, without any attempt being made to commiserate them, and after an acquaintance has been fairly established with them. But, what are properly called their affections must, in the position which they occupy, always remain with their tribe. As for the other part of the race—those whose habits are unexceptionable—it is for us to convince them that no prejudice is entertained for them on account of their being Gipsies; but that it would rather be pleasing and interesting for us to know something of them as Gipsies, that is, about their feelings as Gipsies, and hear them talk some of this language which they have, or are supposed to have.

But how different is the position which the Jews occupy towards the rest of the world! They are, certainly, quiet and inoffensive enough as individuals, or as a community; whence, then, arises the dislike which most people have for them? The Gipsies may be said to be, in a sense, strangers amongst us, because they have never been acknowledged by us; but the Jews are, to a certain extent, strangers under any circumstances, and, more or less, look to entering Palestine at some day, it may be this year, or the following. If a Christian asks: "Who are the Jews, and what do they here?" the reply is very plain: "They are rebels against the Majesty of Heaven, and outcasts from His presence." They are certainly entitled to every privilege, social and political, which other citizens enjoy; they have a perfect right to follow their own religion; but other people have an equal right to express their opinion in regard to it and them.

The Jew is an enigma to the world, unless looked at through the light of the Old and New Testaments. In studying the history of the Jews, we will find very little about them, as a nation, that is interesting, to the extent of securing our affections, whatever may be said of some of the members of it. What appears attractive, and, I may say, of personal importance, to the Christian, in their history, is, not what they have been or done, but what has been done for them by God. "What more could I have done for my vine than I have done?" And "Which of the prophets have they not persecuted?" "Wherefore, behold! I send unto you prophets, and wise men, and scribes; and some of them ye shall kill and crucify; and some of them shall ye scourge in your synagogues, and persecute from city to city." And thus it always was. "Elias saith of them, Lord, they have killed thy prophets, and digged down thine altars, and I am left alone, and they seek my life." Indeed, the whole history of the Jews has given to infidels such occasion to rail at revelation, as has caused no little annoyance to Christians. What concerns the Christian in the Jewish history is more particularly that which refers to the ways of God, in preserving to Himself, in every generation, a seed who did not bow the knee to Baal, till the appearance of Him in whom all the nations of mankind were to be blessed. Beyond this, we find that the Jews, as a nation, have been the most rebellious, stiff-necked, perverse, ungrateful, and factious, of any recorded in history. How different from what might have been expected of them! Viewing the history of the Jews in this aspect, the mind even finds a relief in turning to profane history; but viewing their writings as the records of the dispensations of God to mankind, and they are worthy of universal reverence; although the most interesting part of them is, perhaps, that which reaches to the settlement of the race in Palestine. And to sum up, to complete, and crown the history of this singularly privileged people, previous to the destruction of their city and temple, and their dispersion among the nations, we find that the prophet whom Moses foretold them would be raised up to them, they wickedly crucified and slew; "delivering up and denying him in the presence of Pilate, when he was determined to let him go. But they denied the Holy One and the Just, and desired a murderer to be granted unto them; and killed the Prince of Life, whom God hath raised from the dead." And Pilate "washed his hands before the multitude, saying, I am innocent of the blood of this just person: see ye to it. Then answered all the people, and said, His blood be on us and on our children." And his blood is on their children at the present day; for while he is acknowledged by three hundred millions of mankind as their Lord and Master, the Jew teaches his children to regard him as an impostor, and spit at the very mention of his name. How great must be the infatuation of the poor Jew, how dark the mind, how thick the veil that hangs over his heart, how terrible the curse that rests upon his head! But the Jew is to be pitied, not distressed; he should be personally treated, in ordinary life, as his conduct merits.

The manner in which the Jew treats the claims of Jesus

Christ disqualifies him for receiving the respect of the Christian. He knows well that Christianity is no production of any Gentile, but an emanation from people of his own nation. And so conceited is the Jew in this respect, that he will say: "Jesus Christ and his apostles were Jews; see what Jews have done!" He regards the existence of his race as a miracle, yet looks with indifference upon the history and results of Christianity. People have often wondered that Jews, as Jews, have written so little on the inspiration of the Old Testament; but what else could have been expected of them? How could they throw themselves prominently forward, in urging the claims of Moses, who was "faithful in all his house as a servant," and totally ignore those of Christ, who was "a son over his own house?" So far from even entertaining the claim of the latter, the Jew proper has the most bitter hatred for the very mention of his name; he would almost, if he dared, tear out part of his Scriptures, in which the Messiah is alluded to. Does he take the trouble to give the claims of Christianity the slightest consideration? He will spit at it, but it is into his handkerchief; so much does he feel tied up in the position which he occupies in the world. He cannot say that he respects, or can respect, Christianity, whatever he may think of its morals; for, as a Jew, he must, and does, regard it as an imposture, and blindly so regards it. But all Jews are not of this description; for there are many of them who believe little in Moses or any other, or give themselves the least trouble about such matters.

The position which Jews occupy among Christians is that which they occupy among people of a different faith. They become obnoxious to people everywhere; for that which is so foreign in its origin, so exclusive in its habits and relations, and so conceited and antagonistic in its creed, will always be so, go where it may. Besides, they will not even eat what others have slain; and hold other people as impure. The very conservative nature of their creed is, to a certain extent, against them; were it aggressive, like the Christian's, with a genius to embrace *all* within its fold, it would not stir up, or permanently retain, the same ill-will toward the people who profess it; for being of that nature which retires into the corner of selfish exclusiveness, people will naturally take a greater objection to them. Then, the keen, money-making, and accumulating habits of the Jews, make them appear selfish to those around them; while the greediness, and utter want of principle, that characterize some of them, have given a bad reputation to the whole body, however unjustly it is applied to them as a race.

The circumstances attending the Jews' entry into any country, to-day, are substantially what they were before the advent of Christ; centuries before which era, they were scattered, in great numbers, over most part of the world; having synagogues, and visiting, or looking to, Jerusalem, as their home, as Catholics, in the matter of religion, have looked to Rome. In going abroad, Jews would as little contemplate forsaking their own religion, and worshipping the gods of the heathen, as do Christians, to-day, in Oriental countries; for they were as thoroughly persuaded that their religion was divine, and all others the inventions of man, as are Christians of theirs. Then, it was a religion exclusively Jewish, that is, the people following it were, with rare exceptions, exclusively Jews by nation. The ill-will which all these circumstances, and the very appearance of the people themselves, have raised against the Jews, and the persecutions, of various kinds, which have universally followed, have widened the separation between them and other people, which the genius of their religion made so imperative, and their feelings of nationality—nay, *family*—so exclusive. Before the dispersion, Palestine was their home; after the dispersion, the position and circumstances of those abroad at the time underwent no change; they would merely contemplate their nation in a new aspect—that of exiles, and consider themselves, for the time being, at home wherever they happened to be. Those that were scattered abroad, by the destruction of Jerusalem, would, in their persons, confirm the convictions of the others, and reconcile them to the idea that the Jewish nation, as such, was abroad on the face of the earth; and each generation of the race would entertain the same sentiments. After this, as before it, it can scarcely be said that the Jews have ever been tolerated; if not actually persecuted, they have, at least, always been disliked, or despised. The whole nation having been scattered abroad, with everything pertaining to them as a nation, excepting the temple, the high-priesthood, and the sacrifices, with such an ancient history, and so unequivocally divine a religion, so distinct from, and obnoxious to, those of other nations, it is no wonder that they, the common descendants of Abraham and Sarah, should have ever since remained a distinct people in the world; as all the circumstances surrounding them have universally remained the same till to-day.

A Jew of to-day has a much greater aversion to forsake the Jewish community than any other man has to renounce his country; and his associations of nationality are manifested wherever a Jewish society is to be found, or wherever he can meet with another Jew. This is the view which he takes of his race, as something distinct from his religion; for he contemplates himself as being of that people—of the same blood, features, and feelings, all children of Abraham and Sarah—that are to be found everywhere; that part of it to which he has an aversion being only such as apostatize from his religion, and more particularly such as embrace the Christian faith. In speaking of Jews, we are too apt to confine our ideas exclusively to a creed, forgetting that Jews are a race; and that Christian Jews are Jews as well as Jewish Jews. Were it possible to bring about a reformation among the Jews, by which synagogues would embrace the Christian faith, we would see Jewish Christian churches; the only difference being, that they would believe in Him whom their fathers pierced, and lay aside only such of the ceremonies of Moses as the Gospel had abrogated. If a movement of that kind were once fairly afoot, by which was presented to the Jew, his people as a community, however small it might be, there would be a great chance of his becoming a Christian, in one sense or other: he could then assume the position of a protesting Jew, holding the rest of his countrymen in error; and his own Christian-Jewish community as representing his race, as it ought to exist.

At present, the few Christian Jews find no others of their race with whom to form associations as a community; so that, to all intents and purposes, they feel as if they were a sort of outcasts, despised and hated by those of their own race, and separated from the other inhabitants by a natural law, over which neither have any control, however much they may associate with, and respect, each other. It requires a very powerful moral influence to constrain a Jew in embracing the Christian faith—almost nothing short of divine grace; and sometimes a very powerful immoral one in professing it—that which peculiarly characterizes Jews—the love of money. Were a community of Christian Jews firmly established, among whom were observed every tittle of the Jewish ceremonial, excepting such as the dispensation of Christ had positively abolished; or ever observing most of that, (circumcision, for example,) as merely characteristic of a people, without attaching to it the meaning of a service recommending themselves, in any way, to the mercy of God; and many Jews would doubtless join such a society. They could believe in Christ as their Messiah—as their prophet, priest, and king; receive baptism in His name; and depend on Him for a place of happiness in a future state of existence. To such, the injunction, as declared by St. Paul, is: "If thou shalt confess with thy mouth the Lord Jesus, and shalt believe in thine heart that God hath raised him from the dead, thou shalt be saved." (Romans x. 9.) And when they contemplate death, they might lay their heads down in peace, with the further assurance, as also declared by St. Paul: "For if we believe that Jesus died and rose again, even so them also which sleep in Jesus will God bring with him." (I Thess. iv. 14.) This is the kind of Messiah which the Jew should contemplate, and seek after. He will find his conception and birth more particularly recorded in the two first, and his death, resurrection, and ascension, more fully detailed in the two last, chapters of the Gospel according to St. Luke. A person would naturally think that a Jew would have the natural curiosity to read this wonderful book called the "New Testament;" since, at its very lowest estimate, it is, with the exception of the writings of St. Luke, altogether a production of people of his own nation. Among the Jews, there are not a few who believe in Christ, yet, more or less, appear at the synagogue. They have no objections to become "spectacles to angels;" but they are not willing to make themselves such to men, by placing themselves in that isolated position which a public profession of Christianity would necessarily lead to. But, all things considered, one is rather apt to fall into Utopian ideas in speaking of the conversion of Jews, as a body, or even as individuals, unless the grace of God, in an especial degree, accompanies the means to that end.

It is no elevated regard for the laws of Moses, or any exalted sense of the principles contained in the Old Testament, that leads a Jew to lend a deaf ear to the claims of Christianity; for his respect for them has always been indifferent, even contemptible, enough. Indeed, the Talmud, which is the Jew's gospel, may be characterized as being, in a very great part, a tissue of that which is silly and puerile, obscene and blasphemous. It is with the Jew now, as it was at the advent of Christ. "They have paid tithe of mint, and anise, and cummin, and omitted the weightier matters of the law—judgment, mercy, and faith." "Laying aside the commandment of God, they have held the tradition of men, as the washing of pots and cups, and many other such-like things;" "making the word of God of none effect through their traditions which they have delivered." "Full well have they rejected the commandments of God, that they might keep their own traditions." "In vain do they worship me, teaching for doctrines the commandments of men." The main prop of a Jew for remaining a Jew, in regard to religion, rests much more upon the wonderful phenomena connected with the history of his nation—its antiquity, its associations, its universality, and the length of time which it has existed, since its dispersion, distinct from the rest of the world, and so unique, (as he imagines,) that he at once concludes it must have the special approbation of God for the position which it occupies; which is very true, although it proceeds from a different motive than that which the Jew so vainly imagines. The Jew imagines that God approves of his conduct, in his stubborn rebellion to the claims of Christianity, because he finds his race existing so distinct from the rest of the world; whereas, if he studies his own Scriptures, he will see that the condition of his race is the punishment due to its rebellion. Who knows but that the mark which is to be found upon the Jew answers, in a sense, the purpose of that which every one found upon Cain? Did not his ancestors call a solemn imprecation upon his head, when they compelled Pilate to crucify the "just person," when he was determined to let him go; with no other excuse than, "His blood be on us, and on our children?" Will any genuine Jew repudiate the conduct of his ancestors, and say that Christ was not an impostor, that he was not a blasphemer, and that, consequently, he did not deserve, by the law of his nation, to be put to death?

The history of the Jews acts as a spell upon the unfortunate Jew, and proves the greatest bar to his conversion to Christianity. He vainly imagines that his race stands out from among all the races of mankind, by a miracle, wrought for that purpose, and with the special approbation of God upon it, for adhering to its religion; and that, therefore, Christianity is a delusion. But we must break this spell that enchants the Jew, and "provoke him to jealousy by them that are no people." And who are this people? The Gipsies? Yes, the Gipsies! For they are numerous, though not as numerous, and ancient, though not as ancient, as the Jews.*

As to the Gipsy population, scattered over the world, I think that the intelligent reader will agree with me, after all that has been said, in estimating it as very large. There seems no reason for thinking that the Gipsies suffered so greatly, by the laws passed against them, as people have imagined; for the cunning of the Gipsy, and the wild, or partly uncultivated, face of all the countries of Europe would afford him many facilities to evade the laws passed against him. We have already seen what continental writers have said of the race, relative to the laws passed against it: "But, instead of passing the boundaries, they only slunk into hiding places, and, shortly after, appeared in as great numbers as before." And this seems to have been invariably the case over the whole of Europe. Mr. Borrow, as we have already seen, speaks of every Spanish monarch, on succeeding to the crown, passing laws against the Gipsies. If former laws were put in force, there would be no occasion for making so many new ones; the very fact of so many laws having been passed against the Gipsy race, in Spain, is

* It would almost seem that the Gipsies are the people mentioned in Deut. xxxii. 21, and Rom. x. 19, where it is said: "I will provoke you, (the Jews,) to jealousy, by them that are no people, and by a foolish nation I will anger you." For the history of the Gipsy nation thoroughly burlesques that of the Jews. But the Jews will be very apt to ignore the existence of the present work, should the rest of the world allow them to do it. Yet, excepting the Gipsies themselves, none are so capable of understanding this subject as the Jews, there being so much in it that is applicable to themselves.

sufficient proof of each individual law never having been put to much execution, but rather, as has already been said, (page 394,) of its having been customary for every king of Spain to issue such against them. It does not appear that any force was employed to hunt the Gipsies out of the country, but that matters were left to the ordinary local authorities, whom the tribe would, in many instances, manage to render passive, or beyond whose jurisdiction they would remove for the time being. The laws passed against the nobility and commonalty of Spain, for protecting the Gipsies, (page 114,) is a very instructive commentary on those for the extermination of the body itself. But the case most in point is in the Scottish laws passed against the Gipsies. Upon the passing of the Act of James VI., in 1609, we find that the Gipsies "dispersed themselves in certain secret and obscure places of the country"; and that, when the storm was blown over, they "began to take new breath and courage, and unite themselves in infamous companies and societies, under commanders" (page 114). The extreme bitterness displayed in Scots acts of parliament against the best classes of the population, for protecting and entertaining the tribe, and, consequently, rendering the other acts nugatory, has a very important bearing upon the subject. We find that the Gipsies wandered up and down France for a hundred years, unmolested; and that, so numerous had they become, that, in 1545, the King of France entertained the idea of embodying four thousand of them, to act as pioneers in taking Boulogne, then in possession of England. The last notice which we have of the French Gipsies was that made by Grellmann, when he says: "In France, before the Revolution, there were but few, for the obvious reason, that every Gipsy who could be apprehended, fell a sacrifice to the police." Grellmann, however, had not studied the subject sufficiently deep to account for the destiny of the race. If they were so very numerous in France, in 1545, the natural encrease, in whatever position in life it might be, must have been very great during the following 235 years. I have learned, from the best of authority, that there are many Gipsies in Flanders.* If the

* This information I obtained from some English Gipsies. Thereafter, the title of the following work came under my notice: "Historical Researches Respecting the Sojourn of the Heathens, or Egyptians, in the

Gipsies in England were estimated at above ten thousand, during the early part of the reign of Queen Elizabeth, how many may they not be now, including those of every kind of mixture of blood, character, and position in life? If there is one Gipsy in the British Isles, there cannot be less than a quarter of a million, and, possibly, as many as six hundred thousand; and, instead of there being sixty thousand in Spain, and constantly *decreasing*, (*disappearing* is the right word,) we may safely estimate them at three hundred thousand. The reader has already been informed of what becomes of all the Gipsies. As a case in point, I may ask, who would have imagined that there was such a thing in Edinburgh as a factory, filled, not merely with Gipsies, but with *Irish* Gipsies? The owner of the establishment was doubtless a Gipsy; for how did so many Gipsies come to work in it, or how did he happen to know that his workmen were *all* Gipsies, or that even *one* of them was a Gipsy?

Even to take Grellmann's estimate of the Gipsies in Europe, at from 700,000 to 800,000, and the race must be very numerous to-day. Since his time, the Negroes in the United States have encreased from 500,000 to 4,000,000, and this much is certain, that Gipsies are, to say the least of it, as prolific as Negroes. The encrease in both includes much white blood added to the respective bodies. Some of the Gipsies have, doubtless, been hanged; but, on the other hand, many of the Negroes have been worked to death. There is a great difference, however, between the wild, independent Gipsy race and the Negroes in the New World. I should not suppose that the Gipsy race in Europe and America can be less than 4,000,000. It embraces, for certainty, as in Scotland, men ranging in character and position from a pillar of the Church down to a common tinker.*

Christians not only flatter but delude the Jew, when they say that his race is "purity itself;" they greatly flatter and

Northern Netherlands. By J. Dirks. Edited by the Provincial Utrecht Society of Arts and Sciences. Utrecht: 1850. pp. viii. and 160."

Indeed, the Gipsies are scattered all over Europe, and are to be found in the condition described in the present work.

* There are, probably, 12,000,000 of Jews in the world. I have seen them estimated at from ten to twelve millions. It is impossible to obtain anything like a correct number of the Jews, in almost any country, leaving out of view the immense numbers scattered over the world, and living even in parts unexplored by Europeans.

delude him, when they say that the phenomenon of its existence, since the dispersion, is miraculous. There is nothing miraculous about it. There is nothing miraculous about the perpetuation of Quakerdom; yet Quakerdom has existed for two centuries. Although Quakerdom is but an artificial thing, that proceeded out from among common English people, it has somewhat the appearance of being a distinct race, among those surrounding it. As such, it appears, at first sight, to inexperienced youth, or people who have never seen, or perhaps heard, much of Quakers. But how much greater is the difference between Jews and Christians, than between Quakers and ordinary Englishmen, and Americans! And how much greater the certainty that Jews will keep themselves distinct from Christians, and all others in the world! It must be self-evident to the most unreflecting person, that the natural causes which keep Jews separated from other people, during one generation, continue to keep them distinct during every other generation. A miracle, indeed! We must look into the Old and New Testaments for miracles. A Jew will naturally delude himself about the existence of his race, since the dispersion, being a miracle; yet not believe upon a person, if he were even to rise from the dead! A little consideration of the philosophy of the Jewish question will teach us that, perhaps, the best way for Providence to preserve the Jews, as they have existed since their dispersion, would have been merely to leave them alone—leave them to their impenitence and unbelief—and take that much care of them that is taken of ravens.

The subject of the Gipsies is a mine which Christians should work, so as to countermine and explode the conceit of the Jew in the history of his people; for that, as I have already said, is the greatest bar to his conversion to Christianity. Still, it is possible that some people may oppose the idea that the Gipsies are the "mixed multitude" of the Exodus, from some such motive as that which induces others not merely to disbelieve, but revile, and even rave at some of the clear points of revelation.* What objection could

* It is astonishing how superficially some passages of Scripture are interpreted. There is, for instance, the conduct of Gamaliel, before the Jewish council. (Acts v. 17–40.) The advice given by him, as a Pharisee, was nothing but a piece of specious party clap-trap, to discomfit a Sadducee. St. Paul, who was brought up at the feet of this Pharisee, and, doubtless,

any one advance against the Gipsies being the people that left Egypt, in the train of the Jews? Not, certainly, an objection as to race; for there must have been many captive people, or tribes, introduced into Egypt, from the many countries surrounding it. Pharaoh was a czar in his day, transplanting people at his pleasure. Of one of his cities it was said,

> "That spreads her conquests o'er a thousand states,
> And pours her heroes through a hundred gates:
> Two hundred horsemen, and two hundred cars,
> From each wide portal, issuing to the wars."

That the "mixed multitude" travelled into India, acquired the language of that part of Asia, and, perhaps, modified its appearance there, and became the origin of the Gipsy race, we may very safely assume. This much is certain, that they are not Sudras, but a very ancient tribe, distinct from every other in the world. With the exception of the Jews, we have no certainty of the origin of any people; in every other case it is conjecture; even the Hungarians know nothing of their origin; and it is not wonderful that it should be the same with the Gipsies. Everything harmonizes so beautifully with the idea that the Gipsies are the "mixed multitude" of the Exodus, that it may be admitted by the world. Even in the matter of religion, we could imagine

well versed in the factious tactics of his party, gives a beautiful commentary on the action of his old master, when, on being brought before the same tribunal, and perceiving that his enemies embraced both parties, he set them by the ears, by proclaiming himself a Pharisee, and raising the question, (the "hope and resurrection of the dead,") on which they so bitterly disagreed. (Acts xxiii. 6–10.) There was much adroitness displayed by the Apostle, in so turning the wrath of his enemies against themselves, after having inadvertently reviled the high priest, in their presence, and within one of the holy places, in such language as the following: "God shall smite thee, thou whited wall: for sittest thou to judge me after the law, and commandest me to be smitten, contrary to the law." As it was, he was only saved from being "pulled in pieces" by his blood-thirsty persecutors—the one sect attacking, and the other defending him—by a company of Roman soldiers, dispatched to take him by force from among them. Nothing could be more specious than Gamaliel's reasoning, for it could apply to almost anything, and was well suited to the feelings of a divided and excited assembly; or have less foundation, according to his theory, for the very steps which he advised the people against adopting, for the suppression of Christians, were used to destroy the false Messiahs to whom he referred. And yet people quote this recorded clap-trap of an old Pharisee, as an inspiration, for the guidance of private Christians, and Christian magistrates!

Egyptian captives losing a knowledge of their religion, as has happened with the Africans in the New World, and, not having had another taught them, leaving Egypt under Moses, without any religion at all.* After entering India, they would, in all probability, become a wandering people, and, for a certainty, live aloof from all others.

While the history of the Jews, since the dispersion, greatly illustrates that of the Gipsies, so does the history of the Gipsies greatly illustrate that of the Jews. They greatly resemble each other. Jews shuffle, when they say that the only difference between an Englishman and an English Jew, is in the matter of creed; for there is a great difference between the two, whatever they may have in common, as men born and reared on the same soil. The very appearance of the two is palpable proof that they are not of the same race. The Jew invariably, and unavoidably, holds his "nation" to mean the Jewish people, scattered over the world; and is reared in the idea that he is, not only in creed, but in blood, distinct from other men; and that, in blood and creed, he is not to amalgamate with them, let him live where he may. Indeed, what England is to an Englishman, this universally scattered people is to the Jew; what the history of England is to an Englishman, the Bible is to the Jew; his nation being nowhere in particular, but everywhere, while its ultimate destiny he, more or less, believes to be Palestine. Now, an Englishman has not only been born an Englishman, but his mind has been cast in a mould that makes him an Englishman; so that, to persecute him, on the ground of his being an Englishman, is to persecute him for that which can never be changed. It is precisely so with the Jew. His creed does not amount to much, for it is only part of the history of his race, or the law of his nation, traced to, and emanating from, one God, and Him the true God, as distinguished from the gods and lords many of other nations: such is the nature of the Jewish theocracy. To persecute a Gipsy, for being a Gipsy, would likewise be to persecute him for that which he could not help; for to prevent a person being a

* Tacitus makes Caius Cassius, in the time of Nero, say: "At present, we have in our service whole nations of slaves, the scum of mankind, collected from all quarters of the globe; a race of men who bring with them foreign rites, and the religion of their country, *or, probably, no religion at all*."—*Murphy's Translation.*

Gipsy, in the most important sense of the word, it would be necessary to take him, when an infant, and rear him entirely apart from his own race, so that he should never hear the "wonderful story," nor have his mind filled with the Gipsy electric fluid. An English Gipsy went abroad, very young, as a soldier, and was many years from home, without having had a Gipsy companion, so that he had almost forgotten that he was a Gipsy; but, on his returning home, other Gipsies applied their magnetic battery to him, and gipsyfied him over again. A town Gipsy will occasionally send a child to a Gipsy hedge-schoolmaster, for the purpose of being extra gipsyfied.

The being a Gipsy, or a Jew, or a Gentile, consists in birth and rearing. The three may be born and brought up under one general roof, members of their respective nationalities, yet all good Christians. But the Jew, by becoming a Christian, necessarily cuts himself off from associations with the representative part of his nation; for Jews do not tolerate those who forsake the synagogue, and believe in Christ, as the Messiah having come; however much they may respect their children, who, though born into the Christian Church, and believing in its doctrines, yet maintain the inherent affection for the associations connected with the race, and more especially if they also occupy distinguished positions in life. So intolerant, indeed, are Jews of each other, in the matter of each choosing his own religion, extending sometimes to assassination in some countries, and invariably to the cruelest persecutions in families, that they are hardly justified in asking, and scarcely merit, toleration for themselves, as a people, from the nations among whom they live. The present D'Israeli doubtless holds himself to be a Jew, let his creed or Christianity be what it may; if he looks at himself in his mirror, he cannot deny it. We have an instance in the Cappadoce family becoming, and remaining for several generations, Christians, then returning to the synagogue, and, in another generation, joining the Christian church. The same vicissitude may attend future generations of this family. There should be no great obstacle in the way of it being allowed to pass current in the world, like any other fact, that a person can be a Jew and, at the same time, a Christian; as we say that a man can be an Englishman and a Christian, a McGregor and a Christian, a Gipsy and a Christian, or a Jew and a Christian, even should he not know when his ancestors attended the synagogue. Christianity was not intended, nor is it capable, to destroy the nationality of Jews, as individuals, or as a nation, any more than that of other people. We may even assume that a person, having a Jew for one parent, and a Christian for another, and professing the Christian faith, and having the influences of the Jew exercised over him from his infancy, cannot fail, with his blood and, it may be, physiognomy, to have feelings peculiar to the Jews; although he may believe them as blind, in the matter of religion, as do other Christians. But separate him, after the death of the Jewish parent, from all associations with Jews, and he may gradually lose those peculiarly Jewish feelings that are inseparable from a Jewish community, however small it may be. There are, then, no circumstances, out of and independent of himself and the other members of his family, to constitute him a Jew; and still less can it be so with his children, when they marry with ordinary Christians, and never come in intimate contact with Jews. The Jewish feeling may be ultimately crossed out in this way; I say ultimately, for it does not take place in the first descent, (and that is as far as my personal knowledge goes,) even although the mother is an ordinary Christian, and the children have been brought up exclusively to follow her religion.

Gipsydom, however, goes with the individual, and keeps itself alive in the family, and the private associations of life, let its creed be what it may; the original cast of mind, words, and signs, always remaining with itself. In this respect, the Gipsy differs from every other man. He cannot but know who he is to start life with, nor can he forget it; he has those words and signs within himself which, as he moves about in the world, he finds occasion to use. A Jew may boast of the peculiar cast of countenance by which his race is generally characterized, and how his nation is kept together by a common blood, history, and creed. But the phenomenon connected with the history of the Gipsy race is more wonderful than that which is connected with the Jewish; inasmuch as, let the blood of the Gipsy become as much mixed as it may, it always preserves its Gipsy identity; although it may not have the least outward resemblance to an original Gipsy. You cannot crush or cross out the Gipsy race; so thoroughly subtle, so thoroughly adaptable, so thoroughly capable, is it to evade every weapon that can be forged against it. The Gipsy soul, in whatever condition it may be found, or whatever may be the tabernacle which it may inhabit, is as independent, now, of those laws which regulate the disappearance of certain races among others, as when it existed in its wild state, roaming over the heath. The Gipsy race, in short, absorbs, but cannot be absorbed by, other races.

In my associations with Gipsies and Jews, I find that both races rest upon the same basis, viz.: a question of people. The response of the one, as to who he is, is that he is a Gipsy; and of the other, that he is a Jew. Each of them has a peculiarly original soul, that is perfectly different from each other, and others around them; a soul that passes as naturally and unavoidably into each succeeding generation of the respective races, as does the soul of the English or any other race into each succeeding generation. For each considers his nation as abroad upon the face of the earth; which circumstance will preserve its existence amid all the revolutions to which ordinary nations are subject. As they now exist within, and independent of, the nations among whom they live, so will they endure, if these nations were to disappear under the subjection of other nations, or become incorporated with them under new names. Many of the Gipsies and Jews might perish amid such convulsions, but those that survived would constitute the stock of their respective nations; while others might migrate from other countries, and contribute to their numbers. In the case of the Gipsy nation, as it gets crossed with common blood, the issue shows the same result as does the shaking of the needle on the card—it always turns to the pole: that pole, among the Gipsies, being a sense of its blood, and a sympathy with the same people in every part of the world. For this reason, the Gipsy race, like the Jewish, may, with regard to its future, be said to be even eternal.

The Gipsy soul is fresh and original, not only from its recent appearance in Europe, without any traditional knowledge of its existence any where else, but from having sprung from so singular an origin as a tent; so that the mystery that attaches to it, from these causes, and the contemplation of the Gipsy, in his original state, to-day, present to the

Gipsy that fascination for his own history which the Jew finds in the antiquity of his race, and the exalted privileges with which it was at one time visited. The civilized Gipsy looks upon his ancestors, as they appeared in Europe generally, and Scotland especially, as great men, as heroes who scorned the company of anything below a gentleman. And he is not much out of the way; for John Faw, and Towla Bailyow, and the others mentioned in the act of 1540, were unquestionably heroes of the first water. He pictures to himself these men as so many swarthy, slashing heroes, dressed in scarlet and green, armed with pistols and broadswords, mounted on blood-horses, with hawks and hounds in their train. True to nature, every Gipsy is delighted with his descent, no matter what other people, in their ignorance of the subject, may think of it, or what their prejudices may be in regard to it. One of the principal differences to be drawn between the history of the Gipsies and that of the Jews, is, as I have already stated, that the Jews left Palestine a civilized people, while the Gipsies entered Europe, in the beginning of the fifteenth century, in a barbarous state. But the difference is only of a relative nature; for when the Gipsies emerge from their original condition, they occupy as good positions in the world as the Jews; while they have about them none of those outward peculiarities of the Jews, that make them, in a manner, offensive to other people. In every sense but that of belonging to the Gipsy tribe, they are ordinary natives; for the circumstances that have formed the character of the ordinary natives have formed theirs. Besides this, there is a degree of dignity about the general bearing of such people, rough as it sometimes is, that plainly shows that they are no common fellows, at least that they do not hold themselves to be such. For it is to be remarked, that such people do not directly apply to themselves the prejudice which exists towards what the world understands to be Gipsies; however much they may infer that such would be directed against them, should the world discover that they belonged to the tribe. In this respect, they differ from Jews, all of whom apply to themselves the prejudice of the rest of their species; which exercises so depressing an influence upon the character of a people. Indeed, one will naturally look for certain general superior points of character in a man who has fairly emerged from a wild and barbarous state, which he will not be so apt to find in another who has fallen from a higher position in the scale of nations, which the Jew has unquestionably done. A Jew, no matter what he thinks of the long-gone-by history of his race, looks upon it, now, as a fallen people; while the Gipsy has that subdued but, at heart, consequential, extravagance of ideas, springing from the wild independence and vanity of his ancestors, which frequently finds a vent in a lavish and foolish expenditure, so as not to be behind others in his liberality. A very good idea of such a cast of character may be formed from that of the superior class of Gipsies mentioned by our author, when the descendants of such have been brought up under more favourable circumstances, and enjoyed all the advantages of the ordinary natives of the country.

In considering the phenomenon of the existence of the Jews since the dispersion, I am not inclined to place it on any other basis than I would that of the Gipsies; for, with both, it is substantially a question of people. They are a people, scattered over the world, like the Gipsies, and have a history—the Bible, which contains both their history and their laws; and these two contain their religion. It would, perhaps, be more correct to say, that the religion of the Jews is to be found in the Talmud, and the other human compositions, for which the race have such a superstitious reverence; and even these are taken as interpreted by the Rabbis. A Jew has, properly speaking, little of a creed. He believes in the existence of God, and in Moses, his prophet, and observes certain parts of the ceremonial law, and some holidays, commemorative of events in the history of his people. He is a Jew, in the first place, as a simple matter of fact, and, as he grows up, he is made acquainted with the history of his race, to which he becomes strongly attached. He then holds himself to be one of the "first-born of the Lord," one of the "chosen of the Eternal," one of the "Lord's aristocracy;" expressions of amazing import, in his worldly mind, that will lead him to almost die for his *faith;* while his *religion* is of a very low natural order, "standing only in meats and drinks, and divers washings, and carnal ordinances," suitable for a people in a state of pupilage. The Jewish mind, in the matter of religion, is, in some respects, preëminently gross and material in its nature; its idea of a Messiah rising no higher than a conqueror of its own race, who will bring the whole world under his sway, and parcel out, among his fellow-Jews, a lion's share of the spoils, consisting of such things as the inferior part of human nature so much craves for. And his ideas of how this Messiah is to be connected with the original tribes, as mentioned in the prophecies, are childish and superstitious in the extreme. Writers do, therefore, greatly err, when they say, that it is only a thin partition that separates Judaism from Christianity. There is almost as great a difference between the two, as there is between that which is material, and that which is spiritual. A Jew is so thoroughly bound, heart and soul, by the spell which the phenomena of his race exert upon him, that, humanly speaking, it is impossible to make anything of him in the matter of Christianity. And herein, in his own way of thinking, consists his peculiar glory. Such being the case with Christianity, it is not to be supposed that the Jew would forsake his own religion, and, of course, his own people, and believe in any religion having an origin in the spontaneous and gradual growth of superstition and imposture, modified, systematized, adorned, or expanded, by ambitious and superior minds, or almost wholly in the conceptions of these minds; having, for a foundation, an instinct—an intellectual and emotional want—as common to man, as instinct is to the brute creation, for the ends which it has to serve. We cannot separate the questions of race and belief, when we consider the Jews as a people, however it might be with individuals among them. It was as unreasonable to persecute a Jew, for not giving up his feelings as a Jew, and his religion, for the superstitions and impostures of Rome, as it was to persecute a Gipsy, for not giving up his feelings of nationality, and his language, as was specially attempted by Charles III., of Spain: for such are inherent in the respective races. The worst that can be said of any Gipsy, in the matter of religion, is, when we meet with one who admits that all that he really cares for is, "to get a good belly-full, and to feel comfortable o' nights." Here, we have an original soil to be cultivated; a soil that *can* be cultivated, if we only go the right way about doing it. Out of such a man, there is no other spirit to be cast, but that of "the world, the flesh, and the devil," before another can take up its habitation in his mind. Bigoted as is the Jew against even entertaining the claims of Christ, as the Messiah, he is very indifferent to the practice, or even the knowledge, of his own religion, where he is tolerated and well-treated, as in the United States of America. Of the growing-up, or even the grown-up, Jews in that country, the ultra-Jewish organ, the "Jewish Messenger," of New York, under date the 19th October, 1860, says that, "with the exception of a very few, who are really taught their religion, the great majority, we regret to state, know no more of their faith than the veriest heathen:" and, I might add, practise less of it; for, as a people, they pay very little regard to it, in general, or to the Sabbath, in particular, but are characterized as worldly beyond measure; having more to answer for than the Gipsy, whose sole care is "a good meal, and a comfortable crib at night."*

Amid all the obloquy and contempt cast upon his race, amid all the persecutions to which it has been exposed, the Jew, with his inherent conceit in having Abraham for his father, falls back upon the history of his nation, with the utmost contempt for everything else that is human; forgetting that there is such a thing as the "first being last." He boasts that his race, and his only, is eternal, and that all other men get everything from *him!* He vainly imagines that the Majesty of Heaven should have made his dispensations to mankind conditional upon anything so unworthy as his race has so frequently shown itself to be. If he has been so favoured by God, what can he point to as the fruits of so much loving-kindness shown him? What is his nation now, however numerous it may be, but a ruin, and its members, but spectres that haunt it? And what has brought it to its present condition? "Its sins." Doubtless, its sins; but what particular sins? And how are these sins to be

* The following extract from "Leaves from the Diary of a Jewish Minister," published in the above-mentioned journal, on the 4th April, 1862, may not be uninteresting to the Christian reader:

"In our day, the conscience of Israel is seldom troubled; it is of so elastic a character, that, like gutta percha, it stretches and is compressed, according to the desire of its owner. We seldom hear of a troubled conscience. . . . . Not that we would assert that our people are without a conscience; we merely state that we seldom hear of its troubles. It is more than probable, that when the latent feeling is aroused on matters of religion, and for a moment they have an idea that 'their soul is not well,' they take a homœopathic dose of spiritual medicine, and then feel quite convalescent."

put away, seeing that the temple, the high-priesthood, and the sacrifices no longer exist? Or what effort, by such means as offer, has ever been made to mitigate the wrath of God, and prevail upon Him to restore the people to their exalted privileges? Or what could they even propose doing, to bring about that event? Questions like these involve the Jewish mind in a labyrinth of difficulties, from which it cannot extricate itself. The dispersion was not only foretold, but the cause of it given. The Scriptures declare that the Messiah was to have appeared before the destruction of the temple; and the time of his expected advent, according to Jewish traditions, coincided with that event. It is eighteen centuries since the destruction of the temple, before which the Messiah was to have come; and the Jew still "hopes against hope," and, if it is left to himself, will do so till the day of judgment, for such a Messiah as his earthly mind seems to be only capable of contemplating. Has he never read the New Testament, and reflected on the sufferings of him who was meek and lowly, or on those of his disciples, inflicted by his ancestors, for generations, when he has come complaining of the sufferings to which his race has been exposed? He is entitled to sympathy, for all the cruelties with which his race has been visited; but he could ask it with infinitely greater grace, were he to offer any for the sufferings of the early Christians and their divine master, or were he, even, to tolerate any of his race following him to-day.

What has the Jew got to say to all this? He cannot now say that his main comfort and support, in his unbelief, consists in his contemplating what he vainly calls a miracle, wrapt up in the history of his people, since the dispersion. That prop and comfort are gone. No, O Jew! the true miracle, if miracle there is, is your impenitent unbelief. No one asks you to disbelieve in Moses, but, in addition to believing in Moses, to believe on him of whom Moses wrote. Do you really believe in Moses? You, doubtless, believe after a sort; you believe in Moses, as any other person believes in the history of his own country and people; but your belief in Moses goes little further. You glory in the antiquity of your race, and imagine that every other has perished. No, O Jew! the "mixed multitude" which left Egypt, under Moses, separated from him, and passed into

India, has come up, in these latter times, again to vex you. Even it is entering, it may be, pressing, into the Kingdom of God, and leaving you out of it. Yes! the people from the "hedges and by-ways" are submitting to the authority of the true Messiah; while you, in your infatuated blindness, are denying him.

What may be termed the philosophy of the Gipsies, is very simple in itself, when we have before us its main points, its principles, its bearings, its genius; and fully appreciated the circumstances with which the people are surrounded. The most remarkable thing about the subject is, that people never should have dreamt of its nature, but, on the contrary, believed that "the Gipsies are gradually disappearing, and will soon become extinct." The Gipsies have always been disappearing, but where do they go to? Look at any tent of Gipsies, when the family are all together, and see how prolific they are. What, then, becomes of this encrease? The present work answers the question. It is a subject, however, which I have found some difficulty in getting people to understand. One cannot see how a person can be a Gipsy, "because his father was a respectable man;" another, "because his father was an old soldier;" and another cannot see "how it necessarily follows that a person is a Gipsy, for the reason that his parents were Gipsies." The idea, as disconnected from the use of a tent, or following a certain kind of life, may be said to be strange to the world; and, on that account, is not very easily impressed on the human mind. It would be singular, however, if a Scotchman, after all that has been said, should not be able to understand what is meant by the Scottish Gipsy tribe, or that it should ever cease to be that tribe as it progresses in life. In considering the subject, he need not cast about for much to look at, for he should exercise his mind, rather than his eyes, when he approaches it. It is, principally, a mental phenomenon, and should, therefore, be judged of by the faculties of the mind: for a Gipsy may not differ a whit from an ordinary native, in external appearance or character, while, in his mind, he may be as thorough a Gipsy as one could well imagine.

In contemplating the subject of the Gipsies, we should have a regard for the facts of the question, and not be led by what we might, or might not, imagine of it; for the latter course would be characteristic of people having the moral and intellectual traits of children. The race might, to a certain extent, be judged analogously, by what we know of other races; but that which is pre-eminently necessary, is to judge of it by facts: for facts, in a matter like this, take precedence of everything. Even in regard to the Gipsy language, broken as it is, people are very apt to say that it *cannot* exist at the present day; yet the least reflection will convince us, that the language which the Gipsies use is the remains of that which they brought with them into Europe, and not a make-up, to serve their purposes. The very genius peculiar to them, as an Oriental people, is a sufficient guarantee of this fact; and the more so from their having been so thoroughly separated, by the prejudice of caste, from others around them; which would so naturally lead them to use, and retain, their peculiar speech. But the use of the Gipsy language is not the only, not even the principal, means of maintaining a knowledge of being Gipsies; perhaps it is altogether unnecessary; for the mere consciousness of the fact of being Gipsies, transmitted from generation to generation, and made the basis of marriages, and the intimate associations of life, is, in itself, perfectly sufficient. The subject of two distinct races, existing upon the same soil, is not very familiar to the mind of a British subject. To acquire a knowledge of such a phenomenon, he should visit certain parts of Europe, or Asia, or Africa, or the New World. Since all (I may say all) Gipsies hide the knowledge of their being Gipsies from the other inhabitants, as they leave the tent, it cannot be said that any of them really deny themselves, even should they hide themselves from those of their own race. The ultimate test of a person being a Gipsy would be for another to catch the internal response of his mind to the question put to him as to the fact; or observe the workings of his heart in his contemplations of himself. It can hardly be said that any Gipsy denies, at heart, the fact of his being a Gipsy, (which, indeed, is a contradiction in terms,) let him disguise it from others as much as he may. If I could find such a man, he would be the only one of his race whom I would feel inclined to despise as such.

From all that has been said, the reader can have no difficulty in believing, with me, as a question beyond doubt, that the immortal John Bunyan was a Gipsy of mixed blood. He was a tinker. And who were the tinkers? Were there any itinerant tinkers in England, before the Gipsies settled there? It is doubtful. In all likelihood, articles requiring to be tinkered were carried to the nearest smithy. The Gipsies are all tinkers, either literally, figuratively, or representatively. Ask any English Gipsy, of a certain class, what he can do, and, after enumerating several occupations, he will add: "I can tinker, of course," although he may know little or nothing about it. Tinkering, or travelling-smith work, is the Gipsy's representative business, which he brought with him into Europe. Even the intelligent and respectable Scottish Gipsies speak of themselves as belonging to the "tinker tribe." The Gipsies in England, as in Scotland, divided the country among themselves, under representative chiefs, and did not allow any other Gipsies to enter upon their walks or beats. Considering that the Gipsies in England were estimated at above ten thousand during the early part of the reign of Queen Elizabeth, we can readily believe that they were much more numerous during the time of Bunyan. Was there, therefore, a pot or a kettle, in the rural parts of England, to be mended, for which there was not a Gipsy ready to attend to it? If a Gipsy would not tolerate any of his own race entering upon his district, was he likely to allow any native? If there were native tinkers in England before the Gipsies settled there, how soon would the latter, with their organization, drive every one from the trade by sheer force! What thing more like a Gipsy? Among the Scotch, we find, at a comparatively recent time, that the Gipsies actually murdered a native, for infringing upon what they considered one of their prerogatives—that of gathering rags through the country.

Lord Macaulay says, with reference to Bunyan: "The tinkers then formed a hereditary caste, which was held in no high estimation. They were generally vagrants and pilferers, and were often confounded with the Gipsies, whom, in truth, they nearly resembled." I would like to know on what authority his lordship makes such an assertion; what he knows about the origin of this "*hereditary* tinker caste," and if it still exists; and whether he holds to the purity-of-Gipsy-blood idea, advanced by the Edinburgh Review and

Blackwood's Magazine, but especially the former. How would he account for the existence of a hereditary caste of any kind, in England, and that just one—the "tinker caste"? There was no calling at that time hereditary in England, that I know of; and yet Bunyan was born a tinker. In Scotland, the collier and salter castes were hereditary, for they were in a state of slavery to the owners of these works.* But who ever heard of any native occupation, so free as tinkering, being hereditary in England, in the seventeenth century? Was not this "tinker caste," at that time, exactly the same that it is now? If it was then hereditary, is it not so now? If not, by what means has it ceased to be hereditary? The tinkers existed in England, at that time, exactly as they do now. And who are they now but mixed Gipsies? It is questionable, very questionable indeed, if we will find, in all England, a tinker who is not a Gipsy. The class will deny it; the purer and more original kind of Gipsies will also deny it; still, they are Gipsies. They are all *chabos*, *calos*, or *chals*; but they will play upon the word Gipsy in its ideal, purity-of-blood sense, and deny that they are Gipsies. We will find in Lavengro two such Gipsies—the Flaming Tinman, and Jack Slingsby; the first, a half-blood, (which did not necessarily imply that either parent was white;) and the other, apparently, a very much mixed Gipsy. The tinman termed Slingsby a "mumping villain." Now, "mumper," among the English Gipsies, is an expression for a Gipsy whose blood is very much mixed. When Mr. Borrow used the word *Petulengro*,† Slingsby started, and exclaimed: "Young man, you know a thing or two." I have used the same word with English Gipsies, causing the same surprise; on one occasion, I was told: "You must be a Scotch Gipsy yourself." "Well," I replied, "I may be as good a Gipsy as any of you, for anything you may know." "That may be so," was the answer I got. Then Slingsby was very careful to mention to Lavengro that his *wife* was a white, or Christian, woman; a thing not necessarily true because he asserted it, but it implied that *he* was different. These are but instances of, I might say, all the English tin-

* See pages 111 and 121.

† *Petul*, according to Mr. Borrow, means a horse-shoe; and *Petulengro*, a lord of the horse-shoe. It is evidently a very high catch-word among the English Gipsies.

kers. Almost every old countrywoman about the Scottish Border knows that the Scottish tinkers are Gipsies.*

* Various of the characters mentioned in Mr. Borrow's "Lavengro," and "Romany Rye," are, beyond doubt, Gipsies. Old Fulcher is termed, in a derisive manner, by Ursula, "a *gorgio* and basket-maker." She is one of the Hernes; a family which *gorgio* and basket-maker Gipsies describe as "an ignorant, conceited set, who think nothing of other Gipsies, owing to the quality and quantity of their own blood." This is the manner in which the more original and pure and the other kind of English Gipsies frequently talk of each other. The latter will deny that they are Gipsies, at least hide it from the world; and, like the same kind of Scottish Gipsies, speak of the others, exclusively, as Gipsies. I am acquainted with a fair-haired English Gipsy, whose wife, now dead, was a half-breed. "But I am not a Gipsy," said he to me, very abruptly, before I had said anything that could have induced him to think that I took him for one. He spoke Gipsy, like the others. I soon caught him tripping; for, in speaking of the size of Gipsy families, he slipped his foot, and said: "For example, there is our family; there were (so many) of us." There is another Gipsy, a neighbour, who passes his wife off to the public as an Irish woman, while she is a fair-haired Irish Gipsy. Both, in short, played upon the word Gipsy; for, as regards fullness of blood, they really were not Gipsies.

The dialogue between the Romany Rye and the Horncastle jockey clearly shows the Gipsy in the latter, when his attention is directed to the figure of the Hungarian. The Romany Rye makes indirect reference to the Gipsies, and the jockey abruptly asks: "Who be they? Come, don't be ashamed. I have occasionally kept queerish company myself." "Romany *chals!* Whew! I begin to smell a rat." The remainder of the dialogue, and the *spree* which follows, are perfectly Gipsy throughout, on the part of the jockey; but, like so many of his race, he is evidently ashamed to own himself up to be "one of them." He says, in a way as if he were a stranger to the language: "And what a singular language they have got!" "Do you know anything of it?" said the Romany Rye. "Only a very few words; they were always chary in teaching me any." He said he was brought up with the *gorgio* and basket-maker Fulcher, who followed the caravan. He is described as dressed in a coat of green, (a favourite Gipsy colour,) and as having curly brown or black hair; and he says of Mary Fulcher, whom he married: "She had a fair complexion, and nice red hair, both of which I liked, being a bit of a black myself." How much this is in keeping with the Gipsies, who so frequently speak of each other, in a jocular way, as "brown and black rascals!"

I likewise claim Isopel Berners, in Lavengro, to be a *thumping* Gipsy lass, who travelled the country with her donkey-cart, taking her own part, and *wapping* this one, and *wapping* that one. It signifies not what her appearance was. I have frequently taken tea, at her house, with a young, blue-eyed, English Gipsy widow, perfectly English in her appearance, who spoke Gipsy freely enough. It did not signify what Isopel said of herself, or her relations. How did she come to speak Gipsy? Do Gipsies *teach* their language to *strangers*, and, more especially, to strange women? Assuredly not. Suppose that Isopel was not a Gipsy, but had married a Gipsy, then I could understand how she might have known Gipsy, and yet not have been a Gipsy, except by initiation. But it is utterly improbable that she, a strange woman, should have been taught a word of it.

In England are to be found Gipsies of many occupations; horse-dealers,

The prejudice against the name of Gipsy was apparently as great in Bunyan's time as in our own; and there was, evidently, as great a timidity, on the part of mixed, fair-haired Gipsies, to own the blood then, as now; and great danger, for then it was hangable to be a Gipsy, by the law of Queen Elizabeth, and "felony without benefit of clergy," for "any person, being fourteen years, whether natural born subject or stranger, who had been seen in the fellowship of such persons, or disguised like them, and remained with them one month, at once, or at several times." When the name of Gipsy, and every association connected with it, were so severely proscribed by law, what other name would the tribe go under but that of tinkers—their own proper occupation? Those only would be called Gipsies whose appearance indicated the pure, or nearly pure, Gipsy. Although there was no necessity, under any circumstances, for Bunyan to say that he was a Gipsy, and still less in the face of the law proscribing, so absolutely, the race, and every one countenancing it, he evidently wished the fact to be understood, or, I should rather say, took it for granted, that part of the public knew of it, when he said: "For my descent, it was, as is well known to many, of a low and inconsiderable generation; my father's house being of that rank that is meanest and most despised of all the families of the land." Of whom does Bunyan speak here, if not of the Gipsies? He says, of *all* the families of the land. And he adds: "After I had been thus for some considerable time, another thought came

livery stable-keepers, public-house keepers, sometimes grocers and linen-drapers; indeed, almost every occupation from these downwards. I can readily enough believe an English Gipsy, when he tells me, that he knows of an English squire a Gipsy. To have an English squire a Gipsy, might have come about even in this way: Imagine a rollicking or eccentric English squire taking up with, and marrying, say, a pretty mixed Gipsy bar or lady's maid, and the children would be brought up Gipsies, for certainty.

There are two Gipsies, of the name of B———, farmers upon the estate of Lord Lister, near Massingham, in the county of Norfolk. They are described as good-sized, handsome men, and swarthy, with long black hair, combed over their shoulders. They dress in the old Gipsy stylish fashion, with a green cut-away, or Newmarket, coat, yellow leather breeches, buttoned to the knee, and top boots, with a Gipsy hat, ruffled breast, and turned-down collar. They occupy the position of any natives in society; attend church, take an interest in parish matters, dine with his lordship's other tenants, and compete for prizes at the agricultural shows. They are proud of being Gipsies. I have also been told that there are Gipsies in the county of Kent, who have hop farms and dairies.

into my mind, and that was, whether we, (his family and relatives,) were of the Israelites or no? For, finding in the Scriptures, that they were once the peculiar people of God, thought I, if I were one of this race, (how significant is the expression!) my soul must needs be happy. Now, again, I found within me a great longing to be resolved about this question, but could not tell how I should; at last, I asked my father of it, who told me, No, we, (his father included,) were not."* I have heard the same question put by Gipsy lads to their parent, (a very much mixed Gipsy,) and it was answered thus: "We must have been among the Jews, for some of our ceremonies are like theirs." The best commentary that can be passed on the above extracts from Bunyan's autobiography, will be found in our author's account of his visit to the old Gipsy chief, whose acquaintance he made at St. Boswell's fair, and to which the reader is referred, (pages 309–318.) When did we ever hear of an *ordinary Englishman* taking so much trouble to ascertain whether he was a *Jew*, or not? No Englishman, it may be safely asserted, ever does that, or has ever done it; and no one in England could have done it, during Bunyan's time, but a Gipsy. Bunyan seems to have been more or less acquainted with the history of the Jews, and how they were scattered over the world, though not publicly known to be in England, from which country they had been for centuries banished. About the time in question, the re-admission of the Jews was much canvassed in ecclesiastical as well as political circles, and ultimately carried, by the exertions of Manasseh Ben Israel, of Amsterdam. Under these circumstances, it was very natural for Bunyan to ask himself whether he belonged to the Jewish race, since he had evidently never seen a Jew; and that the more especially, as the Scottish Gipsies have even believed themselves to be Ethiopians. Such a question is entertained, by the Gipsies, even

* Bunyan adds: "But, notwithstanding the meanness and inconsiderableness of my parents, it pleased God to put it into their hearts to put me to school, to learn me both to read and write; the which I also attained, according to the rate of other poor men's children."

He does not say, "According to the rate of poor men's children," but of "*other* poor men's children:" a form of expression always used by the Gipsies when speaking of themselves, as distinguished from others. The language used by Bunyan, in speaking of his family, was in harmony with that of the population at large; but he, doubtless, had the feelings peculiar to all the tribe, with reference to their origin and race.

at the present day; for they naturally think of the Jews, and wonder whether, after all, their race may not, at some time, have been connected with them. How trifling it is for any one to assert, that Bunyan—a common native of England—while in a state of spiritual excitement, imagined that he was a Jew, and that he should, at a mature age, have put anything so absurd in his autobiography, and in so grave a manner as he did!

Southey, in his life of Bunyan, writes: "Wherefore this (tinkering) should have been so mean and despised a calling, is not, however, apparent, when it was not followed as a vagabond employment, but, as in this case, exercised by one who had a settled habitation, and who, mean as his condition was, was nevertheless able to put his son to school, in an age when very few of the poor were taught to read and write." The fact is, that Bunyan's father had, apparently, a town beat, which would give him a settled residence, prevent him using a tent, and lead him to conform with the ways of the ordinary inhabitants; but, doubtless, he had his pass from the chief of the Gipsies for the district. The same may be said of John Bunyan himself.

How little does a late writer in the Dublin University Magazine know of the feelings of a mixed Gipsy, like Bunyan, when he says: "Did he belong to the Gipsies, we have little doubt that he would have dwelt on it, with a sort of spiritual exultation; and that of his having been called out of Egypt would have been to him one of the proofs of Divine favour. We cannot imagine him suppressing the fact, or disguising it." Where is the point in the reviewer's remarks? His remarks have no point. How could the fact of a man being a Gipsy be made the grounds of any kind of spiritual exultation? And how could the fact of the tribe originating in Egypt be a proof of Divine favour towards the individual? What occasion had Bunyan to mention he was a Gipsy? What purpose would it have served? How would it have advanced his mission as a minister? Considering the prejudice that has always existed against that unfortunate word Gipsy, it would have created a sensation among all parties, if Bunyan had said that he was a Gipsy. "What!" the people would have asked, "a *Gipsy* turned priest? We'll have the devil turning priest next!" Considering the many enemies which the tinker-bishop had to contend with, some of whom even sought his life, he would have given them a pretty occasion of revenging themselves upon him, had he said he was a Gipsy. They would have put the law in force, and stretched his neck for him.* The same writer goes on to say: "In one passage at least—and we think there are more in Bunyan's works—the Gipsies are spoken of in such a way as would be most unlikely if Bunyan thought he belonged to that class of vagabonds." I am not aware as to what the reviewer alludes; but, should Bunyan even have denounced the conduct of the Gipsies, in the strongest terms imaginable, would that have been otherwise than what he did with sinners generally? Should a clergyman denounce the ways and morals of every man of his parish, does that make him think less of being a native of the parish himself? Should a man even denounce his children as vagabonds, does that prevent him being their father? This writer illustrates what I have said of people generally—that they are almost incapable of forming an opinion on the Gipsy question, unaided by facts, and the bearings of facts, laid before them; so thoroughly is the philosophy of race, as it progresses and develops, unknown to the public mind, and so absolute is the prejudice of caste against the Gipsy race.†

* Justice Keeling threatened Bunyan with this fate, even for preaching; for said he: "If you do not submit to go to hear divine service, and leave your preaching, you must be banished the realm: And if, after such a day as shall be appointed you to be gone, you shall be found in this realm, or be found to come over again, without special license from the king, you must stretch by the neck for it. I tell you plainly."

Sir Matthew Hale tells us that, on one occasion, at the Suffolk assizes, no less than thirteen Gipsies were executed, under the old Gipsy statutes, a few years before the Restoration.

† Perhaps the following passage is the one alluded to by this writer: "I often, when these temptations had been with force upon me, did compare myself to the case of such a child, whom some Gipsy hath by force took up in her arms, and is carrying from friend and country." *Grace abounding.* The use of a simile like this, confirms the fact that Bunyan belonged to the tribe, rather than that he did not; unless we can imagine that Gipsies, when candid, do not what every other race has done—admit the peculiarities of theirs, while in a previous and barbarous state of existence. His admission confirms a fact generally believed, but sometimes denied, as in the case of the writer in Blackwood's Magazine, mentioned at page 375.

Bunyan, doubtless, "dwelt on it with a sort of spiritual exultation," that he should have been "called"—not "out of Egypt," but—"out of the tribe," when, possibly, no others of it, to his knowledge, had been so privileged; but it was, certainly, "most unlikely" he would say that "he belonged to that class of vagabonds."

I need hardly say anything further to show that Bunyan was a Gipsy. The only circumstance that is wanting to complete the evidence, would be for him to have added to his account of his descent: "In other words, I am a Gipsy." But I have given reasons for such verbal admission being, in a measure, impossible. I do not ask for an argument in favour of Bunyan not being a Gipsy, but a common Englishman; for an argument of that kind, beyond such remarks as I have commented on, is impracticable; but what I ask for is, an exposition of the animus of the man who does not wish that he should have been a Gipsy; assuming that a man can be met with, who will so far forget what is due to the dignity of human nature, as to commit himself in any such way. That Bunyan was a Gipsy is beyond a doubt. That he is a Gipsy, now, in Abraham's bosom, the Christian may readily believe. To the genius of a Gipsy and the grace of God combined, the world is indebted for the noblest production that ever proceeded from an uninspired man. Impugn it whoso list.

Of the Pilgrim's Progress, Lord Macaulay, in his happy manner, writes: "For magnificence, for pathos, for vehement exhortation, for subtle disquisition, for every purpose of the poet, the orator, and the divine, this homely dialect—the dialect of plain working men—was perfectly sufficient. There is no book in our literature on which we would so readily stake the fame of the old, unpolluted, English language," as the Pilgrim's Progress; "no book which shows, so well, how rich that language is in its own proper wealth, and how little it has been improved by all that it has borrowed." "Though there were many clever men in England, during the latter half of the seventeenth century, there were only two great creative minds. One of these minds produced the Paradise Lost; the other, the Pilgrim's Progress"—the work of an English tinkering Gipsy.

It is very singular that religious writers should strive to make out that Bunyan was not a Gipsy. If these writers really have the glory of God at heart, they should rather attempt to prove that he was a member of this race, which has been so much despised. For, thereby, the grace of God would surely be the more magnified. Have they never heard that Jesus Christ came into the world to preach the Gospel to the poor, to break the chains of the oppressed, and raise up the bowed-down? Have they never heard that the poor publican who, standing afar off, would not so much as lift up his eyes to heaven, but smote his breast, and exclaimed: "God be merciful to me, a sinner," went down justified rather than him who gave thanks for his not being like other men, or even as that publican? Have they never heard that God hath chosen the foolish things of the world to confound the wise; and the weak things of the world to confound the things which are mighty; and things which are despised, yea, and things which are not, to bring to naught things that are: that no flesh should glory in his presence? I shall wait, with considerable curiosity, to see whether the next editor, or biographer, of this illustrious Gipsy will take any notice of the present work; or whether he will dispose of it somewhat in this strain: "One of Bunyan's modern reviewers, by a strange mistake, construes his self-disparaging admissions to mean that he was the offspring of Gipsies!"

Sir Walter Scott admits that Bunyan was most probably a "Gipsy reclaimed;" and Mr. Offor, that "his father must have been a Gipsy."* But, with these exceptions, I know not if any writer upon Bunyan has more than hinted at the possibility of even a connexion between him and the Gipsies. It is very easy to account for all this, by the ignorance of the world in regard to the Gipsy tribe, but, above all, by the extreme prejudice of caste which is entertained against it. Does caste exist nowhere but in India? Does an Englishman feel curious to know what caste can mean? In few parts of the world does caste reign so supreme, as it does in Great Britain, towards the Gipsy nation. What is it but the prejudice of caste that has prevented the world from acknowledging Bunyan to have been a Gipsy? The evidence of the fact of his having been a Gipsy is positive enough. Will any one say that he does not believe that Bunyan meant to convey to the world a knowledge of the fact of

* It is interesting to notice what these two writers say. If Bunyan's father was a Gipsy, we may reasonably assume that his mother was one likewise; and, consequently, that Bunyan was one himself, or as Sir Walter Scott expresses it—a "Gipsy reclaimed." A Gipsy being a question of race, and not a matter of habits, it should be received as one of the simplest of elementary truths, that once a Gipsy, always a Gipsy. We naturally ask, Why has not the fact of Bunyan having been a Gipsy stood on record, for the last two centuries? and, echo answers, Why?

his being a Gipsy? Or that he does not believe that the tinkers are Gipsies? Has any writer on Bunyan ever taken the trouble to ascertain who the tinkers really are; and that, in consequence of his investigations, he has come to the conclusion that they are *not* Gipsies? If no writer on the subject of the illustrious dreamer has ever taken that trouble, to what must we attribute the fact but the prejudice of caste? It is caste, and nothing but caste. What is it but the prejudice of caste that has led Lord Macaulay to invent his story about the tinkers? For what he says of the tinkers is a pure invention, or, at best, a delusion, on his part. What is it but the prejudice of caste that has prevented others from saying, plainly, that Bunyan was a Gipsy? It would be more manly if they were to leave Bunyan alone, than receive his works, and damn the man, that is, his blood. It places them on the level of boors, when they allow themselves to be swayed by the prejudices that govern boors. When they speak of, or write about, Bunyan, let them exercise common honesty, and receive both the man and the man's works: let them not be guilty of petit larceny, or rather, great robbery, in the matter.

Southey, in his life of Bunyan, writes: "John Bunyan has faithfully recorded his own spiritual history. Had he dreamed of being 'forever known,' and taking his place among those who may be called the immortals of the earth, he would probably have introduced more details of his temporal circumstances, and the events of his life. But, glorious dreamer as he was, this never entered into his imagination.* Less concerning him than might have been expected has been preserved by those of his own sect; and it is not likely that anything more should be recovered from oblivion." Remarks like these come with a singular grace from a man with so many prejudices as Southey. John Bunyan has told us as much of his history *as he dared to do.* It was a subject upon which, in some respects, he doubtless maintained a great reserve; for it cannot be supposed that a man occupying so prominent and popular a position, as a preacher and writer, and of so singular an origin, should

* Although Bunyan probably never anticipated being held in high estimation by what are termed the "great ones" of the earth, yet what Southey has said cannot be predicated of him, if we consider the singularity of his origin and history, and the popularity which he enjoyed, as author of the

have had no investigations made into his history, and that of his family; if not by his friends, at least, by his enemies, who seemed to have been capable of doing anything to injure and discredit him. But, very probably, his being a tinker was, with friends and enemies, a circumstance so altogether discreditable, as to render any investigation of the kind perfectly superfluous. In mentioning that much of himself which he did, Bunyan doubtless imagined that the world understood, or would have understood, what he meant, and would, sooner or later, acknowledge the race to which he belonged. And yet it has remained in this unacknowledged state for two centuries since his time. How unreasonable it is to imagine that Bunyan should have said, in as many words, that he was a Gipsy, when the world generally is so apt to become fired with indignation, should we *now* say that he was one of the race. How applicable are the words of his wife, to Sir Matthew Hale, to the people of the present day: "Because he is a tinker, and a poor man, he is despised, and cannot have justice."

Had Southey exercised that common sense which is the inheritance of most of Englishmen, and divested himself of this prejudice of caste, which is likewise their inheritance, he never could have had any difficulty in forming a proper idea of Bunyan, and everything concerning him. And the same may be said of any person at the present day. John Bunyan was simply a Gipsy of mixed blood, who must have spoken the Gipsy language in great purity; for, considering

Pilgrim's Progress; a work affecting the mind of man in every age of the world. Of this work Bunyan writes:

"My Pilgrim's book has travelled sea and land,
Yet could I never come to understand
That it was slighted, or turned out of door,
By any kingdom, were they rich or poor.
In France and Flanders, where men kill each other,
My Pilgrim is esteemed a friend, a brother.
In Holland, too, 'tis said, as I am told,
My Pilgrim is, with some, worth more than gold.
Highlanders and Wild Irish can agree
My Pilgrim should familiar with them be.
'Tis in New England under such advance,
Receives there so much loving countenance,
As to be trimmed, new clothed, and decked with gems,
That it may show its features, and its limbs.
Yet more, so public doth my Pilgrim walk,
That of him thousands daily sing and talk."

the extent to which it is spoken in England, to-day, we can well believe that it was very pure two centuries ago, and that Bunyan might have written works even in that language. But such is the childish prejudice against the name of Gipsy, such the silly incredulity towards the subject, that, in Great Britain, and, I am sorry to say, with some people in America, one has nearly as much difficulty in persuading others to believe in it, as St. Paul had in inducing the Greeks to believe in the resurrection of the dead. Why seemeth it unto thee incredible that Bunyan was a Gipsy? or that Bunyan's race should now be found in every town, in every village, and, perhaps, in every hamlet, in Scotland, and in every sphere of life?*

To a candid and unprejudiced person, it should afford a relief, in thinking of the immortal dreamer, that he should have been a member of this singular race, emerging from a state of comparative barbarism, and struggling upwards, amid so many difficulties, rather than he should have been of the very lowest of our own race; for in that case, there is an originality and dignity connected with him personally, that could not well attach to him, in the event of his having belonged to the dregs of the common natives. Beyond being a Gipsy, it is impossible to say what his pedigree really was. His grandfather might have been an ordinary native, even of fair birth, who, in a thoughtless moment, might have "gone off with the Gipsies;" or his ancestor, on the native side of the house, might have been one of the "many English loiterers" who joined the Gipsies on their arrival in England, when they were "esteemed and held in great admiration;" or he might have been a kidnapped infant; or such a "foreign tinker" as is alluded to in the Spanish Gipsy edicts, and in the Act of Queen Elizabeth, in which mention is made of "strangers," as distinguished from natu-

* Bunsen writes: "Sound judgment is displayed rather in an aptness for believing what is historical, than in a readiness at denying it. . . . . . Shallow minds have a decided propensity to fall into the latter error. Incapability of believing on evidence is the last form of the intellectual imbecility of an enervated age."

A writer who contributes frequently to "Notes and Queries," after stating that he has read the works of Grellmann and Hoyland on the Gipsies, adds: "My conclusion is that the tribes have no more right to nationality, race, blood, or language, than the London thieves have—with their slang, some words of which may have their origin in the Hebrew, from their dealings with the lowest order of Jews."

ral born subjects, being with the Gipsies. The last is most probable, as the name, *Bunyan*, would seem to be of foreign origin. It is, therefore, very likely, that there was not a drop of common English blood in Bunyan's veins. John Bunyan belongs to the world at large, and England is only entitled to the credit of the formation of his character. Be all that as it may, Bunyan's father seems to have been a superior, and therefore important, man in the tribe, from the fact, as Southey says, of his having "put his son to school in an age when very few of the poor were taught to read and write."

The world never can do justice to Bunyan, unless it takes him up as a Gipsy; nor can the Christian, unless he considers him as being a Gipsy, in Abraham's bosom. His biographers have not, even in one instance, done justice to him; for, while it is altogether out of the question to call him the "wicked tinker," the "depraved Bunyan," it is unreasonable to style him a "blackguard," as Southey has done. He might have been a blackguard in that sense in which a youth, in a village, is termed a "young blackguard," for being the ringleader among the boys; or on account of his wearing a ragged coat, and carrying a hairy wallet on his shoulder, which, in a conventional sense, constitute any man, in Great Britain, a blackguard. Bunyan's sins were confined to swearing, cursing, blaspheming, and lying; and were rather intensely manifested by the impetuosity of his character, or vividly described by the sincerity of his piety, and the liveliness of his genius, than deeply rooted in his nature; for he shook off the habit of swearing, (and, doubtless, that of lying,) on being severely reproved for it, by a loose and ungodly woman. Three of the kindred vices mentioned, (and, we might add the fourth, lying,) more frequently proceed from the influence of bad example and habit, than from anything inherently vicious, in a youth with so many of the good points which characterized Bunyan. His youth was even marked by a tender conscience, and a strong moral feeling; for thus he speaks of himself in "Grace Abounding:" "But this I well remember, that though I could myself sin, with the greatest delight and ease, and also take pleasure in the vileness of my companions, yet, even then, if I had, at any time, seen wicked things in those who professed goodness, it would make my spirit tremble. As, once above all the rest, when I was in the height of vanity, yet hearing one swear that was reckoned for a religious man, it had so great a stroke upon my spirit, that it made my heart ache." He was the subject of these experiences before he was ten years of age. It is unnecessary to speak of his dancing, ringing bells, and playing at tip-cat and hockey. Now, let us see what was Bunyan's *moral* character. He was not a drunkard; and he says: "I know not whether there be such a thing as a woman breathing under the copes of heaven, but by their apparel, their children, or by common fame, except my wife." And he continues: "Had not a miracle of precious grace prevented, I had laid myself open even to the stroke of those laws which bring some to disgrace and open shame, before the face of the world." The meaning of this is, evidently, that he never stole anything; but that it was "by a miracle of precious grace" he was prevented from doing it. In what sense, then, was Bunyan a blackguard? There was never such occasion for him to say of himself, what John Newton said of himself, as a criminal passed him, on the way to the gallows: "There goes John Bunyan, but for the grace of God." But such was the depth of Bunyan's piety, that hardly any one thought and spoke more disparagingly of himself than he did; although he would defend himself, with indignation, against unjust charges brought against him; for, however peaceable and humble he might be, he would turn most manfully upon his enemies, when they baited or badgered him. "It began, therefore, to be rumoured, up and down among the people, that I was a witch, a Jesuit, a highwayman, and the like. . . . . I also call those fools and knaves that have thus made it anything of their business to affirm any of these things aforesaid of me, namely, that I have been naught with other women, or the like. . . . My foes have missed their mark in this their shooting at me. I am not the man. I wish that they themselves be guiltless. If all the fornicators and adulterers in England were hanged up by the neck till they be dead, John Bunyan, *the object of their envy*, would be still alive and well." The style of his language even indicated the Gipsy; for English Gipsies, as Mr. Borrow justly remarks, speak the English language much better than the natives of the lower classes; for this apparent reason, that they have not the dialect of any particular part of England, which would be, were they always to have resided in a particular place. It must have been more so before the middle of the seventeenth century, upwards of a hundred years after the arrival of the Gipsies in England; for, in acquiring the English language, they would keep clear of many of the rude dialects that so commonly prevail in that country. But Bunyan's language was, doubtless, drawn principally from the Scriptures.

The illustrious pilgrim had many indignities cast upon him, by the lower and unthinking classes of the population, and by Quakers and strict Baptists. 'Twas a man like John Owen who knew how to appreciate and respect him; for, said he to Charles II.: "I would readily part with all my learning, could I but preach like the tinker." And what was it that supported Bunyan, amid all the abuse and obloquy to which he was exposed, as he obeyed the call of God, and preached the gospel, in season and out of season, to every creature around him? When they sneered at his origin, and the occupation from which he had risen, he said: "Such insults I freely bind unto me, as an ornament, among the rest of my reproaches, till the Lord shall wipe them off at his coming." And again: "The poor Christian hath something to answer them that reproach him for his ignoble pedigree, and shortness of the glory of the wisdom of this world. I fear God. This is the highest and most noble; he hath the honour, the life, and glory that is lasting."*

In Great Britain, the off-scourings of the earth can say who they are, and no prejudices are entertained against

* That the rabble, or "fellows of the baser sort," should have pelted Bunyan with all sorts of offensive articles, when he commenced to preach the gospel, is what could naturally have been expected; but it sounds strange to read what he has put on record of the abuse heaped upon him, by people professing to be the servants of Him "in whom there is neither Jew nor Greek, bond nor free, male nor female." See with what Christian humility he alludes to such treatment, as contrasted with the manly indignation which he displayed in repelling slanders. He speaks of "the Lord wiping off such insults at his coming;" when his enemies, with the utmost familiarity and assurance, may approach the judgment-seat, and demand their crowns. "Lord, Lord, have we not prophesied in thy name? and in thy name have cast out devils? and in thy name done many wonderful works?" And it may be answered unto them: "I never knew you; depart from me, ye that work iniquity."

them. Half-caste Hindoos, Malays, Hottentots, and Negroes, are "sent home," to be educated, and made pets of, and have the choice of white women given to them for wives; but the children of a Scottish Christian Gipsy gentleman, or of a Scottish Christian Gipsy gentlewoman, dare not say who they are, were it almost to save their lives. Scottish people will wonder at what caste in India can mean, deplore its existence, and pray to God to remove it, that "the gospel may have free course and be glorified;" yet scowl—silently and sullenly scowl—at the bare mention of John Bunyan having been a Gipsy! Scottish religious journals will not tolerate the idea to appear in their columns! To such people I would say, Offer up no more prayers to Almighty God, to remove caste from India, until they themselves have removed from the land this prejudice of caste, that hangs like an incubus upon so many of their fellow-subjects at home. It is quite time enough to carry such petitions to the Deity, when every Scottish Gipsy can make a return of himself in the census, or proclaim himself a Gipsy at the cross, or from the house-top, if need be; or, at least, after steps have been taken by the public to that end. But some of my countrymen may say: "What are we to do, under the circumstances?" And I reply: "Endeavour to be yourselves, and judge of this subject as it ought to be judged. You can, at least, try to guard against your children acquiring your own prejudices." To the rising town generation, I would look with more hope to see a better feeling entertained for the name of Gipsy. But I look with more confidence to the English than Scottish people; for this question of "folk" is very apt to rankle and fester in the Scottish mind. I wish, then, that the British, and more especially the Scottish, public should consider itself as cited before the bar of the world, and not only the bar of the world, but the bar of posterity, to plead on the Gipsy question, that it may be seen if this is the only instance in which justice is not to be done to a part of the British population. With the evidence furnished in the present work, I submit the name of Bunyan, as a case in point, to test the principle at issue. Let British people beware how they approach this subject, for there are great principles involved in it. The social emancipation of the Gipsies is a question which British people have to consider for the future.

The day is gone by when it cannot be said who John Bunyan was. In Cowper's time, his *name* dare not be mentioned, "lest it should move a sneer." Let us hope that we are living in happier times. Tinkering was Bunyan's *occupation*; his *race* the Gipsy—a fact that cannot be questioned. His having been a Gipsy adds, by contrast, a lustre to his name, and reflects an immortality upon his character; and he stands out, from among all the men of the latter half of the seventeenth century, in all his solitary grandeur, a monument of the grace of God, and a prodigy of genius. Let us, then, enroll John Bunyan as the first (that is known to the world) of eminent Gipsies, the prince of allegorists, and one of the most remarkable of men and Christians. What others of this race there may be who have distinguished themselves among mankind, are known to God and, it may be, some of the Gipsies. The saintly Doctor to whom I have alluded was one of this singular people; and one beyond question, for his admission of the fact cannot be denied by any one. Any life of John Bunyan, or any edition of his works, that does not contain a record of the fact of his having been a Gipsy, lacks the most important feature connected with the man that makes everything relating to him personally interesting to mankind. It should even contain a short dissertation on the Gipsies, and have, as a frontispiece, a Gipsy's camp, with all its appurtenances. The reader may believe that such a thing may be seen, and that, perhaps, not before long.

It strikes me as something very singular, that Mr. Borrow, "whose acquaintance with the Gipsy race, in general, dates from a very early period of his life;" who "has lived more with Gipsies than Scotchmen;" and than whom "no one ever enjoyed better opportunities for a close scrutiny of their ways and habits," should have told us so little about the Gipsies. In all his writings on the Gipsies, he alludes to two mixed Gipsies only—the Spanish half-pay captain, and the English flaming tinman—in a way as if these were the merest of accidents, and meant nothing. He has told us nothing of the Gipsies but what was known before, with the exception, as far as my memory serves me, of the custom of the Spanish Gipsy, dressing her daughter in such a way as to protect her virginity; the existence of the tribe, in a civilized state, in Moscow; and the habit of the members of the race possessing two names; all of which are, doubtless, interesting pieces of information. The Spanish Gipsy marriage ceremony was described, long before him, by Dr. Bright; and Twiss, as far back as 1723, bears testimony to the virtue of Gipsy females, inasmuch as they were not to be procured in any way. Twiss also bears very positive testimony on a point to which Mr. Borrow has not alluded, viz.: the honesty of Spanish Gipsy innkeepers, in one respect, at least, that, although he frequently left his linen, spoons, &c., at their mercy, he never lost an article belonging to him. He alludes, in his travels, to the subject of the Gipsies incidentally; and his testimony is, therefore, worthy of every credit, on the points on which he speaks. In Mr. Borrow's writings upon the Gipsies, we find only sketches of certain individuals of the race, whom he seems to have fallen in with, and not a proper account of the nation. These writings have done more injury to the tribe than, perhaps, anything that ever appeared on the subject. I have met with Gipsies—respectable young men—who complained bitterly of Mr. Borrow's account of their race; and they did that with good reason; for his attempt at generalization on the subject of the people, is as great a curiosity as ever I set my eyes upon. How unsatisfactory are Mr. Borrow's opinions on the Gipsy question, when he speaks of the "decadence" of the race, when it is only passing from its first stage of existence—the tent. This he does in his Appendix to the Romany Rye; and it is nearly all that can be drawn from his writings on the Gipsies, in regard to their future history.

I do not expect to meet among American people, generally, with the prejudice against the name of Gipsy that prevails in Europe; for, in Europe, the prejudice is traditional—a question of the nursery—while, in America, it is derived, for the most part, from novels. American people will, of course, form their own opinion upon the tented or any other kind of Gipsies, as their behaviour warrants; but what prejudice can they have for the Gipsy race as such? As a race, it is, physically, as fine a one as ever came out of Asia; although, at the present day, it is so much mixed with the white blood, as hardly to be observable in many, and absolutely not so in others, who follow the ordinary vocations of other men. What prejudice can Americans have against

Gipsy blood as such? What prejudice can they have to the Maryland farmers who have been settled, for at least two generations, near Annapolis, merely because they are Gipsies and speak Gipsy? If there is any people in the world who might be expected to view the subject of the Gipsies dispassionately, it ought to be the people of America; for surely they have prejudices enough in regard to race; prejudices, the object of which is independent of character or condition—something that stares them in the face, and cannot be got rid of. If they have the practical sagacity to perceive the bearings of the Gipsy question, they should at once take it up, and treat it in the manner which the age demands. They have certainly an opportunity of stealing a march upon English people in this matter.

Part of what I have said in reference to Bunyan, I was desirous of having inserted in a respectable American religious journal, but I did not succeed in it. "It would take up too much room in the paper, and give rise to more discussion than they could afford to print."—"Perhaps you would not wish it to be said that John Bunyan was a Gipsy?"—"Oh, not at all," replied the editor, colouring up a little. I found that several of these papers devoted a pretty fair portion of their space to such articles as funny monkey stories, and descriptions of rat-trap and cow-tail-holder patents; but for anything of so very little importance as that which referred to John Bunyan, they could afford no room whatever. Who cared to know who John Bunyan was? What purpose could it serve? Who would be benefited by it? But funny monkey stories are pleasant reading; every housewife should know how to keep down her rats; and every farmer should be taught how to keep his cows' tails from whisking their milk in his face, while it is being drawn into the pail. Not succeeding with the religious papers, I found expression to my sentiments in one of the "ungodly weeklies," which devote their columns to rats, monkeys, and cows, and a little to mankind; and there I found a feeling of sympathy for Bunyan. Let it not be said, in after times, that the descendants of the Puritans allowed themselves to be frightened by a scare-crow, or put to flight by the shake of a rag.

I am afraid that the native-born quarrelsomeness of disposition about "folk," and things in general, which characterizes Scottish people, will prove a bar to the Gipsies owning themselves up in Scotland. Go into any Scottish village you like, and ascertain the feelings which the inhabitants entertain for each other, and you will find that such a one is a "poor grocer body;" that another belongs to a "shoemaker pack," "another to a "tailor pack," another to a "cadger pack," another to a "collier pack," and another to a "low Tinkler pack;" another to a "bad nest," and another to a "very bad nest." And it is pretty much the same with the better classes. Now, how could the Gipsy tribe live amid such elements, if it did not keep everything connected with itself hidden from all the other "packs" surrounding it? And is it consonant with reason to say, that a Scotchman should be rated as standing at the bottom of all the various "packs" and "nests," simply because he has Gipsy blood in his veins? Yet, I meet with Scotchmen in the New World, who express such a feeling towards the Gipsies. This quarrelling about "folk" reigns supreme in Scotland; and, what is worse, it is brought with the people to America. It is inherent in them to be personal and intolerant, among themselves, and to talk of, and sneer at, each other, and "cast up things." In that respect, a community of Scotch people presents a peculiarity of mental feeling that is hardly to be found in one of any other people. When they come together, in social intercourse, there is frequently, if not generally, a hearty, if not a boisterous, flow of feeling, and, if the bottle contributes to the entertainment, a foam upon the surface; but the under-tow and ground-swell are frequently long in subsiding. Even in America, where they are reputed to have the clanishness of Jews, we will find within their respective circles, more heart-burnings, jealousies, envyings, and quarrellings, (but little or no Irish fighting, for they are rather given to "taking care of their characters,") than is to be found among almost any other people. At the best, there may be said to be an armed truce always to be found existing among them. Still, all that is not known to people outside of these circles; for those within them are animated by a common national sentiment, which leads them to conceal such feelings from others, so as to "uphold the credit of their country," wherever they go. It will be a difficult matter to get the Gipsies heartily acknowledged among such elements as equals; for it makes many a native Scot wild, to tell him that there are Scottish Gipsies as good, if not better, men than he is, or any kith or kin that belongs to him.

And yet, it is not the Scottish gentleman—the gentleman by birth, rearing, education, mind, or manners—who will be backward to assist in raising up, and dignifying, the name of Gipsy. No; it will be the low-minded and ignorant Scots; people who are always either fawning upon, or sneering at, those above them, or trampling, or attempting to trample, upon those below them. It is very apt to be that class which Lord Jeffrey describes as "having a double allowance of selfishness, with a top-dressing of pedantry and conceit," and some of the "but and ben" gentry, who will sneer most at the word Gipsy. It is the flunkey, who lives and brings up his family upon the cast-off clothes and broken victuals of others, and but for whom such things would find their way to the rag-basket and the pigs; 'tis he and his children who are too often the most difficult to please in the matter of descent, and the most likely to perpetuate the prejudice against the Gipsy tribe.

I have taken some trouble to ascertain the feelings of Scotchmen in America towards the Scottish Gipsies, such as they are represented in these pages; and I find that, among the really educated and liberally brought up classes, there are not to be discovered those prejudices against them, that are expressed by the lower classes, and especially those from country places. It is natural for the former kind of people to take the most liberal view of a question like the present; for they are, in a measure, satisfied with their position in life; while, with the lower classes, it is a feeling of restless discontentment that leads them to strive to get some one under them. No one would seem to like to be at the bottom of any society; and nowhere less so than in Scotland. A good education and up-bringing, and a knowledge of the world, likewise give a person a more liberal cast of mind, wherewith to form an opinion upon the subject of the Gipsies; and it is upon such that I would mainly rely in an attempt to raise up the name of Gipsy. Among the lower classes of my own countrymen, I find individuals all that could be desired in the matter of esteeming the Gipsies, according to the characters they bear, and the positions they occupy in life; but they are exceptions to the classes to which they belong. Here is a specimen of the kind of Scot the most difficult to break in to entertaining a proper feeling upon the subject of the Gipsies:

By birth, he is a child of that dependent class that gets a due share of the broken victuals and cast-off clothes of other people. His parents are decent and honest enough people, but very conceited and self-sufficient. Any person in the shape of a mechanic, a labourer, or a peasant, appears as nobody to them; although, in independence, and even circumstances, they are not to be compared to many a peasant. The "oldest bairn" takes his departure for the New World, "with the firm determination to show to the world that he is a man," and "teach the Yankees something." The first thing he does to "show the world that he is a man," is to sneer, behave rudely, and attempt to pick quarrels with a better class of his own countrymen, when he comes in contact with them. Providence has not been over-indulgent with him in the matters of perceptors or reflectors; for, what little he knows, he has acquired in the manner that chickens pick up their food, when it is placed before them. But he has been gifted with a wonderful amount of self-conceit, which nothing can break down in him, however much it may be abashed for the moment. No one boasts more of his "family," to those who do not know who his family are, although his family were brought up in a cage, and so small a cage, that some of them must have roosted on the spars overhead at night. No one is more independent, none more patriotic; no one boasts more of Wallace and Bruce, Burns and Scott, and all the worthies; to him there is no place in the world like "auld Scotland yet;" no one glories more in "the noble qualities of the Scot;" and none's face burns with more importance in upholding, unchallenged, what he claims to be his character; yet the individual is a compound of conceit and selfishness, meanness and sordidness, and is estimated, wherever he goes, as a "perfect sweep." Although no one is more given to toasting, "Brithers a' the world o'er," and, "A man's a man for a' that," yet speak of the Gipsies to him, and he exclaims: "Thank God! there's no a drap o' Gipsy blood in me; no one drap o't!" Not only is he unable to comprehend the subject, but he is unwilling to hear the word Gipsy mentioned. In short, he turns up his nose at the subject, and howls like a dog.*

* It is interesting to compare this feeling with that of the lowest order

It is the better kind of Scottish people, in whatever sphere of life they are to be found, on whom the greatest reliance is to be placed in raising up and dignifying the word Gipsy. This peculiar family of mankind has been fully three centuries and a half in the country, and it is high time that it should be acknowledged, in some form or other; high time, certainly, that we should know something about it. To an intelligent people it must appear utterly ridiculous that a prejudice is to be entertained against any Scotchman, without knowing who that Scotchman is, merely on account of his blood. Nor will any intelligent Scotchman, after the appearance of this work, be apt to say that he does not understand the subject of the Gipsies; or that they cease to be Gipsies by leaving the tent, or by a change of character or habits, or by their blood getting mixed. It will not do for any one to snap at the heels of this question: he must look at it steadily, and approach it with a clear head, a firm hand, and a Christian heart, and remove this stigma that has been allowed to attach to his country. No one in particular can be blamed for the position which the Gipsies occupy in the country: let by-gones be by-gones; let us look to the future for that expression of opinion which the subject calls for. This much I feel satisfied of, that if the Gipsy subject is properly handled, it would result in the name becoming as much an object of respect and attachment in many of the race, as it is now considered a reproach in others. There is much that is interesting in the name, and nothing necessarily low or vulgar associated with it; although there is much that is wild and barbarous connected with the descent, which is peculiar to the descent of all original tribes. It is unnecessary to say, that in a part of the race, we still find much that is wild, and barbarous, and roguish.

The latter part of the Gipsy nation, whether settled or itinerant, must be reached indirectly, for reasons which have already been given; for it does not serve much purpose to interfere too directly with them, as Gipsies. We should bring a reflective influence to bear upon them, by holding up to their observation, some of their own race in respectable positions in life, and respected by the world, as men,

of Spaniards, as described by Mr. Borrow. "The outcast of the prison and the *presidio*, who calls himself Spaniard, would feel insulted by being termed Gitano, and would thank God that he is not." *Page* 386.

though not known to be Gipsies. I could propose no better plan to be adopted, with some of these people, than to give them a copy of the present work, along with the Pilgrim's Progress, containing a short account of the Gipsies, and a Gipsy's encampment for a frontispiece. The world may well believe that the Gipsies would read both of them, and be greatly benefited by the Pilgrim's Progress; for, as a race, they are exceedingly vain about anything connected with themselves. Said I to some English Gipsies: "You are the vainest people in the world; you think a vast deal of yourselves." "There is good reason for that," they replied; "if we do not think something of ourselves, there are no others to do it for us." Now since John Bunyan has become so famous throughout the world, and so honoured by all sects and parties, what an inimitable instrument Providence has placed in our hands wherewith to raise up the name of Gipsy! Through him we can touch the heart of Christendom! I am well aware that the Church of Scotland has, or at least had, a mission among the itinerant Scottish Gipsies. In addition to the means adopted by this mission, to improve these Gipsies, it would be well to take such steps as I have suggested, so as to raise up the name of Gipsy. For, in this way, the Gipsies, of all classes, would see that they are not outcasts; but that the prejudices which people entertain for them are applicable to their ways of life, only, and not to their blood or descent, tribe or language. Their hearts would then become more easily touched, their affections more readily secured; and the attempt made to improve them would have a much better chance of being successful. A little judgment is necessary in conducting an intercourse with the wild Gipsy, or, indeed, any kind of Gipsy; it is very advisable to speak well of "the blood," and never to confound the race with the conduct of part of it. There is hardly anything that can give a poor Gipsy greater pleasure than to tell him something about his people, and particularly should they be in a respectable position in life, and be attached to their nation. It serves no great purpose to appear too serious with such a person, for that soon tires him. It is much better to keep him a little buoyant and cheerful, with anecdotes and stories, for that is his natural character; and to take advantage of occasional opportunities, to slip in advices that are to be of use to him.

What is called long-facedness is entirely thrown away upon a Gipsy of this kind.

I am very much inclined to believe that a Gipsy, well up in the scale of Scottish society, experiences, in one respect, nearly the same feelings in coming in contact with a wild Gipsy, that are peculiar to any other person. These are of a very singular nature. At first, we feel as if we were going into the lair of a wild animal, or putting our finger into a snake's mouth; such is the result of the prejudice in which we have been reared from infancy; but these feelings become greatly modified as we get accustomed to the people. The world has never had the opportunity of fairly contemplating any other kind of Gipsy; hence the extreme prejudice against the name. But when we get accustomed to meet with other kinds of Gipsies, and have associations with them, the feeling of prejudice changes to that of decided interest and attachment. I have met with various Scottish Gipsies of the female sex, in America, and, among others, one who could sit any day for an ideal likeness of the mother of Burns. She takes little of the Gipsy in her appearance. There is another, taking greatly after the Gipsy, born in Scotland, and reared in America; a very fine motherly person, indeed. I cannot, at the present stage of matters, mention the word Gipsy to her, but I know very well that she is a Gipsy. It takes some time for the feeling of prejudice for the word Gipsy to wear off, when contemplating even a passable kind of Gipsy. That object would be much more easily attained, were the people to own "the blood," unreservedly and cheerfully; for the very reserve, to a great extent, creates, at least keeps alive, the prejudice. But that cannot well take place till the word "Gipsy" bears the signification of gentleman, in some of the race, as it does of vagabond, in others.

Some of my readers may still ask: "What is a Gipsy, after all that has been said upon the subject? Since it is not necessarily a question of colour of face, or hair, or eyes, or of creed, or character, or of any outward thing by which a human being can be distinguished; what is it that constitutes a Gipsy?" And I reply: "Let them read this work through, and thoroughly digest all its principles, and they can *feel* what a Gipsy is, should they stumble upon one, it may be, in their own sphere of life, and hear him, or her, admit the fact, and speak unreservedly of it. They will then feel their minds rubbing against the Gipsy mind, their spirits communing with the Gipsy spirit, and experience a peculiar mental galvanic shock, which they never felt before."* It is impossible to say where the Gipsy soul may *not* exist at the present day, for there is this peculiarity about the tribe, as I have said before, that it always remains Gipsy, cross it out to the last drop of the original blood; for where that drop goes, the Gipsy soul accompanies it.†

It is the Christian who should be the most ready to take up and do justice to this subject; for he will find in it a very singular work of Providence—the most striking phenomenon in the history of man. In Europe, the race has existed, in an unacknowledged state, for a greater length of time than the Jews dwelt in Egypt. And it is time that it should be introduced to the family of mankind, in its aspect of historical development; embracing, as in Scotland, members ranging from what is popularly understood to be Gipsies, to those filling the first positions in Christian and social

* Let us suppose that a person, who has read all the works that have hitherto appeared on the Gipsies, and noticed the utter absence, in them, of everything of the nature of a philosophy of the subject, thoroughly masters all that is set forth in the present work. The knowledge which he *then* possesses puts him in such a position, that he approximates to being one of the tribe, himself; that is, if all that is contained therein be known to him and the tribe, only, it would enable him to pass current, in certain circles of Gipsydom, as one of themselves.

† There is a point which I have not explained so fully as I might have done, and it is this: "Is any of the blood *ever lost?* that is, does it *ever cease to be Gipsy*, in knowledge and feeling?" That is a question not easily answered in the affirmative, were it only for this reason: how can it ever be ascertained that the knowledge and feeling of being Gipsies become lost? Let us suppose that a couple of Gipsies leave England, and settle in America, and that they never come in contact with any of their race, and that their children never learn anything of the matter from any quarter. (Page 418.) In such an extreme, I may say, such an unnatural, case, the children would not be Gipsies, but, if born in America, ordinary Americans. The only way in which the Gipsy blood—that is, the Gipsy feeling—can possibly be lost, is by a Gipsy, (a man especially,) marrying an ordinary native, (page 881,) and the children never learning of the circumstance. But, as I have said before, how is that ever to be ascertained? The question might be settled in this way: Let the relatives of the Gipsy interrogate the issue, and if it answers, *truly*, that it knows nothing of the Gipsy connexion, and never has its curiosity in the matter excited, it holds, beyond dispute, that "the blood" has been lost to the tribe. For any loss the tribe may sustain, in that way, it gains, in an ample degree, by drawing upon the blood of the native race, and transmuting it into that of its own fraternity.

society. After perusing the present work, the reader will naturally pass on to reconsider the subject of the Jews; and he will perceive that, instead of its being a miracle by which the Jews have existed since the dispersion, it would have been a miracle had they been lost among the families of mankind. It is quite sufficient for the Christian to know that the Jews now exist, and that they have fulfilled, and will yet fulfill, the prophecies that have been delivered in regard to them, without holding that any miracle has been wrought for that end. A Christian ought to be more considerate in his estimate of what a miracle is; he ought to know that a miracle is something that is contrary to natural laws; and that the existence of the Jews, since the dispersion, is in exact harmony with every natural law. He should not maintain that it is a miracle, for nothing having the decent appearance of an argument can be advanced in support of any such theory; and far less should he, with his eyes open, do what the writer on the Christian Evidences, alluded to, (page 459,) did, with his shut—gamble away both law and gospel.* He might give his attention, however, to a prophecy of Moses, quoted by St. Paul, in Rom. x. 19, from Deut. xxxii. 21, wherein it is said of the Jews: "I will provoke you to jealousy by them that are no people, and by a foolish nation I will anger you;" and lend his assistance towards its fulfillment.† The subject

* It was the nature of man, in ancient times, as it is with the heathen to-day, to *worship* what could not be understood; while modern civilization seems to attribute such phenomena to *miracles*. It is even presumptuous to have recourse to such an alternative, for the enquirer may be deficient in the intellect necessary to prosecute such investigations, or he may not be in possession of sufficient data. If the European will, for example, ask himself, 1stly: what is the idea which he has of a Gipsy? 2ndly: what are the feelings which he entertains for him personally? And 3dly: what must be the response of the Gipsy to the sentiments of the other? he cannot avoid coming to the conclusion, that the race should "marry among themselves," and that, "let them be in whatever situation of life they may, they all" should "stick to each other." (*Page* 369.)

† Viewing the Gipsies as they are described in this work, and contrasting their history with that of the nations of the world in general, and the Jews in particular, and considering that they have no religion peculiar to themselves, yet are scattered among, and worked into, all nations, but not acknowledged by, or even known to, others, we may, with the utmost propriety, call them, in the language of the prophet, "no people," and a "foolish nation;" yet by no means a nation of fools, but rather more rogues than fools. Of all the ways in which the Gipsies have hoaxed other people, the

of the Gipsies is certainly calculated to do all that the prophet said would happen to the Jews; if Christians will only do their duty to them, and, by playing them off against the Jews, *provoke* and *anger* Israel beyond measure. That the Jews have existed, since the dispersion, by the Providence of God, is what can be said of any other people, and more especially of the Gipsies for the last four centuries and a half in Europe. It is as natural for the Gipsies to exist in their scattered state, as for other nations by the laws that preserve their identity; and although their history may be termed remarkable, it is in no sense of the word miraculous, notwithstanding the superstitious ideas held by many of the Gipsies on that head, in common with the Jews regarding their history. A thousand years hence the Gipsies will be found existing in the world; for, as a people, they cannot die out; and the very want of a religion peculiar to themselves is one of the means that will contribute to that end.* It is the Christian who should endeavour to have the prejudice against the name of Gipsy removed, so that every one of the race should freely own his blood to the other, and make it the basis of a kindly feeling, and a bond of brotherhood, all around the world.

I may be allowed to say a word or two to the Gipsies, and more especially the Scottish Gipsies. I wish them to believe, (what they, indeed, believe already,) that their blood and descent are good enough; and that Providence may reasonably be assumed to look upon both with as much complacency and satisfaction, as He does on any other blood and descent. All that they have to do is to "behave themselves;" for, after all, it is behaviour that makes the man. By all means "stick to the ship," but sail her as an honourable merchantman. They need not be afraid at being discovered to be Gipsies; they should feel as much assured on the subject now, as before the publication of this work, and never entertain the least misgiving on that score. They

manner in which they have managed to throw around themselves a sense of their non-existence to the minds of others, is the most remarkable.

* The prejudice of their fellow-creatures is a sufficiently potent cause, in itself, to preserve the identity of the Gipsy tribe in the world. It has made it to resemble an essence, hermetically sealed. Keep it in that position, and it retains its inherent qualities undiminished; but uncork the vessel containing it, and it might (I do not say it *would*) evaporate among the surrounding elements.

will have an occasion to cultivate a proper degree of confidence in respect to themselves, and be so prepared as never to commit themselves, if they wish not to be known as Gipsies. I know there are few people who have nerve enough so to deport themselves, as to prevent moral detection, who have committed murder, when they are confronted with the objects of it; but if the individuals are perfectly satisfied of there being no evidence against them, they may confidently assume an appearance of innocence. It is so with the Gipsies in settled life, as to their being Gipsies. Generally speaking, their blood is so much mixed as almost to defy detection; although, for the future, some of them will be very apt to look at themselves in their mirrors, to see whether there is much of the "black de'il" in their faces. But it rests with themselves to escape detection, and particularly so as regards the fair, brown, and red Gipsies.

I may also be allowed to say a word or two to the Church, and people generally. It says little for them, that, although two centuries have elapsed since Bunyan's time, no one has acknowledged him. It surely might have occurred to them to ask, *1stly*: What was that particular family, or tribe, of which Bunyan said he was a member? *2ndly*: Who are the tinkers? *3dly*: What was the meaning of Bunyan entertaining so much solicitude, and undergoing so much trouble, to ascertain whether he, (a *common Englishman*, forsooth!) was a Jew, or not? *4thly*: Was John Bunyan a Gipsy? Let my reader reply to these questions, like a man of honour. Aye or nay, was John Bunyan a Gipsy? "He *was* a Gipsy."

In modern times people will preach the gospel "around about Illyricum," compass sea and land, and penetrate every continent, to bring home Christian trophies; while in Bunyan they have a trophy—a real case of "grace abounding;" and yet no one has acknowledged him, although his fame will be as lasting as the pyramids. John Bunyan was evidently a man who was raised up by God for some great purposes. One of these purposes he has served, and will yet serve; and it becomes us to enquire what further purpose he is destined to serve. It is showing a poor respect for Bunyan's memory, to deny him his nationality, to rob him of his birth-right, and attempt to make him out to have been that which he positively was not. To gratify their own prejudices, people would degrade the illustrious dreamer, from being this great original, into being the off-scourings of all England. People imagine that they would degrade Bunyan by saying that he was a Gipsy. They degrade themselves who do not believe he was a Gipsy; they doubly degrade themselves who deny it. Jews may well taunt Christians in the matter of evidences, and that on a simple matter of fact, affecting no one's interests, temporal or eternal, and as clear as the sun at mid-day; for by Bunyan's own showing he was a Gipsy; but if any further evidence was wanted, how easily could it not have been collected, any time during the last two hundred years!

I have hitherto got the "cold shoulder" from the organs of most of the religious denominations on this subject: time will show whether it is always to be so. The Church should know what is its mission: it rests on evidence itself, and it should be the first to follow out its own principles. It should fight its own battles, and give the enemy no occasion to speak reproachfully of it. In approaching this subject, it would be well to do it cheerfully, and gracefully, and manfully, and not as if the person were dragged to it, with a rope around his neck. No one need imagine that by keeping quiet, this matter will blow over. For the Gipsy race cannot die out; nor is this work likely to die out soon; for unless it is superseded by some other, it will come up centuries hence, to judge the present generation on the Gipsy question. May such as have written on the great dreamer never lift up their heads, may his works turn to hot coals in their fingers, may their memories be outlawed, if they allow this unchristian, this unmanly, this silly, this childish, prejudice of caste to prevent them from doing justice to their hero. Nor need any one utter a murmur at the prospect of seeing the Pilgrim's Progress prefaced by a dissertation on the Gipsies, with a Gipsy's camp for a frontispiece. Such a feeling may be expressed by boors, snobs, and counterfeit religionists; but better things are to be expected from other people.

Let the reader now pause, and reflect upon the prejudice of caste that exists against the name of Gipsy, and he will fully realize how it is that we should know so little about the Gipsies, and why it is that the Gipsies, as they leave the tent, should hide their nationality from the rest of the world, and "stick to each other."

In bringing this Disquisition on the Gipsies to a close, I may be allowed to say a word or two to some of the critics. In the first place, I may venture to assert, that the *subject* is worthy of a criticism the most disinterested and profound. I am well aware that the publication of the work places me in a position antagonistic alike to authors and critics who have written on the subject, as well as to the prejudices of mankind generally. If critics call in question any of the facts contained in the production, they must give their authorities; if they controvert any of the principles, they must give their reasons. It will not do to play the ostrich instead of the critic. For as the ostrich is said to hide its head in the sand, or in a bush, or, it may be, under its wing, and imagine that because it sees no one, so no one sees it; so there are people, sometimes to be met with, who will not only imagine, but assert, that because they know nothing of a thing, or because they do not understand it, therefore, the thing itself does not exist. This was the way in which Bruce's travels in Africa were received. But we are not living in those times. Procedure such as that described, is playing the ostrich, not the critic. I refer more particularly, however, to what is contained in this Disquisition. Taking the work all through, I think there are sufficient materials contained in it, to enable the critics to settle the various questions among themselves.

To place myself in a position a little independent of publishers, (for I have had great difficulty in finding a publisher,) I had the Introduction, (pages 55–67), printed, and circulated among some acquaintances in Canada, for subscribers.* A copy of it fell into the hands of an intelligent Scottish newspaper editor, in a small community, where every one knows every other's business nearly as well as his own, and where all about the Prospectus was explained to those to whom it was given. It seems to have frightened and en-

* The MS. of this work has undergone many vicissitudes. Among others, it may be mentioned that, in the state in which it was left by the author, it was twice lost, and once stolen; on which last occasion it was recovered, at an expense of one shilling! Then the original copy, in its present form, was stolen, and never recovered. In both instances did that happen under circumstances that such a fate was most unlikely to befall it. Then a copy of it was sent to Scotland, and never acknowledged, although I am in hopes it is now on its return, after a lapse of nearly three years; in which case, I will be more fortunate than the author, who gave the MS. to an individual and never got, and never could get, it back.

raged the editor to such an extent, that I entertain little doubt he did not sleep comfortably, for nights in succession, on finding that subject brought to light at his own door, which has been considered, by some, as well-nigh dead and buried long ago. He imagines the circulation of the Prospectus to be confined pretty much to his own neighbourhood; and so he must crush the horrible thing out. But what can he say about it? How put it down? A capital idea occurs to him; he will father it upon Barnum! Let the reader glance again at the Introduction, and imagine how a Scotchman, well posted up on Scotch affairs, past and present, should credit Barnum with the production. He heads his criticism, "The science of humbug," and, in some long and bitter paragraphs, pitches into what he calls American literary quackery; the substance of which is, that the work represented by the Prospectus, is a rare tit-bit of genuine, Barnumized, American humbug!

He finds, however, that he has gone much too far in his description of the Prospectus; so he comes tumbling down a long way from the high position which he took at the start, and continues: "Now, we do not, at present, venture the assertion that the forthcoming 'Scottish Gipsies' is a Yankee get-up, a mere American humbug; but we say the Prospectus savours strongly of the Barnum school; and our reasons for so saying are the following: *Firstly:* It would be nothing less than a literary miracle, that a Scottish work of sufficient merit to command the highest commendations of Sir Walter Scott, and Blackwood's Magazine, should be published, first of all in America, thirty years afterwards—published, by subscription, at one dollar, in a book of 400 pages. We assert, positively, that of such a work William Blackwood, alone, could have disposed of five thousand copies, at double the proposed price. [He is well acquainted with the prices of books in the two countries.] *Secondly:* There is no evidence to connect Sir Walter Scott's note to Quentin Durward with Walter Simson, or any other particular individual; and the same may be said of the *jingle* of Professor Wilson, and the other allusions in Blackwood's Magazine. *Thirdly:* There is neither danger nor difficulty in writing anything you please, and telling the public it is an extract of a private letter you had from some particular man of eminence, thirty years ago, provided your eminent friend has been many years in his grave. Such a fraud is not easily detected. And *Fourthly:* The reason assigned for publishing the 'Scottish Gipsies' . . . . . is totally upset by the simple fact, that *there are no such people in existence, in so far as Scotland is concerned.* [What an audacity he displays here! What a liberty he takes with the Scotch settlers in his neighbourhood! He is evidently afraid that he has gone too far; so he qualifies what he has said, by adding:] There are, it is true, a few families of itinerant tinkers, or *Tinklers*, according to our peculiar vernacular, who stroll the country, and subsist by making horn-spoons and sauce-pans, which they barter with the rural peasantry, for potatoes and other eatables. They are generally wild, reckless, and dishonest, and are a terror to children and old women. In nineteen cases out of twenty, they are natives of Ireland; and were any person idle enough to trace their genealogy, he would discover that their ancestors, not more than three generations back, were honest brogue-makers, pig-drovers, or, it may be, members of some more elevated occupation. [He has been 'idle enough' to give us a very odd account of the descent, in two senses of the word, of the Irish tinkering Gipsies now in Scotland.] The writer of these remarks is well acquainted with almost the whole Lowlands, and a portion of the West Highlands. He has been familiar with the shires of Fife and Linlithgow, with Annandale, the Upper Ward of Lanarkshire, and the other fabulously reputed haunts of the Gipsies [he seems to have done a little *tramping* in his time]; and he never saw twenty Scottish *Tinklers* in his whole life, nor *one single individual* corresponding to the description we have received of the Gipsies. [He has told us who the *Irish Tinklers* in Scotland were originally, but does not venture to say anything of the *Scottish* ones. He will not admit that there is a *Gipsy* in Scotland, or ever has been; and virtually denies that there are Gipsies in England; for he continues:] The nearest approach to the character is the hawkers from the Staffordshire potteries, who are found living in tents by the way-side, throughout the North Riding of Yorkshire, and the five northern counties of England. These are a kind of savages, who live in families, strolling the country, in large caravans, consisting frequently of half a dozen canvas-covered wagons and twice that number of horses. . . . . .

These characters often cross the Border, at Langholm and Gretna Green, and infest Annandale, Roxburghshire, Dumfries-shire, and the Stewartry of Kirkcudbright. [He will not allude to the *tented Gipsies* in England.]

"These two classes of foreign vagrants [why does he call them *foreign* vagrants? why not say *Gipsies?*] which we mention, are to be found, occasionally, in certain localities of Scotland, [still nothing said of the *Scottish Tinklers*,] and are to be found as a dreaded, dangerous nuisance. But the idea of a race of Scottish Tinklers, or Scottish Gipsies, existing as a distinct and separate people, possessing a native, independent language, and peculiar habits, rites, and ceremonies, and bearing, in many features of their barbarous customs, and outcast destiny, a resemblance to the vagabond Jews; such an idea, we say, has as little foundation in fact, as has Swift's story of the Lilliputians, or the romance of Guy Mannering itself! [It is astonishing what he would not attempt to palm upon the public. Still, he is evidently afraid that the subject will, somehow or other, bite him; and, after all that he has said, he concludes:] Still, we do not, *at present*, assert that the Prospectus we have received is another 'cute move of American humbug; but we do say, if there is a James Simson in existence, who possesses such a manuscript, and such commendations of it as are set forth in this Prospectus, he has already erred sufficiently far to ensure his identification with Yankee quackery. He has been Barnumized into an egregious blunder." [He is bound to discredit the whole affair, under any circumstances, even at the expense of the plainest consistency.]

Well might a brother editor reply to the foregoing, thus: "The bile of our excellent friend has just been agitated after a pestilent fashion. . . . . . . The announcement [of the intended publication] hath all the ungenial effects upon our gossip that the exhibition of a pair of scarlet decencies produces upon a cranky bull. . . . . . Now, just listen to us quietly for a little. More than two years ago, the manuscript of the above-mentioned treatise on the Scoto-Egyptians came under our ken. We perused the affair with special appetite, and were decidedly of opinion that its publication would be a grateful and important boon to the republic of letters. Mr. Simson is neither a myth nor a disciple of Barnum." Upon the back of this, the first editor writes: "We are pleased to be informed that the work is a *bona fide* production, and that Mr. Simson is no Yankee fiction. [As if he did not know that from the first.] And albeit he, [the other editor,] furnisheth neither facts nor arguments to satisfy us that our notions of the Gipsies of Scotland are heretical, we willingly accept his recommend that the 'Scottish Gipsies' will be, at least, an entertaining book, and reserve all further remarks till we see it."[!]

The foregoing is a very curious criticism; and although I could say a great deal more about it, I refrain from doing so.

INDEX.

* The song of "Johnny Faa, the Gipsy Laddie," appears in the Waverly anecdotes. It might have been included in the Minstrelsy of the Scottish Border.

PAGE

Ever since entering Great Britain, about the year 1506, the Gipsies have been drawing into their body the blood of the ordinary inhabitants and conforming to their ways; and so prolific has the race been, that there cannot be less than 250,000 Gipsies of all castes, colours, characters, occupations, degrees of education, culture, and position in life, in the British Isles alone, and possibly double that number. There are many of the same race in the United States of America. Indeed, there have been Gipsies in America from nearly the first day of its settlement; for many of the race were banished to the plantations, often for very trifling offences, and sometimes merely for being by "habit and repute Egyptians." But as the Gipsy race leaves the tent, and rises to civilization, it hides its nationality from the rest of the world, so great is the prejudice against the name of Gipsy. In Europe and America together, there cannot be less than 4,000,000 Gipsies in existence. John Bunyan, the author of the celebrated *Pilgrim's Progress*, was one of this singular people, as will be conclusively shown in the present work. The philosophy of the existence of the Jews, since the dispersion, will also be discussed and established in it.

When the "wonderful story" of the Gipsies is told, as it ought to be told, it constitutes a work of interest to many classes of readers, being a subject unique, distinct from, and unknown to, the rest of the human family. In the present work, the race has been treated of so fully and elaborately, in all its aspects, as in a great measure to fill and satisfy the mind, instead of being, as heretofore, little better than a myth to the understanding of the most intelligent person.

The history of the Gipsies, when thus comprehensively treated, forms a study for the most advanced and cultivated mind, as well as for the youth whose intellectual and literary character is still to be formed; and furnishes, among other things, a system of science not too abstract in its nature, and having for its subject-matter the strongest of human feelings and sympathies. The work also seeks to raise the name of Gipsy out of the dust, where it now lies; while it has a very important bearing on the conversion of the Jews, the advancement of Christianity generally, and the development of historical and moral science.

LONDON, *October 10th*, 1865.

Ever since entering Great Britain, about the year 1506, the Gipsies have been drawing into their body the blood of the ordinary inhabitants and conforming to their ways; and so prolific has the race been, that there cannot be less than 250,000 Gipsies of all castes, colours, characters, occupations, degrees of education, culture, and position in life, in the British Isles alone, and possibly double that number. There are many of the same race in the United States of America. Indeed, there have been Gipsies in America from nearly the first day of its settlement; for many of the race were banished to the plantations, often for very trifling offences, and sometimes merely for being by "habit and repute Egyptians." But as the Gipsy race leaves the tent, and rises to civilization, it hides its nationality from the rest of the world, so great is the prejudice against the name of Gipsy. In Europe and America together, there cannot be less than 4,000,000 Gipsies in existence. John Bunyan, the author of the celebrated *Pilgrim's Progress*, was one of this singular people, as will be conclusively shown in the present work. The philosophy of the existence of the Jews, since the dispersion, will also be discussed and established in it.

When the "wonderful story" of the Gipsies is told, as it ought to be told, it constitutes a work of interest to many classes of readers, being a subject unique, distinct from, and unknown to, the rest of the human family. In the present work, the race has been treated of so fully and elaborately, in all its aspects, as in a great measure to fill and satisfy the mind, instead of being, as heretofore, little better than a myth to the understanding of the most intelligent person.

The history of the Gipsies, when thus comprehensively treated, forms a study for the most advanced and cultivated mind, as well as for the youth whose intellectual and literary character is still to be formed; and furnishes, among other things, a system of science not too abstract in its nature, and having for its subject-matter the strongest of human feelings and sympathies. The work also seeks to raise the name of Gipsy out of the dust, where it now lies; while it has a very important bearing on the conversion of the Jews, the advancement of Christianity generally, and the development of historical and moral science.

LONDON, *October 10th*, 1865.

www.ingramcontent.com/pod-product-compliance
Lightning Source LLC
Chambersburg PA
CBHW022126020426
42334CB00015B/773

* 9 7 8 3 7 4 2 8 2 3 2 2 9 *